AMERICA'S *Favorite* INNS, B&Bs & SMALL HOTELS

Fifteenth Edition

The South

States Covered in This Edition

Alabama	Louisiana
Arkansas	Mississippi
Florida	North Carolina
Georgia	South Carolina
Kentucky	Tennessee

Also in this Series

America's Favorite Inns, B&Bs & Small Hotels, U.S.A. and Canada
America's Favorite Inns, B&Bs & Small Hotels, New England
America's Favorite Inns, B&Bs & Small Hotels, The Middle Atlantic
America's Wonderful Little Hotels & Inns, The Midwest
America's Wonderful Little Hotels & Inns, The Rocky Mountains and The Southwest
America's Favorite Inns, B&Bs & Small Hotels, The West Coast

AMERICA'S *Favorite* INNS, B&Bs & SMALL HOTELS

Fifteenth Edition

The South

Edited by Sandra W. Soule

Associate Editors:
Nancy P. Barker, Kathy Banak,
Audrey S. Levine
Amy Phillipps, Hilary Soule
Contributing Editors:
Mary Ann Boyle, Suzanne Carmichael,
Rose Ciccone, Gail Davis, Nancy Debevoise, Linda
Goldberg, Abby Humphrey, Betty Norman, Pam Phillips,
Joe Schmidt, Susan Schwemm, Diane Wolf
Editorial Assistants:
Meghan Morris, Sarah Phillipps

St. Martin's Griffin
New York

This book is dedicated to the people who take the time and trouble to write about the hotels and inns they've visited, and to my children—Hilary and Jeffrey—my husband, and my parents.

 For information, address St. Martin's Press, 175 Fifth Avenue, New York, N.Y. 10010.

ISBN 0-312-16767-9

First St. Martin's Griffin Edition: December 1997

10 9 8 7 6 5 4 3 2 1

Contents

Acknowledgments

I would like again to thank all the people who wrote in such helpful detail about the inns and hotels they visited. To them belong both the dedication and the acknowledgments, for without their support, this guide would not exist. If I have inadvertently misspelled or omitted anyone's name, please accept my sincerest apologies.

I would also like to thank my helpful and supportive editor Anne Savarese; to my wonderful colleagues Nancy Barker, Kathy Banak, Audrey Levine, Amy Phillipps, Suzanne Carmichael, Rose Ciccone, Nancy Debevoise, Gail Davis, Linda Goldberg, Betty Norman, Pam Phillips, Susan Schwemm, and Diane Wolf; and to faithful respondents Peg Bedini, Donna Bocks, Judith Brannen, Sherrill Brown, James and Pamela Burr, Marjorie Cohen, Dianne Crawford, Lynne Derry, Gail DeSciose, Brian Donaldson, Sally Ducot, Lynn Edge, Ellie and Robert Freidus, Lynn Fullman, Connie Gardner, Gail Gunning, B. J. Hensley, Lisa Hering, Emily Hochemong, Tina Hom, Stephen Holman, Linda Intaschi, Christopher Johnston, Keith Jurgens, Arleen Keele, Peggy Kontak, Bradley Lockner, Bill MacGowan, Myra Malkin, Celia McCullough, Mark Mendenhall, Michael and Dina Miller, Carolyn Myles, Eileen O'Reilly, Marilyn Parker, Julie Phillips, Adam Platt, Penny Poirier, Jill Reeves, Stephanie Roberts, Glenn Roehrig, Duane Roller, Marion Ruben, Lori Sampson, Joe and Sheila Schmidt, B. J. and Larry Schwartzkopf, Robert Sfire, Fritz Shantz and Tara O'Neal, Nancy Sinclair, Mary Jane Skala, Ruth Tilsley, Susan Ulanoff, Wendi Van Exan, Hopie Welliver, Tom Wilbanks, Beryl Williams, Susan Winner, Rose Wolf, Karl Wiegers and Chris Zambito, Susan Woods, and the many others who went far beyond the call of duty in their assistance and support.

Introduction

Reading the Entries

Each entry generally has three parts: a description of the inn or hotel, quotes from guests who have stayed there, and relevant details about rooms, rates, location, and facilities. Please remember that the length of an entry is in no way a reflection of that inn or hotel's quality. Rather, it is an indication of the type of feedback we've received both from guests and from the innkeepers themselves.

Wherever a location is of particular tourist interest, we've tried to include some information about its attractions. In some areas the magnet is not a particular town but rather a compact, distinct region. Travelers choose one place to stay and use it as a base from which to explore the area. But because this guide is organized by town, not by region, the entries are scattered throughout the chapter. When this applies, you will see the name of the region noted under the "Location" heading; check back to the introduction for a description of the region involved. Cross-referencing is also provided to supplement the maps at the back of the book.

The names at the end of the quotations are those who have recommended the hotel or inn. Some writers have requested that we not use their names; you will see initials noted instead. *We never print the names of those who have sent us adverse reports, although their contributions are invaluable indeed.*

Although we have tried to make the listings as accurate and complete as possible, mistakes and inaccuracies invariably creep in. The most significant area of inaccuracy applies to the rates charged by each establishment. In preparing this guide, we asked all the hotels and inns to give us their 1998–1999 rates, ranging from the least expensive room in the off-season to the most expensive peak-season price. Some did so, while others just noted the current rate.

Some of the shorter entries are marked "**Information please**" or "**Also recommended**." These tend to be establishments that are either too large or too small for a full entry, or about which we have insufficient information to complete a full entry.

Please remember that the process of writing and publishing a book takes nearly a year. *You should always double-check the rates when you make your reservations; please don't blame the inn or this guide if the prices are wrong*. On the other hand, given the current level of inflation, you should not encounter anything more than a 5% increase, unless there has been a substantial improvement in the amenities offered or a change of ownership. Please let us know immediately if you find anything more than that!

If you find any errors of omission or commission in any part of the entries, we urgently request your help in correcting them. We recognize that it takes extra time and effort for readers to write us letters or fill in report forms, but this feedback is essential in keeping this publication totally responsive to consumer needs.

The Fifteen Commandments of Vacation Travel

We all know people who come back from a vacation feeling on top of the world, and others who seem vaguely disappointed. Here's how to put yourself in the first category, not the second.

1. Know yourself. A successful vacation is one that works for the person you are, not the person you think you should be. Confirmed couch potatoes who resent having to walk from the far end of the parking lot will not find true fulfillment on a trek through the Himalayas. If privacy is a top priority, a group tour or communal lodge will turn fantasy into frustration. Acknowledge your own comfort levels. How important is it for you to be independent and flexible? Structured and secure? How essential are the creature comforts when it comes to sleeping, eating, and bathing? Would you rather have one week of luxury travel or two weeks of budget food and accommodation? And remember that while your personality doesn't change, your needs do. The type of vacation you plan for a romantic getaway is totally different from a family reunion.

2. Know your travel companions. Adjust your plans to accommodate your travel partners. Whether you are traveling with friends, spouse, children, and/or parents, you'll need to take their age, attention span, agility, and interests into account. If you're traveling with the kids, balance a morning at an art museum with an afternoon at the zoo; if you're spending time with elderly parents, make sure that they can stroll a country lane while you go rock-climbing; if your group includes skiers and non-skiers, pick a resort that has appealing shops and other activities.

3. Plan ahead: anticipation is half the fun. Enjoy the process. The more you know about an area you're going to visit, the more fun you'll have. Skim a guidebook; get a calendar of events; write to the local chambers of commerce and tourist offices; read a novel set in the region; talk to friends (or friends of friends) who have been there recently.

4. Don't bite off more than you can chew. Keep your itinerary in line with the amount of time and money available. Focus on seeing a smaller area well, rather than trying to cover too much ground and seeing nothing but interstate highways. Don't overprogram; allow yourself the luxury of doing nothing.

5. Avoid one-night stands. Plan to stay a minimum of two nights everywhere you go. A vacation made up of one-nighters is a prescription for exhaustion. You will sleep poorly, spend most of your time in transit, and will get only the smallest glimpse of the place you're visiting. If it's worth seeing, it's worth spending a full day in one place.

6. Travel off-season. Unless your vacation dates are dictated by the school calendar, off-season travel offers many advantages: fewer crowds, greater flexibility, and a more relaxed atmosphere. Learn to pick the best dates for off-season travel; typically these are the weeks just before and after the rates change. Off-season travel offers big savings, too; for example, most ski areas are delightful places to visit in summer, and offer savings of 50% or more on accommodations.

7. Book well ahead for peak season travel. If you must travel during peak periods to popular destinations, make reservations well in advance for the key sites to avoid aggravation, extra phone calls, and additional driving time.

8. Take the road less traveled by. Get off the beaten path to leave the crowds behind. Instead of booking a room in the heart of the action, find a quiet inn tucked in the hills or in a neighboring village. If you visit the Grand Canyon in August, at the height of the tourist season, stay at the North Rim, which attracts 90% fewer visitors than the South Rim.

9. Ditch the car. Sure you need a car to get where you're going. But once you're there, get out and walk. You'll see more, learn more, experience more at every level, while avoiding crowds even at the most popular destinations. We promise. Car travel is an isolating experience, even when you're in bumper-to-bumper traffic.

10. Hang loose. The unexpected is inevitable in travel, as in the rest of life. When your plans go astray (and they will), relax and let serendipity surprise you. And keep your sense of humor in good working order. If possible, travel without reservations or a set itinerary.

11. Carpe diem—seize the day. Don't be afraid to follow your impulses. If a special souvenir catches your eye, buy it; don't wait to see if you'll find it again later. If a hiking trail looks too inviting to pass up, don't; that museum will wait for a rainy day.

12. Don't suffer in silence. When things go wrong—an incompetent guide, car troubles, a noisy hotel room—speak up. Politely but firmly express your concern then and there; get your room changed, ask for a refund or discount, whatever. Most people in the travel business would rather have you go away happy than to leave grumbling.

13. Remember—being there is more than seeing there. People travel to see the sights—museums and mountains, shops and scenery—but it is making new friends that can make a trip memorable. Leave a door open to the people-to-people experiences that enrich travel immeasurably.

14. Don't leave home to find home. The quickest way to take the wind out of the sails of your trip is to compare things to the way they are at home. Enjoy different styles and cultures for what they are and avoid comparisons and snap judgments.

15. Give yourself permission to disregard all of the above. Nothing is immutable. If you find a pattern that works for you, enjoy it!

The Inngoer's Bill of Rights

Although nothing's perfect, as we all know, inngoers are entitled to certain reasonable standards. Of course, the higher the rates, the higher those standards should be. So, please use this Bill of Rights as a kind of checklist in deciding how you think a place stacks up on your own personal rating scale. And, whether an establishment fails, reaches, or exceeds these levels, be sure to let us know. We would also hope that innkeepers will use this list to help evaluate both the strong points and shortcomings of their own establishments, and are grateful to those who have already done so.

The right to suitable cleanliness: An establishment that looks, feels, and smells immaculate, with no musty, smoky, or animal odors.

The right to suitable room furnishings: A firm mattress, soft pillows, fresh linens, and ample blankets; bright lamps and night tables on each side of the bed; comfortable chairs with good reading lights; and adequate storage space.

The right to comfortable, attractive rooms: Guest rooms and common rooms that are as livable as they are attractive. Appealing places where you'd like to read, chat, relax.

The right to a decent bathroom: Cleanliness is essential, along with reliable plumbing, ample hot water, good lighting, an accessible electric outlet, space for toiletries, and thirsty towels.

The right to privacy and discretion: Privacy must be respected by the innkeeper and ensured by adequate sound-proofing. The right to discretion precludes questions about marital status or sexual preference. No display of proselytizing religious materials.

The right to good, healthful food: Fresh nutritious food, ample in quantity, high in quality, attractively presented, and graciously served in smoke-free surroundings.

The right to comfortable temperatures and noise levels: Rooms should be cool in summer and warm in winter, with windows that open, and quiet, efficient air-conditioning and heating. Double windows, drapes, and landscaping are essential if traffic noise is an issue.

The right to fair value: Prices should be in reasonable relation to the facilities offered and to the cost of equivalent local accommodation.

The right to genuine hospitality: Innkeepers who are glad you've come and who make it their business to make your stay pleasant and memorable; who are readily available without being intrusive.

The right to a caring environment: Welcoming arrivals with refreshments, making dinner reservations, providing information on activities, asking about pet allergies and dietary restrictions, and so on.

The right to personal safety: A location in a reasonably safe neighborhood, with adequate care given to building and parking security.

The right to professionalism: Brochure requests, room reservations, check-ins and -outs handled efficiently and responsibly.

The right to adequate common areas: At least one common room where guests can gather to read, chat, or relax, free of the obligation to buy anything.

The right of people traveling alone to have all the above rights: Singles usually pay just a few dollars less than couples, yet the welcome, services, and rooms they receive can be inferior.

The right to a reasonable cancellation policy: Penalties for a cancellation made fewer than 7-14 days before arrival are relatively standard. Most inns will refund deposits (minus a processing fee) after the deadline only if the room is rebooked.

The right to efficient maintenance: Burnt-out bulbs and worn-out smoke detector batteries are the responsibility of the innkeeper—not the guest. When things go wrong, guests have the right to an apology, a discount, or a refund.

Of course, there is no "perfect" inn or hotel, because people's tastes and needs vary so greatly. But one key phrase does pop up over and over again: "I felt right at home." This is not written in the literal sense—a commercial lodging, no matter how cozy or charming, is never the same as one's home. What is really meant is that guests felt as welcome, as relaxed, as comfortable, as they would in their own home.

What makes for a wonderful stay?

We've tried our best to make sure that all the inns listed in this guide are as special as our title promises. Inevitably, there will be some disappointments. Sometimes these will be caused by a change in ownership or management that has resulted in lowered standards. Other times unusual circumstances will lead to problems. Quite often, though, problems will occur because there's not a good "fit" between the inn and the guest. Decide what you're looking for, then find the place that suits your needs, whether you're looking for a casual environment or a dressy one, a romantic setting or a family-oriented one, a vacation spot or a business person's environment, an isolated country retreat or a convenient in-town location.

We've tried to give you as much information as possible on each property listed, and have taken care to indicate the atmosphere each innkeeper is trying to create. After you've read the listing, request a copy of the establishment's brochure, which will give you more information. Finally, feel free to call any inn or hotel where you're planning to stay, and ask as many questions as necessary.

Inn etiquette

A first-rate inn is a joy indeed, but as guests we need to do our part to respect its special qualities. For starters, you'll need to maintain a higher level of consideration for your fellow guests. Century-old Victorians are noted for their nostalgic charms, not their sound-proofing; if you come in late or get up early, remember that voices and footsteps echo off all those gleaming hardwood floors and doors. If you're going to pick a fight with your roommate, pull the covers up over your head or go out for a walk. If you're sharing a bath, don't dawdle, tidy up after yourself, and dry your hair back in your room. If you've admired the Oriental carpets, antique decor, handmade quilts, and the thick fluffy towels, don't leave wet glasses on the furniture, put suitcases on the bed, or use the towels for removing make-up or wiping the snow off your car. After all, innkeepers have rights too!

Hotels, inns ... resorts and motels

As the title indicates, this is a guide to exceptional inns, B&Bs, and small hotels. Generally, the inns have 5 to 25 rooms, although a few have only 2 rooms and some have over 100. The hotels are more often found in the cities and range in size from about 50 to 200 rooms.

The line between an inn or hotel and a resort is often a fine one. There are times when we all want the extra facilities a resort provides, so we've added a number of reader-recommended facilities. We've also listed a handful of motels. Although they don't strictly fall within the context of this book, we've included them because readers felt they were the best option in a specific situation.

Although we do not provide full coverage of hotel chains, we do want to point out that the Four Seasons and Ritz-Carlton hotels are almost impossible to beat at the luxury end of the spectrum. Readers consistently rave about their unbeatable combination of unparalleled service and plush accommodation; weekend rates make them an exceptional value.

What is a B&B anyway?

There are basically two kinds of B&Bs—the B&B homestay and the B&B inn. The homestay is typically the home of an empty nester, who has a few empty bedrooms to fill, gaining some extra income and pleasant company. B&B inns are run on a more professional basis, independently marketed and subject to state and local licensing. Guests typically have dedicated common areas for their use, and do not share the hosts' living quarters, as in a homestay. We list very few homestays in this guide. Full-service or country inns and lodges are similar to the B&B inn, except that they serve breakfast and dinner on a regular basis, and may be somewhat larger in size; dinner is often offered to the public as well as to house guests. The best of all of these are made special by resident owners bringing the warmth of their personalities to the total experience. A B&B is *not* a motel that serves breakfast.

Rooms

All guest rooms are not created equal. Although the rooms at a typical chain motel or hotel may be identical, the owners of most of the establishments described in this book pride themselves on the individuality of each guest room. Some, although not all, of these differences are reflected in the rates charged.

More importantly, it means that travelers need to express their needs clearly to the innkeepers when making reservations and again when checking in. Some rooms may be quite spacious but may have extremely small private baths or limited closet space. Some antique double beds have rather high footboards—beautiful to look at but torture for six-footers. Most inns are trading their double-size mattresses in for queens and kings; if you prefer an oversize bed, say so. If you want twin beds, be sure to specify this when making reservations and again when you check in; many smaller inns have only one twin-bedded room. If you must have a king-size bed, ask for details; sometimes two twin beds are just pushed together, made up with a king-size fitted sheet.

Some rooms may have gorgeous old bathrooms, with tubs the size of small swimming pools, but if you are a hard-core shower person, that room won't be right for you. More frequently, you'll find a shower but no bathtub, which may be disappointing if you love a long, luxurious soak. If you are traveling on business and simply must have a working-size desk with good lighting, an electric outlet, and a telephone jack for your modem, speak up. Some rooms look terrific inside but don't look out at anything much; others may have the view but not quite as special a decor. Often the largest rooms are at the front of the house, facing a busy highway. Decide what's important to you. Although the owners and staff of the hotels and inns listed here are incredibly hard-working and dedicated people, they can't read your mind. Let your needs be known, and, within the limits of availability, they will try to accommodate you.

Our most frequent complaints center around beds that are too soft and inadequate reading lights. If these are priorities for you (as they are for us), don't be shy about requesting bedboards or additional lamps to remedy the situation. Similarly, if there are other amenities your room is lacking—extra pillows, blankets, or even an easy chair—speak up. Most innkeepers would rather put in an extra five minutes of work than have an unhappy guest.

If you really don't like your room, ask for another as soon as possible, preferably before you've unpacked your bags. The sooner you voice your dissatisfaction, the sooner something can be done to improve the situation. If you don't like the food, ask for something else—since you're the guest, make sure you get treated like one. If things go terribly wrong, don't be shy about asking for your money back, and be *sure* to write us about any problems.

What is a single? A double? A suite? A cottage or cabin?

Unlike the proverbial rose, a single is not a single is not a single. Sometimes it is a room with one twin bed, which really can accommodate only one person. Quite often it is described as a room with a standard-size double bed, in contrast to a double, which has two twin beds. Other hotels call both of the preceding doubles, although doubles often have queen- or even king-size beds instead. Many times the only distinction is made by the number of guests occupying the room; a single will pay slightly less, but there's no difference in the room.

There's almost as much variation when it comes to suites. We define a suite as a bedroom with a separate living room area and often a small kitchen, as well. Unfortunately, the word has been stretched to cover other setups, too. Some so-called suites are only one large room, accommodating a table and separate seating area in addition to the bed, while others are two adjacent bedrooms which share a bath. If you require a suite that has two separate rooms with a door between them, specify this when you make reservations.

Quite a few of our entries have cabins or cottages in addition to rooms in the main building. In general, a cabin is understood to be a somewhat more rustic residence than a cottage, although there's no hard-and-fast rule. Be sure to inquire for details when making reservations.

Making reservations

Unless you are inquiring many months in advance of your visit, it's best to telephone when making reservations. This offers a number of advantages: You will know immediately if space is available on your requested dates; you can find out if that space is suitable to your specific needs. You will have a chance to discuss the pros and cons of the available rooms and will be able to find out about any changes made in recent months—new facilities, recently redecorated rooms, nonsmoking policies, even a change of ownership. It's also a good time to ask the innkeeper about other concerns—Is the neighborhood safe at night? Is there any renovation or construction in progress that might be disturbing? Will a wedding reception or bicycle touring group affect use of the common areas during your visit? If you're reserving a room at a plantation home that is available for public tours, get specifics about the check-in/out times; in many, rooms are not available before 5 p.m. and must be vacated by 9 a.m. sharp. The savvy traveler will always get the best value for his accommodation dollar.

If you expect to be checking in late at night, *be sure to say so;* many inns give doorkeys to their guests, then lock up by 10 p.m.; often special arrangements must be made for late check-ins, and a handful of inns won't accept them at all.

We're often asked about the need for making advance reservations. If you'll be traveling in peak periods, in prime tourist areas, and want to be sure of getting a first-rate room at the best-known inns, reserve at least three to six months ahead. This is especially true if you're traveling with friends or family and will need more than one room. On the other hand, if you like a bit of adventure, and don't want to be stuck with cancellation fees when you change your mind, by all means stick our books in the glove compartment and hit the road. If you're traveling in the off-season, or even midweek in season, you'll have a grand time. But look for a room by late afternoon; never wait until after dinner and expect to find something decent. Some inns offer a discount after 4:00 p.m. for last-minute bookings; it never hurts to ask.

Payment

The vast majority of inns now accept credit cards. A few accept credit cards for the initial deposit but prefer cash, traveler's checks, or personal checks for the balance; others offer the reverse policy. When no credit cards are accepted at all, you can settle your bill with a personal check, traveler's check, or even (!) cash.

When using your credit card to guarantee a reservation, be aware that most inns will charge your card for the full amount of the deposit, unlike motels and hotels which don't put through the charge until you've checked in. A few will put a "hold" on your card for the full amount of your entire stay, plus the cost of meals and incidentals that you may (or may not) spend. If you're using your card to reserve a fairly extended trip, you may find that you're well over your credit limit without actually having spent a nickel. We'd suggest inquiring; if the latter is the procedure, either send a check for the deposit or go elsewhere. If you have used American Express, Diners Club, MasterCard, or Visa to guarantee your reservation, these companies guarantee if a room is not available, the hotel is supposed to find you a free room in a comparable hotel, plus transportation and a free phone call.

Rates

All rates quoted are per room, unless otherwise noted as being per person. Rates quoted per person are usually based on double occupancy, unless otherwise stated.

"Room only" rates do not include any meals. In most cases two or three meals a day are served by the hotel restaurant, but are charged separately. Average meal prices are noted when available. In a very few cases no meals are served on the premises at all; rooms in these facilities are usually equipped with kitchenettes.

B&B rates include bed and breakfast. Breakfast can vary from a simple continental breakfast to a full breakfast. Afternoon tea and evening refreshments are sometimes included as well.

MAP (Modified American Plan) rates are often listed per person and include breakfast and dinner; *a 15% service charge is typically added to the total.* Full board rates include three square meals a day, and are usually found only at old-fashioned resorts and isolated ranches.

State and local sales taxes are not included in the rates unless otherwise indicated; the percentage varies from state to state, city to city, and can reach 20% in a few urban centers, although 10–15% is more typical.

When inquiring about rates, always ask if any off-season or special package rates are available. Sometimes discounted rates are available *only* on request; seniors and AAA members often qualify for substantial discounts. During the week, when making reservations at city hotels or country inns, it's important to ask if any corporate rates are available. Depending on the establishment, you may or may not be asked for some proof of corporate affiliation (a business card is usually all that's needed), but it's well worth inquiring, since the effort can result in a saving of 15 to 20%, plus an upgrade to a substantially better room.

A number of companies specialize in booking hotel rooms in major cities at substantial discounts. Although you can ask for specific hotels by name, the largest savings are realized by letting the agency make the selection; they may be able to get you a discount of up to 65%. **Hotel Reservations Network** (8140 Walnut Hill Lane, Dallas, Texas 75231; 800–96–HOTEL) offers discount rates in over 20 U.S. cities plus London and Paris; **Quikbook** (381 Park Avenue South, New York, New York 10016; 800–789–9887) is a similar service with competitive rates. **Express Reservations** (3800 Arapahoe, Boulder, Colorado 80303; 800–356–1123) specializes in properties in New York City and Los Angeles. For California, try **San Francisco Reservations** (22 Second Street, Fourth Floor, San Francisco, California 94105; 800–677–1500), or **California Reservations** (3 Sumner Street, 94103; 800–576–0003).

Another money-saving trick can be to look for inns in towns a bit off the beaten path. If you stay in a town that neighbors a famous resort or historic community, you will often find that rates are anywhere from $20 to $50 less per night for equivalent accommodation. If you're travelling without reservations, and arrive at a half-empty inn in late afternoon, don't hesitate to ask for a price reduction or free room upgrade. And of course, watch for our ¢ symbol, which indicates places which are a particularly good value.

If an establishment has a specific tipping policy, whether it is "no tipping" or the addition of a set service charge, it is noted under "Rates." When both breakfast and dinner are included in the rates, a 15% service charge against the total bill—not just the room—is standard; a few inns charge 18–20%. A number of B&Bs are also adding on a service charge, a practice which sits poorly with us. If you feel—as many of our readers do—that these fees are a sneaky way of making rates seem lower than they really are, let the innkeeper (and us) know how you feel. When no notation is made, it's generally expected that guests will leave $1–3 a night for the housekeeping staff and 15% for meal service. A number of inns have taken to leaving little cards or envelopes to remind guests to leave a tip for the housekeepers; most readers find this practice objectionable. If you welcome a no-tipping policy and object to solicitation, speak up.

While the vast majority of inns are fairly priced, there are a few whose rates have become exorbitant. Others fail to stay competitive, charging top weekend rates when a nearby luxury hotel is offering a beautiful suite at a lower price. No matter how lovely the breakfast, how thoughtful the innkeepers, there's a limit to the amount one will pay for a room without an in-room telephone, TV, or a full-size private bathroom. One B&B has the nerve to charge $125 for a room with shared bath, then asks you to bring your own pool towels during the summer (it's not listed here!).

Deposits and cancellations

Nearly all innkeepers print their deposit and cancellation policies clearly on their brochures. Deposits generally range from payment of the first night's stay to 50% of the cost of the entire stay. Some inns repeat the cancellation policy when confirming reservations. In general, guests canceling well in advance of the planned arrival (one to four weeks is typical) receive a full refund minus a cancellation fee. After that date, no refunds are offered unless the room is resold to someone else. A few will not refund *even if the room is resold,* so take careful note. If you're making a credit card booking over the phone, be sure to find out what the cancellation policy is. We are uncomfortable with overly strict refund policies, and wish that inns would give a gift certificate, good for a return visit, when guests are forced to cancel on short notice.

Sometimes the shoe may be on the other foot. Even if you were told earlier that the inn at which you really wanted to stay was full, it may be worthwhile to make a call to see if cancellations have opened up any last-minute vacancies.

Minimum stays

Two- and three-night minimum weekend and holiday stays are the rule at many inns during peak periods. We have noted these when possible, although we suspect that the policy may be more common than is always indicated in print. On the other hand, you may just be hitting a slow period, so it never hurts to call at the last minute to see if a one-night reservation would be accepted. Again, cancellations are always a possibility; you can try calling on a Friday or Saturday morning to see if something is available for that night.

Pets

Very few of the inns and hotels listed accept pets. When they do we've noted it under "Extras." On the other hand, most of the inns listed in this book have at least one dog or cat, sometimes more. These pets are usually found in the common areas, sometimes in guest rooms as well. *If you are allergic to animals, we strongly urge that you inquire for details before making reservations.*

Children

Some inns are family-style places and welcome children of all ages; we've marked them with our symbol. Others do not feel that they have facilities for the very young and only allow children over a certain age. Still others cultivate an "adults only" atmosphere and discourage anyone under the age of 16. We've noted age requirements under the heading "Restrictions." If special facilities are available to children, these are noted under "Facilities" and "Extras." If an inn does not exclude children yet does not offer any special amenities or rate reductions for them, we would suggest it only for the best-behaved youngsters.

Whatever the policy, you may want to remind your children to follow the same rules of courtesy toward others that we expect of adults. Be aware that the pitter-patter of little feet on an uncarpeted hardwood floor can sound like a herd of stampeding buffalo to those on the floor below. Children used to the indestructible plastics of contemporary homes will need to be reminded (more than once) to be gentle with antique furnishings. Most importantly, be sensitive to the fact that parents—not innkeepers—are responsible for supervising their children's behavior.

State laws governing discrimination by age are affecting policies at some inns. To our knowledge, both California and Michigan now have such laws on the books. Some inns get around age discrimination by limiting room occupancy to two adults. This discourages families by forcing them to pay for two rooms instead of one. Our own children were very clear on their preferences: although they'd been to many inns that don't encourage guests under the age of 12, they found them "really boring"; on the other hand, they loved every family-oriented place we visited.

Porterage and packing

Only the largest of our listings will have personnel whose sole job is to assist guests with baggage. In the casual atmosphere associated with many inns, it is simply assumed that guests will carry their own bags. If you do need assistance with your luggage, don't hesitate to ask.

If you're planning an extended trip to a number of small inns, we'd suggest packing as lightly as possible, using two small bags rather than one large suitcase. You'll know why if you've ever tried hauling a 50-pound oversize suitcase up a steep and narrow 18th-century staircase. On the other hand, don't forget about the local climate when assembling your wardrobe. In mountainous and desert regions, day- and nighttime temperatures can vary by as much as 40 degrees. Also, bear in mind that Easterners tend to dress more formally than Westerners, so pack accordingly.

Meals

If you have particular dietary restrictions—low-salt, vegetarian, or religious—or allergies—to caffeine, nuts, whatever—be sure to mention these when making reservations and *again* at check-in. If you're allergic to a common breakfast food or beverage, an evening reminder will ensure that you'll be able to enjoy the breakfast that's been prepared for you. Most innkeepers will do their best to accommodate your special needs, but be fair. Don't ask an innkeeper to prepare a special meal, and then, when it's being served, say: "I've decided to go off my diet today. Can I have the luscious peaches-and-cream French toast with bacon that everyone else is eating?"

In preparing each listing, we asked the owners to give us the cost of prix fixe and a la carte meals when available. An "alc dinner" price at the end of the "Rates" section is the figure we were given when we requested the average cost of a three-course dinner with a half bottle of house wine, including tax and tip. Prices listed for prix fixe meals do not include wine and service. Lunch prices, where noted, do not include the cost of any alcoholic beverage. Hotels and inns which serve meals to the public are noted with the ✕ symbol.

Dinner and lunch reservations are always a courtesy and are often essential. Most B&B owners will offer to make reservations for you; this can be especially helpful in getting you a table at a popular restaurant in peak season and/or on weekends. Some of the establishments we list operate restaurants fully open to the public. Others serve dinner primarily to their overnight guests, but they also will serve meals to outsiders; reservations are essential at such inns, usually 24 hours in advance.

A few restaurants require jackets and ties for men at dinner, even in rather isolated areas. Of course, this is more often the case in traditional New England and the Old South than in the West. Unless you're going only to a very casual country lodge, we recommend that men bring these items along and that women have corresponding attire.

Breakfast: Breakfast is served at nearly every inn or hotel listed in this guide, and is usually included in the rates. Whenever possible we describe a typical breakfast, rather than using the terms "continental" or "full" breakfast.

Continental breakfast ranges from coffee and store-bought pastry to a lavish offering of fresh fruit and juices, yogurt and granola, cereals, even cheese and cold meats, homemade muffins and breads, and a choice of decaffeinated or regular coffee, herbal and regular tea. There's almost as much variety in the full breakfasts, which range from the traditional eggs, bacon, and toast, plus juice and coffee, to three-course gourmet extravaganzas.

We've received occasional complaints about breakfasts being too rich in eggs and cream, and too sweet, with no plain rolls or bread. A dietary splurge is fun for a weekend escape, but on a longer trip we'd advise requesting a "healthy breakfast" from your innkeeper. You can be sure that they don't eat their own breakfasts every day! Equally important to many guests are the timing and seating arrangements at breakfast. Some readers enjoy the friendly atmosphere of breakfast served family-style at a set time; this approach often enables innkeepers to serve quite spectacular three-course meals. Other readers much prefer the flexibility and privacy afforded by breakfasts served at tables for two over an extended time period.

Lunch: Very few of the inns and hotels listed here serve lunch. Those that do generally operate a full-service restaurant or are located in isolated mountain settings with no restaurants nearby. Many inns are happy to make up picnic lunches for an additional fee.

Dinner: Meals served at the inns listed here vary widely from simple home-style family cooking to gourmet cuisine. We are looking for food that is a good, honest example of the type of cooking involved. Ingredients should be fresh and homemade as far as is possible; service and presentation should be pleasant and straightforward. We have no interest in the school of "haute pretentious" where the hyperbolic descriptions found on the menu far exceed the chef's ability.

Drinks

With a very few exceptions (noted under "Restrictions" in each listing), alcoholic beverages may be enjoyed in moderation at all of the inns and hotels listed. Most establishments with a full-service restaurant serving the public as well as overnight guests are licensed to serve beer, wine, and liquor to their customers, although "brown-bagging" or BYOB (bring your own bottle) is occasionally permitted, especially in dry counties. Bed & breakfasts, and inns serving meals primarily to overnight guests, do not typically have liquor licenses, although most will provide guests with setups, i.e., glasses, ice, and mixers, at what is often called a BYO (bring your own) bar.

Overseas visitors will be amazed at the hodgepodge of regulations around the country. Liquor laws are determined in general by each state, but individual counties, or even towns, can prohibit or restrict the sale of alcoholic beverages, even beer.

Smoking

The vast majority of B&Bs and inns prohibit indoor smoking entirely, allowing it only on porches and verandas; a few don't allow smoking anywhere on the grounds. Larger inns and hotels usually do permit smoking, prohibiting it only in some guest rooms, and dining areas. Where prohibitions apply we have noted this under "Restrictions." We suggest that confirmed smokers be courteous or make reservations elsewhere. If there is no comment about smoking under "Restrictions," those allergic to smoke should inquire for details.

Physical limitations and wheelchair accessibility

We've used the well-known symbol ♿ to denote hotels and inns that are wheelchair accessible. Where available, additional information is noted under the "Extras" heading. Unfortunately, what is meant by this symbol varies dramatically. In the case of larger hotels and newer inns, it usually means full access; in historic buildings, access may be limited to the restaurant and public rest rooms only, or to a specific guest room but not the common areas. *Call the inn/hotel directly for full details and to discuss your needs.*

If you do not need a wheelchair but have difficulty with stairs, we urge you to mention this when making reservations; many inns and small hotels have one or two rooms on the ground floor, but very few have elevators. Similarly, if you are visually handicapped, do share this information so that you may be given a room with good lighting and no unexpected steps.

Air-conditioning

Heat is a relative condition, and the perceived need for air-conditioning varies tremendously from one individual to the next. If an inn or hotel has air-conditioning, you'll see this listed under "Rooms." If it's important to you, be sure to ask when making reservations. If air-conditioning is not available, check to see if fans are provided. Remember that top-floor rooms in most inns (usually a converted attic) can be uncomfortably warm even with air-conditioning.

Transportation

A car is more or less essential for visiting most of the inns and hotels listed here, as well as the surrounding sights of interest. Exceptions are those located in the major cities. In some historic towns, a car is the easiest way to get there, but once you've arrived, you'll want to find a place to park the car and forget about it.

If you are traveling by public transportation, check the "Extras" section at the end of each write-up. If the innkeepers are willing to pick you up from the nearest airport, bus, or train station, you'll see it noted here. This service is usually free or available at modest cost. If it's not listed, the innkeeper will direct you to a commercial facility that can help.

Parking

Although not a concern in most cases, parking is a problem in many cities, beach resorts, and historic towns. If you'll be traveling by car, ask the innkeeper for advice when making reservations. If parking is not on-site, stop at the hotel first to drop off your bags, then go park the car. In big cities, if "free parking" is included in the rates, this usually covers only one arrival and departure. Additional "ins and outs" incur substantial extra charges. Be sure to ask.

If on-site parking is available in areas where parking can be a problem, we've noted it under "Facilities." Since it's so rarely a problem in country inns, we haven't included that information in those listings. Regrettably, security has become an issue in most cities. Never leave anything visible inside the car; it's an invitation for break-in and theft.

Christmas travel

Many people love to travel to a country inn or hotel at Christmas. Quite a number of places do stay open through the holidays, but the extent to which the occasion is celebrated varies widely indeed. We know of many inns that decorate beautifully, serve a fabulous meal, and organize all kinds of traditional Christmas activities. But we also know of others, especially in ski areas, that do nothing more than throw a few token ornaments on a tree. Be sure to inquire.

Is innkeeping for me?

Many of our readers fantasize about running their own inn; for some the fantasy will become a reality. Before taking the plunge, it's vital to find out as much as you can about this demanding business. Begin by reading *So You Want to Be an Innkeeper*, by Pat Hardy, Jo Ann Bell, and Mary Davies. Hardy and Bell are co-directors of the Professional Association of Innkeepers, International (PAII—pronounced "pie") which also publishes *Innkeeping Newsletter,* various materials for would-be innkeepers, and coordinates workshops for aspiring innkeepers. For details contact PAII, P.O. Box 90710, Santa Barbara, CA 93190; 805–569–1853, or visit their internet website at www.paii.org. Another good book is *How to Start and Run Your Own Bed & Breakfast Inn* by long-time innkeepers Ripley Hotch and Carl Glassman, covering everything from financing to marketing to day-to-day innkeeping responsibilities ($14.95; Stackpole Books, P.O. Box 1831, Harrisburg, PA 17105;

800–732–3669). Another excellent source, especially in the East, are consultants Bill Oates and Heide Bredfeldt. Contact them at P.O. Box 1162, Brattleboro, VT 05301; 802–254–5931 to find out when and where they'll be offering their next prospective innkeepers seminar. Bill and Heide are highly respected pros in this field and have worked with innkeepers facing a wide range of needs and problems; his newsletter, *Innquest*, is written for prospective innkeepers looking to buy property. An equally good alternative is Lodging Resources Workshops, 98 South Fletcher Avenue, Amelia Island, FL 32034; 888–201–7602. Director Dave Caples owns the Elizabeth Pointe Lodge in Amelia Island, and has been conducting workshops throughout the U.S. since 1992.

For more information

The best sources of travel information in this country and in Canada are absolutely free; in many cases, you don't even have to supply the cost of a stamp or telephone call. They are the state and provincial tourist offices.

For each state you'll be visiting, request a copy of the official state map, which will show you every little highway and byway and will make exploring much more fun; it will also have information on state parks and major attractions in concise form. Ask also for a calendar of events and for information on topics of particular interest, such as fishing or antiquing, vineyards or crafts; many states have published B&B directories, and some are quite informative. If you're going to an area of particular tourist interest, you might also want to ask the state office to give you the name of the regional tourist board for more detailed information. Most states have toll-free numbers; call 800–555–1212 to get the numbers you need. If there's no toll-free listing, call the information operators for the relevant states, and ask them to check for the number under the state's capital city. Many states have also established websites on the Internet; use search engines to see what you can find.

You may also want to contact the local chamber of commerce for information on local sights and events of interest or even an area map. You can get the necessary addresses and telephone numbers from the inn or hotel where you'll be staying or from the state tourist office.

If you are one of those people who never travel with fewer than three guidebooks (which includes us), you will find the AAA Tour Guides to be especially helpful. The guides are distributed free on request to members, and cover hotels, restaurants, and sightseeing information. If you're not already an AAA member, *we'd strongly urge you join before your next trip;* in addition to their road service, they offer quality guidebooks and maps, and an excellent discount program at many hotels (including a number listed here).

Guidebooks are published only once every year or two; if you'd like to have a more frequent update, we'd suggest one of the following:

Country Inns/Bed & Breakfasts (P.O. Box 182, South Orange, NJ 07079; 800–877–5491), $23, 6 issues annually. You know what they say about a picture being worth a thousand words. A must for inngoers.

The Discerning Traveler (504 West Mermaid Lane, Philadelphia, PA

19118; 800–673–7834 or 215–247–5578), $50, 6 issues annually, $8 single copy. Picks a single destination in the New England, Mid-Atlantic, or Southern states and covers it in real depth—sights, restaurants, lodging, and more. The authors have published three delightful books on the subject as well.

Easy Escapes (P.O. Box 120365, Boston, MA 02112–0365), $47, 10 issues annually, $6 single copy. Covers inns, hotels, and resorts in the U.S. and the world; exceptionally honest and forthright. Each issue usually covers one or two destinations in a breezy, informal style.

Harper's Hideaway Report (Box 300, Whitefish, MT 59937), $125, 12 issues annually. Covers the best (and most expensive) inns, hotels, resorts in the U.S. and abroad.

The Internet: Those of you with on-line access will want to check out the huge amount of travel information found on the World Wide Web. Start with our own website, at http://www.inns.com, where you'll find thousands of listings and photographs. From there, take a look at some of the other inn directories, as well as the many sites devoted to state and regional travel information. Of equal interest are the chat rooms and bulletin boards covering bed & breakfasts; you can find them on the internet as well as on the proprietary services like America on Line and Prodigy.

Where is my favorite inn?

In reading through this book, you may find that your favorite inn is not listed, or that a well-known inn has been omitted from this edition. Why? Two reasons, basically: In several cases, establishments have been dropped because our readers had unsatisfactory experiences. Feel free to contact us for details. Other establishments have been omitted because we've had little or no reader or innkeeper feedback. This may mean that readers visiting these hotels and inns had satisfactory experiences but were not sufficiently impressed to write about them, or that readers were pleased but just assumed that someone else would take the trouble. If the latter applies, please, please, do write and let us know of your experiences. We try to visit as many inns as possible ourselves, but it is impossible to visit every place, every year. So please, keep those cards, letters, and telephone calls coming! As an added incentive, we will be sending free copies of the next edition of this book to our most helpful respondents.

Little Inns of Horror

We try awfully hard to list only the most worthy establishments, but sometimes the best-laid plans of mice and travel writers do go astray. Please understand that whenever we receive a complaint about an entry in our guide we feel terrible, and do our best to investigate the situation. Readers occasionally send us complaints about establishments listed in *other* guidebooks; these are quite helpful as warning signals.

The most common complaints we receive—and the least forgivable—

are on the issue of dirt. Scummy sinks and bathtubs, cobwebbed windows, littered porches, mildewed carpeting, water-stained ceilings, and grimy linens are all stars of this horror show.

Next in line are problems dealing with the lack of maintenance: peeling paint and wallpaper; sagging, soft, lumpy mattresses; radiators that don't get hot and those that make strange noises; windows that won't open, windows that won't close, windows with no screens, decayed or inoperable window shades; moldy shower curtains, rusty shower stalls, worn-out towels, fluctuating water temperatures, dripping faucets, and showers that only dribble, top the list.

Food complaints come next on this disaster lineup: poorly prepared canned or frozen food when fresh is readily available; meals served on paper, plastic, or worst of all, styrofoam; and insensitivity to dietary needs. Some complaints are received about unhelpful, abrasive, or abusive innkeepers, with a few more about uncaring, inept, or invisible staff. Complaints are most common in full-service inns when the restaurant business preoccupies the owners' attention, leaving overnight guests to suffer. Last but not least are noise headaches: trucks and trains that sound like they're heading for your pillow, and being awakened by the sound of someone snoring—in the next room. More tricky are questions of taste—high Victorian might look elegant to you, funereal to me; my collectibles could be your Salvation Army thriftshop donation. In short, there are more than a few inns and hotels that give new meaning to the phrase "having reservations"; fortunately they're many times outnumbered by the many wonderful places listed in this guide.

Pet peeves

Although we may genuinely like an inn, minor failings can keep it from being truly wonderful. Heading our list of pet peeves is inadequate bedside reading lights and tables. We know that there is not always room for a second table, but a light can always be attached to the wall. For reasons of both safety and comfort, a lamp should be at every bedside. Another reader is irked by inadequate bathroom lighting: "I think it must be an innkeepers' conspiracy to keep me from ever getting my makeup on properly." *(SU)* Other readers object to overly friendly innkeepers: "The innkeeper chatted with us all during breakfast, and was disappointed that we didn't plan to go in to say goodbye after we loaded up the car. Innkeepers should remember that the guests are customers, not long-lost relatives." *(KW)* Another common gripe concerns clutter: "Although pretty and interesting, the many collectibles left us no space for our personal belongings." And: "Instructions were posted everywhere—how to operate door locks, showers, heat, air-conditioning, and more." Anything you'd like to add?

Glossary of Architectural and Decorating Terms

We are not architectural experts, and when we started writing this series, we didn't know a dentil from a dependency, a tester from a transom. We've learned a bit more since then, and hope that our primer of terms, prepared by associate editor Nancy Barker, will also be helpful to you.

Adam: building style (1780–1840) featuring a classic box design with a dominant front door and fanlight, accented by an elaborate surround or an entry porch; cornice with decorative moldings incorporating dentil, swag, garland, or stylized geometric design. Three-part Palladian-style windows are common.

antebellum: existing prior to the U.S. Civil War (1861–1865).

Arts and Craft movement: considered the first phase of the Modern movement that led to the Prairie style (1900–20) of Frank Lloyd Wright in Chicago, and the Craftsman style (1905–30) of the Greene brothers in Southern California. In the Arts and Craft style, historical precedent for decoration and design was rejected and ornamentation was "modernized" to remove traces of its historic origins. It features low-pitched roofs, wide eave overhangs, and both symmetrical and asymmetrical front façades.

beaded board: simple ornamented board, with a smooth, flat surface alternating with a half-round, rod-like carving (bead) running the length of the board. Common wainscoting or panelling in Victorian-era homes.

carpenter Gothic: *see* country, folk Victorian.

chinoiserie: imitation of Chinese decorative motifs; i.e., simulated Oriental lacquer covering pine or maple furniture. See also Chinese Chippendale below.

Chippendale: named for English furniture designer, Thomas Chippendale, of the Queen Anne period (1750–1790); the style varies from the Queen Anne style in ornamentation, with more angular shapes and heavier carving of shells, leaves, scrolls. Chinese Chippendale furniture employs chiefly straight lines, bamboo turnings, and as decoration, fluting, and fretwork in a variety of lattice patterns.

Colonial Revival: building style (1880–1955) featuring a classic box design with a dominant front door elaborated with pilasters and either a pediment (Georgian-style) or a fanlight (Adam-style); double-hung windows symmetrically balanced.

corbel: an architectural member that projects from a wall to support a weight and is stepped outward and upward from the vertical surface.

Corinthian: column popular in Greek Revival style for support of porch roofs; the capitals are shaped like inverted bells and decorated with acanthus leaves.

cornice: projecting horizontal carving or molding that crowns a wall or roof.

country, folk Victorian: simple house form (1870–1910) with accents of Victorian (usually Queen Anne or Italianate) design in porch spindlework and cornice details. Also known as carpenter Gothic.

Craftsman: building style (1905–1930) with low-pitched, gabled roof and wide, unenclosed eave overhang; decorative beams or braces added under gables; usually one-story; porches supported by tapered square columns.

dentil: exterior or interior molding characterized by a series of small rectangular blocks projecting like teeth.

dependencies: buildings that are subordinate to the main dwelling; i.e., a detached garage or barn. *See* also garçonniere.

Doric: column popular in Greek Revival style for support of porch roofs; the simplest of the three styles, with a fluted column, no base, and a square capital.

Eastlake: architectural detail on Victorian houses, commonly referred to as "gingerbread." Typically has lacy spandrels and knob-like beads, in exterior and interior design, patterned after the style of Charles Eastlake, an English furniture designer. Eastlake also promoted Gothic and Jacobean Revival styles with their strong rectangular lines; quality workmanship instead of machine manufacture; and the use of varnished oak, glazed tiles, and unharmonized color.

Eclectic movement: architectural tradition (1880–1940) which emphasized relatively pure copies of Early American, Mediterranean, or Native American homes.

eyebrow dormer: a semi-circular, narrow window over which the adjoining roofing flows in a continuous wave line; found on Shingle or Richardsonian Romanesque buildings.

faux: literally, French for "false." Refers commonly to woodwork painted to look like marble or another stone.

Federal: *See* Adam.

Franklin stove: metal heating stove which is set out into the room to conserve heat and better distribute it. Named after its inventor Benjamin Franklin; some designs resemble a fireplace when their front doors are open.

four-poster bed: variation on a tester bed but one in which the tall corner posts, of equal height, do not support a canopy. Carving of rice sheaves was a popular design in the Southern states, and signified prosperity.

gambrel roof: a two-slope, barn-style roof, with a lower steeper slope and a flatter upper one.

garçonniere: found on antebellum estates; a dependency housing unmarried male guests and family members.

Georgian: building style (1700–1830) featuring a classic box design with a dominant front door elaborated with pilasters and a pediment, usually with a row of small panes of glass beneath the crown or in a transom; cornices with decorative moldings, usually dentil.

Gothic Revival: building style (1840–1880) with a steeply pitched roof, steep gables with decorated vergeboards, and one-story porch supported by flattened Gothic arches. Windows commonly have pointed-arch shape.

Greek Revival: building style (1825–1860) having a gabled or hipped roof of low pitch; cornice line of main and porch roofs emphasized by a wide band of trim; porches supported by prominent columns (usually Doric).

half-tester bed: a bed with a low footboard and a canopy projecting from the posts at the head of the bed. Pronounced "half tee'stir."

Ionic: column popular in Greek Revival style for support of porch roofs; the caps of the column resemble the rolled ends of a scroll.

Italianate: building style (1840–1885) with two or three stories and a low-pitched roof with widely overhanging eaves supported by decorative brackets; tall, narrow windows arched or curved above with elaborate crowns. Many have a square cupola or tower.

keeping room: in a Colonial-era home, the equivalent of a modern family room; it was usually warm from proximity to kitchen, so infants and the ill were "kept" here.

kiva: stuccoed, corner beehive-shaped fireplace common in adobe homes in Southwestern U.S.

latillas: ceiling of unpeeled, rough sticks, supported by vigas (rough beams); seen in flat-roofed adobe homes.

Lincrusta (or Lincrusta-Walton): an embossed, linoleum-like wallcovering made with linseed oil, developed in 1877 in England by Frederick Walton.

lintel: horizontal beam, supported at both ends, that spans an opening.

mansard roof: having two slopes on all sides with the lower slope steeper than the upper one.

Mission: building style (1890–1920) with Spanish mission-style parapet; commonly with red tile roof, overhanging, open eaves, and smooth stucco finish. In furniture, the Mission style is best represented by the work of designer Gustav Stickley. Using machine manufacture, he utilized simple, rectangular lines and favored quarter-sawn white oak for the rich texture of the graining.

Palladian window: typically a central window with an arched or semicircular head.

Pueblo Revival: building style (1910 to present) with flat roof, parapet above; corners and edges blunted or rounded; projecting vigas, stepped back roof lines, and irregular stucco wall surfaces. Influenced by the flat-roofed Spanish Colonial buildings and Native American pueblos; popular in Arizona and New Mexico; common in Santa Fe and Albuquerque.

Pewabic (tile): glazed tiles made in the Detroit, Michigan, area, in the first half of the 1890s, whose unique manufacturing process has been lost.

pocket doors: doors that open by sliding into a recess (pocket) in the wall.

portal (or portale): in Spanish-style homes, the long, narrow porch that opens onto an internal courtyard; it functions as a sheltered passageway between rooms.

post and beam: building style based on the Medieval post-and-girder method, where upper loads are supported by heavy corner posts and cross timbers. In contemporary construction, the posts and beams are often left exposed on the interior.

Prairie: building style (1900–1920) with low-pitched roof and widely overhanging eaves; two stories with one-story wings or porches; façade detailing that emphasizes horizontal lines; massive, square porch supports.

Queen Anne: building style (1880–1910) with a steeply pitched roof of irregular shapes; an asymmetrical façade with one-story porch; patterned shingles, bay windows, single tower. In furniture design the Queen Anne style was prevalent from 1725 to 1750, characterized by a graceful, unadorned curve of the leg (known as cabriole) and repeated curve of the top crest and vase-form back (splat) of a chair.

quoin: wood, stone, or brick materials that form the exterior corner of a building and are distinguishable from the background surface because of texture, color, size, or material.

rice-carved bed: *See* four-poster bed.

Richardsonian Romanesque: building style (1880–1900) with massive masonry walls of rough, squared stonework and round-topped arches over windows, porch supports, or entrances; round tower with conical roof common.

Second Empire: building style (1855–1885) with mansard roof adorned with dormer windows on lower slope; molded cornices above and below lower roof, and decorative brackets beneath eaves.

Shaker: style of furniture which represents the Shaker belief in simplicity. The finely crafted pieces are functional, without ornamentation. Chairs have ladder backs, rush seats, and simple turned legs; tables and cabinets are angular, with smooth surfaces.

Sheraton: named for English furniture designer, Thomas Sheraton, of the Federal period (early 1800s); style marked by straight lines, delicate proportions, wood inlays, and spare use of carving; characteristically tapered legs.

Shingle: building style (1880–1900) with walls and roofing of continuous wood shingles; no decorative detailing at doors, windows, corners, or roof overhang. Irregular, steeply pitched roof line and extensive porches common.

shotgun: simple 19th century house form suited to narrow urban lots, featuring a single-story, front gable building one room wide. Rooms and doorways are in a direct line, front to back; theoretically, a bullet fired through the front door would travel through the house unobstructed.

spandrel: decorative trim that fits the top corners of doorways, porches, or gables; usually triangular in shape.

Santa Fe: *see* Pueblo Revival.

Spanish Colonial: building style (1600–1900) of thick masonry walls, with low pitched or flat roof, interior wooden shutters covering small window openings, and multiple doorways. Pitched roof style often has half-cylindrical tiles; flat style has massive horizontal beams embedded in walls to support heavy roof of earth or mortar. Internal courtyards or cantilevered second-story porches are common.

Stick: building style (1860–1890) with a steeply pitched, gabled roof, usually with decorative trusses at apex; shingle or board walls interrupted by patterns of boards (stickwork) raised from the surface for emphasis.

Territorial: a variation of the Spanish Colonial building style found in New Mexico, western Texas, and Arizona. The flat roof and single story are topped by a protective layer of fired brick to form a decorative crown.

tester bed: a bed with a full canopy (the tester), supported at all four corners by tall posts. Pronounced "tee'stir."

transom: usually refers to a window placed above a doorway.

trompe l'oeil: literally, French for "to trick the eye." Commonly refers to wall paintings that create an optical illusion.

Tudor: building style (1890–1940) with steeply pitched roof, usually cross-gabled; decorative half-timbering; tall, narrow, multi-paned windows; massive chimney crowned with decorative chimney pots.

vergeboard: decorative trim extending from the roof overhang of Tudor, Gothic Revival, or Queen Anne-style houses.

vernacular: style of architecture employing the commonest forms, materials, and decorations of a period or place.

viga(s): exposed (interior) and projecting (exterior) rough-hewn wooden roof beams common in adobe homes in Southwestern U.S.

wainscoting: most commonly, narrow wood paneling found on the lower half of a room's walls.

widow's walk: a railed observation platform built above the roof of a coastal house to permit unobstructed views of the sea. Name derives from the fate of many wives who paced the platform waiting for the return of their husbands from months (or years) at sea. Also called a "captain's walk."

Windsor: style of simple chair, with spindle back, turned legs, and usually a saddle seat. Considered a "country" design, it was popular in 18th and early 19th century towns and rural areas.

For more information:

A Field Guide to American Houses (Virginia and Lee McAlester, New York: Alfred A. Knopf, 1984; $19.95, paperback) was an invaluable source in preparing this glossary, and is highly recommended. Its 525 pages are lavishly illustrated with photographs and diagrams.

Clues to American Architecture (Marilyn W. Klein and David P. Fogle, Washington, D.C.: Starrhill Press, 1985; $7.95, paperback) is a handy, affordable 64-page pocket guide to over 30 architectural styles, from the Colonial period to contemporary construction. Each is clearly described in easy-to-understand language, and illustrated with numerous detailed sketches. Also in the same style and format is *Clues to American Furniture* (Jean Taylor Federico, Washington, D.C.: Starrhill Press, 1988; $7.95), covering design styles from Pilgrim to Chippendale, Eastlake to Art Deco. If your bookstore doesn't stock these titles, contact Starrhill directly at P.O. Box 32342, Washington, D.C. 20007; 202–387–9805.

Regional itineraries

Contributing editor Suzanne Carmichael has prepared these delightful itineraries to lead you from the best-known towns and cities through beautiful countryside, over less-traveled scenic highways to delightful towns and villages, to places where sights both natural and historic outnumber the modern "attractions" which so often litter the contemporary landscape.

To get a rough idea of where each itinerary will lead you, take a look at the appropriate map at the back of this book. But to really see where you'll be heading, pull out a detailed full-size map or road atlas, and use a highlighter to chart your path. (If you're hopeless when it comes to reading maps, ask the AAA to help you plan the trip with one of their Triptiks.) Some of our routes are circular, others are meant to be followed from one end to another; some are fairly short, others cover hundreds of miles. They can be traveled in either direction, or for just a section of the suggested route. You can sample an itinerary for a weekend, a week, or even two, depending on your travel style and the time available. For information on what to see and do along the way, refer to our state and local introductions, and to a good regional guidebook. For a list of places to stay en route, see the list of towns at the end of each itinerary, then refer to the entries in the state chapters for full details.

Ocean Auto Cruise: Cruise back roads cooled by sea breezes, loll on ocean beaches, and explore both historic southern towns and barrier islands along the South's prettiest stretch of ocean. Begin in gracious Charleston, South Carolina, where pastel houses peek out from behind lacy iron gates and horse-drawn carriages clomp by on cobblestoned streets. Visit revolutionary era and 19th-century homes, stroll the walkways at Charles Towne Landing park, and peruse items for sale at City Market (especially the Gullah Blacks' sweetgrass baskets).

Head south on Route 17 to South Carolina's Low Country and resort islands, with a stop in historic Georgetown. Pause in Beaufort, where Spanish explorers arrived 100 years before the Pilgrims landed at Plymouth Rock. Absorb the town's 18th century atmosphere as you walk past palmetto trees and moss-covered oaks. Before turning south, take Route 21 to Hunting Island State Park, where you can climb to the top of a 140-foot lighthouse for superb island, ocean, and mainland views.

Continue south on Route 170 to Route 17 and the Georgia border, detouring if you wish on Route 278 to Hilton Head Island, the largest sea island between New Jersey and Florida and a popular, though crowded, resort area. Savannah welcomes you to Georgia. A town of public squares (21 of them) with the country's largest urban historic district, Savannah was founded in 1733 as the seat of our 13th colony.

Route 17 now meanders slowly south through sleepy villages, across river channels and towards the area's famous Sea Islands. Turn east from Victorian Brunswick to visit Saint Simons Island, a vacation center with lush resorts and sophisticated shops. Or continue south, then turn east on Route 50 to Jekyll Island where you can "hyde" away on golden beaches or bicycle through stands of stately palms. Another detour, just north of the Florida border, is to take Route 40 to St. Marys where you can ferry to Cumberland Island National Seashore to glimpse wild horses, collect shells, and swim on pristine beaches.

It's time to explore northeastern Florida. To maintain your vacation mentality, leave Route 17 and skirt north of urban Jacksonville by turning east at Yulee on Route 200, to Route A1A which runs south along barrier beaches for 105 miles. Turn north first to Fernandina Beach, famous for its Victorian architecture and infamous as an early 19th-century haven for pirates and smugglers. South on Route A1A is Amelia

Island, the only area in the U.S. to have been governed under eight different flags.

Follow Route A1A to St. Augustine, the end of your ocean auto cruise. A center of Spanish influence since 1513, St. Augustine is the oldest U.S. city. Be sure to visit the restored Spanish quarter, as well as Castillo de San Marcos, a rock fortress made from coquina, a local limestone of shells and coral.

Appalachian Highland Routes: North Carolina's Highland area is known for its beauty: ancient weathered and rounded mountains, gentle pastures, waterfalls and tumbling trout-filled streams, hillsides vivid with wild flowers. Equally enduring are the legacies of the Cherokee Indians and the craft traditions of the area's Appalachian residents. We suggest both a northern and a southern loop route, both starting in Asheville.

Before setting off on either journey, pause in Asheville to visit the impressive Biltmore Estate, with its gardens and winery. Start your northern journey by following I-40 and Route 70 onto the Blue Ridge Parkway, a 470-mile road tracing mountain ridges north to Virginia. Numerous overlooks and attractions dot the parkway. Look particularly for The Folk Art Center (Milepost 382; ½ mile north of Route 70) which offers an excellent introduction to regional crafts, and Craggy Gardens (Milepost 364.6, 17 miles northeast of Asheville), which are spectacular in spring.

Take short detours from the parkway to see the double waterfalls at Linville Falls, and Blowing Rock's unusual rock formation. Leave the parkway at Route 16 to head northwest through Glendale Springs, then turn south on Routes 221 and 194. Wind through small Appalachian hamlets such as Banner Elk, continuing south on Route 19E. Pass through Spruce Pine, then take a short detour north to Penland, home of the famous Penland School of Crafts and its impressive gallery. Return to Route 19E, continuing past Burnsville to Mars Hill. Follow Route 213, then Route 251 back to Asheville (or drop south from Mars Hill on Route 19 for a high-speed return to the city).

Begin your southern loop in Asheville by heading west on Route 19 through the picturesque Great Smoky Mountain foothills and small towns such as Clyde. Detour several miles south to Waynesville for a peek at the Museum of North Carolina Handicrafts, then return to Route 19. Continue to Cherokee, home of the eastern branch of the Cherokee tribe. Just north, on Route 441, visit Oconaluftee Indian Village, a reconstructed 1750 Cherokee town where residents create top-notch crafts (available for purchase at Qualla Arts & Crafts, next door).

From here you may want to detour south on Route 441 along the Tuckasegee River to Dillsboro, and Sylva (note the architecture of the county courthouse). Return to (or continue on) Route 19 through Bryson City, at the southern edge of the Great Smoky Mountains National Park. Just past Lauada, turn north on Route 28 to Robbinsville, on the shore of Lake Santeetlah, near excellent white-water rafting on the Naantahala River. From here follow Route 129 south, turning (south again) on Route 141 to Brasstown, home of the John C. Campbell Folk School, best known for its stable of talented woodcarvers.

Go north from Brasstown to Route 64 and head east. You'll pass through scenic countryside and, just before Highlands, near five waterfalls in the Cullasaja River Gorge. Farther along, Cashiers and Lake Toxaway are popular resort areas. Continue north passing through Brevard, known as "Land of the Waterfalls." Follow Route 280 which runs alongside the southern boundary of the Pisgah National Forest back to Asheville.

Lower Mississippi River Route: Bustling river cities and small, languid towns, Confederate and Acadian-French historical sites, plantation mansions and sugarcane fields all vie for travelers' attention along the lower Mississippi River. Our route takes you from Jackson, Mississippi, to New Orleans through a variety of settings. Plan to spend three to five days on this route, leaving yourself plenty of time to enjoy New Orleans too.

Begin in Jackson, the state's capital, where you can see Confederate trenches in Battlefield Park, and visit Mynelle Gardens botanical park. Head west on Route 20, a superhighway that will whisk you to Vicksburg and your first glimpse of the mighty Mississippi. Known for its Civil War sites, Vicksburg also has several plantation mansions open to the public.

Turn south on Route 27 to the Natchez Trace Parkway, which stretches 500 miles from Natchez to Nashville, Tennessee. Originally a footpath used by rivermen to "trace" their way back north after taking goods down river, today the two-lane road passes green fields, forests, huge rhododendrons, and flocks of wild turkeys. Take the parkway south to Natchez, stopping to see Port Gibson's historic homes. Overnight in Natchez, and tour plantation homes, Natchez-Under-the-Hill, and the Grand Village of the Natchez Indians.

Head south on Route 61, driving past pecan orchards and oak trees dripping with Spanish moss. Make your first Louisiana overnight in St. Francisville to see Rosedown Plantation, then take a short detour up Route 965 to the Audubon State Commemorative Area. Leave St. Francisville via Route 10 south continuing to the river's edge. Board a small car ferry here to cross the Mississippi, then follow Route 10 to Route 415 which winds behind river dikes, through sugarcane fields and rice paddies, and past signs advertising "fried pig tails."

Turn east on Route 190, following it through Baton Rouge, then picking up Route 30 south of the Old State Capitol. Turn south on Route 75 which follows the river's oxbow turns. At Carville head again to river's edge and another car ferry which will take you across the Mississippi to White Castle. From here scenic Route 1 travels along Bayou Lafourche past Napoleonville to Thibodaux in the heart of Louisiana's "sugar belt."

Take Route 24 south to Houma, a historic Cajun city laced by seven bayous and more than 50 bridges. Walk through the local historic district, embark on a boat tour of nearby bayous and swamps, or stroll by the Intercoastal Waterway which begins south of Tallahassee, Florida, and stretches to Brownsville, Texas. Before heading to New Orleans on Route 90, an optional detour (128 miles round-trip) is for those who like to "go to the end of the road." Take Route 1 south as it parallels Bayou Lafourche and ends at Grand Isle State Park on the Gulf of Mexico, near the entrance to Barataria Bay.

Criteria for entries

Unlike many other guides, inns cannot pay to be listed in this book. All selections are made by the editors, based on guest recommendations and personal visits. Entries are written and compiled by the editors, not the inns. When we update a regional guide, inns that received full entries in the previous edition, and that will also appear in the new edition are charged a processing fee to help defray our research costs. There is no fee for new entries, and no fee for listing in our *U.S.A & Canada* edition. If we receive significant complaints or insufficient recommendations about a particular property, we omit their listing. As always, what matters most to us is the feedback we get from you, our readers.

About our Name

We've changed our name from *America's Wonderful Little Hotels & Inns* to *America's Favorite Inns, B&Bs, & Small Hotels*. Why? First, we felt that it better reflects what we're all about. Properties listed here are *your* favorites—if you don't like them, we don't include them. Since the majority of our entries are inns and B&Bs, the new title better reflects their importance. Last but not least, reasons connected with the copyright were also a factor.

Free Copy of INNroads Newsletter

Want to stay up-to-date on our latest finds? Send a business-size, self-addressed, stamped envelope with 55 cents postage and we'll send you the latest issue, *free!* While you're at it, why not enclose a report on any inns you've recently visited? Use the forms at the back of the book or your own stationery.

Key to Abbreviations and Symbols

For complete information and explanations, please see the Introduction.

¢ Especially good value for overnight accommodation.
Families welcome. Most (but not all) have cribs, baby-sitting, games, play equipment, and reduced rates for children.
Meals served to public; reservations recommended or required.
Tennis court and swimming pool and/or lake on grounds. Golf usually on grounds or nearby.
Limited or full wheelchair access; call for details.
Rates: Range from least expensive room in low season to most expensive room in peak season.
Room only: No meals included; European Plan (EP).
B&B: Bed and breakfast; includes breakfast, sometimes afternoon/evening refreshment.
MAP: Modified American Plan; includes breakfast and dinner.
Full board: Three meals daily.
Alc lunch: A la carte lunch; average price of entree plus nonalcoholic drink, tax, tip.
Alc dinner: Average price of three-course dinner, including half bottle of house wine, tax, tip.
Prix fixe dinner: Three- to five-course set dinner, excluding wine, tax, tip unless otherwise noted.
Extras: Noted if available. Always confirm in advance. Pets are not permitted unless specified; if you are allergic, ask for details; *most innkeepers have pets.*

We Want to Hear from You!

As you know, this book is effective only with your help. We really need to know about your experiences and discoveries. If you stayed at an inn or hotel listed here, we want to know how it was. Did it live up to our description? Exceed it? Was it what you expected? Did you like it? Were you disappointed? Delighted? Have you discovered new establishments that we should add to the next edition?

Tear out one of the report forms at the back of this book (or use your own stationery if you prefer) and write today. *Even if you write only "Fully endorse existing entry" you will have been most helpful.*

Thank You!

Alabama

The Victoria, Anniston

There's much to see and do in Alabama, from Huntsville's Alabama Space and Rocket Center to historic Mobile, and the gorgeous gardens at Bellingrath. To sample Gulf Coast beaches, drive south from Mobile to Dauphin Island, a scenic sliver of land where you can rent boats, swim, and watch huge ships enter Mobile Bay. In northern Alabama visit Russell Cave National Monument, an enormous limestone cave that was used as a seasonal shelter by people beginning in 6500 B.C. Birmingham, a major commercial center, is also known for the unusual "geologic walkway" carved into a mountain at Red Mountain Museum.

If you'd really like an in-depth look at Alabama's B&Bs, pick up a copy of *And to Y'all a Good Night* (Seacoast Publishing, P.O. Box 26492, Birmingham AL 35226; $8 plus $1.50 p/h) written by frequent contributor Lynn Edge. Lynn describes dozens of B&Bs, along with recipes for their breakfast favorites.

ALEXANDER CITY

Also recommended: Built by the founder of the town's first bank, **Mistletoe Bough** (497 Hillabee Street, 35010; 205–329–3717) is an imposing Queen Anne Victorian mansion, complete with stained glass windows, a grand staircase, original oak and pine woodwork, and brass chandeliers. The inn sits on over an acre, studded with azaleas, camellias, gardenias, fruit, pecan, and magnolia trees. B&B double rates for the four guest rooms range from $70–90, and include welcoming refreshments and a full breakfast. "Beautifully restored by Jean and Carlise Payne. Delightful hosts, delicious breakfasts." *(Lynn Edge)* Alexander City is located in east central Alabama, approximately 45 miles from Auburn and Montgomery.

ALICEVILLE

Information please: A quiet village in western Alambama, about 45 miles west of Tuscaloosa, Aliceville was the site of a German POW Camp during World War II. The Edwardian-style **Willowbrooke** (501 Broad Street 35442; 205–373–6133) was built in 1911, with beautifully restored woodwork and antique furnishings. B&B rates for the three guest rooms are $50–60, including a generous continental breakfast. Guests are welcome to relax in the hot tub, or take a bicycle out for a spin.

ANNISTON

Textile mills and blast furnaces were built in Anniston after the Civil War to help the region recuperate from the ravages of war. Today it's better known as the home of Fort McClellan; although the fort's Chemical Corps Training Command is off-limits to civilians, those intrigued by peculiar museums can make an appointment to visit the Chemical Corps Museum, tracing the history of chemical warfare. More appealing is Anniston's Museum of Natural History, best known for its bird collection (but the kids will prefer the Egyptian mummies). Anniston is located in northeastern Alabama, one hour's drive east of Birmingham via I-20, and about two hours west of Atlanta, Georgia.

The Victoria ¢ 🚶 ✕ — *Tel:* 205–236–0503
1604 Quintard Avenue, P.O. Box 2213, 36202 — 800–260–8781
Fax: 205–236–1138

Built in 1888 and listed on the National Register of Historic Places, The Victoria wears its name well, with a three-story turret, beautiful stained and etched glass windows, a conservatory, and colonnaded verandas. Restored in 1985 and expanded in 1996, the inn consists of the original building, housing a restaurant and three suites, plus two hotel wings which wraps around the courtyard and swimming pool. Breakfast includes bagels, English muffins, home-baked breads, eggs on request, cereals, fresh fruit and juice; a complete Southern breakfast is served on weekends. Lunch favorites include chicken with dumplings, fettucini with shrimp, or salmon salad on croissant. Among the dinner entrees are crab cakes with wild rice, grilled veal with garlic mashed potatoes, and beef tenderloin with blue cheese crust.

"Though bordered by busy commercial streets, the hilltop setting surrounded by trees and well-kept flower beds insulates it from traffic noise. Our room in the annex had a king-size bed with a brass headboard, complemented by white wicker furniture—a chaise longue, glass-topped table and several chairs." *(Jeanne Smith)* "Best public restaurant in the area, with outstanding soups. Also on the property is a century-old carriage house, restored as a lovely art gallery called the Wren's Nest, emphasizing artwork by well-known local wildlife artist

Larry Martin." *(Carol Flaherty)* "Impeccable service, from the valet parking to the attentive waiters in the lovely restaurant, to the pub-style bar with working fireplace." *(Debbie Trueblood)* "Delightful food, service, accommodations. *(Stanley Krawiec)*

Open All year. Restaurant closed Sun.
Rooms 1 cottage, 3 suites in main house, 56 doubles in annex. All with private bath, telephone, TV, air-conditioning.
Facilities Restaurant, bar/lounge, swimming pool, art gallery, valet parking.
Location 60 m E of Birmingham. From I-20, take Exit 185 (Oxford/Anniston); go 4 m N on Quintard (Hwy. 21/431) to inn. Make a U-turn at 17th St. & enter from Quintard.
Credit cards Amex, CB, DC, Discover, MC, Visa.
Rates B&B, $129–299 suite, $74 double, $64 single. Extra person, $10. Children under 12 free. Alc lunch, $10–13; dinner, $25–35.

AUBURN

Information please: In eastern Alabama, between Montgomery and Columbus is the university town of Auburn, and **The Crenshaw Guest House** (371 North College Street, 36830; 334–821–1131). Built in 1890, this six guest room B&B is shaded by giant oak and pecan trees. B&B rates of $50–80 include a continental breakfast; each of the well-equipped rooms has a private bath, telephone with data port, television, and working desk; some have a kitchenette.

BIRMINGHAM

Information please: Built in 1914, the **Tutwiler** (Park Place at 21st Street North, 35203; 205–322–2100 or 800–HERITAGE) was restored in elegant and luxurious style, with antique reproduction furnishings created especially for the hotel. The hotel restaurant serves classic American cuisine in an environment meant to simulate that of a private club. Heritage Club rates include use of the Club Lounge, with free breakfast and evening hors d'oeuvres. "Just as wonderful on a return visit. Everything is beautifully maintained by a caring staff; courteous service by all. The restaurant continues to be one of the best in the South. Exceptional duck. Everything we tried from the large menu was excellent."*(HJB)* Double rates for the 148 guest rooms ranges from $145–155 double, $175–650 suite.

DECATUR

Hearts and Treasures B&B *Tel:* 205–353–9562
911 7th Avenue Southeast, 35601

Whether you're a business traveler looking for a safe and friendly haven, a snowbird in search of a place to stay en route to Florida, or weary Alabamian in search of pampering, consider Hearts and Treasures B&B, built in 1918, and restored as a B&B in 1991 by Lukie Pressley. Two guest rooms are available in the main house, with another three in the restored Victorian cottage. High ceilings and polished wood floors are graced by Lukie's lovely antiques and collectibles. Breakfast, served 8–9 A.M. at the dining room table, includes fresh fruit, home-baked muffins, breads, or biscuits, plus bacon, ham, or sausage, and oven-baked pancakes, casseroles, or omelets. A continental breakfast of fruit and muffins is also available midweek from 7–8:30 A.M.

"Relaxing setting, hospitable innkeeper, excellent breakfast. I felt like I was visiting my grandparents' home in the country." *(Kyle Pannell)* "The spacious, well-lit living room was a fine place to get some paperwork done. Ample supplies of soaps and toiletries in the bathroom." *(Robert Hardcastle)* "More than adequate storage space for clothing." *(Jim Syrdal)* "Mrs. Pressley is very knowledgeable about the historic area. Soft drinks, coffee, tea and cocoa are always available, and she even made us a tasty fruit cobbler as a special treat. Spotless throughout." *(Margaret Pennington)* "Lukie Pressley is a wonderful hostess who has furnished her home with many lovely antiques and collectibles." *(Janis Harrison-Hutchinson)* "Excellent restaurant and sightseeing suggestions." *(Candace King)* "Enjoyed relaxing in a rocking chair on the front porch, sipping an icy glass of lemonade." *(MW)* "Loved the hand-painting, and the peach French toast." *(Robert Sharkey)*

Open All year.
Rooms 5 doubles—3 with private shower and/or tub, 2 with private half-baths share whirlpool tub/shower. All with clock/radio, air-conditioning, ceiling fan. 4 with desk. 3 rooms in Victorian cottage. Telephone on request.
Facilities Dining room, living room with fireplace, family room; guest refrigerator, laundry; porches. Cottage with fireplace, TV/VCR. Off-street parking. 2 ½ blocks to Delano Park with tennis courts, swimming pool, walking trail. Point Mallard Park nearby for golf, wave pool, ice skating.
Location N central AL. 120 m S of Nashville, TN; 75 m N of Birmingham. 1 block off Hwy. 31; approx. 5 m off I-65. From Hwy. 31 N (6th Ave.,) turn right at 5th St., to inn on right.
Restrictions No smoking. Children over 9 preferred.
Credit cards MC, Visa.
Rates Room only, $65 double, $55 single. Extra person, $8. B&B, $72–75 double, $60–65 single. Extra person, $10. 10% senior, AAA discount. Corporate rate midweek, $55 single with continental breakfast. "No tipping necessary."
Extras Airport pickup, $10.

EUFAULA

Eufaula is located on the Chattahoochee River, at the Georgia border, about 50 miles south of Columbus, Georgia.

Reader tip: "Eufaula is an intriguing town with many gorgeous antebellum homes in Greek Revival, Italianate, and Victorian styles. Destruction was avoided during the Civil War, because news of the war's end reached Union troops before an attack was launched." *(Suzanne Carmichael)*

Also recommended: One of Alabama's finest B&Bs, **Kendall Manor Inn** (534 West Broad Street, 36027; 334–687–8847) was built in the 1860s by James Turner Kendall, and is listed on the National Register of Historic Places. Restored by Barbara and Timothy Lubsen in 1993, this Italianate-style home has sixteen-foot ceilings, gold leaf cornices, Italian marble fireplaces, and ruby-colored glass windows. An open porch wraps around three sides of the house with 52 carved supporting columns; the two-story home is topped by a belvedere (or cupola) which bears the names, dates, and comments of the five generations of Kendalls who lived here. The six guest rooms are furnished with antiques and Oriental rugs; most have four-poster queen or king-sized beds. The B&B double rates range from $89–109. "Comfortable common rooms with a handsome library. We stayed in the spacious, high-ceilinged Alabama room, with butter-yellow walls and wall-to-wall carpeting." *(Suzanne Carmichael)* "Tim and Barbara welcomed us with freshly baked cookies and hot chocolate. Evening turndown service with brownies left at our bedside was a thoughtful touch. Wonderful breakfast of scones with jams, French toast with fresh strawberries and syrup, country bacon, juice, and coffee." *(Kelly & Lane Atchley)* "Barbara knows everything about the history of her home and the area." *(Lynn Edge)*

EUTAW

Kirkwood ¢ 🚸 *Tel:* 205–372–9009
111 Kirkwood Drive, 35462

Construction of this antebellum plantation house was halted in 1860 by the Civil War. Although continuously occupied, the building was not completed until it was bought and restored by Mrs. R.A. Swayze in 1972. Now listed on the National Register of Historic Places, this American Greek Revival mansion has a roof supported by eight massive Ionic columns, two stories high. The rooftop cupola—built in 1860, removed in the 1900s, and rebuilt in 1973—can be reached from the third floor billiard room. Inside are Carrara marble mantels, Waterford crystal chandeliers, and windows with the original 9-over-9 with wavy glass. Furnished primarily with original antiques, the bedrooms have four-poster beds.

"Mary Swayze lives here with her daughter and granddaughter in a separate part of the house. They rarely spend time in the main part of the house, which made me feel like I was in this big plantation home alone. The two upstairs bedrooms share a huge, nicely decorated bath, although I didn't have to share. Breakfast was delicious and plentiful and included scrambled eggs, bacon, fried tomatoes, ham, and fresh orange juice. Homemade waffles on the second morning were a special treat. During the day I took a walking/driving tour of the town to see the many fascinating antebellum homes." *(Bill Novack)* "A most interesting home; delightful hostess." *(MR)*

Open All year.
Rooms 2 doubles share 1 bath. Both with radio, fan, fireplace, balcony.
Facilities Dining room, breakfast room, living room, family room with books, TV; guest laundry, screened porch. 8 acres with children's swing set, gardens, woods. Swimming pool, tennis nearby.
Location W AL, 32 m SW of Tuscaloosa, 100 m NW of Montgomery. From I-20/59, take Exit 40 (Hwy 14). Drive E 2½ m, turn left on Kirkwood Drive.
Restrictions No smoking.
Credit cards None accepted.
Rates B&B, $75 double, $38 single. Children's rate.
Extras Airport/station pickup. Pets by prior arrangement.

FAIRHOPE

Fairhope makes an ideal base for touring Mobile and the Alabama coast. It's a charming little town, with appealing shops, a lovely park and fishing pier on Mobile Bay, and several enjoyable restaurants. Within an easy drive are the sugar sands of the Gulf beaches, Fort Morgan and the ferry across the bay, and the dozens of factory outlet shops of Riviera Centre. Golf (five courses nearby), tennis, and horseback riding are all available as well.

Fairhope is located on the Eastern Shore of southern Alabama, 15 miles southeast of Mobile. Take I-10 E across Mobile Bay to Route 98 south. Follow 98 south for 8 miles, then turn right at sign for Fairhope/Point Clear, and follow road (Section Street) into Fairhope.

Reader tips: "Fairhope is a quiet residential community. The pier and cozy village streets are ideal for an evening stroll. Several sidewalk cafes offer dining under the stars." *(Joe Schmidt)* "A jewel of a town, with unusual shops and restaurants. At night the main streets twinkle with tiny white lights, and by day the flower beds and hanging baskets are equally lovely." *(Nancy McFadden)*

Information please: Although not a small hotel at over 300 rooms, we wanted to share some comments about the elegant old **Grand Hotel Resort and Golf Club** (Route 98, Point Clear 36564; 800–544–9933 or 800–228–9290) on the bay in nearby Point Clear, owned by Marriott since 1981. According to the hotel, Marriott has invested $10 million into renovations, including the refurbishing of all guest rooms. Double rates range from $114–249, with golf and tennis packages available. Facilities include several restaurants, two 18-hole golf courses, 8 tennis courts, swimming pool, boating, horseback riding, and children's programs. "Grounds are beautiful, with live oaks and magnolias everywhere. Public areas are lovely, with water views and vaulted ceilings." *(SHW)* "Our corner room had spectacular sunset and water views. The Boardwalk offers a mile-long walk between the water and beautiful homes; you can also rent a bike and take the two-mile path into town." *(Glen Lush)* Also: "Comfortable rooms, good facilities, big-hotel atmosphere." *(Rita Langel)* And: "I thought it needed re-doing and new young blood; lots of conferences." *(HC)*

Information please: Built in 1902, **The Guest House** (63 South Church Street, 36532; 334–928–6226 or 334–928–0720) enjoys a quiet but convenient location, just a short walk from Fairhope's lovely main street. The five lovely guest rooms are beautifully decorated with antiques, and the B&B double rate of $85 includes a breakfast of eggs and bacon or waffles, with fresh fruit and juice. "The Garden Room was very private, with a large bay window, a taupe and white color scheme, toile print wallpaper, and a black metal queen-size bed, and an antique wardrobe. Lovely gardens, too." *(MR)* Current reports welcome.

Bay Breeze Guest House/Church Street Inn ♿ ¢ *Tel:* 334–928–8976
742 South Mobile Street, 36533 *Fax:* 334–990–1493

As you might expect from its name, the Bay Breeze Guest House sits right on Mobile Bay, offering lovely water views from its common rooms, a beach to explore, and decks for fishing and crabbing. Owners Bill and Becky Jones welcome guests to their stucco home, built in the 1930s, now restored, remodeled, and enlarged. Furnished with family heirlooms and period antiques dating back five generations, the decor includes wicker, stained glass, hooked and Oriental rugs. Under the same ownership is the **Church Street Inn**, listed on the National Register of Historic Places, and offering three guest rooms ($85 double) with turn-of-the-century ambiance just steps from Fairhope's charming shops and galleries. A full breakfast is served at both properties, and includes fresh fruit and juice, plus such entrees as French toast or omelets and Southern-style apples.

About Bay Breeze: "Ideal for peace, quiet, and a charming waterfront location, with friendly hosts, cheerful common areas. The long dock is a focal point for many activities, including breakfast." *(Joe & Shelia Schmidt)* "Becky and Bill Jones make you feel like invited guests. The flower-filled yard has a winding entrance bordered with hundred of narcissus. Sunsets are notable, and can be viewed from the glassed-in sunroom. Little touches include miniature pralines at bedside, and fresh flowers in the rooms. Breakfast began with fresh fruit garnished with homemade sorbet, followed by perfect eggs Benedict." *(Nancy McFadden)* "Blooming camellias, azaleas, well-maintained gardens; food available to feed dozens of wild ducks. Plenty of good coffee, served promptly at breakfast." *(Patricia Waters)* "The beautiful Magnolia Room had white wicker furnishings with quilted cushions, and a comfortable bed with a lovely old quilt and a ruffled eyelet bedskirt. The bathroom was sparkling and tidy. The Joneses shared some pointers about good local restaurants while we enjoyed wine, toasted pecans, and a view of the bay at sunset." *(Fran Langley)* "Beautifully decorated with antiques, family heirlooms, quilts, and plants, enhanced by fragrant gardens, birdsong, and the bay waters lapping at the shore." *(Kenneth Blad)* "Good jogging route along the beach, pier, and city parks." *(Janet Wright)* "The comfortable Camellia room was large and sunny, with white wicker contemporary furnishings, a little TV, and a bathroom added to what had been two little closets. Becky took our hands and greeted us very warmly; she joined eagerly in our conversations at breakfast." *(SC)* "Becky and Bill are delightful hosts. Homey, comfortable rooms, highlighted by family antiques; wonderful food. Nothing does more to relieve stress than strolling through Becky's wonderful gardens to the pier, feeding the ducks and sea gulls and watching the world go by." *(Lynn Edge)* **About Church Street Inn:** "Beautiful antiques provided warmth, character and comfort. Coffee always available. Enjoyed the charming courtyard with a fountain and comfortable seating, and the front porch with wicker furniture. Delightful in-town location." *(Dr. Evelyn Laycock)* "Lovely innkeeper, Alayne; delightful food and conversation at breakfast. Different place settings each day. Best of all was the freezer stocked with Blue Bell Ice Cream, always available." *(Kelly Heath)*

Open All year.
Rooms 1 cottage suite with kitchenette, 3 doubles—all with full private bath and/or shower, clock, TV, air-conditioning, fan. 2 with telephone, radio, desk.
Facilities Dining room, sitting room with fireplace, piano; living room with books, family room with TV/VCR; sun porch, family kitchen. 3 acres with camellia, azalea gardens. On beach with private pier; fishing, crabbing.
Location To Bay Breeze: At 3rd light (Magnolia Ave.), turn right. Go 4 blocks, turn left on S. Mobile St. at Municipal Pier. Go approx. 1 m to inn on right. To Church St.: From U.S. Hwy. 98 exit right onto Scenic/Alt. Hwy. 98 at "Welcome to Fairhope" sign. At 4th light (Fairhope Ave.), go right. go 1 block & turn left on Church St. to inn on next corner.
Restrictions No smoking. Facilities for children very limited.
Credit cards Amex, MC, Visa.
Rates B&B, $100 suite, $95 double. Extra person, $10. Some weekend minimums.
Extras 1 cottage wheelchair accessible. Limited Spanish spoken.

FLORENCE

Also recommended: In the northwestern corner of Alabama is the **Wood Avenue Inn** (658 North Wood Avenue, 35630; 205–766–8441), an imposing Queen Anne mansion with octagonal and square towers, wraparound porch and fourteen-foot ceilings. Each of the five guest rooms has a private bath, and the B&B double rate of $60–90 includes a full breakfast. "Friendly, accommodating hosts; beautiful grounds with wisteria arbors and antique roses. Beautiful fresh floral bouquets in each room. Careful attention to detail; comfortably restored home with many collectibles. Lovely breakfast; charming, old-fashioned porch. Enjoyed the comfortable bed in the honeymoon suite. Florence is a lovely, clean town with interesting historic neighborhoods." *(MR)*

GULF SHORES

For an additional area inn, see **Orange Beach**.

Also recommended: Named for the dolphins that can be seen frolicking in the surf from this B&B's porches, the **Grey Dolphin** (5928 Beach Boulevard, Kiva Dunes, 36547; 334–540–7308) is an eclectic beach house, complete with stained glass windows, carved doors, antiques, and memorabilia. B&B double rates for the three guest rooms range from $105–125. "Beautifully decorated and immaculate, with ample common space. Our bedroom had a king-sized bed, private deck and stairs leading to a walkway to the beach. Great outdoor shower. Hospitable, accommodating owners Bob and Wanda Bell. Wanda enjoys preparing delicious breakfasts, as well as afternoon snacks; wonderful home-baked breads. They know the area well and give excellent directions to local attractions and restaurants." *(Lillie Galvin)*

GUNTERSVILLE

For additional area inns, see **Mentone** and **Pisgah.**

Lake Guntersville B&B ¢ *Tel:* 205–505–0133
2204 Scott Street, 35976 *Fax:* 205–505–0133

"They don't make 'em the way they used to," is a phrase that certainly could be applied to the construction of the Lake Guntersville B&B, built in 1910 by Alexander Hooper. Mr. Hooper owned a local brick factory, and built his house with double brick construction, using rock-hard solid cedar columns to support the double verandas that wrap around the house. Restored as an inn in 1992, this B&B was purchased by Carol Davis in 1995, who reports that "Guntersville is a lovely town, built on a peninsula within the Tennessee River valley. It's surrounded by Lake Guntersville, Alabama's largest lake, with 950 miles of shoreline, and framed by the foothills of the Appalachian mountains. The lake is ideal for all water sports, especially bass fishing. Also of interest in the area is outlet shopping in Boaz, and the Space Center in Huntsville." Breakfast is served at the dining room table or at individual tables on the veranda, at 7:30 A.M. weekdays, and 8:30 A.M. on weekends. Entrees include egg and cheese strata or perhaps European-style pancakes with fresh fruit, plus hot rolls, bacon, sausage, and breads.

"Comfortable and attractively decorated. Carol is an excellent host." *(James Martin)* "Relaxed on the lovely white wicker chairs on the veranda, looking out through the trees to the lake beyond. We missed our own cat, and were happy to meet Carol's cat, Sauci." *(MW)* "Historic setting, pampering atmosphere. Delicious food, lovely room, charming innkeeper." *(GR)* "Although the house itself is very spacious, even better are the wonderful porches, with views of the city and lake. Carol is delightful innkeeper; delicious European baked pancake for breakfast." *(Lynn Edge)*

Open All year.
Rooms 4 suites—1 with full private bath, 3 with maximum of 4 people sharing bath. All with radio, clock, TV, air-conditioning, balcony, private entrance. Some with telephone, desk, ceiling fan, refrigerator. 1 with kitchenette.
Facilities Dining room, living room, family room, library, wraparound verandas with hammock. ½ acre with off-street parking, lawn games. Lake for bass fishing, swimming, boating. Walking trail along lake; hiking nearby.
Location NE AL. 45 min. SE of Huntsville, 90 min. NE of Birmingham. 1 block to shops, restaurants; historic area. 1 block from Chamber of Commerce on right after bridge. From Hwy 431 S, take 2nd right onto Scott St. after crossing river bridge; from Hwy 431 N, 1.9 m after McDonald's, take left on Scott St. Go 2 blocks up hill to inn sign.
Restrictions No smoking. Prefer children over 16.
Credit cards MC, Visa.
Rates B&B, $70 double. 10% senior, AAA discount. Weekly, corporate rates. Spa, sailing, shopping packages.
Extras Limited wheelchair access. Marina pickups.

HUNTSVILLE

Located in north central Alabama, Huntsville is known as the birthplace of the United States space program, and a visit to the U.S. Space and Rocket Center is a must.

Information please: The Twickenham Historic District, close to Courthouse Square, is one of the state's largest antebellum residential districts. You can stay in the heart of this area at the **Stockton House** (310 Green Street, Southeast, 35801; 205–539–3195), owned by the Stockton family since 1945. You can relax on the wide porch of this brick Queen Anne home, built in 1910, or in the spacious living areas, complete with intricately carved paneling, Tiffany stained glass windows, plus family antiques and Oriental rugs. Two of the three guest rooms have a private bath, and the B&B double rates of $80–120 include a continental breakfast tray, brought to your room or served on the porch.

JEMISON

Jemison is roughly halfway between Birmingham and Montgomery, just off I-65.

Also recommended: For Southern hospitality in the heart of an old-fashioned small town, try the **Jemison Inn** (212 Highway 191, Jemison, 35085; 205–688–2055 or 800–438–3042). The three guest rooms are furnished with antiques and queen- or king-size beds, with fresh flowers and fruit to welcome you; the rates range from $65–85, including a full breakfast. Guests will enjoy the formal gardens and swimming pool. "Southern hospitality at its best. Incredible attention to detail in the decor; fabulous breakfasts. While owners Joe and Nancy Ruzickas have decorated with antiques, they've provided such modern luxuries as a swimming pool for guests' use and a guest room with a double whirlpool tub. Their gardens are incredible. Well worth a detour to this treat." *(Lynn Edge)*

LEESBURG

Also recommended: Offering a panoramic view of two states is **the secret—Bed & Breakfast Lodge** (2356 Highway 68 W, Rte. 1, Box 82, 35983–9732; 205–523–3825). Each of the four guest rooms have queen-size beds, private baths, TVs, and balconies; B&B double rates of $95–115 include a full breakfast. "Carl and Diane Cruickshank are charming hosts; the views are incredible. From their rooftop swimming pool, one can see cities in Georgia and Alabama, as well as Mount Cheaha, the highest point in Alabama, and Weiss Lake. Delicious breakfasts; twelve acres with resident deer and llamas add to the feel that you've really gotten away from it all." *(Lynn Edge)* This B&B is located in northeastern Alabama, about nine miles from I-59, and almost equidistant from Birmingham, Chattanooga, and Atlanta.

MARION

Information please: Surrounded by five acres of Victorian gardens, **Myrtle Hill** (303/305 West Lafayette Street, 36756; 334–683–9095) incorporates two restored antebellum homes, listed on the National Register of Historic Places, and furnished with 18th and 19th century antiques. B&B double rates for the six guest rooms (three with private bath) start at $65, including a full breakfast. Marion is located in central Alabama, 80 miles northwest of Montgomery.

MENTONE

For additional area inns, see **Guntersville** and **Pisgah.**

Reader tip: "The beautiful Little River Canyon is a hidden treasure unknown even to most native Alabamians." *(MR)*

Also recommended: In neighboring Valley Head is **Winston Place** (Route 117, P.O. Box 165, Valley Head 35989; 205–635–6381 or 888–4–WINSTON). B&B double rates for the five suites range from $85–200. "Renovated as a decorator's show house, so the interior is just the way you'd want it to be. Leslie Bunch is a delightful hostess and visiting husbands love to talk Alabama football with her Jim Bunch. Winston Place has been in Leslie's family for years and was the site where the Union soldiers gathered before the Battle of Chickamauga. Rich history and Leslie knows a lot about it." *(Lynn Edge)*

Information please: Set on Lookout Mountain in northeastern Alabama, **Mountain Laurel Inn** (East River Road, P.O. Box 443, 35984; 205–634–4673 or 800–889–4244) overlooks the Little River; a trail behind the inn leads to DeSoto Falls, a ten-minute walk. Accommodations are found in a separate guest home with four appealing guest rooms, and a small apartment, each with private bath, private entrance, and porch with rockers. The B&B double rate of $85–115 includes a full breakfast. "Located on Little River Canyon below DeSoto Falls, and next to Mentone's Wedding Chapel in the woods, is this lovely guest house, just down the path from the main house where innkeeper Sarah Wilcox lives." *(MR)*

MOBILE

For additional area accommodations, see **Fairhope. Information please:** In the downtown Leinkauf historic district is the **Portman House Inn** (1615 Government Street, 36604; 334–471–1703 or 800–471–1701), built in 1922 and restored as an inn in 1995. B&B double rates for the nine guest rooms range from $129–209, including a continental breakfast. All rooms have a private bath, telephone, and TV; some have a double Jaccuzzi tub, fireplace, and kitchenette. Additional amenities include on-site parking and a garden picnic area. "Marvelous Mediterranean Revival-style architecture; small European hotel ambiance; comfortable accommodations. Convenient location on tree-lined Government Street." *(William Wells)*

MONTGOMERY

State capital of Alabama, Montgomery also served as the first capital of the Confederacy; today it is equally renowned for its role in the Civil Rights movement. For evening entertainment, call 800–841–4273 for information on the Alabama Shakespeare Festival, which offers high quality repertory theater by the Bard as well as contemporary playwrights. Montgomery is located in central Alabama, 85 miles south of Birmingham, 160 miles north of Mobile.

Lattice Inn ¢ ♿
1414 South Hull Street, 36104

Tel: 334–832–9931
800–525–0652
Fax: 334–264–0075

Michael Pierce welcomes guests to the Lattice Inn, built in 1906, and restored as a B&B in 1993; he notes that he "strives to be attentive without intruding on guests' privacy."

"We were made to feel welcome from the first minute. Our wonderful room had a king-size bed with a good reading light on each side. Delicious breakfasts of smoked sausage with apple pancakes one day, turkey and tomato omelets the next. Michael and his nephew Richard were most helpful with tips and advice on restaurants, sights, and the excellent Shakespeare Theater. Our favorite dinner was at the Vintage Year restaurant, just five minutes away." *(Ian & Irene Fisher)* "Michael, the consummate host, accommodates dietary needs without sacrificing taste." *(David Clark)* "The parrot Rene, and the dogs, Alexandra and Katie, make wonderful, relaxing companions." *(Tina Wyatt)*

"Our favorite place to stay during the Alabama Shakespeare Festival. Exquisite yet comfortable furnishings, highlighted by the host's personal collections." *(MR)* "Delicious homemade cookies; beautiful, tasty fruit basket in our room. Michael willingly shares his recipes." *(Jane & Walter Little)* "A beautiful dining room and two living areas where guests can watch TV, read or chat. Ideal location, in a historic neighborhood three blocks from the Governor's Mansion, charming for jogging or walking. A large deck and swimming pool offer privacy and comfort in the shade of lovely hardwood trees. Breakfasts are a highlight, with a bowl of fresh-cut fruit (kiwi, raspberries, blackberries, and more), and an array of delicious homemade muffins." *(Joy Satterlee)*

"The neighborhood is quiet and unhurried, yet conveniently located for access to the interstates, downtown or suburbs. Michael is witty, urbane, erudite, and charming." *(David Clark)* "The rooms have high, beamed ceilings, four-poster beds, antiques, and an elegant country feel." *(Vicki Ford)* "Michael provided a bag of cookies for the ride home. Wonderful breakfast with fresh fruit, great coffee, eggs Benedict, and macadamia French toast." *(Laura Ward)* "Michael's rooms are immaculate, his breakfasts are superb. More than that, though, Michael is gracious host, determined to meet his guests' needs. He has earned the nickname 'The Cookie Man,' and leaves wonderful cookies in each room along with fresh fruit." *(Lynn Edge)*

Open All year.
Rooms 1 cottage, 4 doubles—all with full private bath, radio, clock, desk, air-conditioning, fan. 2 with telephone (on request), fireplace, deck; 1 with refrigerator, TV. Cottage with living room, kitchen.
Facilities Dining room, living room with fireplace, library with TV, fireplace; porch, decks. Gazebo, swimming pool, fish pond, patio, hot tub, off-street parking.
Location 1 m from downtown in historic garden district. Exit I-85 at Union St., & go W on service rd. to Hull. Go S on Hull to inn on right, between Maury & Earl.
Restrictions No smoking. Children welcome in cottage.
Credit cards Amex, MC, Visa, Discover.
Rates B&B, $65–85 cottage, double. Extra person, $5–10. 5% senior, AAA discount.
Extras Limited wheelchair access.

Red Bluff Cottage ¢ *Tel:* 334–264–0056
551 Clay Street, P.O. Box 1026, 36101 *Fax:* 334–262–3054

Anne and Mark Waldo built Red Bluff Cottage in 1987 to offer a base to those visiting the city for business or pleasure. Mark is a retired Episcopal minister, and together the Waldos have raised six children, making them old hands at extending Southern hospitality to family and friends. Situated in a neighborhood of 19th century cottages, and pre- and post-Civil War homes, the Waldos built their home in the traditional style of a raised cottage; the decor is highlighted by family antiques. The bedrooms are on the ground floor, and are furnished with queen or twin-size beds, while the common rooms are on the upper level. Breakfast is served in the dining room, or on the front porch overlooking the river plain; menus change daily, but might include fresh-squeezed orange juice, chili-cheese sausages, sausages, fresh-baked whole wheat bread, and bran muffins, or perhaps hot peach cobbler with vanilla ice cream and crisp bacon.

"Convenient location, close to many cultural events. The congenial atmosphere and stimulating breakfast table conversations will ensure our return."*(EC)* "Clean and comfortable; delicious breakfast." *(Cynthia Blakely)* "Well furnished with antiques and historical memorabilia." *(Mary Morgan)* "Gracious, kindly, warm owners. Lovely antiques, Oriental rugs, interesting books; ample common areas in which to relax." *(Margaret Powell)* "Atmosphere, cleanliness, location, and particularly, the friendliness of the owners are all first-rate." *(Daniel Reinker)*

Open All year.
Rooms 1 family suite, 3 doubles—all with private bath and/or shower, air-conditioning, fans. Some with desk.
Facilities Dining room, family room with fireplace, music room with harpsichord, porch. Off-street parking.
Location Central AL. From I-65, take Exit 172. Take Herron St. (downtown) 1 block to Hanrick. Go left 100 ft. Parking area on right.
Restrictions No smoking. Special arrangements for children under 8.
Credit cards MC, Visa.
Rates B&B, $75 suite, $65 double, $55 single.
Extras Crib. Airport pick-up by arrangement.

ORANGE BEACH

"The most beautiful beach in the USA," is how a long-time contributor describes Perdido Beach, and having seen its sugar-fine white sand and clear Gulf waters, we've placed it high on our list of favorites, too.

For an additional area B&B, see **Gulf Shores**.

The Original Romar House
23500 Perdido Beach Boulevard

Tel: 334–974–1625
800–48–ROMAR
Fax: 334–974–1163
E-mail: original@gulftel.com

If you're looking for a relaxing beachside getaway where you can let your hair down and put your feet up, where you can gently sway in a hammock, caressed by soft Gulf breezes, go directly to the Original Romar House. Built in 1924, the house takes its name from its first owner, Spurgeon Roach and his best friend, Carl Martin. The wood to build the house had to be brought in by water, since there were no roads; the lumber was floated down the beach, pulled by a mule team. Later, as the area was developed, Romar Beach took its name from the house. Jerry M. Gilbreath bought the house in 1980 and restored it as Alabama's first seaside inn in 1991; Darrell Finley has been the innkeeper since 1996.

The house is primarily decorated Art Deco style, but its eclectic charms include many stained glass windows, an 1800s tiger oak bar from a New Hampshire inn, and cypress doors and wainscotting from a turn-of-the century New Orleans home. Each of the guest rooms has a queen-size bed, and an original bedroom set from the 1920s. Breakfast, served 8:30–9:30 A.M., can be enjoyed at the dining room table, hand-crafted of heart pine by the original owner, or on the deck overlooking the beach. You might enjoy an egg casserole with sausage, ham, cheese grits, and hot biscuits one day, and peach pancakes, bacon, hash browns, and pastries the next. Complimentary wine and cheese is served at sunset in the Purple Parrot bar.

"Outstanding features: the location on the beach, the magnificent views, the delightful host, early morning coffee, the attention to detail, the way each guest room was decorated in honor of a local festival, and the privacy each room provided. A huge outlet mall is nearby for a rainy day." *(Frank Craig)* "Clean, comfy, and homey. We were given the run of the house, and felt comfortable and welcomed. Enjoyed the generous porch overlooking the Gulf and roomy common areas." *(Alan Schroeder)* "Excellent value; delicious breakfast prepared by Darrell." *(Gail Takara)* "Our cozy room, #4, had an excellent queen-size bed, unusual green lamps, and furnishings with delicate wood inlays and carvings. Beautiful woodwork and stained glass throughout the inn." *(Karl Wiegers & Chris Zambito)* "Hospitality and housekeeping excellent; convenient location. The manager was helpful in answering questions, making reservations, and providing directions." *(Jack Carroll)*

Open All year. Bar closed Sun.
Rooms 1 suite, 4 doubles, 1 single—all with private shower and/or tub, clock/radio, air-conditioning, ceiling fan. 2 with balcony. 1 cottage with kitchen, refrigerator, TV/VCR.
Facilities Dining room; living room with fireplace, TV; bar/lounge; deck/porches with hammock, swing; hot tub, courtyard with fountain; off-street parking. 6 golf courses within 5 miles, on beach for swimming, diving, sailing.
Location Gulf Coast. 35 m S of Mobile, 25 m W of Pensacola, FL. From I-10, go S on Highway 59. Turn left on Highway 182. Go 4.1 miles to inn.
Restrictions Smoking permitted only in bar, on decks. Children 12 & over.
Credit cards Amex, MC, Visa.
Rates B&B, $79–120 suite, double. Extra person, $15. 2-night weekend minimum.

PISGAH

For additional area inns, see **Guntersville** and **Mentone.**

The Lodge on Gorham's Bluff ✕
101 Gorham Drive, P.O. Box 160
Gorham's Bluff 35765

Tel: 205–451–3435
Fax: 205–451–7403

Buying an inn is no small matter; building one is a major undertaking. Now imagine developing a complete town! That's the daring vision that Bill McGriff and his daughter Dawn decided to pursue in 1992. Using the 186 acres of land they owned in the foothills of the Appalachian Mountains, the McGriffs hired architect Lloyd Vogt as a master planner. Starting in 1993 with a few houses, shops, a wedding pavilion, and a performance amphitheater, The Lodge at Gorham's Bluff opened in 1995. Cultural activities include a summer theater, story-telling, and chamber music festivals.

The Lodge is built Southern cottage style, with common areas and guest rooms opening to the first and second floor verandas which wrap around the white clapboard structure. Inside, the common area walls are done in cream-painted clapboard, with hardwood floors, enormous fieldstone fireplaces, Oriental rugs, and traditional furnishings with lots of soft, comfortable couches. The spacious guest rooms are no less lovely; most have queen- or king-size beds. The Woods Suite is done in soft reds and pale greens, with two double beds, and two overstuffed chairs before the lovely stone fireplace. The romantic Parton Suite has a pencil post canopy bed, Impressionist prints, and a Victorian wardrobe, with a mauve and soft floral color scheme. The Lodge on Gorham's Bluff is managed by Stan Hanby. Breakfast is served at 8:30A.M., and includes fresh fruit and juice, bacon, eggs or a casserole, grits, and biscuits.

"A five-star inn; an incredible find." *(Hillary Cheney)* "If Dorothy and Toto had been blown from Kansas to Gorham's Bluff instead of Oz, they couldn't have been more amazed than we were by this elegant, beautifully designed retreat, set on a high bluff overlooking the Tennessee River." *(MW)*

Open All year. Restaurant closed Mon.–Wed.
Rooms 2 suites, 4 doubles—all with full private bath with single or double whirlpool tub, telephone, clock, desk, air-conditioning, ceiling fan, working fireplace. 4 with balcony/deck. TV on request.
Facilities Living room with fireplace, dining room with fireplace, den with TV, guest kitchen/refrigerator, porches, decks. 180 acres with gazebo, lawn games, hiking trails, bicycling, fishing at West Lake. Overlooking Tennessee River for water sports.
Location NE AL. 1 hr. from Huntsville & Chattanooga, 2 hrs. from Altnata & Birmingham; 3 hrs. from Nashville. 3 m N of town. From Pisgah, follow Jackson Cty. Rte. 58 for 2.2 m. Turn left onto Cty. Rte. 357 & go 1.2 m. Go left onto Cty. Rte. 457. Follow for 7⁄10 mile & go right onto Main Street.
Restrictions No smoking. Children 12 and over.

Credit cards Amex, MC, Visa.
Rates B&B, $140–165 suite, $110–140 double. Extra person, $10.
Extras Wheelchair access to common areas, restaurant, public bathroom.

SELMA

Information please: Combining Greek Revival neoclassicism with Victorian trends, **Grace Hall** (506 Lauderdale Street, 36701; 334–875–5744) is listed on the National Register of Historic Places. B&B double rates for the six guest rooms, each with private bath, range from $79–125, including refreshments on arrival, a tour of the mansion, and a full breakfast. "Wonderful fountain and gardens to wander in, quiet setting, pets to make you feel at home, sumptuous linens on the four-poster bed, and French toast to die for!" *(Debbie Trueblood)* "Joey and Coy Dillon do a great job of making their guests feel welcome. Their B&B is in a wonderful, historic structure and they have made the most of the setting. My room was lovely and well equipped. Breakfast with the other guests was delightful." *(Lynn Edge)*

TALLADEGA

Information please: A Greek Revival plantation-style home, **Orangevale** (1400 Whiting Road, 35160; 205–362–3052) was built in 1852, and remains a working livestock and fruit farm. Guests are accommodated in three guest rooms in the main house, plus an additional four in the restored summer kitchen, smokehouse, well house, and a log cabin. The B&B double rate of $85–95 includes a full breakfast; guests can pick their own fruit in season.

A good choice for an in-town location may be **Somerset House B&B** (701 North Street East, 35160; 205–761–9251 or 800–701–6678), a fully renovated turn-of-the-century home with four guest rooms, each with private bath. The B&B double rate of $55–80 includes a full breakfast. "Innkeeper Rodger Adams was the perfect host, welcoming yet unobtrusive. Cold drinks were always available, as was area information. Tasty breakfasts, especially the biscuits. The second-floor veranda was lovely for relaxing. Our room was spacious and spotless, with television, ceiling fan, and gas fireplace. Ample off-street parking; convenient location in the historic Silk Stocking district." *(Kathleen Ransom)*

The Governor's House ¢

Embry Cross Road, Lincoln
Mailing address:
500 Meadowlake Lane, Talladega 35160

Tel: 205–763–2186
Fax: 205–362–2391

When people mention a "mobile home," they usually don't have an 1850 Greek Revival house in mind, but that's just what the Governor's House became for the short trip from downtown Talladega to its present location on Meadowlake Farm, overlooking Logan Martin Lake. Built by Alabama Governor Lewis Parsons, Mary Sue and Ralph Gaines moved the building onto their farm in 1990, restoring it as a B&B and furnishing it with family antiques and quilts. Guests enjoy watching the farm's horses, Hereford cattle, chicken, and pet goats, trying their luck at fishing in the bass-stocked pond, or going out for a patio boat ride on the lake. A typical breakfast might include fresh fruit and juice, eggs or a cheese soufflé, garlic grits, fresh-baked biscuits, and sweet rolls with homemade jellies and strawberry butter, plus bacon, ham, or sausage.

"Enjoyed meeting the gracious, hospitable, gentle Gaines family." *(Janice Baker Clarke)* "Rolling green meadows, lush foliage, split rail fences, grazing cattle, ripples on the lake, and wispy cotton-puff clouds are a welcome change from the city. Unwind with a glass of wine, seated on an antique wicker love seat on the veranda, accompanied by a gentle breeze, the chirping birds, an occasional lightning bug. We awoke to the sound of cows mooing and the song of a bobwhite." *(Jackie & Larry Pryor)* "Enjoyed morning walks along the winding road of the farm. Lovely roses at my bedside." *(Jamie Ison)* "Candles in every window welcome you 'home' at night; in the morning, you can watch a beautiful sunrise from the front porch swing." *(Sheri Knaebel)* "The breakfast table was appointed with the finest china, silverware, and appliqued or shadow-worked linens. Genuine Southern hospitality." *(Dr. Becky Thomasson)* "Juice and coffee are served on the veranda; a dinner bell summoned us to a wonderful country breakfast. The house is furnished with antiques, quilts, and family heirlooms." *(Judy Fairchild)*

"Lovely setting, on a knoll overlooking the lake, surrounded by rolling pastureland where cattle graze." *(Cheryl Stone)* "Squeaky clean; beautifully furnished. Guest refrigerator loaded with juices, cheese, breads, wine and soft drinks." *(Milly Cowles)* "We were welcomed with a just-baked pecan pie, and helped with dinner reservations. Around the house are framed newspaper clippings which explain the history of the farm, antique shop, and the house itself." *(Staci Valentine)*

Open All year.
Rooms 1 guest house, 3 doubles—1 with private shower bath, 2 with maximum of 4 sharing bath. All with radio, desk, air-conditioning, fan.
Facilities Dining room with fireplace, living room with electric fireplace, TV, books, porch with swing. 7-acre grounds with tennis court, antique shop; 157-acre farm. Lake adjacent to farm with boat ramp, fishing pier, swimming.
Location E central AL. 35 m E of Birmingham, 15 m W of Anniston, 105 m W of Atlanta, GA. 2 m from I-20. From I-20, take Exit 165, and go S 2 m on Embry Cross Rd. 6 m W of Alabama International Motor Speedway and Hall of Fame.
Restrictions No smoking. No children under 12.
Credit cards None accepted.
Rates B&B, $75–85. Corporate, family rates. Picnic baskets. Prix fixe lunch, $8; prix fixe dinner, $15.
Extras Airport/station pickups, $15.

Arkansas

The Heartstone Inn and Cottages, Eureka Springs

Rugged mountain individualism is one of the first things that comes to mind when Arkansas is mentioned. Although the Ozarks are a very old mountain chain and not terribly high, the terrain is rugged and transportation was, until quite recently, very difficult. Distinctive crafts, cuisine, and culture developed as a result, much of which has been preserved through the Ozark Folk Center, located in Mountain View (see listing). Many famous springs dot this region of northwestern Arkansas as well, particularly Hot Springs National Park, 55 miles southwest of Little Rock, and Eureka Springs, in the north.

If you want to add sparkle to your Arkansas trip, visit Crater of Diamonds State Park, southeast of Hot Springs—it's America's only public diamond-hunting field. Outdoor enthusiasts generally head to the state's rivers for white-water canoeing or a fight with a largemouth bass, while amateur spelunkers visit what experts call the greatest cave find of the 20th century, Blanchard Springs Caves near Mountain View.

Reader tip: "For Appalachian antiques and crafts, avoid the overpriced shops of Eureka Springs, and stop in Van Buren, near Fort Smith and I-40, at the Antique Warehouse and Mall; the shops in the restored downtown area are also worth a look." *(MA)*

CADDO GAP

River's Edge B&B 🚸 ♿ — *Tel:* 501–356–4864
Highway 8 & 240 West, HC 65 Box 5, 71935 — 800–756–4864

Come to River's Edge at Caddo Gap, named for the pass between the mountains, where you can hike beautiful mountain trails, canoe the peaceful river, enjoy any number of area activities, or just lay back and relax in one of the inviting hammocks "T" and Judy Cone have set out for their guests. A contemporary-style lodge built in 1980, River's Edge was restored as a B&B in 1994 by the Cones. Rates include "T's" hearty breakfasts of broiled grapefruit or a a fresh fruit plate, eggs Benedict or perhaps French toast, sausage and biscuits or homefries with gravy, plus juice and coffee, served 7–10 A.M. In good weather, Judy serves breakfast at individual tables on the deck.

"After a busy day, we enjoyed curling up by the fire in the cozy great room, with its two-story windows. Friendly, helpful innkeepers. Judy's collection of lovely antique mirrors can be found throughout the house." *(Mike & Rhonda Hicks)* "Judy's peach dessert was delicious. The Willie Nelson room is my favorite." *(Linda Majura)* "Favorite aspects of this B&B included the fresh flowers in my room; tea and cookies served on a tray on the lovely china; and the quiet places to sit and watch the river." *(Ginger Newmeyer)* "Creative breakfasts, different each day of a week-long stay." *(Peggy Whelan)* "The Victorian decor creates a romantic mood, with many paintings throughout the inn. The beautiful mountain hardwoods surrounding the inn lend it a rustic charm, and buffer sounds from the road. Well-maintained grounds, with many flowering plants and shrubs." *(Anne Lane)* "Biscuits with "T's" award-winning jams and jellies were a treat." *(Cheryl Giblin)* "Down-to-earth, helpful innkeepers. Beautiful rural area; great canoeing from the inn." *(Joe Gannon)* "Beautiful setting with the river, plus azaleas and dogwoods in bloom. Coffee and ice cream in the evening was a thoughtful touch. Magnificent hiking, with beautiful waterfalls in Ouachita National Forest, plus Lake Ouachita for all water sports." *(Kevin Overton)*

Open All year.
Rooms 1 cottage, 1 suite, 4 doubles—all with private bath and/or shower, clock/radio, air-conditioning, ceiling fan. 2 with fireplace, private entrance; 3 with balcony/deck, 1 with TV, kitchenette.
Facilities Dining room, living room with TV/VCR, stereo, books, fireplace; great room with fireplace, piano; guest refrigerator, laundry; deck. 3 acres on river with hammocks, fishing, swimming; canoe rental next door. Hiking, golf, lakes, horseback riding nearby.
Location E AR. 35 m SW of Hot Springs. 6 m N of Glenwood at intersection of Hwy 8 & 240 W.
Restrictions No smoking.
Credit cards MC, Visa.
Rates B&B, $85–125 suite, $85–110 double, $40–55 single. Extra person, $15; no charge under 6. Senior, AAA discount. $25 dinner.
Extras Limited wheelchair access. Crib.

EUREKA SPRINGS

Eureka Springs is the site of natural springs first discovered by the Indians, then lost for decades until rediscovered in the 1850s by a local doctor. The curative powers of the spring waters soon became renowned, and by the 1880s this hillside town boasted dozens of hotels. As the decades passed and medicine advanced, the town was forgotten and its Victorian charms thus preserved. The local Historic District Commission now stands guard to make sure that nothing is changed without its approval.

Local attractions include dozens of art galleries and mountain craft shops, the steam train ride through the Ozarks, the Passion Play, and the Pine Mountain Jamboree. Beaver Lake and the Buffalo and White rivers are nearby for swimming, boating, fishing, and canoeing.

Eureka Springs is located in northwest Arkansas, 50 miles northeast of Fayetteville, 200 miles northwest of Little Rock. From Missouri, it's approximately 100 miles south of Springfield, and 50 miles southwest of Branson. It is best reached via Highways 62 or 23.

Reader tip: "Parking on Eureka Springs' narrow, hilly streets ranges from difficult to impossible. Once you have found a space on the street or at your inn, leave your car and get around on the convenient trolley, which stops in front of many inns." *(GR)*

Also recommended: On 20 wooded acres you'll find the three cottages of **Bonnybrooke Farm Atop Misty Mountain** (Route 2, Box 335A, 72632; 501–253–6903). "Owner Bonny Pierson has thought of everything—wood for the fireplace, ample hot water for the Jacuzzi, convenient electrical outlets, plush towels, large bars of soap, hair dryer, beautiful flowers, and soft music for our arrival. A generous basket of fresh fruit and muffins, with tea and coffee, awaited us in the fully equipped kitchen." *(Elaine & David Miller)* "Although only four miles from town, it's completely quiet, private, and serene. Two-story cathedral windows provide a dramatic valley and mountain panoramas." *(Gordon Johnson & Kathy Pressly)* B&B rates range from $95–155.

The **Bridgeford House** (263 Spring Street, 72632; 501–253–7853) is an Eastlake-style Queen Anne home built in 1884, with four newly redecorated guest rooms. B&B double rates range from $85–110. "Beautiful gardens. Our room was romantic without being over-done, with floral patterns in blues, greens, and dusty rose. Located on one of the main streets downtown, the inn was far enough away to be quiet and secluded, yet within comfortable walking distance of the historic area." *(Laurie & David Myers)*

Information please: A 60-year-old Tudor-style B&B, the **Ellis House** (1 Wheeler Street, 72632; 501–253–8218 or 800–243–8218) is decorated with local art and antiques. Some guest rooms have double whirlpool tubs, king- or queen-size beds. "Secluded location with a spectacular view overlooking the town. The grounds were full of honeysuckle, irises, peonies and lilies of the valley. When we arrived, a note invited us to help ourselves to tea, coffee, and treats. Breakfast included fresh strawberries, cheese omelets, sausages, muffins and juice." *(Karla Riley)* Current reports appreciated.

The **Red Bud Valley Resort** (Rock House Road, Route 1, Box 500, 72632; 501–253–9028) enjoys a secluded setting 1.5 miles from town. The 18 log cabins include both two- and three-bedroom well-equipped family units, as well as romantic honeymoon cabins with heart-shaped whirlpool tubs and fireplaces. Activities include trail rides, and swimming and fishing in the spring-fed lake. "Beautiful valley setting, with lovely gardens and walking trails. We love to relax on our cabin's front porch swing, watching the hummingbirds at the feeders." *(Bob Roller)* Double rates range from $79–135.

Arsenic and Old Lace B&B ♿ *Tel:* 501–253–5454
60 Hillside Avenue, 72632 800–243–5223
Fax: 501–253–2246

Sometimes the names of B&Bs slip from our memories, but an inn called Arsenic and Old Lace is hard to forget! In 1994, Gary and Phyllis Jones left longtime careers at IBM to follow a new path as innkeepers. Built as a B&B in 1992, Arsenic and Old Lace was constructed in the Queen Anne style following a set of century-old blueprints. State-of-the-art plumbing in spacious bathrooms and up-to-date insulation were combined with period moldings and cornices, tin ceilings, and antique doors, mantles, and stained glass windows. The elegant furnishings include antiques and period reproductions; most guest rooms have a queen-size bed. Phyllis serves a three-course breakfast at 9 A.M., with such entrees as baked eggs with three cheeses or apple pecan pancakes, in addition to a fruit course, and home-baked breads and muffins.

"Peaceful setting, relaxing atmosphere. The romantic Tree Top Suite in the turret has an octagonal shape with two-story floor-to-ceiling windows, and breathtaking views over the valley. In the morning, the sun rises over the Christ of the Ozarks statue, illuminating the room through stained glass windows. Comfortable brass canopy king-size bed. The wonderful breakfasts include just-brewed coffee with delicious Grand Marnier French toast." *(Jeffrey Thompson)* "The rooms overlook lovely gardens." *(Susanne Bunn)* "Phyllis makes sure home-baked cookies, tasty snacks, and a large variety of beverages are always available. Excellent selection of movies (including *Arsenic and Old Lace*, of course), books, and games. We enjoyed reading through the binder of restaurant menus and other recommendations." *(Maggie Thompson)* "Delightful innkeepers, plus their great dog, Bear. Wonderful balance of antiques with modern convenience. We spent one evening playing a board game in front of the parlor fireplace, sipping elderberry wine, and another on the porch swing. Excellent restaurant recommendations." *(Chrys Hydo)* "Not only was the inn wonderful, but I lived to tell about it!" *(MW)*

Open All year.
Rooms 5 doubles—all with private bath, clock/radio, TV/VCR, air-conditioning, ceiling fan, robes, hair dryer. 4 with single or double whirlpool tub, 3 with fireplace, 2 with balcony.
Facilities Dining room, living room with fireplace, piano; library with games, books, videotapes; guest pantry; wraparound verandas with swing. 1 acre with patio, perennial gardens, off-street parking. Golf, tennis, swimming privileges at nearby country club.

Location Historic district. Take Hwy.23 (N. Main St.) to RR station at N end of town. Turn on Hillside Ave.& go 2/10 m to inn on right; watch for tower, stone wall.
Restrictions No smoking. Children 14 and over.
Credit cards Amex, Discover, MC, Visa.
Rates B&B, $100–160 double, $85–145 single. Extra person, $15. 10% senior, AAA discount. Tipping not encouraged.
Extras Limited wheelchair access. Local airport pickup.

Dairy Hollow House
515 Spring Street, 72632

Tel: 501–253–7444
800–562–8650
Fax: 501–253–7223
E-mail: frontdesk@dairyhollow.com

When the doors of Dairy Hollow House opened in 1981, it was one of the first bed & breakfast inns in the state. Since then, innkeepers Crescent Dragonwagon (she adopted the name after moving to Arkansas at age 18) and her husband, Ned Shank, developed a nationwide reputation for their "Nouveau Zarks" cuisine, combining classic French with the Ozarks' best regional ingredients. Guests can savor their specialties at quarterly special occasion feasts, or buy a copy of one of Crescent's wonderful cookbooks.

The Dairy Hollow House encompasses the Farmhouse in the Hollow, a fully renovated 1880s farmhouse, housing three guest rooms, all with fireplaces, handmade quilts and period antiques; the Main House, with three suites with fireplaces; and the Restaurant at Dairy Hollow, on the garden level of the Main House. The central reception area is here also. Breakfast specialties (delivered to your room) include fresh fruit or juice, German baked pancakes with fresh berry sauce, or perhaps feathebed eggs and chicken-apple sausages, accompanied by homemade jams and jellies, gingerbread muffins, or blueberry coffee cake. Rates also include a check-in beverage and homemade cookies.

"Genuine concern for guests' comfort and scrupulous attention to detail, while maintaining a casual, easygoing atmosphere. It's rustic in style, luxurious in service. The old-fashioned cast-iron bedstead with colorful quilt and a surfeit of pillows covers a top-of-the-line mattress. Wooden floors and calico curtains make the bathroom look homey, but a spanking clean, perfectly functioning Jacuzzi makes one feel pampered. The huge breakfast delivered to your door is much more civilized and sensible than forcing everyone to socialize early in the day. The food itself was exceptional, accenting the region and its specialties." *(Ronni Lundy)* "Delightful town off-season, great for walking and relaxing. The Spring Garden Suite has a lovely sun room, full of wicker furniture, a perfect spot to enjoy the amazing breakfasts. The Summer Meadows suite has a large inviting living room. Rooms in the Farmhouse are smaller, but charming and quiet." *(LI)*

Open Feb. through Dec. Restaurant open for seasonal dinners only.
Rooms 3 suites, 3 doubles—all with private bath and/or shower, air-conditioning, fireplace, mini-refrigerator, coffee maker. 4 rooms with desk. 2 rooms

with Jacuzzi, kitchenette. 1 with deck. Rooms in 2 buildings. Telephone on request.
Facilities Restaurant, lobby. Music entertainment holidays/festivals. 1 acre with flower gardens, woods, hot tub, children's games. 15 min. to water sports.
Location 1 m from downtown.
Restrictions Smoking restricted. BYOB.
Credit cards Amex, DC, Discover, MC, Visa.
Rates B&B, $165–205 suite, $135–165 double, plus optional $2–5 daily for service. Extra person, $10. 2-3 night minimum weekends/holidays. Off-season discount for longer stays. Mystery, gardener, winter honeymoon/anniversary weekend packages. Prix fixe dinner, $49–59 plus service.
Extras Restaurant wheelchair accessible. Crib, babysitting.

Five Ojo Inn ¢ — *Tel:* 501–253–6734
5 Ojo Street, 72632 — 800–656–6734
Fax: 501–253–8831

Built in 1890, this comfortable Victorian home was bought by Paula Kirby Adkins a century later. The four buildings on the property were redone as "painted ladies," and are painted in shades of mauve, with burgundy and dark green accents. The elegant candlelit breakfast is served in the dining room at 9 A.M., and might include fresh fruit, eggs Benedict, sausages, parsley potatoes, muffins, cheesecake, juice, tea or coffee. Afterwards, guests can relax on the front porch before walking or taking the short trolley ride downtown.

"Paul Adkins has the gift of hospitality, and makes sure that her guests are made to feel welcome, extremely comfortable, and highly pampered. This B&B is down-to-earth, cozy and a bit nostalgic. Although the atmosphere encourages privacy, the delicious breakfasts give guests a chance to get to know one another. While extremely convenient, the location is just far enough from downtown to avoid crowds and congestion; off-street parking is ample and easy." *(Randy & Marilyn McGuire)* "Orderly, neat, and clean throughout. Splendid breakfasts served by a courteous, competent staff; dietary needs accommodated without a problem." *(Bill & Felicia Schnittker)* "Homey and welcoming, decorated in lace, florals, and antiques." *(Bonnie Gatewood)*

"In the evening we unwound in the Jacuzzi and enjoyed a peaceful chat by the fire." *(Denise & Pat Bembenek)* "Our immaculate suite was stocked with snacks and beverages; ample lighting.Paula kindly delivered an early breakfast on our departure day." *(V.L.Hollister)* "Paula is a wonderful, energetic woman who serves scrumptious breakfasts, and provides excellent suggestions for places to shop, sight-see, and eat. I liked to sit in the swing on our private porch in the mornings and look off to the woods, watching for deer." *(Kelli Walker)*

Open All year.
Rooms 1 cottage, 4 suites, 5 doubles—all with private bath and/or shower, radio, TV, air-conditioning, fan, refrigerator, coffee-maker. 6 with double whirlpool tub; 1 with fireplace, deck. Rooms in 3 buildings.
Facilities Dining room, living room/common area with piano, books, games. 1½ acres with gardens, hot tub housed in gazebo, picnic area, off-street parking.
Location Historic District.

Restrictions No smoking. Well behaved children welcome.
Credit cards Amex, Discover, MC, Visa.
Rates B&B, $109 cottage, $89–129 suite, $85–109 double. Extra person, $25. Tipping appreciated. 2-3 night weekend/holiday minimum.

The Heartstone Inn and Cottages ¢
35 Kingshighway (Highway 62B), 72632

Tel: 501–253–8916
800–494–4921
Fax: 501–253–6821

A long-time reader favorite, innkeepers Iris and Bill Simantel have owned The Heartstone since 1985. Guest rooms are decorated with antique and reproduction furniture and decorative Victorian touches—including plenty of hearts; most have queen- or king-size beds.

"Delicious meals, gracious atmosphere, lovely decor, good-natured innkeepers and staff." *(Virginia Ozarzak)* "Iris and her assistant prepared the wonderful breakfasts, which were served by Bill. He was friendly and genuinely concerned that everyone was having a good time and had everything needed. Lovely scent to the room, sheets, and towels." *(Debbie Chilcout)* "Comfortable and clean, lots of antiques, quilts, nicely coordinated wallpaper, plenty of light and hot water." *(Judy Glantz)* "The Simantels were delightful, available, and accommodating." *(Patricia Thomas)*

"Fully endorse entry. The owners care, and it shows in the impeccable cleanliness and careful attention to detail throughout the inn. Helpful with restaurant recommendations and area hints. Each breakfast was different, all delicious. A wonderful breakfast room and great deck for relaxing with iced tea or lemonade, watching the birds at the feeders." *(HJB)* "Friendly owners; great location, off the main drag, yet close enough to walk almost everywhere. Delicious breakfasts, not high in fat." *(Regina Donnell)* "Iris is from England and has an extensive collection of Torquay pottery." *(Joanne Ashton)*

"Iris and Bill provided candid restaurant suggestions, gave us accurate directions, and supplied us with blankets for an outside event. In the morning, guests gather for coffee on the deck overlooking the wooded hollow behind the house. Promptly at nine, all are invited to breakfast in the dining room." *(Linda Logsdon)* "Hanging pots of Boston ferns sway lazily above the long front porch, and huge crocks spill over with salmon-colored geraniums. The Bridal Suite has an old lace wedding dress and dried bridal bouquet; a queen-size bed was covered with a red, white, and blue quilt in the double wedding-band pattern." *(Mr. & Mrs. J.D. Rolfe)* "The inn is a beautiful pink Victorian with white trim. We breakfasted on delicious German apple pancakes with bacon, fresh fruit, and chocolate chip muffins." *(Howard & Rebecca Harmon)* "No need for a car with the trolley stop directly in front of the inn." *(Michael Kavanaugh)*

Open Feb. 1–late Dec.
Rooms 1 2-bedroom cottage, 1 1-bedroom cottage, 2 suites, 8 doubles, all with full private bath, TV, radio, air-conditioning, ceiling fans. 1 with Jacuzzi. 4 rooms in annex.

Facilities Dining/breakfast rooms, guest lounge with piano, stereo, games, veranda, decks, gazebo; massage therapy; gift/pottery shop. Off-street parking. Live music during May, Sept. festivals. Golf privileges.
Location Historic district, 4 blocks to downtown. Trolley stop near house.
Restrictions No smoking. Limited facilities for older children.
Credit cards Amex, Discover, MC, Visa.
Rates B&B, $97–117 cottage, $95–120 suite, $65–85 double. Extra person, $15. 2-3 night weekend/holiday minimum. Tipping envelopes.

Pond Mountain Lodge and Resort ¢ 👪 ♿ *Tel:* 501–253–5877
Route 1, Box 50, Highway 23 South, 72632 800–583–8043

Built in 1954 and transformed into an inn by Judith Jones in 1992, Pond Mountain Lodge has a beautiful setting high above the valley floor. Pond Mountain was noted as a geological mystery in the early 1900s because its two spring-fed ponds are located at the highest points of Carroll County, in apparent violation of the laws of gravity. Guests can explore the inn's extensive grounds, enjoy the 25-mile vista, relax by the swimming pool, or take a trail ride on horseback. Breakfast, served buffet style from 8:30–10 A.M., include a fruit compote, a hot entree, just-baked breads, and freshly ground coffee.

"A hike to the top of the mountain revealed a dock stretching over a glorious spring-fed pond. One could fish, picnic or just take in the view." *(Erda Williams)* "We picked out a movie from Judy's extensive video library, and watched it in the privacy of our suite." *(Nancy Eaton)* "Spectacular hiking in the fall, as the leaves turn throughout the valley. In the winter, the great room is decorated for the season and a welcome fire burns in the fireplace. Hot cider and coffee is always available, as are games and books. Judy's wonderful breakfast of homemade breads and muffins, rich quiches, and blueberry or pecan pancakes is served on the veranda in warm weather, or by the fire when it's cold." *(Laurie Sanda)*

Open All year.
Rooms 1 2-bedroom cabin, 4 suites, 2 doubles—all with full private bath, clock/radio, TV/ VCR, air-conditioning, refrigerator. 5 with whirlpool tub; 4 with desk, fan, kitchenette, balcony/deck; 3 with fireplace.
Facilities Great hall/breakfast room with fireplace, piano, VCR library; game room with billiards, exercise equipment; deck, veranda. 150 acres with swimming pool, gardens, hiking trails, fishing ponds, horseback riding. 20 min. from Beaver Lake.
Location 2.2 m to historic district. 2 m S on Hwy. 23 S from junction with Rte. 62 E.
Restrictions No smoking. Some family-friendly suites, cabin.
Credit cards Discover, MC, Visa.
Rates B&B, $126–169 cabin, $64–125 suite, $60–80 double. Extra person $10. 5–10% midweek, AARP, extended stay, educator discounts. 2-night minimum special events. Picnic lunch, $10. Dinner with prior notice.
Extras Limited wheelchair access.

Singleton House ¢
11 Singleton, 72632

Tel: 501–253–9111
800–833–3394

Barbara Gavron, who has owned the century-old Singleton House since 1984, describes her light and airy guest rooms as being "whimsically decorated with an eclectic collection of antiques, folk art, and unexpected treasures." Served on the breakfast balcony overlooking the bird-filled garden and the goldfish pond, the morning meal differs each day; in addition to fresh fruit and juice, breakfast might include blueberry almond pancakes, baked French toast, or an egg casserole.

"Homey, simple, clean, with an old-fashioned Victorian charm. The highlight for me is the little Victorian garden, complete with rock paths lined with wild flowers and perennials, arches with morning glories, a weeping willow over the goldfish pond, and a wonderful collection of bird houses. From the garden, a shaded path leads down the hill to shops and cafes." *(Diane Minden)* "Though small, my room was bright and comfortable; the entire house is extremely clean. Barbara Gavron is warm, witty, professional and entertaining." *(Patsy Maxwell)* "Peaceful, relaxing environment. Wonderful innkeepers. Our darling room was done in pinks and florals." *(Carol Ann Guun)*

Open All year.
Rooms 1 suite, 4 doubles—all with private bath and/or shower, air-conditioning, TV, ceiling fan, balcony, Jacuzzi. Some with ceiling fan. Cottage at separate location with kitchen, Jacuzzi.
Facilities Breakfast balcony, living room with TV, nature library, guest kitchen; porch with swing, rockers. Garden with fishpond, picnic area, off-street parking.
Location Historic district, off Rte. 62B; Singleton is between Pine and Howell. 1 block to shops, trolley.
Restrictions No smoking inside.
Credit cards Amex, Discover, MC, Visa.
Rates B&B, $95–125 cottage, $65–85 suite, double. Discount for multi-night stay. 3-night minimum holiday/festival weekends. 2-night minimum in cottage.

FAYETTEVILLE

Also recommended: Although a Clarion Carriage House property, the **Inn at the Mill** (3906 Greathouse Springs Road, P.O.Box 409, Johnson 72741; 501–443–1800 or 800–CLARION) is far from being a typical chain motel. Listed on the National Register of Historic Places, the mill dates back to 1835; the modern renovation and adjoining 48-room hotel structure was completed in 1991. Continental breakfast can be enjoyed in your room, the parlor or on the deck overlooking the pond and water wheel; complimentary wine and hors d'oeuvres, and evening turndown and cookies are also included in the $80–90 double rates. "The original mill building houses the lobby area highlighted by Frederick Remington bronzes, a 1895 Frank Lloyd Wright stained glass window, antiques and contemporary quilts. Guest rooms are spacious with hand-stitched quilts and marble bathrooms." *(KM)* "Unusual, artistic decor; excellent service and accommodations. Friendly, helpful staff. Pleasant country location, just six miles north of Fayetteville." *(Duane Roller)*

FORT SMITH

Beland Manor Inn ¢ ♿
1320 South Albert Pike, 72903

Tel: 501–782–3300
800–334–5052
Fax: 501–782–7674
E-mail: belandbnb@ipa.net

Business travelers are delighted that they can come "home" to Beland Manor; those looking to re-charge their batteries with a weekend getaway will be equally pleased with the relaxing atmosphere, good food, and comfortable accommodations offered by Mike and Suzy Smith. Beland Manor is a 6,200-square-foot Colonial-style home constructed in 1950. Built of red brick with white trim, a front veranda runs across the front of the house, supported by six columns, each thirty feet high. Furnishings are traditional, and each guest room has a different decorating theme, from the king-size four poster rice bed and Queen Anne furnishings in the suite, to the queen-size Santa Fe four poster bed and Native American prints of the Frontier Room.

Suzy is an accomplished chef who takes justifiable pride in her recipes, combining the freshest possible ingredients with careful presentation. Breakfast served at individual tables 7–9 A.M. weekdays; from 8:30–10 A.M. weekends. A fresh fruit plate with crème fraiche is followed by such entrees as ginger pancakes with lemon sauce, wild rice pancakes with apple cranberry sauce, or eggs Benedict with sauteed mushrooms, and possibly accompanied by peppered bacon, cinnamon rolls, and lemon blueberry bread. On weekends, dinner is served by advance reservation, with homemade pasta on Friday nights, and such Saturday dinner menus as curried yellow squash soup, mushroom salad, a choice of pork tenderloin with cranberry chutney or trout with almonds, with cinnamon bread pudding for dessert.

"Quiet, convenient location. Generous service and hospitality from Suzy and Mike. Impeccable cleanliness and housekeeping; excellent facilities." *(Philip Manners)* "Mike and Suzy are a gracious and caring young couple. Delicious food, comfortable bed, relaxing atmosphere." *(GR)* Comments welcome.

Open All year.
Rooms 1 suite, 6 doubles—all with shower and/or tub, telephone, clock/radio, TV, air-conditioning, ceiling fan. 4 with desk, 1 with double Jacuzzi.
Facilities Breakfast room, dining room with fireplace; great room with TV/VCR, books, magazines, games, stocked guest refrigerator; foyer with piano; reception room; veranda. 1½ acres with patio, herb garden, berry picking, gazebo, off-street parking. Woods, gardens across street for walking.

Location E AR, at TX border. 157 m NW of Little Rock. 2 m to town. Take I-40 to I-540 W. Go 8 m to Rogers Ave. exit. Go W on Rogers Ave. to inn at corner of Rogers & S. Albert Pike.
Restrictions No smoking inside. Children 7 and over.
Credit cards Amex, Discover, MC, Visa.
Rates B&B, $110 suite, $69–110 double. Extra person, $10. Weekend getaway packages. Weekend dinners by advance reservation, $14–22.
Extras Limited wheelchair access. Airport/station pickups.

HARDY

Olde Stonehouse Inn ¢
511 Main Street, 72542

Tel: 870–856–2983
800–514–2983
Fax: 870–856–2983
E-mail: pvolland@centuryinter.net

"Hardy, a tiny town in the northeast Arkansas region called the Ozark Gateway, offers breathtaking scenery, rich local culture, and friendly people," reports Peggy Volland, owner of the Olde Stonehouse Inn. An old railroad town, Hardy is known for its antique auctions; nearby Spring River offers good canoeing and trout fishing.

Constructed of native Arkansas stone, the inn was built in 1928 and was renovated 1992. The focal point of the living room is the rock fireplace, set with fossils, minerals, and unusual stones. A floral theme in dusty blue and soft pink colors with lace accents compliments the inn's antique and reproduction furnishings. Guest rooms have queen-size beds with firm, new mattresses—as Peggy says, "antique beds are fun, antique mattresses aren't!" Breakfast includes orange juice or muscadine grape juice, fresh fruit, yogurt, homemade granola, muffins with strawberry butter, and baked apple pancakes or perhaps cornbread-sausage bake. Rates also include an evening snack of homemade brownies or cookies, with coffee or juice.

"Gorgeous architecture; warm, rich woodwork throughout. Lovely antique furnishings, yet still homey. Feeling of the Old South." *(Sherie Calderon)* "You can stroll through town, visit the shops, walk along the river, then return to your quiet room or have a friendly chat with Peggy in the living room. Delicious food, comfortable beds." *(Jerry Clifton)* "The inn is clean, quiet, and tidy, with ample parking and a great location." *(Diane Weisenberg)* "Gracious innkeeper, great breakfast, clean and homey accommodations." *(Kathryn Terrell)* "Loved sitting in the wicker furniture on the veranda and on the front porch in the big rockers. Beautiful flowers. We visited in the living room with the other guests, and enjoyed the grandfather clocks and player piano. Good security. Delicious breakfast, beautifully served." *(Gladys & Cecil Henderson)*

Open All year.
Rooms 2 suites in separate cottage, 7 doubles—all with private bath and/or shower, air-conditioning, ceiling fan, clock/radio. Telephone on request. Some

with desk, electric fireplace, refrigerator, porch. Suites with TV/VCR, mini-refrigerator, coffee maker.
Facilities Dining room, living room with fireplace, player piano; sitting room with books, games, stereo; porch with rockers. Off-street parking, lawn games. Golf, tennis, fishing, swimming, canoeing, rafting.
Location NE AR. 130 m N of Little Rock. In historic "Old Hardy Town"; near shops.
Restrictions No smoking inside. No children. Dry county; byo wine.
Credit cards Amex, Discover, MC, Visa.
Rates B&B, $85–99 suite, $65–75 double. Extra person $15. Breakfast in bed, $5 extra. 2-night weekend minimum May–Oct. 10% midweek, AAA, senior discount. Picnic lunch, $15. Fly fishing packages.
Extras Bus station pickup.

HEBER SPRINGS

Water is the underlying theme of Heber Springs, located in the foothills of the Ozarks, 60 miles north of Little Rock. The eponymous springs are downtown, plus there's excellent trout fishing and canoeing on the Little Red River, and more water sports on 40,000-acre Greet Ferry Lake.

Information please: The **Anderson House Inn** (201 East Main Street, P.O. Box 630, 72543; 501–362–5266 or 800–264–5279) was purchased by Jim and Susan Hildebrand in 1995. The oldest portion of the building dates to the 1880s, when the town's founder built it as a theater. The inn offer a front porch and balcony, a living room with fireplace and TV, and 16 guest rooms with private baths and ceiling fans. The B&B double rates of $68–98 include a buffet breakfast—perhaps an egg and bacon casserole, cheese garlic grits, cinnamon rolls, biscuits with sausage gravy, and fruit. Guests can enjoy lemonade and cookies on the porch in the afternoon, or in cooler weather, sip cider or hot chocolate in front of the beautiful stone fireplace in the great room. Reports appreciated. Inquire about golf, fly fishing, and romance packages.

Oak Tree Inn ¢ 🚶 *Tel:* 501–362–7731
Vinegar Hill and Highway 110 West, 72543 800–959–3857

Freddie Lou and Jerry Quist, owners, report that although the inn's design is a New England-type Colonial, all materials used in its 1983 construction are from Arkansas. Rooms are decorated with antiques and traditional furnishings. The inn is an adults-only retreat, but the Quists also offer family-style accommodation in their river cabins. Inn rates include evening cookies and coffee, and a full breakfast served between 8:30 – 9:30 A.M.

"Beautifully decorated with antiques and reproductions; comfortable beds; well equipped bathrooms with plush towels, scented soaps and bath salts; delicious breakfasts. Lovely brick patio; warm, inviting living room." *(Carlita Drennan)* "Soothing colors and textures, fresh flowers, delightful chiming clock and the crackling fires in winter. Rooms are large with quality linens, imported soaps, live plants, antiques and quality reproductions. Service was impeccable but unobtrusive. Ample well-lighted parking. The grounds were well landscaped with colorful shrubs and lots of birds to watch. Superb breakfasts of eggs Benedict, Belgian waffles, and omelets." *(Larry Hughes & Lynda Gayle)* "Gracious hostess, lovely and interesting guests, and a comfortable, homelike atmosphere. Desserts and coffee are enjoyed in the evening around the fireplace." *(Mrs. David Garrett)* "Our room had a lovely bathroom, wonderful queen-size bed, beautiful Oriental rug, a ceiling fan, wood shutters, and sofa." *(Phyllis Berlin)*

Open All year.
Rooms 4 doubles—all with full private bath with whirlpool tub, fireplace. 1 2-bedroom, 2-bath cottage with kitchen, fireplace, laundry, porch, grill, hammock.
Facilities Common room. 1 acre with garden; swimming pool, 2 tennis courts adjacent. Swimming, boating, fishing in Greers Ferry Lake 1 block away. Tennis, hiking, trout fishing nearby.
Location Ozarks, 60 m N of Little Rock. From Little Rock, take Rte. 67 NE to Hwy. 5, then N to Rte. 25 to Heber Springs. About 1 m W of Heber Springs on Rte. 110.
Restrictions Smoking, children permitted in cottage.
Credit cards Discover, MC, Visa.
Rates Room only, $120–170 cottage. B&B, $85 double. Extra person, $10. 2-3 night weekend/holiday minimum June 1–Oct.31 (year-round in cottage).
Extras Airport pickup.

HELENA

Edwardian Inn ¢ 👪 ♿
317 Biscoe, 72342

Tel: 870–338–9155
800–598–4749
Fax: 870–572–9105

In 1904 cotton broker William A. Short built his family their dream house at the then-extraordinary cost of over $100,000. The Shorts were not the only prosperous family in town; Helena is known for its historic houses, both antebellum and postbellum. Listed on the National Register of Historic Places and built in the Colonial Revival style, exceptional features include the handsome quarter-sawn oak woodwork in the floors, ceilings, staircases, paneling, and columns, as well as the fine hardware, and beveled and leaded glass. Rates include a breakfast of home-baked breads, pastries, cereals, and fresh fruit. Cathy Cunningham is the managing partner.

"Excellent accommodations, warm hospitality, welcoming atmosphere." *(Carol Green)* "Well maintained; nicely decorated and extremely clean; wonderfully friendly staff; varied, tasty breakfasts; good outside lighting and parking. We arrived relatively late for dinner, and the innkeepers called a local restaurant to ask them to stay open for us." *(Rebecca Daley)* "Our beautiful room had a king-sized bed with a headboard made from a church pew, an enormous bath, a glassed-in sitting area with a window seat, and access to the balcony porch. We took our delicious breakfast of homemade cinnamon rolls and carrot cake outside, and sat down in a rocking chair to eat." *(SG)* "Especially enjoyable is the sunny kitchen/dining room, complete with linen tablecloths and napkins, and fresh flowers." *(Margaret Holaway)*

Open All year.
Rooms 5 suites, 7 doubles—all with full private bath, telephone, radio, TV, air-conditioning, fan. Some with desk, fireplace.
Facilities Breakfast room, garden room with fireplace. Veranda, porches. Near Mississippi Riverfront park.
Location SE AR, on Mississippi River, 70 m S of Memphis, TN.
Restrictions Smoking permitted in two guest rooms. Well behaved children welcome.
Credit cards Amex, DC, Discover, MC, Visa.
Rates B&B, $69 suite, $59 double. Extra person, $15. No charge for children under 16.
Extras Wheelchair access. Crib.

HOT SPRINGS

A visit to Hot Springs will allow you to take your place in a long line of tradition; records indicate that the Indians used this site 10,000 years ago. The springs reached their height of popularity in the 19th century, and the area became a national park in 1921. The bath houses are still well worth a visit; the naturally hot water will soothe your aching muscles after a day of hiking or horseback riding in the surrounding Zig Zag Mountains. And the price is right—call the historic Buckstaff (501–623–2308), where steaming, soaking, and massage costs under $30 (tips extra). Several lakes—Catherine, Hamilton, and Ouachita—are nearby for all water sports. Hot Springs is located in central Arkansas, 55 miles southwest of Little Rock.

Also recommended: Though too large for a full entry with almost 500 rooms, readers are pleased with **The Arlington Resort Hotel & Spa** (Central Avenue and Fountain Street, P.O. Box 5652, 71902; 501–623–7771 or 800–643–1502). "The Arlington is an old-fashioned historic hotel with a large staff and excellent service at moderate prices. Fine location overlooking the national park. Large and well appointed room; buffet breakfast included in the reasonable rates." *(Duane Roller)* "This 70-year-old hotel has been updated with bright yellow flowered wall paper, and brightly painted corridors. Our room was large and clean, with a comfortable king-size bed. Breakfast was served with flowers and a smile at a reasonable price." *(Martha Banda)* Rates range from $58–180 for a double and $150–350 for a suite.

Information please: A Queen Anne home built in 1907, **Vintage Comfort** (303 Quapaw, 71901; 501–623–3258 or 800–608–4682) has four guest rooms, each with private bath; the B&B double rate ranges from $65–95. The inn is just a short walk from Bathhouse Row and the historic district. "Clean, neat, decorated in period. Wonderful, professional innkeeper. Delicious breakfasts of home-made waffles, muffins, fresh fruit and wonderful egg dishes. Tasty snacks each afternoon." *(Bill Perry)*

Ten miles north of Hot Springs village is **Mountain Thyme B&B** (10860 Scenic Byway 7 North, Jessieville, 71949; 501–984–5428), a newly constructed inn which opened late in 1997, owned by Rhonda and Mike Hicks, and Polly Felker. Each of the eight guest rooms has a full private bath, and B&B double rates range from $70–120, including breakfasts of biscuits and gravy with scrambled eggs, or blueberry pancakes and bacon. The entrance to Ouachita National Forest is just a half-mile away, for excellent hiking and bird-watching. Longtime B&B travelers, Rhonda notes that "we have put everything we look for in our B&B: good lights on both sides of every bed for reading, quality beds and linens, 24-hour guest pantry, extra sound-proofing, ceiling fans, individual room controls for heating and cooling, and bath tubs you can actually lie down in. We are sensitive to travelers' needs for privacy and conversation."

Stillmeadow Farm ¢ *Tel:* 501–525–9994
111 Stillmeadow Lane, 71913

If you get the feeling that you've arrived in 18th century New England—instead of 20th century Arkansas—when you reach Stillmeadow Farm, don't be surprised. Although it was built as a B&B in 1985 by Gene and Jody Sparling, this post-and-beam saltbox style house, complete with a central brick chimney, is an authentic reproduction of a typical Cape Cod home, and was inspired by the Sparling's travels in New England. Inside the decor continues the early American atmosphere, with simple country antiques and reproductions, including pencil post beds, hand stenciling, braided rugs, and tabbed gingham curtains. The Sparling's collections of baskets, duck decoys, and crockery are equally appropriate to the era. Breakfast, served 8–9:30 A.M. at the dining room table, varies daily, but might include lemon bread, oatmeal biscuits, bran muffins, fresh preserves, baked apples, scrambled eggs, country ham, and sauteed mushrooms.

"Beautiful Shaker-style furniture, and a wonderful walk-in hearth. Though convenient to town, the inn feels like it is away from it all. The Sparlings are experienced, generous, and helpful innkeepers." *(Mike & Rhonda Hicks)* "Delightful hosts, lovely home, delicious breakfast, pleasant conversation. Appreciated such thoughtful touches as the toiletries, fresh fruit and flowers, and help with directions. Peaceful setting with pond and woods." *(GR)*

Open All year.
Rooms 1 cottage with kitchen, 1 suite, 2 doubles—all with shower/tub, clock, air-conditioning, desk.
Facilities Dining room with fireplace, living room with TV, fireplace; family room, library. 70 acres with herb garden, walking trails, stocked fishing pond, off-street parking, guided trail rides.

Location 10.5 m S of Bath House Row; 5.3 m S of Hot Springs Mall; 3.8 m S of Lake Hamilton. From Hot Springs, take Hwy 7 S to Hwy 290 E. Turn left (E). Go 1½ m to Meadowlark Trace. Turn right. Go to 1st road, turn right and go up hill.
Restrictions Absolutely no smoking. Children 12 and over.
Credit cards MC, Visa.
Rates B&B, $65–70 suite, $65 double, $55 single. No tipping.

Stitt House B&B
824 Park Avenue, 71901

Tel: 501–623–2704
Fax: 501–623–2704

A 6,000 square-foot Italianate Victorian mansion, the Stitt House was built in 1875 by Samuel Stitt, and is listed on the National Register of Historic Places. Said to be Hot Springs' oldest home, it remained in the Stitt family until 1983, when it was purchased by Linda and Horst Fischer, who lived in the house with their four children, and also ran it as a well-known restaurant from 1983 to 1991. Horst is also the manager of the Arlington and Majestic Hotels, and Linda has operated both restaurants and retail clothing shops.

In 1995, the Fischers restored Stitt House as an elegant B&B, complementing the original crystal chandeliers, hand-carved oak staircase, and imposing mahogany and cherry wood fireplace mantles with period antiques and reproductions. Named for the Fischers' grown children, each of the guest rooms is individually furnished in period, and has a king-size bed and sitting area. Guests can select the time, place, and menu for breakfast. The meal is served 8–10 A.M., and can be enjoyed at the dining room table, on the veranda, or in bed. Guests can select one of two entrees—perhaps eggs Benedict with French crepes or a quiche with paprika potatoes, accompanied by their preference of fresh squeezed orange or grapefruit juice, fresh fruit, bacon or sausage, toast or English muffins.

"Horst and Linda were exceptionally helpful in identifying hiking trails and in making restaurant recommendations and reservations. Our lovely room had a high four poster bed with fresh, crisp sheets, and comfortable sitting areas. Lovely swimming pool, perfect temperature. Scrumptious breakfast, served on the veranda." *(Kelly Welsh)* "Among the highlights was a welcoming glass of wine on arrival." *(Linda Clinger)* "The Fischers came to greet us as we rode up the driveway. Exceptionally clean and well maintained. Pampering touches included complimentary beverages, shampoo, toiletries, plus soft white terry robes. At breakfast, the dining room was set with beautiful china and silver." *(Janis & Ed Tidwell)* "This beautiful Victorian home sits atop a hill surrounded by lush greenery; we viewed the lovely scenery from the front porch." *(Nancy Bingamon)* "Impeccably appointed rooms; ours had a canopied king bed with Battenburg lace linens. Warm, hospitable innkeepers." *(Julie R. Salmon)* "Early each morning, tea and coffee is set out on a sideboard close to the guest rooms; the upstairs refrigerator is stocked with soft drinks, and fruit, crackers, and cookies are available for munching. At night, beds are turned down, and there are chocolates." *(Kim James & Philip Snyder)*

Open All year.
Rooms 1 suite, 3 doubles—all with full private bath, radio, clock, TV, desk, air-conditioning, robes. 3 with ceiling fan; 1 with double whirlpool tub.
Facilities Living room with fireplace, piano, TV/VCR, books; family room, library with fireplace, books; guest refrigerator; porch. 2 acres with off-street parking, heated swimming pool. ¾ m to Natl. Park for hiking.
Location Historic district; 1 m to center of town. N end of town on Scenic Hwy. 7.
Restrictions No smoking or chewing tobacco. Children 12 and over.
Credit cards Amex,Discover, MC,Visa.
Rates B&B, $110 suite, $95 double. Extra person, $15. 10% senior, AAA discount. 2-3 night weekend/holiday minimum.
Extras Airport/station pickups, $20. German spoken.

Williams House ¢
420 Quapaw, Hot Springs National Park, 71901
Tel: 501–624–4275
800–756–4635
Fax: 501–624–4275

Listed on the National Register of Historic Places, this imposing 1890 brownstone-and-brick Victorian mansion was purchased by David and Karen Wiseman in 1996. Early morning coffee is followed by breakfast, served between 7:30 and 9 A.M., and includes fresh fruit, homemade bread and muffins, raspberry-stuffed French toast, egg and sausage dishes, or another daily special.

"Karen was helpful from my initial call to make our reservations. The inn's atmosphere is peaceful, private, and secure. The rooms are large with comfortable furniture and beds. Our upstairs room had a spacious private bath, just outside our room; great shower. The large upstairs sitting area was well supplied with books and magazines. It opens to a large porch, overlooking a corner of the property. An outside staircase offered total privacy, if desired. Creative, tasty and relaxing breakfasts were served each morning. When we wanted to talk or visit, Karen and David were friendly and informative about sightseeing and restaurants; if we wanted privacy, they were invisible. David gave us a tour of the rest of the house so we could learn its history, and view the other rooms. An excellent value, too." *(Susan Novek-Fraser)* "Friendly, hospitable, knowledgeable innkeepers. House beautifully restored; clean, comfortable rooms with wonderful antiques." *(C.R. Davies, also Gail Blaylock)* "Both the house and grounds are first-rate." *(Ron Weddel)* "Within walking distance of Bath House Row and downtown Hot Springs, perfect for shopping and sightseeing, or catching the trolley to Oaklawn Park for the horse races." *(Terri Bertschy)* "Our private, two-bedroom suite in the carriage house had ample sitting and reading areas. The bathroom offered a large tiled shower, a good shower head, and excellent water pressure." *(John Blewer)*

Open All year.
Rooms 2 suites, 3 doubles—all with private bath and/or shower, radio, air-conditioning. 2 rooms in carriage house.
Facilities Dining room, living room with fireplace, baby grand piano; sitting room with games, TV; porches. ½ acre with patios, hammock, picnic table. In-

door heated pool at Quapaw Comm. Center next door. Walking distance to Bath House Row. Fishing, swimming, boating, hiking, golf nearby.
Location 4 blocks to National Park headquarters. At corner of Orange and Quapaw. From Bath House Row, go S on Central Ave., right on Prospect, left on Quapaw.
Restrictions No smoking. No children. Daytime traffic noise.
Credit cards MC, Visa.
Rates B&B, $95–105 suite, $80–90 double, $60–75 single. Extra person, $20. 2-night weekend minimum March, April, Oct., holidays.

JASPER

Information please: In northwestern Arkansas, about two hours east of Fayetteville, is **Brambly Hedge Cottage** (Scenic Highway 7, HCR 31, Box 39, 72641; 501–446–5849 or 800–BRAMBLY). At the top of Sloan Mountain, it offers views of the Little Buffalo and Buffalo National River valleys. Owners Billy and Jacquelyn Smyers can advise on area hiking and craft shops. B&B double rates for the guest rooms range from $55–75. "Small, lacy, and magical. Jacquelyn played her harp and psalteries for us, and served us tea and decadent cookies. Wonderfully peaceful." *(Rhonda & Mike Hicks)*

LITTLE ROCK

Little Rock is the capital of Arkansas and its largest city. Bill Clinton lived here when he was Governor of Arkansas, and the city soon adjusted to the unaccustomed glare of media attention after his election as President of the United States. The oldest section of the city is the Quapaw Quarter, which has many fine antebellum and Victorian homes; typical for a historic district, some houses are beautifully restored, others are still run down.

A short drive from the city are ample opportunities for golf, hiking, plus lakes for water sports.

Located in central Arkansas, Little Rock is two hours west of Memphis, Tennessee, and five hours northeast of Dallas.

Reader tip: "Little Rock is like any other city: do not leave valuables visible in the car."

Also recommended: Although it has only two guest rooms, **The Carriage House** (1700 Louisiana, 72206; 501–374–7032) is enthusiastically recommended: "The spacious second floor guest rooms are simply furnished, each with a double bed with an excellent mattress and pillows. Downstairs, the comfortable sitting room has a good selection of games, books, and local restaurant menus. The delicious and healthfully prepared breakfast of fruit salad, Grand Marnier French toast, and Canadian bacon was served on the sunporch of the adjacent beautifully restored Eastlake Queen Anne Victorian mansion. Soft music complemented the spectacular array of flowers and plants."

(John Blewer) The Carriage House is located in the downtown residential Quapaw District; the double rate is $89.

Built in 1876, **The Capital Hotel** (111 West Markham, 72201; 501–374–7474 or 800–766–7666) is listed in the National Register of Historic Places. The spectacular two-story lobby has a stained glass ceiling panel, a mosaic tiled floor, marble walls, faux marble columns, and a marble grand staircase leading to the mezzanine. Ashley's Restaurant offers regional specialities, fresh seafood, and continental dishes. The 123 guest rooms are furnished with period reproductions, and some have canopy beds; double rates range from $85–145, suites to $365.

The Empress of Little Rock *Tel:* 501–374–7966
2120 Louisiana Street, 72206 *Fax:* 501–375–4537

Shunned from proper society because of his occupation as a saloon keeper, James Hornibrook flaunted his success by building an 7,500-square-foot Queen Anne Gothic mansion in 1888. Now listed in the National Register of Historic Places, the mansion is the best example of ornate Victorian architecture in Arkansas. A private home for just a decade, the mansion was used as a women's college, a nursing home, and then as apartments until its restoration as a B&B in 1995 by Robert H. Blair and Sharon Welch-Blair. Architectural highlights include the fine floors and woodwork, the divided stairway of cypress and walnut, the lofty corner tower, the 64-square-foot stained glass skylight, and octagonally shaped rooms. Done in camellia pink and green, the original master bedroom—The Hornibrook Room—has a mahogany bedroom suite, a queen-size half-tester bed, and an original soaking tub. The Murray Room in the tower has an Austrian walnut king-size bed with matching marble-topped end tables. Smoking jackets are provided for male guests, with reproduction Victorian dressing gowns for the ladies.

Breakfast, served 7:30–8:30 A.M. weekdays, 9A.M. on weekends, includes such menus as ham and asparagus in puff pastry with hollandaise sauce, home-baked sweet rolls or perhaps orange oatmeal pie, fresh or sherried fruit, and sausage. A continental breakfast is available for early departures.

"Be sure to take the narrow staircase, under a gorgeous stained glass skylight, across the attic and into the top tower, which houses the small, round card-playing room bathed in light from the stained glass in the tower windows. The Murray room has three long windows in the tower, overlooking quiet gardens, golden leafed trees, and the fountain. The huge wraparound porch overlooked the lovely grounds, bright with fall foliage." *(Bill & Cherry Hill)* "Carefully selected antiques throughout. The candlelight delicious breakfast included orange-flavored croissants, glazed grapefruit, bacon, and freshly squeezed juice." *(Ashley Courtney Feldman)* "A memorable experience, from the history of the mansion to the beautiful decor; from the congenial hosts to the outstanding accommodations and breakfasts." *(Howard Catchings)* "Sharon and Bob are friendly and accommodating. I am in the customer service field, and believe me, these two know what they're doing." *(Rebecca Hullum)*

Open All year.
Rooms 2 suites, 3 doubles—all with private shower and/or tub, telephone with data port, clock/radio, TV, air-conditioning, individual climate control, ceiling fan. 4 with desk. 1 with fireplace.
Facilities Dining room with fireplace, ladies' parlor with piano and fireplace, gentlemen's parlor with fireplace, sitting hall with books, fireplace; card room, guest refrigerator, card room. Victorian jewelry shop. Fax, copier, laundry service. Patio, garden swing, pond with fountain, off-street parking. Exercise trail, gym nearby.
Location Quapaw Quarter historic district. From I-30, take I-630 W, to Main St. Exit. Go left on Main to 22nd. Turn right on 22nd St. Go 1 block to inn at corner of 22nd & Louisiana.
Restrictions No smoking. Children 10 and over.
Credit cards Amex, MC, Visa.
Rates B&B, $125–140 suite, $85–140 double. Extra person, $50. $5 per night service.

Hotze House ¢ *Tel:* 501–376–6563
1619 Louisiana Street, P.O 164087, 72206 *Fax:* 501–374–5393

While many business travelers love to stay at B&Bs, they fear being inconvenienced by a lack of needed modern conveniences. Not so at Hotze House, a magnificent 4,000 square-foot Renaissance Revival mansion, built in 1900. When Suzanne and Steven Gates bought Hotze House in 1993, they used their own experiences as corporate travelers to ensure that guests would have everything needed, from in-room telephones and cable television to modern plumbing, electricity and heating/cooling systems. Suzanne's mom, Peggy Tooker, is the resident innkeeper. Breakfast, served 7–9 A.M., can be enjoyed in the formal dining room or the sunny conservatory, and might include minted blueberry souffle, melon slices, and sausage; or poached pears with pecans, mushroom-tomato quiche, potato casserole, honey-glazed ham, and biscuits.

"Restored to its original beauty with all modern amenities; careful attention to detail in every lovely room; accommodating, gracious staff. We were given a wonderful tour on arrival, and visited with Peggy, our host. Parking was private and well protected." *(Gary & Judy Toche)* "Initially attracted by the inn's beauty, I was then entranced by the warm hospitality. Unusually luxurious bathrooms, huge closets." *(Pamela Johnson)* "Beautiful woodwork, especially the mahogany staircase and elaborate parquet floors. Comfortable queen-size rice four-poster beds." *(MW)* "Wonderful breakfast waffles. Requests are willingly accommodated and preferences remembered." *(Jana Rucker)* "Exceptionally sensitive to the needs of corporate travelers." *(John Hodges)* "Exquisite antiques; beautiful mansion." *(Tina Hunzicker)*

Open All year.
Rooms 4 doubles—all with private shower and/or tub, telephone, clock, TV, desk, air-conditioning, ceiling fan, gas fireplace, individual climate control.

Facilities Dining room, living room, family room, library, music room, conservatory, guest pantry; verandas. ⅓ acre with off-street parking.
Location Governor's Mansion District; Quapaw Quarter Historic District. From I-30, take I-630 W, to Main St. Exit. Go left on Main to 17th & turn right. Go 1 block to inn at corner of 17th & Louisiana.
Restrictions No smoking inside. Children over 5. Traffic noise possible midweek.
Credit cards Amex, DC, Discover, MC, Visa.
Rates B&B, $90–100 double. Senior, AAA discounts. Tipping not encouraged.
Extras Airport/station pickups.

Pinnacle Vista Lodge
7510 Highway 300, 72212

Tel: 501–868–8905
Fax: 501–868–8905
E-mail: pinnaclevista@aristotle.net

If you'd like a peaceful country getaway just ten miles from downtown Little Rock, call the Pinnacle Vista Lodge, a log lodge built in 1925 and restored as a B&B in 1995 by Linda Westergard. Guests can relax on the deck, with its great view of Pinnacle Vista Mountain, or make themselves at home in the inviting great room, complete with exposed log walls, vaulted ceiling, stone fireplace, comfortable couches, and antique pool table. Guest rooms include the Greenery, done with dark green colors and 1920s walnut twin beds (converts to a king); the Victorian Rose, done in soft florals and turn-of-the-century oak furnishings; and Nana's Retreat, done in white iron and wicker, with Battenburg lace and handstitched quilts, and a blue and white color scheme. Breakfast, served 7:30–9:30 A.M., is offered at the common room table, or at individual tables on the deck, and includes fresh fruit and juice, peppered bacon or perhaps sausages, plus such entrees as Belgian waffles, apple-stuffed French toast, or savory eggs with cheddar.

"Peaceful, serene, and relaxing, with wonderful views from the front porch. Interesting antiques complement the charms of this rustic log lodge. Immaculate housekeeping; gracious, accommodating, knowledgeable hostess. We visited Little Rock's historic sights, and hiking up the mountain. The great room offers lots to do, and soft drinks and snacks are always available. Delicious egg souffle for breakfast." *(Patricia Hager)* "Charming lodge; cozy guest rooms; great mountain views." *(Rhonda Hicks)* "We missed our own pet back home, so Linda's friendly dogs kept us company." *(BAB)*

Open All year.
Rooms 1 suite, 2 doubles—all with private shower bath, clock, TV, air-conditioning, ceiling fan, robes. 1 with telephone, deck, coffee maker.
Facilities Great room with pool table, pinball machine, juke box, bar, TV, player piano, stereo, fireplace, stocked guest refrigerator. Dining room, bar/lounge, deck. 23 acres with hammock, adult swings, barn, lawn games, stocked fishing pond, nature trails, bird-watching. ¼ m to riding stable for trail rides, lessons. Lake nearby for boating, fishing. 1 m to Pinnacle Mt. State Pk. for hiking, fishing, canoeing; 15 min. to golf.
Location 10 m W of downtown Little Rock. From Little Rock, go N on I-430. Exit at Hwy. 10, Cantrell Ave. & W on 10. Go right (N) on Hwy. 300 to lodge sign on right.

Restrictions No smoking. Children 6 and over.
Credit cards MC, Visa.
Rates B&B, $95–125 double. Extra person, $15 (suite only). Antique shopping/lunch tour, $25. Romance weekend packages.
Extras Airport, train, bus pickup, $10. Limited German, French.

MAGNOLIA

Information please: Magnolia is located in southwestern Arkansas, 55 miles east of Texarkana, Texas. The **Magnolia Place B&B** (510 East Main Street, 71753; 501–234–6122 or 800–237–6122) is a 1910 Craftsman-style four-square home, restored as a B&B in 1994 by Ray Sullivent and Carolyne Hawley. Each of the five guest rooms has a private bath, in-room telephone, and TV, and is furnished with turn-of-the-century pieces. The B&B double rate of $89–129 includes a full breakfast.

MOUNTAIN VIEW

It's hard to imagine how isolated Mountain View was until the beginning of the 1970s—no paved roads, no trains, no scheduled buses. Then, in 1973, the Ozark Folk Center opened, bringing with it improved transportation. Dedicated to preserving the local culture, the center offers daily demonstrations of indigenous crafts, music and dance, storytelling, and cooking. Summer weekends, especially Saturday nights, see many impromptu outdoor concerts and dancing on the courthouse lawn. The perfect balance to a day spent absorbing cultural history is a good dose of natural history, exploring the fantastic formations in the Blanchard Springs Caverns, 15 miles northwest of town, in the Ozark National Forest. Also of interest is trout fishing on the White River, float trips on the Buffalo River, or shopping in local craft and antique shops.

Also recommended: A neo-Victorian-style home, built by Carole and Jerry Weber as a B&B in 1993, the **Country Oaks B&B** (Highway 9, HC 70, Box 63, 72560; 870–269–2704 or 800–455–2704) is located just a mile from town. Set on 69 acres with a private lake, it offers three spacious guest rooms, each with queen-size bed and private bath. The B&B double rates of $75 include full breakfast, and access to the guest pantry, stocked with soft drinks and cookies or brownies. "Inviting B&B; Carole is a wonderful innkeeper." *(RH)*

Information please: A motel alternative is the **Ozark Folk Center Lodge** (State Rte. 382, 72560; 870–269–3851 or 800–264–3655). "The single-level octagonally shaped buildings have a bungalow feel, many with a private view of the woods from two walls of windows. It's an easy walk to the crafts area, music show, and restaurant." *(Carol Moritz)* Double rates for the 60 guest rooms range from $35–55.

The Inn at Mountain View
307 West Washington Street, 72560

Tel: 870–269–4200
800–535–1301
Fax: 870–269–4200

In 1886, John Webb, Civil War veteran, successful businessman, and Mountain View's first postmaster, opened his rambling Victorian home to traveling salesmen, circuit riders, and other weary travelers, calling it the Dew Drop Inn (really). Re-named and restored as a B&B in 1977, the Inn at Mountain View is owned by Bob and Jenny Williams. The original carved woodwork and wainscotting are enhanced by period antiques, handmade quilts, and embroidered linens. Family-style breakfasts are set on the lazy Susans in the center of the oversized round oak tables in each dining room, and include homemade biscuits with sausage gravy, Belgian waffles topped with fruit, scrambled eggs, fresh fruit and juice.

"Exquisitely decorated in period, and reflective of the personality of the town. The bedrooms are beautiful, comfortable, and each has a theme. Violet's Arbor has a queen-size bed and sitting area, and is delicately done in white, purple, and green; Mallard's Rest is a corner room with two queen-size beds and a sitting area, and features jewel tones and a duck motif; and the private Grandmother's Attic has a king-size bed with an antique patchwork quilt, and 'Grandmother' herself (a large antique doll). Attention to detail is seen in the guest book in each room; pasted in the front of each book is an antique photograph of a fictional 'original occupant' of the room. Another thoughtful touch is the early morning coffee, in mugs printed 'Good Morning from Bob and Jennie!' The grounds are beautifully landscaped, and the wide wraparound porch is furnished with rocking chairs in which one can relax and enjoy the folk music that wafts from the square. The wonderful breakfast included waffles with vanilla praline syrup, sliced tomatoes with basil, and a fresh fruit cup. Bob has an inexhaustible fund of yarns and anecdotes, and the breakfast table conversation was lively indeed." *(Marcia Hecker, also Sidney Flynn)* "Friendly, helpful owners. Beautifully decorated with antiques, with lovely quilts and fine linens. Quiet location. Exceptionally clean and neat, with fresh paint, handsome landscaping, and careful attention to detail. Superb quality and quantity at breakfast." *(Carol Moritz)*

Open All year.
Rooms 3 suites, 7 doubles—all with private bath and/or shower, air-conditioning, ceiling fan.
Facilities 2 dining rooms, living room with fireplace, music room with piano, wraparound porch with rockers, gardens.
Location 1 block W Court House Square. From Main St., go N on Peabody, around Courthouse Sq., then left (W), on W. Washington St.
Restrictions Absolutely no smoking.
Credit cards Discover, MC, Visa.
Rates B&B, $60–100 suite, $65–80 double, $50–60 single. 2-3 night weekend/holiday minimum; no single rate on weekends. Extra person, $18.

Wildflower Bed & Breakfast ¢ 👪 — *Tel:* 870–269–4383
Courthouse Square, P.O. Box 72, 72560 — 800–591–4879

When the Wildflower B&B was built in 1918 to accommodate commercial (i.e. business) travelers, it was appropriately called The Commercial Hotel. Restored in 1982, it was renamed to "reflect what the inn is today rather than what it once was," and was purchased by LouAnne Rhodes in 1997. Listed on the National Register of Historic Places, this craftsman-style inn has a relaxed and welcoming atmosphere. The comfortable guest rooms are named for wildflowers—Azalea, Columbine, Foxglove, and so on, and the decor frequently reflects this theme. The furnishings include simple handmade curtains and dust ruffles, fluffy comforters, and original iron beds and dressers. The buffet breakfast, served in the lobby, includes fresh fruit and juice, breads, muffins, and jams, plus endless pots of coffee. Mountain View is a mecca for local musicians, many of whom congregate on the hotel's front porch.

"An inviting haven in the middle of the Ozark's fiddle-pickin' capital. Handsome, well-fitted rooms are tended with care." *(Janet Smith)* "The proximity to the wonderful mountain music played around the square at night beckons you to join in the fun." *(Susan & John Brant)* "Authentic period feel. LouAnne was attentive but never overbearing." *(Robert Grossmann)* "We've been coming to Mountain View and the Wildflower for years, and were delighted to find that LouAnne is just as friendly and caring as the previous owners. Immaculately clean, too." *(Pat Feeny)*

Open All year.
Rooms 3 suites, 5 doubles—6 with private shower bath, 2 rooms share 1 bath. All with air-conditioning. 1 with kitchenette.
Facilities Lobby, wraparound porch with frequent live music. 1 shaded acre. Pool, tennis, hiking, caves, rock-climbing nearby. Short drive to White River, Sylamore Creek, Greers Ferry Lake, for fishing, swimming, float trips.
Location N central AR, Stone Cty. 100 m N of Little Rock, 150 m W of Memphis, TN. Hwys. 66, 9, 5/14 all lead to Courthouse Sq.; Inn on sq. at corner of Washington and Peabody Sts. 1 m from Folk Center.
Restrictions No smoking. "Dry county."
Credit cards Amex, Discover, MC, Visa.
Rates B&B, $66–86 suite, $42–66 double, $37–48 single. Extra person, $6.
Extras Crib.

Key to Abbreviations and Symbols

For complete information and explanations, please see the Introduction.

¢ Especially good value for overnight accommodation.
Families welcome. Most (but not all) have cribs, baby-sitting, games, play equipment, and reduced rates for children.
Meals served to public; reservations recommended or required.
Tennis court and swimming pool and/or lake on grounds. Golf usually on grounds or nearby.
♿ Limited or full wheelchair access; call for details.
Rates: Range from least expensive room in low season to most expensive room in peak season.
Room only: No meals included; European Plan (EP).
B&B: Bed and breakfast; includes breakfast, sometimes afternoon/evening refreshment.
MAP: Modified American Plan; includes breakfast and dinner.
Full board: Three meals daily.
Alc lunch: A la carte lunch; average price of entree plus nonalcoholic drink, tax, tip.
Alc dinner: Average price of three-course dinner, including half bottle of house wine, tax, tip.
Prix fixe dinner: Three- to five-course set dinner, excluding wine, tax, tip unless otherwise noted.
Extras: Noted if available. Always confirm in advance. Pets are not permitted unless specified; if you are allergic, ask for details; *most innkeepers have pets.*

Florida

Elizabeth Pointe Lodge, Amelia Island

There *is* a real Florida apart from giant theme parks, condo developments, and endless chains of cloned hotels and motels. Although theme parks, beaches, and retired relatives are three popular reasons for visiting Florida, we'd like to suggest some less-well-known Florida highlights. In the southeast, visit the tranquil Japanese flower gardens at the Morikami Cultural Complex west of Delray Beach, or drop by a professional polo match. On the Gulf Coast, travel back roads to find isolated coastal inlets, drop by the Salvador Dali Museum in St. Petersberg, or visit unspoiled Honeymoon and Caladesi islands that are maintained as state parks.

Although best known for its theme parks, Central Florida also boasts miles of grassy prairies, flowering fruit groves, horse farms, 1400 lakes and the world's largest sandy pine forest. In Northeast Florida don't miss the Spanish flavor of St. Augustine, the oldest city in the United States. The Florida Panhandle, in the northwest, offers miles of sugar-white sand, rolling hill country near Tallahassee, the Alaqua Vineyards (one of only four wineries in the state), and an unusual mixture of Creole, Victorian and other architecture in Pensacola's Seville Historic District.

Peak season rates in most of Florida generally extend from December 1–15 through May 1–15; off-season rates are considerably lower. Do remember that August and September are the height of the tropical storm/hurricane season, so it keep this in mind when planning a trip.

AMELIA ISLAND

Amelia Island's only town is Fernandina Beach, at its north end, but since the two addresses are used interchangeably, and the island name is better known, we've listed our entries here. Amelia Island is located in the northeast corner of Florida, just south of the Georgia border, and 35 miles north of Jacksonville. Area activities focus on the area's wide sandy beaches, with ample opportunities for swimming, boating, and fishing, but golf and tennis are available as well. Many flags of sovereignty have flown over Amelia: France, Spain, England, Mexico, Confederate, and U.S.

Reader tips: "The historic district of Fernandina Beach feels the way Key West did 25 years ago. Friendly people; interesting shops and good places to eat." *(Joe & Sheila Schmidt)* "The Kingsley Plantation south of Amelia Island is worth visiting, as are the state parks at Little Talbot Island and Fort Clinch, where there are reenactments of military drills of the 1860s." *(April Burwell)* "The historic district is compact, making walking delightful." *(SWS)*

Also recommended: Although it's far too big for a full entry with hundreds of rooms, dozens of swimming pools and tennis courts, and 45 holes of golf, we've had good reports on the **Amelia Island Plantation** (3000 First Coast Highway, P.O. Box 3000, Amelia Island 32035-1307; 904–261–6161 or 800–874–6878). Set on 1,300 acres with miles of hiking trails and beautiful beaches, it's an excellent choice for families. No meals are included with the $125–405 double rate, so be sure to ask about special packages.

Information please: In Fernandina Beach's downtown historic district is the **Hoyt House B&B** (804 Atlantic Avenue, 32034; 904–277–4300), a restored Queen Anne-style Victorian home. There are three inviting common areas for guests, in addition to the dining room and the garden gazebo. The nine guest rooms have king- and queen-size beds, antique and reproduction furnishings, custom window treatments, and private baths. Rates of $100–139 double occupancy include a full breakfast.

For additional area entries, see **Jacksonville** and **Orange Park;** in **Georgia,** look under **Cumberland Island** and **St. Marys.**

The Amelia Island Williams House ♿
103 South 9th Street, 32034

Tel: 904–277–2328
800–414–9257
Fax: 904–321–1325

History buffs will have a hard time finding a B&B with a past more enticing than that of the Williams House. Built in 1856, the house was once part of the Underground Railroad for runaway slaves, complete with a secret room that's still in existence. Jefferson Davis stayed here when he was president of the Confederacy, and Union troops later used the home as an infirmary. When Dick Flitz and Chris Carter restored the inn in 1993, they returned it to its original elegance, refinishing over 6,500 square feet of woodwork and hanging over 350 rolls of rich Victorian reproduction wallpaper. Architectural highlights of this 500-square-foot mansion include a sweeping cherry and mahogany staircase, lined with original stained glass windows. Museum quality antiques range from a carpet that belonged to Napoleon Bonaparte to a silk robe worn by the last Emperor of China. Additional accommodations are available in the home next door, built circa 1860; each guest room is decorated with antiques, and with decorating themes honoring different countries—perhaps France, China, or England.

Breakfast is served in a warm and informal atmosphere between 8:30 and 9:30 A.M. in the dining room, complete with an inlaid wood dining room table, Chippendale chairs, and a magnificent crystal chandelier. A typical meal might include stuffed baked croissants with raspberry sauce, egg souffle, or French toast, served on antique china and silver.

"Outstanding accommodations, impeccable service." *(Tom Wilson & Cynthia Hermes)* "Probably the most exquisitely decorated B&B I've ever seen. Formal, but not overdone or cluttered, and where Dick and Chris didn't use antiques, they used authentic reproductions to great effect. One spacious guest room has a pair of turn-of-the-century-style stained glass lamps mounted bedside, plus an authentic Tiffany lamp on a side table. Bathrooms, especially in the newly renovated building, are extravagant." *(SWS)*

Open All year.
Rooms 2 suites, 6 doubles—all with private bath, telephone, radio, clock, TV/VCR, desk, air-conditioning, ceiling fan, balcony. 4 in adjacent house. 2 with whirlpool tub.
Facilities Dining room with fireplace, living room with fireplace, piano; double wraparound verandas with swings. Book/video library. Gardens, hot tub, off-street parking. 2 blocks to tennis; 1 m from beach; 9 blocks to charter fishing.
Location Historic district. Take Exit 129 off I-95. Go E to Fernandina Beach, where A1A becomes two lanes. Go right on Ash St. to inn at corner of Ash and 9th.
Restrictions No smoking. Children 12 and over.
Credit cards MC, Visa.
Rates B&B, $155 suite, $135–165 double. Extra person, $20. Senior discount.
Extras Wheelchair access; 1 room specially equipped. Airport pickup. German spoken.

Bailey House ♿

28 South 7th Street, 32034

Tel: 904–261–5390
800–251–5390
Fax: 904–321–0103
E-mail: bailey@net-magic.wet

When steamship agent Effingham Bailey and his new bride Kate MacDonell built their family home, they acquired mail-order plans from a Tennessee architect, and hired local ship carpenters to complete their Queen Anne home in 1895. Now listed on the National Register of Historic Places, it features a wraparound porch, turrets, widow's walk, stained glass windows, heart pine floors, a grand staircase, and antique period furnishings. Owned by the Bailey family for almost 70 years, the home was restored as an inn in 1983, and purchased by Jenny and Tom Bishop in 1993. Breakfast is served at the dining room table from 8:15 to 9:15 A.M., and includes a hot entree, fresh fruit, homemade breads and cereals.

"Warm and helpful innkeepers Tom and Jenny keep the house immaculately clean. Wonderful breakfasts of homemade granola, yogurt, bran muffins, and fresh-squeezed juice." *(Vicky Matalon)* "The exterior of the house is lovely, and is equally appealing on the inside, with lovely stained glass windows in the common areas. A new wing containing four additional guest rooms was under construction when I visited." *(SWS)*

Open All year.
Rooms 5 doubles—all with private bath and/or shower, telephone, clock, TV, air-conditioning, ceiling fan. 3 with fireplace.
Facilities Dining room with fireplace, living room, wraparound veranda. Rose garden, off-street parking, bicycles.
Location Historic disrict. Located 7th Street, off of Ash Street.
Restrictions No smoking. Children 8 and over.
Credit cards Amex, MC, Visa.
Rates B&B, $85–115. Extra person, $15. 10% AAA discount.
Extras Limited wheelchair access. Crib.

Elizabeth Pointe Lodge
98 South Fletcher Avenue, 32034

Tel: 904–277–4851
800–772–3359
Fax: 904–277–6500
E-mail: Eliz.Pt.@worldnet.att.net

Constructed in an 1890s Nantucket shingle style with a maritime theme, the Elizabeth Pointe Lodge is owned by David and Susan Caples. Just steps from the sand dunes, the inn has a large porch with comfy rocking chairs and a cheery sunroom where a generous buffet breakfast of fresh juice and fruit, cereal, home-baked muffins and pastries, grits, and scrambled eggs is served from 7 to 9 A.M. Rates also include the afternoon lemonade, and wine and cheese from 6–7 P.M.

"Hotel-style convenience with inn-style caring; the staff was friendly, helpful, and professional. Lovely water views from most common areas, guest rooms and porches. The cool ocean breezes allowed me to open the windows wide and sleep like a baby to the sound of the waves lapping the shore. My room had an extremely comfortable queen-size sleigh bed, lamps and tables at either side, rattan chair with reading light and phone adjacent, and a custom-built, well-designed storage unit with space for hanging and folded clothes, plus a TV. Spacious bathroom, with excellent lighting and a double-size deep soaking tub. You can enjoy your breakfast in the dining room or on the porch, chatting with the other guests or in privacy, as you prefer. The evening social hour was set up in the library, with fresh fruit and sliced cheese, spinach dip and crackers; we took our glasses and snacks out to the porch to enjoy the ocean air." *(SWS)*

"Our room had a king-size bed with a warm throw and the windows, framed by simple lace panels, gave a direct view out to the dunes. Fresh flowers, Crabtree & Evelyn toiletries, and the morning paper at our door were all thoughtful touches." *(Rebecca Bowers)* "The roaring fire in the library fireplace was appreciated on a stormy night. An elevator takes you directly from the convenient parking area to room level." *(Marlene Jewwett)* "Good provisions for the beach—baskets for shelling, towels, and an outside shower. The porch is a good place for enjoying high tide, when the water almost reaches the steps." *(BA)* "The light lunch menu, available until midnight, was convenient after a day's sightseeing." *(Madge Harlan)* "Shelves are placed conveniently in the bathrooms for cosmetics. The kitchen refrigerator is always open for juice, milk, and tea; coffee is close at hand." *(Beth & Jay Childress, also Diana & Jim Inman)*

Open All year.
Rooms 3 suites, 22 doubles—all with full private bath, telephone, radio, TV, air-conditioning. 7 with whirlpool tub; some with desk, refrigerator, deck. 1 suite in cottage, 4 rooms in annex.
Facilities Dining room, living room, library with fireplace, books, games; porch. Beach with swimming; beach equipment, rental bikes. Off-street parking. Innkeeping seminars.
Location At seaport of Fernandina. 1.5 m from Historic District.
Restrictions No smoking.
Credit cards Amex, MC, Visa.
Rates B&B, $125–195 double. Extra person, $20. Children under 6 free. Senior, AAA discount. Alc lunch, $7. Thanksgiving, Christmas, special event packages.
Extras Wheelchair access; bathroom specially equipped for the disabled. Airport, station pickup, $22. Crib, babysitting. German, Spanish spoken.

The Fairbanks House ♿
227 South Seventh Street, 32034

Tel: 904–277–0500
800–261–4838
Fax: 904–277–3103
E-mail: fairbanks@net-magic.net

Most people think of Florida architecture in terms of high-rise hotels and pastel-colored bungalows, which makes the magnificent Italianate architecture of the Fairbanks House even more striking. Built in 1885 and listed on the National Register of Historic Places, the inn was restored by Nelson and Mary Smelker, and opened in 1994. The inn's exterior is painted in shades of gray-green with burgundy accents, and is highlighted by a Romanesque-style tower, numerous arches and pilasters; the inside offers polished hardwood floors, intricately carved moldings, and fireplace tiles with scenes from Shakespeare and Aesop's Fables. The guest rooms are appointed with antiques, Oriental rugs, and four-poster or canopy king-, queen-, or twin-size beds. Mary made all the drapes, bedspreads and pillow shams, and has done a first-rate job of balancing period charm with modern preferences for comfort and lightness. The breakfast of homemade breads, fresh fruit, and juice is served on silver, china, and crystal, and can be enjoyed in the dining room or on the patio; rates also include evening refreshments.

"Spectacular restoration, lavish decor. Cordial owners and staff. The location is perfect, a few pleasant blocks from the main street. Beautiful gardens, with a lovely swimming pool—the only in-town B&B that has one." *(SWS)* "Each morning's breakfast was a different surprise—homemade muffins, baked apples, fried bananas, all wonderfully presented and served." *(Stephen & Ellen Filreis)* "Beautiful mansion with high ceilings, spacious rooms. In the entry, layers of old paint were stripped away to reveal the beautiful wood underneath. Spacious, attractive grounds." *(Don & Karen Jones)* "The owners were never too busy to stop and chat or offer information of local interest." *(Belinda Barrow)* "Friendly owners, charming grounds, interesting architecture, impeccably maintained. Our creamy-colored cottage had four tall windows, coordinating fabrics, comfortable seating and good reading materials, a well-supplied kitchen, comfortable bedroom and a large bathroom equipped with wonderful-smelling hand lotion. The inn is just a few blocks' walk from the center of Amelia Island, with lots of little shops, leading down to the water. A very friendly place, especially appealing midweek." *(SC, also Mrs. & Mr. George Basior)*

Open All year.
Rooms 3 cottages, 3 suites, 6 doubles—all with private bath and/or shower, telephone, TV, air-conditioning. Nine with fan, fireplace; some with whirlpool tub, refrigerator, balcony.
Facilities Dining room with fireplace, living room with fireplace, books; porches. 1 acre with flower gardens, patios, off-street parking, swimming pool, gazebo, lawn games, beach chairs, bicycles. 1 m to ocean; 7 blocks to river.
Location 2 blocks from town in historic district.
Restrictions No smoking.
Credit cards Amex, Discover, MC, Visa.
Rates B&B, $99–185 double. Extra person, $20. Senior, AAA discount. Corporate rates. Romance, event packages.
Extras Wheelchair access; bathroom specially equipped for the disabled. Airport pickup.

Florida House Inn ✕ ♿ *Tel:* 904–261–3300
20 & 22 South 3rd Street 800–258–3301
P.O. Box 688, 32034 *E-mail:* innkeepers@floridahouseinn.com

One-time Florida resident Thomas Alva Edison is said to have remarked that: "Invention is 1% inspiration, 99% perspiration." When you see the "before" and "after" pictures of the Florida House, you may decide that restoring an old inn follows a similar ratio. In 1991, Karen and Bob Warner completed a total renovation of the Florida's oldest surviving (but just barely) hotel. During the 19th century, its many famous guests included General Ulysses S. Grant, Jose Marti, plus assorted Rockefellers and Carnegies; in those days, the inn had 25 guest rooms and no indoor plumbing—now all have private baths, many with luxurious double Jacuzzi tubs! Rates include a full Southern breakfast, served from 8 to 9:30 a.m.; also available is a restaurant offering "boarding house" dining—fried chicken and catfish with fresh Southern-style vegetables, served family-style at tables for twelve.

"Karen, Bob and their staff will cater to your every whim, making your stay exactly as you want it. After a wonderful breakfast of French toast and other treats, served on beautiful china, I love to finish my coffee on the patio, enjoying the breeze, with a fuzzy kitten curled into my lap." *(Lisa Kittrell)* "Southern hospitality; down-home cooking." *(Eleanor Smith)* "Good lighting and strong showers. An excellent breakfast is served on the back porch or in the sunny breakfast room. Sipping afternoon lemonade on the wooden rockers of the second floor porch was equally pleasant." *(Shirley Hall)* "The shade of time-twisted oaks makes the porch an inviting place to gather over evening wine." *(Michael & Jeanne Green)* "The annual May seafood festival is conveniently located right at the inn's front door." *(Mr. & Mrs. John Cheetham)* "Extensive insulation added during the renovations kept our room extremely quiet." *(Robert & Donna Jacobson)* "Crisp cotton sheets; clean, spacious bathroom; warm hospitality." *(SW & AB)*

"Karen and Bob have done a wonderful job of preserving the inn's historic charm, while adding all modern conveniences. Lunch and dinner are very reasonably priced; along with gallons of iced tea, I sampled delicious sweet and sour cabbage, collard greens, chicken and dumplings, candied yams, and cornbread, and even found room for a bite of apple crisp. The fun, low-key, cozy pub has an incredible collection of bottled brews that are well worth a detour for beer lovers. Antique quilts line the hallway walls, and accent the simple but pleasing furnishings of the guest rooms. Color schemes are soothing and uncomplicated, rooms uncluttered. The two least expensive rooms are small, but a super value." *(SWS)*

Open All year.
Rooms 1 suite, 14 doubles—all with private bath and/or shower, telephone, radio, TV, air-conditioning, ceiling fan. Most with desk; 10 with fireplace, double Jacuzzi tub. 12 rooms in North Bldg; 3 rooms in South Bldg.
Facilities Breakfast room, restaurant, pub with fireplace, TV; parlor with fireplace, games. Gazebo, garden courtyard with fountain. Fax, copier, laundry facilities. Off-street parking. Tennis, golf nearby. 5 min. from Atlantic Ocean for boating, fishing, swimming; 2 blocks from marina.
Location Historic District. From I-95, take Exit 129 and follow Rte. A1A to Amelia Island, Fernandina Beach. Rte. A1A turns into 8th St. on island. Follow 8th St. to the intersection of 8th St. & Atlantic/Centre St. (Shell gas station on left). Turn left on Atlantic/Centre St. Go 5 blocks to S 3rd St. & turn left. Florida House Inn is ½block from Centre on left.
Restrictions Smoking only in pub, on porches, patio.
Credit cards All major.
Rates B&B, $135 suite, $70–140 double. Extra person, $10. 2-night weekend minimum.
Extras Limited wheelchair access. Some pets by arrangement. Local airport/marina pickups. Limited Spanish spoken.

APALACHICOLA

Although once a major Gulf port, Apalachicola (known locally as Apalach) is now a sleepy town in the Florida Panhandle, with shrimp and oysters being the primary cash crops.

Information please: A magnificently renovated 1905 Victorian home, the **Coombs House Inn** (80 Sixth Street, 32320; 904–653–9199) is located in the historic district, minutes from the bay. The ten guest rooms in the main house are beautifully done with elegant antiques and fine reproductions, English chintz fabrics, and Oriental carpet atop gleaming hardwood floors. More casual in decor are the eight rooms in the restored 1907 Coombs Cottage annex. B&B double rates of $69–$125 include a continental breakfast served from 8 to 11 A.M. and use of the inn's bicycles.

A Greek Revival-style plantation home built in 1838, **Magnolia Hall** (177 5th Street, 32320; 904–653–2431) has a swimming pool and rose garden for guests' relaxation. The two guest rooms occupy the entire second floor; each has a gas log fireplace and private bath. The B&B double rates are $150 for the first night, $100 the second, including wake-up coffee, a full breakfast, and afternoon wine and cheese.

Gibson Inn ¢ ✕
51 Avenue C, 32320

Tel: 904–653–2191
904–653–8282

A large blue building surrounded by two-story white verandas and topped by a cupola, the turn-of-the-century Gibson Inn dates from the town's glory days. Restored in 1983, the inn overlooks the water and St. George Island. Rooms are furnished in period, with four-poster beds, ceiling fans, antique armoires, brass and porcelain bathroom fixtures, and claw-foot tubs. Its popular restaurant serves three meals a day, from a full range of standard breakfast favorites, to a lunch of fried oysters, to a dinner of seafood gumbo; shrimp and scallop Dijon; and chocolate bourbon pecan pie.

"Most rooms have four-poster beds; ours had a TV in the armoire, two chairs, and a writing table." *(April Burwell)* "Our beautiful third-floor corner room had a luxurious bath and excellent bedding." *(Imogene Tillis)* "The friendly desk clerk offered helpful suggestions, and we enjoyed a dinner of fresh local snapper. The staff was quick to fix a slow drain in our bathtub." *(HB)* "Well prepared dinner, excellent service, charming hostess." *(Bill Novak)* "The dinner was wonderful, rooms clean and fresh. Excellent renovation." *(JW)* Comments welcome.

Open All year.
Rooms 2 suites, 29 doubles—all with private bath, telephone, TV, air-conditioning, ceiling fan.
Facilities Restaurant, bar with weekend entertainment, verandas, gift/craft shop. Swimming, shelling, fishing, marina nearby.
Location FL Panhandle. Center of town, 1 block from waterfront. 75 m SW of Tallahassee, 60 m SE of Panama City, at corner of Hwy. 98 and Avenue C.
Credit cards MC, Visa.
Rates Room only, $85–115 suite, $70–80 double. Extra person, $5. Senior, group, AAA, military discounts. Package rates. Alc breakfast, $3–7; alc lunch, $7–13; alc dinner, $20–40. 2-night holiday minimum.
Extras Crib. Pets, $5 per night.

AVON PARK

Information please: Built in 1925 in the revivalist style, the **Hotel Jacaranda** (19 East Main Street, 33825; 941–453–2211) was renovated by

South Florida Community College and the SFCC Foundation in 1988. Lunch and dinner feature regional favorites: fried chicken, barbecued ribs, ham, roast beef, southern-style vegetables and desserts. B&B double rates for the 60 hotel rooms range from $40–55. "The second-floor sitting porch is a wonderful place to read and relax. The hot tub and swimming pool are clean and well-maintained, and the staff is friendly. There is a 4,000-book library in the lobby, and a fine antique store specializing in glass and china." *(Bill McGowan)* "My favorite rooms are the mini-suites which open on the balcony via French doors. Fascinating history, immaculately clean." *(Imogene Tillis)*

BIG PINE KEY

Also recommended: To escape the bustle of Key West, consider a visit to tropical, unspoiled Big Pine Key, 15 miles southwest of Marathon, and 33 miles northeast of Key West. Two delightful B&B options are **The Barnacle B&B** (Long Beach Drive, Route 1, Box 780A, Big Pine Key 33043; 305–872–3298) and the adjacent **Casa Grande** (Long Beach Drive, P.O. Box 378, 33043; 305–872–2878). Both B&Bs offer quiet oceanside settings, charming tropical architecture and landscaping, knowledgeable owners, pleasant breakfasts and reasonable rates. "You share the beach with Key deer and long-legged water birds. Tim Marquis of the Barnacle is an accomplished dive instructor and can arrange trips on his 35-foot Luhrs power boat. Excellent seafood is available at KD's, Montes, or Mango Mama's." *(Joe & Shelia Schmidt)*

CAPTIVA ISLAND

For a change of pace from shell collecting and lazing on the wonderful beaches, spend time hiking, canoeing, or bicycling in the "Ding" Darling National Wildlife Preserve in Sanibel, or cross the causeway back to Fort Myers to visit the winter home of Thomas Edison. You can see his home, research labs, and 14-acre botanical gardens.

Reader tip: "The one major drawback about the entire Sanibel/Captiva area is the abominable traffic."

Information please: Set on a narrow strip of land between the Gulf of Mexico and Pine Island Sound, **'Tween Waters Inn** (15951 Captiva Road, 33924; 941–472–5161 or 800–223–5865) began as a one-cabin operation in 1926. The hotel now offers accommodations in 83 hotel rooms, plus 10 apartments and 30 cottages. The waterview suites are quite lovely; others seem to be standard motel issue or can be quite close to noisy traffic. "Our room in the main inn had a breathtaking view overlooking the Gulf of Mexico. We had a screened-in deck that allowed us to enjoy the sunsets and cool ocean breezes. Our room was simple in style but comfortable. Best of all was its location just a few minutes' walk from the gorgeous, private, and shell-covered Captiva Beach. To save money, we used our refrigerator to store breakfast and lunch fixings." *(Thomas & Linda Fontana)*

For additional area entries, see **Sanibel.**

CEDAR KEY

Reader tips: "Cedar Key is the way Florida used to be before the tourists found it—quiet, unflashy. Minimal tourist traffic, quaint, uncrowded, a great area for birds and other natural joys. The old cemetery has shell-covered graves, nesting osprey, and historic tombstones. Also good restaurants, shell mounds, wildlife refuges, and historic walking tours. There's a marina, museum, park, fishing pier. A pleasant spot to visit as a destination or as a stopover, and not far from Manatee State Park." *(Celia McCullough & Gary Kaplan)* "The natives like The Cook's Cafe for casual eating; I like their pineapple cheesecake. To see the watery backcountry try the Island Hopper ferry (352–543–5904)." *(Joe & Sheila Schmidt)*

Also recommended: "In the late 1800s several factories were constructed in Cedar Key to produce wood pencils. The **Cedar Key B&B** (3rd and F Streets, 32625; 352–543–9000 or 800–453–5051) was built in 1880 by the Eagle Cedar Mill to house its salesman. Though not large, guest rooms are bright and clean. Shops and restaurants are easily reached on foot." *(Joe & Sheila Schmidt)* The B&B double rate for the five guest rooms, each with private bath, is $65–85, including a full breakfast and afternoon tea and snacks. Lois and Bob Davenport restored this building in 1991 as a B&B.

Information please: The historic **Island Hotel** (2nd & B Streets, P.O. Box 460, 32625; 352–543–5111) was built of cypress faced with tabby, a mixture of lime rock and crushed oyster shells. Originally built as a general store in the 1850's, the building was turned into a hotel in 1910. Much of the structure is still original, with 11-inch walls, and oak floors sloping in every direction. Dawn and Tony Cousins bought the hotel in 1996, planned to renovate it, while preserving its historic charms. The $85–105 rates for the ten guest rooms include a full breakfast served with homemade poppyseed bread, one of the chef's specialties, while seafood is the favorite at dinner. One reader enthused: "Funky, laid-back Jimmy Buffet-type atmosphere; the restaurant is popular with locals. Absolutely delicious food; friendly, accommodating hosts; nice bar; a delightful town to explore." *(Mrs. John T. May)* "I understand that Dawn and Tony plan to add a few rooms in an annex to accommodate TV watchers. The restaurant serves fresh seafood, cooked to enhance its flavors, not fried to death as do so many local eateries. A peaceful spot to stop and relax and take a taste of the past." *(Debbie Bergstrom)*

For a longer stay in this sleepy fishing village, rent an appealing condo at **The Island Place** (P.O. Box 687, 32625; 352–543–5307 or 800–780–6522), next to the city marina. Designed to blend with the local architecture, the buildings have gabled roofs and tiered verandas overlooking the water. Though small, units have one or two bedrooms, bunk beds for the kids, kitchen, living room, and balcony; there's a swimming pool and hot tub on the grounds. Rates range from $75–130.

DEFUNIAK SPRINGS

Also recommended: Convenient to I-10, about 70 miles east of Pensacola is **Sunbright Manor** (606 Live Oak, DeFuniak Springs 32433; 904–892–0656). "After touring the historic district of this small town, we enjoyed cool drinks on the front porch of this 1886 Queen Anne Victorian house. In addition to the inn's tower, a striking architectural feature, are its extensive porches, with some 1,600 spindles and 33 columns. Delicious breakfast of cheese and egg soufflé, fresh fruit, and homemade muffins." *(HB)* The manor has three guest rooms, two with private baths, and the reasonable $75 B&B double rate includes early morning coffee, full breakfast, and evening tea. "A restful stop when travelling Interstate 10. Byrdie Mitchell is a delightful hostess. Her home is spotless and well maintained." *(Joe & Sheila Schmidt)*

DESTIN

Once a sleepy area of the Florida Panhandle best known for the prolific off-shore fishing in the Gulf of Mexico, Destin has boomed into a major resort community. Most visitors today are attracted by the dazzlingly white sand beaches and brilliant greens and blues of the Gulf surf. Known as the "Emerald Coast," the region boasts of 24 miles of beach, more than 12 miles of which are protected from any development. Prices are moderate (relative to the east and west coasts of Florida) in season and a bargain the rest of the year.

Information please: As you might expect from its name, the **Frangista Beach Inn** (4150 Old Highway East, 32541; 904–654–5501 or 800–382–2612) overlooks the beach. The 52 rooms (in two three-story units) have clay tile floors, tongue and groove paneling, color-washed furnishings, and Adirondack chairs; some of the units have kitchens, and double rates range from $90–375. Some units are on the bay side, and others are across the street. "Beautifully decorated and very clean. Our small suite had a separate living room, mini-kitchen area, perfect for fixing breakfast to take outside. It was directly on one of Florida's loveliest beaches. Helpful staff; recently built swimming pool and refurbished restaurant." *(Theresa Bestor)*

With uninterrupted Gulf views from its private beach, the **Henderson Park Inn** (2700 Old Highway 98, 32541; 904–837–4853 or 800–336–4853) sits among the dunes at the eastern boundary of Henderson Beach State Park. The inn is reminiscent of a Victorian hotel, while the adjoining "villa" looks like a beach cottage, with family-style efficiency suites. The 19 inn rooms have reproduction Queen Anne furnishings and designer fabrics; the 18 villa rooms have more of a beach-cottage look. The double rates of $100–225 include a continental breakfast.

For an additional area entry, see **Santa Rosa Beach**.

EVERGLADES CITY

The Ivey House ¢
107 Camellia Street, P.O. Box 5038, 34139

Tel: 941–695–3299
941–695–4666
Summer: 860–739–0791
Fax: 941–695–4155
Summer fax: 860–739–4470
E-mail: NACT1@aol.com

The Tamiami Trail (now Hwy 41), connecting Miami and Naples, was constructed in the 1920s. Everglades City became a boom town during this period, and what is now The Ivey House was built as a recreational center for the road workers. In 1989, it was purchased and renovated by North American Canoe Tours, for use as a B&B. The inn is surrounded by flower beds; inside, the country charm is enhanced by 1930s antiques. Guest rooms are simply furnished with either twin beds, a single bed, or a queen-size bed. Rates include a breakfast of bagels, fresh baked breads and muffins, citrus fruits, cereal, coffee, tea and orange juice; tea is served in the afternoon. Manager Sandee Dagley and her staff are happy to share their years of experience in guiding travelers on canoe adventures through the Everglades and will suggest hikes and canoe trails, visits to the nesting sites of bald eagles, great horned owls, and ospreys.

"Everglades City, at the northwestern entrance to Everglades National Park, has the charm of a small fishing village, with airboat rides, and some pleasant places to eat. At the Ivey House you can rent a canoe, kayak, or motorized skiff and enjoy the haunting beauty of this remote area. The inn is clean and well-maintained." *(Joe & Sheila Schmidt)* "After dinner, guests gather on the porch for a relaxing drink and conversation." *(Mrs. S.M. Gabb)* "Various public areas afford the opportunity to meet the other guests, while still allowing for individual privacy. The staff is extremely knowledgeable about the history, flora, and fauna of the area, and are adept at directing guest to local areas/attractions of interest." *(Nicky Simpson)* "Friendly, anxious-to-please staff; convenient excursions." *(William Bell)* "Knowledgeable hosts. Outstanding hospitality and service; attractive and quiet. Good food, ample servings." *(Michael North)*

Open Nov. 1–April 15.
Rooms 10 rooms—all with air-conditioning. All share men's/women's bathrooms with multiple showers/toilets. 2-room cottage with air-conditioning, shower bath, kitchen, screened porch.

Facilities Living room with TV, books; decks, porches. Bicycles; coin-op laundry. Flower, herb gardens. Airboat rides, canoe, boat rentals, fishing, all-inclusive canoe tours.
Location SW FL, 32 m S of Naples. Everglades Natl Park. From Tamiami Trail (Hwy. 41), go S on Rte. 29. After crossing bridge, turn right at Circle K store & watch for inn on right.
Restrictions Smoking & alcohol on porches only.
Credit cards MC, Visa.
Rates B&B, $50–55 double. 2-night minimum during Seafood Festival. Cottage, $75–105, 2-night minimum.

FT. LAUDERDALE

Shifting away from its "beach-blanket-bingo" spring break reputation, Fort Lauderdale now offers more than the beach. Enjoy its sophisticated international restaurants, the Riverwalk—following the New River past shops, eateries, tropical gardens—and the Museum of Art. In 1998, a state-of-the-art aquarium and entertainment complex will open. It is, however, a metropolitan area, so don't leave your "street smarts" at home.

Information please: A gracious taste of "old Florida" awaits visitors to the **Riverside Hotel** (620 East Las Olas Boulevard, 33301; 954–467–0671). Bordered by Las Olas (the waves) Boulevard, filled with fine shops and restaurants, the shaded grounds of the Riverside have changed little since the hotel was built over 50 years ago. "Guest rooms in the original building, constructed in 1936, are spacious and spotless, with beautiful oak furniture. Lovely hand-painted tiles." *(Diane Wolf)* Double rates for the 109 rooms are $100–229.

La Casa del Mar
3003 Granada Street, 33304–4317

Tel: 954–467–2037
800–739–0009
Fax: 954–467–7439

B&Bs may be spreading through much of Florida quicker than kudzu, but not in Broward County, where La Casa del Mar was the area's first. Built in 1940 as an efficiency hotel, it was restored as a B&B in 1994 by Larry Ataniso and Lee Prellwitz, and enjoys a convenient location, just 300 feet from the beach. Guest rooms are furnished individually, including the Impressionistic Monet room, the Judy Garland room, and the Southwestern Room. Breakfast is served at 9 A.M., usually at tables for two or four in the landscaped fountain courtyard, and includes hazelnut coffee and Florida orange juice, plus a sausage and mushroom casserole, and strawberry scones, or perhaps orange French toast and ham. Every day but Sunday, guests gather by the swimming pool for afternoon wine and cheese.

"Convenient to the many clubs of Ft. Lauderdale's cosmopolitan night-life. Passing through the video-monitored front gate, we entered a community of peace and tranquility. Larry and Lee offer an exceptionally high level of care, concern, and professionalism; they are knowledgeable about local events and services, and provide a safe, spacious, clean home-away-from home. A highlight was the lively and entertaining wine-and-cheese evening with our hosts and the other guests, with cool jazz playing softly in the background. Our immaculate room was charming, spacious, and guest-friendly, with all amenities—towels, soaps, laundry detergent—easily visible and readily replaced. As for quiet—if we hadn't socialized earlier that evening with the other guests—I'd have though the inn was empty. Not a sound from the neighbors above or on either side. Lee and Larry were exceptionally gracious and kind." *(Suzanne Phillips)* "Breakfast is served beside the pool, in the pretty and restful courtyard, under the flowering vines." *(Mary Wardley)* "Great breakfasts; enjoyable social hour with wonderful focaccia. Clean rooms, good service, nice hosts, good location." *(Ellen Nash)* "Convenient to beach and major highways." *(Stephen Casey)*

Open All year.
Rooms 10 doubles—all with private bath and/or shower, telephone, radio, clock, TV/VCR, desk, refrigerator, air-conditioning, ceiling fan. Some with kitchenette.
Facilities Breakfast room, guest laundry. Courtyard with unheated swimming pool, off-street parking. 300 ft. from ocean beach.
Location SE FL. Approx. 25 m N of Miami. Center of town. Half block from Ocean Blvd. (A1A), at corner of Granada & Birch. Granada is approx. halfway between Las Olas & Sunrise Blvds.
Restrictions No smoking in main house, some guest rooms. Children over 13.
Credit cards Amex, DC, MC, Visa.
Rates B&B, $75–135 double. Extra person, $25. Tips appreciated for housekeeping.

GAINESVILLE

Located in north central Florida, Gainesville is home to the University of Florida.

Information please: Built in 1885, **The Magnolia Plantation** (309 Southeast Seventh Street, 32601; 352–375–6653 or 800–201–2379) takes its name from the trees surrounding this Victorian Second Empire mansard-roofed mansion. Each of the six guest rooms has a private bath and gas fireplace, and the B&B double rate ranges from $80–150, including breakfasts of waffles, quiche, or stuffed French toast. "In the historic district, at the edge of downtown, with beautiful gardens, gazebo, and pond with waterfall. Guest rooms are clean, quiet, cozy, and charming." *(Donna & Bob Jacobson)*

Located in the historic downtown area, **The Sweetwater Branch Inn** (625 East University Avenue, 32601; 352–373–6760) offers an acre of fountain-filled gardens. This restored 1885 Victorian has seven antique-furnished rooms priced at $70–125 which include full breakfast of crepes, croissants, fruits, and juices. Reports appreciated.

For additional area inns, see **High Springs** and **Micanopy.**

HAINES CITY

A quiet alternative to the busy Orlando area is Haines City, a small citrus-growing community in central Florida, 20 miles south of Disney World.

Information please: A charming Art Deco-style home built in 1924 at the height of the Florida land boom, the **Holly Garden Inn** (106 First Street South, 33844; 941–421–9867) offers five guest rooms, each with private bath and TV, as well as a tea room open for lunch on weekdays (by reservation). Flowers bloom throughout the house, in floral arrangements and in the decor—wallpaper, comforters and fabrics. The B&B double rate of $79–89 includes a full Southern breakfast; snacks and beverages fill an antique buffet in the hallway. "Charming, energetic young owners; nicely decorated with Victorian antiques; tasty breakfast." *(Lynn Fullman)*

HIGH SPRINGS

Reader tips: "If you love antique shops, craft galleries, and a wide range of outdoor activities, visit High Springs." *(Donna Jacobson)* "Worth a visit in the area are O'Leno State Park for hiking, Ichetucknee State Park for swimming and snorkeling, and Ginny Springs for scuba diving, snorkeling, and swimming. Excellent meals at the Great Outdoors Cafe." *(Bill Novack)*

Grady House ¢ *Tel:* 904–454–2206
420 Northwest First Avenue, 32655

Fine old homes never die—they're just reborn as B&Bs. Although that's not always true, it certainly applies to the Grady House. Built in 1917, it served as High Spring's first bakery, then became a boarding house for railroad workers when the railroad was a major local industry. Later, many locals lived here as young married couples. Fallen on hard times, Diane and Ed Shupe rescued the house in 1992, restoring it as a B&B designed for relaxing getaways. Guests are invited to the dining room table at 9 A.M. each morning for breakfasts of spinach quiche or perhaps grits casserole, with raisin bran muffins or maybe banana bread.

"Grady House is a short walk to downtown shops and galleries. Friendly, hospitable owners Ed and Diane Shupe provided lots of sightseeing tips and gave us a full tour of the inn. Room #5, the Honeymoon Suite, is very romantic in rose and pink tones, lots of flowers, white wicker furniture, king-size bed, and a soaking tub-for-two. Ed shared coffee and conversation while we enjoyed the delicious breakfast of coffee and juice, fruit with granola and yogurt, an egg casserole, sausage and bacon, homemade bread, and toasted bagels." *(Donna Jacobson)* "The decor includes antiques, lace curtains, and an extensive art collection. My room had an antique iron bed with an old trunk at its foot. The Shupes have done a fine job of restoring and refurbishing the house." *(Bill Novack)*

Open All year.
Rooms 2 suites, 3 doubles—all with private bath and/or shower, radio, clock, air-conditioning, fan. 3 with desk; 1 with double soaking tub.
Facilities Breakfast room, living room, library with fireplace, guest refrigerator, art gallery; porch with swing. Gazebo, off-street parking; bicycles. Canoeing on Santa Fe River.
Location N central FL. 22 miles northwest of Gainesville. From Gainesville, go N on US 441 to High Springs.In High Springs, go left on US 27. Inn is on US 27 (First Ave.), 4 blocks beyond 1st traffic light on right.
Restrictions Some traffic noise in front rooms. No smoking. Children over 8.
Credit cards Visa, MC.
Rates B&B, $79–89 suite, $69 double. Extra person, $10. Children free in parents' room.

HOLMES BEACH

For additional area information, see **St. Petersburg** and **Sarasota.**

Harrington House B&B ♿
5626 Gulf Drive, 34217
Tel: 941–778–5444
Fax: 941–778–0527
E-mail: harhousebb@mail.pcsonline.com

If you've scoured the Gulf Coast for a B&B with a beach in its backyard, search no more. The Harrington House, a 1920s-era stucco building on Anna Maria Island, has seven miles of powdery white sand starting only a few feet from its door. If you're chilled after watching a brilliant Gulf sunset from one of the inn's balconies, join owners Jo and Frank Davis for a cup of hot chocolate before the fireplace in their living room with its 20-foot open-beam ceiling, then climb the original pecky cypress staircase to your room. Guest rooms, with names like Renaissance, Sunset, and Primrose, are decorated with floral wallpapers, reproduction furniture, and lace curtains. You'll need to swim a few early morning laps in the pool to work up an appetite for the breakfast of stuffed French toast or perhaps eggs Benedict, served from 8 to 9:30 A.M.; coffee is set out at 7:00 A.M.

"Like having a beach house of your own. Located directly on a beautiful beach, rooms are individually decorated with a variety of 'Old Florida' or cottage-style furnishings. Jo and Frank and their staff are very helpful, yet never intrude on guests' privacy. Wonderful breakfasts overlooking the gulf." *(Susan Woods, also SHW)* "Immaculate rooms; quiet, lovely setting." *(Dr. & Mrs. Graham Burcham)*

Open All year.
Rooms 11 doubles, 1 cottage—all with private bath and/or shower, telephone, TV, desk, air-conditioning, ceiling fan, refrigerator. Some with VCR, deck, Jacuzzi. 4 rooms in Beach House.

Facilities Dining room, living room with fireplace, piano, TV/VCR, stereo, library; porch, decks. 1½ acres on beach with gazebo, heated swimming pool; kayaks, bicycles. Off-street parking.
Location Central Gulf Coast. 45 m S of Tampa, 25 m NW of Sarasota, 5 m W of Bradenton. On Anna Maria Island (the first island south of Tampa Bay). From I-75, take Exit 42B (northbound) or 42 (southbound), & go E on Manatee Ave. (Rte. 64) to end. Go right on Gulf Dr. (Rte. 789) to inn.
Restrictions Smoking outside only. Children over 12.
Credit cards MC, Visa.
Rates B&B, $109–225 double. 2-night weekend minimum.
Extras Limited wheelchair access.

INVERNESS

Information please: The **Crown Hotel** (109 North Seminole Avenue, 32650; 352–344–5555) began its existence as Inverness's first store a century ago. It was rescued from imminent collapse in 1980 with an 18-month, $2,000,000 restoration. The inn is decorated in the Florida version of an English country inn, with brass beds and reproduction Chippendale furnishings; a sweeping free-floating staircase along with a reproduction of the British crown jewels highlight the lobby. The inn's pub serves casual American fare, along with English favorites such as fish and chips and steak and kidney pie; Churchill's restaurant offers continental specialties. B&B double rates are $65–85, $100–120 for a suite. A recent reader report noted that "food and service at Churchill's was very good, but that our room needed sprucing up." *(BH)*

ISLAMORADA

Also recommended: Known for its first-rate facilities for vacationing families as well as its superb fishing, **Cheeca Lodge** (Mile Marker 82, Overseas Highway, P.O. Box 527, 33036; 305–664–4651 or 800–327–2888) has 60 suites and 143 doubles. Despite its size, several well-traveled readers have pointed out that Cheeca is indeed a special place with luxurious rooms, excellent service, and a relaxing atmosphere. Spiffed up by a multi-million-dollar restoration, the double room rates range from $165 to $620, with suites $275–1,150; many packages are available. Extensive facilities include six tennis courts, a nine-hole par-3 golf course, children's programs, deep-sea fishing, on-site dive shop, parasailing, sailing, scuba, snorkeling, and windsurfing. "A well-equipped resort. Our big, beautiful room had island decor and an ocean view. Exceptionally gracious service; everyone in every department was courteous and smiling." *(Nancy Sinclair)* "Friendly place; excellent Sunday brunch." *(Caroline Raphael)*

JACKSONVILLE

Located in northeastern Florida, Jacksonville is a major port and business center. The St. John's River loops through the city, and the Riverwalk area on the South bank has been attractively preserved.

For an additional area entry, see **Orange Park**.

Cleary-Dickert House ¢ ♿ *Tel:* 904–387–4762
1804 Copeland Street, 32204 *Fax:* 904–387–4003

A Prairie-style home in the Riverside district, the Cleary-Dickert House was built in 1914 and converted to a B&B in 1994 by Joe Cleary and Betty Sue Dickert. Just 50 yards from the river, the charming grounds reflect the gardening traditions of its owners—English cottage garden combined with the cool, splashing fountains of the Deep South. English-born Joe and Southern-born Betty Sue delight in offering an authentic English tea in the afternoon, along with wine and cheese. At breakfast, they serve a variety of English and Southern specialties, complemented by an assortment of breads and jams. You can join Joe and Betty in the dining room for breakfast, or on request, enjoy your meal in the privacy of your room. The guest rooms have traditional furnishings accented with floral fabrics. In-room amenities include the daily newspaper, fresh flowers, chocolates, and an evening beverage.

"The first bit of fun are the accents of the owners—Betty was born in Alabama and raised near the Florida Panhandle, and Joe is English—what a wonderful duo they are. Their hospitality is unbeatable; the accommodations are comfortable, quiet, and squeaky clean." *(Bill MacGowan)* Comments appreciated.

Open All year.
Rooms 4 suites—all with private bath and/or shower, telephone, radio, clock, TV, desk, air-conditioning. 1 with working fireplace, 1 with refrigerator. 2 rooms in carriage house.
Facilities Dining room, living room with TV/VCR, books, fireplace. Large gardens; on-street parking.
Location Riverside district. From I-95, take Exit 110, College St. Go S on College St. to Copeland St. & turn left. Continue on Copeland & go 3-4 blocks to inn on right.
Restrictions No smoking. Children over 10.
Credit cards Amex, MC, Visa.
Rates B&B, $85–95 suite. Extra person, $10.
Extras Carriage house suite equipped for disabled. "Working knowledge of French, Greek, Russian, Spanish, Italian."

House on Cherry Street ¢ *Tel:* 904–384–1999
1844 Cherry Street, 32205 *Fax:* 904–384–5013
E-mail: 104410.2322@compuserve.com

Those who have stereotypical ideas of Floridian decor will be amazed when they see the House on Cherry Street, a Colonial-style home built in 1909, overlooking the St. John's River, and owned by Carol and Merrill Anderson since 1984. Its guest rooms are handsomely decorated in rich, deep colors, with period antiques, canopy beds, handwoven coverlets, and Oriental rugs. The historic mood is further enhanced by the owners' collections of tall-case clocks, duck decoys, baskets, and pewter. No less inviting is the screened porch, equipped with an ample supply of old wooden rocking chairs.

"Beautiful house with wonderful river views; a dock, just steps from the back door, is surrounded by azaleas. Our favorite is the Rose Room with a canopy bed, and a day bed in the sitting area." *(Kathryn Stuart)* "Lovely historic neighborhood. Our room had a four-poster bed with a 150-year-old woven coverlet, antique clock, freshly cut flowers, an ice bucket, glasses and a thirst-quenching drink." *(Alice Schalk)* "The Duck Room is decorated with duck paintings, decoys, and wallpaper. It is small but comfortable with its own sitting room across the hall, looking out to the river." *(William Novak)* "Exceptional cherry muffins. Evening wine and hors d'oeuvres give guests the opportunity to meet the Andersons and each other, share stories and recommendations." *(Linda Hardy)* "Great location with easy access to restaurants, shopping, and the Gator Bowl." *(Sheila Herndon)* "Wonderful resident yellow lab, Streak." *(Teresa Bestor)* "Carol is personable and friendly, concerned with her guests' comfort. The delicious breakfast of eggs Benedict, fresh fruit, and homemade biscuits was graciously served in the dining room, at the time requested." *(Lynda Hinshaw)*

Open All year.
Rooms 4 doubles—all with private bath or shower, telephone, radio, TV, desk, air-conditioning, ceiling fan. Some with balcony/deck.
Facilities Dining room, living room, family room, screened porch. 1 acre with lawn games, off-street parking. Fishing, canoeing, kayaking, dockage, tennis, golf nearby.
Location NE FL. Riverside; 10 min. from downtown; 5 min. from I-95; 25 min. from airport. 1 block from St. John's Ave. From I-95, take Exit 113, Stockton St. Go S 12 blocks & turn right on Riverside, go 4 blocks, & go left on Cherry to inn, last building on right at river. On bus rte.
Restrictions No smoking in guest rooms. No children under 10.
Credit cards MC, Visa.
Rates B&B, $85 double, $75 single. Extra person, $10. 2-night minimum special events.

The San Marco Point House — *Tel:* 904–396–1448
1709 River Road, 32207 — *Fax:* 904–396–7760

A Craftsman-style home built in 1923, the San Marco Point House was purchased by Todd Kemp and Linda Olsavsky in 1994. While the building was structurally sound, it needed extensive renovation. After gutting much of the interior, the owners installed new windows and French doors, but kept the original moldings and woodwork. They've decorated the rooms with an English country motif; two guest rooms have queen-size four poster rice beds. Breakfast, which varies daily and might include tomato-basil quiche, blueberry waffles, gingerbread pancakes, or omelets, with fresh fruit, muffins, coffee, and juice, is served 7–8:30 A.M. weekdays, 8–9:30 A.M. weekends.

"Todd and Linda are great hosts. Comfortable accommodations; we enjoyed strolling the streets of San Marco Point; good dinner at the West River Restaurant." *(GR)* Reports appreciated.

Open All year.
Rooms 2 suites, 2 doubles, 1 cottage—all with private bath, telephone, radio, clock, TV, desk, air-conditioning, fan, refrigerator. One with balcony.
Facilities Dining room, living room with fireplace, family/game room, library, guest kitchen, porches. Off-street parking, lawn games.
Location In historic district. From I-95 S, take 1st exit after Fuller Warren Bridge: San Marco Blvd. At 2nd light go right onto San Marco Blvd. Go ¾m & turn right onto Riviera St. Go left onto River Rd. to inn on left. From I-95 N, take Exit 107, Prudential Dr. Go left & go 2 lights. Turn left onto San Marco Blvd. & follow directions above.
Restrictions No smoking. No children under 16.
Credit cards MC, Visa.
Rates B&B, $90–100 suite, $75–85 double. AAA discount.

KEY LARGO

Information please: Not far from John Pennekamp Underwater Park, **Largo Lodge** (101740 Overseas Highway, 33037; 305–451–0424 or 800–IN–THE–SUN) consists of six duplex concrete-block cottages, set far back from the road, each with a kitchen/dining and living room area, a separate bedroom with two double beds, and a screened porch. The long dock has many comfortable lounge chairs, and is romantically lit at night. The double rate is $85–105. "A delightful, idiosyncratic place. The decor was established sometime in the '50s and no need to change it has ever arisen. The lodge grounds are entered through a dense, well-tended tropical garden. There is also a sandy beach and lovely places to sit and read. Nearby are restaurants, shops, and all manner of places to dive, snorkle, and visit marine parks." *(EH)* "Our unit had a screened ceramic tiled porch, huge living room, kitchen, big bedroom and bath in a lush, tropical setting. Shady, cool, and pretty, with a lovely pier and lawn chairs. Excellent value." *(Andrew Arntfield)*

KEY WEST

Key West is the southernmost city in the continental United States, located 161 miles south of Miami. The completion of the Overseas Highway in 1938 brought major changes to Key West. No longer a sleepy fishing village, the town is often filled with tourists and hustlers. International travelers discovered its allures, and are providing a foreign accent to the goings-on. Its gay population is estimated at 25 percent.

If the sun and water overwhelm, some other Key West sights of interest include Ernest Hemingway's Home, Key West Lighthouse Museum, Wrecker's Museum, and Mel Fisher's exhibit of sunken treasure. Those who feel their stay will be incomplete without a taste (or two or three) of key lime pie may want to sample the offerings at the Deli Restaurant, the Buttery, Pier House, or Sloppy Joes; remember the real thing is *never* green or thickened with gelatin—it's yellow, creamy, and sweet.

A word of advice about navigating in the Keys—the Florida Keys' Overseas Highway (U.S. 1) is studded with 126 mile markers starting at the corner of Fleming and Whitehead streets in Key West and ending near Florida City. Watch for the small green signs with white writing, found on the right shoulder of the road, since they're often used as reference points when directions are given.

Budget travelers should note that hotel rates are substantially lower from June through November, with the exception of holiday weekends.

Reader tips: "On your way to or from Key West, stop at Montes in Summerland Key for excellent seafood, inexpensively served in a casual setting. Camille's on Duval offers delicious breakfasts and lunch at very reasonable prices." *(Sheila & Joe Schmidt)* "The streets of Key West are narrow and congested, making car travel a problem. Park your car and walk!" *(Howard Addis)* "Tour the Audubon House using the recorded tape; actors portray the actual lives of the family. Beautiful old Florida mansion filled with wonderful James Audubon prints." *(Christopher Johnston)* "We got bitten up by no-see-ums during our early June visit; bring insect repellent! Not all inns supply beach towels, so bring your own, along with a hat and suntan lotion. We rented bicycles and rode to the beach at Ft. Zachary Taylor park. Lots of wonderful restaurants in town, though the really imaginative ones have entrees priced at $25–30." *(Carolyn Myles)* "Key West is great for shoppers, and bar and restaurant lovers who enjoy the beautiful weather and stars, but I don't think it's great for kids." *(MP)*"Water pressure is not great anywhere in Key West, and can be a minor annoyance at some inns." *(MW)*

Also recommended: Formerly a private residence, the **Gardens Hotel** (526 Angela Street, 33040; 305–294–2661 or 800–526–2664) was refurbished as a luxury hotel in 1993. The 17 guest rooms overlook a half-acre garden of fragrant flowering plants. Double B&B rates range from $155–625. "Ample places to sit in shade or sun, with as much privacy as you desire. Everything is immaculate and totally first class, including the splendid continental breakfast buffet. Our attractive room in the main house facing Angela Street had a porch and comfy chairs. The staff is extraordinarily friendly and helpful." *(Judith Brannen)* "Once the island's largest estate, now a luxurious retreat from nearby Duval Street." *(Joe Schmidt)*

Bananas Foster B&B (537 Caroline Street, 33040; 305–294–9061 or 800–653–4888) is a Classic Revival home, built in 1888, one block from Duval Street. B&B double rates range from $100–190, and include continental breakfast and afternoon refreshments. Rooms have antique furnishings, private bath, TV, air-conditioning, and telephone. "Our room had a king-size and twin-size bed, good reading lights, chest of drawers, and hooks for hanging clothes. Breakfast consists of fresh fruit, muffins, bagels, cereal, coffee cake, juice and coffee. The dipping pool/Jacuzzi was delightful after riding the bicycles the inn rents for a nominal fee." *(Carolyn Myles)*

Information please: The **Banyan Resort** (323 Whitehead Street, 33040; 305–296–7786 or 800–225–0639) consists of six historic Conch homes now converted into 38 luxury suites, with rates ranging from $135–275. Each comes decorated in soothing neutral shades, with comfortable couches and lots of natural wicker, and all have fully equipped kitchens. "Exceptionally beautiful garden and pool areas; helpful staff." *(MDM)*

One block from Duval Street is the **Heron House** (512 Simonton Street, 33040; 305–294–9227), a small enclave surrounded by coquina walls. Rooms feature contemporary tropical decor, highlighted by beautiful teak, cedar, or oak woodwork, stained glass, tiled floors, and whirlpool tubs set in granite. Decks, balconies, patios and walkways are framed by the orchid and tropical gardens. B&B double rates of $149–249 for the 23 rooms and suites include a continental breakfast served poolside, and light beverages available throughout the day. Reports appreciated.

Three guest houses sharing a private tropical garden make up the **Island City House** (411 William Street, 33040; 305–294–5702 or 800–634–8230). The mansion house was built in the 1880s as the private home of a wealthy Charleston family; the casual Arch House was originally built as a carriage house; the recently built cypress Cigar House takes its architectural style from a cigar factory that once occupied this site; the well-equipped rooms have contemporary decor. The double rates of $95–210 include a continental breakfast, served from 8 to 10:30 A.M. in the garden.

An affordable alternative in increasingly pricy Key West is the **Southernmost Point Guest House** (1327 Duval Street, 33040; 305–294–0715), built in 1885, and restored 102 years later by the Santiago family. Children are welcome, and the B&B double rate ranges from $55–175, including a continental breakfast. Facilities include a garden hot tub, barbecue grills, and a guest laundry, and guest rooms have private baths, TV, telephone, refrigerator, and coffee maker.

Center Court Historic Inn & Cottages ♿ 👪 *Tel:* 305–296–9292
916 Center Street, 33040 800–797–8787
Fax: 964–294–4104
E-mail: centerct@aol.com

A cluster of cottages, the Center Court combines Key West's rich history with modern comfort and convenience. Restored in 1994 by owner/manager Naomi Van Steelandt, the compound includes the Main Guest House, built in 1873 by a ship captain, and captures the style of the early settlers who built their homes much like their ships. Additional buildings reflect such vernacular historic styles as eyebrow conch, shotgun, and cigarmakers' cottages. Naomi is a registered nurse who retired from caring for the sick and now devotes herself to caring for the well, with comforting touches as down comforters, feather pillows, and luxury towels. The self-serve breakfast is available from 7:30 A.M. to noontime, and includes yogurt, juice, coffee, tea, fresh fruit, bagels, English muffins, cereals, jellies, and cream cheese.

"Through hard work and careful attention to detail, Naomi has created a quiet oasis just moments from the busy streets of Key West. Our room was bright and cheerful with ample storage. The pool area invites a quick swim or a chance to read the interesting volumes stored nearby. Fitness buffs can even use the inn's Stairmaster, treadmill, and weights. The guest kitchen is well stocked with complimentary beverages, snacks, and fruit." *(Joe Schmidt)* "Lovely, super-clean rooms. The staff was well informed about local activities, events, restaurants, and always took the time to answer any questions. Great location, within walking distance of historic homes, the harbor, and the glorious sunset." *(MP, also Ken & Margaret Schneider)* "While not large, our room was extremely comfortable and attractive. Friendly, attentive staff, helpful with bike rentals, sailing reservations, and restaurant recommendations. Delicious coffee and fresh fruit at breakfast. Guest and common areas always extremely neat and clean." *(KS)*

Open All year.
Rooms 5 suites, 7 doubles, 3 cottages—all with private bath and/or shower, telephone, radio, clock, TV, desk, air-conditioning, ceiling fan. Most with refrigerator, deck, hair dryer; cottages with kitchen. Rooms in 7 buildings.
Facilities Dining room, living room, TV room, guest kitchen & laundry. Free on-street parking; 2 off-street spaces. Heated swimming pool, hot tub, exercise equipment, gazebo.
Location ½ block off Duval St.
Restrictions No smoking. Children welcome in cottages.
Credit cards Amex, Discover, MC, Visa.
Rates B&B, $118–298 suite, cottage; $78–148 double. Extra person, $15. Breakfast not included in cottages. Weekly rates.
Extras 1 cottage fully accessible. Crib, babysitting (with notice). French spoken.

Colours Guest Mansion *Tel:* 305–294–6977
410 Fleming Street, 33040 800–459–6212
Fax: 305–292–9030

A luxurious Victorian mansion built in traditional Key West architecture, Colours was built in 1886 by a renowned Cuban cigar magnate to lure his young bride to the island. She must have liked it—the locals say her ghost still moves through the house at night—and the mansion is on the daily Key West ghost tour. An inn since 1975, it was purchased and redecorated by Roger Mills in 1996, who reports "our gardens are highlighted by many orchid varieties and exotic palms, and our guest rooms are elegantly furnished with antiques and Oriental carpets. Our poolside areas are clothing optional, and we cater to a gay clientele; however, all are welcome." Rates include a breakfast of fresh baked muffins, non-fat Danish, fresh fruit, cereal, juices, coffee and teas served at individual tables from 8:30–11 A.M.

"Our room was on the main floor and must have originally been a dining room. The ceiling height and architectural details were striking. Excellent art is displayed throughout the inn. The pool and Jacuzzi area at the back was very private and inviting; some rooms have direct access. My husband and I were delighted with our visit." *(Bev McVeigh)*

Open All year
Rooms 1 cottage, 3 suites, 8 doubles—10 with private bath and/or shower, 2 with a maximum of 4 people sharing bath. All with telephone, radio, clock, air-conditioning, fan. 10 with refrigerator, 9 with TV, deck. Cottage with orchid garden.
Facilities Dining room, living room with TV, games; porch/deck areas. Heated swimming pool, hot tub; patio with TV/VCR, orchid gardens. On-street metered parking.
Location Historic district. ½block from Duval St., behind Fast Buck Freddys.
Restrictions No smoking indoors. "Poolside areas clothing optional." No children.
Credit cards Amex, MC, Visa.
Rates B&B, $120–190 cottage, suite; $85–150 double. Extra person, $20.
Extras French, Spanish, German, Italian, Polish, Russian, Czech, Flemish & Swahili spoken.

Duval Gardens
1012 Duval Street, 33040

Tel: 305–292–3379
800–867–1234
Fax: 305–294–7470
E-mail: DUVALG@aol.com

Built as a single-family home in the 1920s and converted into apartments in the 1940s, Duval Gardens was restored as an inn in 1994 by Brian and Andrea Markus O'Grady. Andrea brought her talents in marketing, cooking, and foreign languages to her new career, while Brian's experience restoring Victorian homes in Washington, D.C. was a helpful asset. Undisturbed by the renovations were the five cats who came with the house, who continue to supervise the resident humans. From 8:30 to 10:30 A.M., guests can help themselves from the breakfast buffet, and sit at tables in the garden or on the veranda, enjoying such dishes as cinnamon-vanilla French toast; baked scrambled eggs with bacon, tomato, Hollandaise, and cheese; or perhaps banana maple pancakes topped with whipped cream and strawberries, plus coffee, juice, and assorted pastries. A different tropical punch is served each evening on the second floor veranda, accompanied by light snacks.

"Homey, pampering atmosphere. The staff took care of dinner reservations, mailing postcards, fixing us gourmet pancakes, and countless other details. Fresh flowers in our room each day complemented the attractive rattan furnishings and floral fabrics." *(Holly Harris Hendrix)* "Located at the quiet end of Duval Street. Knowledgeable owners, informative about local attractions and restaurants. Comfortable atmosphere. Excellent breakfasts served outside each morning. Enjoyed use of the nearby beach club, a five-minute walk away." *(Mary Goodwin)* "Just far enough from the action to be quiet, yet close enough to walk everywhere. Clean, comfortable rooms; bright tropical decor.

Guests socialize at sunset over cocktails and snacks." *(Dave & Jennifer Stodden)* "The deck is a relaxing place to watch the stars. Andrea and Brian give a real attention to details; a warm, cheerful home-away-from-home. Immaculate, too." *(Donna Steele)*

Open All year.
Rooms 2 efficiency apts., 4 doubles—all with private bath and/or shower, telephone, radio, clock, TV, air-conditioning, ceiling fan, refrigerator. Some with desk, balcony, kitchen.
Facilities Wraparound verandas, hot tub, garden patio, limited off-street parking. Rate includes beach club membership 5 blocks away with private beach, swimming pool, health club.
Location Historic District. Take U.S. Rte. 1 S to Duval St. & turn left to inn on 1st block, on right.
Restrictions Street noise possible during special events. No smoking in rooms.
Credit cards Amex, Discover, MC, Visa.
Rates B&B, $109–260 1-2 bedroom apt; $79–145 double.
Extras Crib. Spanish, French, Hungarian spoken.

Duval House
815 Duval Street, 33040

Tel: 305–294–1666
800–22–DUVAL
Fax: 305–292–1701
E-mail: duvalhse@key.net

Choosing just the right spot for relaxing may be the most difficult part of your stay at Duval House. Will it be poolside or under the century-old banyan tree? In the lounge, or on the balcony to watch the rest of Key West stroll by? This inn, formed by a cluster of Victorian homes, is furnished with a comfortable mix of wicker and antiques, freshened by hibiscus flowers, picked daily. The inn has been owned by Richard Kamradt since 1989, and is managed by James Renner.

"The yard in back is secluded and relaxing, with a huge banyan and palm trees; sunny spots for basking are balanced with lots of shade. James anticipated our needs, providing towels for the pool, making reservations for dinner and sailing, even offering an outside shower to use after check-out. Breakfast consisted of fresh fruit, Danish, English muffins, juice, and tasty cinnamon coffee. Every day, the staff updated a chalkboard with the low temperatures of the guests' hometowns." *(Christina Grillo)* "The pool was lovely and clean; one would never suspect the tranquility of the inn's 'backyard' could exist in the center of town." *(Catherine Cipollone)* "Our small room was simply furnished and spotless. Coffee is available throughout the day. The pool is located in a tropical garden surrounded by a deck (where breakfast is served), with enough chairs for all the guests." *(Michael & Dina Miller)* "The location is central, so we parked the car and walked everywhere." *(Glenn & Lynette Roehrig)*

Open All year.
Rooms 3 suites, 26 doubles—all with private bath and/or shower, air-conditioning, ceiling fan, deck. Some with desk.
Facilities Lounge with TV, books, games; breakfast room. Swimming pool, gazebo, hammock. Golf nearby. Snorkeling, swimming nearby.

Location Historic district. 120 m S of Miami, 90 m N of Havana, Cuba. Bus. Rte. #1 to Duval St., right on Duval.
Restrictions Light sleepers could be affected by traffic noise in two rooms. Children 12 and over.
Credit cards Amex, DC, Discover, MC, Visa.
Rates B&B, $120–265 suite, $90–185 double. Extra person, $10. 3-night holiday minimum.

Marquesa Hotel ✗ ♿

600 Fleming Street, 33040

Tel: 305–292–1919
800–869–4631
Fax: 305–294–2121

Listed on the National Register of Historic Places, the Marquesa is comprised of two 1880s boarding houses rescued from near destruction by hard work, good taste and $3,000,000, plus the vision of owner/manager Carol Wightman. A waterfall, two swimming pools and a variety of flowering plants enhance this intimate outdoor retreat. A concierge tends to your every whim, and your senses will be soothed by bedtime Godiva chocolates, fresh flowers, and Caswell Massey toiletries. The hotel restaurant, the Cafe Marquesa, offers a creative menu, with such dishes as smoked conch and mussel cake with mango aioli; followed by Caribbean prawns with grilled pineapple, black bean salsa, and couscous; concluded with tangerine flan.

"The enlarged Marquesa is even nicer than before. The decor, porch, furnishings, amenities and overall comfort of our new junior suite were exceptional." *(Sheila & Joe Schmidt)* "Quiet, elegant hotel, with ample parking. Well-appointed rooms, all meticulously maintained. The service is highly professional, attentive without being obsequious." *(James White)* "The rooms are bright, cheerful, and most have porches overlooking the pool. Each morning the *New York Times* was delivered to our door and when we went out to dinner, the bed was turned down, the towels changed and waste baskets emptied." *(JS)* "Perfect location, on a quiet street off Duval, just a short walk to Mallory Square. Beautiful antiques and marble baths. Wonderful breakfast, served in the room or by the pool and fountain." *(Bill & Kim Barnes)* "The excellent restaurant has an imaginative menu and style that is reminiscent of the San Francisco-style of dining." *(Stephen & Ellise Holman)* "Great food. Quality abounds, with tasteful colors and fine furnishings." *(Christopher Johnston)*

Open All year.
Rooms 27 suites, doubles—all with full private bath, telephone, TV, air-conditioning, stocked mini-bar. 17 with deck. Rooms in two buildings.
Facilities Lobby, restaurant, terraces, decks, 2 heated swimming pools. Full concierge service. Off-street parking.
Location Historic district, corner Fleming and Simonton Sts. 5 blocks from Gulf, 10 blocks from Atlantic, 1 block to center.
Credit cards Amex, DC, MC, Visa.
Rates Room only, $180–295 suite, $120–240 double. Extra person, $15. 2–3 night weekend, holiday minimum.
Extras Wheelchair access.

The Paradise Inn ♿
819 Simonton Street, 33040

Tel: 305–293–8007
800–888–9648
Fax: 305–293–0807

Everyone has a different vision of paradise, but for some Key West visitors, it's found at one of the town's newer inns. The Paradise Inn opened in December 1995, and offers accommodations in several renovated one and two-bedroom cigar makers' cottages, as well as in two authentically reproduced Bahamian-style houses with vine-covered porches, sun decks, and shaded balconies. The elegant and uncluttered decor complements natural wood, marble, and fiber with soothing shades of ivory and pale yellow. The traditionally styled furnishings include king-size beds in each room. Shel Segel is the managing partner. Rates include a breakfast of fresh-squeezed orange juice, coffee, tea, milk, cereal, pastries, croissants, bagels and cream cheese, served 8–11 A.M.

"Although located in Old Town, it is off the beaten path and beautifully luxurious, understated and tranquil. The oak floors, high ceilings, marble bathrooms, and beautiful tropical landscaping add to its charms. Shel greeted us on arrival, and never forgot our names. He even supplied us with umbrellas when we were caught in a cloudburst." *(AS)* "Quiet and peaceful, yet just a block from the action on Duval. Walking distance to the harbor and fabulous restaurants. Rooms were sparkling clean, the beds comfortable, the towels soft, and bathrobes provided. Superb hospitality and service. The staff was delighted to make tour or restaurant reservations. On-site parking was a huge bonus. The beautiful swimming pool surrounded by gorgeous tropical plants was wonderfully relaxing. Breakfast was a treat." *(Anita & Tim McBride)* "The friendly courteous staff went out of their way to make us feel comfortable; they were attentive to our needs, responsive to our questions." *(JCN)* "No detail is overlooked; even the tropical plants around the pool are perfectly groomed." *(Juliet Rundle)*

Open All year.
Rooms 15 suites, 3 cottages—all with full private bath, telephone, radio, clock, TV, desk(table), air-conditioning, fan, refrigerator, safe, balcony/deck. 3 with whirlpool tub.
Facilities Dining room, deck. One acre with off-street parking, gardens, lotus pond, unheated swimming pool, hot tub.
Location Historic district. 1 block E of Duval. Follow U.S. 1 to historic area of Key West (name changes to Truman Ave.). After St. Mary's Star of the Sea Catholic Church on left, go right at next traffic light onto Simonton St. Inn is 1st driveway on right after caution light.
Restrictions Smoking *permitted.*
Credit cards All major credit cards.
Rates B&B, $225–475 cottage, $160–295 suite. Extra person, $20. Senior, AAA discount.
Extras Wheelchair accessible; bathroom specially equipped. Crib, babysitting. Spanish, Czech, Portuguese, German spoken.

William Anthony House ♿
613 Caroline Street, 33040

Tel: 305–294–2887
800–613–CAROLINE
Fax: 305–294–9209
E-mail: AMinore@aol.com

Built in 1895 and renovated in 1994 by Anthony Minore and William Beck, the William Anthony House is one of a pair of "mirror twin" homes. To provide additional guest quarters, Tony and Bill have constructed a board-and-batten replica of a traditional outbuilding, and connected it to the original house with an upper level sun deck. Also part of the property is the Conch Cottage, a Cuban conch home that has been expanded and restored. Rates include a breakfast of fresh fruits, juices, cereals and pastries, coffee and tea served from 8:30–11 A.M., and an afternoon social hour.

"Friendly, knowledgeable hosts who are helpful with planning day trips. Large, clean, well-furnished room. Excellent continental breakfast and cocktail hour. Quiet location." *(JEC)* "Tony takes pride and care in everything he does; he's friendly and professional. Everything is immaculate, from the room to the landscaping. Delicious fresh bagels and muffins at breakfast; superb happy hour with great cheeses and dips." *(Georgie Lowe)*

Open All year
Rooms 1 cottage, 4 suites, 2 doubles—all with private bath and/or shower, telephone, radio, clock, TV, desk, air-conditioning, fan, deck, refrigerator, microwave, coffee maker. Cottage has 2-bedroom unit on ground level, apartment on 2nd floor; both with kitchen.
Facilities Dining area, porches, sun deck with hot tub.
Location In Old Town.
Restrictions No smoking inside; no cigars or pipes on property. "Well-behaved children over 12."
Credit cards Amex, Discover, MC, Visa.
Rates B&B, $100–200 cottage, apartment; $95–245 suite, $79–125 double. Extra person, $25. 2-night weekend minimum. 3-night minimum in season.
Extras One guest room equipped for disabled. "Spanish spoken when Bill's here."

KISSIMMEE

Should you wonder, the name of this town is pronounced "ki-SIM-ee." For additional area inns, see **Haines City** and **Orlando.**

Also recommended: If you are spending your days at theme parks or on business, but prefer a quiet, safe, and homey envirnment at night, call **The Unicorn Inn** (8 South Orland Avenue, Kissimmee 34741; 407–846–1200 or 800–865–7212). B&B double rates for the six well-equipped guest rooms, each with telephone, clock-radio, TV, and air-conditioning, are $85. Owners Don and Fran Williamson come from innkeeping families in Yorkshire, and created their "little piece of England" when they opened the Unicorn in 1994. "Don is a trained carpenter, and has transformed an ordinary Florida house, adding gingerbread trim outside, and wainscotting and distressed beams inside. On the second floor with the guest rooms is a small guest lounge and a pantry with coffee, tea, and soft drinks. Breakfast is served from 7–10 A.M. in the dining room. The night before, you note the time you'd like to eat and your requested menu: choices include ham or bacon; eggs scrambled, poached, or fried; tomatoes or mushrooms; toast or English muffins. My room was traditionally furnished, clean and comfortable, with a king-size bed. Don's directions for getting around Orlando were excellent." *(SWS)*

LAKE HELEN

Lake Helen is located in northeastern Florida, 20 miles southwest of Daytona Beach, and 35 miles north of Orlando.

Information please: An 1890 Victorian home, **Clauser's B&B** (201 East Kicklighter Road, 32744; 904–228–0310 or 800–220–0310) has lots of inviting porches, well supplied with rockers and wicker furnishings. The eight guest rooms are decorated with family heirlooms, handmade quilts and afghans; each room has a different decorating theme—English garden, Pennsylvania Dutch, and Old West. Owned by longtime Florida residents Marge and Tom Clauser, they offer early morning coffee on the porch; a country breakfast is served at 9 A.M. The B&B double rates of $70–120 also include afternoon fruit, beverages, and home-baked treats, plus evening sherry or port.

For an additional area inn, see **New Smyrna Beach.**

LAKE WALES

Reader tips: "Take time to see the Bok Tower Gardens, off Alternate Route 27 of Tower Boulevard. The tower is striking (pink Georgia marble with tile work at top), the carillon is worth hearing, and the gardens are pleasant. The coffee shop is surprisingly good and you can eat outside. Visitors are encouraged to buy food for the carp and squirrels, which kept our kids busy while we enjoyed the grounds. What a change from Disney World."*(Diane Wolf, also LG)* "The old railroad depot with its interesting memorabilia is also worth a look." *(HB)*

Chalet Suzanne
U.S. Highway 27 and Chalet Suzanne Drive
3800 Chalet Suzanne Lane, 33853

Tel: 941–676–6011
800–433–6011
Fax: 941–676–1814

Amid the orange groves and alligators of central Florida is the Chalet Suzanne, set on beautiful green lawns and bordering a lake. Over sixty years ago Bertha Hinshaw turned her home into an inn and restaurant, to support the family after her husband died. The inn soon gained a reputation for good food and lodging and was included in Duncan Hines's first *Guide to Good Eating*. During World War II the main building, including the kitchen and many dining rooms, burned down completely. No building materials were available, so the stables, rabbit hutches, and chicken coops were added to existing structures. Additional rooms have been built since then, and the delightful result is an unlikely hodgepodge of munchkin-size towers, turrets, and gables that ramble in all directions on fourteen levels.

Bertha Hinshaw made eighteen trips around the world, bringing back glass, china, tiles, and stained glass windows; the chalet's Swiss, Scandinavian, French, Oriental, Spanish, and Turkish architecture was inspired by what she saw. Guest rooms vary dramatically in size and decor, although most are spacious, with cozy seating areas and thirties-era decor; some bathrooms are dated but functional, others have been updated with whirlpool tubs, and many have stunning hand-painted tiles. Carl and Vita Hinshaw now operate the inn, with the help of their children, Tina and Eric.

"Service is attentive but unobtrusive, professional yet relaxed. The menu never changes: you start with their signature broiled grapefruit with chicken liver, followed by the peppery romaine soup, a seasonal salad, and their addictive potato rolls. Entrees include roast chicken, shrimp curry, lobster Newburg, shad roe, crabmeat in herb butter, lamb chops, and filet mignon." *(SWS)* "The charm here is the inn's quirkiness—a quality that doesn't necessarily appeal to everyone." *(Diane Wolf)* "In-room touches include fresh flowers, a fruit basket with chocolates and hard candy, and a decanter of sherry. My small room also had a little sitting area, two bureaus, two small closets, and a double bed; the bath had a skylight and was beautifully tiled." *(Mary Morgan)* "Our room was large and comfortable, with good bedside lighting. Swedish pancakes were a treat—especially since you could eat anytime from 8–11 A.M." *(Robert & Ellie Freidus)* "Attractive decor, firm beds. Lots of pretty tiling inside and outside our room. Ample assistance with luggage at check-in and check-out." *(HBJ)* "Charming ambiance, welcoming innkeeper, delightful room." *(Wallace & Nina Harris)* Reports welcome.

Open All year. Restaurant closed Mon.
Rooms 4 suites, 26 doubles, 1 single—all with private bath and/or shower, telephone, TV, air-conditioning. Some with radio, desk, fan, balcony, courtyard or patio, Jacuzzi tub.
Facilities Restaurant, bar, lounge, living room, wine dungeon, library, patio, gift shop, antique shop. Pianist or accordionist in restaurant. 70 acres with swimming pool, private lake, badminton, croquet. Mystery weekends. Private airstrip. Self-tours of soup cannery. Tennis, golf nearby.
Location Central FL; Polk County. 1 hr. SW of Orlando, 40 min. S of Disney World, 4 m N of Lake Wales. From I-4, take Rte. 27 S to Chalet Suzanne Dr. & go E to inn.
Credit cards Amex, CB, DC, Discover, JCB, MC, Visa.
Rates B&B, $135–195 suite, double, single; extra person, $12. Prix fixe lunch,

$29–45; prix fixe dinner, $56–79 per person. 18% service. MAP packages May–Nov.; honeymoon packages.
Extras Wheelchair access. Airport/station pickups. Pets by arrangement. Crib, babysitting.

LITTLE TORCH KEY

Information please: If you'd like to escape to a private tropical island, complete with hand-thatched bungalows, luxurious South Seas–style decor, and gourmet French cuisine—just 120 miles from Miami—read on. Occupying the whole of a five-acre island, a twenty-minute boat ride from the mainland, **Little Palm Island** (Mile Marker 28.5, 28500 Overseas Highway, Little Torch Key 33042; 305–872–2524 or 800–343–8567) is located at the western end of the Newfound Harbor Keys. Originally known as Little Munson Island and long used as a private family retreat and fishing camp, it was converted into a luxury resort in 1988. Little Palm was purchased by Noble House Hotels & Resorts in 1996; long-time managing partner Ben Woodson is still in charge. The original fishing lodge is now the Great House, home to the restaurant and two suites. Most guests are accommodated in bungalows holding two suites, all with whirlpool bath, air-conditioning, and all the amenities you'd expect at B&B double rates of $240–695. Also included are launch service to/from the island, and use of the resort's boats, snorkel and fishing gear. Meals can be ordered a la carte or included in the meal plan of $115 per person per day. Reports needed.

MAITLAND

For additional area inns, see **Winter Park.**

Thurston House
851 Lake Avenue, 32751

Tel: 407–539–1911
800–843–2721
Fax: 407–539–0365
E-mail: jball54@aol.com

This sprawling 1885 Queen Anne Victorian home overlooking small but deep Lake Eulalia, was restored as an inn in 1992 by Carole and Joe Ballard. Architectural features include the cross gable roof and corbeled brick chimneys, while the inside is highlighted by the beautifully restored pine and curly cypress woodwork and floors. The rooms are spacious and airy, furnished with an attractive balance of Victorian antiques, Colonial reproductions, and traditional pieces. The Hirsch Room is done in blue and white, with sponge-painted walls in Wedgwood blue, a Sheraton-style highboy, and a queen-size tester bed, while the Cubbedge Room is painted apple green, with a beautiful hand-stitched quilt in a fan pattern. In addition to juice, tea, and coffee, a typical breakfast might include honey peaches, granola, French toast casserole with maple syrup, raisin scones, and zucchini bread, or perhaps melon and kiwi, citrus puffs, cranberry muffins, and buttermilk biscuits.

"Wonderful location, conveniently located just a few miles north of Orlando, and minutes from the charming village of Winter Park, yet tucked away on a quiet lane in a charming country setting overlooking a small lake. I couldn't believe I was still in Florida! In addition to the idyllic screened porch, there's an inviting, comfortable back parlor, a slightly more formal front parlor, and a dining room with three or four small tables where guests enjoy breakfast. The beautiful curly cypress woodwork throughout the downstairs was all painted when the Ballards bought the inn; Carole stripped it all. Guest rooms are clean, bright and fresh, with sponge-painted walls beautifully done in rich colors." *(SWS)* "Fantastic location—near downtown and all the attractions, yet tucked away. Great hosts." *(Paul Dyllor)* "Charmingly and lovingly restored, the inn sits amidst acres of greenery overlooking the lake. Birds, flowers, serenity abound. A beautiful spot to relax and take long walks." *(Patricia Bothwell)* "The screened porch overlooking the lake was a highlight; beautiful azaleas, camellias, and palm trees. Pleasant, helpful innkeepers; excellent breakfast with home-baked breads and muffins." *(NCF)*

Open Sept. 1–July 31.
Rooms 4 doubles—all with private bath and/or shower, telephone, clock, desk, air-conditioning, ceiling fan.
Facilities Dining room, front parlor with fireplace, back parlor with TV/VCR, stereo, books; screened porches. 5 acres with off-street parking, fruit trees, herb garden; on Lake Eulalia for fishing, croquet.
Location Central FL. 5 m N of downtown Orlando. From I-4, exit at Lee Rd. & go N on Wymore Rd. to Kennedy Blvd. Go right to inn on left, where road jogs right & changes name to Lake Ave.
Restrictions No smoking. Children over 12.
Credit cards Amex, MC, Visa.
Rates B&B, $100–110 double. Extra person, $10. 10% AAA, senior discount. 2-night holiday minimum.
Extras Station pickup.

MARATHON

Also recommended: On Walker's Island, just off Little Conch Key, are the **Conch Key Cottages** (RR 1, Box 424, Marathon, 33050; 305–289–1377 or 800–330–1577) offering nine one- and two-bedroom beachside cottages, with screened porches, air-conditioning and full kitchens. Daily rates range from $80–245, with weekly rates available. Dockage is free to all guests, restaurants are nearby, there's quick access to the coral reefs and fishing, and children and pets are welcome. A heated swimming pool and hot tub are also available. "Rustic but appealing." *(Sheila & Joe Schmidt)* "Little cottages in an idyllic, secluded location, complete with rattan and wicker furnishings, inviting hammocks, and surrounded by flowering bushes." *(AA)*

MIAMI/MIAMI BEACH

Most small hotels are found in the section of Miami Beach known as South Beach or SoBe. This mile-square Art Deco district encompasses 800 buildings dating from the 1930s and 1940s, and has grown immensely popular in recent years. Wander Ocean Drive and Collins Avenue between 5th and 15th streets to see the best of them. Many have been restored as hotels, as noted below. In general, rooms in the Art Deco hotels are considerably smaller than most modern hotel rooms are today, and remember that water view rooms on Ocean Drive in SoBe are *noisy*—day and night.

Don't forget that Miami is a big city, where the twin scourges of crime and drugs can quickly sour the vacation of any traveler who isn't citywise. Consult your hotel staff about which neighborhoods are safe, and which routes to walk.

Reader tips: "Miami, once known for Jackie Gleason on Saturday night, bathing beauties on the beach and a new showplace hotel each year (in 1955, a night at the Fontainebleau Hotel cost an astronomical $55), has become a sophisticated sub-tropical city. Leading attractions are the beach and lighthouse at Bill Baggs State Park, the dolphin show at the Seaquarium, and the tropical Fairchild Garden. In the winter there is opera, in summer a film festival. For strolling and sidewalk cafes, try the Art Deco area of Miami Beach, Coconut Grove or Bayside. The elegant Grand Bay Hotel, a short walk from downtown Coconut Grove, serves high tea in the lobby and has one of Miami's best restaurants. The Biltmore Hotel, restored to its 1920s glory, is a reminder of old Miami; a special treat is the Sunday brunch. Your visit will not be complete without a dinner at Joe's Stone Crab Restaurant in Miami Beach. Close to 400,000 diners annually enjoy terrific seafood year-round; stone crabs are in season from mid-October to mid-May. Sport enthusiasts will find the Dolphins, the Heat, the Marlins, Grand Prix, Lipton Tennis, and the Doral Open. Hialeah Racetrack is one of the country's most beautiful. You don't have to bet; have lunch and enjoy the scenery. The best buy is a half-hour ride around downtown on the rubber wheeled people-mover, which stops conveniently near the Bayside shops. On Saturday afternoon, park on the MacArthur Causeway and watch the parade of departing cruise ships. South Miami Beach and Coral Gables have many outstanding ethnic restaurants; check the 'Weekend' section of the Friday *Miami Herald* for a good list." *(Joe Schmidt)*

"In South Beach, shoppers should not miss the boutiques, galleries, restaurants, and cafes on Collins, between 7th and 9th; the recently renovated Lincoln Mall, parallel to Collins and Ocean near 17th Street; and Espagnola Way, just west of Washington Avenue between 14th and 15th Streets. Also worth seeing is the Wolfsonian Museum of Decorative Arts. Best of all is people watching and roller blading on the east side of Ocean Drive." *(GC)*

Worth noting: Come to South Beach for tropical excitement—not peace and quiet. Traffic and people noise at all hours will disturb light sleepers in the rooms of many hotels, although some have invested in surprisingly effective sound-proofing. Ask for a quiet room when making reservations, and bring ear plugs. Rooms at most of the Art Deco hotels are small, and rates vary with the view or lack thereof.

Information please: Minutes away from South Beach, in Coconut Grove, is the **Mayfair House Hotel** (3000 Florida Avenue, Coconut Grove 33133; 305–441–0000 or 800–433–4555), offering 185 elegant and individually decorated suites, each with a private terrace with a Japanese spa tub or an in-suite soaking tub. In addition to the rooftop sundeck, offering views of Biscayne Bay, the hotel has several restaurants, including the Mayfair Grill.

Among SoBe's many Art Deco hotels, here are some intriguing choices (in alphabetical order):

At the heart of the action is the **Cardozo Hotel** (1300 Ocean Drive, 33139; 305–535–6500 or 800–782–6500), a 44-room hotel built in 1939, and newly refurbished in vibrant Art Deco colors. "Owned by Gloria Estefan, it's a favorite with musicians, models, photographers, and foreign tourists. Although street noise forced us to keep our windows closed and the air-conditioning on, this was also part of the hotel's appeal. The excellent restaurant, Allioli, has a large outdoor cafe, a perfect spot for watching roller bladers of all sizes, ages, shapes, sexes, and passing media types. Informal, helpful, and friendly staff. The guest rooms were well-maintained but small." *(Steve Holman)* Doubles range from $120–145; suites $195–$385, including continental breakfast.

One of SoBe's hottest new hotels is the icy cool 238-room **Delano Hotel** (1685 Collins Avenue, Miami Beach; 305–672–2000 or 800–555–5001), opened in 1995 by hotelier Ian Schrager. "Imagine a hotel done all in white. Now add a balmy Miami evening with that famous moon floating over the ocean. Four-story floor-to-ceiling draperies in the lobby billow in the breeze. Plus a wonderful restaurant, done in African wicker with huge white pillows, overlooking the swimming pool. Flickering white candles line the garden paths." *(Chris Johnston)* Fantasy has its price; rates range from $200–600, and some may not think it's worth it. Quiet and elegant, **The Greenview** (1671 Washington Avenue, 33139; 305–531–6588) offers 45 guest rooms with custom-designed, hand-crafted furnishings and mid-century Modernist collector's pieces. Double rates range from $75–150, including continental breakfast.

For a real taste of Art Deco style, try the **Indian Creek Hotel** (2727 Indian Creek Drive, 33140; 305–531–2727), overlooking its namesake waterway. Built in 1936 in the Pueblo Deco style, this 61-room hotel has retained all its original Art Deco furnishings, fixtures, and even dishes, though all modern conveniences have been added. Located in "Mid" Miami Beach, the hotel is one block from the boardwalk, and ten blocks to Lincoln Road and the Deco District of SoBe. The hotel's intimate Pan Coast restaurant serves tempting Pan-Asian/Caribbean cuisine; outside is a Key West-style garden and swimming pool. B&B double rates range from $90–120.

Two blocks from the water, the sleek **Hotel Astor** (956 Washington Avenue, 33139; 305–531–8081 or 800–270–4981) has an outstanding restaurant, 42 well-equipped guest rooms, marble baths, and a tropical garden courtyard with a mosaic spa pool. Double rates range from $95–195, with suites from $185–550. Plusses at the **Hotel Impala** (1228 Collins Avenue, 33139; 305–673–2021 or 800–646–7252) include its intimate size, attentive staff, luxurious if compact rooms and baths. Double rates range from $159–269, and include a continental breakfast. Effective sound-proofing is a big plus at the **Ocean Front Hotel** (1230-38 Ocean Drive, 33139; 305–672–2579), with 27 guest rooms individually furnished in a 1930s Mediterranean theme. Double rates range from $155–225, with suites to $450. For a wonderful restaurant, a beautiful swimming pool, and even more beautiful sunbathing models, try **The Raleigh** (1775 Collins Avenue, 33139; 305–534–6300 or 800–223–5652), known for its beautiful swimming pool, white sand beach, well-equipped guest rooms, and excellent restaurant. Double rates are $170–400.

Lafayette Hotel ✕ ♿
944 Collins Avenue, 33139

Tel: 305–673–2262
800–673–2262
Fax: 305–534–5399

An eclectic Mediterranean-style hotel built in 1935 and listed on the National Register of Historic Places, the Lafayette was purchased by the Cattarossi family in 1991. The original red tile floors and stairs, hand-wrought iron railing and vintage elevator were restored, and all new wiring, plumbing, doors and windows were added, along with strong make-up lights in the sparkling white bathrooms. Fresh flowers, solid wood furniture, tropical plants, and water fountains extend the Mediterranean feel throughout the hotel.

"Superb location, in the heart of a square mile of Art Deco buildings, many restored, and just a block from the beach. Nicely appointed, spotless, spacious rooms. Felt more like house guests than hotel customers." *(Dr. Richard Groves)* "The large lobby has comfortable seating and magazines to borrow. Efficient, cordial staff is always in the know about current restaurants and happenings in South Beach." *(Don Chappell)* "Beautiful tile throughout. Coffee, tea, fruit, fresh-baked rolls, croissants, cereal, and juice are served at the flower-filled back terrace. Rooms are done in understated elegance, with a few well-made maple pieces. Comfortable bed, clean and modern bathroom with fluffy towels." *(Corinne Vita)* "Mercifully quiet setting." *(GR)* "Graziella Cattarossi was accommodating, charming, and genuinely kind." *(Palma Rose Venezia)* "Close to Ocean Drive and to the quieter area of Washington Avenue. Courteous and discreet staff." *(Marc Biscayart)* "The entire staff has an attitude of 'nothing is too much trouble.' " *(Mrs. A. Thompson)* "Good library. A delicious coffee blend and the newspapers (both American and European) were always available." *(Veronica Parada)* "A warm and welcoming oasis in a lively and colorful area." *(Carol Jordan)*

Open All year.

Rooms 5 suites, 49 doubles—all with private bath and/or shower, telephone with voice mail, TV, air-conditioning, closet safe. Some suites with VCR. Voicemail.

Facilities Lobby, bar/lounge, rooftop garden, meeting room, patio with fountain. Room service, concierge. Translation, export services. Beach towels. Close to beach, health club (discount rate), golf, tennis nearby. Valet parking, $14/day; public parking 2 blocks away.
Location Take I-95 & exit at MacArthur Cswy (I-395). Go E across bay to Miami Beach. Stay in center or right lane. In Miami Beach, continue on 5th St. to Washington Ave. (7 blocks). Go left (N) on Washington Ave. Go 5 blocks to 10th St. & go right. Go right again on Collins to hotel between 9 and 10th Sts.
Restrictions Some non-smoking rooms.
Credit cards Amex, DC, MC, Visa.
Rates B&B, $135–245 suite, $99–148 double. Corporate rates.
Extras Limited wheelchair access. Crib. French, Italian, Spanish, German spoken.

MICANOPY

Lest you think Florida is only theme parks, interstates, and strip malls, take a quick detour off I-75 for a visit to sleepy little Micanopy and a taste of Old Florida. Micanopy (pronounced Mick-uh-NO-pea, not "my canopy") is but a few blocks long, spread along a broad and shady boulevard, and consists primarily of antique and collectibles shops.

Herlong Mansion ¢
402 NE Cholokka Boulevard
P.O. Box 667, 32667

Tel: 352–466–3322
800–HERLONG
Fax: 352–466–3322

Although the Herlong Mansion dates back to 1845, it was completely rebuilt in 1910 in the Colonial Revival style, with a wide veranda supported by four massive Roman-style columns. It sits back from the street, surrounded by old oak and pecan trees. A 1987 restoration (requiring 162 gallons of paint stripper) showcases this home's leaded glass windows, mahogany, oak, and maple inlaid floors, and "tiger oak" paneling. In 1990, H.C. "Sonny" Howard purchased the mansion and has done a great deal to enhance the inn's charms. Breakfast might include Herlong decadent bread—a type of bread pudding—accompanied by fresh fruit, juice, and bran-and-buttermilk muffins.

"Sonny makes you feel right at home, with an open kitchen, great sherry hour, lots of wonderful stories, warm introductions to fellow guests, and maps to local restaurants." *(Richard & Jaclin Farrell)* "In the heart of this sleepy turn-of-the-century village, convenient to antique shops and a bookstore, housed in original old buildings." *(HB)* "During breakfast, conversation among the guests stopped as we all sat and listened to Sonny's entertaining stories about the house and its history." *(SC)* "On the walls are fascinating letters and genealogical information about the Herlong family. Our room had two double brass beds with good reading lights." *(April Burwell)* "Enjoyed Sonny's account of how his son kept alive the story of the mansion's ghost by sitting in one of the dormer windows at night with a sheet and flashlight. Sonny is a real story-teller in the old Southern tradition." *(Bill MacGowan)* "The Inez

Suite on the third floor was immaculate, with a romantic free-standing Jacuzzi under the leaded-glass skylight." *(Donna Jacobsen)* "The house is graciously proportioned, with beautiful Arts & Crafts-style oak woodwork in the downstairs common rooms. Eclectically furnished with many handsome pieces ranging from Victorian to Mission." *(SWS)*

Open All year.
Rooms 4 suites, 6 doubles, 2 cottages—all with private bath and/or shower, radio, air-conditioning. 10 with gas fireplace, 4 with balcony, double Jacuzzi. 1 with kitchenette.
Facilities Parlor, dining room, living room, library, all with fireplace; conference room; veranda. 2 acres with garden and gazebo.
Location 12 m S of Gainesville, 24 m N of Ocala; take Micanopy exit off I-75 or Rte. 441 to Cholokka Blvd. & inn in center of town.
Restrictions No smoking.
Credit cards Amex, MC, Visa.
Rates B&B, $110–160 suite, $55–110 double, $115–125 cottage. Extra person, $15. Rollaway bed, $5. No charge from children under 2.
Extras Airport pickups, $25.

MONTICELLO

Also recommended: Just 26 miles east of Tallahassee, and a few minutes from I-10, is the charming little town of Monticello and the **Palmer Place B&B Inn** (625 West Palmer Mill Road, P.O. Box 507, 32345; 904–997–5519). Built in 1830, the inn offers rooms furnished with antiques, five guest rooms with private baths, and delicious breakfasts of home-baked breads, fresh fruit, eggs and sausage, served informally on the sunporch. B&B double rates range from $55–85. "Charming B&B, surrounded by acres of gardens, all in bloom when we visited in February." *(BJ Hensley)*

MOUNT DORA

Reader tips: "This delightful community is known for its antique shops and is sought after for nearby lakes, and hills for bicyclers. Special shows and programs, devoted to the arts in February, antique boats in April, and antique cars in the fall provide amusement all year." *(Joyce Wood)* "One of Florida's few communities retaining its turn-of-the-century charm, and a welcome refuge from the hustle of Disney and Orlando. *(Sheila & Joe Schmidt)*

Information please: We need current reports on the **Lakeside Inn** (100 North Alexander Street, 32757; 352–383–4101 or 800–556–5016), a historic inn built in the 1880s and updated in the 1920s, when it was a fashionable resort frequented by F. Scott Fitzgerald, among others. Saved from the wrecking ball in the 1980s, renovation and refurbishing has been extensive and on-going. Now listed on the National Register of Historic Places, the hotel has a lovely, quiet setting, overlooking the swimming pool and lake beyond. Its extensive porches have plenty of old-fashioned rockers, perfect for reading or conversation. Inside, the inn is decorated with Laura Ashley fabrics and wall coverings and period reproduction furnishings; the color scheme is ivory, dusty rose, and soft blue or green. The hotel has 87 guest rooms, and double rates range from $85–170. "The restaurant is good and the hotel is close to the antique stores. Be sure to take the sunset cruise of Lake Dora." *(Teresa Bestor)*

A reproduction Queen Anne home, the **Darst Victorian Manor** (495 Old Highway 441, 32757; 352–383–4050) is close to antique shops and restaurants. B&B double rates of $115–200 include a full breakfast and afternoon tea; each of the six guest rooms has a private bath, and some have a lake view and/or a fireplace.

Built in 1910 as a merchant's home, the **Mount Dora Historic Inn** (221 East Fourth Avenue, 32757; 352–735–1212 or 800–927–6344) is just a two minute walk from charming shops and restaurants. Rooms are furnished with turn-of-the-century antiques, and the B&B double rates of $85–110 include a home-cooked breakfast and evening turndown service.

The Emerald Hill Inn
27751 Lake Jem Road, 32757

Tel: 352–383–2777
800–366–9387
Fax: 352–383–6701

The prevalence of stone in the construction of their 1941 Florida ranch-style home inspired innkeepers Diane and Michael Wiseman to name their B&B "Emerald Hill" when they opened in 1994: the walls are buff-colored Ocala limestone blocks; both the living room and Florida room (as Floridians call their sunrooms) have coquina rock fireplaces. Each of the guest rooms is named for a different gemstone; the cozy Ruby has red floral fabrics, the Sapphire has blue and yellow predominating in its stripes and plaids, while the Peridot is tailored and elegant with soft green and touches of pink. Throughout the house, the furnishings are vintage, with a few antiques. The beds are queen- or king-size and the curtains are lace; some bathrooms are original, and one even has a square bat hub. Breakfast, served 8–9:30 A.M. in the Florida room, might feature lemon meringue pancakes, mushroom herb quiche, or baked apple-cinnamon French toast, with ginger carrot bread or dried berry scones.

"For warmth on winter days, curl up by the giant coquina fireplace in the living room. The secluded dock is ideal for fishing or meditation. Guest rooms are simple, comfortable, and clean." *(Joe Schmidt)* "Attentive to guests' needs. Excellent breakfast, immaculate housekeeping. Romantic, peaceful gardens." *(Aurea Leal)* "Attractive decor, good water pressure in the shower. Delicious afternoon tea and cookies. Innkeepers helpful with directions, suggesting activities, and in making dinner reservations." *(Van Speas)* "Diane welcomes you to her spotless, peaceful house. Delightful innkeepers. Loved the Florida room and the lovely grounds and lake. Good books for reading and ample information on local restaurants. At breakfast, soft music plays in the background.

Guests are asked if they have dietary needs or preferences; breakfasts were varied, nourishing, and delicious—lemon waffles, baked grits with three kinds of cheese, breads and muffins made from scratch." *(Frances Paul)* "While Diane and Michael were out-of-town, they had an excellent inn-sitter, Barb, who really made our stay perfect." *(Barbara & Bob Dixon)* "Helpful, bright and personable hosts." *(Ginger Brown, and others)*

Open All year.
Rooms 1 suite, 3 doubles—each with private bath and/or shower, radio, clock, air-conditioning, fan. 2 with deck, 1 with desk.
Facilities Florida room with fireplace, stereo; living room with fireplace, piano, library; family room with TV/VCR, video library; guest refrigerator. 2¼ acres with croquet, lakefront for fishing. Boat ramp nearby.
Location Central FL. Lake Jem, 10 min. from Mt. Dora. From Hwy. 441, go W on Sadler Ave. for 2½ mi. Turn right on E. Lake Jem Rd., then at stop sign, turn right on Lake Jem Rd. to inn on left.
Restrictions No smoking. Children 10 and over.
Credit cards MC, Visa.
Rates B&B, $150 suite, $85–115 double. Extra person, $25. 2-night festival weekend/holiday minimum. AAA discount.

Magnolia Inn
347 East Third Avenue, 32757

Tel: 352–735–3800
800–776–2112
Fax: 352–735–0258
E-mail: Ljohnson@mail.cde.com

The Magnolia Inn, built in 1926 by the wealthiest citizen of Mount Dora, is designed in an unusual Georgian Mediterranean style—classic Greek columns frame the entry while the roof is topped with red tile. Gerry and Lita Johnson gave the inn its name when they purchased it in 1996, inspired by the majestic magnolia tree on the lawn. They report that "we enjoy pampering our guests, and offer afternoon beverages and hors d'oeuvres. Guests enjoy relaxing on the large wooden swing, hammock for two, or on the terrace, observing our aviary with parakeets, doves, and finches." The guest rooms are furnished with king-, queen- or twin-sized beds; Victorian antiques and reproductions, swag curtains over lace panels, and floral comforters figure prominently in the decor. Breakfast is served at guests' convenience between 7 and 10 A.M., at either individual tables or a large one, and includes fresh fruit and juice, and such entrees as blueberry cinnamon French toast, eggs Benedict, or spring vegetable strata, with home-baked muffins.

"Located in a quiet residential area, just a short walk from downtown shops and restaurants. Our room was bright and clean with ample storage. In the evening, cookies and coffee were available in the parlor. We still talk about the sumptuous French toast served at breakfast. Highly recommended." *(Joe Schmidt)*

Open All year.
Rooms 4 doubles—all with private bath and/or shower, air-conditioning, fan.

Facilities Dining room, living room, family room with TV/VCR, stereo, library; screened gazebo with stereo, wet bar, TV, Jacuzzi tub. 1 acre with terrace, aviary, hammock, gardens, fountains. 3 blocks to lake for fishing, boating, nature trail.
Location Central FL. 2 blocks from center. Take Hwy. 441 to Mount Dora, then go S on Donnelly St. to downtown. Turn left on 3rd Ave. Go 2 blocks to inn on left.
Restrictions No smoking inside; permitted in gazebo. Children over 8.
Credit cards Amex, MC, Visa.
Rates B&B, $90–120 double. Extra person, $20.

NAPLES

An elegant community of gracious homes and trendy shops and restaurants, Naples' key attraction is its seven miles of white sand beaches, ideal for sunning, swimming, and shelling. Visitors can choose from a full menu of water sports, visits to nature sanctuaries, golf, and tennis.

Information please: Listed in past editions, we need current reports on the **Inn by the Sea** (287 11th Avenue South, 33940; 941–649–4124 or 800–584–1268). Built as a tourist house in 1936, it was restored as a B&B in 1989, when it was featured as a designer showcase. Decorator elements have been combined with such "old Florida" touches as heart pine and cypress woodwork, white iron and brass beds, wicker furnishings, and floral fabrics. Surrounded by tropical plantings of coconut palms, birds of paradise, and bougainvillea, the inn is listed on the National Register of Historic Places. Breakfast includes homemade muffins, granola, fruit, and fresh-squeezed orange juice. B&B double rates for the five guest rooms, each with private bath, range from $80–165.

NEW SMYRNA

New Smyrna is located 15 miles south of Daytona, and 50 miles east of Orlando.

Information please: The porches of the **Riverview Hotel** (103 Flagler Avenue, 32169; 904–428–5858 or 800–945–7416) provide the perfect vantage point for surveying the yacht traffic on the Intracoastal Waterway. Built in 1885, this bridgetender's house was restored as an 18-guest-room inn in 1990. The decor provides a tropical flavor with wicker furnishings, louvered wooden shutters, and brightly painted Haitian art. The adjacent restaurant, Riverview Charlie's, features a wide variety of seafood. B&B double rates of $70–150 include continental breakfast.

For additional area inns, see **Cocoa Beach** and **Lake Helen.**

NORTH HUTCHINSON ISLAND

For additional area entries, see **Palm Beach** and **Stuart.**

Villa Nina Island Inn
3851 North A1A, 34949

Tel: 561–467–8673
Fax: 561–467–8673
E-mail: ninab&B@metrolink.net

"Privacy with a personal touch" could easily be the motto of the Villa Nina Inn. Breakfasts of fresh fruit and juice, with home-baked breads and muffins, are delivered to the door each morning, ideal for inngoers who enjoy silence with their morning coffee. Innkeepers Glenn and Nina Rappaport report "we excel in eco-tourism—with a natural, pristine beach, the wonderful fish-filled Indian River, hiking and bicycling trails, and parks all around." The inn, constructed in 1994, is contemporary Mediterranean in style, with large windows, pale pink stucco walls, and a Spanish tile roof. The guest rooms have cool, white tile floors and white walls accented with colorful stencilling; the furnishings are white or natural wicker, with contemporary oak tables, and pastel bed linens.

"Innkeepers helpful with directions, dinner reservations, and more." *(Patty & Scott Lyon)* "Fastidiously clean rooms. Serene location, relaxed atmosphere. Cordial, welcoming hostess." *(Derrell Gates)* "The beach, across the highway, is one of the best in Florida. The access is easily marked and fun to walk to, even at night. On the other side of the B&B is a lagoon with large nesting birds. We used their canoe to explore the quiet waters and observe the wildlife close at hand. Nina was very helpful in pointing out the local attractions and restaurants; I especially enjoyed the nearby Navy SEAL Museum." *(Fred Schoenberger)*

"Just the right amount of privacy and pampering—from breakfast to turn-down service in the evening." *(Dawn Arthur)* "Quiet, pristine, natural, outstanding hospitality." *(Jane Denner Turner)* "The lovely all-white decor contrasts beautifully with the designs of tropical fish, lighthouses, and sailboats that Nina has stenciled along the ceiling. On the grounds you may see a raccoon, tortoise, even a bobcat." *(Alvina Martin)* "Scrumptious muffins, coffeecakes, and pastries prepared from scratch, plus little tidbits to feed the birds. Nina, a high school science teacher, made us feel right at home, and taught us a little about the local flora and fauna; we saw pictures of otters visiting the swimming pool at night." *(Eileen & Tim Malone)*

Open All year
Rooms 3 doubles—all with private bath and/or shower, telephone, TV, clock/radio, desk, air-conditioning, ceiling fan, kitchenette with microwave, coffeemaker, toaster oven; barbecue grill, private entrance.
Facilities Porch, guest laundry. 3½ acres with heated swimming pool, canoe, rowboat, private beach across the street. Tennis, golf nearby. On beach for snorkeling, scuba.
Location Barrier island, just S of Vero Beach, N of Ft. Pierce inlet. From Vero

Beach, go S on I-95 to Okeechobee Rd. & go E. At Rte. 1, turn N & go to North A1A Bridge. Cross bridge & continue to Rte. A1A. Turn N to inn on left.
Restrictions Smoking allowed in outdoor areas. Children over 12.
Credit cards Discover, MC, Visa.
Rates B&B, $85–125 double. No tipping.
Extras Some Italian, Spanish spoken.

OCALA

The center of Florida's thoroughbred racing industry, many streets in Ocala's historic district are lined with gracious Victorian mansions, shaded by moss-draped oak trees. Nearby is the town of Silver Springs, famous for its crystal clear waters. Ocala is located in north central Florida, about 28 miles south of Gainesville, and about 55 miles northwest of Orlando.

Reader tips: "Although nearby Silver Springs is the area's best-known attraction, our favorite was Ocala's Appleton Museum, with wonderful objects from many parts of the world." *(Robert Freidus)* "Although the countryside north of Ocala is absolutely beautiful, with gently rolling hills, and rich green fields where horses graze, the town itself is fairly ordinary in appearance." *(MW)*

Also recommended: A gracious, three-story Queen Anne Victorian home built in 1888, the **Seven Sisters Inn** (820 S.E. Fort King Street, 32671; 352-867-1170 or 800-250-3496) is painted pink with white and blue trim, accented in turquoise, lavender, and royal blue. Inside, such period details as handmade quilts, antique wicker chairs, armoires, and brass and iron and four-poster beds, are highlighted by a light and sunny atmosphere. Breakfast includes such entrees as cheese-stuffed French toast with ginger peaches, baked apple walnut oatmeal, or tomato zucchini quiche. B&B double rates for the seven guest rooms ranges from $85–145. "Friendly innkeepers; great attention to detail." *(BJ Hensley)* "The finest linens, comforters, quilts, canopies, and mattress pads—you feel like you're sleeping on a cloud." *(Susan Winner)*

ORANGE PARK

The Club Continental ¢
2143 Astor Street, P.O. Box 7059, 32073
Tel: 904-264-6070
800-877-6070
Fax: 904-264-4044

A beautiful waterfront location, a choice of either contemporary or historic accommodations, fine food, good sports facilities, reasonable prices, a welcome to both kids and pets—who says you can't have your cake and eat it too? Built in 1923 as the private winter estate of Caleb Johnson, founder of the Palmolive Soap company, the property was converted from a private residence to country club in 1964, and guest rooms were soon added. Now owned and run by the brother/sister team of Caleb Massie and Karrie Stevens, Johnson's great-grandchildren, the inn has expanded to include the River Suites, completed in 1993. Rooms are also available in the Inn at Winterbourne, an 1870 Victorian frame building on the Club's grounds, while the dining and sitting rooms are in the Spanish-style clubhouse building. Bordering the St. John's River, the complex also includes the Riverhouse Pub, an antebellum waterfront cottage, with decks overlooking the water. Guests at the inn enjoy all the club's facilities.

"The inn and grounds are stunning, imposing, and make you feel for a moment that you have entered the fairy-tale world of the rich and famous. We had a lovely third floor river suite with a comfy king-size bed, wet bar, large sitting room with wicker desk, beautiful wicker sofa, rocking chair, and a coffee table laden with appealing magazines. Our oversized soaking tub/shower had great water pressure and lots of hot water; towels were thick and thirsty. A remote-control TV was tucked in an armoire, and there were great reading lights on both sides of the bed, at the sofa, and the desk. Everything was immaculate. Served in the manor house, breakfast consisted of a lovely array of bagels, Danish, fresh fruit, cereal, coffee, tea, and juice. The coffee was excellent, as was the view through the French doors overlooking the gardens and river. A truly lovely, restful inn." *(Perri & Michael Rappel)*

"Old-style Southern charm with modern convenience. Beautifully manicured grounds. Staff always willing to please. Elegant dining." *(Patricia Johnson)* "Have enjoyed both the Tower Apartment at Winterbourne and the River Suite accommodations. Wonderful setting with superb views of the wide St. John's River, and 200-year-old oak trees draped with Spanish moss." *(Wayne Disch)* "Make reservations ahead for the Sunday brunch." *(LC)* "The French Room has painted headboards and white eyelet sheets. Harriet Beecher Stowe wintered here." *(Teresa Bestor)*

Open All year. Restaurant Tues.–Friday, plus Sunday brunch.
Rooms 7 suites, 15 doubles—all with full private bath, telephone, TV, desk, air-conditioning. 8 with whirlpool tub, 18 with refrigerator, microwave, balcony. 2 with fireplace. 7 rooms in 1870 mansion; 15 in River Suites.
Facilities Restaurant, Riverhouse pub with weekend entertainment. Gardens, 3 swimming pools, 7 tennis courts (2 lighted), lawn games, marina, fishing.
Location 10 m S of Jacksonville. From I-10 or I-95, take I-295 to Hwy. 17. Go S on 17 to Kingsley Ave. & go left, then right on Astor St. to inn on left.
Restrictions Some nonsmoking rooms.
Credit cards Amex, MC, Visa.
Rates B&B, $140 suite, $95–145 double. Extra person, $10. Alc lunch, $7–10; alc dinner, $10–20.
Extras Wheelchair access; 1 bathroom specially equipped. Pets with approval. Cribs. Boat dockage with notice.

ORLANDO

Reader tip: "For a fun evening, visit Church Street, a historic railroad depot converted into an entertainment center, with a wild-west saloon and 'opera house,' a ballroom and dessert cafe, a seafood bar, and a wine cellar."

For additional area entries, see **Haines City, Kissimee, Lake Helen, Lake Wales, Maitland, Minneola, Mount Dora, Winter Garden,** and **Winter Park.**

Also recommended: The **Courtyard at Lake Lucerne** (211 North Lucerne Circle East, 32801; 407–648–5188 or 800–444–5289) is comprised of three buildings sharing a common garden courtyard. The 1885 Norment-Parry Inn is Orlando's oldest house, and is furnished with American and English antiques, accented with floral wallcoverings and fabrics. The Wellborn, one of the finest surviving Art Deco buildings in town, has been furnished with the eclectic styles popular in the Twenties. The I.W. Phillips House, a 1916 antebellum-style manor house, has wooden verandas wrapping around three sides and a Tiffany stained glass window. Rates for the 14 suites and 6 doubles range from $75–165 and include a breakfast buffet, plus a welcoming bottle of wine. "Breakfast, served buffet-style in the ballroom of the Phillips House, was abundant—fresh strawberries, orange juice, fruit compote, English muffins, blueberry muffins, bagels and cream cheese, and a selection of cold cereals. Sitting on the veranda, by the gently splashing fountain, smelling the fragrances of the courtyard, it's hard to believe you are right in downtown Orlando." *(NB)*

Perri House ¢ 👪

10417 Centurion Court,
P.O. Box 22005, Lake Buena Vista 32830

Tel: 407–876–4830
800–780–4830
Fax: 407–876–0241

A quiet, secluded country estate adjacent to Disney World, Perri House is surrounded by trees, meadows, and orange groves. Its many feeders, fountains, and baths make it an inviting sanctuary for birds. Designed as a B&B, Perri House was built by Angi and Nick Perretti in 1990; scheduled for opening at the end of 1998 are four deluxe cottages, complete with king-size canopy beds, double whirlpool tubs, and private courtyards. The Perretis have skillfully planned the inn to provide space and privacy for their guests (all rooms have queen- or king-sized beds and outside entrances). The self-serve breakfast, available from 7–10 A.M., includes fresh fruit, muffins, pastries, toast, and cold cereal.

"Just as comfortable, friendly, and convenient to Disney World as it was on our first trip." *(Susan Doucet)* "An excellent choice for avid birders like ourselves." *(Ann Bretnall)* "The spacious breakfast area allowed us to meet the other guests before starting off each day." *(Dan & Elaine Meyers)* "We were welcomed by name, given a tour of the inn, and they helped us with sightseeing and restaurant plans." *(Alison Ogle & Ethan Jewett)* "The bird sanctuary is inhabited by a variety of birds, rabbits, frogs, and lizards." *(Ana Linn)* "Ideal balance of the privacy provided by private entrance to each room with a sociability of a communal breakfast." *(Chris Borglum)* "Our room and bath was exceptionally spacious, with ample room for a king-size bed, chest of drawers, and more." *(Ann Sullivan & Bob Sheets)* "Nick Perretti built the house more or less by himself, and is constantly working to improve it." *(Sid & Ruth Geller)*

"Lots of fun to pin my home city on the Perretti's giant wall map and read the guests' names on the welcome board." *(Ann Christoffersen)* "Nick and Agni were equally accommodating to families with young children as to a retired Japanese businessman." *(Nancy Koudelka)* "You can eat at the long table in the breakfast room, or take a tray to the patio or your room. Our room had good mattresses and towels, with a quiet ceiling fan; handy soap/lotion/shampoo dispenser in the bathtub." *(NB)* "Wonderful country atmosphere, yet minutes from all area attractions." *(SWS)*

Open All year.
Rooms 4 cottages, 8 doubles—all with full private bath, telephone with voice mail & data port, radio, TV, desk, air-conditioning, fan, private entrance. Cottages with with double whirlpool tub, courtyard.
Facilities Breakfast room, laundry, guest kitchen; den with games, books, electric fireplace; deck. 3 acres with swimming pool, hot tub, gazebo, bird sanctuary. Cypress Equestrian center adjacent for riding. Golf nearby.
Location 15 m W of downtown. 3 min. by car to Disney World, EPCOT, Pleasure Island; 10 min. to Sea World, Univeral Studios, Orlando Convention Center; 20 min. to Orlando airport. From I-4, take Exit 27-Lake Buena Vista/Disney Village, turn right. Go to 2nd traffic light (Texaco Station), turn left. Go 3.4 m to inn on right.
Restrictions No smoking.
Credit cards Amex, Discover, MC, Optima, Visa.
Rates B&B, $295–400 cottage, $89–109 double, $79–99 single. Extra adult, $10; child, $5. 10% weekly discount. 2-3 night holiday minimum.
Extras Cribs, babysitting with advance notice. Airport/station pickups, $35–40.

PALM BEACH

For additional area entries, see listings under **Stuart** and **West Palm Beach.**

Information please: A Palm Beach classic, the **Brazilian Court** (301 Australian Avenue, 33480; 561–655–7740 or 800–552–0335) was built in 1926, and was extensively (and expensively) renovated in 1986 and 1996. Its quiet residential location is close to Worth Avenue and the ocean, and many of its charming rooms overlook the flower-filled courtyards. Double rates from $95–315; suites to $850.

Plaza Inn
215 Brazilian Avenue, 33480

Tel: 561–832–8666
800–BED–AND–B
Fax: 561–835–8776
E-mail: plazainn@aol.com

The pale pink, Art Deco-style Plaza Inn, built in 1940, is situated on a palm tree-lined, residential street, close to the beach and the shops and restaurants of famous Worth Avenue. Wicker, mahogany, pine, brass, or oak furnishings are complemented by green and burgundy draperies, linens, and wallpaper. It has been owned by Ajit Asrani since 1990.

"Mr. Asrani is a charming host, ensuring that each guest is comfortable and enjoying their stay. My room was clean, well-maintained, and appealing, with pale green chintz fabric on the double bed and windows. The lobby is furnished with crystal chandeliers, grand piano, silk Iranian rugs, reading materials, and Louis XV-style reception desk, giving it the look of a private drawing room." *(Dr. Marian Fowler)* "Outstanding atmosphere and service, with a small, cozy bar where friends can meet. Breakfast, served in a lovely English-style dining room, includes juice, fresh fruit, cereal, bacon, and muffins, with a choice of delicious omelets, French toast, and pancakes." *(Dorothy Millner)* "Wonderfully central location, yet high hedges and ample landscaping make the pool area lush and private. The outside lighting accents flowers, trees, and the entire building beautifully." *(John Leach)* "Bathrooms contain straw baskets of soaps and shampoos, and plenty of big towels." *(Elaine Williams)* "Comfortable, spotless, and homey." *(Natalie Foster)*

Open All year.
Rooms 2 suites, 47 doubles—all with full private bath, telephone, radio, TV, air-conditioning, ceiling fans, refrigerator. Some with desk.
Facilities Lobby, breakfast room, piano bar with entertainment, heated swimming pool, hot tub, garden with waterfall. Room service. 1 block from public beach. Tennis, golf, fishing, boating nearby.
Location E FL. 60 m N of Miami. 4 blocks from Worth Ave.
Credit cards Amex, MC, Visa.
Rates B&B, $150–255 suite, $85–215 double. Extra person, $15. Weekly, monthly rates.
Extras Airport/station pickup, $10. Small pets permitted. Crib; babysitting arranged. Spanish spoken.

QUINCY

McFarlin House ♿
305 East King Street, 32351

Tel: 904–875–2526

Restoration of the McFarlin House was an extraordinary family effort. Built in 1895 by tobacco planter John McFarlin, this Queen Anne Victorian had been slated for the wrecking ball when purchased by the Fauble family in 1994. Restoration work began immediately, and family members and friends did the majority of the work—electrical, plumbing, central heat and air-conditioning, sprinkler system, interior decoration and exterior painting—the wraparound porch alone has 42 pillars. Innkeepers Richard and Tina Fauble take special pride in their inn's curly pine woodwork, sculptured fireplace mantels, and beveled and stained glass windows; furnishings include antiques appropriate for the period. Breakfast is served in the large, heart-pine panelled dining room, between 8 and 10 A.M., and includes fruit, yogurt, breads, juice, bacon or sausage, and omelets or perhaps waffles.

"Richard and Tina are gracious hosts who will do whatever they can to make your stay both comfortable and enjoyable. The house itself is a treat, lovingly restored by the Fauble family. Breakfasts are hearty and tasty, served in the dining area, one of the showplace rooms in the house. An ideal choice for anyone who is interested in Victorian architecture and the history of North Florida." *(Charlotte Lane)* "A beautiful and immaculate home, with innkeepers who always made time to do the little extras that make you feel special." *(Jim Reddy)* "The parlor is decorated with Coca-Cola memorabilia, and has albums of 'before' and 'after' of the house—it's amazing how much work and determination was involved." *(Laura Rollins)* "We stayed in 'Laura's Loft' on the third floor—it was delightful to wake up to sunshine streaming through the stained glass window above the bed." *(Mary Alice Timmons)* "The Faubles spend time with the guests discussing the area and the inn's history. A relaxing, quiet, intimate place to stay." *(Jim Reddy)*

Open All year.
Rooms 9 doubles—all with private bath and/or shower, clock, TV, air-conditioning. 1 with fireplace, 1 with balcony.
Facilities Dining room, living room with fireplace, TV/VCR; porch, guest refrigerator. 2 acres with garden.
Location NW FL. 20 min. N of Tallahassee. 2 blocks from center of town. Historic District. 10 m W of I-10 on Hwy. 90. From I-10, take Exit 27 & go W on Hwy. 90. Turn N on Love St. & go 3 blocks to inn.
Restrictions Some traffic noise in front rooms. No smoking.
Credit cards All major.
Rates B&B, $75–120 double. Extra person, $15. "Tips accepted & appreciated."
Extras 1 room equipped for disabled. Crib.

ST. AUGUSTINE

St. Augustine, founded in 1565, is the oldest city in North America. With a few interruptions, it was under Spanish rule until 1821; many of its restored Spanish colonial homes were built in the 1700s. The city's architecture also has a strong Victorian component, dating back to the 1880s, when Henry Flagler did much to popularize St. Augustine as a fashionable resort. St. Augustine is on the northeast Florida coast, 30 miles north of Daytona and south of Jacksonville, and 100 miles northeast of Orlando.

As you would expect, parking in this historic city is extremely tight. Ask your innkeeper for specific advice and information. Once you have parked your car, you may not need it again until you leave. The city is compact and delightful for walking, and many restaurants provide free shuttle service in the evening. Given its considerable charms, St. Augustine is a popular destination, and the better inns are often booked well in advance, so make resevations early.

Reader tips: "Many inns include free passes to the Oldest House in their rates." And: "We had a delightful meal at Le Pavillon, including a lovely salad of Bibb lettuce, delicious cheese bread, and Florida-style bouillabaisse." *(SWS)*

Information please: Built in 1885, the **Carriage Way B&B** (70 Cuna Street, 32084; 904–829–2467 or 800–908–9832) is owned by Bill and Diane Johnson. The nine guest rooms have private baths and rent for $70–125. Breakfast includes homemade breads, fresh fruit, and a hot entree; bicycles are available for touring. "Convenient location two blocks from St. George Street; we parked in the inn's lot and never touched it until departure. The Johnsons offered warm hospitality, excellent restaurant advice." *(Karla Larson)*

Listed in past editions, we need current reports on the **Cedar House Inn** (79 Cedar Street, 32084; 904–829–0079 800–CEDAR–INN), built in 1893, and located in the historic district. The inn has ten-foot-high ceilings and polished heart-of-pine floors, and is furnished with queen-size beds, period antiques, and reproductions. Breakfast is served at guests' convenience at individual tables, and includes juice, home-baked muffins or coffee cake, fresh fruit salad, and a hot entree. B&B double rates for the five guest rooms range from $59–150.

Casa de la Paz — *Tel:* 904–829–2915
22 Avenida Menendez, 32084 — 800–929–2915

Location, location, location are the first three rules of real estate, and they make a great starting point for a B&B as well. The Casa de la Paz complements its superb location overlooking Matanzas Bay and the Bridge of Lions with lovely rooms, charming innkeepers, and delicious food. Built in 1915, the "House of Peace" is a Mediterranean Revival-style home, with white stucco walls and a hipped roof, purchased by experience innkeepers Bob and Donna Marriott in 1996. Inside, the original nine-foot ceilings, heart of pine and oak polished floors, and leaded glass windows and doors are enhanced by period decor.

"Owners Donna and Bob Marriott are experienced, knowledgeable, involved, active, personable, and friendly innkeepers. The inn overlooks the bay, with beautiful views from the parlor and front guest rooms. Common areas include the spacious parlor with ample comfortable seating, and Donna's music box collection; early morning coffee is available here at 8:00 A.M. The breakfast buffet is set out from 9:00 to 9:45 A.M., and can be enjoyed at the dining room table, for those who enjoy a communal meal, or at tables for two in the delightful solarium. You can be done in minutes, or linger for an hour, chatting with the other guests, as you wish. The generous array of dishes included fresh fruit, yogurt, granola, cottage cheese, toasted bagels, delicious turkey crepes, and coffee cake. The staff was attentive with refills of caf and decaf coffee. At the back of the inn is a little garden patio, where guests can sit out and enjoy the shade and cool ocean breezes. My room at the back of the inn was delightful and comfortable, with pale lilac walls, soft green colors, lots of white trim, and a white iron Victorian-reproduction queen-size bed. Good lighting at bedside and in the bathroom. Even a small private balcony." *(SWS)* "Thoughtful touches included cold wine and soda in the guest refrigerator, coffee cake in the living room, and sherry in our room. Beautiful antiques throughout the inn; lovely chandelier in the formal dining room. Hospitable innkeepers; delicious, abundant breakfasts." *(Ginette Brainard)* "Bob and Donna are friendly and helpful, yet never intrusive." *(Margie Galiene)*

Open All year.
Rooms 2 suites, 4 doubles—all with full private bath, clock/radio, TV, air-conditioning, ceiling fan, hair dryer.
Facilities Living room with fireplace, dining room, sun room, guest refrigerator. Garden courtyard, off-street parking, bicycles.
Location Historic district. On Ave. Mendenez, just N of Bridge of Lions, S of fort.
Restrictions No smoking. Children over 15.
Credit cards Amex, MC, Visa.
Rates B&B, $109–159 suite, $89–179 double.

Kenwood Inn *Tel:* 904–824–2116
38 Marine Street, 32084 *Fax:* 904–824–1689

This historic neighborhood was already old when the Kenwood was built between 1865 and 1885; just a few blocks away is the Oldest House, built in the early 1700s. This former boarding house was renovated in 1984; Mark, Kerriane, and Caitlin Constant became its owners in 1988. Rooms are decorated in a wide variety of New England styles, from Shaker to country Victorian, but all are light and airy, with soft floral fabrics.

"A favorite room is the upstairs suite, done with lots of quilts and country-style furnishings. Quiet location. A quick dip in the inn's small swimming pool is a treat after a day of sightseeing." *(SWS)* "We especially enjoy Mark and Kerriane's friendly hospitality, as well as the inn's excellent location and the attractive, comfortable guest rooms." *(Roberta Harvey, also Gail Larkin)* "Laid-back, congenial, family atmosphere. Coffee cake, fresh squeezed orange juice, and warm conversation greeted us each morning at breakfast. Complimentary sherry and chocolate chip cookies always await in the homey parlor." *(Mike White)* "The common areas are comfortable, homey, and inviting." *(Ted & Laura Phelps)* "The owners invited us to look at the rooms before choosing our favorite. Delicious lemon-flavored poppy seed cake and date-nut bread." *(Barbara Charlton)* "Mark Constant was most helpful in recommending restaurants and sights." *(Glenn & Lynette Roehrig)*

Open All year. Closed Christmas.
Rooms 4 suites, 10 doubles—all with private bath and/or shower, clock-radio, air-conditioning, fan; some with desk, TV, fireplace, balcony.
Facilities Sunroom with TV, stereo, books, living room with fireplace, dining room with fireplace, TV/game room; wraparounad verandas. Courtyard, swimming pool.
Location St. Johns County. Historic district. 2 blocks S of Bridge of Lions.
Restrictions No smoking. No children under 9. Some street noise in two rooms. On-street parking only; very limited due to narrow streets. Guests leave bags at inn, park 1 block away.
Credit cards Discover, MC, Visa.
Rates B&B, $115–150 suite, $85–150 double, $65–95 single (midweek). Extra person, $10. 2-3 night weekend, holiday minimum. 10% senior, AAA discount Sun.–Thurs.

St. Francis Inn ¢
279 St. George Street, 32084

Tel: 904–824–6068
800–824–6062
Fax: 904–810–5525
E-mail: innceasd@aug.com

The St. Francis Inn was built in 1791 of *coquina,* a limestone formed of broken shells and coral cemented together. The inn was used as a private residence until 1845, when it became a boardinghouse; a guide to St. Augustine published in 1869 describes it as one of the city's best. In 1996, long-time owner Joe Finnegan completed a major renovation of the inn. Although its historic charms were undisturbed, all the plumbing and wiring were replaced, along with the carpeting and wood flooring. In-room telephones and TVs make it a fine choice of the business traveler; fireplaces and double Jacuzzi tubs are appealing for weekend getaways. The brand-new kitchen enables the inn to offer buffet breakfasts of juice and fresh fruit, granola and oatmeal, a hot entree, and pastries and breads from local bakeries. Guests may enjoy their meal in their room, on a balcony or in one of the courtyards, or in the dining room. Rates also include coffee and iced tea at any time, and wine and cheese before dinner.

"Clean and simply furnished, in an interesting, quiet area with ample parking. Lovely entrance, through a patio with fish pond, trees, and wrought iron furniture." *(Jean Robbins)* "Our comfortable third-floor suite included an attractive living room and a convenient kitchenette."*(Robert Smith)* "A visit to the Oldest House, just down the street, was a highlight of our stay; the free tickets a plus." *(Joyce Wood)*

"Decorated throughout with an eclectic assortment of antiques, wicker, and Persian rugs, old and new books." *(Janet Lay)* "On a quiet one-way street, within walking distance of major sights." *(Pamela Allhands)* "Assistant manager Beverly Lonergan is entertaining, thoughtful, and helpful. April Carlton complements the staff with historical insight, a knack for detail, and kindness." *(Barbara Witchell)* "Quiet location off the main street. Spacious, comfortable rooms." *(Lois Dansereau)* "Lovely gardens, wonderful staff." *(Michelle Long)* "Delightful courtyard, friendly atmosphere. Everything in the historic district is within walking distance." *(Bill White)* "Delighted with the results of the recent renovation." *(Kimberly Cook, SWS)*

Open All year.
Rooms 6 suites, 7 doubles, 1 2-bedroom cottage—all with private bath and/or shower, telephone with dataport, TV, air-conditioning. Some with double Jacuzzi tubs, desk, fireplace, kitchenette, balcony. Separate 2-bedroom cottage with kitchen, fireplace, sleeps 4.
Facilities Living/family room with TV, piano, fireplaces, books; breakfast room with fireplace, conference room, balcony. Bicycles. Patio, courtyard with fountain, pond, swimming pool. Ocean swimming and fishing nearby. Ample on-site parking. Free admission to the Oldest House. Sun. courtyard concerts, 5–8 P.M., April–Oct.
Location Historic district; 3 blocks from restored town.
Restrictions No smoking in guest rooms.
Credit cards MC, Visa, Amex, All major accepted.
Rates B&B, $160 cottage (for 4), $110–165 suite, $85–175 double. Extra person, $12. Weekly, monthly rates available. Rate includes admission to Oldest House.
Extras Crib.

ST. PETERSBURG

St. Petersburg is located on the Gulf of Mexico, just across the bay from the city of Tampa, to which it is linked by a series of bridges and causeways. A string of sandy islands (actually keys), separated from the mainland by the Intracoastal Waterway, it offers miles of sparkling beaches and an unlimited supply of condominiums, motels, shops, and restaurants. The separate communities have names like Treasure Island, Madeira Beach, and Pass-A-Grille, and local residents refer to these places just like a New Yorker does in referring to the Upper East Side or the Bronx. St. Petersburg also has a number of interesting museums, ranging from the well-known Salvador Dali museum, to Great Explorations—ideal for families. The Florida International Museum presents major international traveling exhibitions (i.e. the Splendors of Ancient Egypt), so check to see what's in town during your visit.

One of the entries below is in tiny Pass-A-Grille, on the southernmost of St. Petersburg's islands. Building restrictions have limited development, so there are only a couple of buildings that rise more than two stories, and the public beach is lined with parking spaces, not condos. The town, now a National Historic District, is one of Florida's oldest settlements. Bicycling is a popular pastime, along with fishing in Boca Ciega Bay; a handful of restaurants offer a variety of seafood entrees in a casual atmosphere.

Information please: Under new owners in 1997 is the **Mansion House** (105 Fifth Avenue Northeast, 33701; 813–821–9391 or 800–274–7520) located one block from the water, close to the Sunken Gardens, Salvador Dali Museum, and Museum of Fine Arts. Gleaming wood floors contrast with the soft floral patterns of the wallpaper and comforters. B&B double rates for the six guest rooms, each with private bath (some with whirlpool tubs), range from $85–125, including a full breakfast and afternoon refreshments. "Lovely home, beautifully furnished. Bob and Rosemary Ray are the delightful new owners." *(Sue Winner)* For additional area information, see **Holmes Beach** and **Sarasota.**

Bayboro House B&B — *Tel:* 813–823–4955
1719 Beach Drive, Southeast, 33701 — *Fax:* 813–823–4955

For a quiet Victorian seaside holiday, an appealing choice is the Bayboro House, a Queen Anne-style home located in a quiet residential neighborhood overlooking Old Tampa Bay. Built in 1907, St. Petersburg's first B&B has been owned by Gordon and Antonia Powers since 1982. Breakfast is served at the dining room table 7:30–9:30 A.M. and includes fresh fruit and juice, cereal, breads, and muffins.

"Great attention to detail throughout, from the collection of antique teddy bears in the entry to the dolls and carriage on the landing. The entire inn is spotless and has a wonderful veranda facing the bay with lovely wicker chairs and lounges." *(SD)* "Gordon is a consummate host. He greeted us warmly and gave us a brief tour of the inn. The beautiful period furnishings include lace curtains, floral wallpapers, and Oriental rugs, old black-and-white photos in silver frames, painted globe lamps. Gordon's delicious breakfasts included just-baked quiche, scones, and muffins, presented on a table bedecked with fresh flowers." *(CD)* "A charming neighborhood of stately Victorian homes interspersed with stucco cottages and contemporary ranch-style homes. Bayboro House has a superb location with an unobstructed view of Old Tampa Bay. During our early morning walk on the small public beach, we shared the sand with a solitary great blue heron stalking its breakfast and an elderly fisherman digging for bait. Our room overlooked the bay, and had an enviable collection of Victorian light fixtures, an extremely comfortable queen-size bed, and a small, but well-equipped bathroom. The Powers are fun, personable hosts; we were delighted with their recommendation to visit the Pier complex for Spanish-Cuban cuisine at the Columbia Restaurant." *(Nancy Barker)* "Antonia is a delightful hostess. Wonderful suite for special occasions; lovely inn." *(Sue Winner)*

Open All year.
Rooms 1 suite, 3 doubles—all with private bath and/or shower, clock, TV/VCR, air-conditioning, ceiling fan. Suite with sun deck, kitchen.
Facilities Dining room, living room with piano, fireplace, books: family room, guest laundry, veranda with swing. Heated swimming pool, hot tub, off-street parking. Tennis, golf nearby.
Location 2 min. drive from downtown; 10-15 min. to beaches. From I-275, take Exit 9. Go S (right) on 4th St. S to 22nd Ave S, turning E (left). Go 5 blocks to bay. Go left on Beach Dr. to inn.
Restrictions No smoking. No children.
Credit cards MC, Visa.
Rates B&B, $85–125 suite, double. 10% AAA discount.

Bay Gables B&B ¢
136 Fourth Avenue Northeast, 33701

Tel: 813–822–8855
800–822–8803
Fax: 813–824–7223

A pink-and-white turn-of-the-century Key West building, the Bay Gables was restored as a B&B in 1995. It's owned by the Mort Corporation, and Laura Sharpe-Brock is the innkeeper. Breakfast is available from 8–10:30 A.M., and includes juice, cereal, yogurt, pastries, rolls, and muffins. Rates also include wine or sherry on arrival, and turndown service at night. The Bay Gables Tea Room & Garden is open for lunch and afternoon tea. The inn is located a half-block from the downtown waterfront, within walking distance of museums, art galleries, and restaurants.

"Tastefully decorated and immaculately kept. The setting, Laura's friendliness and graciousness, and the proximity of major points of interest combined to make our stay a pleasant and memorable experience." *(Alfredo & Doris Munoz)* "Highlights included the herbal bath salts, fine lotions and shampoos, lots of nice soft towels, quality bed linens, excellent housekeeping." *(Cynthia Bickey)* "Careful attention to guests needs." *(Maxine DeBaer)* "Gracious innkeeper, attractive rooms. Appealing garden area and tea room. Improving neighborhood, ongoing renovation." *(Sue Winner)*

Open All year.
Rooms 4 suites, 5 doubles—all with full private bath, telephone with data port, clock, air-conditioning, ceiling fan. 1 with whirlpool tub, 3 with desk, 4 with kitchenette.
Facilities Breakfast room, manager's office with puzzles, TV/VCR, fax machine; balconies, porches. Off-street parking, gazebo, garden.
Location Historic district, ½ block from waterfront. From I-375, take Exit 10 & go E on 4th Ave. N to inn at corner of 4th Ave. & 1st St.
Restrictions No smoking.
Credit cards MC, Visa.
Rates B&B, $110–135 suite, $85 double. Extra person, $25.
Extras Wheelchair access. 1 room specially equipped.

Island's End Resort
1 Pass-A-Grille Way, St. Petersburg Beach 33706

Tel: 813–360–5023
Fax: 813–367–7890

Since they purchased the Island's End in 1987, Jone and Millard Gamble have created a cozy retreat from the five buildings that form the inn. Weathered cedar siding and palm-shaded decks complement expansive views of the Gulf of Mexico. The cottages have wood-panelled interiors and comfortable contemporary furniture. Tuesday, Thursday, and Saturday mornings, breakfasts of coffee, freshly squeezed orange and grapefruit juice, plus assorted breakfast pastries, are served in the gazebo; on clear nights, you can see spectacular sunsets across the Gulf.

"Charming area and beautiful landscaping make Island's End seem like our own personal paradise. We enjoy visiting with old friends and meeting new ones at breakfast. Well-equipped fishing pier; super dolphin watching, because it's located right on the point between Boca

Ciega Bay and the Gulf of Mexico." *(Cynthia & Jack VanRoden)* "Terrific setting. Modern, clean cottages, surprisingly quiet for a bustling area. The owners and staff were cordial and helpful, and privacy is easily found in this unique setting. People seeking a bit of Old Florida will like Pass-a-Grille. An easy walk to a number of beach front restaurants." *(Susan Woods)* "Plants grow abundantly around the inn. While the island's tallest building (only four floors) lies just to the north, you feel like you've been transported to your own private island." *(NB)* "We walk the seven miles of beaches, and finish up by trying our luck on the fishing dock." *(Chet & Jan Schanhofer)*

Open All year.
Rooms 6 cottages—all with private bath, telephone, TV/VCR, kitchen with microwave. 1 3-bedroom house with heated swimming pool, 2 private baths, telephone, TV, air-conditioning, heat, kitchen with microwave, dishwasher.
Facilities Deck, gazebo, courtyard, laundry room, gas grill, lighted fishing pier.
Location S tip of Pass-A-Grille. 10 m to downtown St. Petersburg, 30 m to Tampa. From I-275 S, take Exit 4 to Rte. 652. Go W on Rte. 652, crossing Pinellas Bayway (toll causeway) to Gulf Blvd./Pass-A-Grille Way & turn left. Go S on Pass-A-Grille Way to end (1st Ave.) & turn right. Inn immediately on left.
Credit cards MC, Visa.
Rates Room only, $61–170 double. Extra person, $8. 4-night holiday minimum.
Extras Crib, babysitting. Lithuanian, Latvian, Russian spoken.

SANIBEL ISLAND

For a change of pace from shell collecting and lazing on the wonderful beaches, spend time hiking, canoeing, or bicycling in the "Ding" Darling National Wildlife Preserve, or cross the causeway back to Fort Myers to visit the winter home of Thomas Edison. You can see his home, research labs, and 14-acre botanical gardens.

Reader tip: "Kayaked through the beautiful Ding Darling Wildlife Refuge. The only drag was the no-see-ums which come out in the morning and before dusk, and eat you alive. Wear plenty of insect repellent!" *(Andrew Arntfield)*

Also recommended: "At the far end of the island just before you cross the bridge to Captiva is **The Castaways** (6460 Sanibel-Captiva Road, 33957; 941–472–1252), a group of cottages, efficiencies, and motel units owned by the same people as 'Tween Waters, in Captiva but less expensive. Had a comfortable efficiency across the road from the beach. Beaches were more or less deserted all day." *(Andrew Arntfield)*

The **Song of the Sea** (863 East Gulf Drive, Sanibel Island 33957; 941–472–2220 or 800–231–1045) is a 30-room European-style seaside inn, made up of a cluster of pink buildings framed by tropical foliage, right on the beach. Each unit has a kitchen, dining area, bathroom, screened porch, ceiling fan, air-conditioning, TV, VCR, and telephone; the decor includes French country furniture, Mediterranean tile floors, and down-filled comforters. The $155–335 rates include wine and flowers, free bicycles, swimming pool and hot tub, laundry facilities, and a breakfast of pastries, bagels, coffee, tea, and juice; golf and tennis privileges are offered at a nearby club. "Excellent breakfast, convenient location, free videos." *(Robert Mandell & Deborah Brown)*

SANTA ROSA BEACH

For additional area inns, see **Destin**.

Information please: Re-opened in 1997 in a new location is **A Highlands House** (P.O. Box 1189, 32459; 904–267–0110), with a layout similar to Joan and Ray Robbins' first inn: a Southern-style raised cottage with wide porches, a private entrance for each guest room, and easy beach access. Guest rooms (B&B $70–135 double) have reproduction four-poster rice beds and wingback chairs, with matching floral drapes and bedspreads; they open onto the wide front porch, where you can catch cooling breezes off the Gulf. Breakfast menus vary daily, but might include cinnamon coffee cake and batter-dipped French toast with sour cream and strawberries. "Joan is a fine hostess; excellent dining recommendations." *(Joe & Sheila Schmidt)*

SARASOTA

For additional area information, see **Holmes Beach** and **St.Petersburg.**

Information please: A cluster of garden apartments overlooking Heron Lagoon make up the **Banana Bay Club** (8254 Midnight Pass Road, Siesta Key 34242; 941–346–0113). Each of the seven units has a private deck, kitchenette, TV, private bath, and tropical decor. Facilities include a swimming pool, bicycles, barbecue grills, a canoe and rowboat. Daily rates range from $100–185, with weekly rates available.

Turtle Bay Beach Resort
9049 Midnight Pass Road
Siesta Key 94242

Tel: 941–349–4554
E-mail: grubi@ix.netcom.com

Turtle Bay Beach Resort was created in 1992 by Gail and David Rubinfeld; the fishing shacks which once occupied this site have been replaced by charming cottages and beautifully landscaped grounds. Gail notes that "our guests love to fish and eat on our dock, watch the dolphins and manatees, and feed the herons and egrets. They can take long romantic sunset walks along the gulf, and then enjoy dinner, music, and dancing at one of four nearby waterfront restaurants." Each unit is decorated differently, from the Country Cottage, done in blue and white, which actually touches the water, to the florals and lace of The Victorian, to the tropical Key West unit.

"Located on the southern, bay side of Siesta Key is this private cluster of single-story stucco buildings, surrounding an inviting swimming pool and deck area overlooking Turtle Bay. Each guest suite has its own private hot tub ingenuously tucked into the narrow property, and flowering plants bloom from every available nook. The cozy cottages are clean and quiet, just across the street from Turtle Beach, the smallest and least known of Siesta Key's municipal beaches." *(Nancy Barker)* "Warm hospitality, comfortable accommodation, excellent restaurant recommendations. Great area for walking, bicycling, and reading. We were fortunate to have a full moon every evening of our stay, reflecting on the water right out our window. Pure romance. Wonderful dinner at Ophelia's next door." *(GR)*

Open All year.
Rooms 3 2-bedroom cottages, 2 studio units—all with private shower and/or bath, telephone clock/radio, TV, air-conditioning, kitchenette, deck, hot tub. 3 with ceiling fan, 1 with VCR.
Facilities Guest laundry, fishing/boat dock, gazebo, hammock, swimming pool, gardens, bay front. Free bicycles, fishing poles, pedal boat, beach chairs. 3 min. walk to beach. Golf, tennis nearby.
Location 7 m of downtown Sarasota. From I-75, take exit 37 (Clark Rd.) & go W 7 m . Cross Stickney Pt. Bridge to Siesta Key. Go left on Midnight Pass Rd (at light). Go 2½ m to inn on left, just before island's end. From airport, go S on U.S. Rte. 41 to Stickney Pt. Rd. Turn right & go over bridge; follow directions above.
Restrictions No smoking.
Credit cards Amex, DC, Discover, MC, Visa.
Rates Room only, $150–275 for 4 people in 2-bedroom cottages, $130–225 studios. Extra person, $15. Children under 18 free. 10% weekly discount May 1–Dec. 15. Weekend getaway packages off-season.
Extras 10% surcharge for pets. Crib, babysitting.

SEASIDE

Seaside is a carefully designed Victorian-style beach community, with strict architectural controls, and a beautiful beach protected by high dunes. Excellent for both families and couples, it offers ample opportunities for walking, bicycling, and relaxing at the beach. You can choose from a variety of accommodations—Honeymoon Cottages and Dreamland Heights (each adults only), The Motor Court (modern reflection of an early motel), a selection of private cottages and homes for rent, and Josephine's (see below). The entire area has won numerous architectural awards and praise. For information and reservations call 904–231–1320 or 800–277–8696.

Reader tips: Although most readers were delighted with their visits to Seaside, one frequent contributor found it artificial and bland; she much preferred the funkier charms of Cedar Key.

"From the shore road, Seaside appears suddenly like a colorful gingerbread town. Owner Robert Davis conceived the development as a planned residential community. Internationally recognized urban architects, Andres Duany and Elizabeth Plater-Zyberk created an oasis of narrow streets, sandy walks and town squares tucked behind the dunes. Playful walkways lead to the pure white sand Gulf beach. Many homes were designed by distinguished architects; most are available for rent." *(Joe Schmidt)* "To avoid endless tourist tackiness, follow Route 30A right along the water and sand dunes, instead of Route 98." *(NB)*

For an additional area entry, see **Santa Rosa**, above.

Josephine's French Country Inn ✗ *Tel:* 904–231–1940
101 Seaside Avenue, P.O. Box 4767, 32459 800–848–1840
Restaurant: 904–231–1939

Built in 1991 in the Greek Revival style, Josephine's offers guest rooms with four-poster beds, settees, balloon curtains, Battenburg lace comforters, and marble bathtubs. The sitting room even has such period touches as beaded tongue-and-groove paneling and heart pine flooring. The breakfast buffet, served 9–11 A.M., includes cereal, mixed fruit, cakes, and breads. Favorite dinner dishes served in the inn's well-known restaurant include Caribbean bouillabaisse, fried green tomatoes with wilted spinach and jumbo Gulf shrimp, fish with artichoke hearts, or grilled filet mignon. Sean Herbert is the manager.

"Located on one of Seaside's town squares, this charming inn is a short walk from the beaches and amenities of Seaside. The rooms are comfortable and clean, the young innkeepers delightful. Exceptionally high levels of maintenance throughout the community." *(Joe & Sheila Schmidt)* "Excellent food, careful attention to detail." *(Mimi Cohen)* "An elegant inn with an exceptional dining room. Our first floor suite was spacious, with a well-stocked refrigerator. Several restaurants nearby." *(Donna Jacobson)* "The welcoming front porch is a great place to sit and read or people watch." *(EE)*

Open All year. Restaurant closed Jan., also Mon., Tues.
Rooms 4 suites, 7 doubles, 2 cottages—all with full private bath, telephone, radio, clock, TV, air-conditioning, fan, refrigerator. Some with whirlpool tub, desk, fireplace, balcony, VCR, kitchenette. Suites in separate building across street.
Facilities Restaurant, breakfast room, living room, verandas. Off-street parking. Beach, heated swimming pools, tennis, golf, playgrounds, nature trails nearby.
Location FL panhandle, halfway between Destin & Panama City. 70 m E of Pensacola. Center of town.
Restrictions No smoking. Children over 12.
Credit cards Amex, MC, Visa.
Rates B&B, $190–220 suite, $117–220 double. Extra person, $20. Tipping encouraged. Senior, AAA discount, 10%. Alc dinner, $50.
Extras Wheelchair access; bathroom specially equipped.

STEINHATCHEE

Steinhatchee Landing Resort *Tel:* 352–498–3513
Highway 51 North, P.O. Box 789, 32359 800–584–1709
Fax: 352–498–2346

Creeping condo—it has overspread Florida quicker than kudzu, making sleepy Taylor County one of Florida's last real backwaters. With the recent development of Steinhatchee Landing, visitors can explore an undeveloped part of Florida in comfort and style. In 1990, Dean and Loretta Fowler began construction of this resort on the shores of the Steinhatchee River, offering accommodation in handsomely built units in three regional styles; additional accommodations are available at the Steinhatchee River Inn, an all-suite motel a half-mile away. The restaurant specializes in seafood, with such entrees as grouper with pecans and lemon butter, Gulf shrimp to taste, and the "world's best" crab cakes.

"On the banks of the placid, picturesque Steinhatchee River may be Florida's last remote and untouched town. Roy's Restaurant is a good place for tasty, well-priced food. Steinhatchee Landing is a well-run resort and a fine place for a family reunion, as President Jimmy Carter discovered." *(Joe & Sheila Schmidt)* "An oasis in the woods. Our little two-bedroom house was immaculately clean, with windows opened to the breeze, and an inviting screened porch off the kitchen. Beautifully landscaped grounds, with winding paths and low lights, leading down to the river where you'll find the dock, swimming pool, playground, shuffleboard court, and comfortable seating. Delicious dinner of freshly made crabcakes, delicious grouper, and rosemary potatoes." *(NB)*

"The well-maintained motel rooms are an excellent value. Steinhatchee (locals call it STEEN-hatchee) itself, a few miles down the road, is a working fishing town, with three seafood restaurants. Good view of tidal marshes and islets." *(Bill MacGowan)* "Check-in took all for 45 seconds, and set the tone for our stress-free stay. Loved being able to use their bicycles at no charge." *(Katie Test)* "We arrived by boat and tied up at their dock. Charming cottage with clean, bright, and fresh-smelling rooms. Delicious dinner of Cajun shrimp and filet mignon. Breakfast was brought at the requested time, and included fresh fruit, eggs and French toast, crisp bacon, and home fries." *(Cheryl Riley)* "Quality, comfort, and outstanding service. Delightful pontoon boat ride along the winding river to the Gulf of Mexico." *(Fred Ayer)* "Excellently furnished housekeeping cottages; lovely setting. Fine fishing; good food." *(Daniel Ruffle)* "Impeccably maintained swimming pool and spa." *(Mary Garratt)*

Open All year. Restaurant closed Mon–Wed.
Rooms 20 1-4 bedroom cottages, 17 motel suites (½m away)—all with full private bath, radio, clock, TV, desk, air-conditioning, ceiling fan, refrigerator. 15 with fan, 7 with fireplace, 15 with porch/deck, telephone, VCR, stereo.
Facilities Restaurant, bar/lounge, kitchen, laundry, porches. 25 acres with nature trails, gardens, 2 pools, 2 hot tubs, exercise room, tennis court, gazebo, lawn games, bicycles, canoes, boats, playground, parking. Scalloping, fishing, diving on river. 3 m from Gulf.
Restrictions Some non-smoking rooms.
Location NW FL, Taylor Cty. 70 m W of Gainesville. Take U.S. Hwy 19 to Tennille Crossing. Go W on Hwy 51 for 8 m to Landing on left.
Credit cards Amex, MC, Visa.
Rates Room only, $115–255 cottage; sleep 4–10. Maid service, $25 daily. 2-3 night weekend/holiday minimum. Motel, $50–70. Alc dinner, $25; Sunday brunch, $10.
Extras Wheelchair access in restaurant only. Airport/station pickup. Pets with approval. Cribs, babysitting.

STUART

Reader tip: "Old Stuart has been restored, and offers a river walk, interesting shops and galleries, and a variety of pleasant places for indoor or outdoor dining. For a snack, try Coffee & Sweets (7 East Osceola); for a meal, check out the Jolly Sailor Pub across the street." *(Joe Schmidt)*

Also recommended: Overlooking the St. Lucie River is the **Harbor-Front Inn** (310 Atlanta Avenue, 34994; 561–288–7289 or 800–266–1127), a restored 1908 home offering clean, comfortable, simply done rooms in a quiet setting. B&B double rates for the five guest rooms, including a full breakfast, range from $65–110.

For additional area entries, see **North Hutchinson Island** and **Palm Beach.**

The Homeplace ¢
501 Akron Avenue, 34994

Tel: 561–220–9148
800–251–5473
Fax: 561–221–3265

Built in 1913 by one of Stuart's first developers, The Homeplace was restored as a B&B in 1989, and was purchased by Suzanne and Michael Pescitelli in 1995. One handsome guest room has wainscotting on the walls and ceiling, a brass bed, and a dark blue and red color scheme; another is more feminine with frills and ruffles.

"Suzanne is a gracious, welcoming hostess. Spotless and full of lovely antiques, this small inn is a short walk from the Stuart waterfront. For warm, lazy days, the inviting swimming pool awaits just outside the back door." *(Joe Schmidt)* "Suzanne and Michael are friendly hosts with great sightseeing suggestions. This immaculate inn is wonderfully decorated with lovely antiques and knick-knacks. The Prissy room is decorated in floral pastels and ruffles, with a wrought iron queen-size bed. Our cool, comfortable room had plenty of windows, with a cozy chair and a basket full of magazines. The bathroom had a clawfoot tub and a stained glass window. The clean and refreshing swimming pool area was quiet, beautifully landscaped, with a hammock strung between two palms. Breakfast included grapefruit from their own tree, cinnamon-flavored coffee, bagels, freshly baked pecan rolls, plus peach-cobbler French toast one morning, and breakfast burritos the next. The kitchen was always open with soda, juice, coffee, tea and fresh baked cookies readily available." *(Frank & Terry Ficara)*

"Suzanne and Michael were warm and gracious hosts. A number of activities are within a few minutes walk or drive, from the shops and restaurant of downtown Stuart to the beautiful beaches of Hutchinson Island." *(Lisa Crawford)* "Ample books and magazines to read. Quiet area, yet within walking distance of the historic downtown and riverwalk." *(Janet Collins)* "Attention to detail included the ever-full cookie jar, access to a refrigerator, and a carafe of decent wine each evening. Conversations with Suzanne and fellow guests were a highlight." *(SCB)* "Top marks for hospitality, housekeeping, and homey atmosphere." *(Sue Reed)*

Open All year.
Rooms 4 doubles—all with full private bath, air-conditioning, fan. Telephone, radio, TV on request.
Facilities Dining room, parlor with piano, TV, books, sun room, porch. 2.5 acres with swimming pool, hot tub, garden, lawn games. 5 min. to tennis, beaches, boating, fishing.
Location SE central FL. 45 min. N of Palm Beach, 2 hrs. S of Orlando. 2 blocks from historic area. At corner of Akron & 5th St., 2 blocks from S.R. 76.
Restrictions Smoking discouraged. No children under 12.
Credit cards MC, Visa.
Rates B&B, $85–95 double, $80–90 single. Extra person, $25. 2-night minimum weekend. May 1–Nov. 30, 3rd night free midweek.

TALLAHASSEE

The capital of Florida, Tallahassee is also home to Florida State University and Florida A&M; other sites of interest include the Tallahassee Junior Museum, a favorite with children, and the Maclay State Gardens, stunning in early spring for their azaleas, camellias, and dogwood.

Reader tips: "For a nice meal, try Chez Pierre, 115 North Adams Street, 904–222–0936." *(Bill MacGowan)*

Information please: Listed in past editions is the **Governors Inn** (209 South Adams Street, 32301; 904–681–6855 or 800–342–7717), occupying two century-old buildings, linked by an atrium. Each guest room is named after a former Florida governor and is furnished with four-poster beds, black oak writing desks, and rock maple armoires. B&B double rates for the 40 guest rooms range from $119–219, including a continental breakfast and evening cocktail hour. Reports welcome.

For additional area entries, see **Monticello** and **Wakulla.**

VENICE

An island surrounded by the Gulf of Mexico and the intracoastal waterway, Venice was originally called Horse & Chaise and was renamed in 1888 by a local businessman who was inspired by the Grand Canal in Venice, Italy.

The Banyan House ¢ *Tel:* 941–484–1385
519 South Harbor Drive, 34285 *Fax:* 941–484–8032

Built in 1926, this Mediterranean-style home, with red-tiled roof and white stucco, was purchased by Ian and Suzie Maryan in 1996. Although the living room is now decorated with formal Victorian parlor furnishings and an Oriental carpet to complement the Italian sculptured fireplace, the setting was not always so posh. Just three years after the house was built, Venice went bankrupt, and Banyan House was abandoned. For three years, tramps slept on its Italian tile floors, cooking their meals in the fireplace. Meals are served with a bit more ceremony these days; at 9:00 A.M., Suzie serves breakfast of fresh fruit, juice, home-baked breads, pancakes, or crepes.

"The lovely tropical grounds are inviting and private, with numerous seating areas and a wonderful hot tub under the banyan tree. Loved being able to walk to the beach, tennis courts, lovely downtown shops, restaurants, churches, and community center. Attentive innkeepers. Special touches include the bouquets of fresh flowers, first quality table linens, lovely breakfasts, daily newspaper, and the snacks of nuts, candy, and spring water." *(Robert & Ellen Elie)* "Guest rooms are clean, quiet, light, and airy. Breakfasts are served in a cheerful, sunny, porch-like setting." *(Jeff & Margaret Thurlow)* "Reminiscent of a Spanish hacienda, in a desirable neighborhood, close to the beach. The well-appointed rooms have bright, modern color schemes with big, sunny windows." *(John & Jutta O'Flaherty)* "Ian and Suzie are very hospitable and make you feel right at home." *(John & Honora McCarthy)*

Open All year.
Rooms 5 1-bedroom apartments, 3 suites, 1 double—all with full private bath, radio, TV, desk, air-conditioning, fan. Most with telephone, desk, balcony/deck, kitchenette. Rooms in main house, carriage house, annex.
Facilities Living room with fireplace, piano; breakfast solarium with stereo, books; laundry facility. Brick courtyard with fountain, decks, swimming pool, hot tub, bicycles, beach chairs. Walking distance to beach. Golf, tennis, fishing, boating nearby.
Location SW FL coast. 40 m S of St. Petersburg, 50 m N of Ft. Myers. 5 blocks from downtown. Take I-75 to Exit 35. Turn right (W) on Venice Ave., left on Harbor Dr. Inn 5 blocks on left.
Restrictions Smoking restricted. No children under 12.
Credit cards MC, Visa.
Rates B&B, $70–115 suite, double. $425–695 weekly minimum for apts. Extra person, $20.

WAKULLA SPRINGS

Also recommended: Readers rave about the charms of Wakulla Springs State Park, donated to the state of Florida by Ed Ball, a real estate millionaire who fell in love with the natural beauty of this area, and preserved the 2,900 acres which now make up the park. He built **Wakulla Springs Lodge** (1 Springs Drive, 32305; 904–224–5950) in 1937 in the Spanish Mission style; the interior is striking for its lavish use of Tennessee marble. Other decorative motifs include the Aztec Indian designs painted on the cypress ceiling beams, the Spanish tiles, and the Moorish archways. Rates for the 27 guest rooms range from $65–90; meals are equally reasonable in price. Although readers lament the uninspired furnishings in the guest rooms, the "expressionless, semi-trained personnel," and the fact that dinner is "not served after 8 P.M.," all agree that the setting and reasonable rates more than compensate, from the jumping fish you can watch from your breakfast table, to the fascinating jungle boat ride. The spring itself produces over 600,000 gallons of water a minute; its basin reaches a crystal-clear depth of 185 feet.

WEST PALM BEACH

Tropical Gardens B&B
(formerly West Palm Beach B&B)
419 32nd Street, 33407

Tel: 561–848–4064
800–736–4064
Fax: 561–848–2422
E-mail: wpbbed@aol.com

A cottage-style Key West home built of pine in 1937, and restored as a B&B in 1989, Emil Scipioni and Robert Rosario purchased this Key West Style guest house in 1997. The inn has a Caribbean decor with a sunshine yellow color scheme, wicker furnishings, hardwood floors, tropical art, and lots of plants. Breakfast is served each morning in the dining room or by the pool, and includes fresh-squeezed orange juice, tropical fruit salad, cereals, muffins, breads, coffee cake, and scones, served buffet style from 8:30–10:30 A.M.

"The Carriage House is next to the pool in the beautifully landscaped backyard. The rooms are immaculate and tastefully decorated. Our refrigerator was stocked with fresh fruits, juice, breads, cereal and a bottle of wine. Our gracious hosts helped with suggestions and directions."*(Ed Adams)* "It was lovely to come 'home' to the casual, relaxing atmosphere of the inn, decorated with fresh flowers and plants." *(Bea Harmon)* "Good parking; safe, well-lighted setting; good showers; spring water for drinking." *(RL)* "Comfortable king-size beds, spotless rooms." *(Mr. & Mrs. Walter Wall)*

Open All year.
Rooms 1 Carriage House suite with kitchenette, 1 cabana cottage, 2 doubles—all with private bath and/or shower, radio, TV, air-conditioning, ceiling fan, fireplace, refrigerator. Some with kitchenette, VCR.
Facilities Living room with fireplace, dining room, garden room with books, TV; breakfast room, deck. TV, stereo in carriage house. Swimming pool, garden, lawn games, off-street parking, bicycles. Golf, tennis, ocean nearby.
Location SE FL. Old Northwood Historic District. From I-95 N or S, exit on 45th St. East to Dixie Hwy. Head S to 32nd St., make right to 3rd house in on right.
Restrictions No smoking. Traffic noise might disturb light sleepers.
Credit cards Amex, MC, Visa.
Rates B&B, $55–85 double. No tipping. 3-night holiday minimum. Weekly rates.

WINTER GARDEN

Meadow Marsh B&B ♿
940 Tildenville School Road, 32787

Tel: 407–656–2064
Toll-free: 888–656–2064

The home of the Tilden family from 1877 until the 1970s, what was once a modest pine dwelling grew over the decades to become a gracious home, with wonderful wraparound porches on two levels. Restored as a B&B in 1996 by Cavelle and John Pawlack, and listed on the National Register of Historic Places, it now offers gracious common areas, and guest rooms furnished with Victorian antiques and quilts. Breakfast is served at 8:30 A.M. at the dining room table, and includes fresh fruit and juice, cereal, and such entrees as French toast with homemade strawberry jam and whipped cream, and bacon; ham quiche and orange muffins; or eggs, cheese grits, ham and biscuits.

"This handsome building grew along with the citrus fortune of the Tilden family. Owner Cavell Pawlack is a non-stop dynamo, and both she and her husband John are warm and gracious hosts. The windows of our cozy room overlooked a giant meadow. Runners, bicyclers, and walkers will enjoy the paved trail bordering the property which follows a converted rail bed. Excellent breakfast of baked apples, granola, sausages, and French toast." *(Joe Schmidt)* "We were given a tour of this beautiful home, and invited to help ourselves to drinks and snacks in the kitchen. The entire house was immaculate, beautifully furnished with antiques, enhanced by modern plumbing. Our lovely room had fresh flowers, soft music, and mints." *(Joy Pulvino)* "The Pawlacks were working in the garden when we arrived, and dropped everything to greet us and join us for a snack of lemonade and cookies. Our comfortable room was complete with a screened porch and delightful antiques. Each morning we walked on the nearby trail, then returned for a delicious breakfast, served on antique china; the hosts joined us when we were the only guests." *(Jack & Bonne Scott)* "Spacious Victoria's Ivy Attic had ample space for a double Jacuzzi tub, writing desk, and sitting area. An outside entrance, via a spiral staircase, made it especially private. Majestic live oaks surround this beautiful country home." *(Susan Smokey)*

Open All year.
Rooms 1 cottage, 2 suites, 2 doubles—all with private bath and/or shower, air-conditioning, ceiling fan, clock/radio, desk, 2 with Jacuzzi, 1 with screened porch, fireplace.
Facilities Dining room, living room with fireplace, piano, TV/VCR, stereo; library with books, TV/VCR; porches with swings. 12 acres with swiming pool, croquet, gardens, woods; bordered by "Rails-to-Trails" path.
Location N central FL. 14 m W downtown Orlando; 35-40 min. NW of Disney World. Near intersection of FL Rte. 545 & 438; close to FL Turnpike & Hwy. 50; call for directions.
Restrictions No smoking. Well-behaved children over 12.
Credit cards Discover, MC, Visa.
Rates B&B, $180–200 suite, $95–125 double. Extra person, $25. Prix fixe lunch, $15; dinner, $40–50.
Extras Limited wheelchair access; one room partially equipped.

WINTER PARK

The town of Winter Park is pretty, charming, and prosperous, with lots of charming little shops, well-tended parks, gardens, and museums.

Rollins College is a beautiful place, with lush grounds, colorful plantings, and Spanish-style buildings.

Reader tip: "Very appealing at Christmas, with lovely decorations in the park and bands playing carols. Winter Park is close enough to Orlando's attractions to partake, and far enough away not to feel like you have the word 'tourist' stamped on your shirt." *(Perri Rappel)* "Trains run right through town, often with whistles blowing, until the wee hours." *(RP)*

For additional area entries, see **Lake Wales, Maitland, Minneola, Mount Dora, Orlando,** and **Winter Garden.**

Information please: Built in 1922, **The Fortnightly Inn** (377 East Fairbanks Avenue, 32789; 407–645–4440) was restored highlighting its original oak and heart of pine floors, original brass hardware and porcelain fixtures, and clawfoot tubs. "Pleasant rooms; fine choice for Rollins College visitors." *(SWS)* Double rates of $75–95 include breakfast of juice, fruit and pastries served between 8 A.M. and 9 A.M., plus in-room sherry. Right on the main shopping street is the **Park Plaza Hotel** (307 Park Avenue South, 32789; 407–647–1072 or 800–228–7220). Downstairs is a lobby and restaurant; upstairs are the guest rooms. Though dark, the better rooms are at the front of the inn, and open to a balcony which runs the length of the building, curtained from the street by lush ferns, creating a lush bower ideal for people-watching. B&B double rates of $90–185 include a light continental breakfast, delivered to the room.

Georgia

The Veranda, Senoia

There's more to Georgia than peaches and peanuts, Jimmy Carter and Scarlett O'Hara. For urban delights, visit Atlanta, one of the country's most sophisticated cities combining contemporary culture and "Old South" charm; tour graceful historic homes in Savannah; or time-travel to Macon's antebellum mansions. In northwestern Georgia, visit New Echota (outside of Calhoun), the former Cherokee capital where Sequoyah developed a written language for his people; then stop by nearby Chatsworth to see the Vann House, a mansion built by a Cherokee chief and noted for its unusually colored interior paint. In northeastern Georgia, tour the mountains, then stop by the spectacular Tallulah Gorge. Want more water? Get your fill canoeing through the Okefenokee Swamp or visiting posh St. Simons Island.

AMERICUS

Also recommended: In the center of Americus is the extraordinary **Windsor Hotel** (125 West Lamar Street, 31709; 912–924–1555), a Romanesque Revival red brick fantasy built in 1888, and restored at a cost of over $5 million in 1990. A Victorian gem, it features 53 guest rooms, including two round tower suites, with king-size beds. B&B rates range from $70–135. The three-story atrium lobby is done in polished golden oak, with marble floors and crystal chandeliers. "Wonderful round tower room; great room service dinner; real Southern hospitality." *(Margaret Kontack)* "Our room had a queen-size bed, a small table and two comfortable chairs, an old-style wardrobe, and a nice bathroom with tub. Pleasant public rooms." *(Duane W. Roller)* "Charming hotel; excellent dinner in the grand dining room." *(BJ Hensley)*

1906 Pathway Inn B&B
501 South Lee Street, 31709

Tel: 912–928–2078
800–889–1466
Fax: 912–928–2078
E-mail: pathway@sowega.net

Combining Victorian and Greek Revival design elements, the 1906 Pathway Inn features a two-story portico and wraparound verandas. Restored by Sheila Judah as a B&B in 1994, it features extensive common areas, highlighted by stained glass windows, as well as individually furnished guest rooms with queen- or king-size beds. Breakfast, served 6:30–9:30 A.M. at the dining room table, consists of fresh fruit and juice; sausages, ham, or bacon; muffins, strudel, or sweet breads; and casseroles, omelets, crepes, or perhaps waffles. Rates also include afternoon wine and refreshments.

"Convenient to downtown; luxurious, quiet, spacious accommodations." *(Robert P. Hornsby)* "We were welcomed warmly and given a tour of the house, sipped wine on the veranda, and visited with Sheila. She was very helpful in giving us directions to good restaurants for dinner. This grand old home has been beautifully and tastefully decorated in period. Delicious candlelit breakfasts were served on the beautifully laid table, and included home-baked muffins, a ham, cheese, and egg casserole, and blueberry crepes. Our spotless bedroom and bath were lovely and most comfortable; we also enjoyed the parlors for reading and relaxing. Wonderful neighborhood for walking, with homes dating from the mid-1800s to early 1900s." *(Margaret Espy)*

Open All year.
Rooms 5 doubles—all with private shower and/or whirlpool tub, telephone with dataport, clock/radio, TV/VCR, desk, air-conditioning, ceiling fan. 2 with fireplace. 1 with refrigerator, deck.
Facilities Dining room, ladies' parlor (living room) with piano and books; men's parlor (family room) with TV/VCR, videos, stereo, books; porch. ¾ acre with off-street parking, hot tub, croquet. Golf nearby.
Location SW GA. 100 m S of Atlanta. Historic district, ¼ m from City Hall. From I-75 N, take Cordele Exit 33; from I-75 S, take Vienna Exit 36. Go W on Hwy. 280 to downtown Americus. Go left (S) on Hwy. 377 (S. Lee St.) Go right on College St. to inn on corner of Lee & College.
Restrictions No smoking in bedrooms; permitted in men's parlor.
Credit cards Amex, Discover, MC, Visa.
Rates B&B, $79–117 double, $70–110 single. Extra person, $20. Corporate rates.
Extras Local airport/station pickups. Pets with prior approval. Babysitting by arrangement.

ATLANTA

Virtually leveled by General Sherman during the Civil War, Atlanta recovered fairly quickly, becoming a major rail hub by the end of the century. Today, Atlanta is a modern city whose population has exploded in the past three decades; its airport is one of the busiest in the country, and its traffic jams rival those of Los Angeles.

Reader tip: Forty minutes east of Atlanta via I-20 is the **Blue Willow Inn** (Highway 11, Social Circle 30279; 770–464–2131) open for lunch and dinner. "The buffet at this restaurant features exceptional, authentic, Southern cooking. Garden-fresh vegetables, perfectly cooked meat and fish dishes, delicious desserts." *(Joe & Sheila Schmidt)*

Also recommended: When you're in the mood for the best in a big city hotel (551 rooms), the **Ritz-Carlton Buckhead** (3434 Peachtree Road NE, 30326; 404–237–2700 or 800–241–3333) "is worth the money for an all-around luxurious yet friendly atmosphere. Wonderful rooms done in antique reproductions, and baths with all the extras, thick fluffy towels and robes, full length mirrors, nightly turn-down service. Ask for a room with the Phipps Plaza view—you can see to the horizon, or splurge on a room on the Concierge Floor. Good food and service in both restaurants too." *(SHW)*

Information please: Located in the Buckhead section is the **Beverly Hills Inn** (65 Sheridan Drive, 30305; 404–233–8520), a European-style hotel with 18 well-equipped suites, all with kitchenettes. B&B double rates of $90–140 include a continental breakfast and welcoming glass of wine. "Quiet neighborhood, yet close to the intersection of Peachtree and Piedmont. Our room had a balcony overlooking the street, sofa and dining area, and large closet. Friendly innkeepers; excellent value." *(Krista Iba-Armstrong)*

For additional area inns, see **Concord, Newnan** and **Senoia**.

Gaslight Inn
1001 Saint Charles Avenue

Tel: 404–875–1001
Fax: 404–876–1001

Taking its name from the flickering gas lanterns outside the inn, as well as the original gas lighting inside, the Gaslight Inn is a Craftsman-style home, built in 1913, and restored as a B&B in 1994 by Jim Moss. Breakfast, served 8:30–10 A.M., consists of fresh baked breads, muffins, croissants, bagels, potato rolls, Danish, fresh fruit and juice, cereals, yogurts and coffee. Guests are ecstatic about the warm yet professional hospitality, the first-rate location, and most of all the exceptionally lovely decor of this B&B.

"Unparalleled elegance, genuine comfort, impressive guest rooms and common areas; an ideal balance of comfort and elegance. The guest rooms are furnished with lovely antiques, queen or king-sized beds, thick terry robes, and thoughtful amenities. The English Suite has a four poster mahogany bed with a draped canopy, and a separate sitting room which opens to a private veranda overlooking the formal gardens. The bathroom has double sinks and a double Jacuzzi for two, a tiled steam shower, and a wet bar. The other guest rooms and common areas are equally impressive. All was furnished under the supervision of Jim's partner, an architect and interior designer. You can relax on the front porch rockers, or in the screened porch overlooking the garden.

Terrific neighborhood, with wonderful shops and restaurants literally around the corner. Host Jim Moss is warm, hospitable, and a knowledgeable Atlanta native." *(Susan Poole)* "My favorite room is the private Ivy Cottage, with its light, bright, informal Nantucket look." *(MW)* "Jim and his staff run a fine establishment." *(Mark Porter)* "Exquisitely decorated. Close to trendy North Highland Avenue." *(Millie Ball)* "We are always treated like visiting royalty." *(Rich Haas)*

Open All year.
Rooms 3 suites, 3 doubles, 1 cottage—all with full private bath, telephone, clock, TV, desk, air-conditioning, ceiling fan, refrigerator. Some with double whirlpool tub, fireplace, radio, wet bar, veranda. Cottage with kitchen, washer/dryer.
Facilities Dining room, living room; both with fireplace. Sun room/den with piano, TV/VCR, stereo, books. Veranda, screened porch. Courtyard garden with fountain, off-street parking.
Location 2 m NE of downtown Atlanta, in Virginia Highlands historic district. From I-75/85, take Exit 96, Freedom Pkwy (Hwy 10 E) to Ponce de Leon Ave. Go left on Fredrica (between bank & library). Go left on St. Charles to inn on right. Walking distance to Emory, Piedmont Park, Callanwolde Fine Arts Center; public transportation nearby.
Restrictions No smoking. Children over 12 years old.
Credit cards Amex, Discover, MC, Visa.
Rates B&B, $149–$195 suite, $95–$125 double, $85–$125 single.
Extras Wheelchair accessible; 1 suite specially equipped.

Oakwood House
951 Edgewood Avenue N.E., 30307

Tel: 404–521–9320
Fax: 404–688–6034
E-mail: OakwoodBnB@aol.com

Named for the huge oak tree in the backyard, the Oakwood was built in 1911, in Atlanta's oldest suburb, Inman Park. Longtime residents Judy and Robert Hotchkiss restored the residence in 1992, furnishing the inn in a comfortable, uncomplicated style. Guest rooms have queen or king-sized beds; some have exposed brick walls and built-in bookcases, filled with hundreds of volumes. The Romance Room on the garden level has a tented queen-sized bed, and French doors opening to a bathroom with an oversize whirlpool tub and original artwork. Breakfast includes fresh baked muffins—perhaps blueberry, chocolate chip, or bran—fresh sliced fruit, orange juice, and hot or cold cereal.

"Careful attention to detail, from the jar of chocolate chip cookies to the basket of herbal teas, from the plush terry robes to the just-baked breakfast muffins. Our room was comfortable and clean; the bathroom bright with great towels. Charming neighborhood with many restored homes. We enjoyed walks to the Jimmy Carter Library and to Little Five Points, an interesting shopping area." *(Nancy Holden)* "Warm and inviting; friendly helpful hosts. After a long day at a downtown conference I felt like I was coming home." *(Richard Anderson)* "Charming young innkeepers. Spotlessly clean; private and quiet. Fresh flowers in every room, every day."*(Neil Winslow)* "Wonderfully high ceilings and beautifully restored original woodwork. Our spacious room had a comfortable king-size bed." *(Paula Hill)* "Downstairs is an inviting library, its shelves brimming with books and magazines." *(Lyndell Anderson)*

Open All year.
Rooms 5 doubles—all with private bath and/or shower, telephone with voice mail, radio, clock, air-conditioning. 1 with whirlpool tub, TV, fan, balcony.
Facilities Common area with TV, books; laundry; fax, copier; kitchen privileges. Porch, decks. Off-street parking, small garden.
Location Inman Park. 2 m east of downtown Atlanta. From I-75/85 N, take Exit 96, Freedom Pkwy. Follow signs to Carter Ctr. & exit onto Hwy 42 connector just after "flat ice roof." Passing Center entrance, turn right at light onto N Highland Ave. Go ½ m to Elizabeth St. Turn left. Go 4 blocks to 2nd light at Edgewood Ave. & turn right. Inn is 4th on left; park on street or in lot on left side of house. 1½ blocks to Inman Park MARTA station; 5-min. ride downtown.
Restrictions No smoking. "Well behaved children welcome."
Credit cards MC, Visa.
Rates B&B, $79–150 double, $70–140 single. 1 child free in parents' room. 3-night minimum major conventions.
Extras Wheelchair access; 1 room specially equipped. Crib.

Shellmont Bed & Breakfast Lodge *Tel:* 404–872–9290
821 Piedmont Avenue N.E., 30308 *Fax:* 404–872–5379

Built in 1891, and listed on the National Register of Historic Places, Shellmont is an excellent example of Victorian design. Stained, leaded, and beveled glass abound, as do intricately carved interior and exterior woodwork, elaborate mantels, mosaic-tiled fireplaces, documented Bradbury and Bradbury wall coverings, and accurately reproduced original stenciling. The inn is furnished throughout with Victorian antiques. Ed and Debbie McCord, owners since 1984, work hard to improve the inn each year, both in terms of the lovely decor and equally important, to ensure guest comfort and convenience; although the beds are antiques, all have new, top-rated queen-size mattresses. The Shellmont is located in midtown; restaurants, live theaters, art cinemas, museums, and shopping are within walking distance. Breakfast is served at 7:30 or 8:30 a.m. on weekdays (an hour later on weekends) and includes cereal, granola, yogurt, fresh fruit, homemade breads, and such entrees as Belgian waffles with whipped cream and fresh strawberries, frittatas, and specialty egg dishes.

"A smooth and efficiently run inn. Well decorated rooms with nice touches and amenities, spotlessly clean." *(Shirley Dittloff)* "This lovely Queen Anne home is painted pale green with cream trim; the carved shell woodwork above the bay window is gorgeous. The parlor sitting room has window seats in the lovely curved windows. At night, the lovely Tiffany window is back lit from inside the house." *(SHW)* "Debbie intuitively knew when solitude was preferred." *(Barbara Cordaro)* "My room had a comfortable antique bed with a matching dresser, a modern tiled shower with tons of hot water, and plush towels. The high ceilings were painted a beautiful shade of dark green with a stenciled border. Scrumptious chocolates were put on the pillow at night; fresh fruit and an assortment of soft drinks were set on the dresser." *(Nina*

Piccirilli) "Debbie is a jewel—sweet, funny, and helpful." *(Dianne Crawford, also Stephanie Roberts)* "Well-maintained inn. Debbie was always available to chat about Atlanta and suggest touring ideas. Delicious breakfast." *(Happy Copley)*

Open All year.
Rooms 1 carriage house suite, 4 doubles—all with private bath and/or shower, telephone, TV, air-conditioning, radio, ceiling fan. Suite with kitchen, steam shower.
Facilities 3 parlors, library, all with books, magazines, games, fireplaces; guest refrigerator/pantry; veranda. Shady garden with fish pond; off-street parking. ¼m to Piedmont Park.
Location Midtown; 1¼ m from city center. Exit I-75/85 N Peachtree to Piedmont; Exit I-75/85 S at North Ave. to Piedmont. MARTA stop nearby.
Restrictions No smoking. Traffic noise in some rooms. Children under 12 in carriage house only. Limited off-street parking.
Credit cards Amex, DC, MC, Visa.
Rates B&B, $115–150 suite, $105–115 double, $85–120 single. Extra person, $23. 2-night minimum weekend stay.
Extras Crib in carriage house.

AUGUSTA

Founded in 1737, Augusta became Georgia's first state capital and grew prosperous from the tobacco and cotton crops. In the past century, the city's mild winters have attracted golfers, and the Masters golf tournament draws big crowds each spring. Augusta is located 150 miles east of Atlanta via I-20, at the South Carolina border.

Also recommended: Just 30 minutes west of Augusta via I-20 is the **1810 West Inn** (254 North Seymour Drive, NW, Thomson 30824; 706–595–3156 or 800–515–1810). Constructed of heart of pine, this Piedmont plains plantation house inn has five guest rooms, with additional accommodation available in several restored Georgia tenant houses and a tobacco barn, set among the magnolias and pecan trees which dot the property. The B&B double rates of $65–105 (higher Master's Week) includes homemade biscuits and quiche, plus afternoon refreshments. "Quiet atmosphere; beautiful decor. Spacious grounds with a lovely country feel, including animals." *(Jansen Chazanof)*

Information please: A grand old hotel overlooking downtown Augusta, the well-known **Partridge Inn Suites** (2110 Walton Way, 30904; 706–737–8888 or 800–476–6888) was built in 1890. A century later, it was retrofitted with 105 suites, each with bedroom, living room, and kitchen; 50 regular rooms are also available. The inn's restaurant offers Southern and continental cuisine served in the dining room or outside on the veranda. Double rates are $79–120; children under 18 stay free. "Our clean, pleasant, king-bedded room had a balcony overlooking the swimming pool. Food in the restaurant was wonderful; enjoyed the jazz combo in the bar at night. A mixup in our reservations was handled well." *(Celia McCullough)*

Just across the river in South Carolina are two beautifully restored 19th century mansions, **Rosemary Hall & Lookaway Hall** (804 Carolina Avenue, North Augusta, SC 29841; 803–278–6222 or 800–531–5578). The $75–150 rates include early morning coffee, full breakfast, and evening hors d'oeuvres. The 23 luxurious guest rooms are furnished with antiques, reproductions, and Oriental carpets; many have sitting areas, private verandas, and whirlpool baths. Guests are welcome to relax in the inviting common areas, on the verandas, or out in the gardens. (Under the same ownership is Kehoe House; see listing under Savannah).

BLACKSHEAR

Information please: Enjoying a quiet country setting among the pines of southeastern Georgia is the **Pond View Inn** (4200 Grady Street, 31516; 912–449–3697 or 800–585–8659), a working cattle farm located near Waycross, Georgia, 90 miles southwest of Savannah, Georgia, and northwest of Jacksonville, Florida. B&B double rates for the four guest rooms range from $60–85; the suite is $140, with reasonable corporate rates offered midweek. Both well-behaved children and pets are welcome. Most guest rooms have either queen- or king-size four poster beds, and all have a private bath. Rates include welcome refreshments, continental breakfast, and evening turndown service with chocolates. Dinner is served Thursday to Sunday, and includes farm raised black Angus beef, home-grown fruits and vegetables, and local fish, crab, and shrimp. "Delicious meals; cordial innkeepers, Sara and David Rollison. Coffee and snacks were always within reach. Pleasant rooms; great collection of local paintings in the common room. Inviting pond for fishing." *(Traci & Michael Lindsey)*

BLAIRSVILLE

For additional area entries, see **Clayton, Dillard,** and **Hiawassee.**

7 Creeks Housekeeping Cabins ¢
5109 Horseshoe Cove Road, 30512

Tel: 706–745–4753
Fax: 706–745–2904
E-mail: mhernden@yhc.edu

Marvin and Bobbie Hernden have restored one old mountain cabin and have built five more over the past three decades.

"Peaceful atmosphere, plus excellent accommodations, cleanliness, parking, location, and attention to detail. The owners were helpful and courteous. We enjoyed the well marked nature trails." *(Pat Pears)* "The cabins are snug and comfortable in the winter, cool and breezy in the summer." *(Larry & Joyce Bradfield)* "Special touches include garden-fresh flowers or vegetables awaiting you on the kitchen table. The well-spaced cabins are set in a beautiful secluded cove with a lovely little spring-fed lake, complete with ducks and fish. Good area hiking; our toddler loved playing with the dog, goats, pony, and cats." *(Linda & Tom Reeder)*

"The pond was directly across from our cabin and the surrounding mountains cast a beautiful reflection on the clear water. Ample wood provided for the fireplace." *(Lucille Cunningham & Myrna Deshazo)* "We sat on the porch and watched the moon come up over the mountains. Our 10-year-old enjoyed exploring on his own." *(Sarah Bigelow)* "Lots of privacy. A symphony of nocturnal creatures serenade you in the evening." *(Teri Kenith)* "Although secluded, convenience stores and other services were an easy drive. Excellent directions were provided by the Herndens, who were readily available to answer questions without intruding." *(Bernice Bilger)*

Open All year.
Rooms 6 1- to 3-bedroom housekeeping cabins, sleep 4 to 8. All with private bath, kitchen, TV, radio, barbecue grill, fireplace, porch.
Facilities 70 acres with hiking trails, private lake for fishing, swimming. Covered picnic area, playground, tether ball, badminton, horseshoes; pottery shop, library, fishing poles, outdoor chapel. White-water rafting, horseback riding, canoeing, golf nearby.
Location N GA. 100 m N of Atlanta, approx. 20 m S of NC border. From Blairsville, go S on Rte. 19/129, E on Rte. 180. Seven Creeks is 1 m S of 180 (Wolfstake Rd. W) on Horseshoe Cove Rd.
Credit cards None accepted.
Rates Room only, $55–65 cabin. Extra person, $5. No charge for children under 6. 2-night minimum. Weekly rates, $350 double. Extra person, $25. (Linens extra.)

BRUNSWICK

Brunswick Manor ¢ *Tel:* 912–265 6889
825 Egmont Street, 31520

Whether you'd like a taste of history en route to the Golden Isles or a delightful stopover when traveling south on I-95, a fine choice is Brunswick Manor, in the port city of Brunswick. Built in 1886, this B&B was restored in 1988 by transplanted New Englanders Claudia and Harry Tzucanow. They have decorated their inn handsomely with Victorian antiques and period reproductions, complementing the original carved oak staircase, high ceilings, and Victorian fireplace mantels with bevelled glass mirrors. The stained-glass "eyebrow" windows on the first floor offer views of the gardens and moss-draped oaks. One elegant guest room is striking in deep blue and wine colors, accented with crisp white linens, lace curtains, and a queen-size bed with a fishnet canopy. A typical breakfast consists of fresh fruit, stuffed French toast with peach honey butter, juice, coffee and tea, served on fine crystal; also included is afternoon tea at 4 P.M., bathrobes, wake-up and turndown service, and the daily newspaper.

"Homey atmosphere, comfortable accommodations, neat and clean, tasty breakfasts. Quiet neighborhood with moss-draped live oaks and palm trees. Claudia and Harry have interesting life stories to share, including their experiences acquiring the period antiques that furnish the house. I felt entirely comfortable in this beautiful but not overly restored Victorian home. Afternoon tea was accompanied by enjoyable conversation, plus wine, cheese, and crackers, served in the elegant living room. The enormous library has extensive information on the restoration of Jaguar automobiles, sailing, and model trains. I also enjoyed relaxing on the enormous wraparound porch with Harry and his two friendly Brittany spaniels." *(Peter Rundel)*

Open All year.
Rooms 3 suites, 5 doubles—all with private bath and/or shower, air-conditioning. 4 doubles in 1890 House. 2 with kitchenette.
Facilities Dining room, parlor, library, veranda with swing. Arbor with hot tub, gardens, patio, greenhouse, fish pond, lawn games. Bicycling; captained day charters on owner's boat. Tennis nearby.
Location Historic Old Town Brunswick, across from Halifax Sq. Halfway between Savannah & Jacksonville; gateway to Golden Isles. From I-95 S, take Exit 7A. Take ramp S to Rte. 341 to Brunswick. Go approx. 5½ m on Rte. 341, turning left on Prince St. Once on Prince St., do *not* turn right to follow Rte. 341 to Jekyll Island. Stay on Prince St. 4 major blocks to Egmont St; house is on corner of Prince & Egmont.
Restrictions No smoking. Children under 12 in 1890 House.
Credit cards MC, Visa.
Rates B&B, $85–100 suite, $65 double. Honeymoon package.

CLARKESVILLE

Clarksville is about 75 miles northeast of Atlanta, in a rural yet historic area, known for its waterfalls, Chattahoochie National Forest, and the Blue Ridge mountains. Area activities include golf, tennis, horseback riding, fishing, canoeing, whitewater rafting, kayaking, hiking, and bicycling. Several national forests, state parks, and lakes are nearby, including the spectacular Tallulah Gorge State Park.

The Burns-Sutton House ✕

124 South Washington Street, 30523
Tel: 706–754–5565
Fax: 706–754–9698

In the heart of historic Clarksville is The Burns-Sutton House, owned by the Burns/Sutton families from its construction in 1901 until the 1970s. This Queen Anne Victorian home was built of heart pine by two master carpenters; their skills can still be seen in the delicate cutwork in the staircase balustrades and the hand-carved fireplace mantels. Additional architectural features include the pierced-brick foundation, seven brick chimneys, wraparound porches, and extensive stained glass windows. Listed on the National Register of Historic Places, the house was fully restored as a B&B in 1988; Jaime Huffman purchased the inn in 1996. Guest rooms are furnished in period antiques, most with four-poster queen-size beds, plus Jaime's collection of nature and travel books.

Breakfast seatings are at individual tables, every half hour between 7:30 and 9:30 A.M.; the meal includes fresh fruit and juice, with omelets to order, or perhaps Jaime's signature almond French toast. The inn is also home to Jeffrey's Restaurant, which opened in 1997. Lunch favorites range from burgers to chicken pot pie to black bean quesadillas. Dinner entrees include rack of lamb with rosemary and Dijon mustard; veal rolled with spinach and Gruyere; and grilled portabella mushrooms with polenta.

"Jaime is a cheerful, friendly innkeeper; she keeps the house spotless, prepares a delicious breakfast." *(Pat Borysiewiez)* "This B&B is like a warm hug. Combines excellent housekeeping and modern conveniences with the charm and history of a Victorian home. Delightful evening snack of just-baked chocolate chip cookies and choice of beverage. Appealing collectibles; thoughtful touches include the bathroom nightlights." *(Charlene Farmer)*

Open All year.
Rooms 2 suites, 5 doubles—4 with full private bath; 3 with maximum of 4 people sharing bath. All with clock/radio, air-conditioning, ceiling-fan. 3 with gas fireplace.
Facilities Restaurant, living room with fireplace, TV/VCR, stereo, games; wraparound porches. 1 acre with patio, barbecue grill, English garden, off-street parking.
Location 75 m N of Atlanta. Take I-85 to I-985. Follow until it becomes Hwy. 365. Stay on 365 N to Rte. 197. Go left onto Rte. 197 N for 4.1 m; inn is on Rtes. 197/441. Historic district, ½ m from town center.
Restrictions No smoking inside. Children over 8.
Credit cards MC, Visa.
Rates B&B, $70–90 suite, $65–80 double, $65–75 single. Extra person, $10. Senior discount. Alc lunch, $7; dinner, $25–35.
Extras Restaurant wheelchair accessible.

Glen-Ella Springs Inn ✕ ♿
1789 Bear Gap Road, 30523
Tel: 706–754–7295
Fax: 706–754–1560
E-mail: Glenella@cyberhighway.net

In the early 1900s, Atlanta tourists came to "take the waters" at the Glen-Ella Springs Inn. When Barrie and Bobby Aycock purchased the inn in 1986, it had essentially been unaltered since its construction, so the Aycocks' restoration started with the addition of indoor plumbing and electricity. Well off the highway on a quiet gravel road, the inn is surrounded by pine forests and meadows of wildflowers. The gardens supply the herbs and vegetables for summertime dining. Breakfasts include fresh fruit compote, homemade granola, cereal, and home-baked breads, and battered French toast with orange sauce or perhaps blueberry granola pancakes—plus coffee, tea, and juice. Favorite dinner entrees might include grilled swordfish with lemon herb butter, duck with roast vegetables and fettucinni, and honey peach-cured pork chops.

"Charming country setting, yet convenient to lots of activities. Although we had the smallest room, it was cozy and comfortable." *(David*

& Linda Ackerson) "Bobby welcomed us warmly. The whole Aycock family works at the inn, and all are kind and cheerful. Delicious, well-prepared food, beautifully served. The rooms were homey and clean and many thoughtful extras. Beautiful grounds." *(Marian Anderson)* "Atmosphere and charm to match the inn's history: heart pine floors, ceilings, and walls; stacked rock fireplaces; primitive antique furnishings." *(Don Depew, also Sharon Bailey)* "The porch overlooks a lovely meadow; you can hear a swift running creek nearby." *(Francine Hollowell)*

"A restorative place, with its wraparound porches and white rocking chairs. The lobby has a variety of chintz-covered sofas, chairs, and loveseats." *(Nancy & John Schultz)* "Our suite was furnished with antiques, handmade quilts and rugs, with a modern bathroom." *(Anna Culligan)* "Our rustic room had plenty of reading material and a checker board." *(Beth Webster)*

Open All year. Restaurant open for dinner by reservation. Hours vary in winter, early spring.
Rooms 2 suites with fireplace, Jacuzzi; 14 doubles—all with full private bath, telephone, radio, air-conditioning, porch with rocking chairs.
Facilities Restaurant, gift shop, living room with fireplace, TV/VCR, games, books; terrace. 17 acres with swimming pool, gardens, nature trails, mineral spring.
Location NE GA. 85 m NE of Atlanta. From Atlanta, take I-85 N to I-985, Exit 45. Becomes GA 365, then US 441 N of Cornelia. Follow US 441 N for 15 m. Go left on G. Hardeman Rd. at Turnerville, then right on Historic Old 441 for ¼ m. Left on The Orchard Rd. Follow signs 2 ½ m to the inn.
Restrictions No smoking in dining room or guest rooms. Limited interior sound-proofing. "Well-behaved children welcome." BYOB.
Credit cards Amex, MC, Visa.
Rates B&B, $180 suite, $120–140 double. Extra person, $10. 2-night weekend minimum May–Nov. Alc dinner $30.
Extras Wheelchair access.

CLAYTON

For additional area entries, see **Blairsville, Dillard, Hiawassee,** and **Rabun Gap.**

Also recommended: In the northeastern corner of Georgia, set among terraced flower gardens, is the **Beechwood Inn** (Box 120, 30525; 706–782–5485), a rustic weathered lodge, set into the hillside, with views of Black Rock Mountain. Each of the five guest rooms has a private bath, queen-size four poster or canopy bed, fireplace, and a balcony or patio. The B&B double rates of $85–135 include a full breakfast. "Owner Marty Lott is a delightful person, accommodating in every way. Breakfasts were memorable; our fellow guests were warm and friendly. The inn is furnished with exquisite Colonial antiques, the result of years of collecting." *(Mimi Cohen)*

CONCORD

Information please: Fans of *Gone with the Wind* will want to take the 45-minute drive from Atlanta to **Inn Scarlett's Footsteps** (40 Old Flat Shoals Road, 30206; 770–884–9012 or 800–886–7355). Built in 1905, this 8,000-square-foot plantation-style Greek Revival mansion is dedicated entirely to Margaret Mitchell's famous novel and the movie it inspired. K.C. Bassham and her husband, Vern, restored this home in 1993, naming and decorating each guest room after a key character. The first floor houses K.C.'s enormous collection of GWTW memorabilia. The B&B double rate ranges from $79–99, and includes a full breakfast; guided tours are available to the public for $5. "A must for GWTW fans." *(LF)* Reports appreciated.

CUMBERLAND ISLAND

The natural beauty of most of Georgia's barrier islands has been overwhelmed by massive hotel and condominium projects, with tennis courts and golf courses. A welcome exception is Cumberland Island, the southernmost and largest at 17½ miles long. Thomas Carnegie (brother to steel magnate Andrew) bought land on Cumberland Island in 1881, and built an imposing mansion, Dungeness. Eventually a total of five mansions were constructed, but most now lie in ruins. In 1972, much of the island was designated as a National Seashore. Only 300 persons at a time are allowed access to the island, to cause minimum disturbance to the wild horses, deer, wild turkeys, armadillos, alligators, birds, and other wildlife that roam the island.

Reader tips: "Fifteen miles of unused beach, great stands of oak, rolling dunes, and a wealth of history about the days of the Carnegies (the museum is in their old ice house). Wild horses, some believed to be descendants of the stock left by the original Spanish settlers, roam the island. Just one shortcoming—during warm weather, ticks are everywhere, so come prepared." *(Joe Schmidt)* "We walked for two hours and saw only one human but lots of wildlife. Gorgeous private beach." *(Lillie Galvin)*

Information please: Listed in past editions, we'd like current reports on the well-known **Greyfield Inn** (8 North Second Street, P.O. Box 900, Amelia Island, FL 32035; 904–261–6408). Double rates of $245–350 for the 13 guest rooms include all meals, round-trip ferry, use of the inn's bicycles, and a guided nature walk. Five rooms have a private bath, the rest share three baths. This imposing four-story white mansion was built in 1901 for a daughter of Thomas Carnegie, and was opened as an inn in the 1960s.

For additional area inns, see **St. Marys**.

DAHLONEGA

Nestled in the foothills of the Blue Ridge Mountains, Dahlonega was the site of the first gold rush in the United States. The old saying "There's gold in them thar hills" refers not to California but to Dahlonega! The name of the town is the Cherokee word for precious yellow metal. Area activities include hiking, rafting, canoeing, fishing, and panning for gold. Dahlonega is located in the North Georgia mountains, 65 miles north of Atlanta; from Atlanta, take Route 19/400 from I-285.

Information please: Listed in past editions, we need current reports on the **Mountain Top Lodge at Dahlonega** (Route 7, Box 150, 30533; 706–864–5257 or 800–526–9754), a gambrel-roofed barn-style inn built in 1985, and purchased in 1995 by Karen Lewan. Guest rooms are decorated with pine furniture, mountain crafts, antiques, and flea market treasures. B&B double rates for the 13 guest rooms range from $70–125; some rooms have double Jacuzzi tubs and gas fireplaces.

DARIEN

Open Gates ¢ *Tel:* 912–437–6985
Vernon Square, P.O. Box 1526, 31305

You can zoom down I-95 to Florida, refueling both body and car at identical gas, food, and sleep stations, or you can slow down here for an authentic slice of Americana. Founded in 1736, Darien soon became a thriving timber port. Burned twice during the Civil War, its Vernon Square historic district is where Open Gates was built in 1876. Restored as a B&B in 1987 by Carolyn Hodges, Open Gates is shaded by massive live oaks, hung with Spanish moss; inside, its high-ceiling rooms are simply decorated in cheerful colors with family antiques and collectibles. The Timber Baron's room has an antique sleigh bed, while the Quilt Room takes its name from the hand-stitched star-patterned quilts that adorn the queen-size bed and the walls. Breakfast, served at a mutually agreeable time, might include fresh fruit compote, pancakes served with assorted syrups, honey and apple butter, herbed shirred eggs with sausage and cheese, Belgian waffles with whipped cream, or baked apples and oatmeal.

A short drive away are the deserted rice islands and marshes of McIntosh County. Owner Carolyn Hodges provides personal tours to her guests' specifications, including boat tours of the Altamaha River Delta and a guided tour of Butler's Island from a botanical as well as historical perspective.

"Carolyn is knowledgeable about area history." *(Joe Schmidt)* "Well-appointed house on a quiet, picturesque square in this old fishing village. Best of all is Ms. Hodges, a former science teacher, avid environmentalist and self-taught historian, who makes you feel welcome immediately. Sitting down to breakfast with her is a feast of local history and politics." *(Judith Bates)* "Clean, comfortable house; delicious, creative breakfast." *(Keith Westphal)* "Comfortable and elegant, with real Southern charm. Carolyn's colorful local stories were unforgettable." *(Anne Travy)*

Open All year.
Rooms 4 doubles—2 with private bath and/or shower, 2 with maximum of 4 people sharing bath. All with clock, air conditioning; some with fan, desk. 1 room over garage with separate entrance.
Facilities Dining room, living room with fireplace, piano, TV, library with regional titles, porch. ½ acre with swimming pool, gardens, croquet. Game refuges, birding, river, barrier island boat trips.
Location SE GA, halfway between Savannah & Jacksonville, FL. Historic district. Take Exit 10 off I-95. Go 1.9 m SE on Hwy. 251.
Restrictions No smoking.
Credit cards None accepted.
Rates B&B, $55–65 double. Extra adult, $15; child over 10, $10. 2-night weekend minimum. 10% discount for 4-day stay. Boat tours, $30–60.
Extras Airport pick-up. Pets possible; inquire.

DILLARD

For additional area entries, see **Blairsville, Clayton, Hiawassee**, and **Rabun Gap.**

Information please: A family-oriented choice in northeastern Georgia is the **Dillard House** (Old Dillard Highway, P.O. Box 10, 30537; 706–746–5348 or 800–541–0671). Overlooking a fertile valley and surrounded by the Blue Ridge Mountains, Dillard House is a year-round family resort run by generations of Dillards since 1794. Rates for the 57 motel-style rooms, Jacuzzi suites, and chalets range from $45–149, and facilities include their well-known restaurant, serving "all-you-can-eat" platters of Southern-style food, three meals a day. In addition to swimming and tennis, trail rides through the woods are a family favorite.

EATONTON

Magnolia Hill Inn

206 North Maple Avenue, 31024

Tel: 706–485–0012
800–569–5211
E-mail: maghill@ix.netcom.com

If you need to recharge your batteries but can only get away for a day or two, escape to the Magnolia Hill Inn, just an hour's drive from Atlanta, where you'll maximize your relaxation time and minimize your drive time.

This Colonial Revival home was built in 1910 by Henry Hearn, and remained in the Hearn family until it was purchased and restored as a B&B in 1995 by Sharon and Graham Clark. Guest room decor combines elegant antiques with heart pine floors and a vibrant color palette: one room is done in ivory and black with gold accents; another in rose and green, and a third has an ivy motif, with deep green walls, yards of white fabric, a queen-sized canopy bed, and a ceiling border of hand-painted pots of ivy. Breakfast is served at guests' convenience at the dining room table, and includes fresh fruit and juice, just-baked muffins or perhaps zucchini bread with peach butter, and such entrees as three-cheese quiche or an omelet. Dinners are available by advance reservation, and a sample menu may consist of spiced shrimp, cream of mushroom soup, chicken breast filet in lemon garlic butter with inn grown green beans and baked potatoes, and German chocolate cake. Rates also include a welcome basket of wine and fresh fruit, and afternoon coffee or tea with freshly baked cookies or cake.

"Refreshing, relaxing atmosphere. Delicious food, elegantly served in the beautiful formal dining room. We loved relaxing on the wonderful wraparound porch, serenaded by the birds." *(Deanna Bredwell)* "Friendly, helpful innkeepers. Our charming room had two comfortable chairs set before the fireplace." *(Sharon Deamer)* "Elegant, yet homey; beautiful period decor throughout; excellent lighting and plumbing. Convenient, in-town location, yet secluded and quiet. We enjoyed walking the grounds, with beautiful plantings: magnolias, wisteria, azaleas, crepe myrtle, dogwoods, and much more. Delicious breakfast of French toast and quiche, cooked to perfection." *(Dan & Teresa Susong)* "Charming, warm, welcoming atmosphere; careful attention to detail by hosts who clearly enjoy what they are doing. Immaculate housekeeping. We slept soundly, with the windows open, lulled by the crisp country air. Ample hot water and fluffy towels in the bathroom." *(Sharon Dimino)*

Open All year.
Rooms 4 doubles—all with private bath and/or shower, air-conditioning, ceiling fan, gas fireplace.
Facilities Dining room with fireplace, living room with fireplace, library with books, games; double foyer with fireplace, stereo; wraparound porch with rockers, swing. 6 acres with coffee/gift shop, lawn games, extensive flower, vegetable gardens; crepe myrtle maze. Golf, lakes nearby for swimming, boating and fishing.
Location Central GA. 1 hr SE of Atlanta; 40 m N of Macon. Take I-20 E to Madison, Exit 51. Go S 18.3 m on Rtes. 441/129 to Eatonton. Go left on Magnolia St., right on Maple to inn, 3 houses down on left.
Restrictions No smoking. Children over 10.
Credit cards Amex, Discover, MC, Visa.
Rates B&B, $100–150 double. Extra person, $20. MAP, $180–230 double, $140–190 single. Prix fixe dinner, $40; reservations required. Extra person, $40. Murder mystery weekends.

GAINESVILLE

The Dunlap House ♿
635 Green Street, 30501

Tel: 770–536–0200
800–276–2935
Fax: 770–503–7857
E-mail: 72347.2251@compuserve.com

The Dunlap House was built in 1910 and was restored in 1985 as a luxury B&B inn; Ann and Ben Ventress took over as innkeepers in

1992. Guest rooms are handsomely decorated with quality reproductions, including floral chintzes and custom-made rice and four-poster queen and king-size beds, plus designer linens, oversize towels, and terry robes. Rates include the morning paper and a breakfast of fresh fruit, cereal, yogurt, muffins, egg dishes, breakfast meats, and freshly squeezed orange juice, served on the porch in good weather.

"Gracious, sincere hosts who exude Southern hospitality. Amenities include the remote controlled cable TV, terrycloth robes, and bottled water." *(Bill Henderson)* "Beautifully appointed rooms. As a business traveler, it is wonderful to stay in a place that feels like home, yet has all modern amenities." *(Loretta Razynaki)* "A charming, elegantly appointed Southern mansion. Large, comfortable, sunny rooms; brass fixtures; beautiful fabrics and wallpapers. Ben and Ann accommodate requests with warmth, charm, and humor, in a comfortable, homey environment." *(Susan Snowe)* "The large porch is a wonderful place to relax; parking is ample and convenient." *(Blanche & Alan Williams)* "Delicious breakfasts; comfortable, well-furnished room; meticulous housekeeping. We ate well at Rudolph's, across the street. Green Street is lined with wonderful Greek revival houses; the one next door is particularly noteworthy." *(Nancy Bernard)*

Open All year.
Rooms 9 doubles—all with full private bath, telephone, TV, air-conditioning. 2 with fireplace.
Facilities Breakfast room, porch. Off-street parking. Tennis, golf nearby. Lake Lanier for all water sports.
Location N GA. 60 m N of Atlanta. From I-985, take Exit 6. Go N 2 m on Rte. 129 (Butler Pkwy); changes name to Green St. at curve to right. Inn on left at corner of Ridgewood.
Restrictions No smoking.
Credit cards Amex, Discover, MC, Visa.
Rates B&B, $85–125 double, $65–115 single. Extra person, $15. 10% senior, AAA discount. Corporate rates; packages.
Extras Wheelchair access.

GRANTVILLE

For additional area entries, see **Concord, Newnan, Palmetto, Pine Mountain, Senoia** and **Warm Springs.**

Bonnie Castle B&B
2 Post Street, P.O. Box 359, 30220

Tel: 770–583–3090
800–261–3090
Fax: 770–583–3090
E-mail: Bocastle@msn.com

Franklin D. Roosevelt stopped at Bonnie Castle on his way to Warm Springs, and you can too—or you can make this imposing 1896 Romanesque Revival mansion your base for visits to nearby Callaway Gardens, the Little White House, and Warm Springs. Although the private home of the prominent Colley family in Roosevelt's day, Bonnie Castle was restored as a B&B in 1993 by Patti and Darwin Palmer. The original stained glass windows, gilded ceilings, massive pocket doors, hardwood floors, detailed fretwork, and oak paneling is enhanced by the Palmers' collection of period antiques, original art, quilts, regional Georgia pottery and furniture. The Colley's collection of Loveleigh Novelty Dolls and travel memorabilia from the late 1880s–1950s can be seen in the tower room. Guests are welcomed with iced tea or wine on the veranda. Breakfast, served 7–10 A.M., includes home-baked breakfast cakes, French toast, country sausage, and fresh fruit and juice."A unique Victorian home, filled with history. Charming decor with lovely antiques, quality artwork. Wonderful gardens; the wisteria was blooming and smelled heavenly. Patt and Darwin were delightful and gracious in every respect. Convenient to Atlanta and Callaway Gardens." *(MR)*

Open All year.
Rooms 2 suites, 3 doubles—2 with private bath and/or tub, 3 with maximum of 4 people sharing bath. All with clock/radio, desk, air-conditioning, ceiling fan.
Facilities Dining room, living room, TV room, library; guest refrigerator; porches. Gardens, fish pond, off-street parking. Golf nearby.
Location W central GA. 30-40 min. to Atlanta airport, Little White House, Callaway Gardens, Warm Springs. Take I-85 S from Atlanta to Exit 7. Go left (W) on Rte. 29. Go ¼ m & go right onto Griffin St. (just before Amoco station). Go approx. 1 m to downtown Grantville. At train depot, go right on Main St. Inn is on Post St., at end of Main, about 150 yds. from train depot.
Restrictions No smoking inside. "Older well-behaved children welcome." 150 yds. from train tracks.
Credit cards None accepted.
Rates B&B, $80–85 suite, $75–80 double, $50–70 single. Family rate.
Extras Airport pickup, $25. Some German spoken.

HIAWASSEE

For additional area entries, see **Blairsville, Clayton,** and **Dillard.**

Also recommended: Guests are delighted with their stays at **Henson Cove Place B&B and Cabin** (3840 Car Miles Road, 30546; 706–896–6195 or 800–714–5542), with two guest rooms in the main house, plus a three-room cabin. Built in 1940, the B&B was purchased by Bill and Nancy Leffingwell in 1994; Bill is a fine furniture maker, and Nancy, a quilter and rug weaver. The B&B double rate of $60–70, includes a breakfast of apple French toast, baked scrambled eggs, or strata, with fresh fruit and homemade breads. Located in northeastern Georgia, the inn is close to Brasstown Bald, the state's highest point at 4,784 feet. "Immaculate housekeeping, excellent food, perfect location, with lots of waterfalls, hiking trails, and scenic views nearby. Comfortable, quiet suite." *(Diane Saul)* "Our suite had rich wood walls, flannel sheets, soft lighting, quilts and eyelet lace. Inviting and comfortable; extensive library for reading." *(Joi Chevalier)* "Setting is beautiful and peaceful. Great bed. Delicious breakfast, beautifully served." *(Judith Cohen)*

JASPER

For an additional area entry, see **Tate.**

Information please: An hour north of Atlanta is the well-known **Woodbridge Inn** (44 Chambers, 30143; 706–692–6072), long owned by the Rueffert family, and listed in previous editions. The restaurant occupies a historic home dating back to the 1850s. The 12 guest rooms are located in the adjacent contemporary lodge, with views of the mountains, and guests can enjoy the swimming pool and hiking trails. "Delicious dinner of trout, well-prepared vegetables, roast potatoes, and excellent bread. Our table was overlooking blooming roses and a busy bird feeder." *(HJB)*

JEKYLL ISLAND

Jekyll Island Club
371 Riverview Drive, 31527

Tel: 912–635–2600
800–535–9547
Fax: 912–635–2818
E-mail: jiclub@technonet.com

One hundred years ago, the Rockefellers, Morgans, Goodyears, Astors, Pulitzers, and other American millionaires set up a club to relax and get away from the pressures of excessive wealth. Called the Jekyll Island Club, it accepted only society's "crème de la crème," and served as a winter Newport. The club's era ended in the thirties with the Great Depression and it closed at the outset of World War II. After the war, Jekyll Island was purchased by the state of Georgia and opened for public use; most of the island is a state park, and only a third of it can be developed. The club faces the Intracoastal Waterway, while modern construction is primarily on the Atlantic beachfront side of this narrow island.

In 1986, an investment group leased the club (listed on the National Register of Historic Places) from the state of Georgia and spent $17 million restoring and refurbishing it. Ornate woodwork and gold leaf have been returned to their original splendor, while the baths have been modernized. Rooms are furnished with custom-made Queen Anne reproductions.

"An ideal place for relaxing in a genteel yet informal setting. We never felt out of place, under or overdressed, or pressured in any way. Helpful, cheerful staff. The grounds are pristine with ample inviting seating. Our enormous room in the 'apartments' had a king-size bed and lots of comfortable chairs. A Dutch door opened onto an inviting porch. The bathroom was huge and we watched the sun set from the oversize Jacuzzi. Generous supply of toiletries, robes, and towels. We loved the pool, huge and heated; the little bakery shop, and the tour of the hotel and grounds. Scrumptious dinner." *(Penny Poirier)* "Cozy king-bedded room. The grand dining room is elegant and serves excellent food; our flounder was exceptional." *(HJB)* "A lively resort, wonderful for bicycling, with over twenty miles of trails. Relax in wicker chairs on verandas overlooking the river." *(Marjorie Cohen)* "Don't miss the historic tours of the hotel and nearby buildings, or the trolley tour of the historic district. Mansions once owned by the Rockefellers and Pulitzers have been restored and are now open to the public." *(Pat Borysiewicz)*

Open All year.
Rooms 17 suites, 117 doubles—all with full private bath, telephone, TV/VCR, radio, desk, air-conditioning. Most suites with porch, fireplace, Jacuzzi. 24 rooms/suites in Sans Souci Cottage.
Facilities Dining room, room service, delicatessen, snack bar (seasonal) parlors, lounges, verandas. 7 acres with beach club with all water sports, deep-sea fishing, croquet, horseshoes, volleyball, badminton, children's program, swimming pool, fitness center, marina, 8 outdoor tennis courts (5 lighted), 1 indoor court, 63 holes of golf, gift shops, valet parking. Bicycle paths; short walk to ocean.
Location SE GA, Golden Isles. 75 m S of Savannah, 65 m N of Jacksonville, FL. 12 m from I-95. Club is part of 240-acre national historic district, in central part of island, on inland side.
Restrictions Non-smoking rooms available.
Credit cards Amex, CB, DC, Discover, MC, Visa.
Rates Room only, $129–250 suite, $99–125 double, $89–115 single. Extra person, $20. Meal plan, per person, per night, includes tax/gratuity: MAP, $48; full board, $64. Reduced rates for children. Sports, family, romance, murder mystery, off-season packages. Senior discount. Alc lunch, $12; alc dinner, $40. Trolley tour, $10.
Extras Rooms equipped for handicapped; elevator. Airport/station pickups. Shuttle service on island. Crib, babysitting. Spanish, French, Italian, Chinese spoken.

LOOKOUT MOUNTAIN

Information please: The **Chanticleer Inn** (1300 Mockingbird Lane, 30750; 706–820–2015) is a simply furnished 16-room motel, set in attached stone cottages. The B&B double rate ranges from $40–86, with the best room having a queen-sized bed and fireplace. "Could be a real delight with some upgrading, as the grounds and cottages are very quaint. Large clean rooms, adequately furnished; lovely view." *(SW)* Rates include a light serve-yourself breakfast of sweet rolls, juice, and coffee.

MACON

A trading center since its founding, Macon remains a manufacturing center to this day. Much of the downtown business area and the College Hill residential neighborhood has been designated as a historic district. The city is located in central Georgia, 82 miles southeast of Atlanta.

Reader tip: "Of the three restaurants we've tried in Macon, the best is Natalia's on Riverside Drive, a five-minute drive away, located in the shopping plaza behind Wendy's. Excellent continental/Italian food and fine service." *(HJB)*

1842 Inn ♿
353 College Street, 31201

Tel: 912–741–1842
800–336–1842
Fax: 912–741–1842

The 1842 Inn consists of an imposing antebellum Greek Revival mansion, restored in 1984, and an adjacent Victorian cottage. The luxurious rooms are furnished handsomely with Oriental rugs, antiques, and quality reproductions; Phil Jenkins is the managing partner. Rates include a light breakfast, brought to your room with the morning paper; shoeshine; afternoon coffee or iced tea; pre-dinner hors d'oeuvres; and evening turndown service.

"Exceptionally lovely garden, parlors, front porch and guest rooms. Appreciated extras included fresh flowers in our room, a pleasant cocktail hour with plentiful hors d'oeuvres, nightly turndown service with pillow chocolates, and the friendly, helpful staff. An added plus is its proximity to the Hay House and the surrounding historic district with self-guided, illuminated, walking tour." *(Sona Nast)* "The facility is beautifully decorated with a mixture of antiques and reproductions; our room had cut flowers in the bathroom and a live orchid on the desk. Service is solid with a well trained staff." *(B. Crawford Hitt)* "As pleased with our stay in the cottage as we were with our room in the main house. The breakfast of juice, muffin or croissant, and tea or coffee was brought to our room at the time requested; we could have had it brought to a table in the garden. Immaculate rooms, excellent condition, gracious and helpful staff; warm greeting by Phil Jenkins." *(HJB, also Donna Jacobson)*

"This beautiful Southern mansion sits on a street of beautiful houses, in a city of beautiful streets. Double-floor columns extend across the front, with splendidly proportioned rooms inside." *(Robert Freidus)* "Within walking distance of many fine antebellum homes and the fabulous Hay House home museum." *(Celia McCullough & Gary Kaplan)*

Open All year.
Rooms 21 doubles—all with full private bath, telephone, radio, TV, desk, air-conditioning. 9 rooms in annex. Some with whirlpool tubs, gas fireplaces.
Facilities 2 parlors with piano; occasional pianist. 1 acre with garden. Off-street parking. Private club golf, tennis, dining privileges.
Location 1 m from center. Exit 52 off I-75; go left on Forsyth St.; from N, go left on College to inn; from S, go right on Forsyth.

Restrictions Children over 12. Light sleepers should request a second floor room away from lobby, or in adjacent cottage. When booking, inquire if a group will be in residence.
Credit cards Amex, MC, Visa.
Rates B&B, $105–145 double, $95–135 single. Extra person, $10. 10% AARP discount.
Extras Wheelchair access.

MADISON

Located between Atlanta and Augusta, Athens and Macon, Madison is known for its historic district, with many lovely examples of Federal, Greek Revival, and Victorian architecture. The town was spared destruction by General Sherman during the Civil War because of the intervention of Joshua Hill, a Madison resident and former U.S. Senator who had vigorously opposed the conflict.

For an additional area entry, see **Oxford.**

Also recommended: Built around 1830, the two-story Federal-style **Burnett Place** (317 Old Post Road, 30650; 706–342–4034) is typical of Georgia's Piedmont Region, and is listed on the National Register of Historic Places. Each of the three guest rooms has a private bath and TV, and the B&B double rate of $85 includes a full breakfast, afternoon tea, nightly cordial and turndown service, and a guided tour of the historic district, upon request. "Rooms and food are first-rate, but best of all are owners Ruth and Leonard Wallace. Loved their wonderful stories, and the personal tour of the area." *(Valorie Castelli)*

MARIETTA

The Whitlock Inn B&B *Tel:* 770–428–1495
57 Whitlock Avenue, 30064 *Fax:* 770–919–9620

Built in 1900 by Herbert Dobbs, the Whitlock was slated to be torn down, its grounds paved over for use as a parking lot, when Sandy and Nancy Edwards and their daughter Alexis came to the rescue in 1994. They rebuilt the dilapidated mansion, restoring the rich hardwood floors and leaded glass windows and decorating with period antiques and Chinese Chippendale reproductions. Rich colors, floral fabrics, and Oriental rugs are used throughout the inn; most guest rooms have queen-size four poster or canopy beds. Although the inn tends to be busy with weddings most weekends, during the week it's an ideal choice for those interested in exploring the many antique shops of historic Marietta, or in doing business in nearby Atlanta. Breakfast, served 8–10 A.M., includes fresh fruit and juice, just-baked muffins and breads, bacon or mushroom quiche, and hot beverages. You can eat at the elegant dining room table, or have a tray delivered to your room. Rates also include afternoon treats served in the parlor.

"Ideal location just a block from historic Marietta Square, and within walking distance of restaurants, antique shops, and live theater. This graceful Southern Victorian home is shaded by mature trees. Elegant atmosphere; careful attention to detail, with first-quality furnishings and bathroom fixtures; neither frilly nor cluttered. Excellent service and cleanliness, enhanced by sincere thoughtfulness and friendliness—from the loan of an umbrella in a sudden downpour to the use of a computer. Dietary restrictions and work schedules were accommodated with a smile. Although it's the smallest, my favorite room is the Magnolia Room, with a high ceiling, huge lace-covered windows, and a restful, deep green color scheme accented with dark red. A painting of a magnolia is hung over the fireplace, and is repeated in the wallpaper. The armoire hides a full length mirror and small TV. Best of all is the four-poster queen-size canopy bed, with four pillows, the linens, and a perfect mattress. The spacious, well-equipped bathroom has incredibly thick, luxurious towels." *(Susan Schionning)*

Open All year.
Rooms 5 doubles—all with private bath and/or shower, telephone, clock/radio, TV, desk, air-conditioning, ceiling fan.
Facilities Dining room, living room with piano, library with books, guest refrigerator; roof garden, porch. Copier, fax service. Large ballroom for receptions. 1 acre with off-street parking, arbor, gazebo, gardens. Tennis, golf, hiking nearby.
Location 20 m NW of Atlanta. 1 block to Marietta Sq. From Hwy 75, go W on S Loop 120. Go 3 m to Powder Springs Rd. Turn Right (N) Go through 2 lights; turn left on Whitlock Ave. to inn; 1st house on left after bank.
Restrictions No smoking inside. Children over 12. Train noise possible.
Credit cards Amex, Discover, MC, Visa.
Rates B&B, $100–125 double.
Extras Wheelchair access to common areas only.

NEWNAN

Newnan is a historic town, 25 miles southwest of Atlanta, about halfway between the Atlanta airport and Callaway Gardens. For additional area entries, see **Concord, Grantville, Palmetto, Pine Mountain, Senoia** and **Warm Springs.**

Information please: A Greek Revival home built in 1900, the **Southern Comfort B&B** (66 LaGrange Street, 30263; 770–254–9266 or 800–818–0066) is located in a tree-lined neighborhood of historic homes. Architectural features include the two-story portico supported by thirty-foot Corinthian columns, a wraparound porch, twelve-foot ceilings, and stained glass windows. Two of the four guest rooms have a private bath, and the B&B double rate of $90 includes a full breakfast.

OXFORD

For an additional area inn, see **Madison.**

Hopkins House B&B ¢ ♿ *Tel:* 770–784–1010
1111 Wesley Street; 30267 *Fax:* 770–786–3684

Oxford was the birthplace of both Emory University and Georgia Tech. Hopkins House, built in 1847, is named for Isaac Stiles Hopkins, Emory's ninth president (1884-1888). During Reconstruction, Professor Hopkins realized the South's need for better technical training, and he founded Georgia Tech in 1888. The first classes were held in what is now the pool house of the B&B, and he became the school's first president.

Restored in 1995 by Nancy and Ralph Brian, Hopkins House is decorated with both antiques and contemporary furnishings. The Green Room has an Edwardian cherry queen-size bed and English prints, and can be booked as a suite with the Rose Room, done in white wicker, with country quilts on the twin-size beds. The Red Room has a see-through stone fireplace separating the spacious bedroom, with its queen-size antique oak bed, from the cozy library-sitting room. Starting at 7 A.M. midweek, guests are offered a breakfast of home-baked muffins, biscuits, coffee cake or cinnamon rolls with fresh fruit and juice; on weekends, they can sleep in, then relax at the individual tables in the dining room over a meal of caramel apple breakfast pudding and sausages, or mandarin orange salad with an egg and cheese casserole, and Roman apple coffee cake. The bottomless cookie jar is always filled with Nancy's tempting homemade treats.

"Charming, beautiful decor; elegant furnishings, welcoming atmosphere. The chess board, reading materials, and television added to our comfort when we were not lounging by the beautiful pool, complete with pool house, or relaxing with homemade lemonade and chocolate chip cookies on the white wicker rockers of the sun porch. Delicious breakfasts, different each morning, served on fine china, crystal, and silver. Nancy and Ralph were pleased to accommodate our diet and schedules; they welcomed us to the inn, and were extremely helpful with directions, restaurant information, and local assistance with an emergency car repair." *(Lisa Walsh)*

Open All year.
Rooms 4 doubles—all with private shower and/or bath, clock/radio, air-conditioning, ceiling fan. 3 with desk. 1 with fireplace.
Facilities Dining room, living room with fireplace, piano; TV room with fireplace; guest refrigerator; screened porch. 3 acres with off-street parking, swimming pool, horseshoes, croquet. Golf, fishing nearby.
Location 38 m E of Atlanta. Historic district; 3 blocks to Oxford College. Take I-20 to Exit 45. Go E on U.S. 278, to GA 81. Turn left (N) on 81. Go 1.7 m to light at Soule St. & go left. Go 2 blocks to Wesley St. to house on corner.
Restrictions No smoking.
Credit cards Amex, MC, Novus, Visa.
Rates B&B, $85–100 double. Extra person, $15. Senior, off-season discounts.
Extras Limited wheelchair access.

PALMETTO

For additional area inns, see **Grantville, Newnan,** and **Senoia.**

Information please: Just 32 miles southwest of Atlanta is **Seren-be** (10950 Hutcheson Ferry Road, 30268; 770–463–2610) a nearly 300-acre farm, complete with a barn full of farm animals, woods for hiking, stream for wading, pond for fishing, lake for canoeing, and horses for riding. Cool off in the lovely swimming pool, and enjoy the bounty of the flower and vegetable gardens during a delicious full breakfast, served on the glassed in porch. Accommodations are provided in the restored turn-of-the-century farmhouse, wonderfully decorated with owners Marie and Steve Nygren's delightful collection of folk art, plus cheerful, comfortable furnishings. B&B double rates for the three guest rooms and one cottage range from $95–135. Children are welcome and invited for hay rides and marshmellow roasts.

PERRY

Information please: A classic stop on the way to or from Florida is the **New Perry Hotel and Motel** (800 Main Street, P.O. Box 44, 31069; 912–987–1000 or 800–877–3779), known for its good Southern cooking at reasonable prices; at lunchtime, a modest amount buys you baked ham with corn relish, Southern fried chicken, or fried catfish, plus soup, two vegetables, hot rolls and corn sticks, while prices at dinner are only slightly higher. Desserts include your choice of apple pan pie, lemon chess pie, or pecan pie—topped with whipped cream. The hotel dates to 1924, and the motel to 1955, with a total of 57 guest rooms, and double rates of $34–48. Reports?

PINE MOUNTAIN

Located in the foothills of the Appalachians, about 70 miles south of Atlanta, Calloway Gardens was established in the 1930s by a local textile baron, and its 14,000 acres now constitute one of Georgia's best-known and most popular attractions. If visiting during the azalea season or at Christmas, try to avoid weekends unless you enjoy crowds and traffic.

Information please: Readers continue to be delighted with meals at the Verandah and the Gardens restaurants, and with the setting of the cottages at **Callaway Gardens Resort** (Pine Mountain 31822-2000; 706–663–2281 or 800–282–8181), an 800-room complex, but expressed needs for improved communication from the reservations office, better night lighting of the grounds, and a sprucing up of the guest rooms. "Facilities include a golf course and lake with a full complement of water sports." *(SHW)* "Opportunities for walking, bicycling, seeing wildlife. We had a sumptuous breakfast in the Plantation Room overlooking the garden, with interior floral displays. The butterfly house alone makes the trip worthwhile." *(Celia McCullough)* "Nicely furnished cottage in the woods. The screened porch was ideal for playing cards or reading." *(Pat Borysiewicz)*

For additional area entries, see **Concord, Grantville, Newnan, Pine Mountain, Senoia** and **Warm Springs.**

RABUN GAP

Information please: Boasting the second-largest waterwheel in Georgia is the **Sylvan Falls Mill B&B** (Route 1, Box 548, Taylor Chapel Road, 30568; 404–256–2949 or 706–746–7138). Dating back to 1840, this working gristmill is fed by springs from Black Rock Mountain. Restored as a B&B in 1996 by Jan and Ruth Ann Cort, the inn offers three guest rooms, each with private bath. The B&B double rate of $90 includes afternoon refreshments and a full breakfast. The area offers excellent mountain biking, hiking, rafting and canoeing, swimming and fishing, and golf. The Corts are pleased to assist with area activities and dinner reservations.

For additional area entries, see **Blairsville, Clayton, Dillard,** and **Hiawassee.**

ST. MARYS

St. Marys is located at the southernmost corner of Georgia, just north of Amelia Island, Florida, and is the starting point for the ferry to the Cumberland Island National Seashore.

Information please: Owned by Betty and George Krauss, the 1870 **Goodbread House** (209 Osborne Street, 31558; 912–882–7490), is within walking distance of the Cumberland Island ferry. Carefully restored, it offers wide pine floors and antique decor. The rates include afternoon wine and cheese, a continental breakfast, and the morning paper. Double rates for the four guest rooms, each with private bath range from $55–65.

For additional area inns, see **Cumberland Island,** and **Amelia Island, Florida.**

ST. SIMONS ISLAND

For a traditional resort experience, see **Sea Island.**

Little St. Simons Island
P.O. Box 21078, 31522
Tel: 912–638–7472
Fax: 912–634–1811
E-mail: lssi@mindspring.com

A visit to Little St. Simons Island is about as close as most of us will ever come to having our own unspoiled waterfront paradise. Since only 30 people can be accommodated on this 10,000-acre private island, you'll find as much solitude as you desire. With the variety of habitats on the island, and its location in the path of a number of migratory patterns, the opportunities for bird-watching are outstanding. Resident naturalists are available to answer questions, and readers report that their presence really enhances the experience. Debbie and Kevin McIntyre are the long-time managers of both the inn and island's resources.

Rates include three meals a day, evening hors d'oeuvres, wine with dinner, snacks and hot and cold beverages on request, picnic lunches, use of all facilities and equipment, and access to all experts. Guest rooms are located in several cottages, with the main lodge dating back to 1917; the Michael Cottage, built in 1923 and refurbished in 1986; and the historic Helen House built of tabby in 1929 and refurbished in 1996. The two remaining cottages were constructed in the 1980s.

Coffee, juice, yogurt, and cereal are available at 7:30 A.M., with a full breakfast served at 9:00 A.M.—perhaps scrambled eggs, bacon, grits, and biscuits one day, followed by pancakes and sausage, or bagels and cream cheese. Lunch menus range from grilled vegetable salad and steak, to fried chicken and biscuits, to crabcakes with cole slaw. At dinner, you might enjoy duck breast with wild rice and green beans, followed by peach cobbler one night, and garlic shrimp and pasta, plus pecan pie the next. Special dietary needs can be accommodated with prior notice.

"Great bicycling paths, walking trails, deserted beaches, excellent birding, super boating." *(Ronald Daniel)* "Lovely, secluded, private, quiet, and relaxing. The helpful guides are knowledgeable about the environment, history, ecology, and wildlife. Comfortable accommodations; tasty, healthy food." *(Mickey Robbins)* "Outstanding staff, welcoming atmosphere with many caring, loving touches. Family-style meals allow guests to get to know one another." *(Marge Glaser)*

"Great for bird-watchers (the number and variety of birds are incredible), animal-watchers (for the armadillos, alligators, deer, an occasional dolphin or snake), swimmers (seven miles of beach), horseback riders, surf-fishers, boaters, loafers, honeymooners, and anyone who doesn't want an 18-hole golf course or disco." *(Robert Saxon)* "Our room had a king-sized bed, two easy chairs and a table, plenty of closet and drawer space, and a heart-stopping view of the marshes and woods beyond." *(Paula Marcus)* "All needs anticipated; pristine, rustic, pampering." *(Bernadette Nagler)*

Open All year.
Rooms 2 bedrooms in main lodge. Four 2-4 bedroom cabins—all with private bath and/or shower, wood-burning fireplace, ceiling fan, deck, screened porches, living rooms, coffee maker. Some with air-conditioning.
Facilities Dining room, living rooms with library/bar, fireplace; family room. Swimming pool. Slide shows, games, crafts, star-gazing beach walks, oyster roasts, crab boils, cocktail barge cruises. 8 acres for lodge complex; barrier island is 10,000 undeveloped acres, with 7 m of ocean beach. Swimming, saltwater fly-fishing, angling, shelling, boating, bird-watching, hiking, horseback riding, canoeing.
Location SE GA, Glynn County. 70 m S of Savannah, 70 m N of Jacksonville,

FL. Northernmost of the Golden Isles. Nearest mainland town, Brunswick, GA. From I-95, take Hwy. 17 to Brunswick, then follow signs to St. Simons Island. On St. Simons, follow signs to Hampton River Club marina. Ferry for LSSI departs at 10:30 A.M., 4:30 P.M. daily; 20 min. ride.
Restrictions No smoking. Children over 8, Sept.–May; all ages June–Sept. Children must have good table manners. Mosquito repellent advisable in spring.
Credit cards MC, Visa.
Rates Full board, $300–525 double, $275–425 single. Extra person, $125. Full island, $3400–4650. Day trips, Tues., Wed., $75 per person.
Extras Airport/station pickups; varying fee. No charge for boat transportation from St. Simons to Little St. Simons Island.

SAVANNAH

Savannah was founded in the eighteenth century by the English general James Oglethorpe and has been a major port ever since. Today, elegant yachts have replaced the pirate ships and China clippers of the early days, but a surprising number of Savannah's original buildings have survived. In fact, Savannah now claims to have the largest urban National Landmark District in the U.S., with over 1,000 restored homes in an area 2½miles square. Some are now museums; many more are inns and restaurants. In fact, it seems to us that Savannah has more B&Bs these days than you can shake a croissant at!

Savannah is located 255 miles southeast of Atlanta, 136 miles north of Jacksonville, Florida, and 106 miles south of Charleston, South Carolina. It's a 16-mile drive to the Atlantic Ocean beaches. Start your exploration of the town at the Visitors Center on West Broad Street. There's an audiovisual program to introduce you to the city, lots of brochures, and a well-informed staff to answer questions.

Worth noting: Walking at night in some parts of Savannah is inadvisable; ask your innkeeper for advice. Parking in Savannah's historic district can also be a problem. Some inns have a limited number of onsite spaces, while others do not. If you're traveling by car, be sure to get details; ask about city parking passes, which eliminate the constant need to feed meters. The front doors of most historic inns in Savannah are reached by a flight of steps; guest rooms at the ground level look out onto sidewalk at the front of the house and the garden to the back, and usually have exposed brick walls and more rustic furnishings than upstairs guest rooms; these "garden-level" rooms may be dark and sometimes lack privacy.

Reader tips: If you don't mind waiting on line, head for Mrs. Wilkes Boarding House (107 West Jones Street), where enormous Southern-style breakfasts are served at penny-pinching prices. There's no menu, but your table will be covered with a dozen dishes. "I loved the old-fashioned farm-style Southern cooking; you'll have to wait but don't let them rush you once you're seated." *(PP)* And: "Well worth a splurge was dinner at Elizabeth on 37th. Not a neighborhood for strolling, though." *(SWS)* "Wonderful meal at The Olde Pink House (an 18th century mansion) on Abercorn Street at Reynolds' Square; some say it's better than Elizabeth's. Hueys on River Street is a popular casual spot serving New Orleans fare; great beignets at breakfast." *(Rose Ciccone)* "Enjoyed the fine beer, tasty sandwiches, and delightful pub decor at the Six Pence Pub." *(Susan Woods)*

"Read John Berendt's *Midnight in the Garden of Good and Evil* (known locally as 'The Book') before your trip for a different picture of Savannah; the statue on the book's cover has been removed from Bonaventure Cemetery, so don't bother looking for it. Loved the tour of the Green-Mildrem House and the Andrew Low House, but recommend skipping the Hamilton-Turner House. Enjoyed the Art & Craft Center on Bull Street, and the E. Shaver Bookstore in Madison Square. Took a day trip out to Tybee Island for some sunning. Recommend a visit to Fort Pulaski; take time to watch the introductory movie. You can still see shells in the masonry of the fort where it was attacked." *(Penny Poirier)*

Also recommended: A surprising find is recently built 144-room chain property, the **Hampton Inn** (17007 Abercorn Street, 31419; 912–925–1212 or 800–426–7866) directly across from Factor Walk. Double rates of $99–119 include a continental breakfast, and the hotel has both a swimming pool and a parking garage. "Great location, reasonable rates, easy parking." *(Rose Ciccone)*

Overlooking lovely Forsyth Park, at the edge of the historic district, is **Magnolia Place** (503 Whitaker Street, 31401; 912–236–7674 or 800–238–7674), an 1878 mansion with 13 guest rooms; B&B double rates range from $120–195. "Wonderful new owners who really care about their guests. Beautifully decorated. The elegantly served continental breakfast can be enjoyed in the main parlor, on the veranda, or in your room. Convenient off-street parking behind the inn." *(Fran White)*

River tugboats are docked just outside of the **Olde Harbour Inn** (508 East Factor's Walk, 31401; 912–234–4100 or 800–553–6533), a three-story warehouse building along the cobblestone streets of Factor's Walk. Originally planned as condominiums, the inn's 24 one- and two-bedroom suites have living rooms and fully equipped kitchens. Included in the $115–195 double rates are a light breakfast of cereals, muffins, biscuits, juice, and coffee; evening cordials; and turn-down service. "Enjoyed the riverside setting. Courteous, accommodating staff. Tasty breakfasts. Enjoyed meeting the staff and fellow guests over cordials each evening." *(Michaelene McWhinney)*

President's Quarters (225 East President Street, 31401; 912–233–1600 or 800–233–1776) has 16 guest rooms and suites. The double rates of $137–187, include continental breakfast delivered to the room, welcome wine and fruit basket, afternoon tea and cake plus wine and cheese, and nightly turndown service with juice or sherry. "Excellent renovation (not restoration). Each suite is named and decorated for a different president; the luxurious George Washington Suite had fascinating historic prints and documents on the walls. Excellent restaurant, '1790,' around the corner." *(Janet Wright)*

Also recommended: The **River Street Inn** (115 East River Street, 31401; 912–234–6400 or 800–253–4229) is located in the heart of the Landmark district. The inn overlooks the Savannah River and is near all of the downtown attractions. Rates range from $79–139, and include breakfast, wine reception, and evening turndown with homemade chocolates; children under 18 stay free. "Our room was decorated with Oriental rugs, a four poster queen-size bed, two wing chairs, and brass fixtures in the bathroom. Breakfast is served in the restaurant downstairs on the river, and included a choice of eggs, toast and grits, or French toast. Helpful, friendly staff. Hotel was surprisingly quiet, as was the air-conditioning." *(Wendi Van Elan)*

Information please: Listed in many past editions is the well-known **Ballastone Inn & Manor House** (14 East Oglethorpe Avenue, 31401; 912–236–1484 or 800–822–4553), purchased by Jean Hagens in 1997. Built in 1838, the Ballastone was named in recognition of the ballast stones with which much of Savannah had been built. B&B double rates for the 17 guest rooms range from $115–255, and include a welcoming glass of sherry and bowl of fruit, breakfast, fresh flowers, morning paper, brandy and chocolates at bedtime, overnight shoeshines, and terry robes in the bath. Rooms are individually decorated in a variety of styles, with antiques, queen- and king-size beds, modern baths, and TVs with VCRs. Authentic Savannah colors are used throughout, coordinated with Scalamandre fabrics. Late-afternoon tea and cocktails are served in the garden, bar, or in the antique-filled parlor. Reports needed.

Built in 1853 as a cotton warehouse, the **East Bay Inn** (225 East Bay Street, 31401; 912–238–1225 or 800–500–1225) was renovated as a hotel in 1982. Typical of the period, the facade of this sturdy brick building is made of cast iron, as are the interior columns visible in the parlor and some guest rooms. The B&B double rates for the 28 guest rooms include continental breakfast, evening wine and cheese, and evening turndown service with a pillow sweet, and range from $99–139. Rooms are decorated with period reproductions and four poster beds, in addition to all modern conveniences.

Now managed by Holiday Inns, the 122-room **Mulberry** (601 East Bay Street, 31401; 912–238–1200 or 800–554–5544) continues to be a popular hotel. Built in 1860 as a livery stable, and later used as a warehouse and a Coca-Cola bottling plant, it has a convenient location on Washington Square, one block from the river. "Spacious lobby where afternoon tea is served; inviting rooftop hot tub overlooking the river." *(RC)* Double rates range from $125–175 double; ask about off-season specials. For your "own" place in Savannah, consider **Joan on Jones** (17 West Jones Street, 31401; 912–234–3863), a lovely 1883 Victorian townhouse offering two suites at double rates of $115–135. Each well-equipped suite has a sitting area and separate bedroom, and rates include a fix-it-yourself continental breakfast, wine and fruit, and off-street parking.

Eliza Thompson House
5 West Jones Street, 31401

Tel: 912–236–3620
800–348–9378
Fax: 912–238–1920

Opened in 1978 as one of Savannah's first B&Bs, the Eliza Thompson House is an 1847 Federal-style mansion, purchased by Carol and Steve

Day in 1995. The Days are resident, hands-on owners who have completely redecorated the inn, painting the interior in historic colors, refurnishing the rooms with English antiques, and replacing all the linens, as well as the hot water systems. Breakfast, served 8–10 A.M., is enjoyed at individual tables in the courtyard or in the garden room, and includes muffins, bagels, fresh fruit, cereal, homemade granola, juice, milk, coffee and tea, plus such entrees as waffles or pecan pancakes and sausages. Rates also include evening wine and cheese, and bedtime coffee and sweets.

"Located on one of Savannah's prettiest streets, within an easy walk of many sights. Breakfast is usually served in the lovely courtyard, or in an adjacent breakfast room in poor weather. Guests had the opportunity to sit at tables for two or four, depending on whether privacy or conversation was preferred. During the wine and cheese reception (between 5 and 7 P.M.), guests enjoy chatting about the day's activities and sharing dinner recommendations. The excellent young staff are anxious to help with reservations, taxis, and answer questions. Although one of the smallest, our room was beautifully decorated, with a lovely view of Jones Street through large windows. The walls were done in Savannah red; the four poster rice bed had a fishnet canopy, and the quilt and pillow shams were green, rose, and white. Oriental rugs topped the restored pine flooring in many rooms." *(Rose Ciccone)*

Open All year.
Rooms 1 suite, 22 doubles—all with full private bath, telephone, TV, air-conditioning, robes. 15 with desk; 13 with balcony. 10 rooms in attached carriage house.
Facilities Breakfast room, living room with fireplace, conference room, foyer with fireplace, garden courtyard with fountains. On-street parking; parking permits available.
Location Historic district. Go E on I-16 to Montgomery Street Exit. Go right at 1st light on Liberty St. Go right on Whitaker at next light. Go 3 blocks on Jones Street to inn.
Restrictions No smoking. Children over 12.
Credit cards MC, Visa.
Rates B&B, $89–189 suite, double. Extra person, $20. Special occasion packages.
Extras Wheelchair access; 1 room specially equipped.

The Foley House ¢
14 West Hull Street, 31401

Tel: 912–232–6622
800–647–3708
Fax: 912–231–1218

Overlooking lovely Chippewa Square is the Foley House, built in 1896, restored as a B&B in 1982, and refurbished in 1995, when it was bought by Inge Svensson Moore. Decorated in typical Savannah colors of dark reds, and soft greens, guest rooms are beautifully furnished with four-poster Charleston rice beds, antiques and period reproductions, and Oriental rugs; most have either king- or queen-size beds, although a few have two doubles. Guests can enjoy breakfast in their room, the lounge, or the courtyard, selecting serving times between 7:30 and 10:00 A.M.; choices include orange juice or a grapefruit, granola with milk or yogurt, and a basket of just-baked breads. The rates also include afternoon tea, evening hors d'oeuvres with a cash bar, and nightly turndown service.

"The ample common areas include the courtyard and walled garden, as well as the richly decorated parlor. The rooms range from elaborate whirlpool suites with antique four poster beds to our English cottage-style room in the carriage house. It had a king-size bed, pine armoire, and excellent sound proofing. The staff was cordial and helpful. On-street parking was not a problem. A well-run inn with a true feeling of old Savannah, and an excellent value." *(Susan Wood)*

Open All year.
Rooms 19 doubles—all with full private bath, telephone, radio, TV/VCR, desk, air-conditioning. 15 with gas fireplace. Some with double whirlpool tub, balcony. 4 rooms in carriage house.
Facilities Double parlors with fireplaces, videotape library. 2 courtyards with fountain, on-street parking.
Location Center of historic district. On Chippewa Sq., between Whitaker and Bull Sts.
Restrictions On-street parking; city parking passes available. Smoking restricted.
Credit cards Amex, Discover, JCB, MC, Visa.
Rates B&B, $105–200 double. Extra person, $15. 10% AAA & AARP, Children under 12 free.

The Gastonian ♿
220 East Gaston Street, 31401

Tel: 912–232–2869
800–322–6603
Fax: 912–232–0710

Savannah's best known luxury inn was purchased in 1996 by Anne Landers, who is working hard to make a lovely inn even more so. The Gastonian is comprised of two connecting Savannah mansions, built in 1868 in the Regency Italianate style. The interiors are highlighted with fine woods and heart pine floors, decorative moldings and brass, and wallpapers in the original Scalamandre Savannah pattern. Depending on the room, the luxurious decor ranges from French, Italianate, English, Victorian, or Colonial, but both common areas and guest rooms are stunning with authentic antiques, Persian rugs, and rice poster or Charleston canopied beds. Recent improvements include a complete repainting of the inn's interior; replacement of all mattresses, and most draperies and upholstery; resurfacing of all sinks and bathtubs, the installation of an up-to-date telephone system; replanting the gardens and sprucing up the hot tub area. Several king-bedded rooms were added at street level, ideal for those who have difficulty with stairs; breakfast and afternoon tea can be delivered to these rooms on request.

Anne notes that "it is our pleasure to make dinner reservations, arrange tours, and answer questions about this lovely city. A bellman is available to assist with luggage at check-in. Using fine china, crystal, and silver, we serve a beautiful sit-down breakfast between 8 and 10 each morning with home-baked breads and such dishes as German apple pancakes; in the afternoon complimentary wines are available in the parlor; each evening guests may come relax in the candlelit parlor over a glass of port or sherry. Iced tea and lemonade are always available in warm weather, along with chocolate chip cookies. Bottled water is delivered daily to each guest room, and a Savannah praline accompanies evening turndown service.

"Elegant decor, immaculate housekeeping, delicious breakfast, welcoming tea service. Attention to detail includes the fresh flowers in the room, the fire crackling in your room on a chilly evening, and the attentive staff's guidance with restaurant reservations and shopping options. Anne is a delightful innkeeper." *(Pat Conner)* "Located in a quiet residential area near Forsyth Park, the inn is within walking distance of Savannah's attractions." *(Susan Rasmussen)* "Our room was high up in the connecting house, next door, with a four-poster bed and a separate sitting room." *(Lee Todd)* "We stayed one night in one of the most expensive rooms, and the next in one of the least costly; both were wonderful, creatively and comfortably furnished, with every amenity one could wish." *(Sally Schenk)*

Open All year.
Rooms 3 suites, 14 doubles—all with private bath and/or shower, telephone with data port, radio, TV, air-conditioning, fireplace. 9 with whirlpool tub. Some with desk, ceiling fan.
Facilities Kitchen/breakfast room, parlor, dining room, gift shop. Garden courtyard with hot tub. Limited off-street parking.
Location Historic district.
Restrictions No smoking. No children under 12.
Credit cards Amex, MC, Visa.
Rates B&B, $225–350 suite, $185–290 double. Extra person, $25. Midweek corporate rate, $150 (not available spring & fall seasons). 2-night weekend minimum.
Extras Limited wheelchair access.

The Kehoe House ♿ *Tel:* 912–232–1020
123 Habersham Street, 31401 800–820–1020
Fax: 912–231–1587

An imposing mansion built in 1892, The Kehoe House was restored as an inn in 1993, and is owned by Consul Court Property Management; Brenda Giffin is the manager. Rates include breakfast, afternoon tea and evening hors d'oeuvres served at 6 P.M. The inn's common areas include an enormous double parlor, furnished with handsome antiques and highlighted by a beautiful Chinese screen. The beautiful guest rooms are furnished with equal care, luxurious yet not fussy, restfully done in soft colors. Breakfast menus vary daily, but might include scrambled eggs with gravy and biscuits, raspberry pancakes with country ham, or blueberry French toast with sausages. "Exceptional in every way from the young, helpful staff, to our beautifully appointed room, supplied with ice and bottled water; fluffy towels, thirsty robes. Breakfast is graciously served at 8 or 9A.M.; settings are lovely with linen placemats, china and silver. You select an entree the previous evening, and eat at the dining room table, getting acquainted with the other guests. Ideally located on beautiful Columbia Square, just a short walk from the City Market, Bay Street, and River Street, where shops and restaurants abound." *(Shari Thorell)* "Total Southern elegance enhanced by a hospitable, knowledgeable staff." *(Jim Kott)* "Beautiful restoration, excellent furnishings; superb location on an attractive square." *(Don Burd)* "Our suite, overlooking Columbia Square, was beautifully coordinated—from the love seat and armchairs to the handsome queen-size sleigh bed, from the draperies to the wallpaper." *(Jeanne Smith)*

Open All year.
Rooms 2 suites, 13 doubles—all with private bath and/or shower, telephone with dataport, radio, clock, TV, desk, air-conditioning, fan, robes. 10 with balcony. 2 suites in adjoining building.
Facilities Double parlor, music room with piano, conference room. Off-street parking.
Location Historic district, Columbia Square. Take I-16 to end, go right on Oglethrope Ave. Go left of Habersham St. to first square, Columbia.
Restrictions No smoking.
Credit cards Amex, CB, DC, Discover, JCB, MC, Visa.
Rates B&B, $225–250 suite, $165–250 double. AAA, AARP discounts; corporate rates.
Extras Wheelchair access; 1 room specially equipped; elevator.

Lion's Head Inn
120 East Gaston Street, 31401
Tel: 912–232–4580
800–355–LION
Fax: 912–232–7422
E-mail: Lionshead@sysconn.com

Named for the lion's head that appears on the foundation of this 1883 mansion as well as the brass knocker on the front door, the Lion's Head Inn was restored as an inn in 1992 by Christy and John Dell'Orco. The double parlor and dining room are furnished in the formal Empire style of the early 1800s while the guest rooms have four-poster beds and richly colored walls. Breakfast is served in the dining room from 8:30–10 A.M., and includes fresh fruit and juice; croissants, cinnamon rolls, or bagels; and granola and cereal. Rates also include afternoon wine and cheese, and turndown service with cordials and mints.

"Beautiful Empire antiques. Our lovely room had a large, comfortable bed, and robes and thick towels in the bathroom. We borrowed tapes from their collection in the library to watch on our VCR at night. Convenient off-street parking." *(Penny Poirier)* "Easy walking distance to anywhere in historic Savannah. Michigan transplants Christy and John have painstakingly restored the house with beautiful antiques." *(Kip Goldman & Marty Wall)* "Rooms beautifully decorated, immaculately clean." *(Larry Koehn)*

Open All year.
Rooms 2 suites, 4 doubles—all with private bath and/or shower, telephone, radio, clock, TV, desk, air-conditioning. Some with fan, fireplace, refrigerator, VCR.
Facilities Dining room, living room, library with books, stereo, videotapes; all

with fireplace. Veranda with swing, garden courtyard with fountain, pond. 5 off-street parking spaces.
Location Historic district, on E. Gaston between Drayton & Abercorn; ½ block from Forsyth Park. Follow I-16 to end at Montgomery St. Go right at first light. At Liberty St. go right and continue 3 lights to East Gaston. Go right to inn on right.
Restrictions No smoking. No windows in 2 ground level rooms.
Credit cards Amex, Discover, MC, Visa.
Rates B&B, $95–190 (for 4), $140 (for 2) suite; $90–140 double. Extra person, $20. Corporate rate, $80, Sun.–Thurs. Infants free. 2-night weekend minimum.
Extras Limited wheelchair access. Crib, babysitting.

SEA ISLAND

For a back-to-nature experience, see **St. Simons Island.**

Also recommended: For a superbly run traditional resort, it would be hard to top **The Cloister** (Sea Island Road, 31561; 912–638–3611 or 800–SEA–ISLAND), a Spanish-Mediterranean-style resort built in 1928. Occupying 10,000 acres on two of Georgia's Golden Isles, it offers all activities: golf, tennis, horseback riding, fishing, boating, bicycling, spa/fitness center, plus numerous shops and restaurants. A wide variety of packages are available, from golf to tennis, spa to family; regular rates for the 262 guest rooms range from $224–638, including three meals daily (15% service additional). "Superb to say the least, with all amenities." *(Hopie Welliver)* "Like something out of Southern living. Lovely rooms." *(Wendi Van Exan)*

SENOIA

Senoia is located in central Georgia, about 37 miles south of Atlanta. Senoia is 9 miles south of Fayetteville, between Griffin and Newnan, at the intersection of routes 85 and 16, just a half-hour drive to the Atlanta airport.

The Veranda
252 Seavy Street, Box 177, 30276
Tel: 770–599–3905
Fax: 770–599–0806
E-mail: JBBoal@aol.com

A white clapboard building with Doric columns, The Veranda was built in 1907 and is listed on the National Register of Historic Places. Bobby and Jan Boal purchased the house in 1985, and after extensive restoration opened its doors as an inn. Many rooms feature the original tin-covered ceilings and stained-glass windows. Antiques and memorabilia, including Oriental rugs, a player piano, and a bookcase owned by President McKinley, add to the old-fashioned atmosphere. Guest rooms are spacious with high ceilings, armoires, rocking chairs, and handmade quilts. After the beds are turned down at night, guests often discover a small "pillow treat," such as a homemade fruitcake or a miniature kaleidoscope. The gift shop downstairs offers an extensive collection of kaleidoscopes and unique games. Breakfast includes a variety of juices and hot beverages, fresh fruit with strawberry sorbet or stewed dried fruit, granola, and such entrees as cheese souffle with basil and sweet pepper, quiche with chicken and broccoli, or cheddar mushroom omelets with asparagus and seasoned grits. Dinners are no less tempting—a recent meal included corn chowder with corn sticks, salad with edible flowers, smoked trout with watercress and whole wheat sourdough bread, veal with pasta and carrot souffle, and angel cake with raspberries and whipped cream.

"Spacious rooms with careful attention to detail, each with a different decorating theme. Well-maintained and immaculate throughout. Meals on a par with the best restaurants." *(Michelle Ellinas)* "Jan and Bobby are exceptionally gracious innkeepers. Superb food served elegantly, yet in a comfortable, relaxing environment." *(Larry & Linda Young)* "The Boals create a warm, friendly atmosphere that seems to be contagious among the guests. The kaleidoscopes will keep you dazzled for hours." *(Linda Purdy)* "We spent two hours looking over the treasures in the gift shop. Bobby is a superb chef." *(Al & Sue Hagen)* "Jan and Bobby have an amazing memory for guests' names. Sitting on the porch at night, talking with the other guests was so personal and pleasant." *(Vicky Rountree)*

"The many sitting areas come equipped with unusual books and magazines; games provide opportunities for conversation between guests." *(Alice Young)* "Our room had a four poster bed; the immaculate modern bathroom was stocked with toiletries. After a wonderful dinner, the tempting desserts included a cobbler, cheesecake, or fruit tarts. Delicious breakfast of apple crepes with whipped cream, homemade muffins, jam, jelly, and grits." *(Binnie Anne Davidow)* "We stayed in the Bird Watcher room—a soft yellow upstairs room with windows on two sides. After a wonderful night's sleep, crickets and the crowing of roosters awakened us to a royal breakfast." *(MR)*

Open All year. No dinner Sun.
Rooms 9 doubles with full private bath, air-conditioning, clock/radio, robes, hair dryer. 4 with desk. 1 with fan. 1 with whirlpool tub.
Facilities Dining room, parlor, upstairs reading and game area, gift shop with player piano and pipe organ. Conference room.
Location In historic district. ½ block from town center.
Restrictions No smoking. Alcohol only in guest rooms. "Children accepted when accompanied by responsible adult."
Credit cards Amex, Discover, MC, Visa.
Rates B&B, $99–150 double, $80 single. Extra person, $20. Prix fixe dinner, $38 (by reservation).
Extras Wheelchair access. Playpen. Babysitting by arrangement.

TATE

For an additional area entry, see **Jasper.**

Also recommended: An hour north of Atlanta is the **Tate House** (P.O. Box 33, 30177; 770–735–3122 or, inside GA, 800–342–7515) built in 1926 by Colonel Sam Tate, president of the Georgia Marble Company, and designed to exhibit the treasures of his quarry. The Etowah marble exterior of the house is complemented by formal gardens, marble walks, fountains and statues. Restored and opened in 1985 by Ann Laird, guests can also enjoy the tennis courts, swimming pool, and horseback riding. The mansion has five luxurious suites, while the nine log cabins have stone fireplaces, hot tubs, and sleeping lofts. B&B double rates, including tax, are $140–155 for the suites, and $120–135 in the cabins (breakfast not included). "Our spacious first floor room was furnished with a comfortable queen-size bed, two easy chairs, and period antiques. Attractive floral wallpaper; effective air-conditioning. The bathroom fittings were old-fashioned, but in good working order. The cordial, accommodating innkeeper was helpful with luggage and with directions to restaurants and a beautiful waterfall. Beautiful grounds with lovely views. A tray of cheese, crackers, and sparkling non-alcoholic wine awaited our return from dinner." *(HJB)*

THOMASVILLE

Thomasville is centrally located in south Georgia, 28 miles north of Tallahassee, Florida. Once the train lines were repaired after the Civil War, wealthy Northerners traveled here to hunt quail, breathe the pine-scented highland air, and escape the harsh winters; many built lavish "cottages" and "shooting plantations" for the winter season. The mild winter climate hasn't changed over the last century; now travelers detour off I-10 or I-75 to enjoy Thomasville's leisurely pleasures—visits to historic homes and plantations, two challenging golf courses, tennis, and sporting clays. The town's biggest event is the Rose Festival, held the fourth week of April, when reservations are essential.

Reader tip: "Well worth visiting are the Lapham-Patterson House and Pebble Hill Plantation." *(Imogene Tillis)*

Also recommended: Listed on the National Register of Historic Places and overlooking Paradise Park, **Our Cottage on the Park** (801 South Hansell Street, 31792; 912–227–0404) is a Queen Anne Victorian home built in 1893 and opened as a B&B by Connie Clineman in 1992. B&B double rates for the two guest suites are $60 double; children are welcome. "Chocolates are left by your bed at turndown, and the excellent breakfasts include French toast with heart-shaped poached eggs or crepes with peaches and strawberries, served on Royal Doulton china." *(Robert Mast)* "Connie went out of her way to make our visit special, from the comfortable accommodations to the beautifully prepared breakfasts. Her sightseeing advice was invaluable." *(Imogene Tillis)*

The **Serendipity Cottage** (339 East Jefferson Street, 31792; 912–226–8111 or 800–383–7377) is a four-square house built in 1906 by a lumber baron; the interior has handsome oak trim and stained glass windows. Each of the three guest rooms has a private bath, telephone, and TV, and the $70–85 double rate includes made-from-scratch breakfasts of tomato juice, orange ambrosia salad, cream biscuits, jam, and apple Calvados French toast with sourdough bread. "Delicious breakfasts; charming owners, Ed and Kathy Middleton. Wonderful fresh-ground early morning coffee. Excellent lighting, inside and out." *(Nancy Shugart)* "Convenient to historic sights, shops, and restaurants." *(Cathy Ensing)* "Delightful front porch swing; careful attention to detail included the beautifully ironed sheets and evening glass of sherry." *(Kathryn Mickel)* "The warm and welcoming innkeepers made me feel right at home." *(Jill McClung)*

For an additional area inn, see **Monticello, Florida**, 21 miles to the south.

Evans House B&B ¢
725 South Hansell Street, 31792

Tel: 912–226–1343
800–344–4717
Fax: 912–226–0653

Built in 1898, the Evans House is located in an area of late Victorian houses built across from 27-acre Paradise Park, in what was then suburban Thomasville. Its transitional style bridges the asymmetry of the Victorian era and the formality of the emerging Neo-classical style. Lee and John Puskar, who have owned Evans House since 1989, have furnished it with quality Victorian antiques; guest rooms have either queen- or king-size beds. Breakfasts vary daily, but might include fresh squeezed orange juice, baked grapefruit, almond-poppy seed muffins, strawberry crepes with orange sauce, and bacon; or apple cinnamon muffins, bananas and strawberries in cream, crumpets with scrambled eggs and cheese, and sausages. Rates also include evening turndown service with after-dinner liqueurs, sweets, and fresh towels.

"Hospitable, ready-to-please hosts; they made our dinner reservations, and the chef came out to greet us personally. Immaculate and well maintained; carefully manicured grounds. Delicious breakfast; bedtime chocolates and liqueur were a special treat." *(Terry Taylor)* "John and Lee are a charming couple; hospitality and comfort come first here. We especially like the Regency Room with a wonderful king-size bed." *(Donna Jacobson)* "With their security system I felt extremely safe." *(Rita Gable)* "Our room, with twin beds, two comfortable chairs, and good lighting, was clean and quiet. The old-fashioned bathroom was well supplied with towels. Superb breakfast with fresh peach crepes and excellent coffee."*(ELC)* "Lee brought me a plate of homemade brownies and iced tea, and provided helpful information about the area's historic homes." *(Bill Novak)*

Open All year.
Rooms 1 suite, 3 doubles—all with private bath and/or shower, radio, desk, air-conditioning, fan, queen or king size beds.
Facilities Dining room, living room with TV, entrance hall & library with fire-

places, guest kitchen with refrigerator and refreshments. Off-street parking, bicycles. Paradise Park across street.
Location Park Front Historic District. ¼ m from downtown.
Restrictions No smoking.
Credit cards None accepted.
Rates B&B, $125 suite, $75–90 double, $65–85 single. Extra person, $20. Corporate rates.
Extras Airport/station pickups. Wheelchair access; 1 room specially equipped. Pets by arrangement.

The Grand Victoria Inn ¢

Tel: 912–226–7460
817 South Hansell, 31792

Built in 1893, Anne Dodge restored this eclectic Victorian mansion as an inn in 1991. Breakfast menus change daily, but might include freshly squeezed orange juice, fruit compote, pecan-stuffed French toast with raspberry syrup, and bacon.

"We loved to relax on the wonderful front porch, overlooking the park. Historic sights, restaurants, and shops are nearby. Spacious, comfortable guest rooms; delightful innkeeper." *(Cathryn Tyler)* "Anne is exceptionally charming, gracious, and welcoming. Wonderful food, presented with elegance." *(Cynthia Hagist)* "The Sheridan Room has antique walnut furniture and a four-poster king-size bed, with soft down pillows and a floral comforter with a deep burgundy background; there's an adjoining screened sleeping porch with a hammock. The Jenny Lind room has a queen-size wicker bed, oak antiques, and a small sitting area with a fluffy floral couch. We loved sitting on the front porch rockers, overlooking the wooded park, sipping iced tea and chatting with Anne." *(Shannon Mikell)* "The Hoosier Room is decorated in crisp blue and white with an original Hoosier cabinet, a double pencil post canopy bed, down comforter, and luxurious towels. Anne is flexible about the timing of breakfast, trying to accommodate all her guests. Tea, coffee, hot chocolate and soda are always available, and fresh baked goods are often offered." *(Tom & Carol Kehoe)* "Special touches include mints on your pillow, afternoon tea and scones." *(Melissa White)* "Delicious evening snack of chocolate cake and cookies." *(Bob & Anne Huffman)* "Relaxing reading areas—books and magazines everywhere and even a meditation garden outside." *(Caroline San Juan)*

Open All year.
Rooms 4 doubles—all with private bath and/or shower, radio, clock, fan, airconditioning. 2 with gas fireplace, 1 with balcony, screened sleeping porch, whirlpool tub.
Facilities Dining room with piano; living room, family room with TV/VCR, stereo; library; veranda with swing. 1 acre with gardens, patio with fountain, off-street parking. Paradise Park across street.
Location Walking distance to town. From U.S. Rte. 19, go E on U.S. Rte. 319 or Smith Ave. to Hansell St. & turn left to inn on left. On Hansell between Old Monticello Rd. & Smith Ave.
Restrictions No smoking. Alcohol discouraged. Well-behaved children welcome.
Credit cards None accepted.

Rates B&B, $70–90 double, $55–80 single. Extra adult, $10; child under 3, $5. 2-night minimum some weekends.
Extras Crib, babysitting. Picnic baskets.

WARM SPRINGS

For additional area inns, see **Concord, Grantville, Newnan, Pine Mountain,** and **Senoia.**

Reader tip: "Excellent barbecue spot, Mac's BBQ—not fancy but good." *(Sherrill Brown)*

Hotel Warm Springs B&B Inn ¢ ✕
17 Broad Street, P.O. Box 351, 31830

Tel: 706–655–2114
800–366–2771
Fax: 706–655–2771

Best known as the home of Roosevelt's Little White House, Warm Springs attracts visitors for its historic significance as well as its numerous craft shops. Built in 1907, the hotel was restored by Gerrie Thompson in 1988. The town's only hotel in Roosevelt's day, members of the press, secret service, and assorted dignitaries stayed here when Roosevelt was at the Little White House. Breakfast, served 8:30–9:30 A.M., is offered at five large tables in the third floor dining room, complete with elegant chandeliers and Queen Anne furnishings, and includes bacon, ham, sausage, eggs, homemade banana nut bread, ten-day coffee cake, homemade biscuits, cheese grits, fresh fruit and juice. The first floor houses three gift shops, as well as an ice cream parlor featuring homemade peach ice cream and other old-fashioned soda fountain treats; President Roosevelt and his associates came here for ice cream and Coca-Cola.

"When you step into the tiled lobby, with its antique reception desk, cord switchboard, old typewriter, and original telephone booth, you may also be carried back to the days when members of the press used neither a fax nor a modem to get their stories into the 'Final' edition. Most guest rooms can be reached from the second floor guest parlor, complete with 12-foot ceilings, crystal chandelier, and ornate plaster moldings. The room decor varies; the suite has the original English oak furnishings made in Eleanor Roosevelt's Val-Kill Furniture Shop in New York state, while another room is decorated with Victorian heirlooms from Gerrie's family." *(Lynn Fullman)* "We had a comfortable downstairs guest room. Wonderfully copious family-style Sunday morning breakfast." *(Peggy Kontak)* "Impressive renovation. Our comfortable room was furnished with original Val-Kill oak furnishings. Good breakfast served in the recently redone third floor dining room. Gerrie Thompson was friendly, and shared our admiration for FDR. Both the town and the hotel are worth a visit." *(Sherrill Brown)* "We visited during the Olympics and wanted to give Gerrie a gold medal for her cheese grits." *(GR)*

Open All year.
Rooms 2 suites, 12 doubles—all with private bath and/or shower, clock/radio,

TV, ceiling fan, air-conditioning. 7 with desk, 2 with balcony, 1 with double Jacuzzi.
Facilities Lobby, ice cream parlor, gift shops. Dining room, guest parlor, library. Off-street parking, patio, fountain. 8 m to natural spring-fed pool; hiking, horseback riding, fishing in Roosevelt State Park. Golf, tennis nearby.
Location W central GA. 65 m SW of Atlanta. 15 m NE of Callaway Gardens. Take I-85 S to Exit 8, & go S 33 m on Hwy. 27 to inn in center of village. 400 yds. to Little White House Museum.
Restrictions Smoking permitted in some guest rooms. Children 10 and over preferred. Light sleepers should request a quiet room.
Credit cards Amex, Discover, MC, Visa.
Rates B&B, $112–167 suite, $77 double, $50 single. Room only (midweek), $55 double, $40 single. 10% senior, corporate discount. Extra person, $5–10.
Extras Airport/station pickup, $20. Crib, babysitter by arrangement.

We Want to Hear from You!

As you know, this book is effective only with your help. We really need to know about your experiences and discoveries. If you stayed at an inn or hotel listed here, we want to know how it was. Did it live up to our description? Exceed it? Was it what you expected? Did you like it? Were you disappointed? Delighted? Have you discovered new establishments that we should add to the next edition?

Tear out one of the report forms at the back of this book (or use your own stationery if you prefer) and write today. *Even if you write only "Fully endorse existing entry" you will have been most helpful.*

Thank You!

Kentucky

Inn at the Park, Louisville

Kentucky's history is a rich and complex one—Daniel Boone explored and hunted here, Abraham Lincoln was born here, and Stephen Foster and Harriet Beecher Stowe wrote about Kentucky. In the development of the U.S., Kentucky has served as a bridge state: Linking the north and south, it was a slave state but fought for the Union in the Civil War; from Virginia to Missouri, settlers passed through on their way west.

And there is far more to present-day Kentucky than Churchill Downs, the Derby, and horses. A key common denominator is the dominant limestone strata responsible for the state's bourbon (the water), bluegrass (the color), and dramatic scenery (cliffs, canyons, and caves). At Cumberland Falls State Park visitors can walk out on flat limestone slabs to watch a 125-foot-wide, 68-foot-high swathe of water plunge dramatically to the boulders below. During a full moon, the resulting pervasive mist forms a rare "moonbow" visible only here and at Victoria Falls in Zimbabwe, Africa. If you're not claustrophobic, explore some of the 300 miles of charted limestone passages in Mammoth Cave, including some areas used for human habitation over 4,000 years ago.

Other spots to explore: Shaker Village at Pleasant Hill, with its architecturally distinctive buildings where superb design emphasizes stately simplicity; nearby Harrodsburg's Old Fort Harrod—site of the first permanent English settlement west of the Alleghenies; Hodgenville, where visitors can see Abe Lincoln's birthplace and an enormous sinkhole; and the many TVA lakes scattered throughout the state, which offer limitless recreational opportunities.

BARDSTOWN

Bardstown is one of Kentucky's oldest towns, with many historic buildings, and is a center for the growing of tobacco and the distilling of bourbon. Sights of interest include the local historical museum, the Getz Museum of Whiskey History—from colonial days to Prohibition—and My Old Kentucky Home State Park. This park is home to Federal Hill, a mansion that probably inspired Stephen Foster to write "My Old Kentucky Home." From June to early September the "Stephen Foster Story," a musical pageant featuring the composer's melodies, is sung in the park's amphitheater. Bourbon afficionados will want to take the tours of the nearby Jim Beam and Maker's Mark distilleries. Here also is a Trappist abbey that sells a very distinctive (and strong) cheese.

Bardstown is in central Kentucky's Nelson County, 35 miles south of Louisville.

Information please: The well-known **Old Talbott Tavern** (107 West Stephen Foster Avenue, 40004; 502–348–3494 or 800–4TAVERN) is one of Kentucky's most historic inns. Among the tavern's famous visitors were King Louis Philippe of France, Abraham Lincoln, Jesse James, Daniel Boone, Stephen Foster, and James Audubon. Meals include both typical American cuisine and such Kentucky favorites as a "Hot Brown" sandwich, fried chicken with milk gravy, and lamb fries. Seven simply furnished guest rooms are in the tavern, with an additional eight in the neighboring McLean House, at B&B double rates of $55–70.

Two miles from town is **Kenmore Farms** (1050 Bloomfield Road, 40004; 502–348–8023 or 800–831–6159), a Victorian farm house built in 1860, and decorated with period antiques. Each of the four guest rooms has a private bath, and the B&B double rate of $80–90 includes a full, home-cooked breakfast.

Jailer's Inn ¢
111 West Stephen Foster Avenue, 40004

Tel: 502–348–5551
800–948–5551
Fax: 502–348–1852
E-mail: jailersinn@innocent.com

After two centuries as a jail, Fran, Challen, and their son Paul McCoy bought the old jail and jailer's residence at public auction in 1988, and have converted it into an unusual B&B. Five guest rooms have been decorated with antiques and Oriental rugs; the sixth, the former women's cell, is done in prison black-and-white, with framed reproductions of cell-wall graffiti hung on the walls. Public tours are given from 10 a.m. to 5 p.m.; guests may check-in after 2 p.m.

"Fran's suggestions for dining and sightseeing were most helpful; we had an outstanding dinner at the Bardstonian Restaurant." *(Edward Warner)* "The sitting area has an Oriental theme, with a large couch; the breakfast table was set with beautiful china. Our room, #3—The Library—had green walls, a wallpaper ceiling border, red accent curtains, pretty pictures, a king-size bed with a brass headboard, two brocade sitting chairs, and a modern bath." *(Lynne Derry)* "Breakfast was served in the flower-filled fortress courtyard." *(Gail Greco)* "A special breakfast dish was prepared to meet my dietary needs. Interesting collection of jail memorabilia." *(Patricia Davis)*

"Charming and peaceful, relaxed and friendly. We were welcomed warmly, shown to a lovely guest room, and were given the recipe for our breakfast favorite, peach French toast. It's a short walk to the inn's parking area, but we had no problems. Bardstown is an inviting town for evening strolling." *(Richard Miller)* "Paul was an excellent host, both witty and informative. Delightful breakfast." *(JFH)*

Open Feb. 1–Dec. 31.
Rooms 6 doubles—all with private bath, desk, air-conditioning, fan. 2 with double Jacuzzi.
Facilities Breakfast room, TV/VCR room, gift shop, courtyard garden, gazebo, picnic area. Off-street parking. Golf nearby.
Location 35 m S of Louisville. 65 m SW of Lexington. Center of town. Adjacent to Court Square.
Restrictions No smoking in guest rooms. House tours held 10 a.m.–5 p.m.
Credit cards Amex, Discover, MC, Visa.
Rates B&B, $65–95 double. Extra person, $10.
Extras Limited wheelchair access. Crib.

BELLEVUE

For additional area entries, see **Covington**.

Weller Haus B&B ¢
319 Poplar Street, 41073

Tel: 606–431–6829
800–431–4287
Fax: 606–431–4332

While a convenient location, good food, and comfortable accommodations are essential to any B&B, it's the innkeepers themselves that set some places above the rest, and so it is with the Weller Haus. After their children had grown, Mary and Vernon Weller renovated their Victorian Gothic home as a B&B in 1990; in 1992, they purchased the house next door and restored it as well. Inveterate collectors and antiquers, they've decorated each room with a different decor, from Victorian, to French cottage, to Art Deco. Breakfast is served on antique linens, glass, and porcelain, and includes fresh fruit and juice, a hot entree, and home-baked muffins, breads, or coffee cake; cinnamon bread is a specialty.

"Warm, welcoming, and inviting." *(Kathy Banak)* "Though the neighborhood is modest, the restoration is extraordinary. All the rooms are lovely but the Dream Suite, with a double Jacuzzi tub, was my favorite. Incredible breakfast, afternoon treats and well-stocked guest refrigerator." *(Penny Poirier)* "The Wellers anticipate your every need. If they learn that you have a preference—for muffins without nuts, for example—they remember when you return." *(Susan Kirby)* "Wonderful Southern hospitality, in two beautifully restored Victorian homes, decorated carefully in period." *(Janet Wright)* "The Rooftop Suite has lace-veiled French doors leading to the cozy bedroom. The lovely clawfoot tub has a terrific shower, and the comfortable chairs in the living area were ideal for relaxing. The Wellers were unobtrusive but attentive, and suggested area activities, providing excellent directions. Comfortable, inviting common areas; lovely flower gardens behind the house. Lively, intelligent conversation at breakfast; delectable cherry coffee cake." *(Sara Bowling Bernhard)*

Open All year.
Rooms 4 suites, 1 double—all with private bath, radio, TV, desk, air-conditioning, fan. 2 with private entrance; porch, double Jacuzzi.
Facilities Great room with TV/VCR, radio, stereo, books, fireplace; guest kitchen. Garden, on-street parking.
Location Historic Taylor Daughters' District. Just E of Covington; 5 min. from downtown Cincinnati. From Cincinnati, cross river on I-471 (Daniel Carter Beard Bridge). Take Exit 5 (Newport & Bellevue) & bear right to Dave Cowens Dr. (KY. 8). Changes name to Fairfield Ave. in Bellevue. Go right on Washington, right on Poplar to inn on right.
Credit cards MC, Visa.
Rates B&B, $75–130 suite, double, $65–130 single. Corporate rate.

BEREA

Information please: Listed in many past editions is the **Boone Tavern Hotel** (Berea College, Main & Prospect Streets, CPO 2345, 40404; 606–986–9358 or 800–366–9358), founded in 1909 as a guest house for Berea College. Although it's been expanded and modernized many times since then, it's still primarily student-operated. Many of the students are majoring in hotel management, and most of the guest-room furniture has been made by students. Double rates for the 58 guest rooms range from $65–90; the dining room has also been a favorite of many readers. Current reports needed.

COVINGTON

Covington is located in north central Kentucky, on the Ohio River, two miles south of Cincinnati, Ohio, and 90 miles north of Lexington. Of particular interest is the River Center, a mixed-use development project, and home to Covington Landing, a floating entertainment complex with a theater, replica steamboat, and a turn-of-the-century riverfront atmosphere.

Reader tip: "Lots of revitalization work in the waterfront area; attractive historic district just a few blocks away. Other sections of town seemed somewhat rundown." *(KB)*

For an additional area entry, see **Bellevue**.

Also recommended: The **Amos Shinkle Townhouse** (215 Garrard Street, 41011; 606–431–2118 or 800–972–7012) is owned by former Covington mayor Bernie Moorman and his partner, Don Nash. This 1850s brick town house has retained some of the original wall murals, plaster ceiling medallions and cornices, and Rococo Revival chandeliers. The restored carriage house provides rooms ideal for families. B&B double rates for the seven guest rooms range from $75–135, including a full breakfast. "Beautiful room in the Carriage House, with all modern conveniences. Don and Bernie provided terrific information on area sights and restaurants; great breakfast, too." *(Janet Entner)* "Sarah's Room is a favorite, done in mauve and white with dark green accents. It has a beautiful mahogany four poster bed and a huge white armoire, accented with hand-painted ivy leaves." *(Kathy Banak)*

Information please: Overlooking the Licking River in the Historic Riverview District is the **Licking Riverside Historic B&B** (516 Gerrard Street, 41011; 606–291–0191 or 800–GUEST–BB), with a Jacuzzi suite and two queen-bedded double rooms. B&B double rates of $79–120 include a continental breakfast. "The suite has a huge bedroom with fireplace, TV/VCR, and queen-size bed. The enormous bathroom has a double Jacuzzi tub, set in a bay window complete with candles and ferns." *(JH)*

The Summer House B&B (610 Sanford Street, 41011; 606–431–3121 or 800–365–5141) is a 1865 Second Empire home, with three suites and one double room, done in a light, uncluttered Caribbean decor, with lots of white and splashes of bright color. Rooms have queen- or king-size beds, and two have Jacuzzi tubs. The B&B double rates of $79–115 include a full breakfast.

DANVILLE

Also recommended: About nine miles south of Harrodsburg and 35 miles southwest of Lexington is **Twin Hollies** (406 Maple Avenue, 40422; 606–236–8954), a handsome 1836 Greek Revival home in the heart of the Bluegrass Region. Owned by long-time Danville mayor John Bowling and his wife, Mary Joe, this B&B offers three guest rooms at double rates of $75. "Warm Southern hospitality, spacious rooms with antique furnishings. Our attractive room had a fireplace and antique furnishings, including a four-poster bed, chaise, two arm chairs, and tables with lamps. The bathroom was supplied with ample towels, soap, shampoo, and lotions. Effective air-conditioning; excellent lighting. The tasty breakfast included juice, fresh fruit, granola, and freshly baked bread and muffins. The Bowlings are delightful hosts." *(HJB)*

GEORGETOWN

Georgetown is located about ten miles north of Lexington, in the heart of horse country.

Also recommended: If you want to combine plush accommodations with equine attractions, then visit the **Jordan Farm B&B** (4091 Newtown Pike, Georgetown 40324; days, 502–868–9002 or evenings, 502–863–1944), just 11 miles north of the horse park. Located on a 100-

acre working horse farm, the three guest rooms are in a contemporary home and carriage house. Rooms are large, with floral fabrics, dark rose carpeting, and double Jacuzzi tubs, and the very reasonable rates include a continental breakfast brought to your door. Owner Becky Jordan notes: "Our goal is to provide guests with a personal look at the horse business. We've had many guests want to come to the barn to witness the birth of a foal."

Just two miles from I-75 is **Blackridge Hall B&B** (4055 Paris Pike, Georgetown 40324; 502–863–2069 or 800–768–9308). This 10,000-square-foot southern Georgian-style mansion overlooking the rolling bluegrass landscape was built by Jim Black in 1990. B&B double rates for the six guest rooms range from $90–165. "Elegant, beautifully decorated, immaculately clean—a designer perfect environment. Warm hospitality, solicitous innkeeper, excellent breakfasts." *(SHW)*

Information please: A charming country manor house and horse farm, **Bourbon House** (584 Shropshire Lane, 40324; 606–987–8669) dates back to 1820, and overlooks acres of rolling hills and fields. Each of the two spacious guest rooms has a king-size bed, and the B&B rates of $85–125 include a full breakfast. Innkeeper Lynn Lewis is pleased to give guests a tour of the barns and paddocks; in spring, guests may be able to see a foal being born. "Exceptional ambiance and serene setting. Excellent service, cleanliness, lighting, plumbing, and more." *(Marianna Dixon)*

The **Log Cabin B&B** (350 North Broadway; 502–863–3514) is a chinked log cabin built in 1809. Clay and Janis McKnight moved and reassembled this cabin, equipping it with two bedrooms, a living room with fieldstone fireplace, a bathroom, telephone, TV, and a kitchen/dining area, and furnishing it with primitive antiques and quilts. "Set in the innkeepers' backyard, but completely private. You have your own fenced yard, back and front porch, and attentive innkeepers who supply a continental breakfast. We felt perfectly safe and at home." *(C.J. DeSantis)* B&B double rates are $75; pets and children welcome.

GHENT

Ghent is located halfway between Cincinnati and Louisville, close to the Carrollton exit off Interstate 71.

Information please: A restored 1833 Federal-style house, the **Ghent House** (411 Main Street, U.S. Rte. 42, 41045; 502–347–5807) overlooks the Ohio River and is simply furnished with antiques and collectibles from the nearby Amish community. Although steamboats no longer ply the river, guests still enjoy watching the river traffic from the second-floor porches and from the lovely rose gardens, which owners Diane and Wayne Young planted when they restored this B&B in 1990. B&B double rates for the three guest rooms range from $60–110, including welcoming refreshments and a full breakfast.

GLASGOW

For additional area accommodations, see **Mammoth Cave.**

Also recommended: In the rolling hills of southern Kentucky is the **Four Seasons Country Inn** (4107 Scottsville Road [Hwy 31-E], 42141; 502–678–1000), about halfway between Louisville and Nashville. Travelers who enjoy country inn ambiance but are reluctant to sacrifice motel-style comfort will appreciate the Victorian-style Four Seasons, built in 1989. The 21 spacious guest rooms have queen-sized four poster beds and oversized wingback chairs, and most have a hide-away trundle bed to accommodate an extra guest. The breakfast buffet includes pastries, cereal, yogurt, fruit juices, milk, tea, and coffee. Numerous antique shops, Mammoth Cave National Park, the Barren River Lake State Park, and the Horse Cave theater are among the nearby attractions, and good dinners can be had at Bolton's Landing. B&B double rates range from $65–85; the suite is $110.

HARRODSBURG

The Harrodsburg area is home to two of Kentucky's finest inns. If your time in the state is limited, this town, oldest in the state, is probably the one to visit. Sights of interest include Old Fort Harrod State Park, with its historic buildings and amphitheater, featuring dramatizations of the stories of Daniel Boone and Abraham Lincoln; Morgan Row; and Shakertown at Pleasant Hill.

Harrodsburg is located in central Kentucky's Bluegrass Region, 32 miles southwest of Lexington. The recently completely U.S. Route 127 bypass around the town has reduced traffic congestion.

Reader tip: "Mercer County is dry, so come prepared. If you'd like to enjoy a glass of wine with dinner, phone the restaurant in advance to see if it's OK to bring your own."

Information please: Current reports are needed for the **Beaumont Inn** (638 Beaumont Drive, 40330; 606–734–3381 or 800–352–3992), dating back to 1845, and owned by the Dedman family for four generations. Formerly a school for girls, the inn's rooms are spread out over a number of buildings and cottages, including the original main building of the school, a brick building with Greek Revival–style Doric columns. Restaurant specialties include the inn's own Kentucky-cured ham, fried chicken, corn pudding, bread pudding with bourbon sauce, and orange-lemon cake. B&B double rates range from $75–115; three meals are served daily, and are reasonably priced. "Warm hospitality, delicious food, excellent housekeeping, comfortably furnished with many Victorian antiques." *(SHW)* Comments appreciated.

For an additional area inn, see **Danville.**

Shaker Village of Pleasant Hill ¢ 👪 ✕ ♿ *Tel:* 606–734–5411
3501 Lexington Road, 40330 800–734–5611
Fax: 606–734–5411

A longtime reader favorite, Shaker Village preserves 33 original 19th-century buildings, accurately restored and adapted. Visitors take self-guided tours of the buildings where interpreters and craftsmen explain the Shaker approach to life and religion. Shaker music programs are also offered on many weekends. Shakertown at Pleasant Hill is a non-profit educational corporation, listed on the National Register of Historic Places; it is the only historic village offering overnight accommodation in original buildings.

"Well worth a visit; you can really get into the spirit of these extraordinary people. Wonderful musical presentation of the Shaker religious ceremony." *(Robert Freidus)* "The reservationist described the accommodations in detail, helping us to select the East Family Wash-house suite as a good choice. It was airy and light, with seven windows in the bedroom, just a short pleasant walk to the dining hall. Fantastic breakfast buffet; the staff constantly replenished the food." *(Mr. & Mrs. Conrad Schilke)*

"Rolling Kentucky bluegrass, with peaceful vistas in all directions. Tasty down-home cooking with fried fish, fried chicken, and steaks. Family-style vegetables—perhaps green beans with bacon and corn pudding. Furnishings are authentically plain—reproduction Shaker furniture, rag rugs, white walls, dark woodwork. To reach the idyllic Tanyard Brick Shop cottage, you wind through cow pastures down to a small farm pond, surrounded by weeping willows." *(SHW)* "The trundle beds enable a family to share one large room, each with a comfortable bed. Meals are served in the Trustees' House, with spectacular twin spiral staircases." *(Ann Delugach)*

"Our two-room suite in the East Family Wash House was large and private." *(Joyce Ward)* "We enjoyed our stay in the Old Ministry's workshop, with a fireplace and comfortable bed. At night we saw a spectacular sunset over the rolling fence-lined hills." *(Deanna Yen)* "Exceptionally comfortable mattress; excellent home-style cooking at breakfast and dinner." *(Peggy Kontak, also Duane Roller)*

Open All year. Closed Christmas Eve and Day.
Rooms 1 cottage, 2 conference centers, 78 doubles with full private bath, telephone, TV, desk, air-conditioning. Accommodations in 15 restored buildings.
Facilities Sitting rooms, restaurant. 2,700 acres. Riverboat rides on Kentucky River. Craft shops, demonstrations.
Location Central KY, Bluegrass Region. 80 m SE of Louisville, 25 m SW of Lexington, 7 m NE of Harrodsburg, on US Rte. 68. Use caution on winding, hilly road after dark.
Restrictions No alcoholic beverages in dining room (dry county). Traffic noise in North Lot dwelling. Minimal soundproofing; TV noise can sometimes be heard in neighboring rooms.
Credit cards MC, Visa.
Rates Room only, $140–180 cottage, $105–115 suite, $50–80 double, $40–95 sin-

gle. No charge for children under 17 in parents' room. Extra adults, $10. Country buffet breakfast, $7.50; alc lunch, $6.50–9.50; alc dinner, $13.25–17.75. Children's menu. Seasonal, special event packages.
Extras Crib. Dining room, public restrooms wheelchair accessible.

LEXINGTON

A city wealthy from the tobacco industry, Lexington is home to the University of Kentucky, Transylvania University, and many beautiful antebellum and Victorian buildings, a number of which are now open to the public as museums. But the real attraction here is thoroughbred horses. Head for the Kentucky Horse Park, for 1,000 acres of bluegrass, where you can learn everything you ever wanted to know (and more) about equines, then sign up for a tour of the area's best horse farms.

Lexington is located in central Kentucky, 101 miles south of Cincinnati, Ohio, and 78 miles east of Louisville.

Information please: A Federal-style mansion built in 1812, **The Brand House at Rose Hill** (461 North Limestone Street, 40508; 606–226–9464 or 800–366–4942) offers five guest rooms, each with double whirlpool tubs, at B&B double rates of $80–160, including a hearty yet creative full breakfast. Fully restored by Pam and Logan Leet as a B&B in 1995, this 4,000-square-foot mansion has a Greek Revival facade, while the interior combines historically accurate colors and fabrics with exceptional charm and the comfort of queen- and king-size beds and modern plumbing.

What is now the **Camberley Club Hotel at Gratz Park** (120 West Second Street, 40507; 606–231–1777 or 800–555–8000), was originally built as an office building in 1916, then restored as the Gratz Park Inn in 1987. The property changed hands several times from 1987 to 1997, undergoing various financial difficulties. It should now be headed for success under the ownership of the Camberley Hotel Company, which operates a half-dozen other luxury hotels in the U.S. and Canada, including the Camberley Brown Hotel in Louisville. This 44-room hotel, housed in a Georgian Revival–style building, has a lovely lobby and pleasant guest rooms with English antique reproduction furniture, and king- or queen-size pencil post or rice four-poster beds. The hotel restaurant has gathered excellent reviews for its fine cuisine and elegant atmosphere. B&B double rates range from $115–130, including a continental breakfast and evening turndown service with sherry.

For additional area entries, see **Georgetown, Paris** and **Versailles.**

True Inn
467 West Second Street, 40507

Tel: 606–252–6166
800–374–6151
Fax: 606–226–2179

In 1995, lifetime Lexington residents Beverly and Bobby True realized a 20-year dream and opened A True Inn. Built in the Greek Revival style in 1843, their house was remodeled as a Richardsonian Romanesque mansion in 1890, and is listed on the National Register of Historic

Places. Each guest room is named for a famous Lexingtonian, including the infamous Lexington madam, Belle Brezing. Rooms are furnished with antiques, handmade quilts and afghans. Breakfast, served 8–8:30 A.M. weekdays (earlier if necessary) and available at guests' pleasure on weekends, includes fresh fruit and juice, and a full breakfast buffet. Rates also include afternoon and evening refreshments.

"Convenient downtown location. The Trues are Lexington natives, offering genuine Southern hospitality. Cookies, brownies, and lemonade are always available; evening desserts are an occasional treat. The common areas are Victorian in style yet uncluttered, with some antiques, Oriental rugs on the fine hardwood floors, and the original carved mantels and crystal chandeliers. The generous breakfast is usually served at the dining room table, set with fresh flowers and candles, and includes such entrees as thick-cut French toast or pecan pancakes, along with sausage or bacon, an egg dish, and a sweet bread or Danish. The guest rooms are attractive and comfortable. Most luxurious is the Belle Brezing suite, with a lovely, extravagant bathroom, dusty rose fixtures, a double whirlpool tub in an alcove with a stained glass window, and two sinks set in an antique breakfront. The large bedroom has a lovely antique plantation bed, and a fainting couch in the tower area of the room. The John Breckinridge Room has a queen-size rice bed with two wing chairs, an armoire, and a dresser; the private bath for this room is across the hall. The John Hunt Morgan room has a dark green color scheme, a Lincoln bed, and Civil War paintings of the famous southern general. The shower pressure was fabulous, as were the thick, luxurious towels; the bed was comfortable, and I was able to get the rooms dark enough for sleeping in the morning." *(Susan W. Schwemm)*

Open All year.
Rooms 1 suite, 4 doubles—all with full private bath, telephone, clock, TV, air-conditioning. 4 with radio, desk. 1 with whirlpool tub.
Facilities Dining room, living room with fireplace, piano; family room with TV/VCR, books; sun room, verandas. ½ acre with formal gardens, off-street parking, lawn games. 1 block to health club. Golf, tennis nearby.
Location Historic downtown. From I-175/164, take Exit 113 (Paris-Lexington). Drive 2.5 m toward Lexington on N. Broadway. Go right on W 2nd St. to #467 on right. Turn in before brick/iron front wall to off-street parking near the carriage house. Walking distance to Opera House, Rupp Arena, convention hotels.
Restrictions No smoking. Children over 12.
Credit cards Amex, DC, MC, Visa.
Rates B&B, $125 suite, $85–95 double. Extra person, $10.
Extras Free airport/station pick-ups.

LOUISVILLE

Louisville is known best for the Kentucky Derby (the most famous two minutes in sports), and as the state's cultural center year-round, with great jazz clubs, superb live theater, and several truly gracious residential areas where homes date from the 1870s. Louisville is located in the north central part of the state, on the Ohio River, across from Indiana.

Also recommended: Visitors to Louisville are fortunate to have their choice of two lovely, well-maintained, historic luxury hotels, **The Camberley Brown** (4th & Broadway, 40202; 502–583–1234 or 800–555–8000), and **The Seelbach** (500 4th Avenue, 40202; 502–585–3200 or 800–333–3399), each with approximately 300 guest rooms. Although regular double rates at both are in the $140–190 range, ask about weekend packages and promotional rates to AAA members. Comments welcome.

Aleksander House B&B ¢ *Tel:* 502–637–4985
1213 South First Street, 40203 *Fax:* 502–635–1398

Who says you can't have your cake (or croissant) and eat it too? At the Aleksander House, a gracious 1882 Victorian Italianate home restored as a B&B in 1996 by Nancy Hinchliff, you can have all the comforts of home, the elegance of a lovely inn, and the conveniences needed for business travel. Breakfast is served between 7 and 10 A.M., at guests' choice of large or individual tables; the menu varies daily, but might consist of orange juice, oven-baked mushroom omelets with an herbed cheese sauce, bacon, almond croissants, and blueberry bread pudding; or cranberry-orange frappe, baked pears, Grand Marnier French toast with orange butter, and ham.

The decor combines the original light fixtures, fireplaces, hardwood floors, moldings, stained glass windows, and woodwork with period furnishings. The living and dining rooms have a blue and white color scheme with Oriental rugs, while the guest rooms have a pleasing blend of antiques and contemporary pieces. Roxanne's Room is bright and cheerful, with soft yellow walls, white wicker furnishings, and a floral goose-down comforter on the king-size bed, while Katharine's Room is done in dark red and white, with a queen-size four poster bed.

"Convenient to the city center, businesses, stores and theaters, with easy highway access. Parking was always available on the broad, well-lit street. Nancy's taste in art and books was impeccable; first-rate service and housekeeping. Breakfasts excellent in presentation, quantity, and quality." *(Norrie Wake)* "Nancy's warm welcome is followed by wonderful tea and pastries. Beautifully furnished rooms." *(Edward Bryant)* "Coffee, tea, and delicious goodies were left out for us each evening; beautiful music played softly in the background. Enjoyed chatting with Nancy." *(Dan & Nancy Reedy)*

Open All year.
Rooms 1 suite, 3 doubles—2 with private shower and/or tub, 2 with maximum of 4 people sharing bath. All with telephone, clock, TV, desk, air-conditioning, ceiling fan. 2 with fireplace, VCR; 1 with refrigerator.
Facilities Dining room, living room; both with stereo, fireplace, books. Guest refrigerator, deck. Off-street & on-street parking.
Location Take I-65 S to St. Catherine Exit (W). Turn left on 1st St., to inn on right, just past Oak St.
Restrictions No smoking. Children 10 and over.

Credit cards MC, Visa.
Rates B&B, $95–119 suite, $65–85 double. Extra person, $15. Corporate, midweek, weekly rates.
Extras Airport/station pickup, $10. Spanish; limited German, French spoken.

Inn at the Park ¢
1332 South Fourth Street, 40208
Tel: 502–637–6930
800–700–PARK
Fax: 502–637–2796
E-mail: InnatPark@aol.com

In 1886, Russell Houston, president of the L & N Railroad, built a 7,400-square-foot mansion in the massive Richardsonian Romanesque style, with blocks of roughly squared stonework, rounded arches, stone balconies, and more. The interior is equally lavish, with a striking mahogany staircase, rich hardwood floors, 12-foot ceilings, marble fireplaces, and crown moldings. The inn was bought by Sandy and John Mullins in 1995.

The rooms are furnished in period antiques and reproductions. Breakfast is served between 7:30–9:30 weekdays, 8:00–10:00 weekends, and includes freshly baked muffins, croissants, and breads, fresh fruit and juice, coffee and tea, and such entrees as banana-walnut pancakes with maple syrup and bacon, omelets with grilled ham and whole wheat toast, or vanilla yogurt with granola and honey.

"Appealing neighborhood, including the beautiful park with its summer Shakespeare festival and walking tour of Old Louisville, plus convenient access to downtown. The innkeepers love to direct you to local sights and restaurants. The atmosphere is comfortable, casual, and inviting. Delicious coffee is ready for early risers, and Sandy offers a choice of entrees, usually an egg-based dish and waffles or pancakes; plates are garnished with fresh flowers and herbs from her garden. Each room has its own personality and charm, all are very clean, well-lit, beautifully decorated and private. Sandy and John are friendly, outgoing people who truly enjoy being innkeepers. They respect your privacy, but love to share their stories and hear yours." *(Mary Kasik)* "The amenities of a hotel with the ambiance of home. Sandy is helpful, accessible, and friendly." *(FO)* "A gorgeous home in a charming historic neighborhood with an elegant grand stair-case, working fireplaces in every almost room and warm, gracious hospitality." *(Marianna Adams)* "The romantic Parkview Room has a king-size four-poster bed, fireplace, private balcony, and whirlpool tub with a view of the park." *(Pamela Goff)* "Beautifully decorated for Christmas. Delicious omelet with Crimini mushrooms and smoked cheddar cheese; innkeepers accommodating about breakfast times and menus. Well-stocked butler's pantry if you're thirsty or would like a snack." *(Susan Schwemm)* "Elegant, yet comfortable accommodations; well-prepared food, beautifully presented; but best of all is the hospitality and warmth of innkeeper Sandy Mullins." *(Wanda Tate)*

Open All year.
Rooms 3 suites, 4 doubles—all with private bath and/or shower, telephone, radio, clock, TV, air conditioning. Some with ceiling fan, fireplace, desk, dou-

ble whirlpool tub, balcony. 2 suites in adjacent carriage house with double whirlpool tub, dining room, living room with wet bar, kitchen.
Facilities Dining room, living room, meeting rooms; guest pantry; porch; fax, copy service. Off- & on-street parking. Park adjacent for tennis.
Location Historic district, 5–10 min. of downtown, U. of Louisville, Churchill Downs. From I-65, take Exit 135 A & go W (right) on W. St. Catherine St. 4 blocks. Turn S (left) on 4th St. & go 3 blocks to inn at corner of Park & 4th.
Restrictions No smoking. No children.
Credit cards Amex, MC, Visa.
Rates B&B, $79–149.
Extras German spoken.

Old Louisville Inn ¢

1359 South Third Street, 40208
Tel: 502–635–1574
Fax: 502–637–5892
Email: oldlouinn@aol.com

Most people spend 20 years in the corporate world before finding an avocation in innkeeping; Marianne Lesher found her calling a lot sooner. After graduating from college, she set out to explore the U.S. Coming back home to Louisville in 1990, she became the managing partner of Louisville's first bed and breakfast inn, built in 1901 in the Second Empire Beaux Arts style.

"The spacious Celebration Suite on the third floor is prettily furnished with period pieces, with a king-size bed, and Jacuzzi tub in the bathroom. Coffee and tea are set out in the afternoon with freshly baked cookies. At our request, breakfast was brought to our room, and included waffles one day, French toast another, with breakfast breads, juice, yogurt and fruit, and vanilla-flavored coffee. Marianne was helpful, recommended good restaurants, called for reservations, talked when it was clear we were ready for a chat, but didn't intrude when we wanted to be alone. Her terrific cat took a shine to us, and visited through an open window; a real plus." *(Robert Freidus)*

"Iron gates open to a marble alcove just outside the heavy front doors. Inside is a massive entry hall that leads to the wide carpeted staircase. The huge original globe chandeliers are still in place in the hall and the living room. Both rooms also have modern ceiling mythological murals, featuring voluptuous nudes. The dining room has an elaborately carved built-in sideboard; guests sit at individual tables. Room #3 has a four-poster queen-size bed and large bow windows fronting the street. The moss green walls have cornice paper trim, and the enormous original bathroom has marble walls, a deep soaker tub, and a pedestal sink with an Ionic column base." *(SHW)*

"Excellent location in a residential area close to downtown, on a beautiful tree-lined street with stunning architecture. Restaurants, the theater, and Shakespeare in the Park are all within walking distance." *(Arthur Edwards)* "Breakfast, served in the dining room from 7:30 to 10:30 a.m., included granola, yogurt, melon, great popovers and fruit-filled muffins, plus freshly squeezed juice and unlimited coffee and tea." *(Minnie Miller)*

Open All year.
Rooms 3 suites, 7 doubles—all with private bath and/or shower, radio, desk, air-conditioning. 3 with double whirlpool tub.
Facilities Dining room, living room with stereo, game room with TV/VCR, videotape library, books; laundry, porch, exercise room. Courtyard, picnic area, off-street parking. Tennis, golf nearby.
Location Old Louisville. Downtown on 3rd between Ormsby & Magnolia.
Restrictions No smoking in breakfast room, kitchen. Light traffic noise in front rooms.
Credit cards MC, Visa.
Rates B&B, $125–195 suite, $75–95 double, $65–85 single. Extra person, $10. Children 12 & under free.
Extras Crib.

MAMMOTH CAVE

You've seen the bumper stickers for years, so you might as well accept the inevitable and plan a visit to one of "the seven wonders of the New World." In addition to the cave itself, with some 300 miles of cavern corridors, the park offers 80 miles of rugged woodland and 30 miles of river to explore. Bring a sweater even on the hottest day; the cave stays at a steady 54 year-round.

For an additional area inn, see **Glasgow.**

Also recommended: The contemporary brick **Mammoth Cave Hotel** (Mammoth Cave National Park, 42259–0027; 502–758–2225) overlooks a scenic ravine, near the cave entrance, and connects to the National Park Visitor Center by a bridge. Additional accommodations are located at the Sunset Point Motor Lodge and in a variety of cottages. Least expensive are the Woodland Cottages, set in the forest a short distance from the hotel. Double rates in the hotel are $70; the cottages are $50, with family rates available.

"Although the accommodations are ordinary (the rooms small and basic), the scenic location within the park, surrounded by greenery and many hiking and walking trails, is special. The dining room, while unpretentious, serves simple yet tasty Southern food. The place can be rather noisy and crowded during peak season, because of its proximity to the cave entrance. Delightful off season." *(DR)* "We were delighted with our Woodland Cottage, a spacious room with two double beds and private bath. It was a bit old-fashioned, but clean, comfortable, and more quiet and private than the hotel rooms." *(Elisabeth McLaughlin)*

Information please: Built originally in 1933 as the Mammoth Cave Souvenir Shop, **The Wayfarer B&B** (1240 Old Mammoth Cave Road, Cave City, 42127; 502–773–3366) sits at the park border, and offers five guest rooms, each with private bath. B&B double rates range from $65–85, and include a full Southern breakfast, complete with cheese grits, fried apples, and country ham.

MIDDLESBORO

The RidgeRunner ¢ *Tel:* 606–248–4299
208 Arthur Heights, 40965

Susan Richards opened The RidgeRunner, the first B&B in Bell County, in 1989, and is assisted by Irma Gall. A 20-room Victorian built in the 1890s, the house has a massive, 57-foot brick porch across its front, ornate wood paneling, and stained glass windows. The name is derived from the way the house "rides" the ridge overlooking the town, with views of the Cumberland Mountains. A short drive to the southeast is the Cumberland Gap National Historical Park, commemorating the famous Appalachian pass through which Daniel Boone and most of the early pioneers passed on their way west. Susan notes that the "infamous twin tunnels through the Cumberland Gap re-opened in 1996; also worth seeing is the restored P-38 fighter plane, retrieved from Iceland."

Breakfast favorites are pancakes with blueberry sauce, baked eggs with ham and cheese, scrambled eggs with sausage gravy and biscuits, or yogurt with fruit, bran muffins and juice. "We grow our own raspberries, blackberries, strawberries, and raise our own meat, milk, and eggs," reports Susan.

"Our spacious bedroom offered beautiful mountain views, and had an unusually large bathroom for a B&B. Sue and Irma were fascinating and gracious hosts who made us feel most comfortable. Delicious homemade jams were served with the elegant breakfast. Fascinating area tour led by Tom Sattuck." *(Kris & Bob Pearson)* "The innkeepers are not only pleasant and easy to talk to, but quite remarkable women. An enjoyable homestay B&B." *(Susan Woods)*

"Furnished throughout with antiques and memorabilia. Special touches include chocolates on the pillow with turndown service, toiletries in the bathroom, fresh flowers in the room, and fresh mint garnishing the lemonade served on the porch." *(Ann Schell)* "For dinner, we were directed to Ye Olde Tea and Coffee Shoppe, nearby in Cumberland Gap, Tennessee for a superb meal." *(Glenn Roehrig)*

Open All year.
Rooms 5 doubles—2 with private bath and/or shower, 3 with a maximum of 6 people sharing bath. All with radio, desk, fan.
Facilities Dining room, living room with piano, books; library, porch. Picnic area, off-street parking. Golf nearby. Cumberland Gap National Park, Pine Mountain State Park.
Location SE KY, near TN, VA border. 50 m N of Knoxville, TN. 2 m from center. Take Rte. 25 E to Cumberland Ave. & go right on 20th St. for 2 blocks. Turn left on Edgewood Rd and bear right up hill to Arthur Heights & go right to "T" intersection. Go left to 2nd house on left.
Restrictions No smoking. No children under 16.
Credit cards None accepted.
Rates B&B, $55 double, $50 single. Extra person, $15.

PARIS

Amelia's Field ¢ ✕ ♿ *Tel:* 606–987–5778
617 Cynthiana Road, 40361–8859

The perfect ending to a perfect meal is to sip a glass of port, gazing up into a star-studded sky, then retire to a comfortable guest room, without a concern for the drive home. And that's just what you can do at Amelia's Field, a delightful country inn and restaurant owned by Joe Clay and Mark May. These two sons of Kentucky traveled widely in the U.S. and Europe before returning home to restore this handsome red brick 1936 Colonial Revival home, named for Joe's favorite aunt, Amelia Field Clay. Joe is a descendant of Senator Henry Clay, a historic Kentucky family, and Clay family heirlooms decorate some of the rooms. Mark is a trained chef; he studied under chefs in southern France, and owned his own restaurant in New York City. Rates include breakfast with freshly laid brown eggs from the inn's own chickens, with Mark's French country bread.

The Maple Suite is decorated in blue and white, with a bird's eye maple canopy bed and a working Edison gramophone, while the Shaker Bedroom has high maple twin beds with peach patchwork quilts, and woven rag rugs on the hardwood floor. The Georgian Room is done in bright green and soft yellow, with a brass double bed.

"Idyllic pastoral setting in the middle of a working farm; sheep roam the fields between the house and the country road to Cynthiana. We had a superlative meal with excellent presentation and fine service. The butternut squash soup was delectable, thick yet mild in taste, wonderful on a cold night. The delightful mesclun salad featured home-grown produce. The seared salmon entree lay atop braised red cabbage; its mustard glaze was perfect with the natural sweetness of the cabbage. The beef loin was perfectly cooked medium rare, and rested on vegetables with whipped potatoes. Dessert included a delicious walnut tart, cinnamon ice cream, and delicate pear sorbet with fresh raspberries. Well worth the trip for lunch or dinner alone." *(Susan Schwemm)*
Additional reports welcome.

Open All year. Restaurant open Thurs.–Sun.
Rooms 1 suite, 3 doubles—all with private bath and/or shower, air-conditioning. 1 with fireplace.
Facilities Restaurant/sitting room with fireplace, dining terrace. 46 acres with sheep farm, extensive gardens.
Location ½ hr. NE of Lexington. From Lexington, take U.S. 68 (Paris Pike) to Paris. Go left at bypass & go through 2 lights. Turn left onto U.S. 27 (Cynthiana Road). Go 2 to sign for inn on left; turn onto gravel rd.
Restrictions Smoking restricted.
Credit cards Amex, DC, MC, Visa.
Rates B&B, $100–110 suite, $65–85 double. Prix fixe lunch, $15; dinner, $30.
Extras Wheelchair access; 1 room specially equipped.

ROGERS

Information please: One hour southeast of Lexington and seven miles from Natural Bridge is **Cliffview Resort** (900 Cliffview Road, P.O. Box 65, 41365; 606–668–6550), set at the edge of a cliff overlooking the valley below. Two guest rooms are available in the main lodge, with additional accommodations in the five nearby cabins. B&B double rates are $80, with cabins from $125–150. Cliffview's 1,500 wooded acres offer cliffs, a natural arch, and a private lake, with ample opportunities for hiking, fishing, canoeing, or rock climbing. "This log lodge is furnished with modern pine furniture, with chairs of split logs, plus quilts and country touches. Both guest rooms have private entrances to the wraparound porch, complete with a hot tub." *(SHW)*

VERSAILLES

Versailles is located 12 miles west of Lexington, and 45 miles east of Louisville. In addition to Lexington area sights, local attractions and activities include thoroughbred racing at Keeneland, tours of the Labrot & Graham Distillery for fine Kentucky bourbon, the Bluegrass Scenic Railroad, plus stable tours, horseback riding, hiking, llama treks, canoeing, and antiquing.

Reader tip: "Locals call their town 'Vursales.'"

Information please: Built in 1911, the **Sills Inn** (270 Montgomery Avenue, Versailles 40383; 606–873–4478 or 800–526–9801) is a three-story Victorian-style home with five guest rooms furnished with antiques, private baths, telephone, and TV. Rates range from $60–130 and include a full breakfast and afternoon refreshments. Reports welcome.

Rose Hill Inn ¢ 🚸
233 Rose Hill

Tel: 606–873–5957
800–307–0460
E-mail: Rosehillbb@aol.com

Dating back to 1820 and later remodeled in Victorian Gothic style, the Rose Hill Inn was restored as a B&B in 1992 and purchased by Art and Sharon Amberg in 1996. During the Civil War, it may have been used as a hospital; the grounds were bivouac sites for both North and South. Breakfast, served 8:30–9:30 A.M. at guests' choice of the dining room table or a table for two, might include fresh fruit and juice, cranberry muffins, caramel apple French toast or potato pancakes, and bacon or ham.

"Sharon and her daughter Marianne were helpful in every way. This wonderfully restored old home has fourteen-foot ceilings, beautiful hardwood floors, stained glass windows, and working fireplaces, complemented by up-to-date plumbing and electrical systems, with firm mattresses on the queen-size beds." *(Nancy Nash)* "Careful attention to detail: fresh flowers in our room, homemade cookies, and pre-dinner hors d'oeuvres." *(Keith & Laura Elchert)* "Warm, inviting atmosphere, with logs crackling in the fireplaces, puzzles to work on, and plenty of snacks." *(Diane Finley)* "An old-fashioned cookie jar filled with treats, and coffee and hot tea available from morning to late night, plus lots of books and videotapes for the large-screen TV. Art and Sharon were available for pleasant conversation and directions to restaurants and area attractions. They made dinner reservations in advance, an important plus on race weekends. Peaceful location." *(Faye Jendrian)* "Spacious Miss Lucy's Room has a large bathroom with a marble Jacuzzi tub, and plenty of room for personal items near the double sinks." *(Robert Whitehead)* "Ideal mix of friendliness and respect for our privacy. Good area antiquing." *(Gigi Fried)* "Tasty evening hors d'oeuvres gave us a chance to meet the delightful innkeepers, who put a great deal of time and care into their B&B." *(Marilyn Coan)* "Our family loved the rustic charm of the little brick cottage, originally the summer kitchen, complete with colorful quilts on the four poster double bed and a swing on the private porch." *(MW)*

Open All year.
Rooms 1 cottage, 1 suite, 3 doubles—all with full private bath, telephone, clock/radio, TV, air-conditioning, ceiling fan. 4 with desk; 1 with double whirlpool tub. Cottage with kitchen, porch with swing.
Facilities Dining room, living room with TV/VCR, fireplace and books; library with fireplace; sitting room with guest refrigerator, microwave; porch with swing. 3 acres with grape arbor, patio, lawn games. Swimming, golf, park with jogging path, playground nearby. 10 min. to Keeneland Race Track.
Location Rose Hill Historic District, 1 block from downtown. From Lexington, take Rte. 60 W (Versailles Rd.) Follow business rte. to Main St. & go left. At 1st light, go right on Rose Hill (Rte. 62 W) to inn, 4th house on right.
Restrictions No smoking. BYOB. Children welcome in cottage.
Credit cards Amex, Discover, MC, Visa.
Rates B&B, $90–95 cottage, $125 suite, $89–109 double. Extra person, $10. Breakfast in bed, $10 extra.
Extras Airport pickup. Crib, babysitting. Pet OK in cottage with approval.

Tyrone Pike B&B ¢
3820 Tyrone Pike, 40383

Tel: 606–873–2408
800–736–7722
Fax: 606–873–2408
E-mail: tyronebb@uky.campus.mci.net

A handsome contemporary home built in 1992, the Tyrone Pike B&B has been owned by Tim and Jean Forman since 1995. Jean reports "We offer free tours of the horse farm where Derby winner Seattle Slew lives. Trackside Farm is next door, and we are allowed to take our guests there any time." Breakfast, served 8–9 A.M., can be enjoyed at the dining room table or an individual one, and includes such specialties as oatmeal soufflé; Jean is pleased to meet special dietary needs with advance notice.

"Peaceful farmland setting. Although now a full-time innkeeper, Jean is a registered nurse, and considers it her main goal to provide whatever her guests need in terms of tours, comfort, convenience, reservations, or anything else to ensure a pleasant stay. The atmosphere is warm, welcoming and accommodating. I was left alone when I wanted to be alone, and given attention when I felt like visiting. The marvelous breakfast entrees were different each day, and included a baked egg casserole with a choice of either maple syrup or marinara sauce; and a Belgian waffle heaped high with strawberries, blueberries, raspberries, and almonds. The efficiency suite at the back of the house has a private outside entrance through sliding glass patio doors, knotty pine paneling, a soothing beige color scheme, a queen-size canopy bed, a wonderful down duvet, a desk and chair, two overstuffed chairs, and a well-equipped, attractive efficiency kitchen. On arrival, a snack tray with fruit, cheese, crackers, and cookies was delivered to the room. The amenities basket was equipped with a full range of travel necessities. Equally private is the family suite, over the great room, with a sitting area with two wing chairs, a card table, games, and a TV, and two bedrooms—one with a brass queen-size bed, and another bedroom with two twin-size maple beds." *(Susan Schwemm)*

Open All year.
Rooms 2 suites, 2 doubles—all with private shower and/or tub, telephone, clock/radio, color TV, air-conditioning. 3 with desk; 1 with ceiling fan, fireplace, deck; 1 with private entrance, kitchenette.
Facilities Dining room, great room with TV/VCR, piano, games, books; guest refrigerator, deck. Live music some evenings. 5 acres. Fishing, canoeing nearby.
Location Halfway between Frankfort & Lexington. 3 m from downtown. From Lexington, go W on Hwy. 60 to Exit 5-B. Follow business rte. downtown. Go left at Courthouse. Go right on Rte. 62 (Rose Hill Ave.) at next light. Bear left on Tyrone Pike & go 3 m to New Hope Baptist Church on left & B&B on right.
Restrictions No smoking.
Credit cards MC, Visa.
Rates B&B, $125 suite (sleeps up to 5), $98 double, $89 single. 10% senior, student, Canadian discount.
Extras Airport pickup. Pets allowed. Portacrib.

Louisiana

Le Richelieu in the French Quarter, New Orleans

Everybody goes to New Orleans sooner or later, and although it's a big city, you can get a good taste of its delicious food, distinctive architecture, and famous jazz in just a few days' visit. Beyond New Orleans, the state offers a potpourri of cultures and landscapes. North of the city, across Lake Pontchartrain Causeway, horse farms and dense pine forests provide a peaceful contrast to New Orleans' famous excesses. To the south, scenic Route 90 leads to Houma, the heart of Cajun country. Rent a boat here to explore and fish in Louisiana's legendary bayous, swamps and marshes. Continue west on Route 90, then detour to Avery Island, the home of McIlhenny tabasco sauce. Up the road, visit the restored antebellum plantation homes in New Iberia.

Note: You'll frequently hear the words *Cajun* and *Creole* used in Louisiana. The former refers to the French settlers of Acadia (present-day Nova Scotia), who were expelled from Canada by the British in the 1750s and settled in Louisiana, which was then French territory. (The word *Cajun* is derived from the word *Acadian.)* The word *Creole,* on the other hand, describes the descendants of the early French and Spanish settlers of this region. Although time has produced some overlapping, their heritage and traditions are quite different.

ALEXANDRIA

Also recommended: An appealing choice 16 miles southeast of Alexandria is **Loyd Hall Plantation** (292 Loyd Bridge Road, Cheneyville 71325; 318–776–5641 or 800–240–8135), a 640-acre working plantation dating back to 1820, and owned by the Fitzgerald family since 1948. Tours of the 1820 Federal Georgian mansion are offered, while B&B accommodation is found in several restored outbuildings. B&B double rates of $95–135 include a refrigerator stocked with breakfast makings, wine and soft drinks on arrival, mansion tour, and use of the swimming pool. "Beulah Davis conducts the fascinating tours. Ask her to tell you about the ghosts, and what happened to the other 'L' in Loyd. Our suite in the converted Commissary was clean and decorated with antiques. It had a fully stocked kitchen with wine, an apple cobbler, and brownies, plus all the makings for breakfast the next morning. The many animals were a delight to watch." *(Joan O'Brien)* "Two suites are located in the restored carriage house, and another in the commissary. We stayed in the Acadian Cottage, built in 1970. Rustic and private, it has a living room with brick fireplace, TV/VCR, two bedrooms with antique double beds, full kitchen, and even a washer/dryer. Cozy and comfortable, we enjoyed being awakened by Mr. Rooster each morning." *(Sheri & Richard De Bro)*

EUNICE

In the heart of Cajun country, about 70 miles west of Baton Rouge and about 30 miles northwest of Lafayette is the town of Eunice, home of the 1920s-era Liberty Center and its delightful Saturday night radio show, "Rendez-Vous des Cajuns," and of the Prairie Acadian Cultural Center (a U.S. National Park Service project) next door. Modest area clubs are also home to great Cajun and Zydeco music, or ask your innkeeper for recommendations.

Reader tip: "Many local restaurants are closed on Mondays, so try to visit another night." *(Glenn Roehrig)* "Avoid visiting during the oppressive summer heat and humidity." *(Duane Roller)*

Also recommended: Frequent contributor *Duane Roller* wrote to comment on **Potier's Prairie Cajun Inn & Gifts** (110 West Park, 70535; 318–457–0440): "Originally the first hospital in Eunice. Our suite consisted of a large living room with handmade Cajun wood furniture and a TV, bathroom, bedroom, and a kitchen stocked with a selection of coffees and teas." And: "Our suite was bright, clean, and comfortable. An added attraction was the courtyard hot tub. For breakfast, we were given a basket with sweet cereals and pop tarts, plus juice, milk, and coffee in the refrigerator." *(Glenn Roehrig)* B&B double rates for the 10 suites are $60.

JACKSON

Information please: Right in town is **Milbank** (102 Bank Street, P.O. Box 1000, 70748; 504–634–5901), a classic antebellum home furnished with museum-quality antiques, including Mallard tester and hand-carved oak beds, huge old armoires, and more. There is no resident innkeeper, so single travelers may not feel comfortable if he or she is the only guest. B&B double rates are $75. Under the same ownership is the **Old Centenary Inn** (Charter Street, Highway 10, 70748; 504–634–5050), with eight guest rooms, furnished in antiques, each with a television, telephone, and Jacuzzi tub; B&B double rates are $85–95. "Built in 1935 from salvaged brick, columns, and windows of the defunct Cententary College. We enjoyed the Scarlet O'Hara room, with a king-size bed and a balcony overlooking the street. Gracious, helpful innkeeper prepared a tasty breakfast. Pleasant dinner at nearby Bears Corner restaurant." *(DM)*

LAFAYETTE

Located in south central Louisiana, Lafayette is the capital of Cajun country; many Acadians settled here after being driven out of Nova Scotia by the British in 1755. Of particular interest is Vermillionville, a re-creation of the original 18th-century Cajun and Creole village; the Live Oak Gardens, especially beautiful when both azaleas and tulips are in bloom; the Acadian village, a folk museum celebrating 19th-century Acadian life; nearby plantations, and a variety of celebrations and festivals year-round. Lafayette is 131 miles west of New Orleans.

Reader tip: "Great food at Prejean's Restaurant and Enola Prudhomeme's Cajun Cafe; enjoyed the food and zydeco music and dancing at Mulate's in Breaux Bridge." *(MW, also Emily Hoche-Mong)* "Visit Randol's in Lafayette and Robin's in Henderson for great food and music." *(TA)*

Also recommended: Seven miles north of Lafayette is **La Maison de Compagne** (825 Kidder Road, Carencro, 70520; 318–896–6529 or 800–895–0235), offering four guest rooms with private baths, plus a swimming pool, at B&B double rates of $90–110. "Decorated with magnificent Victorian antiques. Careful attention to detail. Each morning, we were greeted with fresh coffee, juice, tea and fresh muffins, which we enjoyed outdoors on rocking chairs on the balcony. At 9 A.M., breakfast was served in the dining room. Fresh baked breads, elegant seafood dishes, superb egg dishes, and wonderful fruit frappes kept us fueled all day." *(Michael Ledger)* "Excellent restaurant and sightseeing suggestions. At departure, we were given a jar of their own honey." *(Martha Banda)* "The delightful McLemores are knowledgeable about area history and attractions. Relaxing setting; spacious grounds with huge oak trees." *(Catherine Lyons)*

A one-story Queen Anne Revival cottage built in 1902, **Alida's** (2631 S.E. Evangeline Thruway, 70508; 318–264–1191 or 800–922–5867) has 12-foot ceilings and hand-hewn cypress casings and doors. "Our lovely room was furnished with an 1860 walnut queen-size bed with matching armoire and marble-topped dresser. Warm, friendly hosts, yet not overbearing. Delicious full breakfast." *(Jack Oehme)* Rates for the four guest rooms, all with private bath and air-conditioning, are $75–150 double.

For additional area inns, see **St. Martinville.**

Belle of the Oaks ¢
122 Le Medecin, Carencro, 70520

Tel: 318–896–4965
E-mail: belleoaks@aol.com

Once a plantation home surrounded by fields of sugar cane, corn, and cotton, Belle of the Oaks was built in 1900, and was restored as a B&B in 1993 by Maxine and Gordon Perkins. Although guests are welcome to relax in the parlor, which features Victorian antiques, a fourteen-foot ceiling, and a walk-out window, the inviting front porch will tempt most guests to sit and rock for a while. Breakfast, served on antique French china 7–10 A.M., includes fresh fruit and juice, plus pecan waffles with blueberry sauce and sausage, or pain perdu with raspberry sauce, and sausages.The Blue Room has a spacious sitting area and a king-size white iron bed, while the Green room has a cypress pencil post double bed, a green double wedding ring quilt, and inviting white wicker chairs.

"This stately plantation home sits magnificently on a landscaped lawn with beautiful old oak trees and flowers, and was carefully renovated to preserve the home's original style. The Blue Room is huge, comfortable, and breezy, with many windows. Sincere and extremely thoughtful owners. Great Southern breakfasts, and an inviting porch with soft breezes." *(Heather & Gerald Allen)* "Comfortable, welcoming atmosphere; wonderful stories told by the innkeepers. Beautiful antiques and handmade quilts; great breakfasts. Best of all are the quiet mornings, sipping coffee in a rocking chair on the gallery looking out at the oak trees." *(Jacque Passow)* "The gracious hosts enjoy visiting with their guests. Our breakfast favorite is the banana pecan pancakes, with nuts picked by the Perkins' grandchildren. We love to sit on the front porch with a glass of wine and a plate of cheese and crackers, socializing under the Louisiana stars." *(Laura Tibodeau)*

Open All year.
Rooms 3 doubles—all with private shower and/or bath, radio, clock, TV, air-conditioning, ceiling fan; 1 with desk.
Facilities Dining room, living room with coal-burning fireplaces, books; porch. 2½ acres with gardens, off-street parking. Boating, fishing nearby.
Location S central LA. 3 m N of Lafayette; 7 m to town center. From I-10, go N on I-49 to Exit 4, Carencro. Go right off exit, & left on Frontage Rd. to inn on right at corner of Le Medecin Rd.
Restrictions No smoking. Children over 12.
Credit cards MC, Visa.
Rates B&B, $85 double, $75 single. Extra person, $20. AAA discount.
Extras Airport/station pickups. French spoken.

Bois des Chenes ¢
338 North Sterling Street, 70501

Tel: 318–233–7816
Fax: 318–233–7816
E-mail: boisdchene@aol.com

Listed on the National Register of Historic Places, this Acadian-style plantation home has been restored to its original 1820 configuration, and is furnished with Louisiana French period antiques, highlighted by Coerte and Marjorie Voorhies' collections of pottery, antiques, and textiles. Part of the Charles Mouton Plantation, the B&B is housed in an 1890 carriage house at the rear of the plantation house. Each guest room has a different antique decor: country Acadian, Louisiana Empire, and Victorian. Rates include breakfast, a welcome bottle of wine, and a plantation house tour. Readers highly recommend signing up for Coerte's boat tour of the Atchafalaya Swamp.

"Our Carriage House room had convenient parking, and was large, exceptionally clean, and attractively furnished, with lovely fresh towels in the bathroom. Marjorie's delicious breakfasts included pain perdu (French toast) with pecans, maple syrup, and boudin sausage the first day, and eggs, sausages, fruit, and biscuits cooked in a skillet with preserves, the next. Coerte joined the guests at the long table, and talked about the local history." *(Beryl & Alex Williams)* "From entertainment and restaurant recommendations, to lessons on the history and culture of the area, to the small, private Atchafalaya Swamp tour, Marjorie and Coerte looked after us well." *(Glenn Roehrig)* "We stayed in the Louisiana Suite, with a high, firm bed. We loved the two family dogs." *(Deborah Ross & Russ Hogan)* "Tons of towels for those multi-shower summer days." *(DS)* "Best of all was the Voorhies' kindness. They provided our toddler with a splendid antique brass child's bed, complete with teddy bear. After breakfast, we got a history and tour of the plantation house, and a slide show of the 'before' pictures." *(Barbara Mast James)*

Open All year. Closed Christmas Eve.
Rooms 3 suites, 3 doubles—all with private bath, radio, TV, air-conditioning, fan, refrigerator. 1 with fireplace. 1 in carriage house.
Facilities Breakfast room, solarium, porch. 2 acres with patio, aviary. Atchafalaya Swamp expeditions.
Location Historic district. From I-10 take exit 103A S to Evangeline Thruway. Go 3 lights to Mudd Ave. Turn left and go 3 blocks to intersection with N Sterling. Inn is on SE corner. Continue on Mudd past inn and enter circular driveway on right at "35 MPH" sign.
Restrictions No smoking.
Credit cards Amex, MC, Visa.
Rates B&B, $115–165 suite, $95 double, $85 single. Extra person, $30. Children under 5 free in parents' room. Crib, $10. 10% senior, AAA discount.
Extras Wheelchair access. Airport/station pickups. Pets by prior arrangement. Crib, babysitting. French spoken.

LAFITTE

Victoria Inn ¢
Highway 45, Box 545 B, 70067

Tel: 504–689–4757
800–689–4797
Fax: 504–689–3399

A visit to Louisiana is more than a trip to New Orleans and a bus tour to a famous plantation. You don't have to go far to experience Cajun life in a Cajun community, where a majority of the people still make their living from fishing and trapping, and weekends are filled with

Cajun music and dance at a local "Fais Do Do." That's the appeal of the Victoria Inn in Lafitte, whose inhabitants are descendants of the pirate Jean Lafitte. This West-Indies style cottage was built in 1884 and was restored as a B&B in 1993 by Roy and Dale Ross. Guest rooms are named after flowers from the garden, and are decorated with antiques. Guests are welcomed with refreshments on arrival and are offered such breakfast choices as pecan waffles and bacon, or a crabmeat omelet; early morning coffee is ready at 6 A.M.

"Tranquil setting; beautiful grounds, filled with flowers and wildlife. The innkeepers made every effort to ensure that we'd feel at home and comfortable. Scrumptious breakfasts. New Orleans is an easy drive if you want to spend the day in the city and retreat to the inn at night." *(Joe & Ann Arena)* "The Rosses care about their guests, yet respect their privacy. Perfect setting for strolling, with a barn full of horses and other animals, and a dock where you can sit and listen to the lapping water. The immaculate Magnolia Suite was furnished with antiques, the quiet broken only by the many area birds." *(Mary Oliveira)*

Open All year.
Rooms 3 suites, 4 doubles—all with private bath and/or shower, clock, TV, air-conditioning, fan. Some with porch.
Facilities Dining room, books, veranda. 6 acres with off-street parking, gardens, lakefront, covered dock, pier for swimming, boating, water skiing, fishing, bird-watching. Swamp tours, fishing charters, Jean Lafitte National Historic Park nearby.
Location S LA. 30 m S of New Orleans. 5 m to town. On Bayou Barataria. From Westbank Expressway, take Barataria Blvd. (LA 45) S to LA 3134 & bear left. Road reconnects with LA 45 at blinking light. Continue S on 45 to bridge across bayou. Continue S 7¼ m until road crosses Goose Bayou, then watch for road for B&B on left.
Restrictions No smoking.
Credit cards Amex, MC, Visa.
Rates B&B, $100–170 suite, $85 double. Extra person, $15. No charge for children under 6.

LIVONIA

Information please: About 20 miles northwest of Baton Rouge, in the little town of Livonia, is one of Louisiana's best eating places. Joe's Restaurant at the Dreyfus Store is known for its shrimp, crawfish, and catfish dishes served etouffee, with remoulade, or in gumbo dishes; most entrees are under $15. Owners Joe and Diane Major also own the **Dreyfus House** (2741 Maringouin Road West, Highway 77 South, 70755; 504–637–2094) next door, so you don't have to worry about driving after a wonderful dinner. This 1850 Louisiana cottage offers rooms decorated with antiques, with B&B double rates of $55–80.

NAPOLEONVILLE

Also recommended: Certainly a visit to Lousiana isn't complete without spending a night on a plantation, but an equally authentic experience is a night in a trapper's swamp cabin. About 15 miles south of Napoleonville is James and Betty Provost's **Wildlife Gardens** (5306 North Bayou Black Drive, U.S. Rte. 90, Gibson 70356; 504–575–3676) located in a natural cypress swamp. The $70 double rate includes a full breakfast; the swamp tour is an additional $8 for adults; children are most welcome. "While a stay here is exciting (a little like staying at the zoo after closing time), we felt safe and comfortable. It is a short walk over well maintained paths to each of the widely spaced cabins. Each clean, simple unit is about 15' by 15,' with a full bath and air-conditioning. Covered front porches overlook the swamp setting; the cabins stand on piers over the water. The porch is a great place to sit and enjoy the beauty, sounds and solitude of the swamp. Guests are given animal food which they are encouraged to feed the small alligators, loggerhead turtles, and the fish which inhabit the swamp area around each cabin. Peafowl, emus, swans, nutria, otters, bobcats and other animals are found in other areas of the large property. Don't miss the two-hour guided walking tour of the property and its many animal and plant inhabitants." *(T. Galt)*

For an additional area entry, see **Vacherie.**

Madewood Plantation House
4250 Highway 308, 70390

Tel: 504–369–7151
800–375–7151
Fax: 504–369–9848

A 21-room Greek Revival mansion, Madewood was designed in 1846 and is a National Historic Landmark. The white-painted mansion has six imposing Ionic columns and was built from bricks produced in the plantation's kiln and from cypress grown on its lands. Madewood was purchased in 1964 by Mr. and Mrs. Harold Marshall and is now owned by their son Keith and his wife Millie. Keith and Millie work in New Orleans during the week, spending many long weekends at Madewood; Janet Ledet is house manager. Rooms are furnished with an extensive collection of antiques, including canopy or half-tester beds, marble fireplace mantels, hand-carved woodwork, and fanned windows. Millie notes that "Madewood is not sophisticated or luxurious, but is a large country mansion. Our food is country cooking, not gourmet; some northerners don't realize that smothered green beans are supposed to be cooked to death." Guest rooms are located in the mansion, an 1820s Greek Revival cottage, and a three-room cabin with more casual country furnishings. Rates include wine and cheese, family-style dinner with wine, coffee and brandy in the parlor, and full breakfast in the dining room. "Probably the most authentic plantation that we have visited; we felt that the experience of staying there was very realistic. Impressive home, with towering Greek Revival columns. The atmosphere of grandeur is echoed by the vast public rooms with their large doorways, high ceilings, and fine Waterford crystal chandeliers. The friendly, efficient staff looked after us well. Our second floor room opened onto the large front balcony, and was pleasantly furnished with antiques. Enjoyable breakfast of eggs, sausage, grits, biscuits, apple sauce, preserves, orange juice, and coffee." *(Beryl & Alex Williams)*

"Beautiful, yet comfortable mansion. We met the other guests over wine and cheese and then went into the perfectly appointed dining room for a fine dinner. The intimate atmosphere gave one the feeling of being an honored guest at a gathering of old friends. The staff cheerfully provided the recipes for my favorite dishes. I loved hearing about my own room during the informative guided tour." *(Rosemary Combs)* "We liked having the run of the house during the hours it was closed to tours." *(Glenn Roehrig)*

Open All year. Closed Thanksgiving, Dec. 24, 25, 31, Jan. 1.
Rooms 1 cottage, 2 suites, 6 doubles with private bath and/or shower, air-conditioning. 3 rooms in annex; 1 2-bedroom cottage. Some with desk, radio, fireplace, refrigerator, balcony.
Facilities Double parlors, dining room, library, music room, verandas. 20 acres with patio, live oaks, bayou. Swamp tours nearby.
Location SE LA. Sugarcane country. 75 m W of New Orleans, 45 m S of Baton Rouge. On Bayou Lafourche, facing LA Hwy. 308. 4 m from town.
Restrictions No smoking. Because of tours, a 5 p.m. check-in and a 10 a.m. check-out is sometimes requested for rooms in the main house.
Credit cards Amex, Discover, MC, Visa.
Rates MAP, $185 double, $150 single. Extra person, $40–50. Reduced rate for small children.
Extras Playpen.

NEW IBERIA

New Iberia is about 20 miles southeast of Lafayette and 10 miles southeast of St. Martinville.

Reader tip: "Be sure to visit nearby Avery Island, home of the McIlhenny Company, manufacturer of Tabasco Sauce, and Jungle Gardens, home to the Bird City sanctuary for nesting herons and egrets." *(Emily Hoche-Mong)*

Information please: Across the street from the famous Shadows-on-the-Teche plantation is **Le Rosier** (314 East Main Street, P.O. Box 11707, New Iberia 70560; 318–367–5306), an elegant restaurant with a romantic B&B. The four guest rooms in this reproduction Acadian raised cottage are furnished with antiques and reproductions, private bath, telephone and TV; the $100 double rate includes a full breakfast. Dinner might include such creative Creole delights as crawfish spring rolls with ginger; duck breast with wild rice and sweet potato hay; and pecan tart with Bourbon whipped cream. Reports appreciated.

NEW ORLEANS

Cognoscenti inform us that the city under discussion here is called *Nu-Aw'luns,* never *New Or-leens'*.

The French Quarter is roughly rectangular in shape, bordered by Canal Street to the west, Rampart Street to the north, Esplanade to the east, and the river to the south. Canal Street forms a border between the French Quarter and the financial district; the big chain hotels—the Sheraton, Marriott, Westin, etc., are all in the area around Canal. Bourbon and Royal Streets run east/west, and can be very noisy in the central section of the quarter; the quietest section is the beautiful residential area to the east, just north of the French Market.

Rates may double and triple during Mardi Gras, Sugar Bowl, Super Bowl, Jazz Festival, and other peak festival times; be prepared to pay *in advance.* Bargain summer rates are generally available from June through September, so ask for details when phoning. Parking can be a problem; if traveling by car, be sure to ask for specifics when reserving your room. A few hotels provide on-site parking; most have arrangements with nearby garages.

Many hotel rooms in the French Quarter tend to be small, with a bed and not much in the way of easy chairs or usable desk space. Although most inns have attractive balconies and courtyards, few offer parlors or dining rooms for guests to gather inside. People come to New Orleans for many reasons, but peace and quiet are not usually among them. It is a noisy city, and light sleepers should stay away from rooms in the commercial sector of the French quarter. Visitors should also be alert to the problem of street crime, a real problem in some areas; ask your innkeeper for advice.

Reader tips: "Be sure to allow plenty of time for just hanging out in front of the Cathedral in Jackson Square, where music is always playing and there's always something going on." *(RSS)* "We enjoyed a delightful afternoon tea at the Windsor Court Hotel, complete with delicious sandwiches, scones, preserves, petits fours and fine tea, delightfully accompanied by harp music." *(Alex & Beryl Williams)* "Wonderful dinner at the Commander's Place included a divine bread pudding soufflé." *(Lynne Derry)* "Once a questionable area with many abandoned homes, the historic Lower Garden District is in transition, with some—but not all—homes beautifully restored. Request secure parking, and expect to encounter street people; caution is especially advisable at night." *(MW)*

"A great day trip from the city is to drive *slowly* down Route 23 to the Mouths of the Mississippi (properly called the Head of Passes). Driving down the levee, the river is on the left, tiny towns and great bays on your right. We stopped at Tom's in Buras for lunch, and returned for an equally delicious dinner of oysters, soft-shelled crabs, and more wonderful seafood. The conversation was as amazing as the food in this untouristed spot. At road's end, in Venice, we saw an amazing variety of bird life at the river's final delta." *(Emily Hoche-Mong)*

Also recommended—hotels: Enjoying a convenient but quiet location in the French Quarter, the **Hotel Provincial** (1024 Chartres Street, 70116; 504–581–4995 or 800–535–7922) is a 97-room hotel occupying several 19th-century buildings. The hotel has five landscaped interior courtyards and patios. The high-ceilinged guest rooms are decorated with Creole antiques, French furnishings, floral fabrics, and modern appointments. Double rates range from $145–225. "Good location with off-street parking. Lovely, accommodating staff; pleasant lobby; nice, small restaurant; delightful little courtyard swimming pool." *(B.J. Hensley, also Stephane Blanc)*

Small and elegant, with an uptown Garden District location, is the **Pontchartrain Hotel** (2031 St. Charles Avenue, 70140; 504–524–0581 or 800–777–6193). Guest room decor varies from library paneling and English antiques, to chintz and wall-to-wall carpeting. Rates for the 100 guest rooms range from $120–600. "Welcoming, helpful staff. Loved the bread pudding and muffins. A wonderful institution!" *(Peggy Kontak)* "Quiet area, pleasant staff; decor in my room a bit tired." *(CB)* "We were upgraded at no extra cost from a regular suite to the enormous Napoleon Suite, with beautiful antiques. Enjoyed the hidden lobby with fountain, and dinner in the Caribbean Room." *(Russ Stratton)*

In the too-big-but-still-wonderful category is the **Windsor Court Hotel** (300 Gravier Street, 70130; 504–523–6000 or 800–262–2662) with 315 suites and doubles (rates of $235–600 double). As the city's first and only 5-diamond hotel, *Alex & Beryl Williams* describe it as "a civilized haven of peace and quiet, with high standards of service and comfort. It boasts a fine collection of original oil paintings; it is worth staying there just to see them. We had a beautifully furnished junior suite with a small balcony. The restaurant is most attractive and the food is excellent." "Although on the list for refurbishing, our room was spacious, comfortable, and quiet amidst Sugar Bowl frenzy." *(SDB)*

Also recommended—inns: In the lower Garden district is the **Fairchild House** (1518 Prytania Street, 70130; 504–524–0154 or 800–256–8096), including an 1841 Greek Revival home and two adjacent guest houses. Each of the 14 guest rooms has a private bath, and the B&B double rate of $75–125 includes free parking, afternoon tea on request, wine and cheese on arrival, and a breakfast of fresh fruit and bread, coffee and tea. "Our comfortable room had effective air-conditioning and heating systems; the inn's small, fragrant garden is lovely for reading. Convenient location, about two blocks to the St. Charles streetcar and the antique shops of Magazine Street. Transitional neighborhood, but the inn seems to have good security systems in place." *(Emily Hoche-Mong)*

On the northeast edge of the French Quarter is **The Garlands** (1129 Rue St. Philip, 70116; 504–523–1372 or 800–523–1060), just a four-minute walk from Bourbon Street. Paula and Kermit Garland's 200-year old Creole cottages offer suites with queen-sized beds, air-conditioning, and fireplaces. The B&B double rate of $150–275 includes a full breakfast, welcoming lemonade, and off-street parking. "Elegant decor, warm hospitality, and great breakfasts of fruit, yogurt, and granola parfaits, followed by French toast, or claret poached pears with cheese and Canadian bacon soufflé. Lovely brick courtyard garden." *(Lucy Guillet-Boyden)*

In a residential section of the French Quarter is the **Hotel Villa Convento** (616 Ursulines Street, 70116; 504–522–1793), dating back to 1848. Although the rooms are rather small and the furnishings modest, most readers feel that these factors are well balanced by the reasonable rates, convenient location, and helpful, knowledgeable owners. "Clean and neat, pleasant atmosphere, ideal location." *(Michele Roedel)* "Great coffee, croissants, and guest conversation in the little breakfast courtyard." *(DS)* B&B double rates for the 24 guest rooms range from $89–225, including continental breakfast.

Popular with straights and gays alike for its reasonable rates, charming courtyard, and quiet location on the northern edge of the quarter near North Rampart Street, is the **New Orleans Guest House** (1118 Ursulines Street, 70116; 504–566–1177 or 800–562–1177), offering 14 guest rooms, each with private bath, telephone, and TV, at B&B double rate of $79–99, including free parking. "Charming rooms, furnished with antiques; fairly clean and comfortable. Delightful courtyard with lush gardens and a fountain where we enjoyed coffee and croissants each morning." *(DFK)*

Information please—reservation service: In operation since 1981, **Bed & Breakfast, Inc.** (1021 Moss Street, P.O. Box 52257, 70152; 504–488–4640 or 800–729–4640) offers reservations in a variety of historic homes in the New Orleans area from suites and intimate cottages to 19th century mansions. Each accommodation is personally reviewed on an annual basis by the staff of the reservation service.

Information please—French Quarter: We'd like more feedback on two of New Orleans' best-known inns, the **Hotel Maison de Ville** (727 Rue Toulouse, 70130; 504–561–5858 or 800–634–1600) and the **Soniat House** (1133 Chartres Street, 70116; 504–522–0570 or 800–544–8808). The Maison de Ville consists of eight buildings, including its well-known restaurant, The Bistro, and the Audubon Cottages, about a block and a half away. Rates, ranging from $195–250 double, $245–545 for the cottages, include a continental breakfast and afternoon cocktails.

The Soniat House is probably New Orleans' best-known B&B inn, and offers 25 lovely guest rooms, a peaceful setting, and a charming courtyard. B&B double rates range from $145–235, suites $235–565; a light continental breakfast is $7 per person, and valet parking, $14 daily; local telephone calls are extra. "Loved it! Our room had twin beds, two wing chairs and a lovely bathroom. The people at the front desk were so helpful." *(BJ Hensley)* "Beautiful flower-filled courtyard 'oasis,' firm beds with top-quality linens, great water pressure, and friendly staff, but would rather save my travel dollars for the great New Orleans restaurants." *(DC)*

If you'd like your own little apartment at the eastern edge of the quarter, try **The Lanaux House** (Esplanade Avenue at Chartres, 70152; 504–488–4640 or 800–729–4640), built in 1879, and opened as a B&B in 1989. Four suites are available, each with a private entrance, sitting room, queen-size bed, bathroom, and kitchenette. A self-serve breakfast is included in the $135–250 rates.

Also on Esplanade is **The Degas House** (2306 Esplanade Avenue, 70119; 504–821–5009 or 800–755–6730), built in 1852 and named for famed French Impressionist Edgar Degas, who lived and painted here during 1872-73 when visiting his brothers. Prints of his work are found throughout the inn. Each of the six guest rooms has a queen- or king-size rice four poster bed, private bath, telephone, and TV. The B&B double rates range from $100–200, including full breakfast of Creole scrambled eggs with cheese grits and home-baked muffins, or blueberry pancakes with hash browns.

An affordable small hotel is the **Chateau Hotel** (1001 Chartres Street, 70116; 504–524–9636) with 46 individually furnished guest rooms surrounding a courtyard with swimming pool and patio. The $100–145 rates include the morning paper, continental breakfast, and valet parking.

The **Maison Dupuy Hotel** (1001 Toulouse Street, 70112; 504–586–8000 or 800–535–9177) is comprised of seven restored French Quarter townhouses. Some rooms overlook the street, while others have French doors opening onto balconies overlooking the lushly planted courtyard and the swimming pool. The furnishings are reproduction French Provincial, and many of its 198 rooms are done in soft pink or aqua tones. "A charming hotel on the corner of Toulouse and Burgundy a few blocks from the French Quarter bustle. Beautiful central courtyard and swimming pool. Rooms are comfortable, and valet parking is provided." *(KM)* Rates for a double range from $210–250.

Information please—business district: An excellent choice in the heart of the central business district is the 226-room **Le Pavillon Hotel** (833 Poydras Street, 70140; 504–581–3111 or 800–535–9095), within a 10-minute walk of the French Quarter (not recommended at night). This elegantly appointed hotel has lovely rooms and good service, original artwork and antiques, marble floors, and a rooftop pool with a spectacular view. Suites range from $195–800; doubles from $110–260; rates include a bedtime snack of milk or cocoa with peanut butter and jelly sandwiches.

Information please—Garden District: Just half a block from the famous Commander's Palace restaurant is the century-old Queen Anne-style **Sully Mansion** (2631 Prytania Street, 70130; 504–891–0457). This B&B features the original stained glass windows, 12-foot ceilings with ornate medallions, 10-foot cypress doors, and heart-of-pine floors. B&B double rates for the seven guest rooms range from $95–195. "Lovely rooms, wonderful fresh breakfast croissants. Long-time owner Maralee Prigmore was very helpful with restaurant and sightseeing suggestions." *(Karen Roseman)*

For additional area inns, see **Lafitte** and **Slidell,** approximately 30 miles from New Orleans.

The Chimes Cottages ¢
1146 Constantinople Street, 70115

Tel: 504–899–2621
800–729–4640
Fax: 504–488–4639
E-mail: bedbreak@gnofn.org

A consistent reader favorite, the Chimes Cottages encircle the brick courtyard belonging to the 1876 Uptown home of innkeepers Jill and Charles Abbyad. In 1985, the Abbyads bought and restored two attached Victorian cottages, with gingerbread detailing and stained and leaded glass windows. Breakfast is served family-style in the dining room, and includes freshly squeezed orange juice, fresh fruit, muffins, rolls, and coffee; guests may opt to take a breakfast tray to their room.

"I would be amazed if anyone, anywhere, does more to make guests special than Charles and Jill. Breakfast conversation is a highlight; great fellow guests. Jill is a gifted decorator, and has created rooms which are beautiful and fun." *(David Evans)* "My room was large, well-lit, and comfortable, with a large clawfoot tub in the bathroom. Convenient and quiet." *(Pam Cook)* "Run with skill by Jill and Charles Abbyad, their children, Alexander and Yasmin, and their resident cats. The small courtyard serves as a gathering place for guests who help themselves to refreshments from the 'honor system' refrigerator. The Abbyads know everything about New Orleans." *(Penny Poirier)*

"Breakfast is hosted by Jill and/or Charles. They introduced the guests and encouraged the exchange of information and suggestions. Their insights made our plans easier, faster, better; they made objective suggestions for dining, tours and activities without imposing." *(Ri Regina)* "Unbeatable restaurant advice. Fresh gardenias from their bushes were placed by the bedside." *(Beth de Anda)* "Our appealing fireplace room had a comfortable queen-size bed and was accessed by a walk-through window in the courtyard. We appreciated the convenience of an in-room phone, and my husband loved having a cable TV with remote control. Jill was helpful and charming, and suggested we walk a few blocks to Copelands for some great crab cakes. Breakfast included just-baked croissants from a local bakery, with fresh fruit, breads, and cheeses." *(Lynne Derry)*

Open All year.
Rooms 2 cottages, 3 doubles—all with private bath and/or shower, telephone with data port, radio, TV, desk, air-conditioning, ceiling fan, refrigerator, coffee-maker. 2 with fireplace. Iron, hair dryer on request.
Facilities Dining room, courtyard with garden trellis, limited off-street parking.
Location Upper Garden district. 2 m from French Quarter; 3 blocks to St. Charles Streetcar. Take I-10 E to Business District which changes to Hwy. 90. Exit at St. Charles Ave. (last exit before Crescent City Connection bridge). Constantinople St. is located between Louisiana & Napoleon on river side of St. Charles.
Restrictions No smoking inside.
Credit cards None accepted.
Rates B&B, $65–125 suite, $50–90 double, 50–75 single. Extra person, $10. 2-3 night weekend minimum Oct.–May.
Extras Pets with approval. Playpen. French spoken.

Dauphine Orleans Hotel
415 Dauphine Street, 70112

Tel: 504–586–1800
800–521–7111
Fax: 504–586–1409
E-mail: dohfq@aol.com

The Dauphine Orleans offers the hospitable atmosphere of a small French Quarter hotel. Amenities include a welcome cocktail with hors d'oeuvres, continental breakfast, morning newspaper, turndown service, afternoon tea, and downtown transportation. Guest rooms were refurbished in 1994; most appealing are the courtyard suites, dating back to the early 1800s.

"Pleasant rooms decorated with period reproductions and custom hotel furnishings. Request one on the courtyard, or overlooking the swimming pool for a little more elbow room; upstairs rooms are quiet. In the sunny kitchen is a buffet breakfast of juice, cereals, fresh fruit, toast, English muffins, bagels, and sweet rolls." *(Stephanie Reeves)* "Neither glitzy nor old-fashioned. Quiet location, yet close to the action on Bourbon Street. Our favorite rooms are in the carriage house; they're spacious and just outside is a pleasant terrace with a small pond, flowers, and shrubbery. Breakfast is served in the main building; the serving ladies are always cheerful and keep the juice, coffee, fruit, cereals, and pastries well stocked. Friendly, well-trained, and hospitable staff who remember us on return visits." *(Frank Conlon)* "Friendly, efficient service from long-time staff members." *(Vernon Ashley)*

Open All year.
Rooms 7 suites, 104 doubles—all with private bath, telephone, radio, TV, desk, air-conditioning, safe, mini-bar. Some with balcony, whirlpool tubs. 18 courtyard rooms.
Facilities Breakfast room, library, bar/lounge, exercise room. Valet parking, swimming pool, hot tub.
Location French Quarter between Conti & St. Louis Sts. 1 block N of Bourbon St.
Restrictions Some non-smoking guest rooms. Street noise in front rooms.
Credit cards Most major cards.
Rates B&B, $165–350 suite, $149–259 double. Extra person, $15. Children under 17 free. Senior, AAA discount.
Extras Transportation (8 A.M.-8 P.M.) in French Quarter, business district. Pets by arrangement. Crib, babysitting. French, Italian, Spanish spoken.

Lafitte Guest House
1003 Bourbon Street, 70116

Tel: 504–581–2678
800–331–7971
Fax: 504–581–2678

Long owned by Dr. Robert Guyton, the Lafitte Guest House is managed by Bobby L'Hoste. Built in 1849, its rooms are furnished with 18th and 19th century antiques. Breakfast is served from 8–11 A.M.; in the evening, wine and hors d'oeuvres are usually served by Dr. Guyton.

"The owner and staff make you feel like you are good friends visiting their elegant mansion." *(Michelle & Bryan Eckert)* "Comfortable sitting areas on the veranda and in the courtyard. Great location, just far enough from the busy part of Bourbon Street to be quiet, yet within easy walking distance to all parts of the quarter." *(Lise Liepman)* "Clean and friendly. Appreciated being able to enjoy breakfast when and where we wished." *(Ali Franki)* "Extra clean bathroom with great water pressure in the shower." *(Daniella Pyle)* "We enjoyed the ghost stories, the other guests, and the wonderful lcoation." *(Mr. & Mrs. Thomas Schwarz)* "The staff really goes out of their way to be helfpul and friendly." *(Perry Bertram)* "Perfectly chilled wine and tasty hors d'oeuvres with true Southern hospitality." *(Nancy Davidson)* "Accolades to the helpful concierge, who always seemed to be on duty." *(Ruth Dunmire)*

"My initial telephone call was answered by a knowledgeable employee providing careful descriptions; confirmation followed promptly." *(Ernest Harmon)* "Rooms are spacious and beautifully furnished with antiques; the parlor is especially pleasant." *(Craig Brummer)* "Fourteen-foot ceilings, fireplaces with mantles, crystal chandeliers, armoires, and four-poster beds." *(David Cooley)* "Breakfast includes fresh fruit, choice of bakery-fresh croissant or Danish, juice, and beverage." *(Elaine Rogers)* "Great advice on which streets are safe to walk at night." *(Martha Ruddell)* "Antique botanicals and fashion prints, canopy beds, flower borders, marble-topped dressers, and flower arrangements all contribute to the atmosphere." *(Mary Webb)*

Open All year.
Rooms 2 suites, 12 doubles—all with private bath and/or shower, telephone, radio, desk, air-conditioning, TV. Many with balcony, fireplace, refrigerator.
Facilities Parlor with fireplace, courtyard, off-street parking (fee).
Location Residential section of French quarter, at corner of Bourbon & St. Philip.
Credit cards Amex, Discover, MC, Visa.
Restrictions Traffic noise in some rooms.
Rates B&B, $265–290 suite, $85–165 double. Extra person, $22; children under 5 free.
Extras Crib ($10), babysitting.

Le Richelieu in the French Quarter
1234 Chartres Street, 70116

Tel: 504–529–2492
800–535–9653
Fax: 504–524–8179

Several restored 19th-century buildings make up Le Richelieu. Longtime owner Frank Rochefort and manager Joanne Kirkpatrick make sure their staff "do their best for guests," which is probably why the hotel has such a high rate of both occupancy and returning guests. Another plus is its "self-service" parking lot, avoiding the inevitable inconvenience of valet parking. Refurbishing is a never-ending job at well-run hotels, and Joanne reports that "18 rooms were just redone with new drapes, coverlets, dust ruffles, and carpeting. Ceiling borders have been added to all rooms, and crown moldings to the suites that didn't have them."

"The front desk staff couldn't have been nicer, taking plenty of time to give directions, marking a handy map for us. Our top-floor room was under the eaves, with a great view of the city skyline. It was clean and tastefully decorated, with dark green walls and coordinating floral bedspreads and drapes. Silent ceiling fans enabled us to leave the windows open on a balmy spring night." *(NB)* "Enjoyed breakfast on the glassed-in porch." *(BJ Hensley)*

"Our spacious room overlooked the courtyard and swimming pool. It had ample room for a king-size bed, armoire for both the TV and drawers for clothing, easy chairs, and a workable desk. The furnishings are quality reproductions, with coordinating drapes, coverlets, and dust ruffles. The bed was firm and comfortable, the sheets soft. The bathroom was functional, with ample storage space and towels. We loved the quiet location, just a block or two from the French Market." *(SWS)* "Being able to drive right into their parking lot is a big plus at night." *(Mary & Sidney Flynn)* "Charming decor, excellent housekeeping, helpful staff." *(GR)*

Open All year.
Rooms 17 suites, 70 doubles—all with full private bath, telephone, radio, TV, desk, air-conditioning, ceiling fan, refrigerator, hair dryer, ironing board. Some with balcony. Irons on request.
Facilities Lobby, cafe, bar/lounge. Courtyard, swimming pool, free private self-park-and-lock lot. Room service. Tour tickets.
Location French Quarter. On Chartres St. in between Gov. Nicholls and Barracks Sts.
Credit cards Amex, DC, Discover, Enroute, Eurocard, JCB, MC, Visa.
Rates Room only, $160–475 suite, $95–150 double, $85–140 single. Extra person, $15. Packages available. Alc breakfast, $5–6; alc lunch or supper, $7–10.
Extras Limited wheelchair access. Elevator. Crib, babysitting. French, Spanish spoken.

The McKendrick-Breaux House ¢
1474 Magazine Street, 70130
Tel: 504–586–1700
Toll-free: 888–570–1700
Fax: 504–522–7138
E-mail: mckenbro@cmq.com

In 1865, Daniel McKendrick—a well-to-do plumber and a Scottish immigrant—built this red brick Greek Revival home in what is now one of the most comprehensive 19th century Greek Revival neighborhoods in the U.S. In 1994, Eddie and Lisa Breaux restored the home, along with an adjacent 1857 home, creating an inviting courtyard and patio between the two buildings. They were able to preserve the original plasterwork, woodwork, and flooring, furnishing the rooms with antiques and family collectibles. Bathrooms are spacious, with clawfoot tubs in the main house, and modern fixtures in the second building. Eddie and Lisa note that "despite its history, this is our home, where we live with our young son Aidan and our dog, Sobaka. We did the restoration work ourselves, with the help of family, friends, and local craftspeople, and we've filled the house with the work of local artists." Rates include a breakfast of fresh fruit, cereal, and pastries, served 8–10 A.M.

"Nice restoration of two old townhouses with comfortable rooms and reasonable prices. Friendly young innkeepers." *(Shirley Dittloff)* "Comfortable accommodations; exceptional hospitality." *(Fran Underwood)* "Well-appointed rooms with all modern conveniences. Clean, homey, yet elegant. Lisa and Eddie's recommendations were first rate." *(Amy Smith)* "Our favorite things: the fresh flowers, Lisa's homemade breads and muffins, soft fluffy towels, huge beds, efficient housekeepers, bath salts, peppermint patties, beautiful furnishings, the deck, insiders' advice on restaurants, music, art, and shopping, Eddie's laugh, endless cups of great coffee, the courtyard plantings, and the incredible intuition of our hosts. The only thing we didn't like was leaving." *(Jan & Steve Warner)* "Lisa and Eddie are informed and gracious hosts, making advance reservations and providing maps. The inn is convenient to the Garden District, the French Quarter, and the antiques district. The courtyard is a comfortable spot to mingle with the hosts and other guests." *(Kathy & Mark Swanson)* "Fascinating history; incredible restoration." *(Phyllis Beinstein)*

Open All year.
Rooms 5 doubles—all with full private bath, telephone, radio, clock, TV, air-conditioning. ceiling fan. Some with desk, balcony. 3 rooms in adjacent town house.
Facilities Dining/living double parlor with books, guest refrigerator, porches, courtyard with brick patio, garden. Off-street parking.
Location Historic Lower Garden District, 2 m from French Quarter. At intersection of Magazine and Race Sts., 4 blocks from St. Charles Ave., & 6 blocks from Pontchartrain Expressway. Close to bus, streetcar stops.
Restrictions No smoking. Children "handled on a case-by-case basis."
Credit cards Amex, MC, Visa.
Rates B&B, $70–130 double. Extra person, $15.
Extras Crib. Spanish spoken.

NEW ROADS

New Roads is a French Creole community dating from 1749, located across the Mississippi from St. Francisville; you can cross by ferry between the "English" and "French" sides. The town is located on the False River, a horseshoe lake created when the Mississippi River changed course.

Also recommended: A 1911 restored Victorian manor house, the **Garden Gate Manor** (204 Poydras Street, 70760; 504–638–3890 or 800–487–3890) has seven guest rooms, named for Louisiana flowers, with period antiques and goosefeather comforters. "Quiet setting, with birds chirping in the trees, beautiful camellias in bloom. Lovely English antiques with bold, colorful fabrics. Lovely Christmas decorations." *(Robbin Calhoun)* "Our room was beautifully decorated in floral prints and lush English fabrics; the bath had a double heart-shaped soaking tub. Breakfast consisted of freshly squeezed orange juice and wonderful French toast and sausage." *(Ri Regina)* B&B double rates for the seven guest rooms are $85–135.

An 1820 Creole plantation house, **Mon Reve** (9825 False River Road, 70760; 504–638–7848 or 800–324–2738) has a front gallery overlooking the False River. Constructed of cypress, old brick and bousillage (mud and moss), this B&B offers guests access to a pier across from the house. "Beautiful antebellum home with lovely decor; gracious hospitality and delicious Southern breakfasts." *(Mrs. Julian Taylor)* "Gorgeous water views; comfortable room with modern bath. Friendly, welcoming owner and cook." *(Sarah Hoffman)* Rates for this B&B start at $55.

SAINT FRANCISVILLE

Settled by the English, St. Francisville is in the heart of Plantation Country, an area much favored by Audubon when he worked in this area during the 1820s, living at Oakley Plantation. "St. Francisville is a truly lovely little town, with quiet streets set off the main highway. Listed on the National Register of Historic Places, the handsome restored historic buildings, lovely gardens, and antique shops make Royal Street well worth exploring. Make it your base to visit the area plantations (less commercial than those closer to New Orleans, two hours away); particular favorites are Rosedown (the showiest), Greenwood, Oakley, and Catalpa, the homiest. Also worth a visit are the lovely gardens at Afton Villa." *(SWS)*

St. Francisville is set on the Mississippi River, two hours north of New Orleans, 25 miles north of Baton Rouge and 60 miles south of Natchez, MS, via Highway 61.

Reader tips: "We had several Po-Boy lunches at Glory B's, and enjoyed dinner at The Cottage." *(Beryl Williams)* "We enjoyed lunch at the Magnolia Cafe, and dinner at Maggie's Restaurant at the Cottage Plantation." *(Ian & Irene Fisher)*

Also recommended: Self-proclaimed as "America's Most Haunted House," **The Myrtles** (Highway 61, P.O. Box 1100, 70775; 504–635–6277) dates back to 1796, and was enlarged in 1834 to create a showplace for lavish parties and balls. Louisiana specialities are served at lunch and dinner in the plantation restaurant. Guest rooms are located in a motel wing; B&B double rates of $95 include a full breakfast and a house tour. "During the tour, we enjoyed learning about plantation's history and all the wonderful ghost stories. A tasty breakfast of scrambled eggs, sausage, biscuits, grits, and fruit were served promptly at 8:30 A.M. in the restaurant." *(Sharon Bielski)* However: "We were disappointed in our motel-style room in the addition." *(SAS)*

Barrow House ¢ *Tel:* 504–635–4791
9779 Royal Street, P.O. Box 700, 70775-0700 *Fax:* 504–635–4769
E-mail: staff@topteninn.com

Built in the saltbox style in 1809 with a Greek Revival wing added in the 1850s, Barrow House is listed on the National Register of Historic Places. Owned by Shirley Dittloff since 1985, it is furnished in 1860s antiques. Across the street is the equally historic Printer's Cottage, dating from the late 1700s; its gazebo has a view of the Mississippi. Other cottage highlights include the 21 original 1840s Audubon bird prints in the sun room, and a growing collection of teddy bears. Dinners are served at 7 P.M. by advance reservation, and include an appetizer (chef's choice), shrimp salad with two sauces, and a choice of chicken stuffed with crawfish and vegetables, shrimp with mustard cream, filet mignon, or rack of lamb with Creole mustard glaze, plus dessert and coffee.

"Our charming room was furnished with antiques; the bathroom was spotless. The common areas are also decorated with lovely antiques. Shirley is delightful, personable, and knowledgeable about the area, including historic spots and wonderful restaurants. Her breakfasts are extraordinary, and she even arranged a special plantation tour for us." *(J. Scott Grisby)* "Our energetic hostess served a variety of breakfasts during our stay: quiche, muffins, and bread pudding with maple syrup, plus eggs with Hollandaise, cheese grits and sweet potatoes; our rooms were made up while we were at breakfast. Shirley is an imaginative cook, and we enjoyed a dinner of crawfish in phyllo, salad, chicken with crawfish and tarragon, and ice cream with praline sauce. The Printer's Cottage is exquisitely furnished and private; breakfast is served at the cottage rather than in the main house. We enjoyed strolling past the well preserved buildings in the historic district." *(Alex, Beryl & Jonathan Williams)*

"We relaxed with a glass of wine on the screened porch to the sound of the splashing fountain. Take a long walk before breakfast the next morning if you're planning to feast on Shirley's full breakfast—poached eggs with beans and rice or grits, accompanied by spicy sausage." *(SWS)* "Everything is provided, from sherry on an antique table, snacks in the refrigerator, and toiletries in the bathroom. Located on a lovely, safe, quiet street of beautiful historic homes." *(Jerome Klinkowitz)* "You can see where a Union cannonball entered and exited the roof of the Printer's Cottage." *(Cindy & Bob Cameron)*

Open All year. Closed Dec. 22–25.
Rooms 3 suites, 5 doubles—all with private bath and/or shower, TV, air-conditioning. 4 with desk, 2 with kitchen. 2 suites, 2 doubles at Printer's Cottage.
Facilities Dining room, living room, screened porch, sunroom. 1 acre with gazebo, camellia collection. Golf nearby.
Location In town, behind the courthouse.
Restrictions "Well-behaved children welcome." Porch conversation can be heard in downstairs guest room.
Credit cards MC, Visa.
Rates B&B, $130–150 suite, $85–105 double, $80 single. Extra person, $25. Full breakfast, $5 extra. Prix fixe dinner, $25–30, with 24 hrs. advance notice.
Extras Port-a-crib.

Butler Greenwood Plantation ¢ *Tel:* 504 635 6312
8345 U.S. Highway 61, 70775 *Fax:* 504–635–6370

In today's mobile society, it's hard to find a family where grandparents and grandchildren still live in the same town. In contrast, Anne Butler is the eighth generation of her family to own the Butler-Greenwood Plantation, established in 1796 and listed on the National Register of Historic Places. Tours of the plantation house, built in the early 1800s and embellished in the 1850s, are guided by knowledgeable family members. Although furnished throughout with antiques, a highlight is the area's finest original Victorian formal parlor.

When Anne took over the plantation in 1991, she restored several outbuildings and built several additional cottages to accommodate guests, combining historic charm, creativity, quiet, and privacy. The 19th century Cook's Cottage has a porch swing, a deck overlooking the pond, and a working fireplace, while the six-sided Gazebo House has three beautiful stained glass church windows and a king-size bed. The Pond House has a hammock on the gingerbread trimmed porch, and the

Treehouse has a three-level deck overlooking the ravine, king-size cypress four poster bed, and fireplace. Each has a kitchen stocked with continental breakfast makings—juice, fruit, cereal, and rolls.

"Beautiful setting among moss-draped live oaks. Owner Anne Butler is a local author. We stayed in the Old Kitchen, built in 1796, and closest to the main house. It had skylights, exposed beams, hand-made bricks, a double Jacuzzi tub, and was comfortable and well-equipped. Enjoyed the house tour, as well as one of Anne's books on area history." *(Ian & Irene Fisher)* "Wonderful privacy and intimacy. The lovely grounds have 200-year-old oaks and many flowers. Mrs. Butler is always hospitable, friendly, informative, and helpful. The Gazebo is our first choice because of the stained glass windows recovered from an old church in central Louisiana. When the sun rises the light coming through the stained glass gives you a feeling of complete serenity. You can sit on the porch, sipping coffee or iced tea, overlooking a pond filled with ducks, geese, and frogs. The Treehouse is our second most favorite, but all the cottages are clean, cool, quiet, and well-equipped." *(Jerome Chauvin)*

Open All year.
Rooms 6 1-2 bedroom cottages—all with full private bath, telephone, radio, lock, TV, desk, air-conditioning, fan, kitchen, coffee maker, porch/deck. 3 with double whirlpool tub, fireplace.
Facilities 55-acre grounds with swimming pool, 19th century formal garden, fishing pond, poolside pavilion, gift shop; 2,200 total acreage. Nature walks, bird-watching. Hiking nearby.
Location 2½ m N of St. Francisville via Hwy. 61.
Restrictions Smoking permitted in cottages. Well-behaved children welcome.
Credit cards America, MC, Visa.
Rates B&B, $90–110 cottage. Extra person, $10.
Extras Pets possible with prior approval. Limited French spoken.

Green Springs Bed & Breakfast ¢ 🚸 *Tel:* 504–635–4232
7463 Tunica Trace (Highway 66), 70775 800–457–4978
Fax: 504–635–3355

Built in 1991 by Madeline and Ivan Nevill, Green Springs was constructed in the Feliciana cottage style reminiscent of the early 1800s, on land that has been in Madeline's family for 200 years. Named for a natural spring in the glen near the house, rooms overlook oak, dogwood, and magnolia trees, a creek-bottom field of Bayou Sara and a 2,000-year-old Indian mound. Inside, the inn is comfortably decorated with handsome antiques and reproduction furnishings. In 1996, the Nevills moved three 1920s era shotgun houses onto their property, and renovated them extensively. The Larkspur House has a queen-size bed and Victorian decor; the Sunflower House has a king-size bed and double Jacuzzi tub, and is furnished in 1950s pieces, with pastel colors and Georgia O'Keefe abstract posters; and the Woodrose Cottage is done in primitives, with a forest-themed decor, including Audubon raccoon prints, and leopard-patterned comforter on the king-size iron pipe tester bed. The family-style breakfast includes coffee, fresh fruit, sausage, eggs, grits, and hot biscuits.

"Beautifully furnished, neither stiff or formal." *(Rebecca Gibson)* "Delicious eggs Benedict served in the charming dining room overlooking a meadow." *(Jackie Freeman)* "Extremely clean and comfortable. Mrs. Nevill is a gracious hostess who makes you feel right at home. Quiet, restful setting, excellent breakfast." *(Mr. & Mrs. Ronald Pope)*

Open All year.
Rooms 3 cottages, 3 doubles—all with private bath and/or shower, radio, clock, air-conditioning, fan. Cottages with Jacuzzi tub, wet bar/kitchenette. TV on request.
Facilities Dining room, family room with TV, porch with swing. 150 acres with hiking trails; Tunica Hill nature area. Bicycling, tennis, golf nearby.
Location From Baton Rouge, take I-110 N to US 61 N. 3 m N of St. Francisville, go left on LA 66 & go ¾ m to sign on left.
Restrictions No smoking.
Credit cards MC, Visa.
Rates B&B, $120–150 cottage, $95 double, $85 single. Extra person, $40. Family rate for 2 rooms, $125–150. Reduced rates for children.
Extras Crib.

ST. MARTINVILLE

Settled by Acadians in the mid-1700s, St. Martinville prospered with the arrival of aristocrats fleeing the French revolution. Immortalized in Longfellow's poem, "Evangeline," the town is where the parted Acadian lovers are said to have met; the centuries-old oak that marks the spot is allegedly the most photographed tree in America. Worth a visit are the Acadian House Museum in the Longfellow Evangeline State Commemorative Area, the St. Martin de Tours Catholic Church, and several other restored buildings and museums.

Reader tip: "This area has lots to offer—historic homes, Cajun food and music, swamp and bayou tours. Sidewalks in St. Martinsville are rolled up around 9:00 P.M. in summer; in July, a lot of Louisiana was on vacation, which meant closed restaurants." *(Christine Grillo)*

Information please: Built in the early 1800s as a hotel, **The Old Castillo Hotel/La Place d'Evangeline** (220 Evangeline Boulevard, P.O. Box 172, St. Martinville, 70582; 318–394–4010 or 800–621–3017) "is a small hotel set on the Bayou Teche, right at the Evangeline Oak. Built in the early 1800s as a hotel, the Castillo served as a Catholic girls' school until it was bought by Gerald and Peggy Hulin in 1987. We stayed in spacious Room #1, with a view of the bayou, antique furnishings, and a wood floor." *(RHM)* B&B double rates of $55–90 for the five guest rooms include a full breakfast. Favorites on the English/French dinner menu include such appetizers as alligator boulettes, popcorn shrimp, or seafood gumbo, and seasonal entrees such as crawfish etouffee, catfish, and broiled frogs' legs. One frequent contributor thought her room could have used a bit of refurbishing; reports appreciated.

Right on Highway 31 is the **Maison Bleue** (417 North Main Street, 70582; 318–394–1215), a Victorian country cottage. The guest rooms have private baths and entrances, with cable TV and a full breakfast. The B&B double rate is $75.

For additional area information, see **New Iberia.**

SHREVEPORT

Set in northwest Louisiana, near the Texas border, Shreveport owes its development to its location on the Old Texas Trail. In fact, the city is a mixture of both states, with many streets named after early Texas heroes. Sights of interest include the Louisiana Downs racetrack and the Louisiana Hayride in neighboring Bossier City, the famous paintings and sculptures of Russell and Remington at the Norton Art Gallery, and the American Rose Society Gardens, a stunning sight from April through November, plus numerous other gardens and historic places of interest. Most of Shreveport's B&Bs are on Fairfield Avenue, in the Highland Historic District.

Reader tip: "The best crawdads in the entire world are at Gerald & Dudley's on East 70th Street. The entire city was there relishing fresh oysters, seafood, and heaping platters of crayfish." *(Nancy Stead)*

Also recommended: A 1905 Victorian, **Twenty Four Thirty Nine Fairfield** (2439 Fairfield Avenue, 71104; 318–424–2424), has guest rooms richly furnished with vintage antiques and wallcoverings, down pillows and comforters, and Amish quilts. B&B double rates for the four guest rooms range from $85–125, and include a full buffet breakfast. "Every corner is filled with something wonderful: antiques, interesting knickknacks, personal photographs, and souvenirs. We appreciated the early morning coffee left outside our door; it was wonderful to sit in a swing on our private balcony, drinking coffee at sunrise in the cool fall air. The bedrooms are spotless, beautifully decorated, with whirlpool baths. Kind and accommodating staff." *(Nancy Sinclair)*

Information please: A 5,200 square-foot home built in 1903, the **Slattery House** (2401 Fairfield Avenue, 71104; 318–222–6577) was restored as a B&B in 1995. Furnished with antiques, each of the six guest rooms has a private bath, telephone, air-conditioning, and TV, and the B&B double rates of $85–165 include breakfasts of biscuits, bacon and sausage, scrambled eggs, cheese grits, Amish bread and muffins, plus mayhaw and muscadine jelly.

Fairfield Place — *Tel:* 318–222–0048
2221 Fairfield Avenue, 71104 — *Fax:* 318–226–0631

After doing extensive renovation and restoration work, Janie Lipscomb opened Fairfield Place in 1983, furnishing it with antiques, fine china and crystal, as well as books and paintings by Louisiana writers and artists. Rates include a full breakfast and afternoon tea.

"Convenient to good, downtown restaurants, the LSU Medical Center, and Louisiana Downs. Breakfast was delicious, with Cajun coffee, fresh fruit and juice, an unusual egg, spinach, and bacon casserole, marmalade muffins, fresh-baked French pastries, and strawberry butter. Janie is a perfect hostess and makes every guest feel right at home."

(Chris Mott) "Rooms are stocked with cold drinks and fruit, and are handsomely decorated." *(MS)* "Our room upstairs in the back was smallish, but impeccably appointed and spotless, with a wonderful European featherbed." *(John Blewer)* "Gracious, well maintained, tree-lined residential area. The downstairs suite is particularly lovely with golden stars upon the ceiling. Thoughtful amenities are the thick robes, private phone line, good collection of books and magazines." *(L. Stovall)* "The sumptuous breakfast is served in the wide center hall." *(Sarah Brown)*

Open All year.
Rooms 9 doubles with private bath and/or shower, telephone, radio, TV, desk, central air-conditioning, fan, refrigerator, hair dryer. 3 rooms in adjacent home.
Facilities Parlor, balcony, porch, courtyard. 1 acre with gardens. Boating, fishing, horse racing, casinos nearby.
Location NW LA, 319 m from New Orleans. Highland Historical Restoration district, 2 m from downtown. From I-20 W, exit at Fairfield, go left 8 blocks. From I-20 E, exit at Line Ave. S, go right on Jordan, left at Fairfield 6 blocks to inn.
Restrictions No smoking. No children under 12.
Credit cards Amex, MC, Visa.
Rates B&B, $112–250 double. Extra person, $14.

SLIDELL

Also recommended: Listed on the National Register of Historic Places, the **Salmen-Fritchie House** (127 Cleveland Avenue, 70458; 504–643–1405 or 800–235–4168) was built in 1895. Breakfast typically includes fresh fruit and juice, blueberry muffins, pecan waffles, and bacon. B&B double rates for the six guest accommodations range from $85–150. "Our first floor suite was large and lovely. The bedroom had creamy trim on powder blue walls and a comfortable bed. The adjoining sun room was idyllic, with rattan couches and soft floral pillows, lots of windows and live plants. Decor throughout this exceptionally lovely home includes genuine antiques and gorgeous hardwood floors. A superb inn in an unlikely area." *(Suzanne Carmichael)* "Sharon and Homer Fritchie are gracious, warm, inviting, and accommodating. Two excellent restaurants nearby." *(Sherri & Richard DeBro)* "Loved the charming privacy of the Carriage House." *(Carol Blodgett)*

VACHERIE

For an additional area entry, see **Napoleonville.**

Oak Alley Plantation
3645 Highway 18, 70090

Tel: 504–265–2151
800–44ALLEY
Fax: 504–265–7035
E-mail: oalley@aol.com

Two rows of majestic 250-year-old live oaks create a quarter-mile-long alley, leading to this 1839 Greek Revival mansion, a National Historic

Landmark. Rescued from decay and restored as a family home in 1925 by Andrew and Josephine Stewart, it has been owned and run as a B&B and restaurant since 1978 by Zeb Mayhew, Jr. Donna Cortez is the long-time manager. The mansion is open only for tours, and guests are accommodated in restored turn-of-the-century Creole cottages, once used by plantation workers. The comfortable, casual furnishings include four poster or brass double beds. Rates include a breakfast of fruit salad, two beignets, coffee or juice, served 8:30 A.M.–10 A.M. in the restaurant; a plantation breakfast of eggs, bacon or ham, grits, orange juice, toast costs extra. The lunch includes such local favorites as chicken and sausage jambalaya, shrimp creole, and crawfish etouffee, plus such desserts as bread pudding, pecan pie, and buttermilk pie.

"Magnificent grounds, peaceful and private once the tours end at five, and the busses depart. Our cottage was bright, neat, clean, and attractively furnished." *(B.J. Hensley)*

Open All year, closed Thanksgiving, Christmas, New Year's.
Rooms 5 1-2 bedroom cottages—all with private bath and/or shower, radio, clock, air-conditioning, ceiling fan, refrigerator. Most with screened porch/deck; 3 with kitchen.
Facilities Restaurant, gift shop.
Location 60 m W of New Orleans. Take I-10 W to Gramercy Exit #194. Cross Mississippi River. Go left 7 ½ m on Hwy 18 (River Road).
Restrictions No smoking. Children over 12.
Credit cards Amex, Discover, MC, Visa.
Rates B&B, $95–$125 double. Extra person, $15. Alc lunch, $7–13. Mansion tour extra. Full breakfast, $6.50.
Extras Some French spoken.

WHITE CASTLE

Reader tip: "Right at foot of the Sunshine Bridge is the Lafitte Landing Restaurant in Donaldsonville. Outstanding dinner, extensive menu." *(BJ Hensley)*

Information please: The largest plantation home in the south, and one of Louisiana's best-known, **Nottoway Plantation** (Mississippi River Road, P.O. Box 160, 70788; 504–545–2730) is a 50,000 square-foot Italianate and Greek Revival mansion, supported by 22 massive cypress columns, saved from Civil War destruction by a Union gunboat officer. Randolph Hall, the plantation's restaurant, serves Cajun cuisine at lunch and dinner. The $125–250 double rates include a welcoming glass of sherry; plantation tour; wake-up coffee, juice, and sweet potato muffins; and a full plantation breakfast. Nine rooms are in the mansion and its wings; four are in the Overseer's Cottage. Understanding that this a business, readers have been pleased with the mansion tour, and lunches or dinners in the Randolph Hall dining room, less so with the accommodations and breakfast room. Reports welcome.

Key to Abbreviations and Symbols

For complete information and explanations, please see the Introduction.

¢ Especially good value for overnight accommodation.
Families welcome. Most (but not all) have cribs, baby-sitting, games, play equipment, and reduced rates for children.
Meals served to public; reservations recommended or required.
Tennis court and swimming pool and/or lake on grounds. Golf usually on grounds or nearby.
Limited or full wheelchair access; call for details.
Rates: Range from least expensive room in low season to most expensive room in peak season.
Room only: No meals included; European Plan (EP).
B&B: Bed and breakfast; includes breakfast, sometimes afternoon/evening refreshment.
MAP: Modified American Plan; includes breakfast and dinner.
Full board: Three meals daily.
Alc lunch: A la carte lunch; average price of entree plus nonalcoholic drink, tax, tip.
Alc dinner: Average price of three-course dinner, including half bottle of house wine, tax, tip.
Prix fixe dinner: Three- to five-course set dinner, excluding wine, tax, tip unless otherwise noted.
Extras: Noted if available. Always confirm in advance. Pets are not permitted unless specified; if you are allergic, ask for details; *most innkeepers have pets.*

Mississippi

Monmouth Plantation, Natchez

Andrew Jackson was one of Mississippi's first heroes. After he defeated the Creek Indian nation and won the Battle of New Orleans, the state's capital was named for him. The Civil War played a major role in Mississippi's history; in addition to the famous siege of Vicksburg, innumerable battles took place across the state, leaving tremendous destruction in their wake.

Today history buffs visit Natchez and Vicksburg in search of antebellum ambience, while beach lovers head south to the Gulf Coast. Plan to spend some time (spring and fall are best) exploring the Natchez Trace Parkway, a 400-mile parkway administered by the National Parks Service. Extending from Natchez nearly to Nashville, Tennessee, it follows the historic trail (or trace) that was one of the region's most frequented roads at the beginning of the 1800s. For the only inn on the Trace, see **French Camp**. "An important wilderness road for over a century, deep cuts still mark the path followed by settlers on wagon, horse and foot. The parkway prides an opportunity to explore the history of the period while enjoying the quiet beauty of the countryside." *(Joe & Sheila Schmidt)*

Gulf Coast: Once known as the "American Riviera," then less favorably as the "Redneck Riviera," Mississippi's Gulf Coast is once again enjoying increased prosperity, fueled by legalized gambling at numerous dockside casinos. Those who want more from a vacation than a turn at the blackjack tables will enjoy beautiful historic homes, appealing antique shops, countless seafood restaurants, beautiful sugar-white sand beaches with warm, shallow waters, and such historic sites as Beauvoir in Biloxi, the restored home of Jefferson Davis, and a museum of the Confederacy; nature lovers can take ferries out to the barrier islands of the Gulf Islands National Seashore. Numerous golf courses, hunting, fishing and water sports are also available.

For area accommodations, see **Biloxi, Gulfport,** and **Pass Christian**.

For additional accommodations in historic private homes and inns, call **Lincoln, Ltd. B&B** (P.O. Box 3479, 2303 23rd Avenue, Meridian 39303; 601–482–5483), a reservation service operated by Barbara Lincoln Hall since 1983. If you're planning to spend some time exploring along the Gulf, pick up a copy of *Ramblin' and Gamblin' on the Mississippi Coast*, an informative guide written by longtime contributors Lynn Edge and Lynn Fullman ($10.50 including postage and handling; Seacoast Publishing, 110 Twelfth Street North, Birmingham, AL 35203, 205–250–8016).

Important note: If you're booking a room in an antebellum mansion that can also be visited by the public, remember that rooms on a tour will rarely be available for occupancy before 5 p.m., and must typically be vacated by 9 a.m. Rooms in adjacent buildings may not be quite as fancy, but have more liberal check-out policies. In addition, public rooms on the tour are usually kept locked.

BILOXI

For additional Gulf Coast accommodations, see **Gulfport** and **Pass Christian.**

Reader tip: "The flashing neon lights and tacky architecture of the nearby casinos stand in sharp contrast to the wonderful old homes lining the street facing the Gulf of Mexico." *(SC)*

Father Ryan House ♿
1196 Beach Boulevard, 39530

Tel: 601–435–1189
800–295–1189
Fax: 601–436–3063
E-mail: frrryan@datasync.com

Dating back to 1841, this B&B is named for Father Abram Ryan—known as the Poet Laureate of the Confederacy—who lived here for several years after the Civil War. Restored as a B&B in 1991 by Rosanne McKenney, this National Historic Landmark, built in 1841, is one of the oldest remaining structures on the Gulf Coast. Many of the antique furnishings are original to the house; most rooms have water views and queen-sized bed with down comforters and pillows. The inn's 60-foot porch looks over the road and white sand beach to the Mississippi Sound beyond. Breakfast is served from 8:00–9:30 A.M., and might include fresh fruit or a fruit crisp; cornbread, cinnamon bread, or perhaps biscuits; and such entrees as vegetable frittata, whole wheat pancakes, or perhaps scrambled eggs in puff pastry with sherry mushroom sauce.

"Charming inn with a fascinating Southern history and intriguing dormer windows, set in a row of wonderful older homes.Our room was lovely, comfortable and elegant. Some original letters written by Father Ryan were displayed under the glass top of a desk. Tasty Southern-style French toast served on an enclosed porch." *(Suzanne Carmichael)* Comments appreciated.

Open All year.
Rooms 3 suites, 8 doubles—all with full private bath, telephone with data port, radio, clock, TV, air-conditioning, ceiling fan, robes. Some with whirlpool tub, desk, fireplace, refrigerator, balcony. 2 suites in adjacent Beach House.
Facilities Dining room, breakfast porch, common area with library, porches. ¾ acre with swimming pool, lawn games, off-street parking. Across from beach for swimming, boating, fishing. Golf nearby.
Location Halfway between New Orleans, LA & Mobile, AL. From I-10, take Exit 46A to I-110. From I-110, take Gulfport-Keesler Exit. From off-ramp, go 6 blocks W to inn on right. 4 blocks W of lighthouse, 2 block E of Keesler Air Force Base. Historic district.
Restrictions No smoking. Children over 12 preferred.
Credit cards Amex, Discover, MC, Visa.
Rates B&B, $130–150 suite, $85–120 double, $70–105 single. Extra adult, $15; extra child under 12, $10. Tips appreciated.
Extras Wheelchair access; 2 rooms specially equipped. Crib. Italian, Spanish spoken.

CORINTH

Rich in history, Corinth was the site of an intense Civil War battle in 1862, and has a national cemetery with over 6,000 graves. Twenty miles north, in Tennessee, is Shiloh National Military Park, where one of the bloodiest battles of the war was fought. It's about the same distance to Pickwick Landing State Park, for water sports and golf. Corinth is located in northeastern Mississippi, 90 miles east of Memphis, 2 miles south of the Tennessee border, 24 miles east of the Alabama border, near the intersection of Highways 72 and 45.

Also recommended: Built in the 1870s, the **Generals' Quarters** (924 Fillmore Street, P.O. Box 1505, 38834; 601–286–3325), furnished with period antiques. B&B rates for the four guest rooms, each with private bath, TV, and telephone, range from $75–85. "Exceptionally friendly, welcoming, and hospitable innkeepers. Our lovely, spacious suite was most comfortable and beautifully decorated with a four poster bed." *(Sharon Bielski)*

Built in 1869, **Robbin's Nest** (1523 Shiloh Road, 38834; 601–286–3109) is a Southern Colonial-style home surrounded by oak and dogwood trees, boxwoods and azaleas. Breakfast includes cereal, fruit, juice, eggs, bacon or sausage, grits, and home-baked breads, served on the back porch in season, where guests can relax in the antique wicker furniture beneath the cooling breezes of the paddle fans. "Highly recommend. The Whytes welcomed us, invited us to join them for refreshments, and chatted with us over a lovely breakfast." *(Frances White)* B&B double rates for the three guest rooms, each with private bath, telephone, and TV are $85.

Samuel D. Bramlitt House ¢

1125 Cruise Street, 38834

Tel: 601–286–5370
Fax: 601–287–7467
E-mail: thom112@AVSIA.com

Named for its original owner, the Samuel D. Bramlitt House is a Queen Anne Victorian home, built in 1892 and listed on the National Register of Historic Places. It's thought to be the first home in Corinth that had indoor plumbing and telephone service. Cindy and Kevin Thomas completed its extensive renovation in 1996, using a picture of the house found at a local museum to recreate the elaborate gingerbread that outlines the house's extensive verandas and gables. Equally detailed oak, pine, and walnut woodwork is found inside, including an unusual keyhole design staircase and elaborate hand-carved fireplace mantels. Rooms are beautifully furnished with Victorian antiques. The spacious Bramlitt room has a double-size brass bed dressed in rose satin, with lace curtains and a sitting area by the decorative fireplace, while the Blue Room is papered in a morning glory pattern with a handmade cross-stitched quilt on the queen-size four poster rice bed.

Cindy notes that "we guarantee the warm hospitality of the old South. Relax with a glass of iced tea or lemonade on the veranda. Enjoy a game of croquet, stroll through the rose garden, or walk downtown to Court Square and visit the soda fountain for a cherry Coke in the state's oldest drug store. "Breakfast, available 6–10 A.M. and served at guests' choice of small or large tables, includes fresh fruit and juice, and perhaps pecan pancakes, with sausages and eggs.

"Beautiful renovation, careful attention to detail. Immaculate housekeeping; quality linens and towels. I awakened each morning to the aromas of just-brewed coffee and sizzling bacon. Lovely gardens." *(Sheri Rouse)* "Even more important than the beautiful decor and careful renovation is the exceptional friendliness and sincere hospitality of the owners." *(Randal Hartnett)* "Guest rooms have beautiful antiques, quality linens, and fresh flowers. Outside is an inviting porch with comfortable wicker chairs and the beautiful rose garden courtyard. Cindy, Kevin and family are gracious, generous, loving, and most of all a fine Christian family." *(Carl & Teresa Clement)* "I was amazed to learn that the Thomases did all the interior restoration work themselves, from refinishing woodwork, to hanging over 100 rolls of wallpaper, to making the draperies." *(Sally Hendrick, also MW)*

Open All year.
Rooms 3 doubles—all with private bath and/or shower, telephone, radio, clock, TV, desk, air-conditioning, balcony. 1 with ceiling fan.
Facilities Dining room, living room with fireplace, antique organ, library with fireplace, TV/VCR, stereo, books; guest kitchen & laundry; wraparound veranda with fans, porches. 1 acre with gardens, arbor, fountain, lawn games. Tennis, lake for water sports, hiking, bicycling nearby.
Location Historic district, 3 blocks to Court Square. From Hwy. 72, at Hardee's and Danver's, turn onto Cass St., & go under train tracks & turn right on Cruise St. Bear left on Cruise St. to inn on left between Kilpatrick & Douglas.
Restrictions No smoking. No alcohol. Well-behaved children welcome. 1 block from train tracks.

Credit cards Amex, MC, Visa.
Rates B&B, $75 double. Extra person, $20. MAP, $100 double, $87.50 single. Extra person, $32.50
Extras Airport/station pickups. Crib, babysitting.

FRENCH CAMP

French Camp B&B Inn ¢
One Blue Bird Lane, 39745

Tel: 601–547–6835
Fax: 601–547–6790

Louis LeFleur, a French Canadian, established an inn on the Natchez Trace in 1812; because of his nationality, the area became known as French Camp. In 1885, a group of Scottish-Irish settlers established a Christian school at French Camp, and in 1950, the French Camp Academy was re-dedicated "to providing a Christian school-home for children with family problems not of their own making." In 1987, two century-old log cabins were moved onto the school's 1,000-acre grounds, and restored as a bed & breakfast inn; Ed and Sallie Williford are the long-time innkeepers. Breakfast is served between 7 and 9 A.M., and includes egg casseroles, sausages, bacon, grits, sauteed apples, banana muffins, home-baked toasting bread, juice and fruit.

"Comfortable, relaxing atmosphere, whether rocking on the veranda or stretched out under a cozy quilt, listening to the hoot owls at night. These two old log cabins retain their original charm, complemented by lots of windows and Miss Sallie's lovely touch with the sturdy, comfortable furnishings. Freshly ironed sheets were a special treat. An electric blanket warded off the night's chill. Clean, quiet, and a terrific value; great location." *(Debbie Trueblood)* "Wonderful area, warm atmosphere, excellent breakfast with homemade jam and home-baked bread. Loved watching the many hummingbirds from our porch. A beautiful base for touring the uncrowded Natchez Trace. Delightful hosts. Our bedroom had a large sitting area with interesting books on Mississippi artists and writers." *(MR)* "Guests of any religious background will enjoy this wonderful place." *(ER)*

Open All year.
Rooms 5 doubles—all with full private bath, air-conditioning, fan, clock; some with telephone, radio, TV. 3 rooms in main house, 2 in cabin.
Facilities Dining room, living room, family room, library, guest kitchen, laundry, decks. School has swimming pool, lake for canoeing, fishing.
Location Central MS, Chotaw Cty. 90 m N of Jackson, 80 S of Tupelo. 2 blocks from Natchez Trace Pkwy.
Restrictions No smoking. No alcohol.
Credit cards None accepted.
Rates B&B, $60 double, $50 single.Extra person, $10. Prix fixe lunch & dinner, $3 at French Camp Academy.
Extras Crib, babysitting.

GULFPORT

Information please: A luxurious Gulf Coast option is the **Magnolia Plantation Hotel** (16391 Robinson Road, 39503-4817; 601–832–8400 or 800–700–7858), close to I-40, Windance Golf Club, and the beach. This renovated plantation-style mansion, built in 1986, offers 32 well-equipped guest rooms, some overlooking a charming pond, complete with swans and ducks. Rooms are decorated with reproduction mahogany furnishings and handmade quilts. B&B double rates include a full Southern breakfast, $85–250. Although designed primarily for corporate groups and weddings,the hotel also welcomes individuals.

For additional area inns, see **Biloxi** and **Pass Christian.**

JACKSON

Located in central Mississippi, Jackson is the state capital and its largest city.

Fairview ✕
734 Fairview Street, 39202

Tel: 601–948–3429
Toll-free: 888–948–1908
Fax: 601–948–1203

Despite its antebellum appearance, Fairview is a Greek Revival-style home built in 1908, and owned by the Simmons family since 1972. This replica of Mount Vernon is listed on the National Register of Historic Places, and was restored as a B&B in 1993 by Carol and William Simmons. The inn is gracious and elegant, with many antiques, while still comfortable and uncluttered. Guest rooms have either queen- or king-size beds. Midweek, business travelers appreciate its convenient location and many amenities; on weekends, Fairview hosts many weddings. The Southern breakfast of bacon, eggs or French toast, grits and biscuits is cooked to order and is served at guests' convenience. Dinners are served by reservation, and a typical menu might include grilled quail with angel hair pasta; green salad with balsamic vinaigrette; beef tenderloin with morels, asparagus, and roasted potatoes; and lemon glory dessert with coffee.

"This beautiful home is framed by fragrant magnolia and brilliant crepe myrtle. We stayed in the honeymoon suite located on the top floor of the renovated carriage house, with a king-size bed and decorated in ivory and beige. Carol is a well-known caterer and William is rooted deeply in Mississippi history. Wonderful Sunday brunch, complete with flowers and a pianist." *(MR)* "We were personally greeted by the hospitable owners; great breakfast." *(Tersa Lawson)* "Longtime owners Bill and Carol Simmons have meticulously maintained Fairview's original charm and comfort; they know everything about Jackson. In the library, virtually unchanged since 1908, Bill has an excellent collection of Civil War books. Exceptionally maintained; every surface glows from cleaning and polishing." *(Joe & Sheila Schmidt)*

Open All year.
Rooms 5 suites, 3 doubles—all with private bath and/or shower, telephone with data port, clock, working desk, air-conditioning, TV. 2 with fan; 1 with fireplace, 2 with Jacuzzi tub. 1 suite in carriage house.
Facilities Dining room, living room; library, foyer with fireplaces, garden room with piano; porch; deck with hot tub. 2 acres with gardens, off-street parking.
Location Old Jackson; near state Capitol Building, medical complexes. From I-55 S, take Exit 98A. Go W on Woodrow Wilson Dr. & turn S (left) on N. State St. Go E (left) at Medical Plaza bldg. on Fairview to inn on left. From I-55 N, take Exit 96C & go W on Fortification St. to N. State & turn right. Turn right on Fairview as above.
Restrictions No smoking. Children over 12.
Credit cards Amex, MC, Visa.
Rates B&B, $150 suite, $100 double. Extra person, $15. Prix fixe dinner by reservations only; menus at $35 & $50 plus 20% service; BYOB.
Extras Wheelchair access; 1 room specially equipped. French spoken.

Millsaps Buie House ♿
628 North State Street, 39202

Tel: 601–352–0221
800–784–0221
Fax: 601–352–0221

Back in the 1880s, Jackson's social elite built mansions along State Street and gathered in each other's homes for dinner parties, tea dances, and croquet. The Millsaps Buie House dates from this period and is listed on the National Register of Historic Places. Its renovation as a bed & breakfast inn began in 1985; the house survived a near disastrous fire and opened fully restored and decorated with period antiques in 1987. Guest rooms have either queen- or king-size beds. The buffet breakfast is eaten at individual tables, and includes freshly squeezed orange juice, fresh fruit, homemade blueberry banana bread and coffee cake, cereals, biscuits and bagels, scrambled eggs, cheese grits, and ham, bacon or sausage.

"Manager Nancy Fleming was very helpful. We particularly enjoyed the comfortable screened porches." *(Joe & Sheila Schmidt)* "We requested help with our bags, which was promptly provided. Interesting magazines and newspapers, with adequate light for reading. Wonderfully comfortable beds. Tasty pralines were placed on our pillows at night." *(HJB)* "Rooms on the first and second floors are furnished with period antiques; those on the third floor have a more contemporary decor." *(Jean Rawitt)* "Our first-floor room had a king-size bed, good lighting, and excellent shower." *(John Blewer)* "Professionally managed with all the amenities a business traveler needs. Wine was served in the parlor in the late afternoon." *(KM)* "Beautiful inn, Southern charm." *(Susan Doucet)* "Comfortable beds, welcoming staff, excellent Southern breakfast, with first-class cheese grits." *(Amanda Jennings)*

Open All year.
Rooms 1 suite, 10 doubles—all with private bath, telephone/computer dataport, radio, TV, air-conditioning. Some with desk.
Facilities Breakfast room, dining room, parlor with grand piano. 1½ acres, patio, off-street parking.

Location Central MS. 1½ blocks from Capitol. From I-55 N, exit at High St. & go W. Turn right at 5th light onto N. State St. House is 4th on the right.
Restrictions No smoking. No children under 12.
Credit cards Amex, DC, Discover, MC, Visa.
Rates B&B, $100–170 double, $85–155 single. Extra person, $15.
Extras Wheelchair access.

LORMAN

Canemount Plantation ✗ ♿
Highway 552 West, Rte. 2, Box 45, 39096

Tel: 601–877–3784
800–423–0684
Fax: 601–877–2010

"We came here for the weekend," claim long-time owners Rachel and Ray Forrest, "and we're still here, 15 years later!" You'll have a hard time leaving Canemount too, once you've experienced the incredible setting, fine food, and comfortable accommodations. Rates include breakfast, dinner, wine and fruit on arrival, a jeep safari through the game preserve, and a tour of the main house, an 1855 Italianate Revival home built in 1855. A highlight of the safari tour is a visit to the majestic stone columns which make up the ruins of Windsor Plantation. Guest accommodations are in three restored cottages, as well as a renovated 1730s carriage house. A country breakfast is served from 9 to 10 A.M., and includes fresh fruit, eggs, bacon, grits, biscuits, with jelly and butter.

"Isolated setting with moss-draped oaks, with trails meandering through the forest. We stayed in the Pond House, complete with a living room with day bed, wet bar, bedroom with king-size bed, and huge bathroom with Jacuzzi tub. While not fancy, it was homey and comfortable. Although you're out in the country on a real plantation, creature comforts abound. Dinner is served in the restored dairy barn; Georgia Jackson is a wonderful cook who whips up incredible meals. The Forrests work closely with the State Department of Wildlife and Fisheries and the local university. A jewel for those with a love for peace, quiet, and nature." *(Sheri & Richard De Bro)* "During our early evening safari, we saw deer, armadillos, and wild boar. Great bird-watching, too, but the highlight was the burned remains of Windsor." *(MW)*

Open All year.
Rooms 3 cottages, 6 doubles in Carriage House—all with full private bath, clock/radio, TV, air-conditioning, ceiling fan, refrigerator. Most with whirlpool tub, fireplace, porch/balcony.
Facilities Restaurant, dining room, bar, family room. 10,000 acre working plantation with heated swimming pool, gardens, stocked fishing pond, hiking trails, jeep safari, bird-watching, bicycling, fishing, deer and wild boar hunting.
Location SW MS. 40 m N of Natchez, 10 m S of Port Gibson. Approx. halfway between Vicksburg & Natchez. From Hwy. 61, take Hwy. 552 & watch for sign.
Restrictions No smoking.
Credit cards Amex, MC, Visa.
Rates MAP, $155–195 double, $135 single. Extra person, $60.
Extras Wheelchair access; 1 bathroom specially equipped.

NATCHEZ

Natchez was founded in 1716. Since then the flags of six nations have flown over the city—France, England, Spain, the sovereign state of Mississippi, the Confederacy, and the U.S. Natchez's greatest wealth and prosperity came in the early 1800s with the introduction of cotton and the coming of the steamboat. Extraordinary mansions were built during this period, which ended with the Civil War. Unlike Vicksburg to the north, Natchez was not of military importance, so although little property was destroyed during the war, further development ceased. As a result, over 500 antebellum mansions survive.

Over half the mansions in Natchez are open to visitors year-round. The others are open during festivals, called Pilgrimages, which are held for four weeks in October, two weeks at Christmas, and five weeks in March and April. The Natchez Opera Festival runs throughout the month of May. If you plan to visit during one of these times, make your reservations six weeks to three months in advance. Alternative bed & breakfast lodging, as well as tickets for the house tours, can be arranged by calling Pilgrimage Tours at 800–647–6742.

Natchez is in southwest Mississippi, on the Mississippi River, 114 miles southwest of Jackson. Try to travel here via the Natchez Trace, once an Indian footpath, now a two-lane parkway run by the National Park Service between Natchez and Nashville, passing centuries of American history en route. Call the Natchez Trace Parkway Visitors Center for more information (601–842–1572).

Reader tips: "For over 100 years, the Natchez Trace was an important wilderness road. Deep wagon cuts still mark the path followed by settlers. Stretching over 400 miles from Nashville, Tennessee to Natchez Mississippi, the superbly landscaped and maintained parkway provides an opportunity to explore the history of the period while enjoying the quiet beauty of the countryside." *(Joe & Sheila Schmidt)* "Explore Natchez-Under-the-Hill, an area wedged in beneath the Mississippi River bluffs that was once home to gamblers, riverboat hustlers and other ne'er-do-wells." *(SC)* "If you're looking for catfish, go across the bridge to Vidalia, Louisiana (right by the Briars and the Ramada), and just over the bridge, turn right to the Sandbar restaurant. Down home atmosphere; clean, inexpensive, friendly, and good fish." *(Frances White)* "Three favorite restaurants on the Mississippi are The Wharfmaster, The Landing, and the Magnolia Bar and Grill; wonderful barbecue and gumbo." *(LR)*

Worth noting: In many plantation homes, the common areas are kept locked, except during tours, because of the value of the antique furnishings. Guests are welcome to relax on the galleries and grounds, but rarely have "free run" of the house itself. Typically, plantation homes are found in neighborhoods where many poor people also live; expect historic Southern neighborhoods to have shacks and mansions next door to each other.

Also recommended: Set on a hill overlooking the Mississippi River is **The Briars Inn** (31 Irving Lane, P.O. Box 1245, 39120; 601–446–9654 or 800–634–1818). This plantation-style mansion was built in the early 1800s and was the site of Jefferson Davis' marriage to Varina Howell in 1845. The 13 guest rooms are elegantly decorated, and the $135–155 B&B double rates include a full breakfast. "Beautiful mansion. We were welcomed graciously and shown the first floor. Our large room opened onto the gallery; it was comfortable and well equipped, with terry cloth robes and hair dryer in the bathroom, and a gas fireplace. Breakfast was very good, served with southern hospitality." *(Frances White)*

A Greek Revival mansion, built in 1855, **Weymouth Hall** (One Cemetery Road, P.O. Box 1091, 39120; 601–445–2304) is set high on a bluff overlooking the Mississippi River. B&B double rates for the five guest rooms are $85, including a hearty plantation breakfast. "Rooms are furnished with the owners' collection of elaborate Victoriana from the 1840s to 1860s. They have tester, four-poster or canopied beds and modern baths; two guest rooms have river views." *(SHW)*

Camellia Gardens *Tel:* 601–446–7944
506 South Union Street, 39120 800–ELEGANS

Named for the dozens of rare old camellia bushes which bloom in the inn's garden, Camellia Gardens is a Queen Anne-style Victorian home built in 1897, and restored in 1990 by Herbert and Marjo Miller. Listed on the National Register of Historic Places, this B&B was completely renovated and refurbished in late Victorian decor. Marjo notes that "the small size of our B&B allows us to provide a personalized stay, with touring and restaurant recommendations. We are also delighted to offer guests a tour of our antique car collection." Breakfast is served at 8:30 A.M., and consists of fruit compote, juice, stuffed French toast with apricot sauce and ham; or perhaps egg soufflé with homemade muffins and sausage patties.Rates also include evening coffee and a tray of homemade desserts for each guest room.

"Tasteful restoration. Outstanding features include the enormous wood pocket doors, original Edison gas/electric lighting, and elegant second floor porches. Weary travelers will appreciate the washer and dryer. Highly recommended." *(Joe Schmidt)*

Open Sept. 1–June. 1.
Rooms 1 cottage, 3 doubles—all with full private bath, radio, clock, air-conditioning. Cottage with TV, desk, refrigerator.
Facilities Dining room, living room, library; each with fireplace. Den with grand piano, sun room with TV; wraparound porches. ½ acre with off-street parking, gardens swimming pool. Golf nearby.
Location Historic Garden District; short walk to downtown & trolley stops. Call for directions.
Restrictions No smoking. Children 12 and over.
Credit cards MC, Visa.
Rates B&B, $100–125 cottage, double.
Extras Spanish spoken.

Linden ♿ *Tel:* 601–445–5472
1 Linden Place, 39120 800–2–LINDEN
Fax: 601–445–5472

Dating back to 1792, most of the present house was constructed between 1818 and 1849, when Linden was bought by ancestors of the current owner, Jeanette Feltus. Nearly all furnishings are original to the house, and Linden is especially noted for its outstanding collection of Federal furniture, including many Hepplewhite, Sheraton, and Chippendale pieces.

"Jeanette, the sixth generation of her family to live at Linden, is constantly on hand with her staff, seeing to her guests' every need. The setting is lovely, surrounded by gardens, well off the main roads with no traffic noise, yet is convenient to downtown. The hearty breakfast was served on the porch at 8:30 A.M. *sharp,* and with grits, sausages, scrambled eggs, and curried peaches one day, then ham, steamed eggs, and apricots the next, with lots of homemade biscuits, orange juice, and coffee. The light and airy guest rooms open to the porch on one side and lawns on the other. Rooms in the garçonniere are a bit smaller, but all are handsome with four-poster beds. The brief tour is interesting and fun, highlighting such features as an enormous lyre-shaped cypress punkah fan above the dining room table, originally pulled by slaves to cool the guests during dinner." *(SHW)* "It was pleasant gathering on the gallery for good conversation with the other guests. Mrs. Feltus is a lovely hostess, and Lily prepares an outstanding Southern breakfast." *(BJ Hensley)* "Breakfast served in the banquet room one morning, and in the back gallery by the courtyard the next. Attentive and pleasant service." *(GH)* "Clean, attractive, and well maintained." *(JS)*

Open All year.
Rooms 7 doubles—all with private bath, air-conditioning.
Facilities Dining room, parlor with piano, porch, galleries. 7 acres with courtyard, gardens.
Location Take U.S. Rte. 61/84 to Melrose Ave.
Restrictions No children under 10.
Credit cards None accepted.
Rates B&B, $90–110 double.
Extras Wheelchair access.

Monmouth Plantation ✕ ♿ *Tel:* 601–442–5852
36 Melrose Avenue at the 800–828–4531
John A. Quitman Parkway, 39120 *Fax:* 601–446–7762
P.O. Box 1736, 39121

Monmouth, a Greek Revival mansion listed on the National Register of Historic Places, was built in 1818 and was purchased in 1826 by John Quitman, who later became governor of Mississippi and a U.S. congressman. Monmouth stayed in the Quitman family until 1905; its restoration began in 1978, when it was purchased by Lani and Ron Riches. Period antiques, including many of the plantation's original furnishings, decorate the rooms, which are also equipped with thick terry robes, English toiletries, and a welcome basket of pralines and cold drinks. In the evening, guests can order freshly mixed mint juleps to accompany the complimentary hors d'oeuvres. Rates also include a full Southern breakfast, house tour, and evening turndown service with chocolates. Five-course candle lit dinners are served (by reservation) in the elegant dining room or gas lit parlors.

"We were warmly welcomed and shown to our Carriage House suite, with a convenient parking space just outside our room. Our request for extra towels was responded to immediately. Though recently built, the architecture of the Carriage House matches the original buildings. Our suite, one of four, had a bedroom with a four-poster bed and armoire, a sitting room with a sofa in front of the fireplace, a private patio, and a well appointed bathroom. Though less grand than the main house rooms, we enjoyed its relaxing privacy. Tasty breakfast of eggs, grits, biscuits and preserves. After breakfast, innkeeper Marguerite Guercio gave us a most interesting and informative house tour. At dinner time, we were seated at the long table in the beautifully furnished dining room, with wonderful period atmosphere. The food was very good, the surroundings lovely, and conversation with our fellow guests delightful.Friendly staff; exceptionally well run." *(Alex & Beryl Williams)*

"The beautiful grounds offer a relaxing setting, with garden gazebos and benches pleasant for playing cards or reading." *(Darrel & Renate Kurtz)* "We had fun being the only Americans at breakfast, surrounded by a French tour group." *(BH)* "After touring all day, it's a treat to sit at one of these formal dinner tables, lights dimmed, and imagine for a moment that you actually live in another time—and in such opulence. The rooms built on the site of the former slave quarters and carriage house are private and elegantly furnished." *(Lynn Fullman, also M. Marsted)* "A highlight of our inngoing experiences." *(Marvin Vernon)*

Open All year. Dinner served Tues.–Sat.
Rooms 13 suites, 12 doubles—all with private bath and/or shower, telephone, radio, TV, desk, air-conditioning, hair dryer, robes. Some with fireplace, Jacuzzi. 6 rooms in mansion, 4 in original kitchen building, 4 in former slave quarters, 4 rooms Carriage House.
Facilities Parlors, study, courtyard patio, gift shop; conference facility (100). 26 acres with gardens, gazebo, fish pond, croquet, walking trails. Golf, tennis nearby.
Location 1 m from downtown. E on State St., at corner of Quitman Pkwy. and Melrose.
Restrictions No smoking. Children over 14.
Credit cards Amex, Diners, Discover, MC, Optima, Visa.
Rates B&B, $150–230 suite, $115–165 double. Extra person, $35. Prix fixe dinner, $38; reservations required. Cocktails, wine not included in rates.
Extras Wheelchair access; some rooms specially equipped.

OXFORD

Oxford is noted as the home of the University of Mississippi, William Faulkner, and John Grisham.

Reader tip: "When visiting Oxford, be sure to tour Faulkner's home and the campus museums. Also worthwhile are the double-decker city bus tours, and Square Books, Oxford's legendary bookstore. Stroll to Court House Square for lunch at Bottletree Bakery, or the City Grocery for dinner." *(Lynn Fullman)*

Barksdale-Isom B&B
1003 Jefferson Avenue, 38566

Tel: 601–236–5600
800–236–5696

Originally built as a log house in 1835, the Barkdale-Isom B&B was long owned by Dr. Thomas Isom. Remodeled in the Greek Revival style, it was substantially expanded over the years to accommodate the growing Isom family. The dining room was extended for another reason: the University of Mississippi's charter was signed here, and the room needed to be large enough to accommodate the entire board of trustees. In fact, Dr. Isom named the town after Oxford University in England as an inspiration to the new school. During the Civil War, Dr. Isom operated a hospital for both Union and Confederate troops on the campus. His kindness to Union soldiers saved the house from destruction when General Smith ordered the town to be burned down in 1864. Later, it served as the setting for a Faulkner short story, "A Rose for Emily"; Faulkner's home, Rowan Oak, is just a few blocks away.

In 1996, the B&B was purchased by Susan Barksdale; rooms were refurbished, and now have queen-, king- or two double beds set in a 19th Century French theme. Most rooms have canopy beds. Rates include morning coffee, and a full Southern breakfast in addition to afternoon wine.

"A special find in that wonderful town where yesterdays shroud today like insulation and authors just keep being born. Attention to detail at this B&B, filled with antiques and masterfully decorated, is incredible. Restoration of this historically significant home is made all the better by attention to creature comforts. Bedside sleep machines make soothing sounds such as crickets, lapping waves, or soft rain, and bathrooms are equipped with terry cloth robes and Caswell-Massey toiletries. The gracious staff makes this a warm and welcoming place. Soft drinks, ice, and home-baked cookies are available anytime." *(Lynn Fullman)* Comments appreciated.

Open All year.
Rooms 5 doubles—all with private bath, telephone, TV, individual thermostat, sleep machine. 4 with fireplace.
Facilities Dining room, living room, library, veranda. Garden, off-street parking.
Location N central MS. Approx. 1 hr. S of Memphis, 1 hr. E of Tupelo. 2 blocks N of Courthouse Square. From Hwy. 6, exit at S Lamar. Go N on S Lamar. At Courthouse Sq. merge right & go to N side of square. Turn right on N Lamar. Go 1 block to Jefferson Ave. Go left to inn, 200 feet on right.
Restrictions No smoking. Children over 12.
Credit cards MC, Visa.
Rates B&B, $150–190. Extra person, $25.

PASS CHRISTIAN

Information please: A turn-of-the-century planter's home a few miles west of Pass Christian, the **Bay Town Inn** (208 North Beach Boulevard, Bay St. Louis 39520; 601–466–5870 or 800–533–0407) is listed on the National Register of Historic Places. Owned by Ann Tidwell, the inn features seven guest rooms, each with a private bath. B&B double rates are $75–85, including a full breakfast, and you can watch the sun come up over the Bay as you sip your morning coffee or relax in the swing under the magnolia tree.

Located in the antebellum seaside community of Pass Christian directly across from the beach and yacht club, the **Harbour Oaks Inn** (126 West Scenic Drive, Pass Christian 39571; 601–452–9399 or 800–452–9399) is a three-story building with covered porches on the first and second floors. French doors open onto the porches facing the Gulf; centuries-old live oak trees, draped with Spanish moss, provide shade. Owners Diane and Tony Brugger have furnished their B&B, built as a hotel in 1840 and listed on the National Register of Historic Places, with family antiques. Guests can relax on the wicker furniture on the verandas with morning coffee or complimentary wine at sunset, or enjoy the card and billiards table in the den. Breakfast is served in the elegant dining room, and includes such menus as strawberry crepes and stuffed pears, or broiled grapefruit and scrambled eggs with chives and avocado. Double rates for the five air-conditioned guest rooms with private baths range from $79–99.

For additional Gulf Coast entries, see **Biloxi** and **Gulfport.**

TUPELO

The Mockingbird Inn ¢
305 North Gloster, 38801

Tel: 601–841–0286
Fax: 601–840–4158

Elvis Presley fans will want to stay at The Mockingbird Inn so they can enjoy the view of the Milam School, where the "King" attended sixth and seventh grade. The rest of us will find many more appealing features: the warm and welcoming innkeepers, the appealing decor, and the delicious food. Named for the Mississippi state bird and symbol of hospitality, The Mockingbird Inn was built in 1925 and restored as a B&B in 1994 by Sandy and Jim Gilmer. Sandy notes that "since our lovely 1925 home is a combination of three architectural styles—Colonial Revival, Prairie, and Arts and Crafts— we didn't restrict ourselves to a specific decor. Although all guest rooms have a queen-size bed, the style of each room was inspired by a different part of the world." Venice has an 1800s tapestry of gondolas and the Doge's Palace, while Mackinac Island has the feel of a white washed cottage with its own porch swing. Africa has faux zebra and leopard skins with mosquito netting over the bed, and Bavaria has a sleigh bed, a featherbed, antique wooden skis, and lace curtains. Breakfast, served 7–8 A.M. weekdays, 8:30–9:30 A.M. weekends, includes fresh fruit and juice, hash browns, and bacon, ham or sausage, plus such entrees as puff pancakes with strawberry preserves, orange French toast, or egg and croissant casserole. Rates also include always-available juice, soft drinks, coffee, tea, and hot chocolate, and an evening snack—perhaps German chocolate cake, cheese and crackers, or popcorn and apples.

"The Gilmers have put heart and soul into this delightful place. The decor is an eclectic mix of antiques and trash-turned-to-treasure chic, artfully mixed with humor, and always focused on guests' comfort." *(Trish Vignati)* "Friendly welcoming atmosphere. Delicious breakfast, attractively presented. I enjoy trying a different room on each visit." *(Jill Penny)* "Everything is always in perfect working order, and there's always ample hot water." *(Diane Monk)* "Helpful staff, familiar with local restaurants and entertainment." *(Sidney Thom)* "Sandy and Jim are warm and friendly people who remember their guests, and go out of their way to make them as comfortable as possible." *(Tiffany Hughes)* "Lots of windows and light. Delicious homemade dessert. Small but beautifully landscaped yard, great for relaxing. Good restaurants close by; enjoyed the area antique stores." *(MR)*

Open All year.
Rooms 7 doubles—all with private shower and/or bath, telephone, clock, TV, air-conditioning, ceiling fan. Some with radio, desk, gas fireplace, double whirlpool tub.
Facilities Dining room, living room with stereo, books, TV; guest refrigerator, sun porch. Fax service. Garden with patio; gazebo with porch swing; off-street parking.
Location N MS. Approx 90 min. SE of Memphis. Halfway between Nashville & Natchez following the Natchez Trace. Walking distance to downtown. 1 block N of Hwy. 6 (Main St.), on Alt. Hwy. 45 (N. Gloster).
Restrictions No smoking. Children over 12. Train noise possible.
Credit cards Amex, Discover, MC, Visa.
Rates B&B, $65–125 double. Extra person, $10. 10% senior, AAA discount. Romance packages.
Extras Wheelchair access; 1 room fully equipped for disabled.

VICKSBURG

When folks talk about "The War" in Vicksburg, it's the Civil War they're referring to, not any of more recent vintage. Because of the town's controlling position, high on the Mississippi River bluffs, Union forces felt Vicksburg's surrender was essential to victory. Repulsed in repeated attempts both from land and water, the town surrendered to General U.S. Grant only after a 47-day siege of continuous mortar and cannon bombardment.

Must-see sights in Vicksburg include the National Military Park and Cemetery and the nearby Cairo Museum, with numerous exhibits and audiovisual programs that bring the history of the battle and the period to life. Amazingly enough, many of Vicksburg's antebellum mansions survived the siege and can be visited today. Check with the Vicksburg Tourist Commission for Pilgrimage dates: 800–221–3536. For a lighter taste of history, stop at the Biedenharn Candy Company Museum to see where Coca-Cola was first bottled in 1894.

Vicksburg is located in southwest Mississippi, 44 miles east of Jackson, via I-20.

Reader tips: "Be sure to visit Vicksburg National Military Park. The battle of Vicksburg was pivotal in the career of General Ulysses S. Grant. It propelled him to command of the Union armies and later to the presidency of the United States. The 15-mile drive through the park travels back and forth between Union and Confederate lines, often only yards apart. The weathered trenches are a reminder of the agony and fury of the battle. During the siege the Union ironside *Cairo* was sunk by a mine. She has been raised from the mud and is the centerpiece of the unique gunboat museum. Nearby, neat rows of white stone monuments mark the National and Confederate Cemeteries. *(Joe & Sheila Schmidt)* "Most riverboat casinos offer excellent, well-priced dinner buffets." *(JS)*

Also recommended: The **Belle of the Bends** (508 Klein Street, 39180; 601–634–0737 or 800–844–2308) is set high on a bluff overlooking the Mississippi. This 1876 brick Italianate-style home is furnished with period antiques and steamboating memorabilia. Double rates for the four guest rooms are $85–150, and includes a country breakfast and afternoon tea. "Beautiful architecture, attractively furnished. The solicitous owner/innkeeper breakfasts with guests; the meal is first class, as is everything about this B&B. Rooms are large and spacious; ours had a river view." *(David Adamson)*

An antebellum mansion built in 1840, **Cedar Grove** (2300 Washington Street, 39180; 601–636–1000 or 800–862–1300) is listed on the National Register of Historic Places. Despite the Union cannonball still lodged in the parlor wall, it survived the Civil War with most of its antiques and architecture intact. The 24 guest rooms are available in the mansion and in the poolside guest cottage; the carriage house has eight suites. Rates of $90–165 include a full Southern breakfast, and a tour of the mansion. Dinners are served in the Garden Room restaurant; grilled chicken, catfish, and filet mignon are among the entrées.

Information please: The **Duff Green Mansion** (1114 First East Street, P.O. Box 75, 39180; 601–636–6968 or 800–992–0037) is a 12,000-square-foot Paladian mansion built in 1856. Once the scene of many parties, the mansion was converted into a hospital during the Civil War. The restoration of the mansion combines antiques and period reproductions with luxurious appointments; B&B double rates for the seven guest rooms range from $75–160, and include a welcoming drink, a full breakfast, and a tour of the house.

The Corners ¢ 🚸 ♿
601 Klein Street, 39180

Tel: 601–636–7421
800–444–7421
Fax: 601–636–7232

Resident owners Cliff, Bettye, and Kilby Whitney will greet you on arrival at the Corners with a complimentary beverage, and you may want to enjoy it in a lazy rocking chair on the wide gallery as you watch the sun set. Built in 1873, The Corners is listed on the National Register of Historic Places and was built in a style combining Greek Revival and Victorian features. The floors are original heart-of-pine boards 20 feet long and the support walls are three bricks thick. Rooms are furnished with period antiques, while baths are modern. The Servants' Quarters houses two guest rooms, with the original brick walls left exposed, fireplaces, whirlpool baths, and a gallery overlooking the back gardens. A typical breakfast includes fresh fruit with yogurt, caramelized French toast with bacon or asparagus ham casserole with banana nut muffins.

"Bettye is a wonderful raconteur and tour guide. We particularly liked the rooms in the old Servants Quarters; those on the first floor of the main house are also light and airy. The four guest rooms in The Galleries next door have exceptional river views." *(Joe & Sheila Schmidt)* "Our lovely room in the Servants' Quarters had individual temperature controls, a wonderful Jacuzzi, and a charming bedroom furnished with antiques." *(Jean Bergmark)* "The Master Suite has two 12-foot windows facing the Mississippi River, a massive canopy bed, an armoire, straight and overstuffed chairs, a tea table, and a dresser. The bath was supplied with thick towels, and imported toiletries." *(SHW)* "Upon arrival, we were served coffee and tea in the parlor while listening to soft-playing music." *(Darel & Renata Kurtz)* "For breakfast, all the guests gathered to feast on pecan banana pancakes, bacon and eggs, and homemade biscuits. Seconds were offered and eagerly accepted." *(Judy & Marty Schwartz)*

Open All year.
Rooms 1 2-bedroom cottage, 1 suite, 13 doubles—all with private bath and/or shower, TV, telephone, air-conditioning. Some with balcony, desk, fan, fireplace, double whirlpool tub, wet bar, microwave. 8 rooms in adjacent buildings.
Facilities Dining room; parlor with 2 fireplaces, piano, library; country kitchen, glassed-in veranda. 1½ acres, parterre gardens, croquet. Boating, golf nearby.
Location 1 m from center. From I-20, take exit 1A. Go N on Washington St., left on Klein St. to inn at corner of Klein and Oak Sts.
Restrictions Smoking in designated areas only. Train noise might disturb light sleepers; some noise in Eastlake room due to location.
Credit cards Amex, MC, Visa.
Rates B&B, $140–160 2-bedroom suite, $85–120 double, $75–95 single. Extra adult, $20; child under age 6, $10–15; infant, free. House tours, $5.
Extras Limited wheelchair access. Pets permitted by prior arrangement.

Stained Glass Manor–Oak Hall
2430 Drummond Street, 39180

Tel: 601–638–8893
Toll-free: 888–VICK–BNB
Fax: 601–636–3055
E-mail: vickbnb@magnolia.net

History and hospitality, food and furnishings—these are the four key components of a memorable B&B, and you'll find them all in abundance at the Stained Glass Manor. Built in 1902 as the home of Fannie Vick Willis Johnson, Vicksburg's greatest individual philanthropist and descendant of the founding "Vick" in Vicksburg, this yellow brick Mission-style home is listed on the National Register of Historic Places. It was restored as an inn in 1985, and purchased by Bill and Shirley

Smollen in 1995. The decor is highlighted (literally and figuratively) by 38 original stained glass windows by Louis J. Millet and other noted stained glass artisans, and by the extensive use of hand-crafted oak woodwork throughout the house. Rooms are furnished with antiques and period reproductions, and are exceptionally spacious—even the entry hall is larger than most contemporary living rooms at 16 by 40 feet. Bill reports that "we offer a family-oriented home-away-from home. Guests love my rich, New Orleans-style breakfasts, learned after years of cooking with the best New Orleans chefs." (Vegetarian and other special dietary needs are accommodated with advance notice). This meal is served at the dining room table, 8:30–11:00, and includes Louisiana-style cafe au lait, home-baked muffins and breads, and quiche Lorraine.

"The Smollens' down-to-earth charm and congenial personalities made us feel instantly at home." *(Karen Davidson)* "Incredibly cordial from the first phone call. Bill welcomed us to his home and treated us like family. He told us which sights in Vicksburg to see, where to shop, where to eat, and taught us about Vicksburg's Civil War history. The Washington room is lavishly decorated, with an extremely comfortable bed. Wonderful breakfast of homemade sourdough bread, mimosas, quiche Lorraine, chocolate fondue, and rich black New Orleans-style coffee." *(John & Maryann Merritt)* "Bill kept us fabulously entertained with stories about his days in New Orleans and with NASA." *(Ron Greene)* "Excellent accommodations; proprietors are gregarious, entertaining, and solicitous." *(Ronald McLaughlin)*

Open All year.
Rooms 1 carriage house suite, 5 doubles—4 with private bath and/or shower, 2 with maximum of 4 people sharing bath, all with telephone, clock, TV, desk, air-conditioning. Some with radio, fireplace, balcony.
Facilities Dining room, living room, family room with TV, library, video collection, kitchen access, hallway with baby grand piano, porches. 2 acres with off-street parking, children's swimming pool.
Location 1 m to downtown. From I-20, take Exit 1A N onto Washington St. Go approx. 1 m to light at Washington & Lee (light marked with small block, #29). Go right onto Lee St. & go 1.3 m through 2 stops signs & 1 light. (Lee, Drummond, & Monroe are all the same street). Inn on left behind iron fence.
Restrictions No smoking in front wing.
Credit cards Discover, MC, Visa.
Rates B&B, $120–140 suite, $60–130 double. Extra person, $20. Senior, AAA, extended stay discounts.
Extras Well-behaved pets with prior approval. Crib. Limited Portugese spoken.

WEST

The Alexander House ¢
210 Green Street, P.O. Box 187, 39192

Tel: 601–967–2417
601–967–2266
800–350–8034

B&Bs do more than provide a warm and welcoming place to stay; innkeepers throughout the U.S. have been instrumental in preserving historic homes that would otherwise have been destroyed. An excellent example is The Alexander House, built in 1880, and abandoned for years. When Ruth Ray and Woody Dinstel heard that the house was to be torn down for scrap lumber, they bought it in 1994 and restored it as a B&B. The Dinstels live a block away, but Ruth Ray is always available to answer guests' questions, or to cook delicious breakfasts of fresh fruit and orange juice, home-baked goods, breakfast meats, plus eggs, French toast, or quiche, served from 8–10 A.M. Rooms are decorated with floral wallpapers, antiques collected over the years, and lovely handmade quilts. Civil War buffs will find the inn makes a good base for exploring nearby sites, while through travelers on I-55 can rest and relax in an inviting setting just minutes from the interstate.

"Charming atmosphere, delicious food, wonderful hospitality, impressive restoration. We loved having the run of the house, since the Dinstels live a block away." *(GR)* "The Dinstels lived all over the world during Woody's career with Exxon, and returned to their home town of West. Although they bought the house for almost nothing, they've spent a fortune restoring it. Lovely antiques, firm mattresses, good reading lights." *(Jimmy Cotten)* "Wonderfully decorated for Christmas. The Dinstels immediately made us feel welcome and comfortable in every way. It was fascinating to hear about the history of the house and its restoration. A restful night's sleep was followed by a candle lit breakfast of fresh fruit medley, home-baked biscuits and cinnamon rolls, bacon and eggs, jams and jellies. The house is immaculate and all plumbing, lighting, heating/cooling systems in top condition. The town of West is small, quiet, and relaxing." *(Rhys Green)*

Open All year.
Rooms 1 suite, 4 doubles—3 with private bath and/or shower, 2 with maximum of 4 people sharing bath. All with radio, clock, desk, air-conditioning, ceiling fan. 1 with TV.
Facilities Dining room, parlor, guest refrigerator, screened porch. 3 acres with gardens; bicycles.
Location Central MS. 1 hr. N of Jackson, 2½ hrs. S of Memphis, TN. 3 m off I-55. Historic district. From I-55, take Exit 164 onto Carrollton St. Go right on Anderson (2nd paved road on right) to inn at corner of Anderson & Green.
Restrictions No smoking.
Credit cards Amex, Discover, MC, Visa.
Rates B&B, $65 double. Extra person, $10. No tipping.Prix fixe steak dinner, $25 each, 10-person minimum.

North Carolina

Lodge on Lake Lure, Lake Lure

Few states offer as much to the traveler as North Carolina—beautiful barrier island beaches and historic towns in the east, breathtaking mountain scenery in the west. Mt. Mitchell, at 6,684 feet the highest point east of the Mississippi, lies in the High Country, in the northwestern part of the state. The center of the state, called the Piedmont, is rich in industry, agriculture, and has some of the state's most beautiful golf courses.

The Blue Ridge mountains in the west are home to artisans who create fine Appalachian crafts while traditional "jugtown" potteries line the roads near Seagrove, south of Greensboro. For an introduction to the region's original residents, visit Cherokee in the southwestern corner of the state. Here you can wander through Oconaluftee Village, a reconstructed 1750 Cherokee town, or purchase top-notch tribal arts at the Qualla gallery.

In North Carolina, liquor is sold only through state-owned "A.B.C." stores, although beer and wine are sold in grocery stores in most counties. Some inns provide setups if you bring your own beverage; others prefer that drinks not be consumed in public. Some counties are completely dry, so be prepared, and watch for the "BYOB" notation under *"Restrictions." State law prohibits pets in commercial accommodations.*

Worth noting: The **Triad** area encompasses the towns of Greensboro, High Point, and Winston-Salem, while the **Research Triangle** includes Chapel Hill, Durham, and Raleigh.

Outer Banks: This string of barrier islands extends from the Virginia border south to Cape Hatteras; next is Ocracoke Island, followed by the Cape Lookout National Seashore. Route 12 runs its length, and road access is available in the north via Route 158, and at Manteo, via Routes 64 and 264. Summer weekend traffic on Route 12 can be bumper-to-bumper; if possible, visit midweek or off-season.

Reader tip: "Don't be disappointed if the sand dunes block your view of the ocean when you're staying in the Outer Banks. Buildings unprotected by sand dunes are soon *in* the ocean." *(DLG)*

For entries in the **Outer Banks**, check under **Beaufort, Cape Carteret, Corolla, Duck, Kill Devil Hills, Manteo, Nags Head,** and **Ocracoke**. For another barrier island escape near Wilmington, see also **Bald Head Island.**

ANDREWS

For additional area entries, see **Murphy** and **Robbinsville.**

Hawkesdene House B&B
Phillips Creek Road, P.O. Box 670, 28901

Tel: 704–321–6027
800–447–9549
Fax: 704–321–5007
E-mail: hawke@dnet.net

Good taste is like the Supreme Court's definition of pornography: we can't define it, but we know it when we see it. And that's what Hawkesdene, built in 1995 by Roy and Daphne Sargent, is all about. Named for the Sargents' first home in Dorset, England, Hawkesdene combines the classic appeal of an English country house with North Carolina country charm. Roy called upon decades of experience in the fields of architecture and furniture in designing and furnishing the inn and cottages, while Daphne's love of gardening is evident both in the inn's gardens and in the appealing color palette she has used to decorate the inn.

Breakfast is served 7:30–9 A.M. at guests' choice of small or large tables, and includes juice, coffee, bacon or sausage, and such entrees as French toast, waffles or baked eggs with Parmesan tomatoes.

"Picturesque setting with the mountains on one side, the creek on the other, and llamas grazing in the pasture. Meticulous housekeeping and maintenance." *(Natalie Morris)* "Cool mountain air, warm hospitality, and wonderful food. Having to leave Roy and Daphne's wonderful home is the only part of our visit that we didn't enjoy." *(Donnie & Patty Roebuck)* "The Sargents are warm, friendly, and most interesting hosts." *(Harry & Kathy Swart)* "Rooms are bright, appealing, and mercifully uncluttered. Windows wrap around much of the great room, and the flowered chintz-covered couch invites you to curl up and watch the flames in the fieldstone fireplace. The Snowbird Room has an iron queen-size bed, and pristine white walls accented by soft gold floral fabrics and ceiling border. Two comfortable upholstered chairs are perfect for reading or taking in the mountain views." *(MW)* "Knowledgeable hosts who entertained us well." *(Michael Gray)*

Open All year.
Rooms 3 2-bedroom cottages, 1 suite, 4 doubles—all with private bath and/or shower, radio, clock, TV, air-conditioning, ceiling fan. Radio on request. Suite with kitchenette; cottages with kitchen, wood-burning fireplace, washer/dryer, screened porch, picnic table, grill.
Facilities Dining room, living room, great room with fireplace, TV/VCR,

stereo, books, games; decks/balconies. 20 acres with croquet, badminton, hiking, llama trekking. Adjoins Nantahla National Forest. Trout/bass fishing, tennis, horseback riding, white water rafting, mt. railroad, gem mines, gold panning nearby.

Location W NC, 90 m W of Asheville. 3 hrs. N of Atlanta. 3 m to town. Take U.S. Rte. 74 to Andrews. Go S on Cherry St./Bristol Rd. (at Wachovia Bank). Go 3.3 m to Phillips Creek Rd & go left ½ m to inn on left.

Restrictions No smoking. Children over 12 welcome in main house; any age in cottages.

Credit cards Amex, Discover, MC, Visa.

Rates Room only in cottage, $125–150. B&B, $95–105 suite, $65–90 double. Extra person, $20. 2-3 night weekend minimum. Weekend, mid-week packages. Llama trek picnics, $45.

Extras Limited wheelchair access. Crib.

ASHEVILLE

Asheville is in western North Carolina, at the juncture of Interstates 26 and 40, 106 miles southeast of Knoxville, Tennessee; it's just an hour's drive to the Great Smoky Mountains National Park. Surrounded by more than a million acres of national forest, Asheville is known for its cool mountain summers. Golf, canoeing, rafting, horseback riding, and hiking are all available nearby. It's also the home of the Biltmore House and Gardens, the Vance Birthplace, the Thomas Wolfe Memorial, and many craft shops and galleries. The Biltmore House is probably its best-known attraction; George W. Vanderbilt (of the railroad/steamship Vanderbilts) was so enamored of the area that he bought 125,000 acres and built this 255-room castle, completed in 1895; many inns sell reduced-rate admission tickets.

Most of Asheville's inns are in the historic Montford district, a charming old residential neighborhood convenient to downtown. Although many beautiful homes had become dilapidated rooming houses, most *(though not all)* have been beautifully restored.

Reader tip: "Although too big (500 guest rooms) and busy with convention business, we had a delightful lunch at the Grove Park Inn, served on the porch overlooking the town and mountains beyond. We also stopped for drink during the holidays, when the inn is beautifully decorated for Christmas." *(RC)*

Also recommended: Carolina B&B (177 Cumberland Avenue, 28801; 704–254–3608) was built around the turn of the century by Richard Sharp Smith, supervising architect for the Biltmore Estate. The home has a stucco exterior, graced by front and rear porches and two pairs of chimneys. The six guest rooms, with large windows and ruffled, organdy curtains, are simply furnished with walnut and brass beds; double rates are $85–100. Breakfasts might include pumpkin-ginger bread, spiced apple rings, and cinnamon French toast.

Built in 1891, the **Cedar Crest Victorian Inn** (674 Biltmore Avenue, 28803; 704–252–1389) offers handsome Queen Anne architecture, enhanced by original oak woodwork and stained and beveled glass windows. B&B rates for the 12 guest rooms range from $120 to $220, and include a full breakfast and afternoon and evening refreshments. "Jack and Barbara McEwan are gracious hosts. The carved woods of master craftsman are enhanced by stunning four poster beds, chintz, lace, stunning wallpaper, and beautiful antiques. Just a quarter-mile from the Biltmore Estate." *(Ken Amato)*

Information please: Built in 1897, **A Bed of Roses** (135 Cumberland Avenue, 28801; 704–258–8700 or 800–471–4182) is a charming Queen Anne Victorian home, complete with an inviting front porch and an hexagonal turret. Located in the historic Montford district, the inn offers five guest rooms and a cottage, each with private bath, air-conditioning, and TV. The B&B double rates of $95–145 include such breakfasts as homemade applesauce, scrambled eggs and ham, and buttermilk biscuits with strawberry preserves plus afternoon tea and home-baked cakes.

For additional area entries, see **Balsam, Black Mountain, Candler, Dillsboro, Flat Rock, Hendersonville, Lake Lure, Maggie Valley, Pisgah Forest, Saluda, Tryon,** and **Waynesville.**

Abbington Green B&B Inn *Tel:* 704–251–2454
46 & 48 Cumberland Circle, 28801 800–251–2454
Fax: 704–251–2872

An English theme pervades Abbington Green, from its guest rooms—all named for London gardens or parks—to its English books, paintings, and furnishings. In 1993, Valerie Larrea restored this Colonial Revival home, built in 1908, as a B&B. Floral themes are evident throughout, creating a light and airy atmosphere. Guest rooms have four-poster, canopy, or draped queen-size beds, with good bedside lighting, terry robes, and beautiful Oriental rugs. Breakfast is served at guests' convenience at individual tables, and consists of homemade cakes, a hot or cold fruit course, and such entrees as cheese crepes with lemon sauce, or quiche Florentine. Tea and other beverages are always available.

"Each morning offered a special surprise, such as hot fruit compote to ward off the autumn chill." *(Susan Recce Lamson)* "Exceptionally comfortable bed." *(Marsha Sutton)* "Lovely English decor with Valerie's beautiful antiques. Wonderful tips on exploring the Ashville area." *(Cliff & Susan Wolfe)* "Breakfast was exquisitely presented on family heirloom china. Valerie Larrea didn't miss a beat preparing a low-fat breakfast." *(Valerie Rubin)* "Valerie was never intrusive, yet was always ready to help with dinner recommendations and reservations." *(Roberta Schoenfeld)* "A beautifully restored house in a lovely, quiet area." *(Roy Farmer, also SWS)* "Spacious grounds and ample parking. Public rooms are comfortable and welcoming." *(J.G. Tyror)* "Tantalizing smells of baked bread and sizzling bacon; delicious cold cherry soup and hot coffee." *(John Schoeni)*

Open All year.
Rooms 1 suite, 5 doubles—all with private bath and/or shower, clock, desk. 3 with gas fireplace, 2 with fan.

Facilities Dining room with fireplace, living room with fireplace, piano, family room/parlor with TV, VCR, fireplace, books, games; porch with swing. Off-street parking, bicycles.
Location Less than 1 m from downtown, historic district. From I-40, take I-240 to Exit 4C. On Montford Ave., go N to traffic light. Go right onto W Chestnut St. At flashing light go left onto Cumberland Ave. Go 2 blocks to Cumberland Circle. Bear right to inn on left.
Restrictions No smoking. Children over 10 preferred.
Credit cards Amex, MC, Visa.
Rates B&B, $160 suite, $105–130 double. Extra person, $40. 2-night minimum most weekends.

Acorn Cottage ¢ 🚸 *Tel:* 704–253–0609
25 Saint Dunsten's Circle, 28803 800–699–0609

Located just a half-mile from the Biltmore Estate, Acorn Cottage is a granite Arts and Crafts home built in 1922, and purchased in 1996 by Sharon Tabor. The Red Room has a Tiffany lamp, mahogany queen-size sleigh bed, and a Chippendale sofa, while the Tree Room has whimsical hand-painted tree murals and floral stenciling. The Green Room has a four-poster queen-size bed piled high with pillows, and the Blue Room is done in crisp blue and white highlighted by a quilted wall hanging. Rates include breakfasts of fruit crepes with plum sauce, blueberry cream cheese strata, or apple puff pancakes with cinnamon cream sauce, plus homemade breads, fruit compote; afternoon tea with hot-from-the-oven cookies; and evening turndown service with bedtime mints.

"Warm hospitality, welcoming innkeeper; peaceful, quiet setting; delicious breakfasts; excellent area advice and information." *(GR)* "A step back in time. The four poster bed was marvelous." *(Margaret Long)* "Clean, comfortable, nicely furnished, and beautifully decorated with a rich color palette." *(William Taylor)* "Delightful wooded setting, yet convenient to the Biltmore Estate." *(Elabeth Fisher)* "Each room is decorated with a mixture of antiques and the comforts of home. There were several quiet spots to read: the sun room, spacious living room, and a comfortable backyard porch overlooking a fountain and flowers. The bed was more comfortable than my own—I hated to leave." *(Lisa Dossett)*

Open All year.
Rooms 4 doubles—all with full private bath or shower, clock/radio, TV, air-conditioning.
Facilities Dining room, living room with fireplace, sunroom, porch with swing. 1 acre with gardens, parking, gazebo. 30 m to hiking, cross country, downhill skiing.
Location 1 m from downtown. From I-40, take Biltmore Estate exit to 25N. Follow Biltmore Ave. 1 ½ m, & go left onto St. Dunstan's Rd. Follow St. Dunston's Rd to Acorn signs at intersection with St. Dunstan's Circle.
Restrictions No smoking.
Credit cards Discover, MC, Visa.
Rates B&B, $85–110 double, $75 single. 10% additional one-night stay weekends or holidays.

Albemarle Inn *Tel:* 704–255–0027
86 Edgemont Road, 28801 800–621–7435

The Albemarle Inn is a Greek Revival mansion built in 1909 and listed on the National Register of Historic Places. Owned by Kathy and Dick Hemes since 1992, it features high ceilings, oak paneling, and a handcrafted oak stairway with a circular landing and balcony. Composer Bela Bartok wrote his Third Piano Concerto here. Breakfast is served from 8–9:30 A.M. at individual tables; a sample menu might consist of juice, grapefruit-strawberry ambrosia, leek and artichoke strata, dill bread, and ham.

"Gracious innkeepers. Many lovely paintings, needlepoint work, and Oriental treasures from the Hemes' years in Hong Kong." *(DB)* "Concern for guests' comfort was evidenced by the ample supplies of hangers, towels, bathroom shelves, nightlights, and comfortable chairs or sofa for relaxing. Kathy and Dick provide excellent advice on local attractions and restaurants. Breakfasts are served on the spacious sunporch, with flowers, lovely table linens, and charming white wicker furniture." *(Louise Wilder)*

"Juliet's Chamber is wallpapered in rich tones of cream, blue, and rose, with a queen-size four-poster bed, dresser, armoire, two wingback chairs, ample lighting, and a clawfoot tub in the bathroom. Small touches created a warm atmosphere: needlepoint pillows, Oriental rugs, inviting seating areas, and more. A warm fire burned in the living room fireplace where guests gathered for pre-dinner wine, cheese, and conversation. Delicious breakfast treats included peach and apple crisps, Mexican quiche, and stuffed French toast." *(David & Deborah Stern)* "Our third-floor room was large, airy and clean, with handsome Victorian furnishings. After breakfast we took a walk and admired the beautiful houses in this historic residential neighborhood." *(Mr. & Mrs. Zack Logan, also SWS)*

Open All year.
Rooms 1 suite, 10 doubles—all with full private bath, telephone, radio, clock, TV, air-conditioning, 6 with fan, 1 with balcony.
Facilities Dining room with fireplace, stereo; living room with fireplace, stereo, books; dining sunporch, veranda. 7/10 acre with off-street parking, swimming pool.
Location 5 min. from downtown. From W on I-40 or S on I-26: take I-240 to Charlotte St.; turn left & go 9/10 m to Edgemont Rd. Turn right & go 2/10 m to inn. From E on I-40: take I-240 to Charlotte St. & go right. Follow as above.
Restrictions No smoking. Children over 13.
Credit cards Discover, MC, Visa.
Rates B&B, $160 suite, $95–160 double. Extra person, $25. 2-night minimum weekends, Apr.–Dec.

Cairn Brae ¢ *Tel:* 704–252–9219
217 Patton Mountain Road, 28804 *E-mail:* CairnBrae@msn.com

Meaning "rocky hillside" in Scottish, Cairn Brae is tucked in the Blue Ridge Mountains above Asheville. Millie and Ed Adams's three-story contemporary home has a secluded setting, with great views and walking trails, yet is close to downtown. Guest rooms overlook the woods or rock garden, and are individually decorated, with king-, queen, or twin-size beds; some have lively floral wallpapers and wicker accents, others with mellow pine walls and furniture.

"Coffee by the fireplace every morning was a special treat, as was the sherry and chocolate by our bed at night." *(Martha Ann Mobley)* "The nature trail and stone patio, with its afternoon tea table, swing, and hammock, offer views of distant ridges and the fresh scents of rhododendron and laurel." *(Richard & Cindy Lacy)* "We especially appreciated the restaurant menus and directions. Plenty of reading materials . Appealing common area for reading, TV, board games, sitting by the fire. Surrounded by acres of woodlands, the loudest noises were the squirrels and birds. Excellent dinner at the Windmill." *(Mitzi Rose)* "Kindhearted hosts. Delicious vegetarian, low-fat breakfasts, at my request included poached pears, melon, waffles, French toast, homemade granola, and vegetable quiche. Afternoon tea, with home-baked cookies and apples; evening sherry and chocolates. Ed and Millie clearly enjoy having guests, and are pleased to assist them." *(Elizabeth McCulloch)* "Inviting garden hammock." *(Terry Brady)* "Comfortable, family atmosphere." *(Yvonne & Jeff Adams)* "Mountain top setting; all you hear is the birdsong and breeze in the trees." *(Loli Gray)*

Open April through Nov.
Rooms 2 suites, 2 doubles—all with private bath and/or shower, radio, air-conditioning, fan.
Facilities Dining room, living room with fireplace, TV, games, phone; deck. 3 acres with walking trails, rock garden, fish pond. Swimming, tennis, golf nearby. Close to river for hiking, fishing, boating, canoeing, whitewater rafting.
Location 12 min. from downtown Asheville. From I-240 W, exit at Charlotte St. Go left onto Charlotte St. Go S to light & turn left on College St. Go left 1 block to Town Mt. Rd. Turn left & go 2 m to Patton Mt. Rd. on left. Follow .8 m to #217 on right. From I-240 E, exit at Charlotte St. & go right; follow directions above.
Restrictions No smoking. Children over 12.
Credit cards MC, Visa.
Rates B&B, $110 suite, $95 double, $70 single. Extra person, $20. 2-night weekend/holiday minimum.

Corner Oak Manor *Tel:* 704–253–3525
53 Saint Dunstans Road, 28803 *E-mail:* vineguy@aol.com

Handstitchery and handicrafts are a special focus at the Corner Oak Manor, an English Tudor-style cottage with a curved roof reminiscent of a thatched cottage. Owners Karen and Andy Spradley have highlighted the decor with the work of local artisans, including that of Karen and her sister Kathie. The house is furnished in soft tones of ivory, rose, blue, and green; guest rooms have antique or reproduction brass or iron beds. Breakfast recipes utilize produce from Karen's garden, and might include tarragon eggs in puff pastry, sauteed ham, baked apples with yogurt, and pecan crumbcake; or whole wheat orange pecan waffles with maple syrup, sausage, fruit salad, and cinnamon ripple muffins, plus fresh squeezed orange juice and fresh-ground coffee.

"Karen and Andy continue to upgrade and improve the inn. They are extremely helpful with restaurant recommendations, reservations, and directions. Delicious breakfasts of herb quiche and spicy roast potatoes, or strawberry stuffed French toast. In the late afternoon, a treat always awaits in the living room. We relaxed in the hot tub in the lovely, private patio area." *(William & Elizabeth Kern)* "Restful atmosphere, comfortable beds." *(Frances & Victor Nagie)* "Well-kept yard with lovely flowers. Welcoming innkeepers introduced guests to one another at breakfast. Our room was clean and fresh, most comfortable." *(Virginia Hoffman)* "Outstanding meals, tasteful presentation, well-rounded menu. Andy works at Biltmore and is delighted to share his knowledge of the town and estate." *(Tricia Palumbo)* "Extra touches in my room included fresh flowers and candy, bath salts, books, handmade quilts and afghans." *(PD)* "Cats and cat memorabilia adorn each room." *(David & Amy Greer)* "Our cozy room had a comfortable queen-size bed, settee, dresser, private bath, and an effective, quiet ceiling fan; a hook was provided for hanging clothing." *(EM)*

Open All year.
Rooms 3 doubles, 1 cottage—all with private shower and/or tub, air-conditioning, ceiling fan. Cottage with radio, TV, refrigerator, gas fireplace.
Facilities Living room with fireplace, baby grand piano, stereo; reading/game room; dining room. Deck with hot tub.
Location 2 m from downtown. From I-40, take exit 50 or 50B. Stay in right lane until Biltmore Ave., then move left & turn left on St. Dunstans Rd. Follow St. Dunstans Rd. 2 blocks to Grindstaff; turn right to inn, 1st driveway on right.
Restrictions No smoking. Night-time train whistle.
Credit cards Amex, Discover, MC, Visa.
Rates B&B, $145–160 cottage, $100–115 double, $75 single. 2-night weekend minimum. Mystery weekend packages.
Extras Limited wheelchair access in cottage.

Flint Street Inns ¢ *Tel:* 704–253–6723
100 and 116 Flint Street, 28801

Lynne and Rick Vogel restored their circa-1915 home in 1981 and opened it as Asheville's first bed and breakfast, expanding to include the English Tudor next door in 1985.

"An excellent example of the B&B tradition. Agreeable room and breakfasts; friendly fellow guests. Marion and Rick Vogel could not do enough to make your stay enjoyable; she supplies endless cookies and lemonade. Wonderful conversation and stories." *(Nicolas Adlam)* "Beautiful dogwoods, redbuds, Rose of Sharon, azaleas, lilacs, wisteria, roses, irises, and tulips. The breakfast table is set with fresh flowers, North Carolina pottery, and of course, a terrific breakfast. Rick, Lynn and Marion can always direct you to a place you'll enjoy and give you some interesting tips. They can recommend restaurants for every taste, and you're welcome to bring leftovers 'home' to reheat." *(Bill Baumbach)* "Pleasant, cheery guest rooms, furnished with floral comforters and country antiques and memorabilia." *(SWS)*

"Inviting living room, with its easy chairs and couch, its cut-glass windows and shelves of period bric-a-brac. If we arrive on a cold, drizzly day we know there will be a fire in the fireplace and hot cider waiting. If we return to the inn on a warm afternoon, they will offer us a glass of iced tea to sip on the porch. The Vogels spend enough time with each guest to get to know their preferences, directing one to the crafts, baskets, and quilts, and another to the best hiking trails." *(Norman & Katherine Kowal)*

"Our room had a queen-size bed; the attached bath was a converted back porch with its own sofa, privacy screen around the toilet, and half-sized tub and a shower. Breakfast, served between 7 and 9 a.m., included juice, grits, biscuits, blueberry pancakes or eggs, bacon or ham. Lynn ran after us with an umbrella when she thought it might rain; Rick greets guests in the parking lot and helps unload the car." *(Julia & Dennis Mallach)*

Open All year.
Rooms 8 doubles—all with full private bath, radio, air-conditioning, fan. 2 with desk, some with fireplace. Inn occupies 2 adjacent buildings.
Facilities Dining rooms, 2 parlors. 1 acre with flower gardens, fish ponds. Off-street parking.
Location Montford Historic District. 3 blocks from Civic Center/downtown.
Restrictions Children 12 and over. No smoking in dining room.
Credit cards Amex, Discover, MC, Visa.
Rates B&B, $95 double, $75 single, plus tax. Extra person, $25. 2-night minimum, peak weekends.

Haywood Park Hotel *Tel:* 704–252–2522
One Battery Park Avenue, 28801 800–228–2522
Fax: 704–253–0481

Asheville's downtown area has experienced a renaissance; many of its lovely Art Deco buildings have been restored or refurbished. The Haywood Park, built as a department store, has been completely renovated, and is now connected to a sunlit atrium, with a variety of shops and restaurants. Guest rooms are exceptionally spacious, elegantly decorated with contemporary decor in shades of pearl gray and soft mauve, and supplied with enough amenities to earn the hotel a four-diamond rating from AAA. Breakfast is delivered to guests' rooms between 7–9:30 A.M. and include guests' choice of coffee or tea, and juice, plus cereal, bagel, croissant, or muffin. Rates also include evening turndown service. The hotel's restaurant offers an elegant, creative menu, accommodating to both carnivores and strict vegetarians. Sample entrees include tempeh and vegetable barbecue with grilled polenta, sea bass with sorrel sauce and spinach custard, and mustard crusted lamb with goat cheese and couscous.

"I was told that the person who designed the guest rooms asked his wife to name everything she could need in a hotel room and these rooms are the result. If the story is true, she is a very thorough woman—I lacked for nothing." *(Lynn Edge)* "Right in the middle of Asheville's restored downtown, close to many appealing shops, galleries, and restaurants. Guest rooms are huge, with the original circular support columns adding a note of architectural interest to the contemporary decor." *(SWS)*

"I appreciated having a wall of windows (that opened), and recessed lighting in the bedroom and spacious bath; thick, plush towels." *(Ann McCrory)* "Our enormous room had a corner seating arrangement with comfortable sofas and a Queen Anne desk. The sensational bathroom had a glass-enclosed double-headed shower." *(Dorothy Van Derveer)* "A very expensively renovated small hotel with huge rooms, a striking modern decor and magnificent bathrooms." *(Judith Brannen)*

Open All year.
Rooms 33 suites—all with full private bath and/or shower, telephone, radio, TV, desk, air-conditioning, wet bar, computer hook-ups. Some with whirlpool tub.
Facilities Restaurant, bar, atrium with shops, fitness center, parking garage. Limousine service. In-room massage.
Location Downtown. Take I-240 to Exit 4C. Continue on Haywood St. to Battery Park Ave. on right.
Restrictions No smoking on some guest floors. Traffic noise in some rooms. Some windows face brick walls.
Credit cards Amex, DC, Discover, MC, Visa.
Rates B&B, $155–295 suite, $130–245 single. Extra person, $15. Children under 12 free in parents' room. 10% AARP discount. Alc lunch, $5–10; prix fixe dinner, $28–30; alc dinner, $25–40.
Extras Wheelchair access; some rooms equipped for disabled. Airport/station pickup. Crib, babysitting.

The Inn on Montford
296 Montford Avenue, 2880

Tel: 704–254–9569
Fax: 704–254–9518
800–254–9569
E-mail: info@innonmontford.com

Designed in 1900 by Richard Sharp Smith, Biltmore's supervising architect, the Inn on Montford is an English cottage interpreted in the Victorian Arts and Crafts style. The inn was purchased by Lynn and Ron Carlson in 1997. Twenty mature boxwoods welcome you to the broad porch that spans the front of the house. Inside is the foyer, with stone fireplace and window seat, a formal sitting room with a double mantle fireplace with French doors opening to the plant-filled sun room, cozy library, and formal dining room. Breakfasts are served here family-style at 9 A.M., with such entrees as baked tomatoes filled with eggs and Brie, Bavarian puff pancakes, or raspberry-filled French toast.

Furnishings include Georgian and Victorian antiques and Oriental carpets; carefully showcased are Lynn's prize collections of Victorian silver napkin rings, tea caddies, Staffordshire china, maps, Baxter prints, and period cut glass. Attention to detail is also evidenced by plenty of plush towels, good lighting, extra pillows, queen-sized beds, and comfortable chairs.

"Large, beautifully furnished rooms; wonderful towels." *(LRS)* "Beautiful furniture, friendly innkeepers, congenial atmosphere." *(AA)*

"Warmth, hospitality, and pampering from our welcome to the helpful directions at departure. Relaxing, comfortable atmosphere; quality information and conversation." *(Linda & Charles Hunter)* Comments appreciated.

Open All year.
Rooms 4 doubles—all with full private bath, radio, clock, desk, air-conditioning, gas fireplace. 3 with whirlpool tub, 1 with TV.
Facilities Dining room, living room, library—all with fireplace; foyer, garden room, porch. ½ acre with gazebo, lawn games.
Location ¾ m from downtown. From I-240, take Exit 4C (Montford Ave.). Go N ¾ m to inn on left.
Restrictions No smoking.
Credit cards Amex, DC, Discover, MC, Visa.
Rates B&B, $115–150 double. 2-night weekend minimum April-Dec.
Extras Airport pickups. French spoken.

North Lodge

84 Oakland Road, 28801
Tel: 704–252–6433
800–282–3602
Fax: 704–252–3034
E-mail: stay@northlodge.com

In 1995, Lois and Herb Marsh completed a lengthy restoration of their beautiful stone and cedar shingle home, built in 1904, and opened North Lodge as a B&B. Oriental rugs top gleaming wood floors, and antique and contemporary art and furniture are showcased by soothing tones of cream and soft gold. The spacious Mahogany Room has a queen-size four poster bed, a cozy loveseat, and a color scheme of soft rose with dark green accents, while the cozy Brass Room has an antique brass double bed and tiny floral print fabrics. Care for guests' comfort is seen in the good bedside reading lights and tables. Breakfast is served in the lovely French country-style dining room or on the inviting sunporch, complete with plants, wicker, and lots of windows. The meal is offered between 8 and 10 A.M., and a typical menu might include warm spiced fruit, Belgian pecan waffles, bacon, biscotti, lemon yogurt bread, scones and preserves; or sliced fresh fruit, eggs Benedict, and blueberry muffins.

"Herb and Lois made us most welcome in their charming home." *(Betty & Don Sands)* "Exceptional hospitality, delicious food in generous quantities." *(Beverly Kennedy)* "Immaculate housekeeping; careful attention to detail. Quiet location near the Biltmore." *(Julie Ralston)* "The innkeepers are delightful people who made us feel right at home and helped us with restaurant selections and sightseeing plans." *(Cathy Walls)*

Open All year.
Rooms 4 doubles—all with full private bath, radio, clock, TV, air-conditioning. Telephone on request.
Facilities Dining room, living room, sun porch, common room with TV/VCR, library/den. 1 acre with gardens, gazebo.
Location 1 m to Biltmore Estate. From I-40, go N on Rte. 25 (Exit 50 or 50B).

Stay in right lane to Biltmore Ave. (2 set of lights). Go up hill past Mission Memorial & turn left on Victoria Rd. Go ½m to Victorian Medical plaza & turn right onto Oakland Rd. Inn 300 yds. down on right.
Restrictions No smoking.
Credit cards Amex, Discover, MC, Visa.
Rates B&B, $90–115 double.
Extras Airport/station pickups, $10.

Richmond Hill Inn ✕ ♿
87 Richmond Hill Drive, 28806
Tel: 704–252–7313
Tel: 800–545–9238
Fax: 704–252–8726

Considering the broken windows, peeling paint, and collapsing porches of Richmond Hill in the 1970s, even a starry-eyed visionary would have been hard put to imagine the extraordinary restoration of this historic mansion. The road to preservation was a long and bumpy one, both literally and figuratively—involving major fundraising efforts by the Buncombe County Preservation Society and moving the 1½-million-pound building 600 feet. A happy ending—or perhaps a new beginning—began in 1987 when Greensboro publishers, Dr. Albert and Marge Michel, bought Richmond Hill and began its renovation as a country inn and restaurant; their daughter Susan Michel is the general manager.

This grand Queen Anne-style mansion overlooks the French Broad River from its hilltop location. Built in 1889 by former congressman and ambassador Richmond Pearson, the guest rooms are named for family members or other prominent figures and authors from Asheville history. Much of the inn's original woodwork was saved, including the native oak of the entrance hall and the cherry-paneled dining room. Guest rooms are decorated with draped canopy beds or four-posters, Victorian antiques, and Oriental rugs. Some retain original claw-footed bathtubs and fireplaces. Completed in 1991 were five attached neo-Victorian cottages housing nine guest rooms; they overlook the croquet courtyard and have pencil-post beds with down comforters, and fireplaces. In 1996, the Garden Pavilion was completed, adding fifteen guest rooms, a gift shop, fitness room, and the Arbor Grille restaurant; rooms offer views of the parterre garden, waterfall, and mansion.

Gabrielle's, the inn's formal dining restaurant, occupies the dining room and the enclosed sun porch of the mansion. Breakfasts include such choices as a ham and cheddar omelet or cinnamon waffles with fresh fruit and whipped cream. A recent menu listed such entrees as grilled venison with onion spaetzle, yellowfin tuna with risotto, and rack of lamb with mushroom potatoes. Menus in the Arbor Grille are equally creative, though more affordable.

"We loved reading and relaxing on the porch of our cottage after a busy day of touring. Superb food, extremely helpful staff." *(Sharon & Howard Fagin)* "An elegant and luxurious country hotel. Guest rooms in the main rooms are extremely spacious, with high-ceilings; those in the cottages are smaller and less formal in decor, done in soothing shades of ivory and taupe." *(SWS)* "The F. Scott Fitzgerald Room has a wicker queen-sized bed, window seat, skylights, and such extras as bathrobes, hair dryer, and chocolates." *(Deanna Yen)* "The Gail Godwin room was quiet, pleasingly bright, and small but not cramped. A choice of feather or foam pillows was accompanied by extra towels." *(JPS)* "Our cottage bedroom contained a queen-size bed, two overstuffed chairs, a stocked refrigerator, and plenty of built-in luggage and counter space. Great bedside reading lights. Spacious, spotless bath with a separate tub and shower and an oversized vanity." *(Ben & Peg Bedini)*

Open All year.
Rooms 3 suites, 33 doubles—all with private bath and/or shower, telephone, radio, TV, heat/air-conditioning control; most with fireplace. 1 suite with fireplace, wet bar, whirlpool tub. 12 rooms in mansion, 15 rooms in garden house. 9 rooms in 5 cottages—all with porch, gas fireplace.
Facilities 2 restaurants, piano entertainment Thurs–Mon.; lobby, drawing room, 2 parlors, formal library, all with fireplace; ballroom, porch with rockers. Meeting facilities. 10 acres with croquet lawn, gardens.
Location 3 m from downtown. From I-240, take North Weaverville exit at Rtes. 19/23. Continue on Rtes. 19/23 to Exit 251/UNC-Asheville. At bottom of ramp, turn left. At 1st stoplight, turn left on Riverside Dr.; turn right on Pearson Bridge Rd. & cross the bridge. At sharp curve, turn right on Richmond Hill Dr. to inn at top of hill. "A bit tricky to find, so follow directions and watch turns carefully."
Restrictions No smoking. Restaurant noise in some rooms.
Credit cards Amex, MC, Visa.
Rates B&B, $285–375 suite, $145–285 double. Extra person, $20. Gabrielle's prix fixe dinner, $50; alc dinner, $45. Arbor Grille, alc lunch, $8, dinner, $15–25.
Extras Wheelchair access, two rooms equipped for disabled. Crib.

BALD HEAD ISLAND

For additional area inns, see **Southport** and **Ocean Isle**.

Theodosia's Bed & Breakfast
Harbour Village, P.O. Box 3130

Tel: 910–457–6563
800–656–1812
Fax: 910–457–6055

In 1812, Aaron Burr's only daughter, Theodosia, sailed from Charleston for New York for a long-awaited reunion with her father. Legend tells that pirates captured the ship, and Theodosia was made to walk the plank. Some say that she made it to the shores of Bald Head Island, and that her restless spirit roams the Outer Banks to this day. Lydia and Steve Love honored Theodosia's memory when they built their B&B in 1995, and assure guests that her ghost is a friendly one, always welcome at the inn. The inn's architecture is neo-Victorian, with many gables, tall chimneys, and gingerbread trim; its many balconies offer views of the harbor below.

Although the inn has many appealing features, guests are especially enthusiastic about its breakfasts. A typical menu might include a choice of omelets to order with salsa, bacon, and hash browns or breakfast tortillas, with home-baked honey wheat bread and almond rolls; or a choice of blueberry, chocolate chip, cinnamon raisin, or bacon and cheese pancakes with sausages and raisin scones.

"Bald Head Island consists of maritime forests with massive live oaks and native palms, rolling dunes, beautiful beaches and picturesque salt marshes. No cars are allowed and all transportation is by foot, bicycle, or electric golf cart." *(Marty Buckingham)* "Delightful ambiance, delicious breakfasts, wonderful island." *(Jerry Ryan)* "One's every need is met by warm and friendly hosts. The rooms are attractively decorated and very comfortable, with private balconies for enjoying the lovely view of the harbor; they're well supplied with blankets, extra pillows, ample storage space, books, magazines, nice towels, and toiletries. Coffee is available in the sitting area outside the rooms at 7 A.M., breakfast 8–9:30 A.M., wine and refreshments 5:30–6:30 P.M., and dessert at 8 P.M. Jelly beans and Oreos are always available." *(Ann Bridgers)* "Our grand room had a private sitting area that overlooked the island's vast wetlands. It was furnished with antiques and was very clean and bright. Breakfast was a highlight of our stay." *(Mike & Karen Huennekens)* "Steve and Lydia make you feel genuinely welcome, and are sincerely concerned for their guests' comfort." *(Gaynelle Glass)*

Open All year.
Rooms 2 suites, 8 doubles—all with private shower and/or bath, telephone, clock, TV, air-conditioning, fan, balcony. 2 with desk. 2 in Carriage House.
Facilities Dining room, living room with piano, fireplace, books. Club membership for swimming pool, tennis, golf, croquet. Beaches for swimming, fishing; canoeing. Bicycles, golf carts included in rate for island transportation.
Location S NC. 40 min. drive S of Wilmington, 60 min. drive N of Myrtle Beach. 20 min. ferry ride from Southport. Entering Southport on Rte. 211 E, go right at light onto W 9th St. Follow to Indigo Plantation Dr., which deadends at marina (1.7 m) & ferry terminal.
Restrictions No smoking. Children 9 and over.
Credit cards Discover, MC, Visa.
Rates B&B, $140–200 suite, $130–150 double, $115–130 single. Extra person, $25.
Extras German, Lithuanian spoken.

BALSAM

Balsam Mountain Inn ✗ ♿ *Tel:* 704–456–9498
Balsam Mountain Inn Road, P.O. Box 40, 28707 800–224–9498
Fax: 704–452–1405

"If you are coming to the mountains come all the way up," read the advertising slogan of the Balsam Mountain Inn when this Colonial Revival structure opened in 1908. In those days, visitors traveled via the Southern Railway to the old Balsam Depot—once the highest railway station east of the Rockies, at an elevation of 3500 feet. Over the years, the inn experienced only minor changes, until an extensive restoration was begun in 1990 by owner Merrily Teasley. Restored hardwood floors, beaded board walls, original art, and Victorian furnishings are among the interior accents. The spacious dining room and kitchen have also been refurbished, while guest rooms are simply decorated with an eclectic assortment of period pieces, brightly patterned fabrics, and walls painted in pastels. In 1996, Merrily created a solarium dining porch with a stunning tiled floor and coordinating violet-patterned Waverly fabrics for the curtains and table linens. Rooms on the third floor were renovated, with lovely suites, king-bedded rooms with sitting areas, and Balsam's only elevator. Breakfast might include eggs strata or cheese soufflé, poppyseed muffins, bacon, fresh fruit, and orange juice. Dinner entrees include grilled swordfish, mountain trout, lamb with lemon and leeks, and chicken marsala.

"Not far from Asheville, the Smokies, and North Georgia; easy to reach from Route 74 and I-40. Friendly staff; immaculate, homey, uncluttered rooms, with simple, elegant furnishings. Breakfast in an elegant sun room off the main dining hall. Friendly dog." (MT) "It's well worth paying a bit extra for the larger rooms. Lots of books and magazines to read, and plenty of inviting couches and porch rockers in which to read them." *(MW)* "Friendly, helpful staff. Good breakfast." *(Barbara Iscrupe)*

"Beautiful restoration job, with great use of color and fabrics. My room, #200, had pale teal-green beaded board walls, dark green floral fabric at the windows and on the king-size bed, coordinating linens and plush towels. Rustic twig furniture created a comfortable seating area. While tiny, the bathroom had good lighting (even a nightlight), a new stall shower, hooks where I wanted them to be, and a shelf next to the antique corner sink. Early morning coffee is available in the game room, one of several comfortable and welcoming common areas." *(NB)* "Two wonderful porches run clear across the front of the inn, with inviting wicker rocking chairs and inspiring mountain views. While the main lobby is large, Merrily has arranged a number of inviting furniture groupings to create an intimate feel." *(Maurice & Jean Feldman)*

Open All year.
Rooms 8 suites, 42 doubles—all with private bath and/or shower; some with desk, 22 with ceiling fan.
Facilities Dining room with piano, pub, living room with fireplaces, library, game room, guest refrigerator, porches; elevator. Dinner music some weekends. 26 acres with trails, creek, springs, pond, lawn games. Tennis, golf, whitewater rafting, fishing nearby.
Location W NC. 35 m SW of Asheville; 100 m E of Knoxville, TN. From Rtes. 74/23, exit ¼ m S of Parkway overpass at green sign marking town limits. Make immediate right, crossing train tracks; continue ⅓ m, cross more tracks before turning into inn's driveway at top of hill.
Restrictions Some non-smoking guest rooms. BYOB for whiskey; wine, beer served.
Credit cards Discover (Novus), MC, Visa.
Rates B&B, \$120–150 suite, \$90–115 double, \$70–95 single. 10% extended stay, senior discount. 2-night high-season holiday minimum. Alc lunch, \$10; dinner, \$15–20.
Extras Wheelchair access, some rooms equipped for disabled; elevator. Crib. French spoken.

BANNER ELK

Information please: The **Archers Mountain Inn** (Beech Mountain Parkway, Highway 184, Route 2, Box 56A, 28604; 704–898–9004) is a rustic contemporary lodge, with 15 guest rooms paneled in pine, some with four-poster beds, others with brass and iron headboards. Guests enjoy relaxing on the old-fashioned porch rockers, with lovely views of the mountains beyond, or in the comfortable living room with equally beautiful views. B&B double rates of $70–150 include a full breakfast. "We prefer the spacious, cedar-beamed rooms in the Hawk's View building, equipped with a cozy eating area with refrigerator and microwave, small sitting area with a large stone fireplace, and two four-poster beds.Indescribable views, especially in the early morning fog. Tasty breakfasts with wonderful birds to watch at the feeders." *(Marcia Hostetter)*

BEAUFORT

Pronounced BO-fort (in contrast to BEW-fort, South Carolina), Beaufort is North Carolina's third oldest town, and is located in the south coastal area, 45 miles south of New Bern, 100 miles north of Wilmington, and 150 miles southeast of Raleigh. There's ample opportunity for tennis and golf, plus fishing, swimming, and boating.

Reader tips: "A charming village; everything is within walking distance." *(Donna Bocks, also Gail Owings)* "Originally a whaling village, founded in 1709, with beautiful old houses, their dates posted outside. Lovely gardens, narrow streets, interesting shops, all right on the water. Fascinating water traffic. Beaches close by." *(Betty Sadler)* "We were delighted with dinner at the Net House, a five-minute walk from the Beaufort Inn." *(Brian Donaldson)* "North Carolina Maritime Museum is well worth seeing. Plenty of mosquitoes; bring insect repellent." *(Bill Novak)*

Also recommended: The **Beaufort Inn** (101 Ann Street, 28516; 919–728–2600 or 800–726–0321) is a new structure, designed to blend in with Beaufort's 18th and 19th century architecture. "Its location on the banks of the Beaufort Channel make it delightful to pull up a rocker on one's private porch and watch the fishing boats, sailboats, yachts, seagulls and pelicans, especially at sunset. Comfortable rooms, furnished with quality reproductions, overlooking the water or the quaint town." *(Betty Sadler)* "Our spacious room, (#301) had a king-size bed, great lighting, nice bath, and a small porch. Many repeat guests. Breakfast at separate tables was identical each morning—juice, cheese and sausage pie, croissants, coffee. Pleasant, helpful staff." *(Peg Bedini)* B&B double rates for the 41 guest rooms range from $50–140.

Information please: Overlooking the harbor since 1768 is **The Cedars Inn by the Sea** (305 Front Street, 28516; 919–728–7036), purchased by

Sam and Linda Dash in 1996, and managed by Veronica Jones. The 12 guest rooms are in two adjacent homes, and each has a TV, air-conditioning, private bath, and balcony; five have working fireplaces, and one has a whirlpool tub. B&B double rates of $75–165 include a Southern-style buffet breakfast and turndown service at 5 P.M.

For an additional area entry, see **Cape Carteret.**

Delamar Inn ¢
217 Turner Street, 28516

Tel: 919–728–4300
800–349–5823
Fax: 919–728–1471

Built in 1866, the Delamar Inn is a Greek Revival home restored as a B&B in 1989 by Mabel and Tom Steepy. In addition to breakfast, rates include complimentary wine, soda, and cookies, plus use of the inn's bicycles and beach equipment.

"Mabel and Tom offer genuine hospitality, warmth, and comfort, in a charming Victorian atmosphere. Breakfast beautifully presented on fine china with crystal and silver." *(Barbara & Tom Hanis)* "Warm welcome, quiet and peaceful. Most activities within walking distance of the inn." *(Stuart Pollock)* "A charming and a gracious hostess, Mabel Steepy offers guests a unique blend of southern and Scottish hospitality. Mornings begin with a good breakfast of homemade breads and muffins, yogurt, fresh fruit, coffee, and herbal tea." *(Bill Novak)* "Immaculate B&B, close to waterfront shops, museums, marina, and restaurants. Comfortable bed, beautiful furnishings, modern bath." *(R. Reach)* "Beautifully restored and furnished with period antiques, family heirlooms, and heart pine floors. But the best part was the warm welcome we received, and the way the Steepys accommodated our needs." *(Jeff Krueck)*

Open All year.
Rooms 3 doubles—all with private bath and/or shower, radio, clock, desk, air-conditioning, ceiling fan.
Facilities Dining room, living room with books, fireplace, stereo; family room with TV; deck, screened porch. Garden, off-street parking. 2 blks. from ocean. Bicycles, beach chairs, coolers.
Location Historic district. 1 blk. off I-70, on Turner St.
Restrictions No smoking. Children over 10.
Credit cards MC, Visa.
Rates B&B, $68–98 double. Extra person, $12. Senior, AAA discounts.
Extras Babysitting.

Langdon House ¢
135 Craven Street, 28516

Tel: 919–728–5499
Fax: 919–728–1717
E-mail: cn3935@coastalnet.com

In 1983 Jimm Prest restored and opened the Langdon House in one of Beaufort's oldest homes. He prides himself on meeting the individual needs of his guests: "This is my home, so we're here to fix you a cup of tea to accompany an evening rock on the porch or supply an antacid if those wonderful hush puppies from dinner are still barking in the night." Breakfast is served in two courses: first, a fruit plate, followed perhaps by eggs with cream and basil with lemon-pineapple-blueberry waffles. Dietary restrictions are accommodated, as are late sleepers (breakfast served until 11 a.m.).

"Appealing details included fresh flowers in our room; true-to-history restoration; personal memorabilia; and a rubber ducky in the bathtub." *(Claire Elise Spampinato)* "Jim was upbeat and entertaining, a great source of advice. He anticipated every need from beach bags with sun block, ice water, and towels, to bicycles, dinner reservations, and fortune cookies with afternoon tea. Rooms were immaculate, furnished with period antiques and eye-catching art. Best of all are the breakfasts: piping hot coffee available upon rising, ricotta-and-apricot stuffed French toast." *(G. Gordon Davis)* "With soothing music playing in the background, Jim, having considered everyone's dietary needs and preferences, artistically presents a delicious breakfast." *(Mindy Oberhardt)* "It's just a short walk to the working waterfront—the restoration of old sailboats, salty dogs living upon the water, and many shops are fun to watch and visit." *(Sally Thomas Kutz)* "Homey atmosphere. Great porch, great food, great company." *(Kathleen Swift)*

Open All year.
Rooms 4 doubles—all with queen-size beds, private bath and/or shower, radio, air-conditioning.
Facilities Dining room; parlor for reading, games, breakfast; guest refrigerator; porch; gardens. Bicycles, fishing equipment, beach baskets, beach towels, small coolers. 1 block to boardwalk, shops, restaurants. Cape Lookout National Seashore nearby. 5 m to ocean.
Location Historic district, corner Craven & Ann Sts. From Hwy. 70, turn at light onto Turner St., then left on Ann St. 1 block to inn at corner.
Restrictions No smoking. No children under 12.
Credit cards None accepted.
Rates Room only (midweek), $73–80 double. B&B, $80–115 double, $75–115 single. 10% discount for 6-day stays. 2-night minimum some weekends. Packages.
Extras Local airport/station pickups.

Pecan Tree Inn *Tel:* 919–728–6733
116 Queen Street, 28516

Those of us getting on in years may be comforted to know that pecan trees do not reach their prime until they're over 75 years old. Named for the 200-year-old pecan trees that grace the property, the Pecan Tree Inn was built in 1866, with Victorian porches and ornamentation added in the 1890s. Restored as an inn by Susan and Joseph Johnson in 1991, the rates include a breakfast of fresh fruit and juice, cereal, with homemade breakfast breads, cakes, and buns.

"Easy walking distance to shops, restaurants, and the waterfront." *(Mr. & Mrs. Jim Garriss)* "Susan and Joe made us feel right at home, from the homemade pecan brittle to the fresh-baked morning pastries. After a day of sun, sightseeing, and shopping, we sipped drinks on the wonderful covered porch, catching the afternoon breeze. The Blue Room was done in a blue floral print with wicker chairs, a lovely antique dresser, and many windows. The other guest rooms and common areas were equally lovely and spotlessly clean. A small refrigerator in the sitting room was filled with an assortment of soft drinks." *(Ellen & Mike Daly)* "The Bridal Suite had a huge lace canopy bed and double Jacuzzi, terry robes, private balcony and entrance. Ample hot water for post-beach showers, plenty of parking. Although the bustling boardwalk is nearby, the inn is always quiet." *(Erin Donnelly & Rick Heeren).* "Delightful breakfast on the porch; outstanding gardens. Joe and Susan are warm, friendly, accommodating, and helpful." *(Peter Loomis)* "Relaxing, refreshing, wonderful." *(John & Debbie Lown)* "Ideal location, one block from the waterfront, across from the best restaurant in town." *(John & Katherine Deal)*

Open All year.
Rooms 2 suites, 6 doubles—all with private bath, radio, clock, air-conditioning, fan. 2 with whirlpool tub, desk; 2 with balcony/deck.
Facilities Dining room, living room, library with books; guest refrigerator, porch; bicycles, coolers, beach towels. Garden, with pond, fountain, parking.
Location Historic district, ½block from waterfront. From I-70 and Hwy. 101, go left onto Queen St.
Restrictions No smoking. Children over 12 preferred.
Credit cards Discover, MC, Visa.
Rates B&B, $110–125 suite, $65–110 double, $55–100 single. Extra person, $15. 5th day free.
Extras Local airport pickup. Spanish spoken.

BELHAVEN

Information please: Current reports are needed on **River Forest Manor** (600 East Main Street, Belhaven, 27810; 919–943–2151 or 800–346–2151), a popular restaurant and inn on the inland waterway. The original mansion dates to 1899, and has hand-carved ceilings, oak mantels for the eleven fireplaces, sparkling cut glass leaded into the windows, crystal chandeliers, and dining room tapestries. In 1947 it was purchased by Axson Smith, whose widow, Melba Smith, still operates the hotel today. The famous 65-dish buffet smorgasbord is served daily from 6–9 P.M., with brunch on Sundays from 10 A.M. to 2 P.M. B&B double rates for the ten guest rooms range from $65–85. One reader was delighted with the inn's charming location, tasty meats, fish, and vegetables at the buffet, and handsome antiques, while another was disappointed with the food, inadequate bathroom in their room, and numerous smokers. Opinions?

For an additional area entry, see **Washington**.

BLACK MOUNTAIN

Information please: An old-fashioned family-owned establishment, the **Monte Vista Hotel** (308 West Sate Street, 28711; 704–669–2199 or 800–441–5400) has a big lobby with lot of comfortable chairs, a porch with rockers, and 60 comfortable guest rooms, updated with fresh paint, cheery fabrics, and new mattresses. Three meals are served daily in the dining room, except Sunday supper. "In the center of beautiful Black Mountain. Old fashioned ambiance with modern comfort at a very reasonable price." *(Betty Norman)*

The Red Rocker Inn ¢ ✕ ♿ *Tel:* 704–669–5991
136 N. Dougherty Street, 28711 *Toll-free:* 888–669–5991

"The Red Rocker Inn is located in a small, friendly mountain town. The innkeepers, Fred and Pat Eshleman, are warm, efficient, and hospitable. The inn is an old-fashioned, three-story beige house with wraparound porch, lined with all sizes of red rockers, and a red swing. The walkway is lined with red impatiens. You are welcomed as you are seated for dinner, then the innkeeper blesses the meal, served by the courteous and youthful staff." *(Ruth Fox & Alice Johnson)* "A quiet inn located at the end of a secluded street, surrounded by huge shade trees." *(Frank Campbell)*

"Elizabeth's Attic, the honeymoon suite, is named for the innkeepers' cat and is especially lovely, done in white wicker, mauve carpeting, and rose floral fabric accents." *(MW)* "Beautiful grounds, quiet residential area, with plenty of off-street parking. Pat and Fred Eshleman are superior hosts who make you feel right at home; outstanding hospitality. The rooms are well lighted, the beds most comfortable, and everything is in good condition and exceptionally clean. Scrumptious meals served by a very friendly and efficient wait staff. Mealtime provides an opportunity to meet other guests, make new friends, and enjoy good fellowship." *(William Nelson)*

"Interesting gift and antique shops a few blocks down the hill in Black Mountain; the lake with walking paths and ducks are in the other direction." *(Jane Thomas)* "From Pat's Belgian waffles to Fred's eggs and grits, breakfasts are a treat, as are the dinners of mountain trout with almond butter, meatloaf, country fried steak, barbecued ribs, grilled chicken, and pork tenderloin. Be careful not to fill up on homemade zucchini muffins, fresh vegetables, salads and soups, or you'll have no room for desserts like Mud Pie, Pea-pickin' cake, homemade cobblers, strawberry shortcake, or spice cake. House guests get priority on dinner reservations, but guests should be sure to tell Fred if they plan to eat in." *(Beth & Jay Childress)*

Open May 1–Oct. 31.
Rooms 18 doubles—all with private bath and/or shower, fan. 2 with fireplace.
Facilities Restaurant, game room with piano; living room with library, fireplace; sun room with games, puzzles, cards; porch. 1 acre with flower garden, swings. Swimming pool, tennis, golf, fishing, hiking nearby.
Location W NC, 17 m E of Asheville. 2 blocks from center. Take Exit 64 off I-40 to center of town, turn left and go 2 blocks, then right on Dougherty St. to inn on top of hill.
Restrictions No smoking, no alcohol in public rooms. Parking limited. Children must be well supervised.
Credit cards None accepted.

Rates Room only, $60–115 double, $55–120 single, plus 17% service. Extra person, $12.50. Full breakfast, $8.00. Alc dinner, $16. Children's menu ½ price.
Extras Limited wheelchair access.

BLOWING ROCK

Blowing Rock is a resort town along the Blue Ridge Parkway, named for a unique rock formation, where air currents from the Johns River Gorge return light objects thrown toward the rock. The town has many attractive craft shops. It's located in northwestern North Carolina's High Country, approximately 7 miles south of Boone, and 110 miles northwest of Charlotte. Blowing Rock is known as the "ski capital of the south." With an elevation of almost 4,000 feet, it also offers cool (though sometimes misty and foggy) summers and beautiful fall foliage.

Area activities include shops and galleries, summer theater and concerts, plus hiking, horseback riding, cross-country and downhill skiing, tennis, golf, canoeing, and whitewater rafting.

Information please: For elegant dining and handsome guest rooms, consider **Crippen's Country Inn** (239 Sunset Drive, P.O. Box 528, 28605; 704–295–3487), in a restored and expanded 1930s summer boarding house. A deliciously creative menu is served in the 70-seat restaurant, and nine luxurious guest rooms offer accommodations at B&B double rates of $80–160.

Under new ownership (with a slightly different name) is the **Inn at Ragged Gardens** (203 Sunset Drive, 28605; 704–295–9703). This turn-of-the-century manor house has a quiet but convenient location, and new owners, Lee and Jama Hyett, who have redecorated the inn's eight guest rooms. B&B double rates of $105–150 include a full breakfast and afternoon refreshments.

For additional area entries, see **Boone**, below.

Gideon Ridge Inn
202 Gideon Ridge Road,
P.O. Box 1929, 28605

Tel: 704–295–3644
Fax: 704–295–4586
E-mail: Gideon Ridge@Skybest.com

The Gideon Ridge Inn was built in 1939 as an elegant yet rustic stone mansion, and offers beautiful views of the Blue Ridge Mountains. In 1983 Cobb and Jane Milner converted this house to an inn, and have furnished the rooms with antiques. Jane says that "our guests leaf through our art books and listen to Mozart and Bach at breakfast; they hike, play bridge, shop for crafts and antiques." A few years ago Cobb and Jane were joined by their son, Cobb, III, and his wife, Cindy; in 1995 they became the innkeepers. For breakfast, enjoy a choice of homemade muesli and fresh fruit, or a hot entree. Rates also include afternoon tea—perhaps cream scones, shortbread cookies, and assorted tea sandwiches.

"Comfortable rooms and attentive service. Cobb and Cindy pay attention to details, from soaps and shampoos to good reading lights."

(Debby & John Wallace) "Elegant atmosphere. The staff gave us good advice on hiking trails." *(Pat Jensen)* "We entered to find a roaring fire in the library and an equally warm greeting from our hosts and their cat." *(Linda Stanley)* "Immaculate and carefully maintained; bedrooms are spacious, comfortable; the baths are thoughtfully provided with ample storage space for cosmetics." *(Elizabeth Rupp)* "The stone terrace that wraps around the inn is a perfect place to watch a harvest moon rise over the mountains, serenaded by the frogs, crickets, and owls." *(Jane & Luther Manners)* "Furnishings and bedding were beautiful, bath towels were nice and thick, and there were big, warm comforters on the beds." *(Debbie Murray)* "The Victorian Room has period antiques, a comfortable bed, working fireplace, chairs with reading lamps, windows that opened, and a door onto the terrace. Blowing Rock is a delightful, scenic town with a variety of great restaurants." *(Judith Brannen)* "Views so wonderful we hated to leave." *(AW)*

Open All year.
Rooms 9 doubles—all with private bath and/or shower, desk, fan, hair dryer; some with gas fireplace, 1 with double whirlpool.
Facilities Dining room, library with TV, fireplace, terraces. 5 acres with wooded paths, formal gardens. Golf, horseback riding, hiking, biking, skiing nearby.
Location 1½ m to town, ¼ m. W of Rte. 321; 3 m S of Blue Ridge Parkway. Call for exact directions.
Restrictions No smoking. No children under 12.
Credit cards Amex, MC, Visa.
Rates B&B, $115–180 double. Single mid-week corporate rate. 2-night weekend minimum summer/fall.

Maple Lodge B&B *Tel:* 704–295–3331
152 Sunset Drive *Fax:* 704–295–9986
P.O. Box 1236, 28605 *E-mail:* Maplelodge@appstate.campus.mci.net

Blowing Rock's oldest continuously operating inn, the Colonial-style Maple Lodge was built in 1946 as a guest house for summer visitors. With a private bath for each room, it was one of the most luxurious places to stay in town. Subsequent owners expanded and improved the inn as Blowing Rock's year-round popularity grew. In 1993, it was bought by Marilyn and David Bateman, who further enhanced the inn by redoing the roof, the plumbing, and the wiring, and redecorated the guest rooms with Oriental rugs, rich fabrics, antiques, four poster and canopy beds with heirloom quilts and goosedown comforters.

Breakfast is served 8:30–10:00 A.M. at individual tables, and includes fresh fruit and juice, home-baked scones and strawberry bread or perhaps orange muffins; and such entrees as sausage frittata, bacon quiche, or blueberry pancakes.

"Warm, welcoming, charming owners; handsome furnishings. A copious breakfast is served in the glassed-in garden room, beautifully done with chintz fabrics." *(Peggy Kontak)* "Delicious food, lovely decor; thoughtful extras included a crystal decanter of sherry in our room, plus chocolate, coffee, and tea makings." *(Betty Summa)*

Open Feb. 14–Jan. 3.
Rooms 1 suite, 10 doubles—all with private bath and/or shower, lock, fan. Some with TV, telephone, desk, air-conditioning, refrigerator.
Facilities Breakfast room with TV/VCR, woodstove; parlor with fireplace, books, games; living room with pump organ, games. Garden, off-street parking. 2 blocks to town park for tennis, basketball, swimming pool.
Location In center of town; ½ block from Main St. (321 Business). From U.S. 321 Bypass, go S on Sunset to inn on left; from U.S. 321 Business, go N on Sunset to inn on right.
Restrictions No smoking. Children over 12.
Credit cards Amex, DC, Discover, MC, Visa.
Rates B&B, $139 suite, $89–129 double. Extra person, $20. Senior, AAA discount midweek.

BOONE

Named for Daniel Boone, this little town high in the Blue Ridge Mountains is home to Appalachian State University and the Appalachian Cultural Museum. In the summer, get tickets for the *Horn in the West*, a musical recounting of Boone's story. Area attractions include hiking, bicycling, fishing, swimming, boating and hunting; in winter, five downhill ski areas are within a 20-minute drive. Boone is located in western North Carolina, roughly 100 miles north of Charlotte, and 80 miles west of Winston-Salem.

Reader tip: "Outstanding dinner at Sam and Stu's." *(Susan Woods)*

Also recommended: A mile from downtown Boone is **The Gragg House** (Kalmia Acres, 210 Ridge Point Drive, 28607; 704–264–7289), a contemporary home in the woods, with mountain views. The two guest rooms share a bath, and the B&B double rate of $75–95 includes breakfasts of apple cobbler, home-baked breads, and a ham and egg casserole. "Clean, comfortable, and quiet, with terrific breakfasts and helpful owners." *(Anne & Wade Barber, and many others)*

Lovill House Inn
404 Old Bristol Road, 28607
Tel: 704–264–4204
800–849–9466
E-mail: innkeeper@lovillhouseinn.com

The Lovill House was built in 1875 by Captain Edward Lovill, a decorated Confederate officer, who helped to draft the founding papers of what is now Appalachian State University. Home to the Lovill family for nearly a century, the building was restored as an inn by Lori and Tim Shahen in 1993. During the renovation, the Shahens preserved the old—rebuilding three of the original fireplaces, and refinishing the floors—while taking care to provide modern comfort. To assure privacy, they double-insulated the guest room walls.

Coffee is set outside guest rooms at 7:30, followed by breakfast served at your choice of 8:15 or 9:15 A.M.; business travelers or early risers may enjoy a continental breakfast tray as early as requested. Typical menus include fresh squeezed juice; baked apples or broiled fruit compote; Belgian waffles, vegetable strata, or eggs Benedict; and sausage, served on fine china at tables for four and six. Rates also include an afternoon social hour with complimentary beverages and appetizers, offered from 5:00–6:00 P.M.

"Delightful innkeepers, delicious food—fresh and plentiful. Attention to detail included the down comforter on the bed, the fresh flowers in the room, and the quality bath essentials. Perfect dinner recommendation." *(Brian Croft)* "Pleasant, quiet atmosphere; exceptional service and hospitality." *(Bryan & Cheryl McSwain)* "Extra large towels, terry cloth robes, lovely Ralph Lauren bed ensemble with matching drapes." *(S. Hirsch)* "Tim welcomed us warmly and gave us a great tour of the inn. Our room was warm and cozy, with a huge bathroom and big fluffy towels. After an excellent dinner (thanks to Tim's advice), we returned for conversation with the other guests in the kitchen. Memorable breakfast with great muffins." *(Linda Mote)* "Well-appointed, carefully sound-proofed B&B with a friendly, sociable atmosphere. Great French toast." *(Susan Woods)*

"We were warmly welcomed by Tim and Lori, and were given a tour of the inn; much care was taken to preserve the unusual woodwork during the renovation. Although convenient to Boone's business district, the inn's location at the edge of the city is private, and the woods behind the inn are ideal for a peaceful walk." *(Cynthia Miller)* "Lovely porch for enjoying your first cup of coffee or for unwinding at the end of the day." *(Ann O'Quinn)* "The furnishings are a pleasing blend of antique and reproduction; our room had a king-size bed, fireplace, and beamed ceiling." *(Robert & Pamela Kreigh)*

Open All year. Closed March & mid-Sept.
Rooms 5 doubles—all with full private bath, TV, telephone, clock, desk, fan, radio. 1 with fireplace.
Facilities Dining room, living room with fireplace, stereo; country kitchen with fireplace, guest refrigerator, laundry, wraparound porch with rockers. 11 acres with hammock, gardens, lawn games, off-street parking, stream, waterfall, berry patches, mt. bicycles.
Location 1 m from old downtown Boone, ASU campus. Hwy. 321/421 becomes W King St. in Boone. Going W, turn right on Old Bristol Rd. to inn on right. Going E, turn left on Old Bristol Rd. to inn immediately on left.
Restrictions No smoking. Children over 12.
Credit cards MC, Visa.
Rates B&B, $85–130 double. Extra person, $20. 2-night minimum holiday weekends.

BRYSON CITY

Located just two miles from the entrance to the Great Smoky Mountains National Park, Bryson City is a center for visitors coming to enjoy hiking, whitewater rafting, canoeing, fishing, swimming, horseback riding, golf, and skiing in the Smokies. For a relaxing, scenic excursion, ride the Great Smoky Mountains Railway west from Bryson City, across Fontana Lake, to the Nantahala Gorge. The town is 60 miles west of Asheville, in western North Carolina.

Reader tips: "Avoid the Indian-style tourist traps and seek out two valid experiences, the Oconaluftee Indian Village, and "Unto These Hills," a dramatic presentation of Cherokee history.

Also recommended: The **Hemlock Inn** (P.O. Drawer EE, 28713; 704–488–2885) is situated on top of a small mountain (elevation 2300 feet) on the edge of the Great Smoky Mountains National Park. The 23 rooms and three cabins (all with private bath) are simply furnished in country antiques and pieces made by mountain craftspeople. Rates of $128–144 double and $132–220 cabin or suite include family-style breakfasts, served at 8:30 A.M., and dinner at 6:00 P.M., with country ham, fried chicken, homemade biscuits, baked apple goodie, and other local favorites. "We appreciated the blessing before meals given by the innkeeper and enjoyed meals served on the lazy Susans in the middle of the large round tables. A homey, pleasant, relaxing inn with most congenial guests. After dinner, it was a pleasant experience to rock on the porch, looking out over the mountain, continuing diner conversations or reading." *(Tom Wilbanks)*

Information please: Built by a lumber baron in 1923, the **Fryemont Inn** (Fryemont Road, P.O. Box 459, 28713; 704–488–2159 or 800–845–4879) offers the rustic charm of open rafters and a huge stone fireplace. Rates for the guest rooms range from $95–175, and include full breakfast and hearty mountain dinner. The main lodge houses 37 rooms, with more luxurious accommodations in the adjacent cottage suites. "Our favorite country inn." *(Kyle Berry)*

For an additional area entry, see **Dillsboro.**

Folkestone Inn ¢
101 Folkestone Road, 28713

Tel: 704–488–2730
Fax: 704–488–0722
E-mail: innkeeper@folkstone.com

Owners Ellen and Charles Snodgrass note that "our inn attracts people who love the outdoors—mountains, streams, rivers, and waterfalls." A farmhouse built in the 1920s and renovated in 1988, the inn has stone floors and pressed tin ceilings in the ground floor guest rooms, and a mix of antiques throughout the house. Porches on both levels of the house provide quiet spots for relaxing. Typical breakfast menus include poached pears, orange thyme pancakes with orange butter, sausage, and eggs to order; or fresh pineapple, French toast stuffed with bananas and walnuts, and bacon. Hot coffee, tea, and cocoa are always available.

"The spacious Rocks and Rills room has a queen-sized bed, comfortable sitting area, and cozy wood-burning stove. The spacious bathroom has a sink cleverly built into an antique sideboard." *(MW)* "Our hosts were friendly but not intrusive. Impeccably clean." *(Keith Rasmussen)* "Charming and distinctive guest rooms. Excellent value."

(Sarah Fox) "Peaceful, beautiful setting on an edge of a forest. A great place to curl up with a book. Delicious breakfasts with corn fritters, apple brown betty, mushroom omelets, and pecan biscuits. Charles and Ellen are ideal innkeepers: quiet, with a sense of humor, and anxious to please. Each room has a different decorating theme, from flowers to fishing. Ours had a bird theme, and was charming but not overdone." *(Rhoda Quarterman)* "Breathtaking scenery." *(Jennifer Culbreth)*

"The inn's decor varies from English pub, to Victorian, to country. The location is delightful, within walking distance of the park entrance, and 15 minutes to Nantahala River rafting." *(Susan Boehlke)* "The wicker rockers on the front porch lull you gently as you look out over the Smokies." *(Sally Hardy)* "We were delighted with the Honeymoon suite with its large bath and expanse of glass in the bedroom." *(Gordon Sutherland)*

Open All year.
Rooms 10 doubles—all with full private bath, fan. 6 with private balcony/deck. 1 with woodstove, private entrance.
Facilities Dining room, living room with woodstove, piano; library with books, game room, porch. 2½ acres with croquet, horseshoes. Fishing, tubing, white water rafting, boating, swimming, hiking nearby.
Location Swain County. 60 m W of Asheville. 150 m NE of Atlanta. 2 m from center of town.
Restrictions No smoking. Well behaved children 6 and older welcome.
Credit cards Discover, MC, Visa.
Rates B&B, $69–90 double, $63–84 single. Extra person, $10. 3-night holiday minimum. 20% discount after 3rd night of stay.

BURNSVILLE

Information please: A rustic mountain lodge, the **Celo Inn** (1 Seven Mile Ridge Road, 28714; 704–675–5132) is owned by Randy and Nancy Raskin. This simple but homey inn is set by a river for swimming and fishing; the area is great for hiking or bicycling. "A meticulously crafted gem in the cottage style. Surrounded by lovely gardens, the inn includes a large main building and an outlying cottage. Much of the post and beam construction is hand-pegged, and the gables feature charming but unorthodox framing. Guest rooms are small but adequate (no phone or TV). Our twin-bedded room had a chest of drawers with mirror, rocker, floor lamp, bedside table and shared reading lamp. The private bathroom across the hall was immaculate. Breakfast on weekends is a casual help-yourself affair in the dining room, featuring fresh fruit, warm scones with butter and jam, homemade granola with raisins, yogurt and coffee. On weekdays, Nancy cooks breakfast to order at reasonable prices." *(Esther Magathan)* Double rates are a modest $30–40 double; breakfast is $4 per person extra.

Nu Wray Inn ¢ ✕ ♿
Town Square, P.O. Box 156, 28714

Tel: 704–682–2329
800–368–9729

Owned by the Wray families for four generations, the Nu-Wray was bought by Doug and Barb Brown in 1996, who plan to honor the inn's long-standing traditions and rich history, while still improving the inn. In operation as an inn since 1833, it is best known for its family-style breakfasts and dinners, both open to the public. Guests are seated family-style at several large tables; a full breakfast is served at 8:30, while the dinner bell rings at 6:30, except on Sunday when it's served at 1:00. Dinner consists of two meats (fried chicken, roast beef, roast turkey, chicken pot pie, baked ham, or barbecue ribs), plus five vegetables, salad, biscuits, beverage and dessert.

"Fresh, seasonal, local produce used to prepare wonderful country-style meals. We relaxed on the front porch in the comfortable rockers, talking quietly and watching cars go around this small town square." *(Sue Ann Spears)* "Exceptional fried chicken. Beautiful antiques throughout." *(Angela Ard)* "We love to sit by the open fireplace in the big den. Breakfast includes country ham, hash browns, grits, sausage, eggs, hot apple sauce, apple butter, honey and biscuits that melt in your mouth, juice, and coffee. Within walking distance are appealing antique shops, art galleries, and craft studios" *(Joyce Wilhelm)* Reports welcome.

Open All year. No dinner Mon.–Thurs., Nov.–April. Closed Dec. 23–25.
Rooms 6 suites, 20 doubles—16 with private bath and/or shower, 10 with shared bath. All with radio, clock, TV, desk, fan.
Facilities Restaurant, lobby with fireplace, games, books; upstairs parlor, guest refrigerator, piano room with baby grand player piano; deck. ½ acre with lawn games. Swimming pool, tennis, golf, hiking nearby. 30 mins. to fishing, canoeing, whitewater rafting.
Location Blue Ridge Mountains. 40 m NE of Asheville. Historic district, on Town Square. From I-40, take Rte. 226 N to Spruce Pine. Go left onto US Rte. 19E. Go 15 m to Burnsville. Go right at 3rd light. ½ block to town square.
Restrictions No smoking.
Credit cards Amex, Discover, MC, Visa.
Rates B&B, $90 suite, $75–95 double, $65–85 single. Extra person, $10. 2-night minimum Oct., some holidays, special weekends. Prix fixe dinner, $15, Sunday brunch, $16. Breakfast, $6. Special weekends: murder mystery, 20K/100K bike rides, barbecue/bluegrass, whitewater rafting; cooking class.
Extras Wheelchair access; public rooms, 1 guest room fully accessible. Crib.

CANDLER

Owl's Nest at Engadine
2630 Smokey Park Highway, 28715

Tel: 704–665–8325
800–665–8868
Fax: 704–667–2539

If you're looking for a lovely country setting just minutes from Asheville and all its attractions, visit the Owl's Nest Inn at Engadine, opened as an inn in 1995 by Jim and Mary Melaugh. Built in 1885, this white frame house has a turret and two-level wraparound porches. It was built with the most modern technology of the day, with electricity, indoor plumbing, and central heating—most unusual in what was then a very remote location. The original owner, John Hoyt, named his home Engadine after one of his favorite places in Switzerland; the Melaughs added the Owl's Nest to reflect Mary's owl collection, found perched around the inn. Breakfast is served at 9 A.M. at the dining room table, and might include fresh fruit cup, jam-filled French toast, apple pecan pancakes, or perhaps a sausage and cheese frittata.

"The Captain's Room has a king-size bed and an old-fashioned claw-foot tub right in the bedroom; you can soak while you enjoy great mountain views right from the tub. Three rooms have the original water closets between the rooms, with a built-in dresser on one side, and the original marble-topped sink on the other. The rooms are sunny and bright, with firm, comfortable beds with lovely linens, plus fresh flowers, books, and magazines. The common areas are equally lovely, with wonderful original woodwork and floors, topped with beautiful Oriental rugs. The pine-paneled dining room is especially attractive. The wraparound porches with wicker seating are perfect for relaxing; the surrounding meadows offer mowed paths for walking and benches for taking in the mountain views. It's a bird watchers' paradise, and in summer, the trees are alight with fireflies. Jim and Mary are friendly, helpful, accommodating, and down-to-earth. In addition to the delicious breakfasts, coffee, tea, soda, and juices are always available; often homemade cookies, too. Ideal alternative to staying in town." *(Deborah Frankel Reese also Bonnie Nigriny).*

Open All year.
Rooms 1 suite, 4 doubles—all with private bath and/or shower, radio, clock, air-conditioning, ceiling fan. 4 with fireplace, 1 with TV, double whirlpool tub.
Facilities Dining room with fireplace, living room with fireplace, TV; den with stereo, piano; porches with swing. 4 acres with patio, gazebo, walking paths. Hiking nearby.
Location W NC. 7 m W of Asheville. Take I-40 to Exit 37. Go S 1/10 m to light at U.S. 19/23 (Smoky Park Hwy). Go right and go 1/2 m to entrance on left.
Restrictions Traffic noise possible in front of house. No smoking. Children 12 and over.
Credit cards Discover, MC, Visa.
Rates B&B, $140–165 suite, $90–135 double, $75–125 single. Extra person, $20. Senior discount midweek.

CAPE CARTERET

Harborlight Guest House B&B
332 Live Oak Drive, 28584

Tel: 919–393–6868
800–62–4–VIEW
Fax: 919–393–6868

Overlooking Bogue Sound and the Intracoastal Waterway, the Harborlight is set on a peninsula with water on three sides. Originally built in 1963 as a restaurant, it then became an apartment house, and was transformed into a B&B in 1993 by Bobby and Anita Gill. The inn's exceptionally spacious guest rooms and suites make them ideal for honeymoons and special occasions. Breakfast is served at 8:30 A.M. at individual tables in the dining room, (or at 9:00 in the luxury suites). The menu might include cinnamon tea rolls, spinach sausage quiche, melon, and croissants; or banana pecan pancakes, sausages, and apple dumplings.

"A charming beach house with lots of decks, access to the shoreline from the front lawn, and large windows everywhere with water views. The lovely dining room has a blackboard that is updated daily with local events, and a refrigerator stocked with soft drinks and snacks. Lovely grounds with palm trees and exotic plants. Our suite had French doors opening onto a private deck, a living room with comfortable seating and even a pair of binoculars. The bedroom had a king-size bed, attractive bedside lamps and tables, and a double Jacuzzi with spectacular water views. We saw most of the guest rooms, and even the smallest are lovely." *(Rose Ciccone)*

"Anita recommended two excellent restaurants which we would never have found on our own." *(Jan Silverman)* "Our romantic suite had a two-person tub and a double shower. We watched the spectacular sunrises and sunsets from our private deck. The Gills were well informed about areas activities, and made reservations for anything needed." *(Donna & Michael Smith)* "Real privacy and careful attention to detail, from umbrellas at the door to the morning newspaper to oversized towels." *(Peggy Gregory)* "Bobby helped with our luggage, and Anita supplied a welcoming tray of fruit for our room. Although the rooms are immaculate, comfortable, and exceptionally well-equipped, one of the best features is the view. You can lie in bed and watch the sun rise over Bogue Sound or watch the spectacular sunset. Bathrooms have both showers and separate tubs, plus ample supplies of plush towels, bubble bath, and soaps. Don't miss Anita's rum raisin French toast with coffee ice cream at breakfast. Many shops and restaurants are in nearby Swansboro, Emerald Island, Beaufort, and Morehead. You can visit secluded Bear Island to hunt sand dollars, or simply ask Bobby and Anita to reserve a tee time at a local course. Superbly relaxing." *(Emily Beasley)*

Open All year.
Rooms 7 suites, 2 doubles—all with private bath and/or shower, radio, clock, TV, air-conditioning, ceiling fan, balcony/deck, private entrance. 4 with double whirlpool tub, gas fireplace, coffee maker, refrigerator.
Facilities Dining room, guest pantry, porches, elevator. 1 acre with garden, hammock, off-street parking. On Bogue Sound. Golf, tennis, swimming pool nearby. 3 m to ocean. Kayaking, boat rentals, horseback riding, fishing charters.
Location Central NC coast. 150 m E of Raleigh/Durham. 4 m E of Swansboro, 20 m W of Beaufort. From Hwy. 24, take Bayshore Dr. Go left on Edgewater Ct., right on Live Oak Dr. to inn.
Restrictions No smoking. Children 16 and older.
Credit cards Amex, MC, Visa.
Rates B&B, $95–175 suite, $75–90 double, $60–110 single. Extra person, $25.
Extras Wheelchair access; 1 unit fully equipped.

CASHIERS

A popular resort town since the 19th century, Cashiers is located in southwest North Carolina, 60 miles southwest of Asheville, and 155 miles north of Atlanta, Georgia, at an elevation of 3500 feet. The name of the town is pronounced CASH'-ers, unlike the people who take your money at the supermarket. The Nantahala National Forest offers 1.3 million acres for hiking, fishing, and rafting; Whitewater Falls is a special favorite.

For additional area entries, see **Highlands** and **Lake Toxaway**, as well as **Salem, South Carolina.**

Information please: Listed in past editions, we'd like current reports on **High Hampton Inn** (Highway 107 South, P.O. Box 338, 28717–0338; 704–743–2411 or 800–334–2551), a traditional family resort, set at an elevation of 3,600 feet. Accommodations are plain and rustic, with walls of sawmill-finished pine and sturdy, mountain-crafted furniture. The food is good, plain Southern country cooking, with homemade breads and pastries and home-grown vegetables. Open April through November, the inn has 130 guest rooms, and the $150–200 double rate includes three meals daily. The resort's 1200 acres offer gardens, a lake for fishing and boating, tennis, 18-hole golf course, archery, hiking, plus a children's program and teen center.

Innisfree Inn *Tel:* 704–743–2946
Highway 107 North, P.O. Box 469, Glenville 28736

Built in 1989 by Henry Hoche, Innisfree is a special-occasion romantic getaway. Henry describes it as being "Victorian and elegant, relaxed and comfortable, private and quiet. We're high on a knoll in the Blue Ridge mountains, overlooking Lake Glenville, the highest lake east of the Rockies. We pamper our guests in every way possible." Breakfast is served 8:30–9:30 A.M., and includes juices, teas, fruit, special breads, jellies, egg dishes, meat, and coffee; it's served in the dining room for guests staying in the inn, or brought to guests' rooms in the Garden House. Rates also include afternoon refreshments, evening Irish coffee, and bedtime Godiva chocolates.

"Beautiful setting, beautiful inn. The lovely rooms in the Garden House are enhanced by classical music playing in the background. Friendly, helpful staff." *(Tom Wilbanks)* "Exuberantly furnished with crystal, gilt, cherubs, Oriental rugs, and rich colors. The guest rooms have every amenity you'd want—firm mattresses, fine linens, plush towels, and good lighting." *(NB)* "A three-story mansion, complete with stained glass dining room tower and full wraparound veranda. Each guest room has different charms, from the flowered wallpaper, brass bed, and mirrored armoire of The Cambridge to the king-size bed and mountain views of Victoria's Suite. The great room with cathedral ceiling and cozy fireplace was perfect for wine or tea in the afternoon, and evening sweets and nightcap. We sipped coffee on the veranda after breakfast, watching the birds at the numerous feeders." *(Elizabeth*

Bryant) "Our room was spotlessly clean, well lighted, with a great view of Lake Glenville and the Smokies." *(Mr. & Mrs. Eugene Bogen)* "Combines the charms of a bygone era with the conveniences of today. Beautiful woodwork and authentic detailing throughout. Furnished in antiques with many windows to bring the spectacular views indoors. The breakfast room is a large open area off the kitchen and great room." *(Louise & Richard Weithas)*

"Even the shower had a mountain view. As dusk fell, we relaxed on our veranda and watched the red sun sink behind the Blue Ridge Mountains." *(Wallace Hoover)* "White birches and red tulips frame this lovely Victorian building. We were welcomed with hot spiced cranberry juice and oatmeal nut raisin cookies. Upon our return from dinner, we were offered Irish coffee and hot chocolate. Wonderful breakfast in the tower." *(Paige Pace)*

Open All year.
Rooms 7 suites, 4 doubles—all with private bath and/or shower, radio, clock, ceiling fan. 5 with Jacuzzi or garden tub. 8 with fireplace; 6 with telephone, TV/VCR, refrigerator, deck. 5 rooms in inn, 6 with Garden House.
Facilities Great room with fireplace, dining room in 25-foot tower, observatory room with TV/VCR, games; gift shop, veranda. 12 acres with dahlia gardens, walking trails, hammock, gazebo. Private beach on lake for water sports; boat rentals, fishing. Tennis, golf, hiking nearby. 15 min. to downhill skiing.
Location W NC. 6 m N of Cashiers on Hwy. 107.
Restrictions No smoking. No children.
Credit cards Amex, Discover, MC, Visa.
Rates B&B, $175–300 suite, $125–150 double. 2-night weekend minimum peak season.

CHAPEL HILL

Located in central North Carolina, Chapel Hill is best known as the home of the main campus of the University of North Carolina.

Also recommended: For luxury hotel amenities, including marble-lined baths, health spa, and limousine service, plus a continental breakfast, choose **The Siena** (1505 East Franklin Street, 27514; 919–929–4000 or 800–223–7379). "Relaxing atmosphere. Our king-bedded corner room was spacious and private, overlooking the front courtyard. After an outstanding dinner at Il Palio, we walked in the semi-residential neighborhood. The weekend rate included a generous buffet breakfast of juice, fruit, eggs, and sausages. A beautifully run small hotel." *(Peg Bedini)* This 80-room hotel was built in the 1920s, and has a decor of stone and stucco, columns and arches, with contemporary Italian designer fabrics and furniture. Its restaurant, Il Palio, serves Northern Italian cuisine. Double rates range from $150–200; inquire about AAA, AARP, corporate, and weekend rates.

Information please: Built in 1924 in the Colonial Revival style and donated to the University of North Carolina, the **Carolina Inn** (211 Pittsboro Street, 27516, Corner of Cameron and Columbia; 919–933–2001 or 800–962–8519) projects an image of the genteel, formal

Old South in its handsome lobby and 140 traditional guest rooms. Readers have been pleased with its key on-campus location, parking facilities (parking on campus is impossible), friendly and accommodating staff, efficient management, small but well-kept guest rooms. A $13.5 million renovation of the hotel has resulted in an updated heating/cooling system, up-to-date telephone and electronic systems, and refurbished decor. Double rates range from $115–135. Comments welcome.

For additional area inns, see **Durham, Hillsborough, Pittsboro**, and **Raleigh.**

The Inn at Bingham School

NC Highway 54 & Mebane Oaks Road,
P.O. Box 267, 27514

Tel: 919–563–5583
800–566–5583
Fax: 919–563–9826
E-mail: Deprez@aol.com.

Dating back to the 1790, The Inn at Bingham School combines Greek Revival and Federalist styles, and provides elegant accommodation in a quiet country setting, amid pecan trees and rolling farmland. Operating from 1845 to 1865, the Bingham School served as a preparatory school for young men seeking entrance to the University of North Carolina. Although the school itself is no longer standing, the headmaster's home, listed on the National Register of Historic Places, was meticulously restored as an inn in 1986, and has been owned by Christina and Francois Deprez since 1995.

Breakfast is served at the dining room table or on the patio 8–9 A.M. and includes a hot entree, plus fresh fruit and biscuits. Rates also include such afternoon treats as herbal iced tea and home-baked goodies, as well as evening wine and cheese, served 5–7 P.M.

"Complete privacy and comfort in the Mill House Suite; welcoming, good-hearted owners, Francois and Christina Depres; incredible breakfasts of apple-cinnamon Dutch soufflés and freshly squeezed orange juice." *(Tory Sally)* "Our country-style room had hardwood floors, rag rugs and quilts, and a high four poster bed. We lounged in the hammock, sipping lemonade, enjoyed afternoon cheese and wine, and munched on homemade cookies at bedtime. Scrumptious German apple pancakes." *(Andrea Lins)* "After a nap in the deliciously cool 1801 Room, I showered using the inn's scented soaps and toiletries, then explored the grounds. Hammocks were strung between ancient trees, and a dog napped beside a weathered barn. Francois led me through the woods to a clearing with a large tree, split by lightning. He had carved seats into the giant branches, and built a platform—the ideal treehouse. The inn is equally enchanting, decorated with period antiques, and well supplied with books, magazines, and videos. Christina and Francois were friendly but unobtrusive, sensitive to guests' needs. The next morning, Christina prepared a mouthwatering breakfast of blueberry lemon waffles." *(Colleen Theis)*

Open All year.

Rooms 1 cottage, 1 suite, 3 doubles—all with private bath and/or shower, radio/clock, TV, air-conditioning, refrigerator. 1 with whirlpool tub, fireplace. Some with telephone, desk, fan.

Facilities Dining room with fireplace, living room with fireplace, TV/VCR, books, movies; porch. 10 acres with patio, play equipment, lawn games. Boating, fishing nearby.
Location 11 m W of Chapel Hill. From I-85/40 E, take Exit 148 S 10.5 m to inn on left at corner of NC Hwy 54 & Mebane Oaks Rd. From I-85/40 W, take Exit 154 & go S on Mebane Oaks Rd. at Hwy 54. From Chapel Hill, take Hwy 54 W, 10 m NW to inn on right.
Restrictions No smoking.
Credit cards Amex, Discover, MC, Visa.
Rates B&B, $120 suite, $75–110 double, $65–110 single. Extra person, $15. Children free under 5 years. Senior discount, 5%.
Extras Spanish, French spoken.

CHARLOTTE

Located in the southwestern part of the state, Charlotte is one of North Carolina's largest cities, as well as a major textile-producing center, with hundreds of factories in the surrounding area. The city is home to a number of museums and parks of interest, as well as the University of North Carolina at Charlotte.

Information please: In the downtown historic district is **The Dunhill Hotel** (237 North Tryon Street, 28202; 704–332–4141 or 800–354–4141), a local historic landmark. The 60 guest rooms are furnished in Chippendale reproductions, plus all expected modern amenities and luxuries. "Lovely room, a little small. Service was friendly and courteous. The attached restaurant, Monticello, was outstanding. Convenient location." *(KM)* Double rates are $89–139.

The Inn on Carmel (4633 Carmel Road, 28226; 704–542–9450) was built in 1967 and was restored as a B&B in 1996 by Tom and Linda Moag. B&B double rates for the four guest rooms ranges from $89–109, and includes breakfast. "Spacious guest rooms with unusual antiques. Comfortable beds, good showers. Gracious, informative hostess; charming, quiet location." *(Judy Henderson)* "Accessible, convenient location in this rapidly growing city. The innkeepers take pleasure in making you feel at home, whether enjoying a cup of tea in front of the fireplace, or awakening to the aroma of fresh-brewed coffee." *(Tanja Bean)*

The Inn Uptown (129 North Poplar Street, 28202; 704–342–2800 or 800–959–1990) is a three-story brick Victorian home, complete with tower, built in 1890. "A real treasure for the corporate traveler. The comfortable rooms have writing desks and phones with modem capability, plus fireplaces, whirlpool tubs, and private balconies. Owner Betty Rich recommended good restaurants and great directions for getting around Charlotte. Beds are turned down at night, and a pretty plate with home-baked cookies await your return." *(Ann Christoffersen)* Six guest rooms are available at double rates of $100–159, including a full breakfast; corporate rates on request.

For an additional area inn, see **Rock Hill, South Carolina,** five miles south via I-77.

The Elizabeth B&B ¢ *Tel:* 704–358–1368
2145 East Fifth Street, 28204

Built in 1920 and restored as a B&B in 1990 by Joan Mastny, The Elizabeth B&B takes its name from its location in Charlotte's second oldest suburb—Elizabeth—begun in 1891, and named for Anne Elizabeth Watts. Joan has decorated beautifully in French country decor. The living room is warm and inviting with soft taupe-patterned wallpaper, couches in cream and black-and-white plaid, a deep red Oriental carpet, and accent pillows in red and black. One of the lovely guest rooms has a four-poster rice bed, with linens, window treatments and wallcoverings in white and dark blue, with cheerful splashes of yellow. Breakfast, served at the dining room table between 7 and 9 A.M., includes fresh fruit and juice, and such entrees as French toast and sausage, pancakes and bacon, or waffles and ham.

"Absolutely immaculate. Each room has a distinct personality without being cluttered. Gracious, helpful, unobtrusive innkeepers who care about guests' comfort; convenient location." *(Wendy & Joe Bell)* "The Garden Room has a private entrance, telephone, and television, making it ideal for business travelers. On-street parking is not a problem in this quiet residential neighborhood. Adequate storage space; updated plumbing, electrical and heating systems. Several good restaurants and coffee houses are within an easy walk." *(Robert Kanze)* "The house is shaded by trees and has a small enclosed courtyard in the back, a pleasant place to sit in spring or summer. Inside are several interesting collections of evening bags, old photographs and advertisements displayed on the walls, plus lots of books and magazines. The Mastnys are careful about security, essential for women travelers. Delicious home-baked bread and fruit for breakfasts; Joan is always ready to refill your coffee cup. The guest rooms have excellent reading lights, comfortable chairs, and good mattresses with plenty of pillows. The bathrooms have extra towels, perfumes for guests to try, and an unfailing supply of hot water." *(Ellen Olson)* "I enjoyed early morning walks in this friendly neighborhood lush with blooming dogwood, azalea, wisteria, and more." *(MT)* "Comfortable chairs are made even cozier with lap blankets and throw pillows." *(Mrs. T. Maxwell Bahner)*

Open All year.
Rooms 1 suite, 3 doubles—all with private bath and/or shower, radio, clock, air-conditioning, fan. Some with telephone, TV, desk, private entrance.
Facilities Dining room, living room with fireplace, library, porch. Garden courtyard, 3 off-street parking spaces; also off-street parking.
Location Historic district, 2 m from downtown. From I-85, take I-7 S. Exit at Trade St. E, heading to downtown. Trade St. becomes Elizabeth Ave. & dead ends at Presbyterian Hospital. Go left on Hawthorne Lane, right on 5th St. Go 3 blocks to Ridgeway Ave. Go left for parking.
Restrictions No smoking. Children 12 and over.
Credit cards MC, Visa.
Rates B&B, $89 suite, $69–84 double, $60–75 single. Extra person, $6. No tipping.

CLINTON

The Ashford Inn ¢
615 College Street, 28328

Tel: 910–596–0961
Tel: 888–AT–THE–INN
Fax: 910–596–2556

Listed on the National Register of Historic Places, Ashford originated as a two-room structure in 1839. In 1869, Colonel John Ashford, who had fought at Gettysburg and Fredericksburg, bought the building and expanded it to its present size and Greek revival style. In 1995, Charlie Harte and Larry Knight restored the building as a B&B.

"Larry greeted us and showed us around the inn. The comfortable sitting room has paneling from the town's old jail, remilled at John Ashford's lumber mill; he also used his mill's best quality work for the floors, doors, and moldings. Our room was furnished with antique and reproduction cherry wood furnishings, including a queen-size canopy bed, ample storage and work space, and an armoire that held a TV, restaurant menus, magazines, and tourist information. The pristine white William & Mary cotton coverlet was from the Colonial Williamsburg collection; an Oriental rug accented the hardwood floor. The walls were painted a deep Colonial red with brass-framed prints and wall sconces. A special touch were the note cards with the inn's name printed on the back and our name in calligraphy on the front. The bed was turned down at night, and wonderful Belgian truffles were left on our pillows. The immaculate and well-lit bathroom had pretty flowered wallpaper and double sinks set in a large white tile vanity, topped by gilt-framed mirrors. Amenities included plush towels and robes, glycerin soap, shampoo, conditioner, and lotion. The upstairs hall has a refrigerator stocked with soda, beer, and bottled water. Charlie offered us cocktails or wine before dinner; Although Clinton is located in a dry county, he suggested two restaurants just over the county line.

"A breakfast menu is provided and you make your selections the night before; the delicious choices included huevos rancheros, Welsh rarebit, and Texas French toast. You select the time you wish to be served, between 7 and 10 A.M., as well as a time for early morning coffee or tea. The morning newspaper awaits at each individual table. The innkeepers are hospitable, pleasant, and flexible, accommodating to both business and pleasure travelers. An incredible value, given its handsome decor, high quality, and attention to detail." *(Rose Ciccone)* "Residential neighborhood surrounded by stately homes. Well furnished, extremely comfortable beds. My breakfast favorite is the sour cream and herb omelet with sausage biscuits. Exceptional service from innkeepers who truly care about their guests' comfort." *(Allan Brittin, and many others)*

Open All year.
Rooms 5 doubles—all with private bath and/or shower, telephone with data port, radio, clock, TV, desk, air-conditioning, hair dryer. 2 with refrigerator.
Facilities Dining room with fireplace, living room with fireplace, library/den;

guest refrigerator, microwave; porch. ½ acre with courtyard garden, off-street parking.
Location SC NC. 60 m SE of Raleigh, NW of Wilmington. 30 E of Fayetteville & I-95, 12 m W of I-40. In historic district, Courthouse Square. From U.S. Rte. 701, take Rte. 24 into Clinton. Inn is on College St., near Beaman St.
Restrictions *Smoking permitted.* Children 12 and over. Dry county; BYOB.
Credit cards Amex, MC, Visa.
Rates B&B, $75 double. Extra person, $15. Corporate rates.
Extras French spoken.

CLYDE

Windsong: A Mountain Inn ♿ *Tel:* 704–627–6111
459 Rockcliffe Lane, 28721 *Fax:* 704–627–8080

Gale and Donna Livengood built their "dream inn" in 1988; they had planned to escape Chicago for a warm sunny island, but were entranced by the mountains of western North Carolina. The rooms are large, bright and airy, with cathedral-beamed ceilings, light pine logs, and Mexican Saltillo tiled floors throughout; large windows and skylights let in the mountain and woodland views. The Livengoods have artfully decorated the rooms with their collection of Native American art, artifacts, and rugs; each guest room has a different theme—African safari, country, Alaska, and Santa Fe. They have a small herd of llamas which they breed and use for wilderness trekking. Breakfast includes fruit and juice, homemade breads and muffins, and a hot entree, perhaps buckwheat banana pancakes or egg-sausage-mushroom strata. Coffee is offered after guests return from dinner.

"The Santa Fe room is a charming mix of Native American, Southwest and Mexican furnishings." *(Sandra Scragg)* "To us, Windsong stands for rejuvenation, peace and pampering. Thoughtful touches include bubble bath and terry robes. The delicious breakfasts are a good time to plan the day and make new friends. Guests can enjoy a shopping spree to nearby Waynesville or Asheville, a picnic and llama trek through the Smokies, or a lazy day on the deck with a good book. Donna and Gale are enthusiastic, flexible, and eager to please." *(Paul & Patrice Phelps)* "With its mountaintop setting, luxurious amenities, and gracious hosts, Windsong is an exceptional experience. Where else can you have your photograph taken with a llama herd?" *(Sheila & Joe Schmitt)*

Open All year.
Rooms 5 doubles—all with full private bath (shower & double soaking tub), fan, fireplace, VCR, patio or deck. Telephone on request. 2-bedroom guest house: living room with wood stove, 2 bedrooms, private bath with double-size tub, deck.
Facilities Dining room, common room with wet bar, VCR, videotape library, pool table, books, games, piano. 25 acres with heated swimming pool, tennis court, hiking trails. 20 min. to downhill skiing. 30 min to Great Smoky Mts. National Park, Biltmore Estate. 40 min. to whitewater rafting. Golf nearby.
Location W NC, Great Smoky Mts. region. 30 m W of Asheville. From I-40 take

Exit 24. Go N on Rte. 209 for 2½ m, & turn left on Riverside Dr. Go 2 m & turn right on Ferguson Cove Loop. 1 m to inn.
Restrictions No smoking. Children over 8; any age in cabin.
Credit cards MC, Visa.
Rates B&B, $140–160 cabin, $99–115 double, $90–102 single. Extra person, $20. 10% discount for 5-night stay. Dinner llama treks, $35; overnight treks, $100 daily.

COROLLA

For additional area entries, see **Cape Carteret, Duck, Kill Devil Hills, Nags Head,** and **Manteo.**

The Inn at Corolla Light
1066 Ocean Trail, P.O. Box 635, 27927
Tel: 919–453–3340
Toll-free: 888–846–6706
Fax: 919–453–6947
E-mail: the-inn@outer-banks.com

"Quiet, romantic, and undiscovered" is how owner Bob White describes the inn he opened in 1995 and expanded in 1997, located in the upscale Outer Banks resort village of Corolla Light. Set among stately water oaks and tall pines along historic Currituck Sound, the inn offers luxurious, well-equipped guest rooms plus a wide choice of activities. Breakfast is served 8A.M.–10A.M. and includes bagels, muffins, pastries, fresh fruit and juice.

"Our room overlooked the Currituck Sound, and had a comfortable king-size bed, well-equipped kitchenette, and a gas fireplace. The area has great restaurants and shops, but no fast food outlets. The Corolla area is just what we thought the Outer Banks would be like (but aren't). Visiting the lighthouse and Whalehead Club gave us a taste of Outer Banks history." *(BNS)* "Welcoming, pleasant laid back atmosphere. Nicely furnished, well-maintained rooms." *(Marsha Reinig-Umanu)* "Wonderful staff; careful attention to detail. Loved Bob's margaritas. Gorgeous water view from the hot tub." *(KH)*

Open All year.
Rooms 3 suites, 38 doubles—all with full private bath, telephone, radio/clock, TV, air-conditioning, refrigerator, hair dryer. Many with whirlpool tub, balcony/deck, gas fireplace, kitchenette.
Facilities Breakfast room, guest laundry. Movies summer weekends. Small garden area, swimming pool, hot tub, deck overlooking Sound, 400-foot pier with gazebo. Kayak, wave runners, paddle boat rentals. Golf nearby. Sports center with 7 outdoor tennis courts, children's swing set, indoor Olympic-size pool, saunas, racquetball, indoor clay tennis courts. Bicycling, jogging paths. Walking distance to ocean beaches, light house, Whalehead club, shopping, restaurants.
Location Outer Banks. 2 hours S of Norfolk, VA. 12 m N of Duck, 15 m S of VA border.
Restrictions No smoking.
Credit cards Amex, MC, Visa.

Rates B&B, $169–269 suite, $75–239 double. Extra person, $15. Off-season senior discount. 2-3 night weekend/holiday minimum. Off-peak packages.
Extras Wheelchair access; 3 rooms specially equipped. Cribs, babysitting.

DILLSBORO

The Chalet Inn ¢ *Tel:* 704–586–0251
285 Lone Oak Drive, Whittier 28789 *Fax:* 704–586–0251

Hanneke and George Ware first met in 1985 in the Netherlands, where she was born and where he was stationed with the U.S. Army. Their dream of opening a mountain inn became a reality in 1993, when they opened the Chalet Inn, an Alpine-style guesthouse in the Blue Ridge Mountains. Carefully built by the Wares using post-and-beam construction, the inn has the overhanging roof and flower-bedecked balconies of an authentic chalet, with natural wood siding that blends perfectly with its forest setting. Breakfast is served 7:30–9 A.M. and includes imported German-style meats, whole-grain breads, authentic *brotchen* (hard rolls), Swiss muesli, yogurt, cereal, home-made pastries, fresh fruit, soft-boiled eggs or perhaps a quiche.

"Warm hospitality; professional innkeepers, wonderful breakfasts." *(Jose Juarbe)* "Hanneke and George provide a special blend of warm Southern comfort with a touch of the Alps, and careful attention to detail. The great room with its massive stone fireplace provides a gathering place to meet old friends or make new ones. Exceptionally clean." *(James E. Shane, Jr.)* "A scenic curving road with lush hardwood forests, rolling hillsides, and quaint towns leads to the inn. We were welcomed by the Wares, given a tour, a hand with the luggage, and were offered a glass of wine or beer. The Wares greeted us the next morning in traditional Bavarian costumes." *(Keith & Sue Bergh)* "Each room has a private balcony overlooking either a small stream and the woods or the Great Smoky Mountains." *(Jodi Fleming)* "The warm and helpful innkeepers are delighted to suggest hikes and area activities. Rooms are well insulated for temperature and noise control." *(Terry Kupers)* "Tucked into a mountain cove, the inn commands a lofty overlook of hills and valleys. The inn's construction reflects an amazing attention to detail and an abundance of hard work; the Wares laboriously hand-cut the intricate design into the wood which trims each balcony. Guest rooms are clean, crisp, and comfortable. George and Hanneke are exceptional sources of information on local activities, from hiking to bicycling, train rides to shopping trips." *(Paula Rebar)* "In the evening we sat by the fire, reading and enjoying a glass of wine or beer." *(Brett & Wendy Grieves)*

Open Late March through New Year's Day; also Valentine's Day.
Rooms 2 suites, 4 doubles—all with private bath and/or shower, clock, ceiling fan, balcony. 1 with whirlpool tub, fireplace, radio.
Facilities Dining area, great room with fireplace, library; balconies. 22 acres with picnic area with grill, lawn games, hiking, pond, brook, waterfall. 10 m S

of Great Smoky Mts. Natl. Park. Whitewater rafting, golf, fishing, horseback riding, gem mining nearby.
Location Western NC. 40 m W of Asheville. 8 min. W of Dillsboro. Short drive E of Bryson City, S of Cherokee. From I-40, take Exit 27, & go W on Rte. 74/441 & go 3 m to Frontier Trading Post. Go left across river at old steel girder bridge, onto Barkers Creek Rd. Go 2⁄10 m & go right on Thomas Valley Rd. Go 1 1⁄10 m & go left on Nations Creek Rd. Go 3⁄10 m to inn on right.
Restrictions Absolutely no smoking. Children 12 and over.
Credit cards MC, Visa.
Rates B&B, $120–150 suite, $70–95 double. 2-night weekend minimum.
Extras Limited wheelchair access. Fluent Dutch, German; limited French.

DUCK

Duck is located on the Outer Banks of northeastern North Carolina, 80 miles south of Norfolk, Virginia.

For additional area entries, see **Cape Carteret, Corolla, Kill Devil Hills, Nags Head,** and **Manteo.**

Advice 5 Cents, A Bed & Breakfast — *Tel:* 919–255–1050
111 Scarborough Lane — 800–238–4235
P.O. Box 8278, 27949 — *E-mail:* advice5@theouterbanks.com

"What's in a name," wrote William Shakespeare. When it comes to inns, you can tell quite a lot. For starters, you can be sure that a B&B called Advice 5 Cents will be neither formal nor pretentious. When Donna Black and Nancy Caviness built their inn in 1995, they took care to create a warm, relaxing atmosphere where guests would feel right at home, while being pampered in a way that highlights any vacation.

Rates include early morning coffee, breakfast served at separate tables, generally 8 A.M.–9 A.M., and afternoon refreshments. [A] typical morning menu includes strawberries and kiwi with lime sauce, orange poppy seed bread, blackberry jam muffins; or sourdough French bread with maple syrup and baked spiced peaches; or citrus compote, apricot almond coffee cake, and Irish oatmeal muffins. Afternoon tea or lemonade features "infamous" gingersnaps as well as other home-baked treats.

"The two friendly proprietors had fun stories to tell while serving up a delicious breakfast. Bedside reading included a fascinating book of lighthouse ghost stories." *(Bunnie Union)* "Delicious afternoon blackberry tea and scrumptious brownies. Squeaky clean. Donna and Nancy's attention to detail is seen in every room." *(Carmen DiSylvestro)* "Everything is topnotch: food, decor, linens, even the beach chairs. Donna and Nancy designed this beach house as a place where you can feel comfortable going barefoot." *(Mark & Paula Kukulich)* "The innkeepers have a wealth of area knowledge, with great suggestions for restaurants, jogging routes, and sightseeing." *(Debera Conlon)* "Wonderfully fresh smelling, and clean, clean, clean!" *(Susan Erika Reynolds)* "The inn is tucked away on a quiet street, yet is within walking distance of everything. The bedrooms are done in soft, appealing colors, with firm, comfortable beds, fluffy pillows and comforters. Natural woods, pastel colors, and overstuffed couches highlight the common room. In addition to the usual beach activities, art galleries and good books are at hand for the occasional rainy day." *(Jamie & Ron Rosas)* "Everything was great, from the peppermint patties left on your pillow (Advice 5 Cents, Peanuts, get it?), to the beautiful Ships Overlook—a small room glassed in on three sides with a beautiful view, from the games cupboard to the menu basket." *(Laura Goyer)* "Innkeepers who cherish your privacy while attending to your every need." *(MW)*

Open All year.
Rooms 1 suite, 4 doubles—all with private bath and/or shower, radio, clock, air-conditioning, ceiling fan, deck. 1 with TV, whirlpool tub.
Facilities Great room with dining area, fireplace, TV, stereo, books; porches with swing; wet bar with icemaker; outdoor showers. Beach equipment; off-street parking. Use of Sea Pines swimming pool, tennis court across street. Five-minute walk to beach, shops, restaurants. Fishing, recreational boating, sailing, kayaking, windsurfing, parasailing, tennis, golf nearby.
Location From N, reach Outer Banks via Rtes. 168 & 158 & cross Currituck Sound at Wright Memorial Bridge. From S & W, take US 64, crossing Pamlico Sound at Manteo & go N on US 158. Duck is 20 m N of 64/158 intersection, 5 m N of Rtes. 158/12 intersection. In Duck, turn right immediately after Duck Blind Art Gallery. Go to crest of hill & inn on right entering Sea Pines.
Restrictions No smoking. Children 16 and over.
Credit cards MC, Visa.
Rates B&B, $105–160 suite, $80–125 double. Special getaway weekends with dinner, wine tasting.

Sanderling Inn
1461 Duck Road, 27949
Tel: 919–261–4111
800–701–4111
Fax: 919–261–1638
E-mail: 74161.40@compuserve.com

As much as we love historic old inns, we are equally delighted when readers enthuse about contemporary inns built with style and distinction. The Sanderling is just such a place. Traditional beach front architecture is blended with a modern sense of space, and the decor combines natural oak with wicker and soft pastel colors. The inn's restaurant is housed in a restored turn-of-the-century lifesaving station; the lunch entrees include pulled pork barbecue sandwiches and ham and swiss rollups in pesto flour tortillas. A dinner selection might begin with foccacia topped with crabmeat and artichokes, fish creole with seafood and sausage, or traditional Carolina crabcakes. Rates include a continental breakfast, afternoon tea, and use of the fully equipped health club.

"Gorgeous scenery, wonderful accommodations, outstanding food, plus substantial off-season discounts. Our ocean-front room (#201) in the main building was huge, with a fully-equipped kitchenette, large balcony, king-size bed, and a sofa bed. There were robes, toiletries, a bottle of wine, and goodies. Afternoon tea was provided with homemade sweets; the breakfast buffet included an assortment of juices, fruits, cereals and pastries. Two small, unusual but nice touches—lockable bureau drawers and a flashlight by the bed." *(Peg Bedini)* "Luxurious common rooms with working fireplaces, current magazines and bestsellers. Second-floor rooms have an outstanding view of the ocean or Currituck Sound." *(Lana Alukonis)* "An extensive collection of bird carvings and Audubon prints highlight the public areas." *(DLG)* "Overlooks a beautiful, vast beach." *(JM)* "We spent relaxing days going from the private beach to the pool to the deck off our room to the rocking chairs on the front porch to the whirlpool." *(Rebecca Anderson)* "The adjacent nature trails are an added treat for wildlife viewing." *(James Burr)*

Open All year.
Rooms 2 3-bedroom villas, 11 suites, 77 doubles—all with full private bath, telephone, TV, radio, desk, air-conditioning, coffee maker, kitchenette or wet bar, porch. 29 rooms in main inn; 26 rooms in South inn with VCR, 6 with Jacuzzi, stereo; 32 rooms in North inn.
Facilities Restaurant, bar, lounges with fireplaces, games, videos; living room with TV/VCR, games; conference center; gallery. Health club with indoor swimming pool. Outdoor swimming pool, hot tub, massage therapy, tennis courts, private beach, jogging trails; 3400-acre nature preserve adjacent. Golf, indoor tennis, birdwatching nearby.
Location NE NC, Outer Banks. 80 m SE of Norfolk, VA. 5 m N of Duck. Take Rte. 158 or 64 onto Outer Banks. From Kitty Hawk, go N approx. 12 m to Sanderling.
Restrictions No cigar or pipe smoking in restaurant. Most 1st floor rooms lack water views.
Credit cards Discover, MC, Visa.
Rates B&B, $254–430 suite, $123–260 double. Extra person, $25. Discount for 7-night stay or 5-night, Sun.–Thurs., except July–Aug. New Year's Eve, July 4, birthday, romance, tennis, golf packages; special value packages. Alc breakfast, $5; alc lunch, $8–15; alc dinner, $15–25.
Extras Wheelchair access; some rooms equipped for disabled. Crib, $10; babysitting.

DURHAM

Located in the Piedmont region of central North Carolina, Durham is the home of Duke University, and is a center for medical education. South of town is an area known as the Research Triangle, a center of industrial research, supported by the area's three major universities—Duke, UNC, and NC State.

Also recommended: B&B&B—bed & breakfast & baseball—awaits you at **The Old North Durham Inn** (922 North Mangum Street, 27701; 919–683–1885). In addition to food and lodging, guests receive free tickets to the Durham Bulls' home games. The inn is located just across the street from the residence filmed in the movie, *Bull Durham*, and is five minutes from the ballpark. A Colonial Revival home built in 1906, the inn has four guest rooms with private baths, ten-foot ceilings, queen-size beds, and period decor. The B&B double rate of $100 also includes a full breakfast and afternoon refreshments. "Had a great time at the Bulls game, then came 'home' to this relaxing place. Loved the special soaps, thick towels, and whirlpool tub." *(Gregory & Grace Munson)*

For additional area inns, see **Chapel Hill, Hillsborough,** and **Raleigh.**

Arrowhead Inn 👪 ♿ *Tel:* 919–477–8430
106 Mason Road, 27712 800–528–2207
Fax: 919–471–8430

The Arrowhead dates from 1775, when it was a large slave-holding property. Owners Jerry and Barbara Ryan have preserved the inn's Colonial architecture, and have decorated the rooms in a homey and comfortable style, ranging from Colonial through Victorian. A five-foot stone arrowhead stands on the lawn; erected sixty years ago, it marks the Great Trading Path to the Smokies, which carried Indians, and then white settlers, to the West. Rates include afternoon refreshments and a full country breakfast.

"Neat, clean, and comfortable. The Ryans are friendly and helpful, yet not overbearing. Delicious food, beautifully presented. We love the comfort and privacy of the log cabin." *(Tim & Cindi Whiteside)* "Spotless and tastefully decorated but not overdone; large rooms with high ceilings, comfortable beds with extra quilts. We enjoyed chatting with the other guests over breakfast." *(Pat Wetzler)* "All business conveniences in a family atmosphere; country setting minutes from the city." *(Natalie Chanin)* "The well-loved appearance of the inn's comfortable furnishings are part of its charm. Carefully planned and prepared breakfast menus, accommodating dietary needs." *(HSI)* "Good selection of local menus. Fluffy towels and bathrobes." *(Celia McCullough)*

Open All year.
Rooms 1 cabin with private bath, fireplace; 1 suite with private bath; 6 doubles with full private bath. All with air-conditioning, radio, desk. Some with telephone, TV. 2 rooms in carriage house.
Facilities Dining room, family room with TV/VCR, games, stereo, fireplace, books, videos; living room with fireplace, guest refrigerator. 4 acres with gardens, picnic area, swings, children's play equipment. Tennis, golf, boating, fishing nearby.
Location Central NC. 8 m N of Durham. 7 m N of I-85. Take Rte. 501 (Duke St./Roxboro Rd.) N; look for West Point on the Eno Park. Go 3 m further N to traffic light at intersection of Rte. 501 and Mason/Snow Hill Rd. to inn on left.
Restrictions No smoking in guest rooms.
Credit cards Amex, DC, MC, Visa, Discover.
Rates B&B, $185 cabin, $145 suite, $95–115 double, $90 single. Extra person, $15. Discount for extended stays.
Extras Wheelchair access to cabin. Crib. French spoken.

EDENTON

One of the colonial capitals of North Carolina, Edenton is filled with tree-lined streets of 18th- and 19th-century houses. It's located in northern coastal North Carolina on the Albemarle Sound, 80 miles southwest of Norfolk, 70 miles west of the Outer Banks, 125 miles south of Richmond, VA, and 150 miles east of Raleigh; it's four hours south of Washington, D.C.

Reader tips: "Edenton is a lovely town off the beaten track. The oldest courthouse in the nation is there, and I would particularly recommend a visit to the charming St. Paul's Episcopal Church (1736)." *(Harrison Gardner)* "We took the worthwhile walking tour originating at the Visitors' Center, with a gracious volunteer guide. Spring and summer are noted for azaleas and crape myrtle displays." *(Peg Bedini)*

Also recommended: Best known for its unusual decor, the **Granville Queen Inn** (108 South Granville Street, 27932; 919–482–5296), has nine guest rooms, each named and decorated for a different "Queen," from the Queen of Egypt room with imported bronze 600-pound sphinxes and tented seating area, to the Peaches and Queen room with ornate Victorian furniture and lacy accents. The five-course breakfast, served weekends from 8–10 A.M., includes apple crunch muffins, fresh fruit cup, yogurt with granola, filet mignon and eggs with rosemary potatoes, and a soufflé or blueberry cream cheese crepe. B&B double rates range from $95–105 on weekends, including evening wine tastings; corporate rates midweek. "Delightful return visit. Same fascinating decor and sumptuous breakfast. Marge and Ken Dunne are the most pleasant hosts. Good reading lamps. Our room had an oversize garden tub with a hand-held shower; a few rooms also have regular stand-up showers." *(Peg Bedini)*

The Lords Proprietors' Inn
300 North Broad Street, 27932

Tel: 919–482–3641
800–348–8933
Fax: 919–482–2432
E-mail: reserv@lordspropedenton.com

Since they first opened The Lords Proprietors' Inn in 1981, Arch and Jane Edwards have renovated three adjacent Victorian buildings and built a restaurant. Rooms are furnished with antiques, and beds have been specially constructed by local cabinetmakers. Chef Kevin Yokley's dinner menus change nightly; a recent meal included crab cakes, salad, veal with red pepper sauce or yellowfin tuna, ending with a signature chocolate dessert or strawberry short cake.

"The guest rooms were all so attractive that it was hard to choose our favorite. They are large, very clean, with bathrooms that have much needed shelf space (a rarity at many inns). The staff was friendly and knowledgeable about area activities. Superb dinner of crawfish tempura, shrimp with sun-dried tomatoes or lamb with dried cherry sauce, and a chocolate soufflé to finish (us) off. Breakfasts were equally wonderful. I enjoyed the feel of a larger inn with several buildings and a separate building for dining." *(Sona Nast)* "Excellent service, charming decor, outstanding cuisine, friendly innkeepers." *(Marguerite Zschiegner)* "Outstanding breakfast by a real Southern cook." *(Anita Fleischer)* "A lovely old inn, tastefully decorated with quality period antiques, supplemented by overstuffed reading chairs in the parlors. Early risers will find the parlors an inviting place for reading." *(John Blewer)* "We breakfasted in a separate one-story dining house, where we enjoyed fresh fruit, orange juice, coffee, and eggs." *(Bruce Campbell)* "I enjoyed canoeing in a nearby mill pond, exploring the world of cypress swamps and beaver dams under a canopy of Spanish moss, then returning at the end of the day to a room in the Pack House. Simple rag rugs from North Carolina's mountains contrast with handsome antiques and fit perfectly with the wide floor boards." *(Rick Larson)* "Our room was comfortable and quiet, even though it is on the main street. Lovely back garden; delicious breakfast of sour cream waffles and sausage. Iced tea and homemade cookies available in the sitting room." *(Julia & Dennis Mallach)*

Open All year.
Rooms 20 doubles—all with full private bath, telephone, TV, air-conditioning. Most with desk. Rooms in 3 adjacent buildings.
Facilities 4 parlors, all with fireplace, 1 dining/meeting room, gift shop, patios, 2 guest kitchens. 1.5 acres. Docks, marinas, golf, tennis, river for fishing, swimming nearby.
Location Center of Historic District. From I-95, take I-295 to Petersburg, VA. Past Petersburg, take Hwy 460 E to Suffolk, Va. At Suffolk, leave 460 & go through town to Hwy 32 S to Edenton. Inn is 6 blocks N of waterfront at corner of Albemarle & Broad Sts.
Restrictions No smoking in dining room or guest rooms. No children under 10 at dinner; babysitting arranged. "Well-behaved children welcome." Central AC; most windows don't open.
Credit cards None accepted.
Rates B&B (Sun.–Mon.) $125–170 double. MAP, (Tues.–Sat.) $185–235 double. Extra person, $20–65. Historic Preservation weekends, Feb., March.
Extras Wheelchair access; 1 room specially equipped. Local airport/marina pickup. Crib, babysitting.

Trestle House Inn at Willow Tree Farm
632 Soundside Road, 27932

Tel: 919–482–2282
800–645–8466
Fax: 919–482–7003
E-mail: thinn@coastalnet.com

Built in 1972, Trestle House takes its name from the 400-year-old California redwood timbers that were used in its construction. They were originally part of a railroad trestle used by the Southern Railroad company, and were left abandoned at what is now the local airport. Purchased at auction, the wood was milled for use as massive support beams throughout the house. Set in a wildlife preserve overlooking a pond and bordered on three sides by water, the inn was purchased by Peter Bogus and Wendy Jewett in 1996. Breakfast is served at 8:30 A.M. at individual tables in the dining room overlooking the canal, and includes orange French toast or perhaps omelets with home-baked breads and muffins. Guest rooms are named for the birds that often can be seen at the inn, and offer a choice of twin-, double-, queen-, or king-size beds; most have water views.

"Very romantic and peaceful, whether you're birdwatching on the deck overlooking the pond, or curled up by the massive fireplace. Tasty breakfast of pancakes and bacon." *(Charles & Gwen Homicki)* "Freshly renovated; bright and cheery rooms; everything in good working order. Hospitable innkeeper welcomed us with wine and coffee. Quiet, serene setting. Homey atmosphere; wonderful fireplace." *(Philip Eckmund)* "Wonderfully calm setting, on a lake populated by bass, turtles, and ducks. The inn itself is filled with books—a paradise for readers. Peter is a most warm and friendly innkeeper, always ready to offer a glass of wine, make a dinner reservation, or tell you about the inn." *(Neil Offen)*

Open All year.
Rooms 1 suite, 4 doubles—all with private bath and/or shower, radio, clock, desk, air-conditioning, ceiling fan.
Facilities Dining room, living room, family room with fireplace, TV/VCR, stereo, books. 6 acres with lawn games. Swimming, boating, fishing, hiking, birding nearby.
Location 3 m from town. From Chesapeake Bay Bridge & Tunnel, take Rte 13S to Rte 64 E, to Exit 84B (Rte. 104 S). Go to Rte 17 S-Bypass (Elizabeth City) to Rte. 17 S-Business to Edenton (85 m). From Edenton, take Rte. 32 S 1.8 m. Go right onto Soundside Rd., & go ⅖ m to inn on right.
Restrictions No smoking. Children 12 and over.
Credit cards Amex, MC, Visa.
Rates B&B, $120–160 suite, $80–100 double, $60–95 single. Extra person, $15. Senior discount.

HENDERSONVILLE

Nestled between the Great Smoky and Blue Ridge Mountains, Hendersonville is both a popular resort and an active farming community. Throughout the 19th century, wealthy southerners took refuge from the summer heat in the fresh mountain air, building summer homes and hotels. Today's visitors enjoy hiking in nearby Chimney Rock Park, as well as the town's many summer festivals, highlighted by the North Carolina Apple Festival, a ten-day event held through Labor Day. There's an excellent theater in neighboring Flat Rock, and on Monday nights, Hendersonville closes sections of Main Street for two hours of clogging and square dancing. The home of Carl Sandburg, also in Flat Rock, is worth seeing. Other activities include golf and white-water rafting. Hendersonville is in western North Carolina, 20 miles south of Asheville via I-26.

Reader tip: "Enjoy dinner in town at Expressions, or drive to Saluda or Green River for barbecue." *(Kerry Smithwick)*

Information please: Listed on the Register of Historic Places, **The Claddagh Inn** (755 North Main Street, 28792; 704–697–7778 or

800–225–4700), has been welcoming guests for almost a century. Each of the 14 guest rooms has a private bath, telephone, and TV. The B&B double rates of $85–109 include a full breakfast. "Old world charm, with spacious hallways upstairs and down. Several first-floor guest rooms a plus for older visitors. Short walk to the main shopping street." *(Betty Norman)*

Two miles south of Hendersonville is the **Highland Lake Inn** (Highland Lake Drive, P.O. Box 1026, Flat Rock 28731; 704–693–6812 or 800–762–1376), built as a private club in 1910. Fifteen cottages and 50 guest rooms are available, with double rates ranging from $69–149, including all activities. Meals are extra, but rates are reasonable. "Our kids loved the many cats, dogs, peacocks, goats, cows, horses, ducks, and geese. Nice swimming pool, lake for canoeing and fishing, big vegetable garden which contributed to the delicious meals, and rocking chairs on the porches of the rustic but comfortable cabins. Safe, fun, and relaxing." *(Celia McCullough)*

For additional area entries, see **Pisgah Forest, Saluda,** and **Tryon.**

Apple Inn ¢ *Tel:* 704–693–0107
1005 White Pine Drive, 28739 800–615–6611

"You'll feel like you're visiting Grandma's," say Pam and Bob Hedstrom, who restored this turn-of-the-century farmhouse in 1994. Although just minutes from town and all area attractions, the quiet country setting makes for a relaxing getaway. Rooms are furnished with period antiques and reproductions, many with beautiful hardwood floors. Breakfast is served at 8:30 at individual tables in the dining room, and includes fresh fruit and juice, and such favorites as apple pancakes, apple cobbler, or fried apples with eggs and bacon.

"Good location, quiet surroundings. Friendly, caring couple who start your day with a hearty, homestyle breakfast." *(Allen Garner)* "Lace curtains, floral bedspreads, rag rugs, crocheted bureau scarves, antiques, and family heirlooms all add to the warm, nostalgic atmosphere. Guest rooms are named for apples; our spacious second-floor room, The York, had good lighting, a comfortable sitting area, and a cozy under-the-eaves atmosphere. The walls were painted a deep red, contrasting handsomely with the sheer white curtains and the dark wooden floor. Terrycloth robes are provided for going from the room to its private hall bath. Caring, concerned innkeepers. Outstanding breakfast of juice, fresh fruit, just-baked muffins, crisp bacon, scrambled egg strudel, delicious fried apples and coffee." *(Betty Norman)*

Open All year.
Rooms 1 2-bedroom cottage, 4 doubles—all with full private bath, clock/radio, ceiling fan, air-conditioning. Cottage with fireplace, TV, desk, kitchen. 2 with electric fireplace.
Facilities Dining room, living room, billiard room, porch. 3½ acres with gazebo, lawn games. Health club privileges. Hiking nearby.
Location 2 m from town. From I-26, take exit for Hwy. 64, Hendersonville. Go W on 64 for 4 m. Go left on Daniels Dr. to inn on left just past White Pine Dr.
Restrictions No smoking. Children over 12.

Credit cards MC, Visa.
Rates B&B, $100–140 cottage, $89–95 double, $69–85 double. Extra person, $10. Weekly rate in cottage, $450.
Extras Station pickups.

Waverly Inn ¢ 🚸
783 North Main Street, 28792

Tel: 704–693–9193
800–537–8195
Fax: 704–692–1010
E-mail: waverlyinn@ioa.com

Built as a boarding house in 1898, the Waverly Inn is the oldest surviving inn in Hendersonville, and it is listed on the National Register of Historic Places. The inn offers spacious porches—upstairs and down—for rocking, a striking Eastlake staircase in the foyer, and guest rooms comfortably decorated with king- and queen-sized lace-canopied rice beds, spindle beds, and white wicker, along with some dressers from its boarding house days. John and Diane Sheiry bought the inn in 1988, and came to it in an interesting way: both had worked in the hotel and restaurant business on the corporate level, and when John went back to school for his MBA, his thesis was on the operation and marketing of country inns. By the time he graduated, the Sheirys were ready to start a new life as innkeepers; they're ably assisted by Darla Olmstead.

"John and Diane create a genuinely warm atmosphere, like being in the home of friends. Excellent recommendations for area activities and restaurants." *(Bill & Jan Gaines, also SWS)* "It's always fun to meet the other guests on the veranda during the wine and cheese hour." *(Kerry Smithwick)* "Friendly but unobtrusive hosts in the best Southern tradition. Breakfast is varied and excellent, a daily social hour provides the opportunity to meet other guests if desired, and some delicious treat and beverage is always available for a snack. My favorite room is at the front of the inn, with a four poster canopy bed, blue patterned quilt, and lace-trimmed bed linens." *(Barbara Cavanaugh)* "Special touches include Darla's just-baked chocolate cookies, the large porches with rockers, huge southern breakfasts, thick fluffy towels, plus the innkeepers easy-going friendliness." *(Jane Edwards)* "Spectacular whole grain blueberry pancakes; the menu choices enable you to eat like a bird or a beast." *(Charles & Martha Jean Liberto)* "The Waverly is located in downtown Hendersonville across the street from a beautiful church. We sat on the front porch, sipping hot chocolate and watching the Christmas parade." *(Michael & Donna Smith)*

Open All year.
Rooms 1 suite, 14 doubles—all with full private bath, telephone, radio, desk, ceiling fan, air-conditioning. Some with TV.
Facilities Dining room, living room, library, 3 TV rooms, porches. ⅓ acre with lawn. Tennis, golf, horseback riding, nearby.
Location 20 m S of Asheville. 2 blocks from Historic District. On Main St. between 7th and 8th Aves.
Restrictions No smoking in dining room. Midweek traffic at 8:00 A.M. & 5:00 P.M.

Credit cards Amex, Discover, MC, Visa.
Rates B&B, $155–185 suite, $89–139 double, $70–80 single. Extra person, $15; no charge for children under 12. Weekend theme packages, wine-tasting evenings.
Extras Crib, highchair.

HICKORY

Hickory B&B ¢
464 Seventh Street SW, 28602

Tel: 704–324–0548
800–654–2961
Fax: 704–324–0443

Known for its many area furniture manufacturers and discount retailers, Hickory is located about halfway between Winston-Salem and Asheville. A Georgian-style home built in 1908, the Hickory B&B was purchased by Bob and Pat Lynch in 1996, and is highlighted by the original high ceilings, wainscotting, crown moldings, bevelled windows, and oak and heart pine floors, complemented by antiques and collectibles from around the world. Rates include a full breakfast and afternoon refreshments.

"Delicious breakfasts wth fresh fruit and locally made syrup." *(Dan Reuter)* "Beautiful, comfortable, and spotlessly clean. Lovely grounds with many feeders to attract the birds. Quiet neighborhood, inviting for morning walks, or an evening stroll to town for dinner. Pat serves afternoon tea and I enjoy mine on the porch or at the poolside gazebo. Pat and Bob are gracious, warm, and interesting, helpful with local directions." *(Alice Andrews)* "Outstanding breakfasts, beautiful grounds." *(Anne Houston)* "Guest rooms are decorated with pretty pastel colors, dhurri rugs, some antiques, and country decor." *(Ann Higgs)* "Spacious rooms with large beds, new mattresses, modern bathrooms." *(SB)*

Open All year.
Rooms 1 suite, 4 doubles—all with private bath and/or shower, clock, fan. 2 with fireplace, 1 with radio, desk.
Facilities Dining room, parlor with piano, TV/VCR; library with fireplace, books; family room; porches. 1½ acres with off-street parking, swimming pool, gazebo. Golf, lake with swimming, fishing, boating nearby.
Location 1 hr. N of Charlotte, 1½ hr. E of Asheville, 1 hr. W of Winston-Salem. 5–10 mins. from town. From Hwy. 70, go right onto 4th St. Go left onto 7th Ave. SW. Go right onto Seventh St. SW.
Restrictions No smoking. Children over 12.
Credit cards MC, Visa.
Rates B&B, $85–105 double.

HIGHLANDS

Highlands is in western North Carolina, 125 miles north of Atlanta, and 60 miles southwest of Asheville. The town has auction galleries, antique shops, and summer theater, along with hiking, tennis, swimming, horseback riding, fishing, white-water rafting, an 18-hole Arnold Palmer golf course, and skiing. Surrounded by national forest lands, it has little of the commercialism found in other tourist areas. Because of its 4000-foot elevation in the Blue Ridge mountains, the mean temperature is around 75°, making for comfortable days and cool nights.

Reader tips: "One of the prettiest towns of the Blue Ridge Mountains. Highlands is a marvelous place in summer—cool, fresh, and with lots of charming little shops. There are many hiking trails nearby, and the people in the hiking store will advise you on the level of difficulty." *(SN)* "This is waterfall country, and Smoky Mountains National Park is just a one-hour drive away." *(ML)* "We were surprised at the high quality of Highlands' restaurants—for such a small town, they were very good and surprisingly sophisticated." *(MS)*

Information please: The **Long House B&B** (Route 2, Box 638, 28741; 704–526–4394 or 800–833–0020) is a completely renovated 75-year-old log cabin with natural wood walls, oak floors, antiques, and handmade quilts. This B&B offers a full breakfast and great views of the surrounding woods; there are four guest rooms with rates of $45–85 double.

The **Old Edwards Inn** (Main Street, Box 1778, 28741; 704–526–5036 or in winter 912–638–8892) is a Victorian inn and restaurant, recommended for its clean, comfortable rooms, good service and superb food. Double rates of $79–99 include a continental breakfast.

Another possibility is **Ye Olde Stone House** (1337 South Fourth Street, 28741; 704–526–5911), offering B&B accommodations in the Tudor-style home, plus a self-catering log cabin and A-frame chalet. "Long-time owners Rene and Jim Ramsdell are friendly and helpful in directing us to local attractions. The chalet is a good choice for families." *(Sona Nast)*

For additional area entries, see **Cashiers,** and **Salem, South Carolina.**

Colonial Pines Inn ¢ *Tel:* 704–526–2060
541 Hickory Street, 28741 *E-mail:* alley@dnet.net

Chris and Donna Alley moved from Atlanta in 1984 and renovated this old farmhouse, adding modern baths and furnishing it with antique and modern country furnishings. Breakfast includes an egg casserole, homemade breads, fresh or baked fruit, cereal, and ham or sausage.

"Low-key, comfortable, and attractive. Our suite extended the length of one side of the house and had two baths, a great place for an extended stay. It was nicely furnished with an emphasis on folk decoration. There's a large inviting lounge and a big, peaceful front porch with a wonderful view. Guests congregate on the porch in the evening, and we enjoyed joining one couple for dinner. Chris Alley is an engaging innkeeper and a good cook. The Alleys provide good information and brochures on scenic drives, hikes, and walks. An ideal choice if you enjoy peace, quiet, comfort, good food, friendly hosts; an excellent value." *(Lucia J. Rather)* "Nice touches include a notebook of local restaurant menus, and the guest pantry stocked with beverages and ice." *(Laura Patterson)* "Just a short walk from the center of town but in a quiet neighborhood. Peach ice tea was always available." *(Betsy Eager)*

"Donna maintains just the right balance between helping her guests and staying out of the way until needed." *(Antonia Bernstein)* "Donna's little extras made our stay delightful—from the constant aroma of cinnamon and fresh-baked bread, to local directions and advice." *(Mark Lampe)*

Open All year.
Rooms 2 guest houses with fireplaces, 1 apt., 2 suites, 4 doubles—all with private bath and/or shower. Some with TV.
Facilities Dining room, living room with TV, grand piano, books; guest pantry; porches. 2 acres with picnic table, berry picking.
Location 80 m SW of Asheville, 130 m N of Atlanta. ½m from town. From Main St. take Hwy. 64 E. Go 6 blocks and turn right on Hickory St. to inn at corner.
Restrictions No smoking. Children over 12 in inn. No charge for children under 12 in apt.
Credit cards MC, Visa.
Rates Guest houses, $105–220 (sleep up to 6). B&B, $105–140 suite, $85–120 double, $55–95 single. Extra person (B&B), $15. Minimum stays peak periods. Winter weekend discounts.

Morning Star Inn *Tel:* 704–526–1009
480 Flat Mountain Estates, 28741

"The brilliance of the morning star signals the promise of a new day," are the words of one of Patricia Allen's favorite hymns. This thought inspired the name of the Morning Star Inn, a handsome mountain home built in 1960 and refurbished as a B&B by Pat and her husband, Patrick Allen, in 1994. In addition to years spent traveling to B&Bs, Pat prepared for her new career by attending cooking school, apprenticing under Chef Tell in the Cayman Islands, and even writing a food critic's column in the *Macon Telegraph.*

Breakfast is served at individual tables in the wicker-filled sun room, 9–9:30 A.M.; a recent meal consisted of homemade granola with apples and yogurt, spinach and mushroom pie, broiled tomatoes, apple-carrot muffins, glazed bacon, orange juice, and Costa Rican coffee. Other favorites include Southwestern chili eggs, cheese grits, and banana praline French toast. Wine, tea, cider and hors d'oeuvres are served at the weekend social hour. A color scheme of rose and green carries through many of the traditionally furnished rooms, with rich floral fabrics, and plush and Oriental rugs. Named for stars, the guest rooms are also beautifully decorated with four poster and sleigh beds with down-filled duvets and antiques.

"The spacious sun room has a wall of windows offering gorgeous mountain views. Pat is an accomplished chef; her breakfasts are fabulous. Exceptional hospitality from the two Pats." *(Jenny Boren)* "Friendly ambiance and welcoming atmosphere. Beautifully presented breakfasts, plus weekend wine and hors d'oeuvres." *(Bonnie Schuler)* "Friendly innkeepers; comfortable, cozy furnishings; homey, welcoming, and romantic." *(Susan Billingsley)*

Open All year.
Rooms 1 suite, 4 doubles—all with private bath and/or shower, clock, fan. Some with radio, TV, air-conditioning, refrigerator.
Facilities Living room with fireplace, sun room with dining area, games; guest refrigerator, porches with swing. 2 acres with rock & perennial gardens, lawn games, hammock.
Location 3½m from town. From traffic light on Main St. in Highlands, go E on US 64 (toward Cashiers) for 2.3 m. Go left on Flat Mt. Rd & go 1.9 m *(watch mileage; no sign)*. Go left on Flat Mt. Estates Rd. & go ½m to inn on left.
Restrictions No smoking.
Credit cards MC, Visa.
Rates B&B, $125–140 suite, $115–130 double. Extra person, $20. Cooking classes fall, spring.

HIGH POINT

The Bouldin House B&B

4332 Archdale Road, Archdale 27263

Tel: 910–431–4909
800–739–1816
Fax: 910–431–4914
E-mail: lmiller582@aol.com

Whether you're heading for High Point because you're in the furniture business or because you want to decorate your own home, you'll be delighted with your stay at the Bouldin House. Named for the family who owned it for decades, this handsome four-square house has a dark red hipped roof, soft yellow clapboards with white trim, and a welcoming plant-lined wraparound porch. Built in 1916, it was extensively restored as a B&B in 1994 by Larry and Ann Miller, who added a new roof, bathrooms, heating and cooling systems, and more. Each guest room has a king-size bed and different decor. The Parlor Room has walnut woodwork and Victorian antiques, while the Weekend Retreat has a peach-and-white beach cottage feel. Breakfast is served 8–9 A.M. in the oak-paneled dining room, and might include pecan-basil pesto omelets, banana-sour cream waffles, or tarragon eggs in puff pastry. Rates also include evening refreshments and home-baked treats.

"Beautiful rooms, clean and comfortable. Excellent breakfasts, with attention to detail in presentation and creativity; homemade pastries. Innkeepers helpful with area attractions and locations." *(Susan Silko)* "Exceptional breakfast of Southwestern-style eggs, with scones and fresh pineapple. Other thoughtful touches include the early morning coffee and tea set outside the rooms each morning, and the treats waiting in the hallway each evening. High quality bedding." *(Trudy Bardes)* "Immaculate housekeeping. The innkeepers are warm and hospitable without being overbearing." *(K.M. Simmons)* "Excellent advice on furniture buying." *(Teresa Imhoff)* "Restaurant suggestions right on target." *(Bradford Martin)* "Larry and Ann made us feel right at home, welcoming us to the inn with iced tea." *(Lorna Romanvich)* "Comfortable beds and pillows, with an understated fresh scent. Interesting conversations with fellow guests and the Millers." *(Jackie Rose)* "The second floor gathering room had interesting books, games and videos, and was a wonderful spot to meet the other guests. The wraparound porch was a comfortable place to enjoy the early morning before breakfast and evening quiet." *(D. Gray)* "Superb breakfasts, tasty evening snacks of homemade cookies and beverages." *(Linda & Ray Holland, and many others)*

Open All year.
Rooms 4 doubles—all with private bath and/or shower, radio, clock, air-conditioning, ceiling fan, fireplace.
Facilities Dining room with fireplace, living room with fireplace, TV/VCR; wraparound porches. 3.5 acres with lawns.
Location Central NC, Piedmont Triad. Approx. 25 m S Winston-Salem & Greensboro. 4 m S of downtown High Point. 1 m from I-85. Take Exit 111, High Point/Archdale & turn N on Rte. 311. At 1st light turn left on Balfour Dr. Go to end & turn right on Archdale Rd. Inn is 2/10 m on left.
Restrictions No smoking. Children 10 and over.
Credit cards Discover, MC, Visa.
Rates B&B, $85–95 double. Extra person, $25. Rates higher during Int'l Home Furnishings Market.

HILLSBOROUGH

Also recommended: For sale at press time was the historic **Hillsborough House Inn** (209 East Tryon Street, P.O. Box 880, 27278; 919–644–1600), owned by the Webb family for over 140 years. Each of the five guest rooms has a private bath, and the romantic cottage (originally the summer kitchen) also has a double Jacuzzi tub and six-foot fireplace. Although the house itself is lovely, readers are especially taken with the charm and talents of its owners, Bev and Katherine Webb, so comments are most welcome. B&B double rates range from $95–105; $175 for the cottage. "Cordial and understanding hosts, available when you needed help or information, but never in the way. Our room was light and airy. The grounds were beautifully maintained, pleasant for strolling. Tasty buffet-style breakfast." *(Michael Hustage)*

KILL DEVIL HILLS

For additional area entries, see **Cape Carteret, Corolla, Duck, Nags Head,** and **Manteo.**

Information please: Just 200 yards from the beach is the **Cherokee Inn** (500 North Virginia Dare Trail, 27948; 919–441–6127 or 800–554–2764), built about 50 years ago as a hunting and fishing lodge. The six guest rooms have private baths and central air-conditioning, and guests can relax in the common room or on the porch. B&B double rates range from $65–105. "Beautiful cypress construction. Rooms are decorated with pastel comforters, light wicker or pine furnishings for a fresh, cheerful look. Our room had cushioned rocking chairs and a really comfortable bed. From the front rooms you can see the ocean;

from the back, the Wright Brothers Memorial. The breakfast of fresh fruit, pastry, muffins, bagels is set in the upstairs hall. Owners Kaye and Bob Combs were helpful with restaurant and sightseeing suggestions. Ample off-street parking. The beach is just across the road, down a short path." *(Chrys Bolk)*

LAKE LURE

In addition to all water sports, the Lake Lure area offers such activities as hiking, golf, tennis, bicyling, and horseback riding, plus antiquing and exploring Chimney Rock state park. Nearby is the Biltmore Estate, Flat Rock Playhouse, the Carl Sandburg Home, and the Brevard Music Festival.

Information please: Built in 1920, the **Lake Lure Inn** (P.O. Box 10, 28746; 704–625–2525 or 800–277–5873) is a 50-room inn decorated with a Euro-Mediterranean touch, plus a swimming pool, gardens and solariums to enjoy. B&B double rates range from $59–109; children under 12 stay free.

Lodge on Lake Lure
Charlotte Drive, Box 519, 28746
Tel: 704–625–2789
800–733–2785
Fax: 704–625–2421

Originally built in 1938 as a refuge for (not from) the North Carolina Highway Patrol, the Lodge at Lake Lure offers rest and relaxation amid spectacular scenery on the shores of this 27-mile-long crystal clear lake in Hickory Nut Gorge; it's been owned by Jack and Robin Stanier since 1990. Especially appealing on chilly evenings is the great room, with its hand hewn ceiling beams, wormy chestnut walls, and enormous stone fireplace with a gristmill stone embedded within it. Hearty breakfasts are served 8–9:30 A.M. on the sunporch, overlooking the lake and mountains beyond. Favorite entrees include scrambled eggs in tortillas, buckwheat banana pancakes with mango sauce, cardamom French toast with red currant syrup, and apple-and-sausage stuffed croissants.

"The comfortable guest rooms are furnished with antiques and quilts, most with lake views. Late every afternoon, wine is served on the backyard patio after guests return from a delightful ride on the inn's pontoon boat, skippered by Jack and accompanied by his black lab, Muffin. A terraced path lined with flowers leads down to the boathouse, which is topped by a large sundeck with plenty of lounge chairs and shaded tables for relaxing in full view of the lake and surrounding cliffs. *Dirty Dancing* and *The Last of the Mohicans* were filmed in this area. Breakfast was different each day with such entrees as Belgian waffles or eggs Benedict, beautifully presented. Jack and Robin were informal and friendly, socializing and introducing guests to one another." *(Adriana Di Cecco)* "Breath-taking setting overlooking the lake and Blue Ridge mountains beyond. Robin and Jack welcomed me warmly, and made me feel immediately at home." *(Betty Norman)*

Open All year.
Rooms 2 suites, 10 doubles—all with private bath and/or shower, fan. 3 with double soaking tubs.
Facilities Living room with fireplace, piano; breakfast sun porch; library room with fireplace, TV, games; veranda with rockers. 3 acres with trails, lake swimming, pontoon boat, canoes, boats for fishing. Tennis, golf nearby.
Location Blue Ridge Mts. foothills. 25 m SE of Asheville, 90 m W of Charlotte. From Hwy. 64/74, turn at Lake Lure fire station opposite the golf course. Follow signs to lodge.
Restrictions Smoking restricted to den. One child per room.
Credit cards Amex, Discover, MC, Visa.
Rates B&B, $125–135 suite, $96–105 double. Extra person, $15. 10% Senior discount. 2-3 night weekend/holiday minimum. Weekly discount.
Extras Crib. Spanish spoken.

LAKE TOXAWAY

Also recommended: About 30 miles east of Highlands is western North Carolina's most luxurious (and most expensive) country inn, a reader favorite, the **Greystone Inn** (Greystone Lane, Lake Toxaway 28747; 704–966–4700 or 800–824–5766). Set on a private lake in a residential resort, the inn complex includes a 1915 mansion, a modern structure, The Hillmont, and the Cottage, with two suites. Double rates for the 33 guest rooms of $280–420 include a full breakfast, afternoon tea, and dinner. Rates include use of most of the resort's sports facilities. A highlight is the lake cruise which leaves every day at 5 p.m., with a skipper to recount tales of the lake's history. Readers rave about the food, rooms, and setting, and are especially impressed with the service.

Information please: A family-friendly, environmentally sensitive mountain escape, **Earthshine Mountain Lodge** (Route 1, Golden Road, 28747; 704–862–4207), is a rustic cedar lodge and farm. Each of its eight guest rooms has handmade quilts, log beds, private baths, and lofts for kids to sleep in. "Glorious location. A mountain retreat where you can breathe fresh air, gaze at spectacular views, eat homemade hearty food, and go without TV. Pack jeans and walking shoes. The staff care about their guests and always have a smile and a kind word." *(Nancy Schultz)*

For additional area inns, see **Cashiers.**

LITTLE SWITZERLAND

Information please: Open from late April until early November, the **Switzerland Inn** (Milepost 334 on Blue Ridge Parkway, Box 399, 28749; 704–765–2153) is a chalet-style complex of lodgings, restaurant, and shops, owned by the Jensen family. Double rates for the 60 guest rooms and chalets range from $85–120, including a full breakfast. "Attractive grounds, excellent food in the restaurant, surprisingly high quality artwork and crafts in the shops. Although we didn't care for a viewless room we were offered in the main lodge, we were delighted with our suite in the Heidi Chalet, with large picture windows and a porch for enjoying the mountain views." *(ABK)* Comments?

Big Lynn Lodge ¢ 👪 ♿ *Tel:* 704–765–6771
Highway 226A, P.O. Box 459, 28749–0459 800–654–5232
Fax: 704–765–0301

Set at an altitude of 3,100 feet, Big Lynn is known for its beautiful views, fine food, comfortable accommodations, and reasonable rates. Named for the 600-year-old Linden tree that once shaded the main lodge, Big Lynn was bought by Gale and Carol Armstrong in 1989. Gale reports that "our elevation keeps us cool and mosquito-free all summer. Our primary market is retired people, but families with pre-teen children also enjoy it here. We take pride in our food service, and extra helpings are offered." While the Armstrongs have upgraded and refurbished a number of the rooms, and have built four spacious condos, most accommodations here are more a "view with a room" than the reverse.

Breakfast includes your choice of juice, fruit, coffee or tea, cereal, eggs to order with toast, grits, pancakes, or waffles. A typical fixed-menu dinner might include broiled trout or chicken, red-skinned potatoes, steamed broccoli and baby carrots, cole slaw, honey wheat rolls, and double chocolate cake with ice cream.

"The fresh trout from a local hatchery was delicious and we were surprised when the owner and chef came to our table to see if we would like seconds." *(Betty Norman)* "Big Lynn is not for those looking for historic buildings, meticulously restored and laden with antiques. My room was plain but comfortable and immaculate. The food is good, old-fashioned, wholesome home cooking. Breads are homemade, and desserts were difficult to refuse; the apple pie had a light, flaky, golden crust, with tart, well seasoned apples. But the best part of our stay was the friendly folks we met. The common rooms and grounds offer many places for spontaneous and spirited conversation." *(Linda Nelson)* "The entire staff is efficient, friendly, and genuinely dedicated to giving excellent service. Our clean, comfortable room was above average in size, comfortably furnished with two rocking chairs, good lighting, with good cross ventilation. Rest and relax, or use the inn as a base for interesting day trips." *(Sam Beckley)* "Each accommodation has a porch with rocking chairs where the tranquility can be truly absorbed and appreciated."*(James and Carol Murphy)*

Open Mid-April–Nov. 1.
Rooms 4 suites, 21 doubles, 5 singles, 12 cabins—all with private bath and/or shower, telephone, radio, desk, fan. Most with porch. Condos with TV, air-conditioning, balcony, kitchen. Rooms in 13 buildings.
Facilities Restaurant, library with player piano, game room with fireplace, TV lounge, gift shop, porch, laundry. 22 acres with lawn games, hiking. Fishing, golf nearby.
Location W NC. 50 m NE of Asheville, on Blue Ridge Parkway; 5 m SW of Spruce Pine.
Restrictions No smoking in dining room; several non-smoking guest rooms.

Credit cards MC, Visa.
Rates MAP, $115 suite, $79 double, $70 single. Extra person, $23. No charge for children under 5. Alc breakfast, $6. Weekly, monthly rates.
Extras Limited wheelchair access. Crib. German spoken.

MAGGIE VALLEY

Also recommended: You don't have to go out West for a quality riding vacation—just mosey over to the **Cataloochee Ranch** (Route 1, Box 500, Maggie Valley, 28751; 704–926–1401 or 800–868–1401). Owned by the same family since 1934, rustic accommodations are available in the historic main lodge, a newer lodge, two- and three-bedroom cabins, and one-bedroom "romance" cabins. Many have wood-burning fireplaces, and are furnished with quilts and primitive or classic antiques. The ranch is open from late March to January 4; double rates of $130–275 include breakfast and dinner, while rides cost $35 for a half-day ride, $80 for a full day. You'll explore the ranch's 1,000 acres, plus adjoining Great Smoky Mountains National Park. Additional activities include tennis, hiking, and trout fishing. Cinnamon puffed toast is a breakfast classic, and dinners typically include a choice of trout or steak, turkey or pork, accompanied by just-baked bread, salad and vegetables with a fruit cobbler for dessert. "Our luxury cabin, The Dogwood, was set off by itself, overlooking mountains and valleys, an incredible autumn sight. We had mountain views from our bed; skylights enabled us to watch the stars. Firewood was delivered daily for the fireplace; the cabin also had a wet bar and double whirlpool tub. Delicious Southern cooking; friendly, helpful staff. I rode while my husband golfed at the three nearby courses nearby." *(Christine Tanguay)*

For additional area entries, see **Waynesville.**

Maggie Valley Resort and Country Club
1819 Country Club Road, P.O. Box 99, 28751
Tel: 704–926–1616
800–438–3861
Fax: 704–926–2906

Beautiful mountain vistas. Cool mountain breezes. A nationally acclaimed 18-hole championship golf course. Plus on-site swimming and tennis, and a myriad of area activities for non-golfing spouses. Can a golfer get any closer to summertime heaven? Guests are kept well fueled for the many activities by the resort's restaurant. During peak season, the extensive breakfast buffet includes separate omelet and waffle stations; off-season, guests order from a menu of morning favorites. Lunch includes the usual sandwiches and burgers, and dinner entrees range from red snapper with spinach and feta cheese in phyllo, to Southwestern chicken lasagna with black beans, to filet mignon with garlic potatoes.

"Very pleasant, nicely landscaped, spacious hotel accommodations with great mountain views from the balcony. Our second-floor room had a vaulted ceiling, handsome pine armoire and headboard. We also stayed in a first-floor room, done in blue-and-white stripes and florals, with white wicker and yellow accents. Tasty breakfast buffet, cordial staff." *(Susan Woods)* "Excellent value. King-size bed, lovely room, fantastic overlooking the first tee to the mountains beyond. With a golf tournament in progress, we enjoyed the competition from our deck. Excellent food. Gorgeous grounds with flower beds everywhere." *(Pat Borysiewisz)*

Open All year. Restaurant closed Christmas Eve.
Rooms 11 cabins, 64 doubles—all with full private bath, telephone, radio, clock, TV, ceiling fan, air conditioning, balcony. Cabins with kitchenettes. Guest rooms in 13 lodges/villas.
Facilities Restaurant, dining room, bar/lounge, snack bar, conference rooms. Some with fireplace, TV/VCR. Evening entertainment Thurs.–Sat. April– Oct. 125 acres with extensive gardens, heated swimming pool, 2 tennis courts, 18-hole golf course, pro shop. Downhill, cross-country skiing nearby.
Location 35 m W of Asheville; 90 m E of Knoxville, TN. 3 m to town center. ½ m from intersection of Hwys. 276 & 19. 6 m S of I-40. From I-40, take Exit 20, & go S on Rte. 276. Go W (right) on Rte. 19. After ½ m, turn right on Moody Farm Rd. Go right on Country Club Dr. to inn.
Restrictions No smoking in public areas.
Credit cards Amex, Discover, MC, Visa
Rates Room only, $69–129 suite, $59–119 double, $49–89 single. Extra person, $10. 17% service charge. Family rates. Golf, ski packages. Alc breakfast, $5–10, alc lunch, $5–8; alc dinner, $25.
Extras Cribs, babysitting by arrangement.

MANTEO

Manteo is located on Roanoke Island of the Outer Banks, 90 miles south of Norfolk, Virginia, and is the long-time mercantile hub and government center of the Outer Banks. Travelers will want to visit the *Elizabeth II* (a reproduction of Sir Walter Raleigh's ship), the Fort Raleigh National Historic Site, and the Elizabethan Gardens; in summer, get tickets for the *Lost Colony*, an outdoor musical drama playing since 1937. Outdoor sports include tennis, golf, swimming, boating, fishing, and windsurfing.

Also recommended: Dating back to the 1860s, **The Roanoke Island Inn** (305 Fernando Street, 27954; 919–473–5511) was restored and renovated as an inn in 1990; Ada Hadley is the longtime manager. B&B double rates of $88–128 for the eight guest rooms include a continental breakfast, plus access to the guests' pantry for beverages and snacks. "Friendly innkeeper, quiet, comfortable room with a bay view. We bicycled through this beautiful little town, and sat on the porch sipping tea and listening to the birds." *(Anke Kohtahl)* "The privacy of outside entrances plus a comfortable common room. Guests can enjoy breakfast or cocktails on a second-floor porch overlooking the waterfront." *(Susan Hedeler)*

Overlooking Shallowbag Bay, the **Tranquil House** (Queen Elizabeth Street, P.O. Box 2045, 27954; 919–473–1404 or 800–458–7069) was built in 1988 in the style of a 19th century inn. Rates include a continental breakfast, plus evening wine and cheese. After a day of exploring, guests relax in the Adirondack chairs on the inn's ample verandas. Dinners are served in the inn's 1587 Restaurant. "Located across the bay from the re-creation of the ship that brought the settlers to the Roanoke Community. Our room had two comfortable queen-size beds with brass headboards, good lighting, thick towels, and English toiletries. Helpful, pleasant staff." *(Amy Peritsky)* B&B double rates for the 25 guest rooms range from $80–170.

For additional area entries, see **Corolla, Duck, Kill Devil Hills,** and **Nags Head.**

MOUNT AIRY

If you remember Andy Griffith's old sitcom, *Mayberry RFD*, you'll be interested to know that Mount Airy was Griffith's hometown and served as the inspiration for the show. Mount Airy is located about 35 miles northwest of Winston-Salem, a few miles south of the Virginia border, in the foothills of Blue Ridge Mountains.

Information please: Built in 1901, the **Merritt House B&B** (618 North Main Street, 27030; 910–786–2174 or 800–290–6290) is a two-story red brick house with a steep hipped roof with bracketed eaves, tall paneled chimneys, wraparound porch, and a tower-like projecting bay. B&B double rates for the four guest rooms—each with private bath—range from $65–90. "Rich and Pat Mangels suggested wonderful area activities, and offered us early morning coffee and afternoon refreshments as we relaxed on the porch, enjoying the quiet neighborhood. Local antiques highlighted our homey room: a four-poster bed, a sitting area with an old cast iron stove as a table, a spinning wheel, and an old quilt hanging from a wooden quilt rack. Outstanding breakfast: egg and cheese casserole with tomatoes and fresh basil, sausages, and blueberry muffins, served on china and crystal." *(Linda Bush)*

Information please: For sale at press time was the **Pine Ridge Inn** (2893 West Pine Street, 27030; 910–789–5034), a sprawling Southern plantation-style mansion built in 1948 and luxuriously decorated with antique and traditional furnishings. The back of the house looks over a swimming pool and the beautiful North Carolina hills. In addition to the inn's six guest rooms, its restaurant prepares such classics as prime rib, chicken Kiev, veal Marsala, and shrimp scampi. B&B double rates range from $60–100.

For an additional area entry, see **Pilot Mountain.**

MURPHY

For additional area entries, see **Andrews** and **Robbinsville.**

Huntington Hall B&B ¢

500 Valley River Avenue, 28906

Tel: 704–837–9567
800–824–6189
Fax: 704–837–2527

Bob and Katie Delong purchased Huntington Hall, a restored 1880s clapboard house, in 1990, and report that "our comfortable inn is decorated in the tradition of an English country garden home. We are avid backpackers and can advise guests on hiking trips in the Great Smoky Mountains, or white-water rafting on the Ocoee River." We heard from many of the Delong's guests, all enthusiastic about the welcoming hospitality, helpful innkeepers, attention to detail, outstanding breakfasts, and exceptional value found at Huntington Hall; many were equally delighted with the inn's murder mystery weekends.

"Immaculate housekeeping. Delicious, healthy breakfast of crepes with apples, raisins, and yogurt sauce." *(Dawn Bush)* "We were free to join the innkeepers and other guests or to have our privacy." *(Ruth Coll)* "Sumptuous breakfast of French toast, bacon, strawberries and cream, bran muffins. Classical music played softly in the background." *(John MacLeod)* "We were welcomed with glasses of wine, and were offered a pot of tea to take up to our room before bedtime. Sinfully good dark chocolates were left on our pillows at turndown." *(Ruth Young)* "Coffee and juice are ready by 6:30 A.M., and breakfast is served at guests' convenience. Delicious vegetarian breakfast of gingerbread pancakes with strawberries, almonds, and real whipped cream." *(Lyn Marion)*

"Restful living room with Oriental rugs; pleasant, sunny breakfast room. My favorite guest room is the Avalon, with a peach and blue color scheme, heart pine floor, Oriental rug, comfortable queen-size bed, reading chairs, and spacious bathroom." *(Suzanne Carmichael)* "Without being cluttered, each cheerful room is artfully accented with art and antiques. The in-town location was extremely quiet with adequate parking." *(Mr. & Mrs. Otto Clarisio)*

Open All year.
Rooms 5 doubles—all with full private bath, TV, desk, air-conditioning, fan.
Facilities Dining room with fireplace, library; living room with TV, breakfast room, screened porch. Swimming pool, tennis, golf nearby. Lakes, rivers nearby for swimming, kayaking, canoeing. Theatre, whitewater rafting, mystery weekend packages.
Location W NC. 90 m E of Chattanooga TN, 90 m W of Asheville, 100 m N of Atlanta. 2 blocks from downtown. From U.S. 64, take Hwy. 19 to downtown area. Turn onto Peachtree St. Then right onto Valley River Ave. Pass Presbyterian Church; inn is on right.
Credit cards Amex, DC, Discover, MC, Visa.
Rates B&B, $85 double, $65 single. Extra person, $10. Murder mystery weekends.
Extras Airport/station pickups. Crib.

NAGS HEAD

In addition to all possible water sports, area activities include exploring the National Seashore, the Pea Island Wildlife Refuge, the Nags Head Woods Preserve, or the North Carolina Aquarium. History buffs will enjoy the Wright Brothers Memorial, the *Lost Colony* outdoor drama, and the *Elizabeth II*, a replica 16th century ship.

For additional area entries, see **Cape Carteret, Corolla, Duck, Kill Devil Hills,** and **Manteo.**

First Colony Inn 👪 ♿
6720 South Virginia Dare Trail, 27959
at U.S. Route 158

Tel: 919–441–2343
800–368–9390
Fax: 919–441–9234
E-mail: first.colony.inn@worldnet.att.net

Innkeeping is a moving experience, and in the case of the Lawrence family, it's been true literally as well as figuratively. The last surviving Nags Head oceanfront hotel, built in 1932, the First Colony Inn was rescued by the Lawrence family and moved 3½ miles to a safer location. Now listed in the National Register of Historic Places, the inn re-opened in 1991 after a three-year renovation, which preserved the inn's historic charms while adding up-to-date plumbing, heating, and cooling systems. The inn's wraparound porches form continuous circles around both the first and second floors, with guest rooms opening onto them; rooms are decorated with English antiques, traditional furnishings, old photographs and prints, and king, queen or extra-long twin beds.

The buffet breakfast changes daily, but might include lemon poppyseed cake, apple and cherry turnovers, chocolate iced sticky buns, croissants stuffed with scrambled eggs, sausages, toasting breads, hot and cold cereal, yogurt, apple sauce, and assorted fresh fruits; rates also include afternoon tea, cookies, cheese and crackers.

"Camille's enthusiasm encompassed not only her inn, but the local area. She led us to our immaculate room and explained where everything was, provided restaurant menus, and made dinner reservations. Breakfast was served in a lovely room overlooking the sand dunes with the ocean beyond. Guests are seated at tables covered by lovely pink tablecloths with a matching flower bouquet. The delicious meal included super-fresh orange juice, bagels, chocolate banana pound cake, and quiche." *(Edna Pike)* "A real family-run inn, with a helpful, friendly staff." *(Lee & Mary Miller)* "Wonderful amenities, especially the hand-held remote control for the heating/cooling system." *(J.F. Hassell)* "Careful attention to detail ranged from the fluffy towels on heated rack, to the ample supply of current magazines in our room." *(Gwen Boyles)* "We watched humpback whales from the beach, then returned to the inn for breakfast." *(Eloise Potter)* "Cozy library with lots of great stuff to read." *(Janet Skinner)*

"Our magnificent top floor room had a king-size poster bed, great mattress, pillows, and comfy linens. Nooks and crannies held comfortable reading chairs and excellent reading lights; there was also ample space for a working desk, beautiful antiques, and our own things. Abundant toiletries in the bath, plus a full-length and a make-up mirror. Even an ironing board and iron in the closet." *(Perri & Michael Rappel)*

Open All year.
Rooms 6 suites, 20 doubles—all with private bath and/or shower, telephone, radio, clock, TV, air-conditioning, refrigerator, microwave, hair dryer. Most with wet bar, microwave, desk. 2 with whirlpool tub, 2 with screened porch. 8 with VCR, 4 with kitchenette with dishwasher.
Facilities Dining room, library with fireplace, organ, books, games; sundeck. Secure bicycle/windsurfer storage. 5 acres with off-street parking, swimming pool; plus 2½ acres on beach side of street with boardwalk, gazebo, swimming, surfing, windsurfing, sailing. Complimentary beach chairs, umbrellas, beach towels, grills, picnic tables. Tennis, golf nearby. Rental boats, party boats, hunting or fishing guides nearby.
Location Outer banks of NC. 80 m SE of Norfolk, VA. Parking E side of US 158 at mile post 16.
Restrictions No smoking.
Credit cards Amex, Discover, MC, Visa.
Rates B&B, $75–250 suite, $120–250 double. Extra person, $30. Babies, $10. 2–3-night weekend/holiday minimum.
Extras First floor wheelchair access. Crib, babysitting service.

NEW BERN

New Bern is located in mid-coastal North Carolina, 2 hours east of Raleigh, at the confluence of the Trent and Neuse rivers. It's a 45-minute drive to the Atlantic Ocean beaches. The town was founded in 1710 by German and Swiss colonists searching for political and religious freedom. New Bern prospered from the production of tar, pitch, and turpentine. When the royal governor of the Carolinas, William Tryon, saw the need for a permanent capital, New Bern was selected as the site. Tryon Palace, completed in 1770, was the Colonial capitol and the first state capitol of North Carolina. New Bern's prosperity continued through much of the 19th century, and many of its finest buildings date from the early 1800s. A number of historic buildings have been restored and are open to the public as museums. On a more commercial note, Pepsi Cola (known originally as "Brad's Drink") was invented here in the 1890s by a local pharmacist, C.D. Bradham.

Also recommended: Built in 1882, **The Aerie** (509 Pollock Street, 28562; 919–636–5553 or 800–849–5553) is decorated in Williamsburg colors, with early American-style furnishings. Located in the historic district just one block from Tryon Palace, the inn offers seven guest rooms, each with private bath and TV, at B&B rates of $79–89 double. "Good combination of comfort and elegance in the decor. Delicious English afternoon tea served on bone china." *(Betty Norman)* "The new owners are doing an excellent job." *(BJ Hensley)*

Close by is the **Harmony House Inn** (215 Pollock Street, 28560; 919–636–3810 or 800–636–3113), built in the 1850s, and furnished with antiques and locally made reproductions. The B&B double rate for the nine doubles is $85–130; each has a private bath, TV, and air-conditioning. "Our spacious room had a comfortable bed, nice linens, thick towels, and good bedside lighting. Delightful breakfast with home-cooked entrees. Friendly owners who recommended area sights and restaurants." *(Amy Pentsky)*

Built in 1848, the **King's Arms** (212 Pollack Street, 28560; 919–638–4409 or 800–872–9306) was restored as an inn in 1980. Breakfast, delivered to your room, includes such baked treats as ham biscuits or perhaps lemon ginger muffins, along with the morning paper; you can also breakfast on the wicker rockers on the back porch. "Richard and Pat Gulley were helpful with restaurant suggestions and reservations. We had privacy, but felt welcome asking for anything." *(CJA)* B&B double rates for the 10 guest rooms range from $90–130.

New Berne House (709 Broad Street, 28560; 919–636–2250 or 800–842–7688), is a restored Colonial Revival home shaded by massive magnolia, pecan, and camelia trees. The seven guest rooms, each with private bath, have an English country decor, accented with antiques. A full breakfast is included in the $80–88 double rate. "Our quiet room at the back of the house had a comfortable bed, lots of pillows, eyelet-trimmed sheets, and a puffy comforter. Owners Howard Bronson and Marcia Drum welcomed us with wine and cheese. Delicious pecan waffles for breakfast, accompanied by Howard's fascinating stories of life in the merchant marine." *(Chris Bolk)*

For an additional area entry, see **Oriental** and **Washington.**

OCEAN ISLE

Information please: We'd like more reports on the **Goose Creek Bed & Breakfast** (1901 Egret Street Southwest, 28469; 910–754–5849 or 800–275–6540), a large, contemporary beach house with extensive decks and a screened porch overlooking Goose Creek. Guests can fish from the dock; the creek flows into the intracoastal waterway, ideal for kayaking or canoeing. Two of the four guest rooms have a private bath, and the B&B double rates of $60–85 include a continental breakfast, served on the screened porch."Quiet, relaxing, spacious deck overlooking the water. Great hospitality; friendly, casual atmosphere. Incredible baked goods." *(Gary & Anne Smith)*

For an additional area entry, see **Tabor City.**

OCRACOKE

Ocracoke is on the Outer Banks of coastal North Carolina, about 1½ hours south of Nags Head, and 40 minutes by ferry from Hatteras village.

Reader tip: "Come to Ocracoke to heighten your awareness of the incredible forces of nature. Violent summer storms sweep through in minutes, and the pounding of ocean waves never ceases. The island is mercifully undeveloped, since most of it is part of the Cape Hatteras National Seashore. There's little to do but relax and enjoy the beautiful uncrowded beaches, fish and swim, rent a bicycle, and explore. The seafood is delicious; some of it familiar, some unusual to Yankee tastebuds." *(MS)*

Information please: Owned by Ocracoke native, Alton Ballance, and managed by Mary Hollowell, the **Crews Inn B&B** (P.O. Box 460, 27960; 919–928–7011) was built in 1908. The inn is decorated with pictures taken from Alton's book about the island and its people. Abundant porches offer views of the surrounding oaks, cedars and pines, and provide a place for breakfast in warm weather. B&B double rates range from $40–60.

Another old-time option is the **Island Inn** (P.O. Box 9, 29760; 919–928–4351), offering a restaurant plus 35 rooms in the main building and the motel annex, at average rates ranging from $48–75. "Delightful off-season visit to this rambling old hostelry; we had Ocracoke to ourselves mid-week. The staff was pleasant, helpful and unobtrusive; the restaurant featured the local catch of the day. Staying here was like becoming part of the island." *(Claude Gaebelein)* Reports?

ORIENTAL

The Tar Heel Inn ¢
508 Church Street, P.O. Box 176, 28571

Tel: 919–249–1078
Fax: 919–249–0005
E-mail: tar_heel_inn@pamlico-nc.com

Named for a 19th-century ship wreck on nearby Hatteras Island, Oriental is the sailing capital of North Carolina, with more world class boats than people in this quiet little village. The Tar Heel Inn, built in 1899 (about the time the town was founded) has been owned by Shawna and Robert Hyde, along with their two young daughters, since 1994. Guest rooms are decorated with Laura Ashley prints, hand stencilling, antiques, and period reproductions, with four poster or canopy beds. Breakfast is served from 8–9 A.M., and might feature such entrees as pecan French toast with cinnamon syrup, crab meat strata, omelets, or blueberry blintzes, plus freshly baked muffins and breads.

"Robert is a congenial host and breakfast chef. He was an excellent source of local information and continually went above and beyond the call of duty to ensure that our stay was pleasant and gracious." *(Ann Ballantine)* Reports appreciated.

Open All year.
Rooms 8 doubles—all with private bath and/or shower, radio, clock, air-conditioning. 1 with ceiling fan, TV.
Facilities Dining room, living room with stereo, books games; guest kitchen, patio. 1.25 acres with off-street parking, lawn games. Sailing, hunting, fishing, golf, tennis nearby.
Location E NC, 25 m E of New Bern, on Pamlico Sound.
Restrictions No smoking.

Credit cards Discover/Novus, MC, Visa.
Rates B&B, $60–90 double, $50–80 single. Extra person, $10.Extended stay discounts.
Extras Wheelchair access; 1 room specially equipped. Local airport pickups. Crib.

PILOT MOUNTAIN

Information please: Built in 1896 by Dr. Flippin, **Flippin's B&B** (203 West Main Street, 27041; 910–368–1183) features a wraparound porch with rocking chairs, and country Victorian decor with heart pine floors. Each of the four guest rooms has a private bath, and the B&B double rates of $75–100 include a full breakfast and afternoon tea.

Pilot Knob Inn *Tel:* 910–325–2502
P.O. Box 1280, 27041

Have you always loved the rustic appeal of an authentic log cabin, but been reluctant to leave behind modern-day comforts? Are you enticed by country inn charm but reluctant to sacrifice personal privacy? At the Pilot Knob Inn, you can have your cake and eat it too. In 1986, Jim Rouse rescued a collection of abandoned chinked-log tobacco barns, and recreated them as luxury cabins. Moved to a lovely, private setting in the woods, each uses the original beams, drying poles, and foundation stones, enhanced by luxuries unknown when these barns were built: air-conditioning, television, and indoor plumbing (let alone double whirlpool tubs). The result is cabins which look virtually unchanged from the outside, while inside is a living room with comfortable seating, antique accents, pine flooring, stone fireplace, and spacious bathroom with double whirlpool tub; upstairs is a queen-size bed and sitting area. A larger barn serves as the inn's common area, with a dining room and spacious library. Breakfast is served at individual tables 8:30–10 A.M., and might include waffles, sausages, and home-baked breads and coffee cake.

"Wonderful cabins with the living room and bathroom downstairs, and the bedroom upstairs. Jim is extremely friendly, and makes everyone feel welcome. Ideal for a romantic getaway." *(William Hunt)* "Perfect setting, with a lovely view of Pilot Knob; tasty homemade breakfasts. Welcoming atmosphere." *(Nicola Smith)* "Clean, quiet, and away from everything." *(Bobbi Gray)*

Open All year.
Rooms 6 cabins—all with full private double whirlpool bath, telephone, radio, clock, TV, desk, air-conditioning, fireplace, refrigerator. 4 with porch.
Facilities Dining room, library/living room with fireplace, sauna, deck. 50 acres with heated swimming pool, hiking; 50-acre lake for fishing; island gazebo. Pilot Mt. State Park adjacent for hiking. Horseback riding, waterfalls nearby.
Location Central NC. 20 m N of Winston-Salem. From I-40, go N on Hwy. 52

& take exit for Pilot Mt. State Pk. Go left off exit & 1st right on New Pilot Knob La. to inn. No sign for inn; call for directions.
Restrictions No smoking in dining room; permitted in cabins. No children.
Credit cards MC, Visa.
Rates B&B, $135 cabin.
Extras German spoken.

PISGAH FOREST

Key Falls Inn ¢
151 Everett Road, 28768

Tel: 704–884–7559
Fax: 704–885–7812

When exploring the "Land of Waterfalls" what could be more appealing than a clean, quiet, cozy B&B to return to and recharge your batteries for another delightful day. The Key Falls Inn was built by Charles Patton, a prominent local citizen, who constructed the first section of his home in 1860, hauling wood, sand, and layered rock from the mountainside behind the homesite; he completed the house in 1868, after the Civil War. Patricia and Clark Grosvenor restored this Victorian farmhouse in 1989, furnishing it with period antiques; Janet Fogleman also assists as an innkeeper. Breakfast is served at the dining room table at 8:30A.M. and includes a breakfast casserole or eggs with sausage or bacon, scones or biscuits, sweet rolls, fresh fruit and juice. Afternoon refreshments are available from 3 to 4 P.M.

"Delicious, plentiful food; spacious, clean, attractively decorated guest rooms with queen-size beds. Guests gather on the large front porch to chat, relax on the wicker rockers, and enjoy the mountain views. We were invited to pick apples from their fruit-laden trees, and made delicious pies when we returned home, for an extended taste of our vacation. Key Falls is within easy walking distance, and many large waterfalls are within a short drive, as is the Pisgah National Forest—a great area for hiking." *(Gregory & Grace Munson)*

Open All year.
Rooms 1 suite, 4 doubles—all with private bath and/or shower, air-conditioning, clock, ceiling fan. 1 with TV.
Facilities Dining room, living room, TV room with games, porches. 30 acres with picnic/cookout area, tennis court, waterfall, stream, fishing pond with docks. 3 m to Pisgah National Forest for hiking, bicycling, horseback riding.
Location W NC. 33 m S of Asheville, 20 W of Hendersonville, 4 m E of Brevard. From I-40, take I-26 E to Exit 9. Go right on Rte. 280 & go approx. 15 m. Cross Rtes.64/276, turning left on Ecusta Rd. Go left on Old Hendersonville Rd., then right on Everett Rd. to inn on left.
Restrictions No smoking. Children over 12.
Credit cards Amex, Discover, MC, Visa.
Rates B&B, $75 suite, $60–75 double, $50–65 single. Extra person, $15.

PITTSBORO

For an additional area entry, see **Siler City**.

The Fearrington House ✕ ♿
2000 Fearrington Village Center, 27312
Tel: 919–542–2121
Fax: 919–542–4202
E-mail: fci@interpath.net

Fearrington Village is a small complex consisting of a well-established first-class restaurant and cafe, a number of small quality shops, and a luxurious country inn. Owned by the Fitch family and managed by Richard Delany, The Fearrington House features rooms individually decorated with English pine antiques and carefully matched designer wallpapers and fabrics. The Fearrington House restaurant is acclaimed for its innovative Southern cuisine under chef Cory Mattson; the menu includes a generous choice among eight appetizers, entrees, and desserts. A recent dinner included sauteed ostrich with apple onion compote on a potato crisp; salad or sorbet; pan-seared duck breast with carmelized pear and quinoa; concluded with hot chocolate soufflé with whipped cream and chocolate sauce. Breakfasts are no less tempting: freshly squeezed orange juice; warm muffins and just-baked breads; and a choice of yogurt, granola, and fresh fruit; banana fritters with Grand Marnier sauce; eggs to order with spicy sausage and fried cheese grits; or French toast with orange cinnamon syrup and hickory smoked bacon.

"Our second floor room was lush and beautiful with a separate sitting room overlooking the beautiful flower gardens and fountains. It was decorated in colorful floral fabrics with a comfortable window seat and two plush soft chairs. The bedroom was done in white pine and florals and was equally lovely. The beds were wonderfully firm with soft comfortable pillows and baby soft sheets. The huge bright spotless bathroom was filled with every possible bath product from soap to lotions, bath salts, hair dryer, and loads of thick soft towels. There were small vases of fresh cut flowers throughout the room and bathroom, as well as chilled bottled water waiting our arrival. Off the front courtyard is a sitting room where guests are welcome to browse through the shelves of books, sip complimentary sodas, nibble fruit and cookies, or just sit and relax. Part of this complex is a working farm with a rare breed of cattle called Belted Galloways, as well as horses and sheep. The cafe serves good food in a casual setting, while the restaurant serves exceptional food in an elegant setting. Breakfast was served on fine china, with fresh flowers and impeccable service." *(Perri & Michael Rappel)* "White exterior with Southern-style pillars, surrounded by beautifully appointed gardens. The restaurant is elegant and sophisticated with excellent cuisine." *(Carole Vesely)*

Open All year.
Rooms 13 suites, 15 doubles—all with private bath and/or shower, telephone, radio, TV, desk, air-conditioning.
Facilities Living room, restaurant, bar/lounge, wine bar, cafe, specialty shops.

60 acres with gardens, bike trails, swimming pool. 8 m to Lake Jordan for swimming, boating, fishing. 15 min. to golf, tennis.
Location Central NC. 8 m SW of Chapel Hill, 20 m to Research Triangle Park. From Chapel Hill, go S on Rte. 15/501 toward Pittsboro & Sanford.
Restrictions Smoking permitted in lounge only. No children under 12. Lobby noise in 1 room.
Credit cards Amex, MC, Visa.
Rates B&B, $275 suite, $165–225 double. Alc lunch, $5–10; prix fixe dinner, $55.
Extras Wheelchair access; some rooms equipped for disabled. Airport/station pickup, $30. Spanish, French, German spoken. Member, Relais et Chateaux.

RALEIGH

Located in central North Carolina, Raleigh was founded in 1792 as the state capital, and was laid out in a grid pattern. Major state museums are here, including the museums of art and natural history.

Reader tip: "We enjoyed the Farmer's Market, and dinners at the Irregardless Cafe and the Wicked Smile. April and May are the nicest times to visit, before it gets too hot." *(Bonnie Burroughs)*

Information please: Within easy walking distance of the Governor's Mansion, State Capitol, and more is the **William Thomas House B&B** (530 North Blount Street, 27604; 919–755–9400 or 800–OLDE–INN), an 1881 Victorian home, restored as a B&B by Jim and Sarah Lofton. B&B double rates for the four guest rooms range from $96–135, and include early morning coffee and the newspaper, a full (or light) Southern breakfast, and afternoon wine and cheese. "Ample common areas, spacious guest rooms, delicious food. Excellent location, plus off-street parking." *(Peg Bedini)*

The Oakwood Inn ¢ ♿ *Tel:* 919–832–9712
411 North Bloodworth Street, 27604 *Fax:* 919–836–9263

Pressured business travelers with appointments in North Carolina's capital city will find a welcome respite at The Oakwood Inn, opened in 1984. Built in 1871 as the Raynor Stronach House, the inn is listed on the National Register of Historic Places, and is located in the historic Oakwood District, home to twenty blocks of Victorian buildings, ranging in style from Greek Revival to Steamboat Gothic. In 1997, the inn was purchased by Bill and Darlene Smith. In addition to juice, fresh or cooked fruit, and just-baked muffins, breakfast entrees might include gingerbread pancakes with lemon syrup, stuffed French toast with orange sauce, or a mushroom and cheese omelet.

"Lovely, tree-lined, quiet historic neighborhood, within easy walking distance of downtown Raleigh and major governmental buildings and offices. The inn itself is a charming town house with beautiful grounds and gardens. Bill and Darlene welcomed us warmly, and told us about the inn and area. Bountiful breakfast served on good china, with good coffee in ample supply. Gracious, informal, friendly service at every turn. The lovely porches with wicker furniture are a real treat."

(Douglas Eason) "Convenient, well-lit, off-street parking. Beautiful decor; efficient plumbing. My spotless room had already been made up by the time I finished breakfast." *(Gloria Cosgrove)* "This Victorian home is more open and bright than many of the period. The Linden Room on the first floor was spacious, appealing, and authentically decorated." *(Bonnie Burroughs)* "The exquisite Polk Room, on the ground floor, has a large private porch and an ample sitting area within the bedroom." *(PD)* "Complimentary soft drinks, cheese and crackers." *(KM)*

Open All year. Closed Thanksgiving.
Rooms 6 doubles—all with private bath and/or shower, telephone, air-conditioning. Many with fireplace. TV on request.
Facilities Dining room, parlor with fireplace, porches. ½ acre with rose garden. Fax, copier service.
Location In historic district. Between Oakwood and Polk Sts.
Restrictions Smoking in designated areas only. "Small children may find us boring."
Credit cards Amex, DC, Discover, MC, Visa.
Rates B&B, $85–120 double, $75–120 single. Corporate, extended stay rates.
Extras Limited wheelchair access.

ROBBINSVILLE

For additional area entries, see **Andrews** and **Murphy**.

Snowbird Mountain Lodge ¢ ✕ ♿
275 Santeetlah Road, 28771

Tel: 704–479–3433
800–941–9290
Fax: 704–479–3473
E-mail: Snbdmtnldg@aol.com

Snowbird is an informal and relaxed place, set atop a low mountain at 2,880 feet. It was built in 1941 of chestnut logs and native stone, and rooms are paneled in butternut, cherry, and other native woods, with matching custom-made furniture. In 1995, the lodge was purchased by Karen and Robert Rankin, who are working hard to make a longtime reader favorite even more appealing..

Breakfast is served 8–9:30 A.M., and include a choice of eggs and bacon, eggs scrambled with veggies, buttermilk pancakes, French toast, or oatmeal. Picnic lunches include fruit, dessert, beverage, and such choices as baked ham and cheese or hummus on wheat bread. Dinner favorites include mountain trout grilled with herb butter, mashed potatoes with horseradish and cream, ribeye steak with grilled red onion, wild mushroom risotto, and fresh apple tart. Vegetarian diets are easily accommodated.

"Robert and Karen are hard-working folk who act like true innkeepers. Robert has focussed on refurbishing and upgrading the structure and grounds, while Karen oversees the kitchen. A choice of five or six breakfast and dinner entrees were offered. Ham and lentil soup was a personal favorite. Lunches are prepared to order, with a choice of sandwiches, plus carrot and celery sticks, juice or soda and a dessert—ideal to take hiking. Scrumptious desserts, too. The recreation building, horseshoe pits, and extensive library in the great room met my expectations and more. Staff was friendly, interested, and hard-working. A quiet place to escape daily pressures." *(Dhon & Sally MacKinnon)* "Our room was simply furnished but comfortable and clean; fantastic food; delightful staff. Delectable trout for dinner; melt-in-your-mouth French toast at breakfast. No fancy frills here, but a gorgeous setting, with the simple pleasures of good people and good meals." *(Jeff Degner)* "We were prepared to rough it, but were delightful with our luxurious room in the recently renovated Wolfe Cottage, complete with cathedral ceiling, fireplace, and even a whirlpool tub." *(MW)* "I've visited Snowbird several times over two decades. The place has never been better and the price is still reasonable." *(Danielle DuRant)*

"Many guests return again and again, and wonderful friendships develop. We enjoy the peaceful, quiet atmosphere, wonderful view of the mountains, and interesting walking trails, particularly the Joyce Kilmer Virgin Forest." *(Laura Smith)* "We greatly enjoyed sitting in the large common room with ancient hand-hewn wooden posts and beams." *(FJH)* "Located miles from anything but natural beauty, with spectacular views in all directions." *(Phil Young)*

Open Mid-April–Nov. Weekends only in Nov. Wolfe Cottage open all year; no meals in winter.
Rooms 22 doubles—all with private bath and/or shower, desk, ceiling fan, coffee maker, clock. 7 rooms in 2 cottages; rest in main lodge. 6 with refrigerator, 7 with deck, 2 with fireplace, whirlpool tub, porch.
Facilities Dining room; great room with games, 2 fireplaces, piano, books. Weekend evening music, storytelling. Shuffleboard, Ping-Pong, pool, lawn games. 100 acres with stream swimming, trout fishing, hiking, bicycling. Canoeing, white-water rafting on Nantahala River. Spring wildflower walks with naturalist. Horseback riding.
Location W NC. 80 m W of Asheville, 80 m S of Knoxville, TN, 160 m N of Atlanta. 14 m NW of Robbinsville; follow Rte. 129 to Joyce Kilmer Virgin Forest.
Restrictions No smoking. Dry county; BYOB. Children 12 and over.
Credit cards MC, Visa.
Rates Full board, $135–200 double, $102–150 single. Extra person, $42. 15% service. 2-3 night weekend/holiday minimum. Prix fixe dinner, $12–20. Hiking, mt. biking, fly fishing, music, theme weekends.
Extras Wheelchair access; bathroom specially equipped. Spanish, German, Italian spoken.

SALISBURY

Salisbury is located in central North Carolina, 42 miles north of Charlotte, and 39 miles south of Winston-Salem. Founded in 1753, it was the site of one of the Confederacy's largest prison camps, and about 5,000 Union soldiers are buried in the National Cemetery here. Pick up information on walking tours of the historic district from the local visitor center, and visit the town's antique shops.

Rowan Oak House *Tel:* 704–633–2086
208 South Fulton Street, 28144 800–786–0437

A Scottish-Celtic legend tells of a magical tree that symbolized beauty, hospitality, privacy, peace, and sanctuary—the Rowan Oak—also an ideal symbol for a B&B. Built in 1901, this blue-gray and cream house was constructed in the Queen Anne style and features a carved oak front door, leaded and stained glass windows, meticulously carved mantels and the original ornate electric and gas light fixtures. Guests may enjoy evening wine in the Victorian parlor or on the wraparound porch, overlooking the gardens and fountains. The breakfast menu changes daily, but might include juice, hot fruit compote, stuffed French toast with strawberry sauce, featherbed eggs, Carolina ham, and home-baked breads.

Barbara and Les Coombs, who bought the inn in 1995, have decorated the guest rooms with Victorian antiques, period wallpapers and window treatments, complemented by fresh flowers and fruit. The inn's convenient location in Salisbury's 14-block historic district puts it within walking distance of several restaurants and antique shops, and an easy drive to furniture shopping in High Point as well as the Charlotte Motor Speedway.

"A lavishly decorated Victorian home. The owners have made sure that each room in the house holds a special interest." *(Susan Stevenson)* "Clean, comfortable, and charming. Barbara and her husband were very accommodating." *(Linda Leavy)* "Exquisitely decorated, immaculately clean, remarkably quiet. Convenient location, within walking distance of the historic downtown. Creative breakfast." *(Jennifer Taylor)*

Open All year.
Rooms 4 doubles—all with private bath and/or shower, telephone, radio, desk, air-conditioning, ceiling fan. 1 with whirlpool bath, gas fireplace; 1 with private porch, double marble shower.
Facilities Dining room, parlor with fireplace, sitting room with TV, games; wraparound porches. ½ acre with English gardens, 4 fountains. Tennis, golf nearby.
Location 3 blocks to center of town. In historic district. From I-85 take Exit 76B. Go W on Innes St. Turn left on Fulton St. Inn on right.
Restrictions No smoking. Children 12 and over.
Credit cards Amex, MC, Visa.
Rates B&B, $85–125 double, $55–85 single. Extra person, $25. 2-night minimum stay some weekends.

SALUDA

Saluda is a quiet, small town in the foothills of the Blue Ridge Mountains of western North Carolina, 30 miles south of Asheville, 10 miles south of Hendersonville, near the South Carolina border. There are many antique and craft shops in the area, along with restaurants serving good mountain cooking, and lots of good hiking trails. The Carl Sandburg National Historic Site is also nearby.

Information please: The **Ivy Terrace** (Main Street, P.O. Box 639, 28773; 704–749–9542 or 800–749–9542) was built in the 1890s, and renovated as an eight guest-room B&B in 1993. Furnished with country antiques and period decor, the B&B double rate of $95–140 includes a full breakfast and afternoon refreshments. "Diane and Herb McGuire were attentive to our needs, and prepared excellent breakfasts. They pampered us with freshly baked cookies each night, and gave us a jar of apple butter to take home. Beautifully decorated guest rooms." *(Evonne Garrett)* "Terraced grounds with beautiful English flower gardens." *(Betty Norman)*

For additional area entries, see **Tryon.**

The Orchard Inn ✕
Highway 176, P.O. Box 725, 28773

Tel: 704–749–5471
Tel: 800–581–3800
Fax: 704–749–9805
E-mail: nsdoty@aol.com

In the early 1900s the Southern Railway Company built a summer mountain retreat, at an elevation of 2,500 feet, for railroad clerks and their families; it is now known as The Orchard Inn, and has been owned by Veronica and Newell Doty since 1993, who describe it as a quiet romantic spot for special getaways. Guest rooms are decorated with antiques and casual country charm, including brass/iron and four-poster queen-size beds, rag and Oriental rugs, and baskets and other craftwork.

Meals served on the airy sunporch which stretches the length of the inn. Breakfast is served 8:30–9 A.M. at guests' choice of small or family-style tables, and includes juice, fruit, homemade granola, muffins, eggs or pancakes, grits, and bacon, ham or sausage. Complimentary hors d'oeuvres are served prior to dinner at 7 P.M.; the menus change nightly, but a recent one included orange fennel soup; salad with maple vinaigrette; a choice of beef filet with lobster and horseradish, chicken with Brie, or salmon with wild mushrooms; concluded with cranberry almond tart or Victoria creams with raspberry sauce.

"Spectacular mountain setting, inviting porch with rockers and a swing, and a spacious common room with lots to read, plus cookies and tea. Warm, welcoming innkeepers. We enjoyed the views from the deck swing, explored the nature trail, and appreciated the friendliness of Lucy, the resident lab. Comfortable, well appointed guest rooms with fresh flowers, bottled spring water, excellent lighting, luggage racks and fluffy towels. Beautifully served, delicious dinner. Morning offered more lovely views from the sun porch, plus a delicious breakfast of raisin bread French toast." *(Betty Norman)* "The large living room has several conversation areas to allow guests to relax privately or in a group. The fireplace is the focal point, but books and many interesting art objects occupy those who would rather browse. The area has a spacious, bright air, with light hardwood floors and Oriental rugs." *(SHW)* "Upon arriving at the inn, you are greeted by a picturesque arrangement of a white board fence, a planter of seasonal flowers, and the inn's colorful sign. The lane to the inn winds up a steep hill through beautiful hardwood trees that offer cool green shade and colorful foliage in the fall; the steps and walkway leading to the inn are bounded by flowers and boxwood." *(John Mathis)*

Open All year. Restaurant closed Sun., Mon. Inn closed "a few days around Christmas."
Rooms 1 suite, 8 doubles, 3 cottages suites—all with full private bath, ceiling fan. Some with whirlpool tub, radio, clock, air-conditioning, fireplace, refrigerator, balcony/deck.
Facilities Restaurant, living room with fireplace, piano; library; porch with swing, deck. 12 acres with nature walks. Golf, tennis, hiking, birding, fishing nearby.
Location SW NC. 30 m S of Asheville. 1 m from town. On Hwy 176, 2 m S of I-26, Exit 28. Historic district.
Restrictions No smoking. Dry county: BYOB. Children over 12.
Credit cards MC, Visa.
Rates B&B, $150–175 suite, $105–130 double, $95–120 single. 10% service. Extra person, $15. 2-night weekend minimum. Prix fixe dinner, $35 (by reservation). Picnic lunches with 24 hour notice.

SILER CITY

Bed and Breakfast at Laurel Ridge ¢ *Tel:* 919–742–6049
3188 Siler City–Snow Camp Rd, 27344 800–742–6049

Whether you live in the Triad or Research Triangle areas, or have come for business reasons, do yourself a favor: recharge your batteries with a stay at Laurel Ridge, bordering the Rocky River and surrounded by native mountain laurel. This peaceful, serene country location is within an hour of all of central North Carolina's major metropolitan areas. Those interested in local crafts will find the area especially rewarding; the studios of dozens of artisans are within a short drive, and literally dozens of potteries can be found in the nearby Seagrove area.

This timber-framed house, with exposed beams throughout, was built in 1983 by area craftsmen, and was restored as a B&B in 1993 by David Simmons and Lisa Reynolds. Lisa is a pediatric physical therapist and David is a professional chef with extensive experience in all phases of the culinary arts. David's breakfasts are served from 8 A.M.–9A.M. and include seven different kinds of pancakes (poppyseed is a speciality), creative soufflés, or original huevos rancheros, plus just-baked breads, homemade sausage, locally roasted coffee, and fresh juices. The meal is served on plates and mugs from the area's exceptional potters. Rates also include afternoon soft drinks and cookies.

"This B&B's rustic exterior blends with the wooded surroundings, while the interior adds a note of luxury, with fine linens and double Jacuzzi tubs. Dave picked fresh edible flowers and herbs to highlight our breakfast of huevos rancheros." *(Bob, Kate, & Elizabeth DeLong)* "Beautifully renovated and redecorated rooms, plus a very private cottage in the woods. Genuine hospitality from owners who go out of their way to make your stay perfect. David is a fantastic chef." *(Andrea C. Teper)*

Open All year.
Rooms 1 cottage, 1 suite, 2 doubles—all with full private bath, telephone, radio, clock, desk, air-conditioning. Some with double whirlpool tub, ceiling fan, balcony/deck.
Facilities Dining room, living room, guest refrigerator, screened/unscreened porch. 26 acres with garden, walking paths, gazebo, lawn games, riverfront, forest.
Location Central NC, between Triad & Research Triangle. Approx. 45–60 min. SW of Durham, Raleigh, SE of Greensboro, High Point. From Chapel Hill/Durham, take US 15-501 S to Pittsboro, then US 64 W toward Siler City. Go N on Pearlyman-Teague Rd., right on Silver City-Snow Camp Rd. to inn on right. From Charlotte, take I-85 N to Exit 96, onto US 64 E. Cross over US 421 intersection & follow directions above.
Restrictions No smoking. Children 10 years.
Credit cards Amex, MC, Visa
Rates B&B, $125 cottage, $99 suite, $74 double, $64 single. Extra person, $10.
Extras Wheelchair access to cottage; bathroom specially equipped. Spanish spoken.

SHELBY

Information please: A majestic 11,000-square-foot Colonial Revival mansion, **The Inn at Webbley** (403 South Washington Street, 28150; 704–481–1403 or 800–852–2346) has been restored to its original elegance by Max Gardner III and his wife, Victoria; they are the fifth generation of the Webb-Gardner family to live here. The eight spacious guest rooms are decorated with French and English antiques and canopy beds. The inn is located in Shelby's historic district, 42 miles west of Charlotte and 72 miles east of Asheville. B&B double rates range from $165–195.

SOUTHERN PINES

Located in the Sandhills of south central North Carolina, Southern Pines is known for its mild winters and exceptional area golf courses (31 within a 20-mile drive) in both Southern Pines and neighboring Pinehurst.

Knollwood House | *Tel:* 910–692–9390
1495 West Connecticut Avenue, 28387 | *Fax:* 910–692–0609

Golf can be the most elegant of sports, and a stay at Knollwood House will certainly supply that quality—even if it is lacking in your swing. Built in 1925, and restored as a B&B in 1992 by Mimi and Dick Beatty, Knollwood is handsomely decorated with late 18th and early 19th century family antiques, soft colors, warm chintzes, tapestry and needlepoint work. Attention to detail includes the starched white eyelet cotton sheets, terry robes, and towels—changed as often as three times daily. The back lawn extends 100 feet to Mid-Pines, a golf course designed by Donald Ross. Dick is knowledgeable about area courses, and arranges tee times for guests. A typical breakfast, might include juice, fresh fruit with yogurt and sour cream sauce, Viennese bread pudding with raspberry puree, baked Canadian bacon, and cranberry coffee cake.

"The owners and staff were discreet and helpful; the atmosphere lush, and the food memorable. Our room was comfortable, quiet and clean." *(Francine Teolis)* "Dick Beatty was a helpful and gracious host. Lovely furnishings—like stepping into the pages of a fine interior decorating magazine. Good shopping nearby in Pinehurst." *(Sona S. Nast)* "Delicious breakfast served in a beautiful dining room. We enjoyed sitting on the terrace alongside the golf course." *(Susan Harris)* "Splendid Christmas decorations enhanced the decor. The hospitable innkeepers anticipate guests' needs and preferences." *(Carole Winding)* "The house is set back from the road, providing a quiet setting." *(J. N. Murphy)* "The Beattys allow guests to feel totally at home in their beautiful inn. Careful attention to detail, plus family heirloom furnishings, delicious breakfasts, and lovely surroundings." *(Philip Miller)*

Open All year.
Rooms 4 suites, 2 doubles—all with private bath, telephone, clock, TV, air-conditioning. Some with desk, wet bar/refrigerator; 1 with fireplace.
Facilities Dining room with fireplace, living room with fireplace, TV/VCR, books, stereo; solarium. 5 acres with gazebo, lawn games. Overlooks Mid-Pines golf course.
Location 3 min. to downtown, in historic district. From I-95, take US 1. Take Midland Rd. exit. Go left on Pee Dee Rd. Bear left onto West Connecticut Ave. Inn on left.
Restrictions Smoking on 1st floor only. Children over 10.
Credit cards Visa.
Rates B&B, $105–150 suite, $90–115 double, $80–90 single. Extra person, $20. No tipping. 2-night weekend minimum or $20 surcharge. Corporate, government rates midweek. Golf packages.
Extras Airport/station pickups.

SOUTHPORT

Information please: If you need a place to stay enroute to or from Bald Head, a good choice might be **Lois Jane's Riverview Inn** (106 West Bay Street, Southport 28461; 910–457–6701 or 800–457–1152), overlooking the Cape Fear River. Built in 1891, guests can watch the ships go by the inn's porches, or stroll the Southport Riverwalk to antique shops, restaurants, and the maritime museum. B&B double rates for the four guest rooms, decorated with antiques, range from $75–90, and include a full breakfast, afternoon hors d'oeuvres, and evening sweets.

Named for the 800-year-old oak tree across the street is the **Indian Oak Inn** (120 West Moore Street, 28461; 910–457–0209), just a block from the river. B&B double rates for the four guest rooms range from $75–90, including a full breakfast buffet and evening coffee and home-baked chocolate chip cookies.

For an additional area inn, see **Bald Head Island.**

STATESVILLE

Also recommended: At the 150-year-old **Cedar Hill Farm B&B** (778 Elmwood Road, 28677; 704–873–4332 or 800–948–4423), owners Brenda and Jim Vernon raise sheep for hand-spinning wool. Fresh eggs, ham and sausage come from a nearby neighbor and their own garden provides herbs and vegetables for breakfast, while fruits from the orchard go into preserves. Guests can stay in the one guest room in the farmhouse ($60); in the renovated granary ($75); or the Cotswold Cottage ($95); all are furnished with country antiques. "The scenery is gorgeous, and the farmyard is full of geese, sheep and a playful dog." *(Ken Letner)* "Gracious Southern hospitality. Our children were warmly welcomed. Flexible breakfast menu and serving time." *(Shelley Gallup)* "Nice place, fine people, terrific porch swing." *(Celia McCullough)* "Their stories about farm life have you roaring. We kept busy with the trampoline, horseshoes, badminton, swimming, swinging, and the hammock." *(Anita & Foy Taff)*

TABOR CITY

Four Rooster Inn ¢
403 Pireway Road, Route 904, 28463

Tel: 910–653–3878
800–653–5008
Fax: 910–653–3878
E-mail: 4rooster@intrstar.net

Although better known as the yam capital of North Carolina, Tabor City is also home to an exceptional B&B, an ideal place to experience the gracious Southern hospitality in a small town setting. Surrounded by camellias and azaleas, this 1949 red brick home was restored as a B&B in 1993 by Bob and Gloria Rogers, and is elegantly appointed with antiques and period furnishings. Served on Limoges china with sterling silver cutlery, the breakfast menu varies daily; perhaps hot sherried fruit, morning glory muffins, eggs Benedict one day; and frozen fruit cup, apricot pecan bread, cheese strata with country ham and grits the next. Rates also include afternoon tea with cucumber sandwiches and lemon currant scones, and evening turndown service with pillow chocolates.

"Well worth the short detour from I-95. This B&B is a beautifully decorated oasis with the utmost comfort of their guests in mind. Afternoon tea or wine on arrival; exceptionally good lighting for relaxing in your room with one of the Roger's current magazines. Cozy terrycloth robes and slippers, even two luggage racks in our room, to name only a few of the many comforts. Don't think you'll be awakened by crowing roosters (ask Bob and Gloria to explain the inn's name). Instead, you will be awakened by Bob's gentle tap on your door, bringing you a carafe of coffee and the morning paper. At the time of your choosing, Gloria will serve you a sumptuous breakfast in the dining room. An outstanding value and a perfect place to escape from stress, while still an easy drive from Myrtle Beach golf, beaches, and country music." *(Betty T. Norman)*

Open All year.
Rooms 1 suite, 3 doubles—2 with private full bath, 2 with maximum of 4 people sharing bath. All with radio, clock, air-conditioning, desk. TV, telephone on request.
Facilities Dining room, living room with fireplace, piano; family room with TV/VCR, books, stereo, guest refrigerator; sun porch, porches. 2 acres with gardens, off-street parking. Tennis, golf nearby.
Location SE NC. 24 m NW of Myrtle Beach, SC. From N Myrtle Beach take SR 9 to US 701. Travel N 4 m following by-pass to 904. Turn W & go 4/10 m to B&B on right. 2 blocks to town center.
Restrictions Smoking only on sun porch, outside. Children by arrangement.
Credit cards Amex, Diners Club, Discover, MC, Visa.
Rates B&B, $75–85 suite, $55–85 double, $45–75 single. Extra person, $15. 5th consecutive night free.
Extras Non-fluent French.

TRYON

Tryon is in the heart of Carolina fox-hunting country; the climate is mild, with golf and horseback riding available year-round. Just a mile from the South Carolina border, Tryon is located in western North Carolina, 100 miles west of Charlotte, 150 miles north of Atlanta. It's 40 miles southeast of Asheville and 30 miles northwest of Spartanburg, South Carolina.

Information please: Just over the state border in South Carolina is **The Red Horse Inn** (3310 North Campbell Road, Landrum, South Carolina 29356; 864–895–4968), set on 190 mountain view acres. The accommodations consist of five recently built Victorian-style cottages, each with a bedroom, bath, kitchen, sleeping loft, living room with fireplace, porch or patio; three have Jacuzzi tubs. B&B double rates of $85 include a breakfast basket. Reports?

Also recommended: Another Inn, just on the border between Tryon and Landrum, South Carolina is the **Lakeshore B&B** (1026 E. Lakeshore Drive, Landrum, South Carolina 29356; 864–457–5330). Situated on a heavily wooded lot on the lakefront, the Inn offers private porch areas and suites that view the lake and surrounding mountains. Prices for double rates are $75–105 including breakfast.

For additional area entries, see **Saluda.**

Pine Crest Inn ¢ 🚸 ✕
200 Pine Crest Lane, 28782

Tel: 704–859–9135
800–633–3001
Fax: 704–859–9135
E-mail: pinecrestinn@compuserve.com

Established by Michigan equestrian Carter Brown in 1917, and listed on the National Register of Historic Places, the Pine Crest was purchased by Jeremy and Jennifer Wainwright in 1990. Originally from Great Britain, the Wainwrights have renovated the main building to evoke the feeling of an English country inn, with leather chairs and richly upholstered furnishings, and a traditional hunt and steeplechase decor. The restaurant is open to the public, serving two meals daily; sample entrees might include lamb with mustard and Madeira sauce, filet mignon with three peppercorn sauce, and Maryland crab cakes.

"Great dinners. Pleasant, helpful innkeeper." *(Yvonne Stoner)* "The atmosphere is posh, but practical, with Ralph Lauren decor supplementing the antiques. The dining room is evocative of Colonial Williamsburg, with small dining rooms of just four to six tables. The Front Pine room has a half-tester paisley canopy, down duvet, and a hunting print over the bed, accenting the dark paneling and shutters and the hunt green and red color scheme. All rooms have thick towels and robes, English soaps and gels in generous portions." *(SHW)* "Secluded setting, yet close to the center of a lovely small town just at the edge of the Blue Ridge Mountains." *(Sandra & Berge Heede)*

"Spacious but cozy rooms; clean, quiet, and tastefully decorated; fresh flowers everywhere. Our cottage had a fireplace, a wide selection of books, and even an iron and ironing board. Nightly turndown service with mints on your pillow and robes laid out on the bed. Breakfast offered a wide selection of cereals, homemade granola, fresh squeezed orange juice, mixed berry muffins, pastries and more. Delicious lamb, veal chop, and salmon at dinner. Ample parking, efficient housekeeping." *(Catherine & Tom Blottman)* "Friendly staff who soon learns your name and ensures your comfort." *(James M. Gorrell)* "An exceptional inn." *(Sibyl Nestor)*

Open All year.
Rooms 35 cottages, suites, doubles—all with private bath and/or shower, telephone, TV, desk, air conditioning. Rooms in 10 buildings and cottages, most with gas fireplace, VCR, hairdryer.
Facilities Restaurant, lobby, den with fireplaces, TV, books, games, puzzles, piano, Ping-Pong; porches. Conference center with fax, copier, computer. 9 acres with swimming pool, golf, tennis, hiking nearby.
Location ½m to town; 4 m from I-26. Take I-26 to Exit 36, Tryon/ Columbus & take NC 108 to Tryon. Go S (left) on Rte. 176. Go into Tryon, & go left on New Market St. to inn.
Credit cards /Amex, MC, Visa.
Rates B&B, $155–555 cottage, $155–185 suite, $135–160 double. Children under 6 free in parents' room. Futon (for children), $10. Alc dinner, $25–50. Golf packages. Additional charge for full breakfast.

Stone Hedge Inn ✗ *Tel:* 704–859–9114
300 Howard Gap Road, P.O. Box 366, 28782–0366 800–859–1974

In 1934, all the fieldstone needed to built this mansion and its outbuildings was brought from a local quarry by horse and wagon. Restored as an inn in 1977, the Stone Hedge has been owned by Tom and Shaula Dinsmore and Gary and Margo Shidaker since 1995. Guest rooms have either queen- or king-size beds; some are decorated with antiques, while others are more rustic with pine panelled walls and a stone fireplace.

Picture windows in the dining room offer guests stunning mountain views. Under the careful hand of Chef Tom, dinner entrees include such specialities as mountain trout with almonds, veal with prosciutto and Parmesan cheese, and spinach-stuffed chicken with red pepper sauce, while the tempting desserts include pecan pie or perhaps New Orleans bread pudding. Rates include a full breakfast, served at individual tables 8:15–9:30 A.M.

"Lovely stone house and cottage. Nice views, comfortable rooms, and delicious breakfast of fruit and French toast." *(Celia McCullough)* "Superb food, charming room, friendly owners—welcoming and full of smiles." *(GR)* "Rural setting on a country road. I saw two guest rooms in the main house; both were comfortable in size with a sitting area." *(Betty Norman)*

Open All year. Restaurant
Rooms 1 cottage, 1 suite, 3 doubles—all with private bath and/or shower, telephone, radio, clock, TV, air-conditioning. Some with ceiling fan, kitchenette, fireplace, desk, deck. Guest rooms in 3 buildings.
Facilities Restaurant with fireplace. 28 acres with patio, swimming pool, horseshoes. Tennis, golf, hiking nearby.
Location 2 m from downtown. Take I-26 to Tryon-Columbus. Exit 36. Take NC 108 toward Tryon. Go 2½ m & turn right on Howard Gap Rd. to inn is 1½ m on right.
Restrictions No smoking. Children 12 or over. BYOB.
Credit cards Visa, MC.
Rates B&B, $100 cottage, $115 suite, $85–100 double. Extra person, $20. Alc dinner, $25.

VALLE CRUCIS

Named for the three streams that cross in this high mountain valley, Valle Crucis is the home of the Mast General Store, dating back to 1883, and several interesting craft stores; it was founded by Scottish Highlanders, and hosts the largest gathering of the clans in the U.S. each summer. The village has been designated a National Historic District, the first rural one in North Carolina, and it encompasses 1,000 acres. Valle Crucis is located in the High Country of northwest North Carolina, midway between Boone and Banner Elk, 100 miles north of Charlotte, and 93 miles west of Winston-Salem. In addition to the Blue Ridge Parkway, within a short drive are such activities as golf, tennis, horseback riding, hiking, fishing, canoeing, downhill and cross-country skiing.

Also recommended: Built as a farmhouse in 1911, the **Inn at the Taylor House** (Highway 194, Box 713, 28691; 704–963–5581) has been restored as a European-style B&B with Oriental rugs and imported duvets. There are seven rooms, each with private bath; the rates of $125–165 double, $165–285 suite, include a full breakfast served at 8:30 A.M.; additional accommodations are offered in five cottages ($105–235; no breakfast). Chip Schwab is the long-time innkeeper; Allison Milligan is the manager. "Beautiful, immaculate room and bath. Delicious, elaborate gourmet breakfast." *(Yvonne Stoner)*

Information please: For an idyllic family getaway, consider the charming **Cottages of Glowing Hearth** (171 Glowing Hearth Lane, Vilas, 28692; 704–963–8800), five spacious dwellings, each with lots of windows to take in the mountain views, a 30-foot porch, well-equipped kitchen, two bedrooms, two baths (one with a double Jacuzzi), great room with stone fireplace and oversize television with cable and VCR, and more. Children are welcome at this family-friendly mini-resort, and will enjoy visiting the barn with dogs, pigs, chickens, goats, donkey, and even a llama.

Mast Farm Inn ✕ ♿
Broadstone Road, P.O. Box 704, 28691

Tel: 704–963–5857
Toll-free: 888–963–5857
Fax: 704–963–6404
E-mail: stay@mastfarminn.com

The Mast Farm dates back to the 1700s, when the original Mast family settled in Valle Crucis. It grew to include a blacksmith shop, a woodwork shop, smokehouse, spring house, wash house, apple house, granary, and barn. All of these outbuildings remain, earning the inn a place on the National Register of Historic Places; some have been converted to guest cottages. Construction of the farmhouse began in 1885; during the first half of the 20th century, it served as a thirteen-bedroom, one-bath guest house. Restored as an inn in 1986, the Mast Farm was bought by Wanda Hinsaw and Lyle Schoenfeldt (and their daughter, Sarah) in 1996, assisted by Wanda's sister, Kay Phillip. While taking care to preserve the inn's country charm, they've worked hard to provide the creature comforts today's inngoer enjoys. Guest rooms have either queen- or king-size beds, and the once-cramped third floor rooms now boast central air-conditioning, double-size bath tubs, and spacious sitting areas. Under the supervision of chef Scott Haulman, the dinner menu now offers a choice of a set menu or a la carte options. On a recent evening, the former featured creamy potato soup, green salad, salmon with garlic-basil sauce, and blueberry apple cobbler. A la carte entrees included cornmeal-encrusted trout, grilled ribeye steak, and roasted quail. Breakfasts are no less tempting, beginning with fresh fruit and yogurt or granola, followed by such entrees as three-grain pancakes, French toast, omelets, egg casseroles, or Dutch baby pancakes.

"Our reception was efficient, cheerful, and warm. As we were led to our dormer room, we were shown where we could fix ourselves a cup of tea. Our charming room had excellent lighting; hot water in the bathroom was ample and almost instant. After a good night's sleep under cozy comforters, we awoke to find a quilted basket containing a thermos of coffee and two mugs. Breakfast included bacon and eggs one morning, and French toast the next. We had a chance to chat with Wanda and Lyle, as well as their staff, and found them to be well-informed and friendly." *(MBB)* "The antiques, beautiful quilts, cozy down comforters, clawfoot tubs, and wonderful meals are just a few of the inn's charming qualities. The innkeepers are wonderfully helpful and pleased to give you a tour of the inn." *(Sue Weed)* "Beautifully manicured grounds and gardens. Welcoming porch with rockers, a perfect place for a hot cup of coffee, a cookie from the bottomless jar, a friendly chat, or a good read. Exceptional attention to detail, from meeting requests to remembering you from a previous visit. Immaculate housekeeping from almost invisible housekeepers. Amenities include robes and toiletries; high quality bedding and bath towels." *(Mary Pergerson)* "Wonderful inn with exceptionally kind-hearted innkeepers." *(Carol Sue Bingham)*

Open All year.
Rooms 4 cottages, 9 doubles—all with private bath and/or shower, radio, fan. Some with fireplace, double soaking tub, air-conditioning.
Facilities Restaurant, parlor with fireplace, sun porch, library/game room. 18 acres with flower, vegetable gardens; river for trout fishing; pond for fishing, swimming. Downhill, cross-country skiing nearby.
Location On SR 1112, 3 m from NC 105.
Restrictions No smoking. No children under 12. Some traffic noise in front rooms. Parking can be tight when the inn is busy with dinner guests. Dry county; BYOB.
Credit cards MC, Visa.
Rates B&B, $125–185 cottage, $100–175 double. Extra person, $25. 2-night weekend minimum. Prix fixe dinner, $17; alc dinner, $22.
Extras Wheelchair access. 1 room specially equipped.

WASHINGTON

Pamlico House Bed & Breakfast ¢
400 East Main Street, 27889

Tel: 919–946–7184
800–948–8507
Fax: 919–946–9944
E-mail: pamlicohouse@coastline.com

A Colonial Revival house built in 1906 as an Episcopal rectory, Pamlico House was restored as a B&B in 1988, and purchased by Jane and George Fields in 1997. They are former airline staffers who enjoyed B&Bs all over the world, and are now putting their experience to work. Guest rooms are individually decorated with antiques and good lighting, one with a queen-size lace canopy bed, another in white wicker, and a third with a hand-painted Victorian cottage set and a beautifully appliqued pink and white floral quilt. Breakfast includes fresh fruit and juice, bacon or sausage, home-baked goods, and such entrees as pancakes, waffles, or French toast.

"A beautiful white house with inviting verandas all around, rocking chairs, and ice provided for your drinks. Our spacious room was nicely furnished, with a comfortable king-size bed, soft pillows and antiques. The bathroom had a selection of creams, bath oils, and more. Jane and George were helpful, friendly, and welcoming, and breakfast was very convivial with the guests sharing a large table. The garden was full of flowers, their scent perfuming the air." *(Nina Davies)* "The charm of an older home with the convenience of new one. Quiet, safe area, ideal for walking." *(Kelly Edens)* "Spacious rooms, high ceilings, lovely antique furnishings, plus modern plumbing and air-conditioning. Location convenient to restaurants, downtown and waterfront." *(Andy Ackland)* "Our room was comfortable and quiet, with no noise from the street or other guests." *(Nancy Hartmann)* "Excellent lighting for desk work or reading in bed." *(Nancy Overton)* "The guest rooms are well spaced for privacy. Snacks and soft drinks are readily available. Potpourri, bathroom soaps and creams, and complimentary postcards are among the many extras." *(Don & Michelle Carll)* "Smooth, silky sheets; four soft pillows. We had our own well-lit reading nook by the fireplace complete with current magazines." *(Lena Fratz)* "Area information readily available." *(Alyne Bruce)* "Delicious fresh strawberries, just-baked muffins, eggs and sausages." *(L. Rieley)*

Open All year.
Rooms 4 doubles—all with private shower bath, telephone, radio, clock, TV, desk, air-conditioning, ceiling fan.
Facilities Dining room, living room with piano, books/stereo; porch with rockers, hammock. ½ acre with garden, off-street parking. Two blocks to river, marina.
Location E NC. 20 m E of Greenville. Historic district. Corner of Main & Academy Sts.
Restrictions No smoking. Children over 5.
Credit cards Visa, MC, AMEX, Discover.
Rates B&B, $75–85 double, $65–75 single. Extra person, $10.
Extras Airport/bus pickup.

WAYNESVILLE

Waynesville is a popular mountain resort, set between the Great Smoky Mountains National Park and the Pisgah National Forest. Known for its quality antique and crafts shops, summer activities also include hiking, fishing, horseback riding, white-water rafting, golf, and tennis, while downhill and cross-country skiing are available nearby in the winter. Waynesville is 25 miles west of Asheville, 130 miles southeast of Knoxville, and 190 miles north of Atlanta.

Information please: Built as a private home in 1880, the **Hallcrest Inn** (299 Halltop Circle, 28786; 704–456–6457 or 800–334–6457) sits atop

Hall Mountain with views of Waynesville and the Balsam Mountains. Guest rooms are simply furnished, highlighted by family antiques; eight guest rooms are in the inn, and four are in a motel-type annex. The reasonable rates of $80–90 include a breakfast of eggs, grits, juice, fruit, biscuits, breakfast meat, and beverage. A typical dinner might include roast beef, brown rice, squash casserole, lima beans, salad, homebaked rolls with apple butter, and homemade ice cream. "Lovely views from the front porch. Fine, family-style dining." *(Joe Schmidt, also MR)*

An inviting country escape, the **Mountain Creek B&B** (100 Chestnut Walk, 28786; 704–456–5509 or 800–557–9766) was built as a corporate retreat in the 1950s. This 4,745-square-foot lodge sits atop a hill, overlooking a huge trout pond, the surrounding landscaped acreage and the mountains beyond. Its inviting great room has wormy chestnut paneling, a stone fireplace, and wraparound windows. B&B double rates for the six well-equipped guest rooms range from $90–130, and include breakfast of strawberry stuffed French toast or cheese-baked eggs, and afternoon refreshments.

For additional area entries, see **Maggie Valley**.

The Old Stone Inn ¢ 👪 ✂

(formerly Heath Lodge) *Tel:* 704–456–3333
900 Dolan Road, 28786–2802 800–432–8499

Surrounded by century-old oak trees, mountain laurel, rhododendron and dogwood trees, the Old Stone Inn was built in 1946. Set at 3,200 feet, it offers pure mountain air, to be enjoyed on wide porches with high-backed rockers. The buildings are constructed of native poplar and stone, and many of the guest rooms have wood-paneled walls and patchwork comforters. Bob and Cindy Zinser, who bought the inn in 1992, celebrated the inn's fiftieth anniversary in 1996 by changing its name and renovating its common areas to create an atmosphere of rustic elegance. In the lounge, inviting conversational groupings tempt guests to linger before the massive stone hearth; in the dining room, the beamed ceiling and stone walls contrast with the white linens and red floral chair coverings. Served at individual tables 8–9 A.M., breakfast is a hearty affair with fruit smoothies, bacon, sausage, freshly baked muffins, and such entrees as quiches, soufflés, breakfast pie, or Scottish pancakes. Dinners are served at individual tables 6–8 P.M., and include a choice of such entrees as peppered pork medallions, salmon trout with lemon caper butter, and smoked Gouda cheese and wild mushroom tart.

"A fire was blazing in the lounge when we arrived and we enjoyed looking at the beautiful quilts and visiting with Cindy and Bob. Exceptional dinner: we enjoyed filet mignon, crisp salad, unusual yellow squash, sweet potato rolls, and for dessert, a chocolate chip torte. Our room in the main lodge was spacious but cozy, with good lighting, handmade quilts, and a comfortable sitting area. Excellent location at the gateway to the Smoky Mountains, convenient for area explorations." *(Lyn Teven)* "Quiet hilltop location, beautiful wooded setting. Warm welcome, well-kept rooms, excellent meals." *(E.K. Loffler)* "Bob and Cindy make your visit both relaxing and enjoyable." *(Kelli Kenison)* "The lodge is a rustic, restful getaway, cooled by enormous trees. We enjoyed the lodge cats, especially Fred, who visited our room. The Zinsers bend over backward to be solicitous of guests' needs." *(Helen Barranger)*

Open Good Friday through Dec. 31.
Rooms 2 suites, 20 doubles—all with private bath and/or shower, TV, desk, fan. Some with clock/radio, desk, balcony. 2 rooms in main lodge, 20 in 4 outlying buildings.
Facilities Restaurant with fireplace; guest lounge with fireplace, games, books. 6 wooded acres with gazebo, herb garden, lawn games, stream. Golf, fishing, hiking, skiing nearby.
Location 1 m to town. From I-40, take Exit 27, Hwy. 19/23. Go 6 m to Waynesville exit and take Hwy. 276 S. Go about ¼m to Kentucky Fried Chicken (opposite Pizza Hut), turn right onto Love Lane. Turn right again onto Dolan to inn on left.
Restrictions No smoking in common areas; permitted in some guest rooms. Children 12 and over.
Credit cards Discover, MC, Visa.
Rates B&B, $139–164 suite, $89–164 double, $74–149 single. Extra person, $39. Alc dinner, $25. Packages.

The Swag 🚸 ♿ | *Tel:* 704–926 0430
Route 2, Box 280-A, Hemphill Road, 28786 | *Fax:* 704–926–2036
E-mail: letters@theswag.com

Innkeeper Deener Matthews reports that a " 'swag' is a dip between two knolls on a high mountain ridge. It is the traditional term used by our mountain neighbors for as long as anyone can recall to designate our particular site." Perched at 5,000 feet, the inn is made of handhewn logs from original Appalachian structures dating back hundreds of years, with a massive stone fireplace in the living room and original North Carolina art work. A recent addition is the outdoor spa, where you can have a relaxing soak while enjoying spectacular 50-mile mountain views on clear days. Each guest room is individually decorated with handmade quilts and woven rugs. Regional cuisine is presented in a healthy, imaginative and innovative style. The dinner menu might include clam chowder, baby greens with tomato dressing, grilled rainbow trout with saffron angel hair pasta, garlic sauted vegetables, cheesy corn muffins, and chocolate mousse with brandy snaps.

"The views were overwhelming and the food wonderful. Expensive but worth it. Good hiking, too." *(Yvonne Stoner)* "Friendly, helpful staff and innkeeper. Careful attention to details; on the nature trails, small signs identify the trees and plants." *(Tom Wilbanks)* "Our room, high under the eaves, was cozy, comfortable, with a remarkable view. The luxurious bathroom was equipped with soft terry cloth robes. For recreation you can step out the door and hike in the Great Smoky Mountains National Park, engage in activities from racquetball to croquet, or sit by the fire and enjoy a book from the extensive library. Several times during the summer naturalists, musicians, and other experts offer programs for the guests." *(Sheila & Joe Schmidt)* "Deener is a warm, gracious hostess; the food is excellent, the grounds beautiful, and the company good." *(Sibyl Nestor)* "Individual log cabins are most private; for conviviality and conversation, there's a high-ceilinged common room and cheerful, all-at-one-table service for the three spectacular meals a day." *(Crescent Dragonwagon)* "Fantastic mountaintop location; superb cuisine; flexible staff who go the extra mile for guests." *(Burt Richmond)*

Open Mid-May through Oct.
Rooms 2 cabins, 12 doubles—all with private bath and/or shower, refrigerator, coffee maker, hair dryer, CD player, robes. Many with balcony. 7 with steam shower, 9 with woodstove or fireplace, coffee maker. 1 cabin with whirlpool tub, refrigerator, wet bar, fireplace.
Facilities Dining room, living room with fireplace, player piano, games, library; porch. 250 acres with woodland, wildflowers, hammock, swing, hiking trails, badminton, croquet, underground racquetball court, sauna, private entrance to Great Smoky Mt. National Park. Golf nearby.
Location W NC. 12 m from Waynesville, 5 m from Maggie Valley, 30 m W of Asheville. From Waynesville, take I-276 N toward Knoxville. Go 2.3 m past intersection with Rte. 19 to Hemphill Rd. Turn left on Hemphill Rd. to inn.
Restrictions No smoking. No children under 7. Dry county, BYOB.
Credit cards MC, Visa.
Rates Full board (for 2 people), $330–510 cabin, $240–510 double. Extra person, $80–90. Prix fixe lunch, $10; prix fixe dinner $35. 15% service. Box lunches. Nature, hiking, special workshops. 2-night minimum.
Extras Wheelchair access; some rooms equipped for the disabled.

Yellow House On Plott Creek Road
610 Plott Creek Road, 28786

Tel: 704–452–0991
800–563–1236
Fax: 704–452–1140

A gracious Colonial Revival home built in the 1890s, the Yellow House was restored as a B&B in 1995 by Ron and Sharon Smith. Their goal is to create a romantic mountain escape with a touch of French country charm. Guest rooms are named for charming and romantic places the Smiths have visited, from France and England, to California and Nantucket, plus North Carolina, of course. Guests can choose breakfast seatings at 8:30, 9:00, or 9:30 A.M., and can enjoy the meal in their room, in the dining room, or on the flower-filled veranda which wraps around the house, and offers lovely views of the foothills of the Blue Ridge Mountains. A favorite menu consists of Swedish pancakes with fresh berries, bacon, croissants, and home-baked bread. Rates also include pre-dinner drinks and hors d'oeuvres, in-room coffee service, terry robes, a stocked refrigerator, and after-dinner port.

"Warm and inviting, elegantly furnished. Each room has a different flavor: with the atmosphere of a New England seaside inn, the S'conset Room is crisp and breezy, done in blue and white with a cherrywood queen-size four poster bed with white Battenburg comforter. The evening social hour is a wonderful way to meet Ron and Sharon and your fellow guests. Wonderful breakfast, served at the guests' preferred time and location. Convenient to sights, shops, and restaurants in the surrounding area." *(Linda & Michael Gill)* "Sharon and Ron are both gracious and efficient, and you will feel welcome at once in their beautiful home. The other staff members are equally gracious, especially Bonnie, who prepared the hors d'oeuvres in the evening and the truly scrumptious breakfasts—request the Swedish pancakes and the caramel apple breakfast pudding. My favorite room is the E'staing Suite, furnished with natural wood queen-size bed, dresser, and shutters, plus a stone fireplace. Its private second-floor balcony under the portico at the front of the house is the perfect spot for an intimate breakfast. The rooms have speakers for classical and popular music with individual controls to suit personal taste. The quiet beauty of the surroundings and the sun coming over the mountains in the morning help create a totally relaxing setting." *(Carol Burgess)*

Open All year.
Rooms 4 suites, 2 doubles—all with full private bath, telephone, clock, gas fireplace, coffee maker, wet bar and/or refrigerator. 2 with double whirlpool tub, desk, balcony.
Facilities Dining groom, living room, library; each with fireplace; wraparound veranda. 3 acres with lily pond, gardens,lawn games.
Location 10 min. from town.
Restrictions No smoking. Children over 12.
Credit cards MC, Visa.
Rates B&B, $150–250 suite, $115–135 double. Extra person, $20. Picnic lunch, $25 for 2. 2-night weekend minimum. Off-season packages.

WILMINGTON

Located in southeastern North Carolina, on the Cape Fear River, 125 miles south of Raleigh, Wilmington is the state's largest port and a major trading center. It's also popular with the film industry and with retirees. The historic district has been restored in recent years, and is now home to appealing shops, restaurants, galleries, and—of course—B&Bs. The city has plenty of charm and several museums of interest, including the U.S.S. *North Carolina* Battleship Memorial; it's just a short drive to the ocean beaches and to several restored plantation homes.

Reader tip: "Dinner at Elijahs on the river was very good." *(Rose Ciccone)*

Also recommended: A 14,000-square-foot Italian Renaissance Revival mansion, the **Graystone Inn** (100 South Third Street, 28401; 910–763–2000) was built in 1906. B&B double rates for the six guest rooms range from $125–175. "Beautifully restored, in the center of the historic district. Exceptional plaster work and antique furnishings. Spacious common areas. Our immaculate room was done in Laura Ashley and Waverly fabrics; the bathroom had ample country space and lovely toiletries. The breakfast buffet consisted of fresh fruit and juice, apple pastry, quiche, and muffins." *(Perri & Michael Rappel)* "Extraordinary common areas with grand interior columns, hand-carved three-story oak staircase, and magnificent openness. Our huge room had soothing green walls, white moldings, ample reading lights, and modern bath. Beautiful breakfast on individual serving trays." *(Zita Knific)*

Information please: A Queen Anne-style home built in 1889, **Camellia Cottage** (118 South Fourth Street at Cottage Lane, 28401; 910–763–9171 or 800–763–9171) has four guest rooms, each with private bath, queen-size bed, and gas fireplace. Rates include wake-up coffee, a full breakfast, and afternoon refreshments. "Lovely porch with comfortable seating, beautiful plants, and hand-painted flowers. Inside, rooms are attractively decorated with charming collectibles. We were delighted to find the innkeeper's cat napping on our bed." *(CR, also Kimberly Cadwallader)*

An 1837 home in the historic district, **The Curran House B&B** (312 South Third Street, 28401; 910–763–6603 or 800–763–6603) offers three spacious, well-furnished guest rooms with king- or queen-size beds, private baths, and telephones. B&B double rates of $75–100 include early morning coffee and a full home-cooked breakfast.

A good choice if you prefer the atmosphere of a small hotel is the **Front Street Inn** (215 South Front Street, 28401; 910–762–6442), a 1923 building, gutted and restored as a nine-suite inn in 1994. The sophisticated decor complements the exposed brick walls and arched windows. A healthy continental breakfast buffet is served in the common room; guests can enjoy also snacks and drinks here on the honor system. In the basement is a pool table and exercise room. B&B double rates range from $85–155. Reports?

The **Taylor House Inn** (14 North Seventh Street, 28401; 910–763–7581 or 800–382–9982) is a turn-of-the-century Victorian home with an elaborate oak staircase, stained glass and leaded windows, and twelve-foot ceilings. Each of the five guest rooms has a different decor, from Jacobean to antebellum. Double rates of $100–110 include a full breakfast and afternoon wine and hors d'oeuvres. The inn is located on a quiet street in the historic district.

For an additional area entry, see **Bald Head Island.**

Catherine's Inn
410 South Front Street, 28401

Tel: 910–251–0863
800–476–0723
Fax: 910–772–9550

Overlooking the Cape Fear River in the heart of the historic district, is Catherine's Inn, built in 1883, and restored in 1994 by Catherine and Walter Ackiss. Breakfast is served at the dining room table from 7–8:30 A.M., and consists of fresh fruit and juice, a breakfast meat and a hot entree. Rates also include early morning coffee, afternoon refreshments, turndown service and sherry.

"Comfortable yet elegant, with beautifully decorated rooms; delightful, helpful innkeepers; delicious, plentiful breakfasts. The screened second-floor porch at the back is the perfect place to watch the ships go by, while drinking an early morning cup of coffee, sipping a glass of wine, or enjoying bedtime sherry." *(Terry Pocklington)* "Catherine and Walter's hospitality is warm and attentive. We also loved the fresh, delicious coffee ready in the hallway at 7:15 sharp. Evening turndown service with chocolate mints topped off the evening." *(Susan Howie)* "Catherine is warm and hospitable, attentive to every detail and sensitive to her guests' needs. I learned more about Wilmington from her than I did from any guidebook." *(Eleanor Price)* "Wonderful breakfast of French toast and bacon, with homemade peach preserves, served on fine china and crystal." *(SM)*

"Conveniently located in the restored historic area, a short and walkable distance to waterfront restaurants, shops, and museums. The inn is charming, decorated with a variety of antiques. Our room had a king-sized bed with a firm mattress, abundant towels and terrycloth robes." *(Diane Mrva)*

Open All year.
Rooms 5 doubles—all with private bath and/or shower, telephone, radio, clock, desk, air-conditioning, ceiling fan.
Facilities Dining room, living room with piano, library with books, TV/VCR, guest refrigerator, wraparound front porch, screened rear porch. Off-street parking, sunken garden.
Location Historic district. From I-40, take hwy. 17 (Market St.) S to Historic District. Go to Front St. & turn left to inn 4 blocks S on right. From Cape Fear Memorial Bridge (Hwy 74-76-17), exit right for Front St. N and Historic Downtown. Go 3 blocks to in on left past Church St.
Restrictions No smoking. Children 10 and over, or by prior arrangement.
Credit cards Amex, MC, Visa.
Rates B&B, $85–98 double, $75 single. Extra person, $20.

The Inn at St. Thomas Court ♿
101 South Second Street, 28401

Tel: 910–763–4933
800–525–0909
Fax: 910–251–1149
E-mail: theinn@wilmington.net

Reconstructed from turn-of-the-century commercial buildings, The Inn at St. Thomas Court combines the privacy and independence of a hotel with some of the ambiance of an inn. Situated in the heart of historic Wilmington, the area is rich with antique and gift shops, museums and galleries.

"The main building is a Charleston-style two-story building with wide porches and wicker chairs. Our spotless one-bedroom suite had wide plank floors. Suites are individually decorated, with furnishings ranging from country French to Southwestern to antebellum, though the layout is the same in each. A pleasant surprise was the abundant lighting, large mirrors and shelf space in the bathroom. Terrific location, two blocks down to the Riverwalk to stroll and shop, with quite a few restaurants in walking distance. Pleasant and helpful staff. There is a small bar for guests. Breakfast which consists of a choice of juice, cereal, pastry or muffins, is ordered at check-in, then delivered to your door in a basket with the newspaper. You prepare your own coffee or tea in your suite. Linen napkins and real china are a nice addition." *(Ben & Peg Bedini)* "Our suite had a mini-kitchen, lavish bathroom, and large comfortable beds. The inn blends historical ambiance and modern comfort, and is close to great restaurants and nightlife. The owners were often around and were happy to talk about the town and their inn." *(David Scott)*

Open All year.
Rooms 34 1-2 bedroom suites—all with private bath, telephone, radio, clock, TV, desk, air-conditioning, fan, refrigerator, deck/balcony. Some with kitchenette, washer/dryer, whirlpool tub, fireplace. Suites in 4 buildings.
Facilities Bar/lounge, guest laundry, books. Conference room, fax, copier, business services. Garden, courtyard, gazebo, off-street parking. Golf, tennis, sailing packages.
Location In downtown historic area. 15 min. to I-40, airport, beaches. On 2nd St. at Dock, 2 blocks from river. Call for directions.
Restrictions No smoking.
Credit cards Amex, DC, MC, Visa.
Rates B&B, $125–195 suite. 2-night minimum holidays/special events.

The Verandas
202 Nun Street, 28401

Tel: 910–251–2212
Fax: 910–251–1396
E-mail: verandas4@aol.com

Those of us who feel we should get a medal for just painting the bedroom walls will marvel at the renovation undertaken by Dennis Madsen and Chuck Pennington. When they first saw The Verandas in 1995, this once-elegant 8,500-square-foot Victorian Italianate mansion, dating back to 1854, was a fire-damaged, boarded-up mess. Dennis' previous experience as a commercial designer on such projects as Washington DC's Willard Hotel and Union Station was put to good use in the renovation process. Although the owners were able to salvage the pine and pin oak floors, staircases, and entrance, the gutting of the house involved the removal of more than 80,000 pounds of plaster, 10,000 pounds of radiators, and enough debris to fill 20 dump trucks. The entire infrastructure of the house was re-done with state-of-the-art wiring, heating, air-conditioning, plumbing, insulation, and sprinkler system. Although the inn opened in 1997, on-going restoration plans include a new patio and garden landscaping as well as the completion of the third floor rooms.

The inn is decorated with English and American antiques, traditional furniture, and Oriental carpets. Each guest room occupies a corner of the inn, and has individual climate control, king-, queen-, or twin-size beds, and a sitting area; the smallest room is a spacious seventeen by twenty feet with a nine-foot ceiling. Bathrooms feature marble floors, oversized soaking tubs, marble vanities, oversize towels, and Caswell-Massey toiletries. Although the inn's common areas provide ample space for guests to relax, the enclosed cupola is a highlight in all senses of the word. One of the highest points in the historic district, it offers a panoramic view of the downtown skyline, the Battleship North Carolina, and dramatic sunsets. Breakfast is served at the dining room table in the winter, and on the patio in good weather. Early serving times during the week accommodate business travelers; on weekends breakfast is served at 9 A.M. A typical menu includes fresh fruit and juice, French bread casserole, croissants, and sausages.

"Easy walking distance to the river, restaurants, and shops. The common rooms are beautifully decorated, light and airy with enormous windows, pale yellow walls, and lots of fresh flowers. Housekeeping is impeccable. The verandas have rocking chairs, Adirondack chairs, and a swing, and overlook the lovely garden. Our room was dramatic in black and gold. The walls were pearl gray, with a border of black and gold, and the bed linens and window treatments repeated these colors in stripes and florals. Furnishings included an Eastlake dresser, lamp table with side chairs, and end tables with brass lamps on both sides of the bed. The housekeeping is exceptional; even the sheets are hand ironed. Wonderful oatmeal almond soap is used along with other Caswell-Massey amenities. Bedside chocolates were a nice touch. Bountiful, well-prepared breakfasts, with excellent coffee and delicious fresh fruit. Dennis and Chuck try to join their guests for coffee and conversation. They are wonderful hosts, thoughtful and attentive; their restaurant recommendations were excellent." *(Rose Ciccone)*

Open All year.
Rooms 8 doubles—all with full private bath with oversize soaking tub, telephone with data ports, radio, clock, TV/VCR, desk, air-conditioning, individual thermostat, veranda access.
Facilities Dining room, living room with fireplace, library, cupola, 4 verandas, terrace, screened porch. Garden. Easy, convenient on-street parking; off-street parking nearby.
Location Historic district, 2 blocks from Cape Fear River/Riverwalk, South on Market St., left on 3rd St., right on Nun to inn at corner of Second and Nun. From Rte. 421 S, go S (left) on 2nd to inn at 2nd & Nun.
Restrictions No smoking. Children over 12.
Credit cards Amex, Discover, MC, Visa.
Rates B&B, $90–165 double, $90–145 single. Extra person, $25. 2-night weekend minimum.
Extras American Sign Language.

The Worth House
412 South Third Street, 28401

Tel: 910–762–8562
800–340–8559
Fax: 910–763–2173
E-mail: worthhse@wilmington.net

A Queen Anne-style home with bay windows, turrets, and porches, Worth House was built in 1893, and has been owned by Frances and John Miller since 1994. The Millers note: "Although our inn has a decidedly Victorian air, comfort and flexibility are the keynotes here. We try to accommodate guests' schedules for check-in, and their preferred time and location for breakfast—in their room, on the porch overlooking the garden, or in the dining room. The washing machine is available if they've been on the road a while, and they're welcome to enjoy a take-out dinner from a local restaurant using our china and silver. Breakfast is usually served between 8 and 9:30 A.M., and consists of fresh fruit and juice, plus waffles, pancakes, French toast or a variety of egg dishes. Guests can also help themselves to complimentary soft drinks and snacks from the guest refrigerators on each floor.

"A painted lady Victorian, done in pastels, with lovely grounds and a pretty garden. The front hall has a beautiful oak staircase and paneling. Ample, inviting common areas with plenty of games, puzzles, and a great video collection. Spacious guest rooms, most with king-size beds. The Rose Suite has a comfortable king-size four-poster bed with quality linens and a fishnet canopy, end tables with reading lamps, and a rocking chair. The attractive exposed brick wall behind the fireplace accented the wood mantle and hearth tiles. Its little sun room had a wicker table and chairs, and a table that held a phone, lamp, and reading materials about the area. The bathroom had both a clawfoot tub and separate shower; the bathroom door had a stained glass panel. While there are lovely antiques and accessories, the rooms are not overdone. Breakfast consisted of fresh-squeezed orange juice, bananas and strawberries with yogurt, apple cinnamon pancakes, scrambled eggs, and Smithfield ham sausage patties." *(Rose Ciccone)* "Comfortable bed and furnishings; creative, delicious breakfasts. Extremely clean. Easy walking distance to main streets." *(Judith Pynchon)*

Open All year.
Rooms 7 doubles—with private shower and/or bath, telephone, radio, clock, air-conditioning, ceiling fan. Some with desk, fireplace, porch.
Facilities Dining room with fireplace, living room with fireplace; library, 3rd floor sitting room both with TV/VCR, video library, games; guest refrigerators, laundry. ⅓ acre with garden, off-street parking.
Location Historic district. 6 blocks to downtown. On Third St. (Rte. 421) between Nun & Church.
Restrictions No smoking. Occasional traffic noise possible in 2 front rooms. Children 8 and over.
Credit cards Amex, MC, Visa.
Rates B&B, $75–115 double, $70–110 single. Extra person, $20. Senior discount. Corporate rates midweek. Off-season rates, packages.

WILSON

Miss Betty's B&B Inn ¢ ♿
600 West Nash Street, 27893

Tel: 919–243–4447
800–258–2058
Fax: 919–243–4447

"Wilson," reports Fred Spitz, co-owner of Miss Betty's B&B inn, "is the antiques and tobacco capital of North Carolina, where 'Eastern Carolina' barbecue is king. Halfway between New England and Florida, and close to I-95, we offer a welcome resting point for the north/south traveler. Our Miss Betty is an interior decorator, an antiques dealer, an excellent cook, and a natural innkeeper." The inn occupies four buildings in the historic district, dating from 1858 to 1943; one is listed on the National Register of Historic Places, and all are furnished with Victorian antiques. Breakfast is served at 7:30 A.M. weekdays, 8:30 on weekends, and includes fresh juice, cereals, eggs, hot cakes, grits, bacon or locally made sausage, English muffins, and homemade pastries.

"Our spacious room had a king-size bed, desk, and two reading chairs with good lighting. Although a few of the antique furnishings were for sale, these are sparingly and tastefully distributed. Although it was one of the coldest nights of the year, we could adjust the heat to our comfort, and supplement it with electric blankets." *(Duane Roller)* "Loaded with charm and Southern hospitality from the minute Fred welcomes you until you check out and he reminds you to drive safely. Miss Betty dresses in period costume and ruffled cap to served a delicious breakfast of fluffy scrambled eggs, carefully browned pancakes, and apple or banana cake." *(Morgan C. Boyd)* "Room #9 was beautifully decorated, and had soft towels and a comfortable bed. Scrumptious breakfast plus enjoyable conversation." *(GR)* "My immaculate room had a beaded board ceiling, attractive wood trim and hardwood floor, plus soft pastel artwork, good reading chair and lamp, and a firm, comfortable double-size white iron bed." *(Mary Williams)* "Lovely grounds with large shade trees and flowering shrubs." *(Barry Fetzer)*

Open All year.
Rooms 3 suites, 7 doubles—all with private bath and/or shower, telephone, TV, air-conditioning. Most with fireplace, ceiling fan. Some with desk. Rooms in 4 buildings.
Facilities Dining room, 4 parlors with fireplaces, TV/VCRs. 1½ acres with lawn games, off-street parking. Swimming, golf, tennis nearby.
Location E NC, 60 m E of Raleigh, 6 m E of I-95, ½ m from town center. From I-95, take Exit 116 to Rte. 42 E into Wilson. Turn left on Nash St. to inn on right.
Restrictions No smoking. No children.
Credit cards AMEX, CB, DC, Discover, MC, Visa.
Rates B&B, $75 suite, $60–75 double, $50–60 single.
Extras Wheelchair access; 1 room equipped for disabled.

WINSTON-SALEM

Winston-Salem is known for its attention to the arts, and is the home of Old Salem, a restored 18th-century Moravian village. Other sites of interest include Reynolds House, the estate of the late R.J. Reynolds, founder of the tobacco firm that bears his name. The residence and gardens are open to the public; the house has an excellent collection of American art. If all that culture makes you thirsty, we suggest a free tour of the Joseph Schlitz Brewing Company; their Winston-Salem facility produces 4 million barrels of beer annually.

Winston-Salem is in central North Carolina, 144 miles east of Asheville, 80 miles north of Charlotte, and 104 miles west of Raleigh.

Also recommended: About 12 miles west of Winston-Salem is the **Tanglewood Manor House** (Highway 158 West, P.O. Box 1040, Clemmons 27012; 910–766–0591). Once the private estate of William and Kate Reynolds, Tanglewood is now operated by Forsyth County as an 1150-acre park. Very reasonably priced accommodations are available in the Manor house, a motel lodge, and cabins; a restaurant is also available. Recreation facilities include 3 golf courses, 9 tennis courts, a swimming pool and lake, horseback riding, and more. "Lovely bucolic setting atop a hill, surrounded by gardens. The Manor is tastefully decorated with antiques and reproductions. Our sunny deluxe double room had two canopy beds, a sitting area, and was done in soothing green and white. The continental breakfast was served on a lovely porch. Delightful in spring; extremely popular in summer and fall." *(Zita Knific)*

Information please: Based in an old cotton mill complex dating back to 1836, the **Brookstown Inn** (200 Brookstown Avenue, 27101; 910–725–1120 or 800–845–4262) offers 71 spacious guest suites, with loft ceilings, exposed handmade brick walls, and rough-hewn beams. The decor mixes Appalachian handmade quilts, traditional pieces, and antiques. The Brookstown is located between Winston's commercial center and the restored Colonial village of Old Salem. "We arrived to a lovely display of wine, cheese, and fruit, and had an enjoyable meal at Darryl's restaurant, part of the inn complex. Our room was clean and comfortable, with good reading chairs, magazines, quality mattresses and pillows, comfy towels and sheets. Breakfast consisted of Moravian buns, Danishes, muffins, a nice array of fresh fruit, cereals, hot chocolate, tea, excellent coffee, and juices; attentive hostess." *(Perri & Michael Rappel)* B&B double rates are $100–145, including breakfast, morning paper, wine and cheese, bedtime milk and cookies, and evening turndown service; non-smoking rooms available on "first-come, first-serve" basis.

For an additional area entry, see **Pilot Mountain.**

The Augustus T. Zevely Inn
803 South Main Street, 27101

Tel: 910–748–9299
800–928–9299
Fax: 910–721–2211

In the heart of Old Salem is The Augustus T. Zevely Inn, built in 1844, and restored as an inn in 1994 with meticulous attention to historic accuracy. The renovation was overseen by co-owner Tom Lantz, who also operates the Thomas Bond House in Philadelphia's Independence National Park, an equally historic structure and a longtime reader favorite. Linda Anderson is the on-site innkeeper. Rooms are furnished with Old Salem collection furnishings, based on originals found in local museums and private homes. Breakfast is served 7–9:00 A.M. weekdays, and 8–10:00 A.M. on weekends; guests have their choice of eating at the large table in the formal dining room, or the individual tables in the breakfast room. The meal includes fruit and juice, cereal, Moravian-style rolls and breads, sugar cake, and blueberry or perhaps apple walnut muffins. On weekends a hot entree is added, perhaps pineapple strata or sausage egg bake. Also included is afternoon wine and cheese, and evening treat. "Considerate, professional staff; comfortable, luxurious rooms; historic setting." *(GR)* Comments appreciated.

Open All year.
Rooms 1 suite, 11 doubles—all with private bath and/or shower, telephone,

radio, clock, TV, desk, air-conditioning. Some with whirlpool tub, fireplace, microwave, refrigerator, balcony.
Facilities Dining room with fireplace, breakfast room, living room with fireplace, stereo; guest pantry; porches. ⅓ acre with off-street parking. Swimming, tennis, fishing, boating nearby.
Location Old Salem historic district, at corner of Main & Blum. 1 m from town center.
Restrictions Smoking allowed only in 2 guest rooms. Well-behaved children welcome.
Credit cards Amex, MC, Visa.
Rates B&B, $205–325 suite, 80–185 double. Extra person, $15. Children under 6 free.
Extras Wheelchair access; 1 room specially equipped.

Colonel Ludlow House
434 Summit & West Fifth Street

Tel: 919–777–1887
800–301–1887
Fax: 910–777–1890
E-mail: innkeeper@bbinn.com

The Colonel Ludlow House consists of two adjacent Victorian homes, the Benjanin Joseph Sheppard House, built in 1895, and the Jacob Lott Ludlow House, dating to 1887. They were restored and converted into luxury B&Bs in 1982 by Ken Land; Constance Creasman has been the innkeeper since 1990. Rooms feature original stained glass windows and are furnished with Victorian antiques, plus *all* modern conveniences. A typical breakfast consists of juice, fresh fruit, quiche, breads, bagels, and pastries, bacon or ham; although it's available between 8–11 A.M. in the dining room or on the porch, most guests choose to have it placed in their rooms the evening before, so they can microwave it at their convenience. Each room is also supplied with complimentary coffee, tea, popcorn and fruit; espresso and cappucino is delivered on request.

"The spacious guest rooms are charming and comfortable. The bedside stereo has extra speakers in the bathroom. At the end of a long business day, it was relaxing to soak in the tub soothed by your favorite music." *(Rebekah Ellis)* "All the comforts of staying at a friend's house with none of the obligations. Loved heating up my own breakfast so I could eat in my robe. Unobtrusive staff; quiet, pleasant neighborhood." (Katherine Gibbs McCombs) "Careful attention to detail included the make-up mirrors, bathrobes, heated towel racks, and oversize towels." *(Jody Mitchell)* "Special perks include the TV/VCR by the hot tub as well as in the bedroom, and the drinks and snacks waiting in the refrigerator along with breakfast." *(Amanda Walker)* "The front doors have intercoms, so only guests can enter. Upon check-in, we were offered a drink and a chance to browse in the sitting room, where we were asked to review the video collection and pick the ones we wanted. We were given the keys to several rooms and could pick the one we liked best, but all were beautiful. On-street parking is available after 6 P.M., and we found that most convenient." *(Teri Beasley)* "From the in-room ironing board and safety pins, everything was there to meet guests' needs." *(Nancy Lewman)* "The staff provided computer printouts to answer our requests for information on local sites and restaurants." *(Nancy Rosenfeld)* "When we called to make reservations, the knowledgeable innkeeper gave us directions to the inn and offered to make dinner reservations for us." *(Robin Brown)* "Convenient to downtown, and right next to one of the city's best (and most expensive) restaurants, the Zevely House. The West End is a pretty neighborhood of 1890s–1920s restored homes, excellent for a stroll." *(Carey Sutton)*

Open All year.
Rooms 5 suites, 5 doubles—all with private bath and/or shower, telephones with data ports, voice mail; stereo, TV/VCR, desk, air-conditioning, ceiling fan, refrigerator, microwave, coffee maker, ironing board; 9 with double whirlpool tub. Some with fireplace, steam bath, deck. 4 rooms in Ludlow House, 6 in adjacent Sheppard House.
Facilities Breakfast room, living room with piano, fireplace; CD & video library, exercise room, billiards room, library, porch. Fax, copier service. 1 acre with off-street parking.
Location Historic West End, 6 blocks from downtown. From Hwy 311, go N onto Hwy 52. From 52, go W onto Business I-40 (not new I-40 bypass). From I-77, go E onto Business I-40 & take Broad St./Downtown Exit. Go right onto Broad. Go 4 lights & turn left onto W 5th St. Go 1 block to Summit St. & inn on left corner.
Restrictions Children 12 and over. Non-smoking guest rooms available.
Credit cards Amex, Discover, MC, Visa.
Rates B&B, $169–209 suite, $139–179 double, $75–95 single (midweek).

Henry F. Shaffner House
150 South Marshall Street, 27101

Tel: 910–777–0052
800–952–2256
Fax: 910–777–1188

Built in 1907, the Henry F. Shaffner House is a handsome Tudor-style Queen Anne mansion restored as an inn by Betty and Henry Falls, Jr. in 1993. The original tiger oak and marbleized woodwork, brass fixtures, and hand-stenciled hardwood floors have been restored, and are complemented by elegant antique and reproduction decor. The guest room furnishings range from the cherry French country garden decor of the Reynolda room to the sophisticated neoclassic style of the Piedmont Room. Breakfast includes fresh fruit, cereal, granola, muffins, waffles, Danish, fresh-squeezed orange juice, yogurt, and such entrees as omelets with spinach, pine nuts, and dried tomatoes. Rates also include evening wine and cheese.

"Rooms were well furnished, staff very friendly and helpful." *(Frances White)* "An elegant, charming place, close to area restaurants and the charm of Old Salem. Convenient to Business I-40." *(Lee Milton)* "Unobtrusive staff. Guest rooms were nicely decorated with reproduction decor; the common areas were handsomely furnished, and the inn was clean, well run and comfortable. The penthouse suite is decorated with 18th-century style Biedermeier-style furnishings and is worth looking at." *(Sona Nast)*

Open All year.
Rooms 4 suites, 4 doubles—all with private bath and/or shower, telephone

radio, clock, TV, air-conditioning, fan. 2 with whirlpool tub, 6 with desk, 2 with wet bar/refrigerator.

Facilities Dining room, living room with piano, library area, sun room, tea room. Off-street parking, Free health club membership. Meeting facilities; weddings, receptions, murder mystery weekends.

Location Border of downtown & Old Salem. 6 blocks to downtown; 3 blocks to Old Salem. 20 min. from airport. From Bus. I-40 E, take Cherry St./Convention Ctr. exit & go left on High St. 2nd left is Marshall; inn is at corner of Marshall & High Sts. From I-40 W, take Cherry St. Exit & go left on 1st St. Left again on Marshall to inn on right.

Restrictions Smoking only on 3rd floor veranda, front porch. Air-conditioning masks traffic noise.

Credit cards Amex, MC, Visa.

Rates B&B, $99–189 double. Extra person, $15. Children under 12 free. 10% senior discount.

Extras Airport/station pickup. Crib.

South Carolina

Brasington House, Charleston

South Carolina's major area of tourist interest is the Low Country, extending from Charleston down along the coast from Beaufort and Hilton Head to Savannah. This area's original wealth came from shipping and rice plantations, and later from cotton. For an interesting side trip, take Route 17 north from Charleston to Mt. Pleasant. A highlight of this drive is the stands lining the highway where sweetgrass baskets are sold. Using skills brought from Africa on slave ships, the local basket makers create intricate pieces from simple trivets to large lacy baskets.

Inland, visitors will find deep forests, the foothills of the Blue Ridge mountains, and the Santee Cooper Lakes. In Aiken, visit Hopeland Gardens' flower-lined paths; in Abbeville, see a play in the restored Opera House; or snap photos of the colorful fields at Greenwood's Park Seed Company gardens.

Important note: Much of coastal South Carolina will be changing from the 803 to the 843 area code in 1998. If you don't get through on one, try the other!

BEAUFORT

The second oldest town in the state, Beaufort (pronounced BYOU-fort) was founded in 1711. Overlooking the Intracoastal Waterway, this historic port town has beautifully restored 18th and 19th century antebellum homes shaded by century-old trees. Beaufort is located in the Low Country of coastal South Carolina, 50 miles northeast of Savannah, Georgia, and 62 miles southwest of Charleston. It's 15 miles to the beaches of Hunting Island State Park on the Atlantic for swimming, fishing, and boating.

Reader tip: "Our favorite restaurant, just short drive from town, was the Gullah House." *(Steve Holman)* "Enjoyable antique shops, art galleries, and carriage rides." *(HJB)*

Also recommended: Overlooking the Beaufort River, just across from Waterfront Park, is the **Cuthbert House Inn** (1203 Bay Street, 29902; 803–521–1315 or 800–327–9275), a beautifully restored plantation home built in 1810. Each of the six guest rooms has a private bath and elegant furnishings, and the B&B double rates of $135–165 include a breakfast and afternoon refreshments, often enjoyed on the first- and second floor verandas. Breakfast is served from 8–9:30 A.M., and might include a fresh fruit medley, pecan waffles, and sausages. "Ideal waterview location, just a block from shops and restaurants." *(RC)* "Beautiful restoration, gracious hospitality, excellent food, careful attention to detail." *(Jim Donaldson)*

Information please: Facing the Intracoastal Waterway is the handsome Greek Revival-style **Bay Street Inn** (601 Bay Street, 29902; 803–522–0050), on a quiet residential street convenient to downtown. Renovated and refurbished in 1997 by new owners, the $125–195 B&B double rates include a full breakfast, afternoon tea, evening social hour, and nightly turndown service.

For a totally private experience, consider the **Craven Street Inn** (1103 Craven Street, 29902; 803–522–1668), in the historic district, one block from the water. Four suites in the main house and carriage house are available, at B&B rates of $125–175. "Lovely suite, furnished in beige, white, and pickled pine, with a king-size bed and kitchenette. Breakfast is included in the rate, but is taken at a nearby deli." *(RC)*

Listed in many past editions is the well-known **Rhett House Inn** (1009 Craven Street, 29902; 803–524–9030), a handsome antebellum mansion, with a beautiful, flower-bedecked veranda, eight guest rooms and a restaurant. Although a darling of the media, and a favorite of movie stars filming in the area, additional reader feedback is requested. B&B double rates are $95–225 double; dinner is approximately $35 per person.

For an additional area inn, see **Hilton Head Island.**

Beautort Inn ✕
809 Port Republic Street, 29902
Tel: 803–521–9000
Fax: 803–521–9500

Although the Beaufort Inn has lovely rooms, excellent food, and an ideal balance of historic charm and modern convenience, what guests like best is the genuine hospitality offered by owners Debbie and Rusty Fielden and their staff. Built in 1897, and run as a hotel in the 1930s, the inn was fully restored by the Fieldens in 1994. Breakfast, served 8–10 A.M., can be enjoyed in the dining room, on the porch, or in guests' rooms. The dinner menu might include such entrees as ginger crusted sea bass with citrus glaze; filet mignon au poivre; or eggplant with grilled shrimp and risotto.

"A gorgeous, well-decorated inn; Debbie and her staff define the term 'Southern hospitality.' Outstanding dinner at the inn's restaurant." *(Susan Sinclair)* "Excellent lighting; comfortable, firm beds. Attentive, helpful innkeepers and staff. Attractive restaurant occupying several first floor rooms, popular with both locals and tourists. The duck with shallot berry sauce was exceptional." *(HJB)*

"A first-class luxury inn in a totally renovated building, complete with wonderful porches, new pine flooring, mahogany moldings, and even an elevator in the atrium addition. Each beautifully decorated and spacious guest room features a picture and description of the Low Country plantation for which it is named. All have a sitting aréa and a good-sized bathroom, supplied with Caswell-Massey amenities. Our room had a queen-size triple-sheeted iron bed, bedside tables, and two glass floor lamps for reading. Between the two matching swivel club chairs was a lamp table that concealed a small refrigerator. The delicate floral striped wallpaper was topped with a border trim of cabbage roses that matched the bedspread, pillow shams, and window swags. Honeycomb venetian blinds ensured complete privacy, and an in-room thermostat guaranteed a comfortable temperature for sleeping. Dinner was outstanding in the quality of food, presentation, and service. Breakfast choices included whole grain French toast stuffed with Brie and sun-dried peaches, pecan pancakes, eggs Benedict with crab cakes, and a light breakfast of cereal, grapefruit, and bagel. Fresh fruit was served along with a basket of biscuits and honey butter." *(Rose Ciccone)*

"Handsome moldings throughout, plus lovely antiques and reproductions. Brilliant crystal chandeliers and a stunning staircase which winds up to the third floor. Our room had a queen-sized bed with carved posts featuring acanthus leaves and pineapple finials. Delicious breakfasts of shrimp omelet, wheat nut bread French toast and fresh-squeezed orange juice." *(Kathryn Hayes)* "The steak-and-eggs breakfast is a must; an afternoon nap a welcome pleasure." *(David Anderson)*

Open All year. Closed Dec. 24–25.
Rooms 4 suites, 9 doubles—all with full private bath, telephone with data port, voice mail; radio, clock, TV/VCR, in-room thermostats, air-conditioning, ceiling fan, refrigerator, coffee maker, robes. Some with whirlpool tub, desk, fireplace, balcony. 2 rooms in Carriage House.
Facilities Restaurant with fireplaces; verandas, courtyard garden with fountain. Video collection. Off-street parking.
Location Historic district, 1 block from bay.
Restrictions No smoking. Children 8 and over.
Credit cards Amex, Discover, MC, Visa.
Rates B&B, $125–185 suite, double. Extra person, $20. 10% AAA, senior discount Sun.–Wed. Prix fixe breakfast (outside guests), $9.50. Alc dinner, $25–40.
Extras Wheelchair access; elevator; 1 room specially equipped. Dutch, German spoken. Airport/station pickups.

TwoSuns Inn Bed & Breakfast ♿
1705 Bay Street, 29902

Tel: 803–522–1122
800–532–4244
Fax: 803–522–1122
E-mail: twosuns@islc.net

A panoramic bay view is one of the most appealing features of this 1917 Neoclassic Revival-style home, complete with 63-foot-long wraparound veranda. Built as a private residence by the Keyserling family, it became a female teachers' residence, known as the Teacherage, during World War I. Following two fires, it was virtually abandoned for over 13 years. Carrol and Ron Kay fully restored it as a B&B, beginning in 1990, and have created an informal ambiance with antiques, collectibles, and Carrol's beautifully made window and bed ensembles. Guests enjoy a different breakfast each morning: perhaps baked pears with cinnamon and brown sugar, strawberry muffins, and German baked eggs with turkey ham one day; followed by fresh fruit compote with vanilla yogurt, cheddar cheese biscuits, and strawberry cheese crepes the next.

"Beautiful bay view. Attractive guest rooms, especially the Art Deco room with the original full body shower. A lovely first-floor guest room is fully wheelchair accessible, unusual in a B&B of this size. The Kays live on the premises and are readily available to guests." *(Rose Ciccone)* "Carrol and Ron take pride in maintaining a pleasant, clean, relaxed home." *(Connie Engelmohr)* "Our room shared a second-story sun porch overlooking the water. The Kays were helpful with area information." *(Pat Malone)* "Breakfasts were healthy and delicious with homemade breads, fruits, and herbs from the garden." *(Janet & Frank Harlan)* "Carrol's creativity is evident in her homemade crafts, draperies, and bedspreads throughout the inn. Equally impressive were Ron's specialty omelets and pancakes. We enjoyed the tea and toddy hour with lively conversation and one of Ron's impromptu song and dance routines." *(Nancy & James Cerar)* "Our large bathroom had the original 'body' shower, with brass piping in a semi-circle to produce spray all around, set in new tiles." *(Patricia Swift)* "Welcoming, friendly host, who organized a croquet and horseshoes competition on the front lawn." *(Steve Holman)*

Open All year.
Rooms 5 doubles—all with private bath and/or shower, radio, air-conditioning, telephone with data port, fan. Cable TV on request. 3 with balcony/deck.
Facilities Dining room, living room with fireplace, books, games; parlor with TV/VCR, porch. Bay-front lot with croquet, horseshoes, bicycles. Boating, fishing, swimming, kayaking, state park nearby.
Location Beaufort County, SC. 45 m N of Savannah, GA. 65 m S of Charleston, SC. 7 short blocks from downtown.
Restrictions No smoking except on veranda, 2nd floor porch. No children under 12.
Credit cards Amex, MC, Visa.
Rates B&B, $120–140 double, $105–125 single. Extra person, $22. No tipping. Corporate rates. Senior, AAA, CAA, AARP discounts. 10% discount for extended stay. 20% discount off-season.
Extras Wheelchair access; 1 room equipped for disabled.

CAMDEN

Information please: Owned by Jack Branham, **The Greenleaf Inn** (130/810 North Broad Street, Camden 29020; 803–425–1806 or

800–437–5874) is composed of two houses: the Colonial-style Reynolds House, built in 1840, and the Victorian-era McLean House. The twelve guest rooms are furnished with antiques and period reproductions; its restaurant, Avanti's, offers classic southern Italian cuisine. B&B double rates are $65–85. "Comfortable, well-equipped room; excellent breakfast of fresh fruit, juice, and pancakes, delivered to my room." *(Betty Norman)*

For additional area inns, see **Hartsville** and **Sumter**.

Candlelight Inn *Tel:* 803–424–1057
1904 Broad Street, 29020

In addition to their respective careers in nursing and with General Motors, JoAnn and George Celani had tried their hand at innkeeping when they lived in Michigan and liked it. In 1994, when they decided to "retire" and move south, they chose Camden as an inviting place for a B&B. Named for the candles that illuminate each window, the Candlelight Inn is a Colonial-style brick home, built in 1930. In addition to family antiques and vintage quilts, plus queen-size four-poster beds, the decor is highlighted by lovely hand-stitchery: needlepoint work done by JoAnn's mother, JoAnn's reproduction samplers, and her daughter's counted cross-stitch. Breakfast is served at the dining room table at guests' convenience, and includes fresh fruit and juice, breakfast cookies, and perhaps an egg and sausage puff, caramel French toast, or featherbed eggs, accompanied by frizzled ham, and peach crumb coffee cake.

"Lovely neighborhood; a wide, brick-lined circular driveway leads to the front door, where JoAnn greeted us warmly. Our room was beautifully decorated and homey, with a private hall bath, just two steps away." *(Betsy Meister)* "Spacious and spotless. Delicious breakfasts, beautifully presented. You could tell the Ceianis enjoy being innkeepers and want their guests to be comfortable, satisfied, and happy (which we were). Sarah's Suite has a wonderful private sitting area with white wicker furniture, a private bath en suite, and a lovely large bedroom with good reading lights and two comfy wing-backed chairs." *(Mr. & Mrs. Douglas Peck)* "Loved the bright white terry cloth bathrobe in the bathroom." *(Annise Brown)* "Always freshly baked cookies to take for a snack. The immaculate bathrooms are equipped with shampoo and bath oils." *(Cheryl Prince)* "Quiet yet convenient location." *(Mary R. Scott)* "The coolest, smoothest bed linens ever." *(Melanie Parker)* "The owners are great conversationalists, yet are not intrusive nor overly chatty." *(Ann Friedrich)*

Open All year.
Rooms 1 suite, 3 doubles—all with full private bath, radio, clock, desk, air-conditioning. 2 with TV, 1 with ceiling fan.
Facilities Dining room, living room, library with books, TV; each with fireplace; sun porch. 2 acres with flower gardens, off-street parking.
Location Central SC. 30 m NE of Columbia. Historic district. From I-20, take

Exit 98, & go N on Hwy. 521 to inn on right. From I-77, take Exit 55 & go S on Hwy 97 to Hwy 521. Go S on 521 to inn on left.
Restrictions No smoking. Children 10 and over.
Credit cards Discover, MC, Visa.
Rates B&B, $85–125 suite, $75–125 double. 2-night minimum race weekends; peak rate applies.
Extras Airport/station pickups.

CHARLESTON

Charleston, founded in 1670, was at one point the wealthiest city in Colonial America; many think that it is still the most beautiful. The Civil War brought major devastation and poverty to the city and halted development. Efforts to preserve the city's priceless heritage began in the 1920s. Restoration work progressed slowly until around 1975, when the American Bicentennial, followed by the founding of Spoleto Festival U.S.A., sparked the restoration and conversion of numerous homes and commercial properties into bed & breakfast inns and restaurants.

Sights of interest in Charleston and the surrounding area include the many restored houses and museums, antique shops, the city market, tours of the river and harbor, the public beaches and resorts (with full golf and tennis facilities) at Folly Beach, Seabrook Island, and Kiawah Island, and last but far from least, the beautiful gardens of Middleton Place, Magnolia Gardens, and Cypress Gardens. Although all three gardens bloom year-round, many think that they are at their most magnificent from late March to early April, when the azaleas are in full bloom.

The peak season in Charleston runs from February to mid-June, from September through October, and other special events. The times of highest demand are in late March and early April for the azaleas, and in late May and early June for the Spoleto Festival. Charleston is located midway along the South Carolina coast, at the confluence of the Ashley, Cooper, and Wando rivers and Intracoastal Waterway. It's 106 miles northeast of Savannah, GA, 113 miles southeast of Columbia, SC, and 94 miles southwest of Myrtle Beach.

Reader tips: "Make your first Charleston stop the Visitor's Center. They have discount coupons for just about every restaurant and shop in town. You can also get special rates on accommodations when booking through the Vistor's Center, including some B&Bs. Charleston has some first-rate restaurants; ask your innkeeper for advice on which ones are 'hot.'" *(Rose Ciccone)* "As in any city, don't leave any packages on the seat of your car." And: "Parking is impossible in season. Park your car and enjoy walking!" *(Hopie Welliver)* "Our favorite restaurant was called Slightly North of Broad (SNOB)." *(GA)* "Don't miss having dinner at Magnolia's." *(Penny Poirier)*

Also recommended: Over 50 private homes and carriage houses within the historic district are listed with **Historic Charleston Bed & Breakfast** (60 Broad Street, 29401; 803–722–6606 or 800–743–3583), a reservation service in business since 1981. "Our wonderful old carriage house came with a kitchen stocked for breakfast; there were two bedrooms and a bath upstairs, and a laundry in a half-bath downstairs. We parked in the driveway to the main house, and enjoyed viewing the courtyard garden and fountain adorned with Christmas lights. Convenient for sightseeing." *(Celia McCullough)*

Located next to the city market, the **Ansonborough Inn** (21 Hasell Street, 29401; 803–723–1655 or 800–522–2073) is a three-story 1901 warehouse with heart pine beams and red brick walls, restored as a 37-suite hotel. Rooms have fully equipped kitchens and are furnished with antique reproductions and cotton chintz fabrics. B&B double rates of $80–180 include a continental breakfast buffet, the morning paper, and afternoon wine. "A terrific value, with charming Low Country decor and lots of striking features—vaulted, beamed ceilings, exposed brick walls, and architecturally interesting atrium lobby. Young, exceptionally personable and well-informed staff. Our third-floor suite had a comfortable, king-sized bed, large armoire, spotless well-appointed kitchen, and queen-bedded sleeping loft with its own TV, closet, and phone. The rooftop hot tub offers a terrific view of Charleston, and the secure off-street parking is a big plus. Though located on the edge of the historic district, we considered the reasonable price, off-street parking, and spacious accommodations to be a fair trade-off." *(Susan Woods)*

Built in 1732, **The Kitchen House** (126 Tradd Street, 29401; 803–577–6362) offers two suites, at B&B double rates of $99–195. "Ideal location in a residential section of the historic district. Accommodating, informative hostess; immaculate room in a charming home." *(Pat Malone)*

A four-diamond hotel in the heart of the historic district, **The Mills House Hotel** (115 Meeting Street, 29401; 803–577–2400 or 800–874–9600) offers 215 guest rooms, with double rates of $170–250 (ask about off-season promotional and AAA rates). "Despite its Holiday Inn affiliation, we had a beautiful room for a reasonable rate, and wonderful personal service from a caring staff." *(Richard & Jaclin Farrell)*

Built as a dry goods warehouse in the 1830s, **The Planters Inn** (112 North Market Street, 29401; 803–722–2345 or 800–845–7082) is now a 62-room hotel with off-street parking; B&B double rates range from $105–225, and fine dining can be enjoyed at the hotel's Peninsula Grill. "Excellent location; spacious, quiet room with reproduction antique furnishings; friendly staff. Rates included in-room continental breakfast and newspaper, plus afternoon wine and cheese." *(Glenn Roehrig)*

Travelers who seek the elegant atmosphere of a fine inn, but who are concerned about privacy will be thrilled with their stay at **Twenty-Seven State Street** (27 State Street, 29401; 803–722–4243), located two blocks from the harbor in the old French Quarter of the original walled city. This beautifully restored home has five suites, three in the main house and two in the Carriage House. Each has one or two bedrooms, private bath, and kitchenette; double rates are $85–145, with an additional charge for breakfast, delivered to your suite the night before. Long-time resident owners Joye and Paul Craven are pleased to provide advice and information about their lovely city.

Under the same ownership as the John Rutledge House (see entry) is the **Victoria House Inn** (208 King Street, 29401; 803–720–2944 or 800–933–5464), a Richardsonian Romanesque home built in 1889. B&B double rates for the 18 guest rooms range from $115–175, and include a light continental breakfast delivered to the room and evening sherry (extra charge for full breakfast and mini-bar refreshments). Rooms in this small hotel are decorated with period reproductions, and have either a king-sized bed or two doubles; some have a fireplace or whirlpool tub. "Pluses include off-street parking and a convenient location in the heart of the historic district, within walking distance of most shops, the Marketplace and restaurants. Spacious, well-decorated rooms with all amenities." *(Rose Ciccone)*

Also recommended—nearby: For a more rural, contemporary setting, consider driving 14 miles north to Middleton Place. Laid out in 1741, its formal, landscaped gardens were the first in America, with sweeping terraces and vast plantings of camellias, magnolias, and roses. Constructed on the grounds in 1986, the **Middleton Inn** (Ashley River Road, 29407; 803–556–0500 or 800–543–4774) won architectural awards for its contemporary concrete, glass, and wood design. A short walk from the inn is the Restaurant at Middleton Place, specializing in Southern plantation cooking. B&B double rates for the 50 guest rooms range from $109–129, and include use of the swimming pool, tennis courts, hiking trails, and visits to the magnificent gardens. "Striking contemporary design. Delicious cooked-to-order omelets at the breakfast buffet. For lunch and dinner, we drove up the Ashley River Road to Summerville, a charming town with lots of antique shops and much better food than at the chain restaurants close to the inn." *(Frances White)*

About 20 miles north of Charleston is **Woodlands Resort** (125 Parsons Road, Summerville, 29483; 803–875–2600 or 800–774–9999), an English-style country house hotel with Southern-style hospitality. A Greek Revival mansion built in 1906, this 42-acre property was restored and expanded in 1994 as a twenty-room luxury inn, with conference center, tennis courts, croquet lawn, and swimming pool. Rooms are beautifully decorated with period antiques and reproductions, and the B&B double rates of $175–325 include continental breakfast, afternoon tea, welcome champagne, and handmade chocolates at turndown. There's also a fine dining restaurant with a sophisticated menu of international and southern favorites, and a full-service spa. "Real elegance. Beautiful dining room with lovely garden view." *(BN)*

Information please: The **Battery Carriage House** (20 South Battery, 29401; 803–727–3100 or 800–775–5575) has been repaired, renovated, and redecorated under the ownership of Katherine and Drayton Hastie. Overlooking the waterfront and White Point Gardens, the inn offers eleven luxurious guest rooms, all with private baths, at B&B rates of $89–219. A continental breakfast is delivered to your room on a silver tray, or can be enjoyed in the garden.

The Elliott House Inn (78 Queen Street, 29401; 803–723–1855 or 800–729–1855) has 26 guest rooms with period decor and Oriental rugs; guests gather in the garden courtyard for iced tea, afternoon wine and cheese, or to relax in the hot tub. The $95–140 rates also include continental breakfast, delivered to guests' rooms, and evening turndown service. "Excellent location, walking distance to everything." *(GA)* **The Indigo Inn** (1 Maiden Lane at Pickney Street, 29401; 803–577–5900 or 800–845–7639) is a 40-room luxury hotel in the historic district, with double rates of $95–165, including breakfast, the morning paper, and parking. "Attractive rooms, pleasant staff." *(Glenn Roehrig)*

For a taste of Low Country plantation life, an easy drive from Charleston, see **Edisto Island** and **McClellanville**.

Ashley Inn/Cannonboro Inn ¢
201/184 Ashley Avenue, 29403

Tel: 803–723–1848 (Ashley)
803–723–8572 (Cannonboro)
Fax: 803–723–9080

The Ashley and Cannonboro Inns were built in 1832 and 1853, respectively, and have been owned by Bud and Sally Allen since 1990. Rates include both breakfast and afternoon refreshments. Breakfast is served between 8–9 A.M., and typically includes grits, cheese and sausage casserole, and buttermilk biscuits, or lemon poppyseed pancakes served with bacon, plus fresh fruit, juice, and coffee.

"Both inns are meticulously clean, tastefully decorated with antiques and reproductions, and are just several houses away from each other, on opposite sides of the street. Bud is a general contractor and Sally, an interior decorator; their combined talents in the inns' restoration and the use of detailing, wallpapers, patterns, and the absence of clutter is wonderful. Delightful staff. Our room at the Ashley had a four-poster queen-size rice bed with a fishnet canopy, one end table and reading lamp, a blanket chest at the foot of the bed, a small loveseat, desk and a built-in closet with a TV shelf. At the Ashley, breakfast is served in the large dining room at a communal table. We enjoyed a choice of juice, a hot fruit compote, stuffed waffles and sausage as well as coffee and tea." *(Rose Ciccone)*

Ashley: "Comfortable common areas for reading and conversation; tea, coffee, cookies, and sherry were always available." *(Solomon Levine)* "The innkeepers always made time to visit with us and answer questions, make reservations, and recommend attractions and restaurants. Delicious breakfasts; special diet requests accommodated. Our top-floor room was clean, attractive, and quiet." *(Caroline Pierson)* "Soft thick towels, wonderful breakfast." *(Mary O'Brien)* "Ample hot water, even with a full house. Fresh flowers in every room." *(Lucy Morison)*

Cannonboro: "Tasty breakfast of almond crêpes with lemon sauce served at individual tables on the veranda, alongside a narrow garden." *(Brad & Babs Rymer)* "Delightful garden, fountain, and fish pond." *(LM)* "Loved coming in from a day of touring to enjoy afternoon tea and cookies, or a glass of sherry and classical music." *(Elizabeth Flaherty, also Shannon Jones)* "Courteous, friendly innkeepers who provided excellent directions and maps." *(Tasha Knight)* "Loved the pineapple streusel at tea-time." *(Dina Fullwood)* "Beautiful, bright and clean. Excellent housekeeper and cook." *(Sarah & John Staples)* "Afternoon treats included a variety of great cookies, sherry, hot and iced tea. Enjoyed using the inn's bicycles to tour the historic area. Our darling cozy room was tucked under the eaves, with a comfortable bed and robes to wear to the adjacent private bath." *(Penny Poirier)*

Open All year.
Rooms 2 suites, 11 doubles—all with private bath, telephone, clock, TV, desk, air-conditioning, fan. Some with balcony/deck, fireplace, refrigerator.
Facilities Dining rooms, living rooms with fireplace, TV, stereo, books, guest refrigerator; porches, terrace. Bicycles, off-street parking.
Location Historic district; 15 min. walk from downtown; approx. 1 m to waterfront. From I-26, follow last exit sign, "Meeting St. Visitor Info" onto Meeting St. Go right onto Calhoun St. Go right onto Ashley Ave. Across from USC medical center. On trolley bus route.
Restrictions Street noise possible in front rooms. No smoking. Children over 10.
Credit cards Amex, Discover, MC, Visa.
Rates B&B, $125–165 suite, $79–135 double. Extra person, $20.
Extras French spoken.

Brasington House *Tel:* 803–722–1274
328 East Bay Street, 29401

The Brasington House is a 1790s "single" house, meaning it's one room wide, two rooms deep, and three stories high, with a corresponding three-story piazza (Charlestonian for porch). It was restored as a B&B in 1987 by Dalton and Judy Brasington. Breakfast is served at 9 A.M., and includes eggs, grits, ham, fruit, yogurt, breads and pastry, presented at the dining room table on fine china, crystal, and silver. Rates also include afternoon wine and evening liqueurs; the bedrooms, all with either king/twin or queen-size beds, have supplies of coffee, tea, and hot chocolate for guests to prepare for themselves.

"Spacious rooms; gracious, charming hosts, ever ready to help with suggestions for sightseeing. Excellent location, a short walk from historic sights." *(AA)* "We were delighted with our nicely furnished second floor room, but would request the top-floor suite, with windows on three sides, on a return visit. Wonderful breakfasts with a variety of fruit, including mango and papaya, plus large sticky buns, eggs and bacon, or grits cooked with ham and cheese. The Brasingtons are ideal B&B hosts, knowledgeable about the city (including tours, restaurants, and transportation), enthusiastic, and relaxed. Mr. Brasington joined us at breakfast and stimulated a lively discussion among the guests. First-rate innkeepers at a real B&B." *(Lucia Rather)* "The Brasingtons rescued this lovely home from a ramshackle state and have restored it to its original 1790s style. Their 'before-and after' albums are fun to peruse." *(Belinda King)* "Our room was large, clean, and nicely decorated. A huge mahogany armoire contained drawers, two wardrobes, and a color TV. The high ceiling and large bathroom contributed to the feeling of spaciousness." *(Karl Wiegers & Christine Zambito)*

Open All year.
Rooms 1 suite, 3 doubles—all with full private bath, telephone, clock, TV, desk, air-conditioning, ceiling fan, coffee/tea maker; 1 with balcony.

Facilities Dining room with fireplace, living room with fireplace; porches. Off-street parking.
Location Ansonborough section of historic district, on East Bay at George St.
Restrictions No smoking. No children.
Credit cards MC, Visa.
Rates B&B, $98–134 suite, double. Extra person, $35. 2-3 night weekend/holiday minimum.

John Rutledge House Inn *Tel:* 803–723–7999
116 Broad Street, 29401 800–476–9741
Fax: 803–720–2615

The John Rutledge House Inn was built in 1763 by one of the fifty-five signers of the U.S. Constitution, John Rutledge, later Chief Justice of the U.S. Supreme Court. Much of the history of South Carolina and the U.S. can be traced to meetings and writings which took place in the ballroom and library here; reminders of Rutledge's service is visible in the Federal eagle and South Carolina's emblem, the palmetto tree, forged in the antebellum ironwork. Of equal significance to some is the fact that Charleston's famous she-crab soup was supposedly invented here.

Meticulously restored and stylishly updated in 1989 by Rick Widman, rooms are furnished in antiques and period reproductions. One of the two carriage houses is a new building, constructed to duplicate the original; rooms in the main house have the most historic feel. Rates include continental breakfast brought to your room or served in the courtyard between 7 and 10 a.m., afternoon tea from 4:30 until 6:00 P.M., plus bedside brandy and chocolates. The breakfast menu includes (in addition to the usual juices, hot beverages, yogurt, cereals, and breakfast breads) Rutledge's biscuits with hot sherried fruit, and for an additional charge, hot entrées such as French toast, shrimp and grits with toast, and eggs cooked to order.

"The Ashley Carriage House was delightful. Nothing was too much trouble for the staff. We were greeted by the owner and served afternoon tea with fellow guests. Excellent in-room breakfast; good parking situation." *(Nicholas Adlam)* "Impressive attention to detail; professional staff; fine service." *(Avery Kant)* "Late afternoon tea, lemonade, fruit, cheese and crackers provided a chance to chat with Linda Bishop—the inn's effervescent innkeeper, review the inn's renovation scrapbook, and meet the other guests. Immaculate, even to the wine cellar where the original tile remains." *(Thomas & Eileen Garberina)* "Our room in the original carriage house was immaculate with two canopied queen-size beds and a modern bathroom. Lovely breakfast in the courtyard." *(Jo-Ann & David Purser)* "A beautiful historic home, efficiently run by a full staff. The suites are extremely large and beautifully decorated." *(Rose Ciccone)*

Open All year.
Rooms 3 suites, 16 doubles—all with full private bath, telephone, radio, TV, desk, air-conditioning, fan, mini-refrigerator. Some with fireplace, deck. Rooms in inn and 2 carriage houses.
Facilities Parlor with fireplace, ballroom with fireplace, games, library. Off-street parking.

Location Historic district. From King St. turn right on Broad St. to inn.
Restrictions Smoking restricted in some guest rooms.
Credit cards Amex, DC, Discover, MC, Visa.
Rates B&B, $240–295 suite, $140–245 double, $125–230 single. Extra person, $15. Children under 12 free in parents' room. 10% senior, AAA discount. 3-night minimum mid-February. Full breakfast, $5–10 plus 15% service.
Extras Limited wheelchair access; some rooms equipped for disabled. Crib, babysitting. Spanish, French spoken.

Lodge Alley Inn
195 East Bay Street, 29401

Tel: 803–722–1611
Inside SC: 800–821–2791
Outside SC: 800–845–1004
Fax: 803–722–1611
E-mail: LodgeAlley@aol.com

Originally built as a series of warehouses, the Lodge Alley offers the amenities of a small luxury hotel, with the warmth of a historic inn. Rooms have the exposed brick walls and pine flooring of the original warehouses, and are individually decorated with Oriental rugs and elegant period reproduction furniture. Rates include morning coffee, daily newspaper, afternoon sherry, and evening turndown service with chocolates. Breakfast choices range from a Southern-style breakfast of eggs, bacon, and grits to vegetable omelets or eggs Benedict. The hotel's restaurant, The French Quarter, also offers a variety of sandwiches and salads at lunch, while the dinner menu includes both Charleston and Italian specialities.

"A small elegant hotel with a perfect location right next to the market. Our attractive, spacious room overlooked the courtyard." *(Brian Donaldson)* "Our two-bedroom, two-bathroom suite included a spacious living/dining room with fireplace and a brick hearth and mantle. Three handsome, tall, deep-set windows looked out on East Bay Street but allowed in no street noise. The wide pine flooring was partially covered with an elegant Oriental rug, and the upholstered sofa and side chairs were attractive and comfortable. The kitchen allowed us to prepare our own breakfasts and snacks. The staff was most accommodating and attractive, and the free valet parking was a plus. Perfectly located for exploration, in the heart of restaurant row and close to Waterfront Park." *(Mark Mendenhall)*

Open All year.
Rooms 61 1-2 bedroom suites, 34 doubles—all with full private bath, refrigerator, telephone, radio, TV, air-conditioning. Most with gas fireplace. Some with kitchen; 8 with whirlpool tub.
Facilities Restaurant, lounge, parlor with fireplace, meeting rooms, landscaped courtyard with fountain. Complimentary valet parking.
Location Historic district. On East Bay St., between Cumberland & Queen Sts.
Credit cards Amex, MC, Visa.
Rates Room only, $135–325 suite, $115–165 double. Extra person, $15. Children under 13 free in parents' room. Full breakfast, $5–9; alc lunch, $10–18; alc dinner, $25–50.
Extras Crib, babysitting.

Rutledge Victorian Inn ¢
114 Rutledge Avenue, 29401

Tel: 803–722–7551
Toll-free: 888–722–7553
Fax: 803–727–0065

An Italianate-style home built in the 1880s, the Rutledge Victorian Inn was restored as an inn in 1989, and was purchased by Lyn Lee-Beam and Norman Beam in 1996; Jeanne Ross is the innkeeper. The original detailed plaster ceiling moldings, mahogany and oak woodwork, and 12-foot-ceilings are complemented by antique and reproduction furnishings. Breakfast, served 8–10:30 A.M., can be enjoyed at the dining room table, on the porch, or in your room, and includes fresh fruit and juice, cereal, and a variety of nut breads, scones, muffins, and pastries.

"Clean and well-maintained; comfortable bed. Warm welcome, friendly atmosphere provided by accommodating innkeeper Jeanne Ross." *(DW, also Ann Bragdon)* "Jeanne Ross is unobtrusive but available. Drinks and snacks are available around the clock in the dining area. Beautiful period decor enhanced by the scent of potpourri. Historic district location is convenient for walking, and was quiet, clean, safe, and friendly." *(Terry Zappellani)* "Ideal lighting, with overhead lights for brightness and small accent lights for atmosphere." *Pamela Bangham)* "Convenient to the Market, museums, shops, and restaurants; knowledgeable staff. We liked having our breakfast and newspaper delivered to our carriage house room each morning. Secure parking behind the inn. Afternoon tea with homemade cookies, fudge, and fruit made us feel at home, and evening sherry was a nice end to the day, as were the pillow chocolates. The immaculate bathroom has bright lighting, along with plenty of clean towels, soaps, and shampoos." *(Evelyn Sobel)* "Staff was helpful with luggage, and suggested walks, activities, and good restaurants." *(Jeanne Senouillet)* "Real Victorian flavor to the antiques and decor. Quiet neighborhood within walking distance of the Market. Loved the decor and the unusual touches painted on the fixtures in Room 5." *(Noreen Kelly)* "A great place to meet fellow travelers, especially at breakfast." *(Karin Boughey)* Just a 15-20 minute walk to anywhere in historic Charleston. Great porch for reading or resting." *(Donna Angel)*

Open All year.
Rooms 1 suite, 10 doubles—7 with private shower and/or bath, 4 rooms share 2 baths. All with telephone, radio, clock, TV, air-conditioning, ceiling fan. Some with desk, fireplace, refrigerator.
Facilities Dining room, living room with piano, TV/VCR, stereo, library; each with fireplace. Wraparound veranda. 8 off-street parking spaces (for rooms with private bath).
Location Historic district. On Rutledge, between Calhoun & Beaufain, across from Roman Columns & Old Museum Park.
Restrictions No smoking.
Credit cards Amex, Discover, MC, Visa.
Rates B&B, $69–150 double. Extra person, $20. Tipping envelope.
Extras Airport/station pickups, $10–20.

Sword Gate Inn
111 Tradd Street, 29401

Tel: 803–723–8518
800–501–6810
Fax: 803–723–8126

Hurricane Hugo brought massive damage to Charleston in 1989, and one of its casualties was the lovely Sword Gate Inn. Fully restored and re-opened in 1996, the inn is now owned by Gordon and Patricia Timmons; Cathy and Norm Gage are the innkeepers. Taking its name from the sword-and-spear design of the wrought iron gates that originally opened onto the property from Legare Street, the Sword Gate is a stucco-over-brick Federal-style building dating back to 1803 and listed on the National Register of Historic Places. Charleston's only "Nationally Registered Ballroom" is found here, with 14-foot ceilings, gold leaf moldings created by Tiffany in 1849, enormous rococo-style gilded mirrors, a hand-carved Carrara marble fireplace, and a heart-pine planked floor. Originally a private home, the building later served as a consulate, and was also a seminary for the daughters of Charleston's elite.

Four guest rooms are on the ground floor, opening off the cobbled courtyard, with queen-size beds and country-cottage decor; the two largest rooms, the Sword Gate and the Honeymoon suites, are on the third floor, and are elegantly furnished with antiques. Breakfast, served 8–10 A.M., includes fresh fruit and juice, buttermilk biscuits, eggs and omelets cooked to order, grits, waffles, pancakes, French toast, bacon, sausage, or country ham with red eye gravy, and a daily chef's special.

"The Bridal Suite has six beautiful windows overlooking this charming neighborhood, a pencil post queen-size bed, and a huge whirlpool tub in the bathroom. Lovely rooms, exceptional wallpapers; delightful fellow guests. Sword Gate is delightful; we left the car and walked everywhere. Many excellent restaurants and historic sights are within easy walking distance." *(Hopie Welliver)* Comments appreciated.

Open All year.
Rooms 6 doubles—all with full private Jacuzzi bath, telephone, radio, clock, TV, air conditioning, refrigerator. 3 with fireplace.
Facilities Dining room, living room with fireplace, piano. Courtyard garden, off-street parking.
Location Historic residential district. On Tradd between Legare & King Sts.
Restrictions No smoking. Children over 5 preferred.
Credit cards Amex, Discover, MC, Visa.
Rates $115–242 double. Extra person, $10. 15% weekly discount.
Extras "Very small" pets permitted with prior approval.

Two Meeting Street Inn
2 Meeting Street, 29401

Tel: 803–723–7322

Built in 1892 as a father's wedding present to his daughter, this Victorian mansion has been owned by the Spell family since 1946; Karen Spell is the innkeeper. A light breakfast of home-baked muffins, fresh fruit, juice, coffee, and tea, is served in the dining room or on the veranda. Rates also include afternoon tea with scones, toffee, cheese wafers, and fruit; the almond poppy bread with raspberry preserves is a guest favorite. This inn is deservedly popular; advance reservations (months ahead in season) are essential.

"The piazzas and gardens are wonderful places to sit, read, people watch, or enjoy the harbor views. The English oak staircase and Tiffany windows are magnificent; fresh flowers were everywhere. Our room on the second floor was decorated with a flower-bird-pagoda patterned fabric, and Queen-Anne style pencil post bed, end tables, chest and dressing table. The spacious bathroom had good lighting and plenty of towels. Our room shared access to the upper piazza with groupings of cushioned wicker furniture." *(RC)* "Gleaming hardwood floors, paneling and many fine antiques. Inviting walk to many restaurants and shops." *(Gayle Gibb)* "Relaxing in one of the porch rockers, feeling the breeze coming through the live oaks, is truly the feel of old Charleston." *(Betty Norman)* "Guests gather around the breakfast table to discuss their plans for the day, while being served a plate of fresh fruit and a muffin (my favorite is the fresh peach); in the afternoon we reassemble for a Low Country tea while watching the horse-drawn carriages pass the veranda. Karen Spell and her entire staff are warm and friendly." *(Judy Sivils)* "Just as delightful on a return visit." *(James & Pamela Burr)*

The Spell family also owns the **Belvedere** (40 Rutledge Avenue, 29401; 803–722–0973), an imposing, turn-of-the-century Colonial Revival home with early Adam-style woodwork brought from the old Belvedere Plantation (circa 1800). Beautifully refurbished by David Spell, the house also has a real "Charleston feel" with period antiques and reproductions—rice beds, ceiling fans, even sweet grass baskets. "Our room had a four-poster bed, fireplace, TV, air-conditioning, beautiful antique furniture, and a private bathroom. Innkeeper Rick Zenger brought us a breakfast tray of pastries, juice, and fruit at the requested time. The inn's lovely furnishings include antique blue and white Chinese porcelains. Quiet neighborhood, easily accessible by car or foot to the major restaurants. An excellent value." *(Deanna Yen)*

Open All year. Closed Dec. 24, 25, 26.
Rooms Two Meeting Street: 9 doubles—all with private bath and/or shower, TV, air-conditioning, ceiling fan. Some with fireplace, balcony. Belvedere B&B: 3 doubles—all with private bath and/or shower, TV, air-conditioning.
Facilities Two Meeting Street: dining room with fireplace, breakfast room, lobby with fireplace, parlor with fireplace, piazzas, formal garden. Belvedere: parlor, dining room, porch; on-street parking. Tennis, golf, picnic area, beaches nearby.
Location Two Meeting Street: historic district, opposite Battery Park. Exit I-26 or Rte. 17 onto Meeting St. Inn is at end of Meeting St., the corner house at the Battery, near Battery Park. Call for directions to Belvedere.
Restrictions No smoking. No children under 12.
Credit cards None accepted.
Rates Two Meeting Street: B&B, $145–275 double. Extra person, $25. Belvedere: B&B, $110 double. Suggested tip: $5 per day. 2-3 night weekend/holiday minimum.
Extras German spoken at Two Meeting Street.

COLUMBIA

Capital of South Carolina for over 200 years, Columbia is located in the center of the state, and is home to the University of South Carolina. Children will enjoy visiting the Riverbanks Zoo and the Criminal Justice Hall of Fame, while history and architecture buffs will enjoy seeing the Hampton-Preston Mansion, a restored antebellum home, and the State House.

For additional area inns, see **Camden** and **Sumter.**

Claussen's Inn at Five Points 🚸 ♿
2003 Greene Street, 29205
Tel: 803–765–0440
800–622–3382
Fax: 803–799–7924

Originally constructed in 1928 as Claussen's Bakery, the structure was rebuilt in 1986 as a small luxury inn by Richard T. Widman (owner of John Rutledge House in Charleston); Dan Vance is the general manager. Rates include a breakfast of coffee, juice, muffins and croissants; afternoon fruit and sherry, and turndown service with chocolates. Many of the building's original architectural features were preserved in the renovation, while skylights and terra-cotta tiling were added. Rooms are decorated with lots of plants, overstuffed furniture, four-poster or iron and brass beds, and traditional furnishings.

"The inn is interesting architecturally and ideally located within easy walking distance of the University of South Carolina. The Five Points area is a mixture of sidewalk cafes, small shops, and good restaurants." *(Pam Hurpootlian)* "Quiet, good service, friendly staff; good area for a morning run." *(William Webster)* "Our room was on two levels, with a large living room and bathroom on the lower, and a sleeping alcove (and second bathroom and TV) on the upper level." *(Robert Freidus)* "Charming inn, friendly staff. We enjoyed a spacious loft-style suite." *(Celia McCullough)* "Plan ahead and reserve one of the suites—it's well worth the modest extra cost." *(SN)*

Open All year.
Rooms 8 suites, 21 doubles—all with full private bath, telephone, radio, TV, desk, air-conditioning. Some with fan, balcony, or loft.
Facilities Lobby with breakfast area, bar, fountain. Hot tub. Off-street parking.
Location Five Points section, near intersection of Saluda, Greene, and Harden Sts., in SE section of city. 4 blocks to center.
Restrictions No smoking in some guest rooms.
Credit cards Amex, DC, Discover, MC, Visa.
Rates B&B, $115–130 suite, $103–118 double, $100–115 single. Extra person, $15. Children under 12 free. 10% AAA, AARP discount. Corporate rate, $75–105.
Extras Wheelchair access; some rooms equipped for disabled. Crib. Spanish spoken.

Richland Street B&B
1425 Richland Street, 29201
Tel: 803–779–7001

A neo-Victorian home built as a B&B in 1992, the Richland Street B&B showcases the design talents of owner Naomi Perryman, and offers the high ceilings, spacious rooms, and grand staircase typical of a Victorian home. The guest rooms are named for South Carolina governors, and have queen- or king-size beds with antique or reproduction decor; color schemes range from the soft peach and green of the Campbell room to the dark wood and deep red of the Hollings room. Breakfast menus include home-baked breads and muffins, with Belgian waffles or an egg and cheese casserole; rates also include afternoon refreshments.

"Naomi and Jim Perryman were friendly and helpful. The inn was built to blend with the architecture of this historic area. The spotless guest rooms are large with lovely furnishings. Delicious breakfast of waffles with bananas. Lemonade is served in summer on the front veranda. Though the inn is on a busy street, we were not aware of any traffic noise. Well-lit off-street parking." *(Susanne Ventura)* "Knowledgeable hosts; great restaurant recommendations. All modern conveniences with wonderful antiques, Oriental carpets, and handmade quilts. Fine linens, sacheted closets with quilted hangars, thoughtful evening turndown and mints, and a cozy comforter for chilly nights. Convenient location; easy interstate access." *(Debbie Trueblood)* "Fully endorse entry." *(Frances White)*

Open All year.
Rooms 1 suite, 6 doubles—all with private bath and/or shower, telephone, TV, air-conditioning. 2 with double whirlpool tub.
Facilities Dining room, living room with fireplace, verandas. Off-street parking.
Location Historic Preservation District. On Richland, between Bull & Assembly Sts. Walking distance to USC, Finley Park, Koger Center.
Restrictions No smoking. Children 12 and over.
Credit cards MC, Visa.
Rates B&B, $135 suite, $79–110 double. Corporate rates.

EDISTO ISLAND

Also recommended: If you need a break from busy Charleston, head south to sleepy Edisto Island and historic **Cassina Point Plantation** (1642 Clark Road, 29438; 803–869–2535.) This restored 1847 plantation home has four guest rooms. Breakfast, served 8–9 A.M., might include juice and coffee, strawberries and cream, French toast with maple syrup, and sausage-stuffed mushrooms; the double rate of $105 also includes afternoon refreshments. "During the Civil War, this house was occupied by Union troops, and much of their graffiti remains on the basement walls. The careful restoration and exquisite furnishings allow one to clearly imagine 19th century plantation life." *(James & Pamela Burr)* "Elegant antique-filled formal parlor; welcoming guest lounge; delightful screened porch. Extensive, beautiful grounds." *(Sibyl Nestor)*

GEORGETOWN

Originally settled in the early 1700s by indigo and rice planters, Georgetown has long been a major port. A variety of tours is available to explore the town: walking, horse and carriage, tram, and water tours cover the historic district, area plantations, the port, and other sights of interest. Beautiful beaches are nearby at Huntington State Park and Pawley's Island, while most of the rice plantations, the area's original source of prosperity, have largely been replaced with golf courses. Georgetown is located on the South Carolina coast, about 10 minutes from the beach, about 30 minutes south of Myrtle Beach and one hour north of Charleston.

Reader tips: "The restored waterfront, with interesting shops and restaurants, is a pleasant place to stroll. For nearly 50 years, in early spring, the women of Prince George Winyah Parish have sponsored visits to pre-Revolutionary and antebellum churches and town houses." *(Joe Schmidt)* "We had an excellent meal at the Rice Paddy restaurant." *(Sibyl Nestor)*

Also recommended: Built in 1770 and renovated in 1989 as a B&B by Chris and Tom Roach, the **Dozier Guest House** (220 Queen Street, 29440; 803–527–1350 or 800–640–1350) was built by a Revolutionary War captain. The double rate for the three king- or queen-bedded guest rooms is $65–75, and children are welcome. "Welcoming innkeeper, Chris Roach. Guest rooms are furnished with comfort in mind—adequate lighting, luggage racks, and comfortable chairs. Convenient private entrances to guest rooms. Short walk to downtown. Inviting porches." *(Betty Norman)*

For an additional area entry, see **McClellanville**.

King's Inn at Georgetown
230 Broad Street, 29440

Tel: 803–527–6937
800–251–8805
Fax: 803–527–6937

Listed on the National Register of Historic Places, the King's Inn is a 7,000 square-foot four-square Federal-style mansion built in 1825. In 1857, double piazzas were added across the front of the house, along with elaborate plaster moldings, cornices, and ceiling medallions in the foyer, and front parlors. In later years, the building served as Union headquarters during the Civil War, then was used as a boarding house, converted to apartments, and even became a church office and Sunday school. In 1994, Marilyn and Jerry Burkhardt moved from Missouri to restore it to its original elegance, complete with handsome period antiques, quality reproductions, and the rich use of exceptionally lovely designer fabrics; Oriental rugs top the original heart-pine floors in many rooms. Breakfast, served 8:30–10 A.M. on fine china and crystal at individual tables, might consist of a fresh fruit cup or strawberries and cream, a pineapple-ham omelet or a wine-and-cheese quiche with grits or potatoes, plus home-baked cornbread or zucchini muffins. Rates also include early morning coffee, afternoon tea and sherry.

"A restored 1825 Federal mansion, handsomely decorated with beautiful fabrics and furnishings; many interesting touches in the public rooms and guest rooms. Breakfast is worth forgetting your diet for. Charming owners who make you feel glad you've come." *(Jean Burbage)* "Although the inn combines elegance and comfort at any season, it's especially lovely when decorated for Christmas." *(MW)* "Friendly, warm atmosphere. Delicious breakfast, beautifully presented. Careful attention to detail." *(Euber & Monty Collins, also Patsy & Fred Detweiler)*

Open All year.
Rooms 7 doubles—all with private bath and/or shower, radio, clock, air-conditioning, robes. Some with TV, double whirlpool tub, desk, balcony.
Facilities Dining room, breakfast room with fireplace, morning room with TV, parlor, music room, screened porch, verandas. Off-street parking, lap swimming pool, croquet.
Location Historic district.
Restrictions No smoking.
Credit cards Amex, MC, Visa.
Rates B&B, $85–125. Extra person, $20.
Extras Crib, babysitting.

1790 House ¢ 👪 ♿ *Tel:* 803–546–4821
630 Highmarket Street, 29440 800–890–7432

Built in 1790 in the West Indies style, when Georgetown's rice planter culture was at its peak, the 1790 House was bought by Patricia and John Wiley in 1992. Breakfast is served in the dining room or on the veranda, and might include fresh strawberries, chicken quiche, cheddar potatoes, fried green tomatoes, and home-baked pumpkin-ginger muffins. Soda and iced tea are always available, and evening wine is served.

"John Wiley was a most hospitable host, who graciously recommended restaurants for dinner, and described an archaeological excavation made on the property. The spacious Indigo Room has a sitting area, twin-size pencil post beds, and a fireplace. The bath was decorated in shades of red and had a modern shower." *(William Novack)* "John is knowledgeable about area attractions. Delightful breakfast." *(Jerry & Barbara Ryan)* "Despite a raging storm, we slept soundly, snug in our comfortable top floor room." *(Joe & Sheila Schmidt)* "Fully endorse entry." *(Frances White)*

Open All year.
Rooms 1 cottage, 1 suite, 5 doubles—all with private bath and/or shower, radio, clock, air-conditioning. Some with desk, fan, fireplace, telephone, TV. Cottage with whirlpool tub, refrigerator, patio.
Facilities Dining room with fireplace, living room with fireplace, piano; family room with fireplace, books; porch; bicycles.
Location Historic district. From Hwy. 17 S, go left onto Screven St. Go left onto Highmarket St. to inn on left.
Restrictions No smoking.
Credit cards Amex, Discover, MC, Visa.

Rates B&B, $125 cottage, $95 suite, $75–95 double. Extra person, $15. Child, senior, AAA discount. Corporate, midweek rates off-season.
Extras Limited wheelchair access. Local airport pickup.

The Shaw House ¢ 🚸 *Tel:* 803–546–9663
613 Cyprus Court, 29440

Mary Shaw describes her B&B as "a recently built two-story Colonial with a large front porch and rocking chairs. Rooms are spacious, furnished with antiques, and our location is ideal—close to town yet very quiet. We serve refreshments on arrival, and a home-cooked Southern breakfast each morning. We turn back beds with a night-time chocolate, and always send guests on their way with 'a little something'—perhaps a recipe, a Christian prayer, or a little jar of jam or jelly."

"We ate breakfast in the den, overlooking the beautiful Willowbank salt marsh." *(Leslie & Pat Rowell)* "Located in a picturesque part of Georgetown, a delightful area for bird lovers." *(Betty Norman)* "Mary's breakfasts were delicious; her enthusiasm for the area left us with wonderful memories." *(Bob & Kathy Van Dyne)* "Our room was unusually large, with a queen-size four poster rice bed, good reading lamps on both sides of the bed, a sofa, and two chairs. The family room overlooking the marsh is ideal for bird watching. The Shaws are both warm, friendly people." *(Sibyl Nestor)* "Like a visit with friends. Mary always makes you feel right at home, and even gives you the freedom to help yourself in the kitchen. Our spacious bedroom had a king-size bed, beautiful antique furnishings, and a large bathroom. Quiet neighborhood, with street lined with oak trees." *(Jan Boggess)*

Open All year.
Rooms 3 doubles—all with full private bath, telephone, radio, TV, air-conditioning.
Facilities Living room with piano, den with TV, games; kitchen, porch. Golf, tennis, marinas nearby.
Location Coastal SC. 30 m SW of Myrtle Beach, 10 m S of Pawley's Island, 60 m NE of Charleston. 4 blocks from center of town. From Hwy. 17, turn W on Orange St. and continue to Cyprus Ct. Turn left on Cyprus to inn. Walking distance to historic district.
Credit cards None accepted.
Rates B&B, $50–75 double. Extra person, $10. 10% senior discount.
Extras Airport/station pickups. Crib, babysitting.

GREENVILLE

Information please: A classic Georgian Federalist home built in the 1920s, **Pettigru Place** (302 Pettigru Street, 29601; 864–242–4529) was restored as a B&B in 1993 by Gloria Hendershot and Janice Beatty, who take care to accommodate the needs of business travelers. Breakfast is served at guests' convenience, and includes fresh fruit and juice, homemade breads, muffins or coffee cake, breakfast meat, and a hot entree. B&B double rates for the four guest rooms range from $90–160, and also include evening turndown service. The simple but elegant guest rooms have queen- or king-size beds, antiques, period reproductions, fresh flowers, featherbeds, and individual flair—some have Victorian decor, while others have either Charleston or African accents.

HARTSVILLE

Also recommended: In northeastern South Carolina is the **Missouri Inn** (314 East Home Avenue, Hartsville, 29550; 803–383–9553). B&B double rates for the five guest rooms, each with private bath, range from $75–85. "A charming turn-of-the-century home which originally belonged to the owner's great-grandmother. Across the street from a well-kept and nicely planted college campus, in a beautiful small Southern town." *(Mary Coker Joslin)*

HILTON HEAD

Named for the English sea captain who "discovered" it, Hilton Head Island developed into a major resort area after the bridge to the mainland was completed in 1956. Rates are highest in summer, with excellent values available from mid-November to early March. This barrier island is located halfway between Beaufort and Savannah, in southeastern South Carolina.

Information please: Although it has thousands of condo and hotel units, Hilton Head's first inn did not open until 1996. **The Main Street Inn** (2200 Main Street, 29926; 803–681–3001 or 800–471–3001) was patterned after the mansions of antebellum Charleston, with wrought iron balconies, louvered shutters, and flower gardens. Each of the 34 individually decorated guest rooms have period reproduction furnishings, handsome artwork, Italian linens, Frette robes, down comforters, and marble bathrooms. Common areas include the elegant tea room, library, and breakfast area. A soothing color palette of taupe and ivory is used throughout the inn. B&B double rates, $115–295, include a continental breakfast, afternoon tea, and evening turndown service with freshly baked cookies or perhaps chocolate dipped strawberries.

For additional area entries, see **Beaufort.**

LATTA

Founded in 1877 with the establishment of a railroad depot, Latta is a small Southern town with 64 buildings listed on the National Register of Historic Places. Also of interest are its several art galleries with resident artists, plus the Dillon County Museum.

Abingdon Manor
307 Church Street, 29565

Tel: 803–752–5090
Toll-free: 888–752–5090

Whether you're traveling north or south on Interstate 95, or are a resident of Columbia or Charlotte looking for a weekend escape, you're guaranteed a memorable respite at Abingdon Manor. This 8,000-square-foot Greek Revival yellow brick home was built in 1902 by plantation owner and State Senator James H. Manning, and features extensive first- and second-floor verandas, supported by 40 Ionic columns from trees cut on Manning's 7,200-acre plantation. The interior is no less impressive, with the original window shutters, hand-crafted maple and mahogany woodwork, and enormous arched pocket doors and pier mirrors. Guest rooms are no less impressive, and are handsomely furnished with antique and reproduction furnishings. The home was restored in 1993, and has been owned by Michael and Patty Griffey since 1995.

Breakfast, served 8:30–10 A.M. at individual tables in the dining room or brought to your room, includes fresh fruit and juice, muffins and breads, and such dishes as baked French toast or cheese omelets with garden-fresh herbs. Rates also include early morning coffee and such evening hors d'oeuvres as herbed breadsticks and hot crab dip, while just-baked chocolate cookies are a possible bedtime treat.

"What fun to find a B&B that is truly a mansion. It's easy to imagine the parties and festivities that took place in the welcoming parlors and spacious verandas of this home that stands in the middle of an entire block. The Griffeys focus on the comfort of their guests, from evening refreshments to soft feather-beds and luxurious bed linens and towels. Enjoyed a tasty breakfast, served in front of the dining room fireplace." *(Betty Norman)* "Hard to imagine when barreling down I-95—only six miles away is this bastion of Southern charm and gentility!" *(MW)*

Open All year.
Rooms 1 suite, 4 doubles—all with full private bath, clock, desk, air-conditioning, fireplace. 4 with TV.
Facilities Dining room, 2 parlors, library, family room with TV/VCR, books, games; each with fireplace. Wraparound verandas with hot tub, exercise equipment. 3 acres with gardens. Golf, fishing, hunting, riding, canoeing nearby.
Location NE SC, Pee Dee Region. 6 m E of I-95. 25 m N of Florence, approx. 55 m N of Myrtle Beach. 12 m S of NC border. Approx. 1½ hrs. from Columbia, Charlotte, Fayetteville. Historic district, 3 blocks from downtown. From I-95, take Exit 181 & go E to Latta on Rte. 917 (becomes Main St.). At 1st light (Marion St.), go left. At Methodist Church, take right fork (Church St.). Go to end & inn on left. From Rte. 301 N, go past Main St. to next light (Academy St.) Go left & go 3 blocks to inn on corner of Church & Academy.
Restrictions No smoking. Children 12 & over. Trains can be heard at night.
Credit cards Amex, Discover, MC, Visa.
Rates B&B, $120 suite, $95 double. Extra person, $25. No tipping.
Extras Airport pickups, $10.

LYMAN

Information please: Conveniently located between Greenville and Spartanburg in northwestern South Carolina is the **Walnut Lane B&B** (110 Ridge Road, 29365; 864–949–7230), a handsome Colonial Revival home. B&B double rates for the five guest rooms range from $60–90, and include a full breakfast and evening refreshments. The spacious rooms of this nearly 7,000 square-foot cotton plantation home are handsomely decorated with period antiques and reproductions. The lushly landscaped grounds have many fruit trees and berries. Close by are antique shops, restaurants, the BMW manufacturing plant, and a manufacturers' discount mall. Reports welcome.

McCLELLANVILLE

Reader tips: "Graham and Company is an old-fashioned general store with a small cafe in the back which serves breakfast, lunch, and dinner. Great Southern food with an eclectic twist. All kinds of hot sauces from all over the U.S., and great grilled fish." *(Natalie Ferrer)*

Laurel Hill Plantation ¢ *Tel:* 803–887–3708
(843 area code after March, 1998) *Toll-free:* 888–887–3708
8913 North Highway 17, P.O. Box 190, 29458

Lee Morrison's family goes back four generations in the McClellanville area; in the early 1980s, he and his wife Jackie moved the 140-year-old family home, Laurel Hill, from Route 17 to a more scenic spot overlooking the water. Destroyed by Hurricane Hugo in 1989 (along with much of McClellanville), the Morrisons rebuilt the home, retaining its historic charm but adding effective insulation and modern conveniences. Breakfast is served at 8:30 A.M., and might include a grits casserole or artichoke strata with Canadian bacon, fruit salad, home-baked Amish bread with herb butter, plus preserves, juice, coffee, and tea.

"We love to sit out with a cup of coffee on the inviting wraparound porch; one of the inn's four outdoor pet cats will probably join you for a snooze. The inn is furnished with simple country antiques, handmade quilts, canopy and spindle beds, and primitive designs. The Gator Gaze room has two antique three-quarter beds and overlooks a fresh-water pond where several alligators (not pets) live. The area abounds with birds and wildlife, and the porch binoculars bring them into close range." *(Phyllis Cline)* "The antique shop has reasonable prices, superb quality." *(Douglas Macfie)*

"A most beautiful inn, set at the end of a long winding sand road. When you leave your car the only sound is the wind moving through the oak trees. From the porch, you can watch the waving marsh grass, like a kaleidoscope, constantly changing color." *(Joe Schmidt)* "The most outstanding features are the hospitable personality of the owners, the breathtaking coastal setting, and the delectable food. Rooms are immaculate and furnished with impeccable taste." *(Margene Odom)* "The landscape of marsh and waterways was beautiful and compelling. The innkeepers had thought of everything to assure guests' comfort—even nightlights in the bathrooms. This inn is run to a high standard by people who clearly care about what they are doing." *(Susan B. Johnson, also Natalie Ferrer)* "Loved Jackie's artichoke strata. Perfect balance of helpful yet unobtrusive innkeeping." *(Lauren Collier-Gorham)* "Jackie and Lee welcome guests as they would family members." *(Jay Daughtry)*

Open All year.
Rooms 4 doubles—all with full private bath, air-conditioning, clock, desk, fan.
Facilities Dining room, living room, common room with piano, fireplace, TV; sunporch, porch with swing, hammock; gift shop. 80 acres with parking, lawn games, swings, freshwater pond, saltwater creek with dock for fishing, boating, crabbing. Cape Romain National Wildlife Refuge.
Location Low Country; 30 m N of Charleston, 25 m S of Georgetown. 5 m to village. From Hwy. 17S, go left onto dirt road across from St. James Santee School. Go approx. 7/10 m to Inn. From Hwy. 17N, go right onto dirt road after fire station (across from St. James School).
Restrictions No smoking. Children at innkeepers' discretion.
Credit cards MC, Visa.
Rates B&B, $85–95 double, $65–75 single. Extra person, $15. No tipping.

MYRTLE BEACH

The largest city on South Carolina's 60-mile-long Grand Strand, Myrtle Beach is a popular tourist destination with the usual complement of boardwalk entertainment, plus water and amusement parks. In addition to swimming, fishing and boating in the Atlantic, the area is home to nearly 100 golf courses, most popular in spring and fall. On rainy days, you can sample innumerable shopping outlets, entertainment malls, country music, and variety theaters. Myrtle Beach is about 90 miles north of Charleston, and about 20 miles south of the North Carolina border.

For additional area entries, see **Tabor City,** as well as **Bald Head Island** and **Ocean Isle, North Carolina.**

Brustman House
400 25th Avenue South, 29577
Tel: 803–448–7699
800–448–7699
Fax: 803–626–2478

Owned by Wendell Brustman since 1984, the Brustman House offers a welcome change from the busy boardwalk area. A Colonial-style home built in 1968, it is furnished throughout with classic 60s and 70s Scandinavian decor; the veranda is a popular gathering spot. Low-fat, heart-healthy breakfasts are a speciality; and are served at guests' convenience (usually at 8:30 and 9:30 a.m.); a meal might include 10-grain buttermilk pancakes, frittata with fresh garden herbs, or organic eggs scrambled with low-fat cream cheese, and fresh fruit. Early morning coffee and the newspaper awaits guests in the garden room.

"The quiet, inviting wooded setting as well as the spacious and comfortable suite would be a most welcome refuge after a day on the beach." *(Betty Norman)* "Afternoon tea and cake, or wine, cookies, nuts and more, were available daily." *(Nancy Hodge)* "Afternoon tea-time is equally pleasant, an opportunity for guests to socialize while enjoying home-baked cakes. The dining room is enhanced by just-cut roses." *(John Norris)* "Clean, quiet, convenient, and well-maintained. The spacious rooms with the whirlpool tubs have lots of drawer space. Excellent breakfasts with fresh fruit, farm-fresh eggs, just-picked herbs, and pancakes with sunflower seeds. Afternoon tea and sweets were a treat." *(Carolyn & Arthur Todd)* "Ample privacy, a priority for us." *(Daniel Anderson)* "Delicious, healthy breakfasts, with seconds offered. Excellent lighting. Peaceful and relaxing, yet close to the beach, shops, and restaurants." *(Amanda Calderone)*

Open All year.
Rooms 1 suite, 4 doubles—all with private bath, telephone, radio, clock, desk, air-conditioning, fan. 3 with double whirlpool tub. 2 with TV. Suite with TV/VCR, full kitchen, private entrance.
Facilities Dining room, guest kitchen, laundry facilities, veranda. 1½ acres with off-street parking, gazebo, rose & herb gardens, lawn games, walking paths, bicycles, beach chairs. 300 yards from ocean beach.
Location S end of Myrtle Beach. From N or Hwy 501, take Business 17S through downtown Myrtle Beach; turn left onto 25th Ave S. From S take Business 17 when it splits from Bypass 17. Go about 8 m. 4 blocks after Jetport runways (on left), turn right at sign for Kingsway Pentecostal Church.
Restrictions No smoking. Children over 10 preferred.
Credit cards MC, Visa to hold reservations only.
Rates B&B, $95–130 suite, $55–95 double, $50–90 single. Extra person, $15; extra child, $5. 10% weekly discount. 2-3 night weekend/summer holiday minimum. Off-season rates.
Extras Airport/station pickup. Pets at management discretion. Crib, rollaway bed. Limited French, German spoken.

Serendipity, An Inn ¢ — *Tel:* 803–449–5268
407 71st Avenue North, 29572 — 800–762–3229

Just 300 yards from the beach, Serendipity is a Spanish–style inn owned by Terry and Sheila Johnson since 1994. Guest rooms are individually decorated with antiques, reflecting different time periods and countries. A breakfast of juice, fruit salad, cereal, hard-boiled eggs, and home-baked bread and muffins is served in the garden room, decorated with white wicker.

"Our room was done in country prints and antique furniture. Terry, Sheila, and their daughter Deborah were always around and never seemed too busy to give directions, offer recommendations, or just chat. Clean and neat swimming pool area with lots of flowers." *(Suzanne Zill)* "Excellent lighting, spotless housekeeping, satisfactory plumbing, ample parking, quiet setting, comfortable room, food fresh and healthy, and delightful owners, who treated us like old friends." *(Paul*

Whittington) "Friendly atmosphere, excellent housekeeping, convenient yet quiet location, tasty breakfast." *(Hilary Sanfey)*

Open Feb.–Nov.
Rooms 2 suites, 12 doubles—all with private bath and/or shower, TV, desk, refrigerator, air-conditioning. Some with radio, fan, balcony, kitchen. 8 rooms in annex.
Facilities Garden room, patio with fountain. Heated swimming pool, Jacuzzi, gas grill, shuffleboard, fountain, garden, Ping-Pong. 300 yds. to ocean beaches, fishing, water-skiing.
Location N coastal SC, Horry County. 90 m NE of Charleston, SC; 40 m NE of Georgetown, SC; 60 m SW of Wilmington, NC. Center of town. Take Hwy. 17 Bus. to 71st Ave. N. Turn E toward ocean; inn is just off Hwy. 17.
Restrictions No smoking in common rooms.
Credit cards Amex, MC, Visa.
Rates B&B, $73–129 suite, $59–99 double. Extra person, $10.

ROCK HILL

Just 25 minutes from downtown Charlotte, North Carolina, is Rock Hill, home to Winthrop University.

Also recommended: Located in the downtown historic district is the **East Main Guest House** (600 East Main Street, 29730; 803–366–1161), a Craftsman-style house built in the early 1900s. Each of the three guest rooms has a private bath, TV, and telephone; two have a fireplace, and one has a double whirlpool tub. B&B double rates of $59–79 include a continental breakfast. "Inviting second floor guest sitting room with TV, games, and books. Nicely decorated, clean rooms; firm mattress. Enjoyed an early morning walk before a breakfast of fruit, juice, cereal, and warm breads and muffins. Owners Jerry and Melba Peterson are available and helpful when needed, but allow their guests ample privacy. Good dinner at Pam's Tavern, a popular local eatery." *(HJB)*

SALEM

Information please: In southwestern South Carolina, close to the North Carolina and Georgia borders, about 20 miles south of Highlands and Cashiers, is **Sunrise Farm** (P.O. Box 164, 29676; 864–944–0121), a 74-acre cattle farm. Guests can relax on the rocking chairs on the wraparound porch and take in the mountain views, or sip hot cider by the fire. Three guest rooms are available in the turn-of-the-century farm house, with additional accommodations in two charming cottages; B&B double rates $65–100. Area attractions include hiking, whitewater rafting, fishing, boating, and golf.

SUMTER

Also recommended: About 40 miles east of Columbia is the **Bed & Breakfast of Sumter** (6 Park Avenue, 29150; 803–773–2903), an 1896 home in the historic district. Each of the five guest rooms have a private bath, and the B&B double rate ranges from $65–70. Suzanne and Jess Begley are friendly and welcoming. They helped us with maps and directions, made dinner reservations, and served a wonderful breakfast of Belgian waffles with strawberries. The deep porch faces a lovely park and the inn is located in a quiet residential neighborhood. *(Frances White)*

Key to Abbreviations and Symbols

For complete information and explanations, please see the Introduction.

¢ Especially good value for overnight accommodation.
Families welcome. Most (but not all) have cribs, baby-sitting, games, play equipment, and reduced rates for children.
Meals served to public; reservations recommended or required.
Tennis court and swimming pool and/or lake on grounds. Golf usually on grounds or nearby.
♿ Limited or full wheelchair access; call for details.
Rates: Range from least expensive room in low season to most expensive room in peak season.
Room only: No meals included; European Plan (EP).
B&B: Bed and breakfast; includes breakfast, sometimes afternoon/evening refreshment.
MAP: Modified American Plan; includes breakfast and dinner.
Full board: Three meals daily.
Alc lunch: A la carte lunch; average price of entree plus nonalcoholic drink, tax, tip.
Alc dinner: Average price of three-course dinner, including half bottle of house wine, tax, tip.
Prix fixe dinner: Three- to five-course set dinner, excluding wine, tax, tip unless otherwise noted.
Extras: Noted if available. Always confirm in advance. Pets are not permitted unless specified; if you are allergic, ask for details; *most innkeepers have pets.*

Tennessee

Richmont Inn, Townshend

Music (from country to bluegrass to rock 'n' roll), whiskey, horses, Davy Crockett, and Appalachian mountain crafts are sounds and images evoked by the name of this state. Yet although we think of Tennessee as a rural state, its major cities—Nashville, Memphis, Knoxville, and Chattanooga—are important manufacturing centers, while Oak Ridge is home to the National Laboratory and other high-tech industries. The key to Tennessee's development dates to the 1930s, when the Tennessee Valley Authority built huge dams all over the state, creating inexpensive electricity for homes and businesses.

Smoky Mountains: Great Smoky Mountains National Park straddles the North Carolina-Tennessee state border, and attracts over 9 million people annually. If you are traveling in the Gatlinburg/Pigeon Forge/Sevierville a weekend in July, August, or October, you may feel that most of them are there on the road with you. Although six lanes wide, Highway 441 into Gatlinburg and the park can resemble an elongated parking lot. *We urge you to study the map and check with your innkeeper for alternate routes to your destination.*

Worth noting: Many of Tennessee's inns are in dry counties; if you enjoy having a glass of wine with your dinner, call ahead or come prepared.

ATHENS

Information please: Halfway between Knoxville and Chattanooga is the **Woodlawn B&B** (110 Keith Lane, Athens 37303; 423–745–8211 or 800–745–8213), an imposing red brick Greek Revival home built in

1858. Used as a hospital for Union soldiers during the Civil War, it has now been restored as a B&B, offering four guest rooms with private baths, and B&B double rates of $75–110, including a full breakfast.

CHATTANOOGA

Chattanooga is located on the Tennessee River, in southeastern Tennessee, at the Georgia border. For an overview of the city, drive or take the incline railway to the top of 2,100-foot high Lookout Mountain, just south of the city. Of particular interest is the Tennessee Aquarium, and the Chickamauga and Chattanooga National Military Park, commemorating several Civil War battles.

Information please: While too large at 300 rooms for a full entry, the **Chattanooga Choo-Choo Holiday Inn** (1400 Market Street, 37402; 423–266–5000 or 800–TRACK–29) has really been enjoyed by readers. Located in the depot of that memorable railway and listed on the National Register of Historic Places, the lobby offers seating beneath the soaring dome of the vestibule. "Most of the rooms are in three different motel sections, but the antique-filled rooms in the old railroad cars are charming, spacious, and romantic; ask for one facing the attractive gardens." *(Ruth & Derek Tilsley)* "Our railroad car had Victorian style furnishings, a queen-size bed, firm mattress, marble stands on each side with hanging lamps, and two comfortable chairs with a marble top table in between, and more. A trolley connects this large complex; parking is tight." *(HJB)* "Great fun to stay in the sleeping cars; book early. Excellent dinner in the diner." *(BJ Hensley)* Hotel rates are $89–175; train car rates are $125, and many packages are available.

Twenty minutes from downtown is **The Captain's Quarters Inn** (13 Barnhardt Circle, Fort Oglethorpe, GA 30742–3601; 706–858–0624 or 800–710–6816) on the edge of Chickamauga National Military Park. Built by the U.S. Army in 1902 as married officers' quarters, the building was auctioned off when Fort Oglethorpe closed in 1946. Restored as a B&B in 1988, and refurbished in 1995, it offers seven guest rooms, with private baths and antique furnishings, at B&B double rates of $79–119, including a full breakfast.

Adams Hilborne ✕ ♿
801 Vine Street, 37403

Tel: 423–265–5000
Fax: 423–265–5555
E-mail: innjoy@worldnet.att.net

Listed on the National Register of Historic Places, the Adams Hilborne is a stone mansion, built for the mayor of Chattanooga in 1889. In 1995, Wendy and David Adams, long time owners of the Adams Edgeworth Inn in Monteagle (see entry), restored it as a small, European-style hotel and restaurant. Local decorators furnished the inn as part of a designer showcase. The 16-foot coffered ceilings with elaborate moldings, original cherry paneling, curved staircase, and Tiffany glass windows are complemented by antiques and period reproductions. Most guest rooms have queen-size beds accented by countless yards of lovely floral fabrics, and some offer mountain views. Rates include a breakfast of muffins, rolls, cakes, fruit, juice, cereals, served at individual tables 7–9:30 A.M. The inn's restaurant, the Porch Cafe, offers casual meals midweek, with more formal dining on weekends; pasta specialties include tortellini with prosciutto and garlic cream sauce, and seafood linguine in saffron sauce. In addition to the regular menu, guest chefs from around the U.S. occasionally host fine dining evenings.

"Beautiful restoration, cordial staff." *(Karen Kitchens)* "Wonderful staff, romantic honeymoon suite. Exceptional dining, including a tasty vegetarian meal." *(GR)* "Personable, helpful innkeeper; knowledgeable staff." *(RC)* Comments appreciated.

Open All year.
Rooms 4 suites, 6 doubles—all with private bath and/or shower, telephone with data port, radio, clock, TV/VCR, desk, air-conditioning, ceiling fan. Some with whirlpool tub, balcony.
Facilities Restaurant, living room, library, bar/lounge with occasional live music, veranda. Off-street parking. Tennessee River for water sports; tennis, golf, hiking nearby.
Location Downtown Fortwood historic district. Across the street from UT-Chattanooga Fine Arts bldg., at corner of Vine & Palmetto.
Restrictions No smoking. Children by arrangement.
Credit cards Amex, DC, MC, Visa.
Rates B&B, $100–275 suite, double. Corporate rate. Senior discount midweek. Alc lunch, $8–12; alc dinner, $23–30.
Extras Wheelchair access; 1 room specially equipped.

Bluff View Inn ✗ ♿

412 East Second Street; 37403
Tel: 423–265–5033
Fax: 423–757–0124

Intrigued by its European and New Orleans-style atmosphere, and its striking cliffside setting overlooking the Tennessee River, Dr. and Mrs. Charles Portera began the revival and restoration of what is now the Bluff View Art District in 1991. Starting with the River Gallery, the district has grown to encompass the Bluff View Scenic Overlook, the Sculpture Garden, Rembrandt's Coffee House, Tony's Pasta Shop and Trattoria, the Back Inn Cafe, Renaissance Commons Conference Center, and of course, the Bluff View Inn. Accommodations are available in three handsomely restored buildings: The C.G. Martin House, a Colonial Revival home built in 1927; The Thompson House, a 1908 Victorian, and the Maclellan House, an 1889 English Tudor mansion set on the bluff's crest. This historic neighborhood is conveniently connected to downtown Chattanooga and the North Shore by the Tennessee Riverwalk and the Walnut Street pedestrian bridge.

Inn guests enjoy a full breakfast in the River Room of Renaissance Commons, served 7–9 A.M. weekdays, 8–10 A.M. weekends. Choices might include French toast made from inn-baked baguettes, topped with strawberry-kiwi glaze, or perhaps an Italian sausage and portabello mushroom omelet. The district's Back Inn Cafe serves casual lunches and dinners with a changing menu that might include salmon-dill ravioli with chive mascarpone sauce, or spinach fettucine with chicken and mushroom-rosemary broth. Other dining options are available at Tony's and Rembrandt's.

"The staff is courteous, hospitable, and extremely accommodating." *(Harvey Moskowitz)* "Fabulous art district overlooking the Tennessee River. Beautifully decorated in elegant antiques; clean and cozy. Parking is safe and located between the two buildings. Fantastic food with vegetarian choices." *(Becki Carroll)* "Charming rooms with four-poster beds. The accommodating chef prepared a low-fat breakfast; river views enhanced my meal. Wonderful shops and a safe, invigorating walking path nearby leading to a pedestrian bridge." *(Betsy Gamlin)* "Delicious breakfasts of French toast with berries or omelets and fresh-squeezed orange juice; if you're in a rush, stop instead at the coffee house for capuccino and a muffin." *(Kimberly Mashburn)* "Beautiful outdoor sculpture garden overlooking the river." *(Lynn Edge)* "The inn is shaded by immense magnolia trees." *(Vanessa Young)* "Wonderful location; surprisingly quiet; many activities within walking distance. Four restaurant choices, all popular with locals; elegantly casual atmosphere. Rooms are decorated with artwork, and are clean and well kept. The art district is a great place to spend the day." *(Daniel Vance)*

Open All year.
Rooms 3 suites, 13 doubles—all with full private bath, telephone, clock, TV, air-conditioning, coffee maker. Some with gas fireplace, single or double-jetted bathtub, sitting area, balcony. Rooms in 3 buildings.
Facilities 4 restaurants, library with fireplace; sitting rooms with river views, music room with piano; private event rooms; conference center. Off-street parking, sculpture garden, art exhibits, special event festivals.
Location Downtown Chattanooga, Bluff View Arts district, along TN Riverwalk. Walking distance from Aquarium, IMAX. From I-24, take Hwy 24 N to 4th St. Exit. Go 7 blocks on 4th /St. Turn left onto High St. Go 2 blocks to East 2nd St. & turn right. Parking on right, check in on left at Maclellan House.
Restrictions No smoking.
Credit cards Amex, Discover, MC, Visa.
Rates B&B, $225–250 suite, $115–185 double. Corporate rates midweek. Alc lunch, $6–15; alc dinner, $10–25.
Extras Wheelchair access to restaurant, banquet hall, public bathrooms.

COLLEGE GROVE

For additional area entries, see **Columbia, Culleoka, Franklin, Nashville,** and **Shelbyville.**

Peacock Hill Country Inn ♿
6994 Giles Hill Road, 37046

Tel: 615–368–7727
800–327–6663
Fax: 615–368–7933

Come home to Tennessee, to a 150-year-old farmhouse on the hill, where you can rock on the porch and look out to the rolling farmland beyond. You can make that fantasy a reality with a visit to Peacock Hill, a working cattle and horse farm, home to several dozen peacocks, plus many wild turkeys and deer. Built in 1853 of cedar and poplar, the original farmhouse was restored and substantially expanded as an inn in 1994 by Anita and Walter Ogilvie. Guest rooms are available in the guest rooms, built during the renovation, plus a cozy log cabin—originally the smokehouse—and a restored granary. Furnishings include high quality country decor, folk art, handmade quilts, and both primitive and Victorian antiques; fresh flowers in every room are typical of the Ogilvies' attention to detail.

Breakfast is served at individual tables 8–10 A.M., and includes fresh fruit and juice, biscuits and sweet rolls, honey-puffed pancakes or perhaps eggs scrambled with vegetables and bacon. Rather than leaving this peaceful haven, guests often prefer to stay in for dinners of perhaps tomato bisque, chicken Tetrazzini, carrots and zucchini, lettuce with oranges and pecans, home-baked rolls, and mocha ice cream torte. Rates also include afternoon refreshments and evening turndown service with a homemade treat.

"Warm and friendly welcome. Our cheerful room had a divinely comfortable bed, fireplace, and an immaculate bathroom with a double whirlpool tub and thirsty white robes. Breakfast was plentiful and imaginative but not overly rich, served in a relaxing setting with soft background music. The guests intermingled easily, and shared common pleasures and interests. Delightful hosts. After breakfast, we were given a tour of the farm by Abbie, their English sheepdog, who had clearly taken this assignment on as her lot in life. We left her lying in the sun on the flower-lined brick walk—obviously well pleased with her day's work." *(Christine Walter)* "Exceptional decor. Fires were blazing in all the inn's fireplaces when we arrived on a cold winter afternoon. We loved the garden feel of the Kathleen Suzanne room, crisp in green and white with floral print fabrics and white wicker." *(Monica Battell Hasewood)* "Calm, serene setting." *(Gloria Parkinson)* "Excellent, creative food; innkeepers were helpful beginning with our first phone call." *(Calvin Shields)* "The best of all worlds—historic ambience with modern conveniences. We loved the Anna Virginia room, with a pencil post canopy bed, wedding ring quilt, and crisp gingham curtains and pillows. Wonderful balance of sophisticated elegance and country comfort." *(MW)*

Open All year.

Rooms 2 cabins, 2 suites, 2 doubles—all with full private bath, clock, desk, air-conditioning. Most with whirlpool tub, ceiling fan; some with radio, fireplace, balcony/deck, refrigerator.

Facilities Dining room, living room, den with TV/VCR, fireplace, books, games; guest refrigerator, sun porch with piano; barn with exercise room. 650 acres with gardens, lawn games, creek fishing, hiking, riding trails. Golf nearby.

Location Middle TN, 20 m S of Nashville, 25 m E of Franklin. From I-65, go E on Hwy 96 for 1.5 m. Go right onto Arno Rd. Go 13.7 m to Giles Hill Rd. Go 2.8 m to inn.

Restrictions Absolutely no smoking.

Credit cards Discover, MC, Visa.

Rates B&B, $175 suite, $110–120 double. Extra person, $20. Prix fixe lunch, $10; dinner, $20; 48 hrs. notice. 2-night weekend minimum.
Extras Wheelchair access; 1 room specially equipped. Pets with approval; horses boarded.

COLUMBIA

For additional area entries, see **College Grove, Culleoka, Franklin, Nashville,** and **Shelbyville.**

Locust Hill B&B ¢
1185 Mooresville Pike, 38401

Tel: 931–388–8531
800–577–8264

Dating back to 1840, the Locust Hill Inn was restored in 1994 by Bill and Beverly Beard. Guest rooms in the main house are furnished with family antiques, lace curtains, embroidered linens, and handmade quilts. For special occasions, guests may prefer the renovated smokehouse, with a loft bedroom, sitting room with fireplace, and a bathroom with a clawfoot tub and oversize shower. Early morning coffee is brought to each room, followed later by breakfast in the dining room, with fresh fruit and juice, country ham, eggs, grits soufflé, homemade biscuits and jam, and home-baked coffee cake.

"Lovely rural setting. This historic home has large, beautifully proportioned rooms, furnished with comfortable and attractive antiques and traditional furniture. Attention to detail can be seen in the carefully ironed cutwork pillowcases. The warmth you sense when you make your reservation is evident in every feature of the house. Exceptionally delicious food at breakfast and dinner. The Beards are delightful people with interesting ideas and backgrounds. Bill lived in France for many years, and both Bill and Bev are accomplished cooks. Columbia is an appealing area, the center of Tennessee Walking Horse country, with rolling hills, and many Civil War historic sites and other places of interest." *(Sibyl Nestor)* "Just as delightful on a return visit." *(SN)*

Open All year.
Rooms 1 cabin, 1 suite, 2 doubles—all with private bath and/or shower, radio, clock, desk, air-conditioning. Some with TV, ceiling fan, fireplace, balcony/deck.
Facilities Dining room with fireplace, living room with fireplace, TV; library with book, sunroom, porches. 8½ acres with flower & herb gardens, hot tub. Golf nearby.
Location Middle TN. 40 m W of Nashville. 4 m from town; 2 ½ m S of Rte. 50 on Mooresville Pike. From I-65, take Exit 46 & go E 9 m on Hwy. 99/412. Go S on Hwy. 31 for 4 m. Go left (E) on James Campbell Blvd. After ½ m, turn right on Mooresville Pike & go 2 ½ m to inn on left.
Restrictions No smoking. Children over 12.
Credit cards Amex, Discover, MC, Visa.
Rates B&B, $100–125 cabin/suite, $80 double, $70 single. MAP, $140–165 suite, $120 double, $90 single. Extra person, $20–40. 10% senior discount. Prix fixe dinner, $20 by reservation only. 2-night weekend minimum.
Extras Fluent French, German.

CULLEOKA

Sweetwater Inn
2436 Campbells Station Road, 38451

Tel: 931–987–3077
800–335–3077
Fax: 615–987–2525

Culleoka is the Choctaw Indian word for "sweet water," and the inspiration for this inn's name, restored as an inn in 1994 by Sandy Shotwell. In fact, you can relax in one of the porch rockers and listen to the sweet waters flowing in a nearby creek. Built in 1900 in the Steamboat Gothic style, the facade of the house is angled, with wraparound verandas on the first and second floors, much like the stern of an 1880s riverboat. The architecture is unusual for this area, and is more typically found in the Mississippi and Ohio river valleys. Breakfast is served at the dining room table at 8:30 A.M., and includes juice, fruit compote, a main dish such as eggs Benedict, and a dessert-like sour cream coffee cake. Dinners are also served by advance reservation; Sandy prepares "Southern gourmet" meals, and promises to extract all calories before dinner is served.

"The main floor has one delightful common area after another: a cozy small parlor with fireplace for cold nights, a sun-filled sitting room for morning coffee and conversation, a sun room for summertime breakfast, a formal dining room, wide verandas all around the house on both floors for sitting and rocking. Captain Campbell's suite was spacious and comfortable, with antique furnishings and a modern bath." *(Emily Hoche-Mong)* "Delightful innkeeper, beautifully restored home with a gracious country setting. All you can see from the inn are beautiful views of fields, old barns, a cemetery, and a church. Superb eggs Benedict." *(Marvin Vernon)* "Sandy took an old house in desperate need of repair and did a marvelous renovation job. The rooms have charming hand-painted borders; the same artist also painted a marvelous 'window' on the wall of one windowless bathroom. Country rock fans will want to know that Alan Jackson's house is about 30 minutes away." *(Susan Sinclair)*

Open All year. Closed Christmas Day, Thanksgiving.
Rooms 2 suites, 2 doubles—all with private shower and/or bath, telephone, radio, clock, TV, desk, air-conditioning, ceiling fan.
Facilities Dining room, living room with piano, den with fireplace, TV/VCR, stereo; sun room, wraparound porches. 10 acres with lawn games; on river for fishing.
Location Middle TN. 45 m S of Nashville, 60 m N of Huntsville. 9 m W of Columbia on Hwy. 373.
Restrictions No smoking. Children over 12.
Credit cards Discover, MC, Visa.
Rates Room only, $100 suite, $75 double. B&B, $125 suite, $100 double. MAP, $175 suite, $150 double. Extra person, $25. 2-night weekend minimum. Senior, AAA discount. Prix fixe dinner, $50, plus 20% service.

ELIZABETHTON

Also recommended: Just across from Tennessee's oldest covered bridge (still in use) is the **Hunter Cottage B&B** (213 South Riverside, 37643; 423–542–9268), a restored 1902 Victorian home decorated with period antiques. The owners, John and Lisa Bunn, spent four years redecorating and remodeling their two guest-room B&B. B&B double rates range from $65–85. "Charming town, delightful riverside setting, wonderful hosts, delicious breakfast." *(Ramsey Pollard)*

FRANKLIN

Founded in 1799, Franklin's downtown is listed on the National Register of Historic Places, with beautiful homes in a variety of architectural styles. In November, 1864, it was the scene of one of the bloodiest battles of the Civil War, resulting in the death of over 8000 soldiers in a single day.

For additional area entries, see **Cottage Grove, Columbia, Culleoka,** and **Nashville.**

Also recommended: As you might guess from its name, **Blueberry Hill** (4591 Peytonsville Road, Franklin 37064; 615–791–9947 or 800–400–4923, code 7929) has a hilltop setting offering breathtaking views of the surrounding hills. Two guest rooms are available in this spacious Federal-style replica home, at B&B double rates of $65–75. "Attractive decor with some lovely antiques; delicious breakfast; extremely comfortable." *(MR)*

Lyric Springs Country Inn ✗
7306 South Harpeth Road, 37064
Mailing address: P.O. Box 120428
Nashville, 37212

Tel: 615–329–3385
800–621–7824
Fax: 615–329–3381
E-mail: patsy@lyricsprings.com

The Lyric Springs Country Inn originated a century ago as a log cabin, and was updated many times over the years without losing its rustic country flavor. Patsy Bruce bought and expanded the house in 1974, opening it as a B&B in 1990. Patsy's collection of beautiful quilts is used to drape tables and upholster chairs; a grouping of antique wrought iron is artistically displayed on one wall, handkerchiefs on another. The inviting "saloon" is filled with memorabilia from Patsy's music and film career; she co-wrote such country hits as *Mammas Don't Let Your Babies Grow to be Cowboys* and *Texas When I Die* here at Lyric Springs. Breakfast is served at guests' convenience, and includes fresh fruit and juice, hot biscuits, honey-baked ham, and such entrees as Tennessee breakfast casserole or Belgian waffles. Rates also include 24-hour access to the ice cream sundae bar, plus popcorn. Dinners are served weekends by reservation, and a recent one included Mandarin orange salad, Italian-style chicken, herbed rice, tomatoes au gratin, and cheesecake.

"Set in beautiful rolling hills beside a small river; great hospitality.

Large rambling house decorated with great flair." *(Laura Patterson)* "A treat for country music fans. Lovely setting." *(Sibyl Nestor)*

Open All year. Closed Dec. 20–Jan. 2.
Rooms 4 doubles—all with private bath and/or shower, radio, clock, desk, air-conditioning, fan, bathrobes. 2 with balcony.
Facilities Dining room, living room, family room with TV/VCR, fireplace; library with books; saloon with pool table, piano; sun porch. 50 acres with garden courtyard with fountain, swimming pool, barn, riding trails. Golf, fishing, hiking, bicycling nearby.
Location 23 m SW of downtown Nashville; 18 m W of downtown Franklin. *Set your odometer.* Take I-40 W to Exit 199, Old Hickory Blvd. & turn left. Go 3.6 m on Old Hickory to Hwy 100 & turn right. Go 7.4 m on Hwy 100 to Hwy 96 & turn left. Go 8/10 m on Hwy 96 & turn right. Go 6.6 m on Old Harding Pike & turn right onto S Harpeth Rd. (Do not turn at 3-way stop at old country store after 5 m). Go 1.1 m to inn. From Franklin, take Hwy 96 W 2.5 m past Natchez Trace bridge & turn left on Old Harding Pike & follow directions above.From I-65, exit at Hwy. 96 & go E 13.9 m to Old Harding Rd. & turn left (SW). Continue to stop sign at Fernvale Grocery. Continue to S. Harpeth Rd. & inn on right.
Restrictions No smoking. Adults.
Credit cards Amex, MC, Visa.
Rates B&B, $135 double. Prix fixe lunch, $10; dinner, $20, weekends by reservation. Theme weekends.
Extras Airport, station pickup, $12.

GATLINBURG

People come to Gatlinburg because it is a convenient starting point for exploring the Great Smoky Mountains National Park. Unfortunately, the road from Knoxville to Gatlinburg is littered with one tourist trap after the next. Gatlinburg itself is no better, with dozens of tacky souvenir shops, no-go traffic, and non-stop people, and precious few parking spaces. Leave the town, and then your car, behind as soon as possible. Spend your time exploring the beauty and peace of the park—easily accessible hiking trails ensure that you won't have to go far on foot to leave the crowds behind. Gatlinburg is located in southeastern Tennessee, 50 miles southeast of Knoxville.

Information please: Breath-taking mountain views are yours from the many porches of the Victorian style **Hippensteal's Mountain View Inn** (Grassy Branch Road, P.O. Box 707, 37738; 423–436–5761 or 800–527–8110), about five miles from town. Built as an inn in 1990, each of the eight guest rooms has a queen-sized bed, reading chairs, full private bath with whirlpool tub, TV, air-conditioning, ceiling fan, and gas fireplace. Vern Hippensteal is a leading area watercolorist, and his works highlight the inn's eclectic decor. There's a spacious wicker-filled living room for guests to relax in, and a dining room where a full breakfast is served each morning. B&B double rates range from $95–125.

If you'd like a downtown location, within walking distance of all Gatlinburg's shops and restaurants, consider the **Olde English Tudor Inn** (135 West Holly Ridge Road, 37738; 423–436–7760 or 800–541–3798).

Each of the seven spacious guest rooms has a private bath and TV. Guests can relax on the patio or in the spacious living room. B&B double rates of $75–110 include a full breakfast, and children are welcome.

For additional area entries, see **Newport, Pigeon Forge, Sevierville, Townshend** and **Walland.**

Buckhorn Inn ✕ ♿

2140 Tudor Mountain Road, 37738
Tel: 423–436–4668
Fax: 423–436–5009
E-mail: buckhorninn@worldnet.att.net

The Buckhorn's white-columned porch overlooks a panorama of Mount LeConte and the blue-gray Smoky Mountains. The spacious living room and dining area are decorated with antiques and country-comfortable sofas. Guest rooms in the inn are furnished simply, with spindle beds and antiques. Breakfast is served from 8–9 a.m. and might include a choice of French toast, pecan pancakes, or broccoli-mushroom-cheese omelet, plus home-fried potatoes, buttermilk biscuits, country ham and sausage, home-mixed muesli and fresh fruit juices. Dinner is served at 7:30 p.m. by reservation only and is different each night; one evening the menu might offer Hungarian mushroom soup, marinated beef tenderloin with twice-baked potatoes, blue Mediterranean salad, and mud pie; another might consist of seafood chowder, trout with toasted almond and sun-dried tomato butter and rice pilaf, and peach cobbler. Special diets can usually be accommodated with advance notice. The Buckhorn has been owned by the Young family since 1979, and is managed by Rachael Young.

"Well-maintained, idyllic setting. Dinner was inventive and delicious." *(LS)* "We stayed in one of the newer cottages, with 60s decor, and a nice view from the back windows." *(Celia McCullough)* "Very close to my Platonic ideal of an inn. Enjoyed the nature trail." *(EA)* "Wonderful place to find, peace, quiet, and southern hospitality at the foothills of the Smoky Mountains, in full view from our high antique bed. Gracious hosts, outstanding food." *(Mary Nelson Wulsin)*

Open All year. Closed Dec. 24, 25. No dinners Sun.
Rooms 2 2-bedroom guest houses, 4 cottages, 6 doubles—all with private bath and/or shower, air-conditioning. Cottages with TV, fireplace, porch, refrigerator.
Facilities Dining/living room with fireplace, piano, books. Conference facilities. 35 acres for hiking, fishing; nature trail. 1 m to swimming, trout fishing. 8 m to downhill skiing.
Location 5 m from town. From Gatlinburg, take Hwy. 321 N 5 m; turn left at Buckhorn Rd. Go 1 m and turn right on Tudor Mt. Rd. to inn.
Restrictions Smoking only in 2 cottages, covered patio. Children 6–10 in cottages; no children under 10 in inn or at dinner.
Credit cards Discover, MC, Visa.
Rates B&B, $175–260 guest house (rate for 4 people), $125–160 cottage, $105–140 double. Extra person, $20. 5% service. 2-night weekend minimum. Prix fixe dinner, $25. Sack lunch by reservation, $8.
Extras Limited wheelchair access.

Butcher House ¢
1520 Garrett Lane, 37738

Tel: 615–436–9457
Fax: 615–436–9457

The Butcher House is a stone and cedar "Swiss chalet-style" home with views extending for miles around; it is elaborately decorated with period antiques and reproductions. Former corporate executives Hugh and Gloria Butcher opened a B&B after choosing early retirement from years of travel throughout the U.S. and abroad. Breakfast consists of French roast coffee, mini-muffins, fresh fruit, almond granola, and fruit yogurt, crêpes, or an egg dish, served on the mountain-view deck, or in the dining room. "Gloria and Hugh were friendly and helpful. The house is clean, well kept; beautiful table set for breakfast. Large windows in our room provided wonderful mountain views." *(Betsy Wilcox)* "The Butchers assisted us with area information, and in getting reservations for shows. We breakfasted on eggs Florentine, croissants, and fruit compote, served on a linen tablecloth with napkins and crystal water glasses." *(Lorraine Koenig)* "When I phoned for reservations, Gloria treated me with great courtesy and kindness. The inn is immaculate, with an ample well-lit parking area. Each day, they suggested different walking trails; in the evening, we returned from dinner to find goodies left out for the guests in the kitchen." *(Gayle Beckner)* "We arose early and were greeted by a beautiful sunrise, as the sun lit the valley below." *(Ralph Conn)*

Open All year.
Rooms 1 suite, 4 doubles—all with private bath and/or shower, TV, air-conditioning.
Facilities Dining room, living room with fireplace, family room with fireplace, TV, books. Guest kitchen, deck. 2 m to cross-country, downhill skiing.
Location 3 m NW of Gatlinburg. From US-441 go S to Gatlinburg, turn right at traffic light 10 on Ski Mtn. Rd. Turn right on Wiley Oakley Rd. At 4-way stop turn left on Ski View Rd., then right on Wiley Oakley Rd. Go N to Garret Dr., turn left. Turn right on gravel road to inn on right.
Restrictions No smoking. No children under 10.
Credit cards MC, Visa.
Rates B&B, $79–129 double, $69–119 single. 2-night minimum stay.
Extras Italian, some French, Spanish spoken.

HAMPSHIRE

Also recommended: A contemporary-style cedar home built in 1979, **Ridgetop** (Highway 412 West, P.O. Box 193, 38461; 615–285–2777 or 800–377–2770) was opened as a B&B in in 1992 by Bill and Kay Jones. Accommodations are in two log cabins, plus one guest room in the main house. Breakfast includes fruit, blueberry muffins, bacon, and such entrees as pancakes with blueberry sauce or pecan waffles. B&B double rates range from $65–90. "We stayed in a restored log cabin, furnished with antiques, and felt as though we'd gone back in time. The owners are charming, friendly, and helpful; wonderful breakfast. Truly a gem!" *(Carol Blodgett)*

JACKSON

Also recommended: An easy drive from I-40, about 75 miles east of Memphis, and approximately 100 miles west of Nashville is the **Highland Place B&B** (519 North Highland Avenue, Jackson 38301; 901–427–1472), a Greek Revival mansion built in 1911, and redecorated in 1995 in a designers' showhouse. Each of the four guest rooms has a private bath, and queen- or king-size bed, and the reasonable rates include a full breakfast.

KINGSTON

Whitestone Country Inn ✗ ♿
1200 Paint Rock Road, 37763

Tel: 423–376–0113
Toll-free: 888–247–2464
Fax: 423–376–4454
E-mail: moreinfo@whitestones.com

If your significant other has resisted your efforts to visit a country inn, drag him or her to the Whitestone Country Inn; we promise any protests will be pacified within minutes of your drive (really) through the entrance barn. The inn was built in 1996 by Paul and Jean Cowell, who took great care to ensure that all those modern comforts sometimes missing from B&Bs are present here in abundance: in-room telephone, television, fireplace, whirlpool tub, king-size bed, and absolutely no antiquated plumbing. A restful color scheme of cream, teal greens, and deep reds is found in many of the spacious guest and common rooms; furnishings are traditional, with coordinating fabrics on the comforters and window swags. While the setting on 39,000-acre Watts Bar Lake, a sanctuary for wildlife and waterfowl, is supremely peaceful, it's an hour or less from all of East Tennessee's major cities and sights.

Breakfast is served at individual tables 8–9:30 A.M., and includes eggs to order, bacon, ham or sausage, biscuits and gravy, and muffins. Set menu dinners are served family style, by reservation, and consist of an appetizer, salad, home-baked bread, iced tea, dessert and coffee, and such entrees as roast beef with mushrooms and baked potatoes, or baked ham with sweet potatoes and lima beans.

"Paul and Jean were warm and welcoming. The joy they find as innkeepers comes across to all who enter their home. Thoughtfully designed, carefully planned construction and decor. Each bedroom is named for a bird, beginning with a stained glass panel of that species above the door; the theme continues throughout the room via colors and more. Sparkling clean. Attention to detail can be seen in the extra heat switch and the nightlights in the bathroom. Muffins and fruit were always on hand. Wonderful view of the Smoky Mountains from the back porch." *(Cheryl Stoller)* "The Cardinal room is understated but luxurious; each need anticipated and fulfilled. The relaxing atmosphere made us feel right at home." *(Karen McCurry)* "Our spacious suite offered a beautiful view of the sun rising over the lake. Peaceful walking trails; gracious Southern hospitality." *(Kay Miles)* "Exceptional decor; tasty meals. An example of the Cowell's careful planning was seen in such a small detail as the electrical outlets in the bathroom." *(J.D. & Sondra Langford)* "Breathtaking view of the moon rising over the lake." *(E. Wayne Law)*

Open All year.
Rooms 5 suite, 7 doubles—all with full private bath, whirlpool tub, telephone, radio, clock TV/VCR, desk, air-conditioning, ceiling fan, gas log fireplace. 8 with balcony, 1 with refrigerator. 4 rooms in barn guest house.
Facilities Dining room, breakfast room, living room with fireplace, piano; library, recreation room with fireplace, pool table, exercise equipment; videotape library; conference room with TV/VCR; porches with swing. 275 acres with hot tub, gazebo, garden, lawn games; 6 m of hiking trails; 7000-foot lake frontage; dock for fishing, boating. Golf nearby.
Location E TN. 1 hr. from Knoxville, Chattanooga, Great Smoky Mts. Natl. Park. 35 m SW of Knoxville. From Knoxville, take I-75 S to Exit 72. Go right 8 m on Rte. 72W to Paint Rock Rd. Go right 4 m to inn on right.
Restrictions No smoking. BYOB. Children 8 and over.
Credit cards MC, Visa.
Rates B&B, $125 suite, double; $85 single. Prix fixe dinner, $13–15, by reservation only.
Extras Wheelchair access; 1 room specially equipped. Airport pickup, $25. Limited Spanish spoken.

KNOXVILLE

Once an outpost of the western frontier, Knoxville is today a manufacturing center and home of the University of Tennessee. Its location in eastern Tennessee, about 50 miles northwest of Gatlinburg, makes it a common starting point for visits to the Smokies.

Reader tip: About 15 miles north of Knoxville is the fascinating Museum of Appalachia (P.O. Box 0318, Norris, 37828; 423–494–0514), where you can observe nearly every Appalachian skill, craft, art, and music—except for the making of moonshine.

Also recommended: About ten minutes south of Knoxville, I-40, and I-75 is the **Wayside Manor B&B** (4009 Old Knoxville Highway, Rockford 37853; 423–970–4823 or 800–675–4823), offering ten guest rooms, most with private baths, in a handsome, red brick, turn-of-the-century country estate and nearby lodge. Guest rooms have antique and modern furnishings, while the grounds offer a tennis court, swimming pool, and more. The $88–175 double rates include a full breakfast and afternoon refreshments. "Wonderfully warm welcome. Our pretty Victorian-style room had flowered wallpaper and lace curtains. Enjoyed welcome refreshments in the comfortable living room. Delicious breakfast of fresh fruit, cheese grits, quiche, apple compote, muffins, and more. The innkeeper was very knowledgeable about the area and the Smokies." *(Brinta Kane-Jaro)*

About 25 miles southwest of Knoxville is the **Mason Place B&B** (600 Commerce Street, Louden 37774; 423–458–3921), a Greek Revival mansion built in 1861. Restored as a B&B in 1991, it offers spacious guest rooms furnished with comfortable period antiques and featherbeds. B&B double rates for the five guest rooms, each with private bath and fireplace, are $96–120. "Sumptuous, delicious breakfast. Beautiful, old-fashioned grounds." *(MR)* "Gracious, hospitable innkeepers Donna and Bob made us feel like family." *(Frances White)* "Impeccably furnished; wonderful featherbeds. Relaxing porches with swings and rocking chairs; delightful swimming pool beside the wisteria-covered arbor." *(Faye Fulton)*

Ten miles east of Knoxville is **Grandma's House** (734 Pollard Road, Kodak 37764; 423–933–3512 or 800–676–3512), a homey B&B with three guest rooms, each with private bath; rates are $75 double. Built in 1990, owners Hilda and Charles Hickman note that "Our guests like to unwind by walking to the river or riding bikes down a country lane. Our large country porch has swings and rockers, or you can sit high on the balcony and watch the sun set over the mountain." The family-style breakfast begins with a Christian prayer around the large dining table and includes eggs, breakfast meat, fresh fruit and homemade jams for the freshly baked biscuits and muffins.

Information please: In historic Maplehurst Park in downtown Knoxville is the **Middleton House Inn** (800 West Hill Avenue, 37902; 423–524–8100 or 888–524–8100), owned by Michael Zwayyed since 1994. The 15 well-equipped guest rooms have either king-size or two double beds, and the double rate of $59–89 includes a continental breakfast, and on occasion, a complimentary evening reception. Reports welcome.

About 30 minutes east of Knoxville via Highway 11 is **Arrow Hill** (6622 West Andrew Johnson Highway [Hwy. 11], Talbot 37877; 423–585–5777), built in 1857, and the site of difficult struggle for control between Union and Confederate forces during the bitterly cold winter of 1863-64. Arrow Hill served as an unwilling host to members of both armies, as it was alternately commandeered as field headquarters and hospital. Now restored as a B&B and listed on the National Register of Historic Places, the inn has three guest rooms, each with a private bath and antique furnishings. B&B double rates range from $55–65.

For an additional area entries, see **Kingston** and **Sevierville.**

Maple Grove Inn ✕
8800 Westland Drive, 37923

Tel: 423–690–9565
800–645–0713
Fax: 423–690–9385

Dating back to 1799, the Maple Grove Inn is a Georgian-style home, restored as an inn in 1992 by Curt Lockett. Guest rooms are named for trees, and range from the cozy Dogwood room, with a four poster queen-sized bed and cheery floral fabrics to the spacious Maple Suite with a queen-size four-poster rice bed, a living room with fireplace, screened veranda, and a marble bath with Jacuzzi tub. Breakfast is served 8–9 A.M. and includes omelets, whole wheat pancakes, ham and bacon, grits, muffins, biscuits, and fresh fruit and juice. Dinners are served to the public on weekends, by reservation; possible entrees are grilled swordfish with orange curry sauce, spinach-filled beef tenderloin, and apple-nut stuffed roast pork.

"Pleasant dinner, nicely served; delicious salads and vegetables. Beautiful old home, with charming guest rooms, individually decorated. Convenient location, about a 20-minute drive from downtown." *(Celia McCullough)* "Great hors d'oeuvres served during the party we attended. The exceptionally charming garden-like sun porch has windows all around, white wicker furnishings, and a tiled floor." *(Deanna Yen)* "The extensive common areas make it ideal for special functions, and the staff was most helpful in assisting us with wedding plans." *(MW)* "Warm, friendly, and exceptionally hospitable. Excellent food." *(James Zarchin)* "Spacious rooms with comfortable beds, attractive furnishings, and clean, roomy bathrooms. Restaurant on a par with the best." *(Eric Ober)*

Open All year. Closed week after Christmas.
Rooms 2 suites, 6 doubles—all with full private bath, clock, air-conditioning. Some with whirlpool tub, telephone, radio, TV, desk, ceiling fan, fireplace, refrigerator, porch.
Facilities Restaurant, living room with fireplace, great room with fireplace, TV/VCR, stereo; sunporch. Conference room; fax service. 20 acres with swimming pool, tennis court, lawn games. Golf, fishing, boating nearby.
Location 10 min. from historic downtown. Exit I-40/75 at West Hills. Go left off exit at light. At next light, turn right onto Morrell. Go through 5 lights. At 5th light, turn right onto Westland. Go 2 m to inn on left.
Restrictions No smoking. Children 12 and over. BYOB.
Credit cards Amex, MC, Visa.
Rates B&B, $150–200 suite, $90–150 double. Weekend dinners by reservation, $25–35.

McMINNVILLE

Historic Falcon Manor ¢ ♿

2645 Faulkner Springs Road, 37110
Tel: 931–668–4444
Fax: 931–815–4444
E-mail: falconmanor@falconmanor.com

From "the finest house in Warren County" to a hospital and rest home, and back to turn-of-the-century elegance is the history of Falcon Manor in a nutshell. Built in 1896, it was bought by George and Charlien McGlothin in 1989, and opened as an inn four years later after extensive renovation. Lowered ceilings and dividing walls were removed; porches, gables and fretwork were reconstructed. Now returned to its original elegance, and listed on the National Register of Historic Places, the decor includes deep, rich Victorian colors, 12-foot ceilings, ornate woodwork, a sweeping staircase, and authentic Victorian antiques throughout, including beautiful hand-carved beds. Breakfast is served in the dining room at 8 A.M., and includes country ham and biscuits, fresh fruit, beignets (French donuts), cereal, milk, juice, coffee and tea; every evening at 8 P.M., George and Charlien gather with their guests for refreshments and conversation.

"A beautiful and charming home, with a warm and welcoming atmosphere." *(Bobby Cobb)* "Breakfast was superb, the honeymoon suite beautiful, and the cookie and mints were a special treat. Best of all is George and Charlien's hospitality." *(GR)* "George and Charlien shared the fascinating history of the house and its restoration. We toured the inn, then gathered for coffee and cake." *(Sue Gatlin)* "Delightful get-together with the owners and other guests each evening. Fascinating collection of both modern and antique books." *(Edmund Wilt)*

Open All year.
Rooms 6 doubles—2 with private bath, 4 rooms with maximum of 4 people sharing bath. All with air-conditioning, ceiling fan. 2 with desk.
Facilities Dining room, parlor with fireplace, 3000-volume library, verandas. 3 acres with Victorian gift shop, parking. Creek across the street for wading. State parks nearby for swimming, boating, fishing, hiking, caving.
Location Central TN. 100 m SW of Knoxville, 71 m SE of Nashville, 71 m NE of Chattanooga. 2½ m from town. From I-24, turn E at Exit 111, (Manchester/McMinnville) onto Hwy. 55. In McMinnville, stay on 4-lane highway.; will become 70S bypass towards Sparta. Go left at 5th traffic light to inn at end of Faulkner Springs Rd.
Restrictions Smoking permitted on verandas. Children over 11 preferred.
Credit cards MC, Visa.
Rates B&B, $75 double. Extra person, $10.
Extras Limited wheelchair access.

MEMPHIS

Come to Memphis to see Graceland, for great blues and barbecue, but don't expect much in the way of accommodations.

Information please: The city's best-known hotel is the 450-room **Peabody** (149 Union Avenue, 38103; 901–529–4000 or 800–PEABODY). Although everybody loves the ducks (stop by at either 11 A.M. or 5 P.M. to see them march through the lobby), past reports lamented ordinary rooms at high prices, inept service, and noise from elevators and conventioneers. Double rates range from $160–295, with suites to $845. Also under the Peabody's management is the 155-room **Ridgeway Inn** (5679 Poplar Avenue, 38119; 901–766–4000 or 800–822–3360), decorated in Country French decor, and located in East Memphis, close to I-240.

A promising possibility in Cordova is **The Bridgewater House** (7015 Raleigh La Grange Road, Cordova 38018; 901–384–0080 or e-mail at kmistilis@aol.com), a few miles east of Memphis. This B&B has two spacious guest accommodations in a converted 1890s Greek Revival schoolhouse. Rooms have 15-foot ceilings, leaded glass windows, faux-painted moldings, and hardwood floors. B&B double rates of $100 include welcoming refreshments and a full breakfast.

MONTEAGLE

Monteagle is an ideal escape from Tennessee's many high-decibel attractions. Listed on the National Register of Historic Places, its Chautauqua Assembly was founded in 1882 and remains active with lectures, concerts, and movies for eight weeks each summer; it was inspired by the original Chautauqua in western New York State. The South Cumberland State Recreation Area is nearby, with wonderful hiking trails in the Cumberland Mountains, as well as trout fishing and canoeing. Natural attractions include the Great Stone Door, Lost Cove Cave, Cathedral Falls, Fiery Gizard Trail, and Sewanee Natural Bridge. Monteagle is 45 miles northwest of Chattanooga, and 85 miles southeast of Nashville. The University of the South is 6 miles away in Sewanee.

Information please: Nancy and Henry Crais invite guests to the **North Gate Inn** (P.O. Box 858–, 37356; 931–924–2799), offering ample common areas, seven guest rooms with private baths, and delicious breakfasts of Belgian waffles or perhaps apple crepes. B&B double rates range from $75–95. "Good accommodations, great meals, and very responsive innkeepers." *(Beth Hardcastle)*

Adams Edgeworth Inn ¢
Monteagle Assembly, 37356

Tel: 931–924–4000
Fax: 931–924–3236
E-mail: innjoy@worldnet.att.net

Wendy and David Adams, owners of the Adams Edgeworth Inn since 1990, report that "our inn is enjoyed by those who love to hike the surrounding mountain trails and enjoy the quiet calm of the mountains." Strolling the picturesque grounds filled with similar gingerbread Victorian cottages, sitting and rocking on the wraparound porch, or gathering by the library fireplace to chat or read a book are delightful options year-round.

The entrance parlor has light poplar walls and white wicker furnishings with flowered cushions. The 1000-book library has comfortable antique chairs and lots of well-read books. Guest rooms are simply furnished with brass or iron beds, country Victorian fabrics, period dressers and chairs. Starting at 7 A.M., guests can help themselves to coffee, tea, and muffins; a full-service breakfast of perhaps sausage strata, raspberry-lime muffins, and fresh berries with cream and granola is offered from 8:00–9:00 A.M. The menu for the five-course candlelit dinner changes nightly, and might consist of spiced plum pudding, salad with blue cheese walnut dressing, sorbet, chicken with apple chutney, green beans, tomato risotto, and summer berry pudding.

"Dinner was a culinary delight, served with beautiful china and silver. Quiet, restful, cool mountain air; we slept with open windows, hearing only chirping of birds." *(Susan James)* "Wonderful sound of rain on the tin roof. We were served cereal with fresh blueberries and hot biscuits and ham; spoonbread and homemade dill bread were a treat on the second day." *(Camille Williams)* "In addition to the Monteagle Assembly program, I enjoyed the many concerts at the nearby University of the South." *(Vivian Scott)* "Welcoming ambiance, friendly staff, peaceful setting." *(Jane Wagner)* "Excellent service; clean, well-decorated rooms; excellent food; lots to do." *(Vicki Keister)*

Open All year.
Rooms 1 suite, 13 doubles—all with private bath and/or shower, fan, desk, air-conditioning. Some with fireplace, refrigerator, microwave, porch.
Facilities Dining room, living room, library with fireplace; sun room, guest kitchen. Wraparound porches with hammock. Golf cart for touring Assembly. ½ acre surrounded by 93-acre Victorian village grounds, with walking trails, tennis. Golf, swimming, hiking, fishing nearby.
Location S central TN, 45 m NW of Chattanooga. From I-24 take Exit 134 to Monteagle. Turn left through gate into Monteagle Assembly. Follow signs to inn.
Restrictions No smoking. Children by prior arrangement.
Credit cards Amex, MC, Visa.
Rates B&B, $135–185 suite, $75–150 double, plus $10 daily gate fee mid-June–mid-Aug. Extra person, $25. 2-night weekend minimum. Weekly rate. Midweek off-season discount. Prix fixe dinner nightly by reservation.

MONTEREY

The Garden Inn at Bee Rock ♿ *Tel:* 931–839–1400
1400 Bee Rock Road, P.O. Box 445, 38574 *Fax:* 931–839–1410
E-mail: hinton@multipro.com

Located at the very edge of the Cumberland Plateau, the Garden Inn takes its name and inspiration from its setting, complete with vegetable and herb gardens, berry patches and a vineyard, plus scenic views, such rock formations as the Bee Rock overlook, and even a natural bridge. Built in 1996 by Dickie and Stephanie Hinton, this handsome, gabled, gray clapboard 9,000-square-foot building offers guest rooms with garden or mountain views, and guest rooms with hand-crafted solid cherry or walnut furnishings and queen-size beds. Breakfast is served at individual tables; guest consensus determines the serving time. A typical meal consists of fresh fruit, breads, meats, and such entrees as French toast or pancakes. Dinners are served Saturday night by advance reservation, and might include the following: hors d'oeuvres of sun-dried tomato cheese balls, spinach and potato puffs; mesclun salad with pears and pecans; grilled pork or Caribbean-style mahi-mahi with asparagus and potatoes; and chocolate-raspberry cake or pineapple cheesecake for dessert.

"Set on the edge of a 90-foot cliff, with beautiful views. The innkeepers spared no expense in decorating the inn. It even has a simulated mountain stream flowing through it, emptying into a goldfish pond. The lovely guest rooms are named after flowers. Our room, Iris, was spacious with a skylight and a whirlpool tub. The leisurely Saturday night dinner was a delicious experience. The dining room has tables for two and four, sofas, books to read and a gas log fireplace; music played softly in the background. Breakfast included home-grown fresh fruit, bacon and cheddar strata, and freshly baked blueberry bread." *(Misty Yates)* "Awesome view of Bee Rock from our room, beautifully furnished with antique reproductions. From our bed, we watched the mountains play hide-and-seek with the clouds. Welcoming hosts, delicious food." *(Frank & Maxine Caster)*

Open All year.
Rooms 10 doubles—all with full private bath, clock, air-conditioning. Some with whirlpool tub, TV, ceiling fan, fireplace, refrigerator.
Facilities Dining room, family room with TV/VCR, refrigerator; library, deck, patio. Conference room. 15 acres with gardens, lawn games. Hiking includes 4,500 adjacent acres.
Location Cumberland Plateau, E central TN. 90 m E of Nashville, 90 m W of Knoxville, 90 m N of Chattanooga, 15 m E of Cookeville. 1 m from town, I-40. Exit I-40 at Monterey. Go W on Hwy. 70 N. Watch for inn sign on left at intersection of Hwy 70 N & Hwy. 84. Call to confirm exact directions.
Restrictions No smoking. Children 12 & over.
Credit cards Amex, Discover, MC, Novus, Visa.
Rates B&B, $95–125 double. Extra person, $15. Saturday night dinner by reservation, $30.
Extras Wheelchair access; 1 room specially equipped.

MOORESBURG

For an additional area entry, see **Rogersville.**

Information please: For a real taste of Tennessee history, plan to stay at **The Home Place** (132 Church Lane, 37811; 423–921–8424 or 800–521–8424). This four guest-room B&B has been owned by Priscilla Rodgers' family since it was built as a log cabin in the 1850s. One of her ancestors settled Mooresburg in 1769, another founded nearby Rogersville; in the late 1800s, Priscilla's great-grandmother rented rooms to traveling salesmen, then called drummers, to supplement the family's income. Rooms are simply furnished with family antiques, and the $45–65 rate includes such breakfasts as zucchini bread, waffles with strawberries, sausage, and fruit salad; children are welcome and the first floor is wheelchair accessible, including the bathroom. Reports welcome.

NASHVILLE

Nashville is both the capital and the commercial center of Tennessee, and, as everyone knows, it's the country music capital of the world. It's also home to seventeen colleges and universities and to tourist attractions ranging from the sublime to the ridiculous, starting and ending, of course, with Opryland. And speaking of which—we've had good reports on the **Opryland Hotel** (2800 Opryland Drive, 37214;

615–883–2211), though most readers are overwhelmed by its size: nearly 2000 rooms.

Reader tip: "Take time for a leisurely tour of the home and grounds of The Hermitage, Andrew Jackson's home." *(MR)*

Also recommended: According to one reader, the 340-room **Loews Vanderbilt Plaza** (2100 West End Avenue, 37203; 615–320–1700 or 800–23–LOEWS) is "the best and most elegant hotel in Nashville." *(Stephanie Roberts)* Some guest rooms have views of the Cumberland River. Double rates are $119–135.

Information please—hotels: Reports are needed for **Union Station** (1001 Broadway, 37203; 615–726–1001 or 800–331–2123), a Romanesque-style fortress built in 1900 as a showpiece for the Louisville & Nashville Railroad, and renovated as a hotel, complete with a clock tower, lofty gables, a barrel-vaulted coffered ceiling, stained glass windows, massive columns, hand-carved oak railings, and wrought iron balconies. Guest rooms are furnished with period reproductions; some look into the lobby through huge arched windows, others overlook the street. The hotel is just blocks from the convention center, Music Row, and Vanderbilt University. Double rates for the 124 rooms range from $129–255. While readers are delighted with the hotel's decor and location, as well as the outstanding meals at Arthur's restaurant, reports on the service have been mixed.

The **Hermitage Hotel** (231 Sixth Avenue North, 37219; 615–244–3121 or 800–251–1908) was built in 1910 at a cost of $1,000,000, with all possible luxuries and amenities. In 1986 the hotel was restored to its early elegance, after years of decay; its original 250 rooms were redone as 120 suites. An additional $4 million were spent on refurbishing in 1994. Double rates of $165 include turndown service, luxury soaps, and the morning paper. The hotel restaurant offers continental cuisine in an elegant atmosphere. Reports needed.

Information please—B&Bs: An 1896 farmhouse, the **Apple Brook B&B** (9127 Highway 100, 37221–4502; 615n646–5082) offers a quiet country setting, complete with swimming pool, barns, and a babbling brook. B&B double rates for the four guest rooms range from $65–75, including breakfasts of apple pancakes with maple syrup. Located in the Belmont-Hillsboro Historic District is **The Hillsboro House B&B** (1933 20th Avenue South, 37212; 615–292–5501 or 800–228–7851). Close to Vanderbilt and Belmont Universities, this 1904 Victorian home offers guest rooms with private baths, queen-size beds, TV, and telephone in the $95 B&B double rate; a full breakfast is also included. Another possibility in the same neighborhood is **Linden House** (1501 Linden Avenue, 37212; 615–298–2701), with two guest accommodations and B&B double rates of $65–85.

For additional area entries, see **College Grove, Columbia, Culleoka, Franklin**, and **Watertown,** all within a 20–30 mile drive.

NEWPORT

For additional area entries, see **Pigeon Forge** and **Sevierville.**

Christopher Place
1500 Pinnacles Way, 37821

Tel: 423–623–6555
800–595–9441
Fax: 423–623–6555
E-mail: TheBestInn@aol.com

When we tour inns, we always make a point of asking to see the least expensive room. Its condition tells you a lot about the innkeepers' attention to detail and concern for quality. At Christopher Place, that room is the Stargazer room, decorated in cream and crimson, with a queen-size bed, red-floral fabrics, and gold accents. In 1995, after Drew Ogle had bought and renovated this 20-year-old inn, that very room won *Country Inn Magazine*'s Waverly's Country Inn Room of the Year. Other guest rooms are equally appealing, and most have a queen- or king-size bed and scenic views. One favorite is Margaret's room, with a king-size four poster bed and an unusual round window with lovely mountain views. Breakfast is served at guests' convenience, 6–10 A.M. at individual tables, and includes ham, eggs, biscuits, and fresh fruit.

Spectacular setting, extensive grounds, spacious rooms, inviting public areas, delightful innkeeper. Excellent location, easy-to-reach from I-40 without traffic problems. From Newport, you can take back roads into Gatlinburg and avoid the four-lane peak season highway congestion. Pristine setting, totally quiet. The inn was built in 1974 as a private mansion; the rear of the inn looks like a brick version of Tara, with six huge white columns, a long second-floor balcony, and third floor dormer windows. Wonderful mountain views. On entering, one immediately notices the fabulous three-story spiral staircase and the enormous largest crystal chandelier. The large wood-panelled game room has a dramatic circular window above the pool table. The library is wood-panelled, with bookcases filled with popular novels and video tapes, and upholstered love seats and wing chairs that invite you to linger. The formal living room has red carpeting, white upholstered Victorian furniture, a grandfather clock, and a grand piano. Delicious dinner, super dessert. Simple breakfasts of ham and eggs, or pancakes. I stayed in the Tournament of Roses room and found it to be exceptionally luxurious and comfortable, with hardwood floors, a wood-burning fireplace, white wicker furniture, a dusty rose double whirlpool tub, queen-size bed, and a well-equipped bathroom. The Roman Holiday room has a white iron bed romantically draped in sheer netting and grapevines, a fireplace, double Jacuzzi tub, and brown and beige shag carpeting; it opens to the balcony that runs the length of the house with those fabulous views. The private bathroom is across the hall. *(SHW)*

"Drew and his staff went out of their way to make sure we were well taken care of. Tim gave us a welcome tour, and we were delighted with the inn's beautiful, peaceful setting. The lovely guest rooms are wonderfully maintained. Both breakfasts and dinners were well prepared and served in a beautiful and relaxed setting." *(Syd & Patti Rodocker)*

Open All year.
Rooms 1 suite, 8 doubles—all with full private bath (some in hallway), radio, clock, air-conditioning. Some with double whirlpool tub, desk, ceiling fan, wood-burning fireplace, refrigerator. 2 rooms in guest house.
Facilities Dining room, living room with fireplace, piano, game room with billiards, TV/VCR, stereo, piano, library with fireplace, books, TV, /VCR, stereo, guest kitchen, exercise room. Evening piano music, singing. 203 acres with heated swimming pool, tennis court, lawn games, hiking. Golf, skiing nearby.
Location E TN. 25 m NE of Gatlinburg. Smoky Mts. 5 m to town, I-40. From I-40, take Exit 435 to Hwy 32 S. Go 2 m to mile marker 22. Go right onto English Mt. Rd. Go 2 m then go right onto Pinnacles Way. Follow to top. From Gatlinburg. Turn at light #3 onto Rte. 321 N. Go 19 m & turn left onto Hwy 32 N at Cosby. Go 11 m to MM 22, & turn left onto English Mt. Rd. & follow as above.
Restrictions No smoking. Children 12 and over. BYOB.
Credit cards MC, Visa.
Rates B&B, $199–209 suite, $99–199 double. Tips appreciated. AAA discount. Prix fixe dinner, $20; byob.
Extras Wheelchair access; bathroom partially equipped.

PIGEON FORGE

Pigeon Forge has so much going on that the ratio of motel rooms to permanent residents is now two to one. Both the eponymous carrier pigeons and the forge are long gone, but what you will find here are "six miles of action-packed entertainment" in the form of innumerable discount shopping outlets, and attractions ranging from Dollywood to the Dixie Stampede, with water parks thrown in for good measure. If you're traveling with kids, either pass through in the dead of night when they're fast asleep, or put your brain on hold and enjoy the fun. As always, avoid visiting in July and August (especially weekends) unless you're nostalgic for rush-hour conditions.

For additional area entries, see **Gatlinburg, Newport, Sevierville, Townshend** and **Walland.**

Day Dreams Country Inn ¢ 🚸 ♿ — *Tel:* 423–428–0370
2720 Colonial Drive, 37863 — *Fax:* 423–428–2622
E-mail: daydreams@sprynet.com

The Day Dreams Country Inn is a contemporary cedar log home with a quiet setting amid weeping willow trees and a babbling creek. Bob and Joyce Guerrera, who bought the inn in 1994, offer a quiet base for exploring the Great Smokies but are also within walking distance of the Pigeon Forge trolley which takes you into town for all activities. They have furnished their home with antiques and reproduction pieces, comfortable couches, and country accents. Breakfast is served at 9:00 A.M., and includes eggs, biscuits and gravy, breakfast meats, fruit, juice, and coffee; rates also include afternoon refreshments.

"Our first B&B and we were hooked! Our room was large, beautifully decorated, quiet, and very clean. We were made to feel right at home, and invited to fix ourselves a drink, roam around, or sit and visit. Parking was convenient, and the front porch had chairs and a swing overlooking a brook with ducks. Amazingly serene setting." *(BJ Schwartzkopf)* "Welcoming ambiance, generous hospitality. Beautiful handmade quilts adorn many of the beds, with old-fashioned braided rugs on the fine wooden floors. A toasty fire in the living room fireplace kept us warm on a cold winter night, enhanced by hot cocoa and Joyce's delicious home-baked brownies. Breakfast starts with a carafe of orange juice and an assortment of seasonal fruits. The hot dishes included scrambled eggs, bacon, biscuits, grits, French toast stuffed with raspberry jam, and home-fried potatoes. Impeccable housekeeping, with lovely glycerin soaps, and fresh towels daily." *(Lyn Lebrewitz)* "Fantastic breakfast, varied each morning. A nice little snack and drink was waiting for us in the evening." *(Vickie & Donald Stulz)* "The charm of an older home with the conveniences of a modern one." *(Erin Lotherington)*

Open All year.
Rooms 2 suites, 4 doubles—all with private bath and/or shower, radio, desk, air-conditioning. 2 with TV.
Facilities Dining room, living room with fireplace, TV/VCR, books; screened porch with swing. 3 wooded acres with creek, picnic area, children's play equipment. 5 m to downhill, cross-country skiing.
Location E TN, 35 m E of Knoxville. ¼m from town center. From I-40, take exit for Rte. 66 S. Go S 13 m to Rte. 441, turn right into Pigeon Forge. Turn right on Wears Valley Rd. Go 1 block, turn left on Florence Dr. Take 3rd right onto Colonial Dr. to inn on right.
Restrictions No smoking.
Credit cards Discover, MC, Visa.
Rates B&B, $99 suite, $79 double. Extra adult, $15; child under 16, $10. 2-night minimum Oct. 10% discount for 4-night stay.
Extras Limited wheelchair access. Crib, babysitting available.

PIKEVILLE

Fall Creek Falls B&B Inn ¢ *Tel:* 423–881–5494
Highway 284, Route 3, Box 298B, 37367 *Fax:* 423–881–5040

Fall Creek Falls Inn is a country manor home built by Rita and Doug Pruett in 1981, and named for the highest waterfall east of the Rockies, located just a mile away. Expanded as a B&B in 1991, the inn's decor combines Victorian and country elements. Breakfast is served at 8 or 8:30 A.M. at individual tables with a different menu each day; perhaps eggs Benedict, strawberry bread and cinnamon rolls, and tropical fruit cup; or stuffed French toast strata with apple cider syrup, sausage patties, and cooked apples.

"Beautiful scenery at nearby Falls Creek State park, with waterfalls and deep gorges; great hiking. Doug and Rita were warm and welcoming, making us feel right at home. Our inviting room had good lighting and a comfortable bathroom. A typically thoughtful touch was the fresh carafe of ice water and glasses in our room. Though a small thing, it communicated a feeling of being personally considered and cared for. Coffee, tea, and cookies were available throughout the evening for guests to help themselves." *(Susan Winner)* "Top marks for cleanliness, warm hospitality, facilities, food, and location. Doug is a wonderful cook; his cinnamon buns are the best, but he's equally happy to accommodate special diets with advance notice. Pastoral setting with horses grazing in the fields." *(Cecilia Fralick)* "Careful attention to detail: night lights, thick terry robes, shower mats, good lighting, good closet space and immaculately clean." *(Bernadette Murphy, also Mary Robbin)* "The beautiful Sweetheart Room has Victorian decor and a bathroom with a red heart-shaped whirlpool tub." *(Margaret & Robert O'Leary)* "Loved the scented soaps, lotions, bubble baths, and body shampoos." *(Wanda Walden)*

Open All year. Closed Jan.
Rooms 2 suites, 7 doubles—all with full private bath, radio, clock, air-conditioning, fan. 2 with double whirlpool tub, gas log fireplace,
Facilities Dining room, living room with TV/VCR; family room with TV, books, games; guest kitchen, porch. 40 acres with 5 acre-yard with picnic area, benches, herb & flower gardens, pond, walk trail. 1 m to Fall Creek Falls State Park; 3 m to golf, swimming, hiking, horseback riding, tennis, fishing.
Location Cumberland Plateau. 50 m N of Chattanooga. 15 m NW of Pikeville. From Rte. 30 or Rte. 111, take Hwy. 284 & call for directions. Inn is off Hwy 284 just S of Rte. 30.
Restrictions No smoking. Children 8 & over.
Credit cards Amex, Discover, MC, Visa.
Rates B&B, $140 suite, $79–119 double, $69–79 single. Extra person, $10. 2-night minimum holidays, Oct. weekends. Picnic lunches.

ROGERSVILLE

For another area inn, see **Mooresburg.**

Hale Springs Inn ¢ ✕ *Tel:* 423–272–5171
110 West Main Street, Town Square, 37857

Rogersville is one of Tennessee's oldest towns, founded in 1786 when this area was still the western frontier. The Hale Springs Inn was built in 1824 and is the oldest continuously running inn or hotel in Tennessee. Presidents Jackson, Polk, and (Andrew) Johnson all stayed here. Originally called McKinney's Tavern, the inn was used as Union headquarters during the Civil War. Confederate headquarters were across the street, in Kyle House. In 1982, Captain Carl Netherland-Brown purchased the inn and began its restoration. Many of the original furnishings are still intact, including several Victorian settees, side chairs, and claw-foot bathtubs. The decor also includes comfortable velvet-covered wing chairs, handsome brass chandeliers, canopied four-poster beds, Oriental carpets, and handmade quilts. Dinner entrees include prime rib, chicken Creole, shrimp scampi and fettucine with chicken, tomatoes, and basil.

"A delightful respite for the business traveler; a quiet, comfortable, and attractive inn with a gracious host who is pleased to share his knowledge of the area's history." *(Leila Niemann)* "Large, comfortable room, good restaurant, and pleasant staff." *(Margaret Sullivan)* "The inn's self-guided walking tour was a highlight of our stay. The restaurant is attractively decorated in period, with good service and food." *(Dana Abdella)* "Cordial welcome and assistance with baggage." *(Helen Hamilton)* "Well maintained and beautifully furnished with genuine antiques. Excellent value. Enjoyed breakfast of juice, cereal, fruit, pastries, and coffee in a sun parlor overlooking the scenic square." *(Betty Norman)*

Worth noting: Three guest rooms have thermostats which control temperature for all.

Open All year. Restaurant closed Sun.
Rooms 4 suites, 5 doubles—all with private shower and/or bath, TV, air-conditioning. Most with desk, fireplace.
Facilities Restaurant, sitting room with fireplace, library; lobby, balcony with rocking chairs. Formal garden with gazebo. Swimming, boating, fishing, tennis, golf nearby.
Location Upper E TN. 65 m E of Knoxville; 30 m W of Kingsport. 16 m NW of I-81 on Rte 11W. In center of town.
Restrictions Traffic, pedestrian noise in front rooms. Dry county; BYOB. No children under 7.
Credit cards MC, Visa.
Rates B&B, $65–90 suite, $45–70 double. Alc lunch, $7.50; alc dinner, $16.

RUGBY

When English author *(Tom Brown's School Days)* and social reformer Thomas Hughes launched his Utopian colony in 1880, he wrote: "For we are about to ... create a new center of human life ... in this strangely beautiful solitude." Unfortunately, his words were more accurate than he had perhaps intended; after reaching a peak population of 450 in 1884, the community foundered, as did most such noble 19th century experiments. A small farming community did survive, and in 1966, Historic Rugby, Inc. was founded to restore the surviving buildings and to encourage historically compatible enterprise. Located on the Cumberland Plateau, the town sits at the southern border of the Big South Fork National River and Recreation Area—a wilderness of high plateaus and rugged river gorges. Contact the Superintendent, Big South Fork National River and Recreation Area (Route 3, Box 401, Oneida 37841; 423–879–3625), for information about recreational opportunities.

Reader tip: "Big South Fork is an undiscovered treasure with high cliffs, natural bridges, deep gorges, and magnificent views. Adults and children will enjoy visiting the wonderfully restored Blue Heron coal mine, best reached by the Big South Fork Scenic Railway. Food prices in the area are very reasonable and the many outdoor activities make it an ideal family vacation spot." *(Joe & Sheila Schmidt)*

Also recommended: The **Grey Gables Inn** (Hwy 52, P.O. Box 52, Rugby 37733; 423–628–5252 or 800–347–5252) is owned by Linda and Bill Jones, closely involved in Rugby's restoration. The $115 double rate includes a hearty country breakfast and an evening meal. Guest rooms are individually decorated with Victorian antiques and American country pieces. An 80-foot veranda encircles the inn, welcoming guests to enjoy the wicker furniture and rustic Tennessee-crafted rockers. "Hosts attentive but not intrusive; the setting peaceful but not boring; the food, extraordinary." *(William Confer)* "Wonderful English high tea, with lovely little sandwiches, scones, cookies, turnovers, and fresh fruit." *(Sibyl Nestor)* "Beautiful, comfortable rooms. Linda made us all feel at home, and Bill's catfish is the best." *(Scott Craig)*

Newbury House at Historic Rugby ¢ ✕ *Tel:* 423–628–2430
P.O. Box 8, 37733

Newbury House, Rugby's first boarding house, was built in 1880 and has been restored as a guest house, decorated with lace curtains and Victorian antiques; additional accommodations are available in the restored Pioneer or Percy Cottages. Three meals a day are served at the Harrow Road Cafe, which serves both traditional English dishes and Tennessee favorites—from shepherd's pie to deep-fried catfish. Room rates include such breakfast choices as buttermilk pancakes with sugar-cured ham, or scrambled eggs with country gravy and biscuits. Take a walking tour of the restored buildings, and browse through the crafts and books at the Rugby Commissary and the Board of Aid Bookshop.

"The area is quiet, a haven for all kinds of birds. Nature trails take you along the river; interesting rock formations." *(Melanie McKeever)* "Small, modest guest rooms; inviting parlor and porch; friendly staff. We visited in July when the waterlilies were blooming in the pond out back, and the bushes were full of ripe blackberries. We took a leisurely walk to the swimming hole for a refreshing dip in the hot humid weather; bring bug spray. We also enjoyed a visit to Tennessee's oldest winery, about 15 miles away." *(Suzie Tolmie)* "The cottage was a comfortable lodging experience for a reasonable price." *(Bill Novack)* Comments appreciated.

Open All year. Restaurant closed Thanksgiving Day, Dec. 24, 25, Jan. 1. No dinner served midweek.
Rooms 2 2-3 bedroom cottages, 1 suite, 5 doubles—3 with private bath, 2 with maximum of 4 people sharing 1 bath. All with air-conditioning, fan. Some with desk, 1 with radio. Pioneer Cottage with screened porch, fully-equipped kitchen.
Facilities Parlor with books. Hiking trails. Canoeing, fishing, swimming nearby.
Location NE TN, 70 m NW of Knoxville. From I-40, take exit for Rte. 27. Go N approx. 32 m to Elgin. Turn left on Rte. 52, go W 7 m to Rugby.
Restrictions No smoking. No children under 12 in inn. Any age fine for cottage. Light sleepers may wish to request a room at the inn instead of in cottage.
Credit cards MC, Visa.
Rates Inn: B&B, $61–84 double, $51–74 single. Extra person, $10. Cottages: room only, $59–64 double. Extra person, $10. Alc breakfast, $3–4, alc lunch $4–6, alc dinner $8–15.
Extras Wheelchair access to restaurant.

SEVIERVILLE

Sevierville, along with Pigeon Forge three miles down the road, has very much become part of the strip of "attractions" lining the route from Knoxville to Gatlinburg. In Sevierville you'll find the Forbidden Caverns, once inhabited by Native Americans, more recently by moonshiners, while Pigeon Forge has so much going on that the ratio of motel rooms to permanent residents is now two to one. Both the carrier pigeons and the forge are long gone, but what you will find are "six miles of action-packed entertainment" in the form of innumerable shopping outlets, and attractions ranging from Dollywood to the Dixie Stampede, with water parks and water shows thrown in for good measure. If you're traveling with kids, either pass through in the dead of night when they're fast asleep, or put your brain on hold and enjoy the fun. Additional area activities include fishing, hiking, white water rafting, horseback riding, and swimming.

As always, avoid visiting in July and August (especially weekends) unless you're nostalgic for rush-hour conditions. Located in east Tennessee, Sevierville is located 30 miles southeast of Knoxville, and 5 miles north of Gatlinburg and the Great Smoky Mountains National Park.

Reader tips: "Our innkeeper had helpful advice on back roads which helped us avoid some of the traffic." *(MW)* "For fairly elegant yet reasonably priced meal, try Five Oaks." *(SHW)*

Important note: Several of the entries below are located on isolated mountain roads, about a mile off Highway 321, between Pigeon Forge and Townshend. *They are not in Sevierville at all,* and while their mountain settings are unparalleled, you will need to drive into town for dinner each night. Be sure to ask whether dinners will be served at the inn during your stay, especially in peak season.

For additional area entries, see **Gatlinburg, Newport, Pigeon Forge, Townsend,** and **Walland.**

Blue Mountain Mist Country Inn ♿ *Tel:* 423–428–2335
1811 Pullen Road, 37862 800–497–2335
Fax: 423–453–1720
E-mail: bluemtnmist@worldnet.att.net

The Blue Mountain Mist Inn, set on a hilltop overlooking meadows and rolling hills with the Smokies as a backdrop, is a delightful country retreat built in 1987 by Norman and Sarah Ball. Guest rooms have a country Victorian look, with lace accented country antiques, collectibles, and beautiful old quilts. Early risers can take a cup of coffee out to one of the porch rockers and watch the sun rise over the misty valleys and mountains beyond. Breakfast is served promptly at 8:30 A.M. at tables for four-to-six people, and typically includes biscuits and gravy, eggs, sausage, bacon, grits, fresh fruit, and coffee cake. Rates also include evening tea or coffee and such desserts as spice cake.

"Beautiful setting, especially lovely during fall foliage. A roaring fire really made the living room especially welcoming, and we noticed that the other guests also felt comfortable relaxing in the inviting common areas, with plenty of comfortable seating. Coffee, tea and snacks are always available, and guests are encouraged to make themselves at home. Our room had a queen-size bed with plenty of pillows, extra blankets, and a writing desk. A friendly, out-going staff member treated us to a tour of the other guest rooms, and each was beautiful, with gorgeous views of the Smokies. The inn is well staffed, with people always around to meet our needs."*(Susan Winner)*

"A neo-Victorian farmhouse with large wraparound porch, filled with white wicker and morning glories winding around the porch posts." *(Joy Hadden)* "The wide porch's rocking chairs were occupied by guests chatting like cousins at a family reunion when I arrived. There was orange cake for the taking in the kitchen. Breakfast included stuffed French toast, eggs and bacon, accompanied by plenty of conversation among the contented guests." *(Millie Ball)* "Our well-equipped cabin had a queen-size bed, and a porch with beautiful mountain views." *(Wayne Cook)* "Cheerful dining room walled with windows overlooks the mountains. Guests can have as much privacy or companionship as they wish. Minutes from outlet shops and Dollywood." *(Nancy Cornell)*

"The inn sits at the top of a small rise, looking out past meadows and woodland to the mountains beyond. The ample commons areas have hardwood floors, Oriental rugs, traditional and Victorian furnishings accented by crocheted doilies, quilts, country crafts, and flowers. The cozy guest rooms are done in pastel colors, and furnished with quilts and floral fabrics. The appealing cottages are individually decorated, with #5 being the most private. Guests assembled in the living room until called into the dining room for a tasty breakfast of fresh fruit with yogurt sauce and pancakes." *(SHW)*

Open All year.
Rooms 5 cottages, 1 suite, 12 doubles—all with full private bath, clock, air-conditioning, fan. 2 with whirlpool bath, 3 with balcony/deck, 4 with desk. Cottages with whirlpool tub, telephones, TV/VCR, books, fireplace, kitchenette, porch.
Facilities Dining room, living room with fireplace, family room with games, TV/VCR, books, videotapes; porch with hammock. Occasional musical entertainment. 60 acres with gazebo, lawn games. Lake, mountain stream nearby. 12 miles to skiing, 10 miles to hiking.
Location 4 m to town. From I-40 take Rte. 66 S. Take U.S. 411 E to Rte. 416S. Go right onto Jay Ell Rd. Go right onto Pullen Rd. Inn on right.
Restrictions No smoking. Children 12 and over.
Credit cards MC, Visa.
Rates B&B, $125 cottage, $95 suite, $79–125 double, $69–115 single. Extra person, $15. Senior discount. 2-night weekend/holiday minimums in October. Off-season rates.
Extras Limited wheelchair access.

Calico Inn *Tel:* 423–428–3833
757 Ranch Way, 37862 800–235–1054

The Calico Inn is a log home built in 1989 by Lill and Jim Katzbeck, and decorated with antiques, folk art, crafts and collectibles. Its hilltop setting offers beautiful views of fields, woods, and the mountains beyond. Breakfast seatings are at 8 and 9 A.M., and the meal includes fresh fruit and juice; home-baked bread, muffins, or biscuits and gravy; bacon, ham or sausage; and quiche with hash browns, puffed apple pancakes or perhaps waffles. Lill promises that "whatever the menu, we keep cooking as long was you keep eating—no one leaves hungry!" Although guests are uniformly delighted with the many charms of this B&B, what they tend to enjoy most of all is the personal warmth and hospitality of the Katzbecks.

"Lemonade on the porch in summer, hot cider by the fire in winter." *(Janet Crecelius)* "The feeling of welcome started in the well-lit parking area, and help with our luggage. Both our room and the front porch offered views of a lake, mountains, grazing horses and cows. Delicious breakfasts, with different menus and china each day. When we returned to the inn each evening, Lill and Jim always had coffee, tea, and a sweet treat waiting." *(Joan Singerman)* "Jim and Lill open their hearts to guests, and make you feel like family." *(Steve Carney)* "My favorite spot was the front porch; in the morning, I sipped coffee, watching the mist on the mountains." *(Janice Balheimer)* "Excellent food, comfortable accommodations, but the best part of the inn is the Katzbecks." *(Robert Bateman)* "Quiet country location, yet convenient to all area attractions." *(Jennifer McCracken)* "After a superb breakfast, a walk through the woods started our day just right." *(Anita Himber)*

Open All year.
Rooms 3 doubles—all with full private bath, radio, clock, air-conditioning, ceiling fan.
Facilities Dinning room, great room with fireplace, TV/VCR, stereo, books; guest refrigerator, porch with swing. 25 acres with hiking trails in woods.
Location 10 minutes to town; 2 m from Hwy. 441. From I-40, take Exit 407 7 go S on Hwy 66 approx. 8 m to Sevierville, & intersection with Hwy 411. Continue on 66/411 S for 2 m & go right on New Era Rd. to end. Go left on Ranch Rd. to inn sign on right.
Restrictions No smoking. Children 6 and over.
Credit cards MC, Visa.
Rates B&B, $89–99. Extra adult, $25; child, $10. Tips welcome.

Little Greenbrier Lodge ¢ *Tel:* 423–429–2500
3685 Lyon Springs Road, 37862 800–277–8100

While any inngoer will enjoy the warm hospitality, good food, comfortable rooms, and lovely setting of the Little Greenbrier Lodge, its most distinctive feature is that it's the closest B&B to Great Smoky Mountains National Park. The little-known Greenbrier entrance and trailhead is just 120 yards away from the inn. The Little Greenbrier Lodge was built as a hotel in 1939, but was run down and vacant in 1993 when Charlie and Susan LeBon bought it and began its restoration. Breakfast is served 8:30–9:30 A.M. and includes egg casseroles, biscuits and gravy, sausage, grits, and pecan pull-apart bread.

"The inn was clean, quaint, and peaceful; the food was well-prepared and generous; and the hospitality was unequalled. The LeBons are wonderful people who make you feel right at home." *(Richard Town-*

shend) "Going directly from the inn to the hiking trails without getting in the car was a treat. We could also drive into the park without having to deal with the traffic of Pigeon Forge or Gatlinburg." *(Betty Kadri)* "Charlie and Susan treat us like family. Susan has a special way of sharing ideas with kindness and a sense of humor. Their sightseeing advice has led us to places the guidebooks don't cover, providing the best memories. In the evenings, guests sit around visiting or playing games. The lodge sits on the side of a mountain with a spectacular view of a valley and lots of surrounding woods. Rooms are furnished with lovely Victorian antiques." *(Chip and Katie Wilt)* "Susan is a great hostess who greets you with friendliness and charm. She offers great tips on local enterprises and has brochures available. The fantastic breakfast kept me going until dinner time." *(Doris Medema)* "Although much of Gatlinburg was wall-to-wall Winnebagos, we hardly saw another soul on our beautiful hike up to spectacular the Ramsey Cascade waterfall." *(MW)*

Open All year.
Rooms 10 doubles—8 with private shower, 2 with maximum of 4 people sharing bath. All with radio, clock, air-conditioning, balcony. Some with desk, ceiling fan; 1 with fireplace.
Facilities Dining room, common room with fireplace, TV/VCR, stereo, books, games; porches. 10 acres bordering natl park. 1⁄16 m to trailhead, road entrance.
Location 9 m W of Pigeon Forge, 10 m W of Gatlinburg, 5 m E of Townshend in Wears Valley. From Pigeon Forge, take 321 for 9.1 m towards Townsend. Go left on Lyon Springs Rd. Follow road for 1.5 m up mountain, to inn on left.
Restrictions No smoking. Children 12 and over.
Credit cards Discover, MC, Visa.
Rates B&B, $80–100 double, $65 single. 5% senior discount.

Von Bryan Inn *Tel:* 423–453–9832
2402 Hatcher Mountain Road, 37862 800–633–1459

The Von Bryan Inn, owned by D.J. and Jo Ann Vaughn since 1988, is a magnificent log home with beautiful mountain views from its windows, porches, decks, and patio. The cathedral-ceilinged living room has a stacked stone fireplace; guests can socialize and relax in the 11-person outdoor hot tub after a day of hiking or shopping. Guest rooms offer a blend of traditional and antique furnishings, with handmade quilts. A typical breakfast might include fresh fruit and juice, cereal, biscuits or popovers, and sausage-egg casserole or rice-asparagus casserole; rates also include afternoon refreshments.

"The inn sits on top of a 2,000-foot mountain, with panoramic views of the Wears Valley, farmland and grazing cows below, and the mountains beyond. Guest rooms are spotlessly clean, comfortably furnished with queen- or king-sized beds, nice sitting areas, and ample closet and drawer space." *(Doris Waters)* "Spent evenings rocking on the porch, relaxing in the hammock swing, or soaking in the hot tub. Most nights the innkeepers sit with a group of guests in the parlor or on the porch to chat in a relaxed, homey atmosphere." *(Mark & Jennifer Gragg)* "Just as lovely on a return trip." *(Sibyl Nestor)*

"Spectacular mountain views, unsurpassed privacy. To sit on the inn's front porches, rocking and watching the cloud patterns pass over the mountain range, observing the 'smoky' mist rising from the valleys, seems as close to heaven as one can get on this earth. The enjoyable breakfast is served at one of two large dining room tables, or at tables for four on the sunporch. Guests can help themselves from the very ample buffet; my favorite was the asparagus rice dish. In the afternoon, the innkeepers set out snacks, veggies, fruit, and a dessert. You could easily spend a relaxing day swimming in the pool, and chatting on the porches. The massive living room with cathedral ceiling is a great place to curl up with a book, and there is a lounge for watching movies.

"The Red Bud Room, located on the first floor behind the main porch, has a king-size bed and a huge red whirlpool tub in the corner. The towels were thick and replenished often. Another first-floor room, the Garden Room, has a steam shower, a wrought iron bed draped with flowers, with a loft sitting area upstairs. The lovely White Oak Room is done in Wedgewood blue and yellow, with white furniture, and a corner whirlpool with a skylight. JoAnn and DJ Vaughn are calm, friendly, and unobtrusive, pleased to offer conversation, directions, restaurant suggestions." *(Susan Schwemm)* "Secluded location, friendly innkeepers, outstanding food. Great feather bed. One night is not enough!" *(Dick Maxwell)*

Open All year.
Rooms 5 doubles—all with private bath and/or shower, radio, air-conditioning, 3 with double whirlpool tub, 1 with steam shower. 3-bedroom, 2-bath cottage with living room with fireplace, kitchen, wraparound porch, TV, hot tub.
Facilities Dining room, living room with fireplace, piano, books, games, TV, stereo; sitting room, hot tub. 6 acres with swimming pool, swings, hammock, English garden. Hiking, skiing, fishing, rafting, tubing, boating, canoeing nearby.
Location From N and E: From I-40 take Exit 407 to Pigeon Forge. Go right onto 321S & 7.2 m to Hatcher Mt. Rd. Turn right & go to top of mountain. From S and W: Exit I 40 at 364 or I-75 at 81 onto 321N. Go through Maryville to Townsend, where 321N turns left. Stay on 321N for 8 more m. Turn left on Hatcher Mt. Rd.
Restrictions Absolutely no smoking.
Credit cards Amex, Discover, MC, Visa.
Rates B&B, $180 cottage, $90–135 double. Extra person, $15. 2-night minimum in cottage. Prix fixe lunch, $11; prix fixe dinner, $20.

SHELBYVILLE

Shelbyville is located in middle Tennessee, about 60 miles south of Nashville, and is the center of Tennessee Walking Horse Country.

For additional area entries, see **College Grove** and **Columbia.**

Also recommended: Built in 1901, the **Taylor House** (300 East Lane Street, 37160; 931–684–3894) is convenient to the historic district and all area attractions. B&B double rates for the three guest rooms, each with private bath, range from $65–75. "Spacious, beautifully restored, and very comfortable. Inviting common areas and a refrigerator stocked with complimentary soft drinks. Generous country breakfast with biscuits." *(MR)* **Information please:** The **Bottle Hollow Lodge** (111 Gobbler Ridge Road, P.O. Box 92, Shelbyville 37160; 931–695–5253) was built in 1990 of brick and fieldstone. Floral wallpapers decorate the spacious guest rooms; the decor includes cherry, walnut, and maple furnishings—both family antiques and hand-crafted period pieces. Breakfast typically includes country ham, biscuits, eggs, preserves, gravy, grits, and fruit. The inn's location on top of a high ridge provides handsome views and a peaceful, quiet setting. B&B double rates for the five guest rooms are $90. "Lovely views, charming inn." *(BJ Hensley)* Current reports welcome.

SMITHVILLE

For an additional area inn, see **Watertown.**

Evins Mill Retreat ✕
Evins Mill Road, P.O. Box 606

Tel: 931–597–2088
Fax: 931–597–2090

Quality time is a concept that's just as important in travel as it is in parenting. When you need a few days for a weekend escape, an off-site business meeting, or some family fun, you can be sure that if your travel time is minimized, your enjoyment will be maximized. Evins Mill, a country inn less than two hours from Nashville, Knoxville, and Chattanooga, is a fine choice on all counts. The oldest building on the property is the gristmill, built in 1824; although the mill is still in operation, with beams and atmosphere intact, the building has been restored as a conference center. Tennessee state senator Edgar Evins purchased the property in 1937. He and his wife built a log-and-stone lodge on the bluff overlooking Fall Creek, complete with massive stone fireplaces and a welcoming cedar porch. When the Lodge was bought and renovated in 1994 by William Cochran and his dad, William, Senior, three guest cottages were built, each with four bedrooms. The inn is popular for business conferences midweek, and for relaxation on the weekends. Appealing theme packages are planned for holiday weekends, plus family getaways Saturdays in summer.

The Evins Mill restaurant serves breakfast 7–9 A.M., lunch 11–1 P.M., and dinner 6–8 P.M. The breakfast menu includes French toast, sausage and biscuits, and eggs and hash browns; lunch favorites include Caesar salad with grilled chicken, or pork barbecue. Slow-roasted pork loin with mushrooms, rosemary roast chicken, and pan-seared tuna are among the dinner entrees. Save room for desserts like peach cobbler, chocolate terrine, and cheesecake with fresh berries.

"Excellent food, service, and ambiance. Gourmet meals, roaring fireplace, impeccably clean rooms." *(James Douglas)* "Magnificent setting. Wonderful gathering place with two huge fireplaces. Careful attention to detail; staff who go the extra mile for guests." *(Jeannie DuBose)* "First-rate hospitality, with helpful but unobtrusive staff. Relaxed atmosphere; fine food, beautifully presented." *(Don Duggen)* "Peaceful grounds; enjoyed the short but steep walk to Carmac Falls, where water cascades down a 90-foot stone 'staircase.'"

Open All year.
Rooms 14 doubles—all with full private bath, radio, clock, desk, air-conditioning, ceiling fan. Most with porch. 2 rooms in main lodge, 12 in 3 adjacent guest cottages.
Facilities Restaurant, bar/lounge, living room, family room with games, videotape collection, den, conference rooms with AV equipment, porches. Grist mill. Occasional weekend entertainment. 40 acres with swimming hole, waterfall, fishing pond, picnic pavilion, hiking/jogging trail, horseshoes, volleyball, ropes course. Lake for boating, golf nearby.
Location Middle TN, 75 m E of Nashville. Approx 2 hrs W of Knoxville, N of Chattanooga. From junction of Hwys 70 & 56 in Smithville, follow Hwy. 70 E 1 ½ m & turn right onto Evins Mill Rd. Go 1 ½ m to inn.
Restrictions Smoking permitted in Stone Room only. Only beer available; BYOB. Children welcome only in summer.
Credit cards Amex, Discover, MC, Visa.
Rates Room only, $70–100 double. B&B, $100–130 double, $85–115 single. MAP, $150–180 double, $115–145 single. Full board, $180–210 double, $130–160 single. Extra adult, $20–95. Children under 6 free, 6–18, $10–50. Tips encouraged. Alc lunch, $10–15; alc dinner, $20–30. Summer family packages; holiday theme weekends.

TOWNSEND

Dubbed Townsend occupies a scenic valley at the entrance to the Cades Cove loop of the Great Smoky Mountains National Park. You can reach it from Knoxville by going south on Highway 129 to Maryville, then east on Highway 321 to Townshend, avoiding all the traffic on Highway 441 to Gatlinburg.

For additional area entries, see **Gatlinburg, Pigeon Forge, Sevierville,** and **Walland.**

Richmont Inn, "On the Peaceful Side of the Smokies" ♿

220 Winterberry Lane, 37882
Tel: 423–448–6751
Fax: 423–448–6480
E-mail: richmontinn@worldnet.att.com

Without exception, guests rave about the distinctive decor and architecture, gracious hospitality, exceptional comfort, attention to detail, beautiful mountain views, outstanding food, and romantic atmosphere of the Richmont Inn, built in 1991 by Jim and Susan Hind. Built in the unusual architectural style of the Appalachian cantilevered barn, with planked wood and slate floors, mortar-chinked log walls, and 13-foot high beamed ceilings, the inn offers pastoral views of the rolling green pastures of Laurel Valley and Rich Mountain. The decor includes 18th century American-English antiques, accented with American-French paintings and prints. Breakfast is served at tables for two in the panoramic dining area where you can watch the morning mist rise from the valley floor; the meal is served at 8:30 weekdays and 8:30 or 9:15 weekends. A typical menu might consist of fresh-squeezed orange juice, granola and yogurt, and such entrees as French toast l'orange with bacon, apple oatmeal cinnamon pancakes, or eggs soufflé with sausage crepes. After dinner, guests return to the inn for such desserts as Grand Marnier soufflé, crème brûlée Kahlua, and bourbon pecan cake, accompanied by flavored decaf coffees and herbal tea.

"Lovely views over the treetops, across the golf course in the valley to the mountains in the distance. The Lucy Morgan Room is accented with dark green fabrics and has a mountain view balcony, wood-burning fireplace, king-size bed, spa tub for two, and five large windows." *(Susan Waller Schwemm)* "The Robert Mize room is named after a local dulcimer musician. The king-size bed was heavenly with white pima cotton sheets and a soft but firm mattress; the soft white robes were perfect after soaking in the whirlpool tub. Soft classical music added to the relaxing atmosphere. We had a private sitting area, and a balcony overlooking the forest, complete with comfortable twig chairs. The delicious candlelight dessert was praline cheesecake and homemade vanilla ice cream with fresh Georgia peaches. The equally delicious breakfast included Danish kringle and Appalachian eggs with sugared bacon. Jim suggested an excellent morning hike, and provided us with a wonderful picnic of smoked trout, Brie, croissants, and biscotti. No detail is overlooked by these hospitable innkeepers."*(Deanna Yen, also MB)* "Quiet and secluded, with rustic, casual charm. Our third-floor room was lovely. Sitting outside on our balcony, looking over the treetops was most relaxing. Excellent breakfast, enjoyed leisurely." *(Carol Blodgett, also Danielle DuRant)*

"Guest rooms are decorated after influential people in the history of the Smokies—a stained glass church window in the circuit rider's room; Native American designs in the rooms honoring Cherokee Indians." *(Linda Smalley)* "Richmont is a 'second honeymoon' every time you visit." *(Charles Torrey)*

Open All year.
Rooms 1 suite, 9 doubles—all with full private bath, air-conditioning, refrigerator, piped-in music, sitting area, coffee maker, hair dryer, robes. Most with double whirlpool tub, desk, gas or wood-burning fireplace, balcony/deck.
Facilities Dining/observation room, living room with fireplace, piano, books; library with VCR; gift shop, deck; conference/family reunion building. 11 acres with patio, green house, lawn games, nature path, waterfall, pond, Chapel in the Woods. Golf, mountain river with fishing, kayaking, canoeing, hiking, skiing nearby. Theme activity weekends: mountain music, flowers, birds.
Location E TN. 35 m S of Knoxville. 3 m to town. 10 min. from Great Smoky Mts. Natl. Park. Enter Townsend city limits from Maryville on U.S. 321 N. Go right on Old Tuckaleecheee Rd. Follow signs to Laurel Valley. Take 1st paved rd. on right, Laurel Valley Rd. Go $\frac{8}{10}$ m, bear right through stone entrance to Laurel Valley. Stay on paved road to crest of hill. Turn left into inn.
Restrictions No smoking. Children over 12.
Credit cards None accepted.

Rates B&B, $145 suite, $95–130 double. Extra person, $35. 2-night minimum holiday weekends & all Oct. Prix fixe dinner, $25 for two. Picnic lunch for 2, $25.
Extras Wheelchair access; 1 bathroom specially equipped.

WALLAND

For additional area entries, see **Gatlinburg, Pigeon Forge, Sevierville,** and **Townsend.**

Also recommended: If an inn called **Blackberry Farm** (1471 West Millers Cove, 37886; 423–984–8166 or 800–862–7610) set in the Smokies, makes you think of country bumpkins and corncob pipes, think again. Built in 1930 of mountain stone, shingles, and slate, Blackberry Farm is the most elegant—and most expensive—inn in Tennessee. All-inclusive double rates for the 30 guest rooms range from $295–575, including three meals daily, afternoon tea, unlimited snacks and beverages, and use of all recreational equipment and amenities. Its handsome rooms are richly appointed with Oriental rugs, flowered chintzes and other fine fabrics, and English and American antiques. Famous for its fine food, the inn's breakfasts always include fresh fruit and just-baked breads, with a choice of thick sliced bacon and blueberry cornmeal pancakes, or perhaps scrambled eggs, homemade sausage, buttermilk biscuits, and sawmill gravy. A typical lunch choice might consist of a leek and ricotta tart served with a salad of hearty greens and citrus, and lentil soup. At dinner, try the potato-horseradish crusted catfish or hickory-smoked loin of pork. "Everything you could possibly wish for is provided, from fishing tackle to golf carts for reaching distant sections of the grounds. If you want instruction in tennis, a pro is ready to help you. The manager met us at the door, welcomed us, and took our bags to our room. Our car was removed as if by magic, and re-appeared the same way when check-out time arrived." *(Sibyl Nestor)* "The winding drive leads past manicured grounds to an elegant white frame manor house with eaves, dormers, and intriguing angles. The guest room decor was designer elegant, and the compact modern bathrooms were sparkling clean." *(Susan Waller Schwemm)*

WATERTOWN

For an additional area entry, see **Smithville.**

Information please: About 35 miles west of Nashville and ten miles south of I-40 is the **Watertown B&B** (116 Depot Avenue, 37184–1404; 615–237–9999), built as the Railroad Hotel in 1898. Located just off the square in historic Watertown, B&B double rates for the five guest rooms range from $55–120. "Charming innkeepers. Wonderful breakfast of individual home-baked brads, scrambled eggs with cream puff shells with Hollandaise." *(BJ Hensley)*

WAYNESBORO

Information please: If traveling along the Natchez Trace, in south central Tennessee, consider a stay at the **Waynesboro Inn** (406 South Main Street, 38485; 615–722–7321), a spacious brick home with three guest rooms. "Welcoming homestay B&B with friendly innkeepers, relaxing atmosphere. Clean and comfortable, tasty pancake breakfast." *(Eric Linden)* The double rate of $55 includes a full breakfast.

Free Copy of INNroads Newsletter

Want to stay up-to-date on our latest finds? Send a business-size, self-addressed, stamped envelope with 55 cents postage and we'll send you the latest issue, *free!* While you're at it, why not enclose a report on any inns you've recently visited? Use the forms at the back of the book or your own stationery.

We Want to Hear from You!

As you know, this book is effective only with your help. We really need to know about your experiences and discoveries. If you stayed at an inn or hotel listed here, we want to know how it was. Did it live up to our description? Exceed it? Was it what you expected? Did you like it? Were you disappointed? Delighted? Have you discovered new establishments that we should add to the next edition?

Tear out one of the report forms at the back of this book (or use your own stationery if you prefer) and write today. *Even if you write only "Fully endorse existing entry" you will have been most helpful.*

Thank You!

MAPS

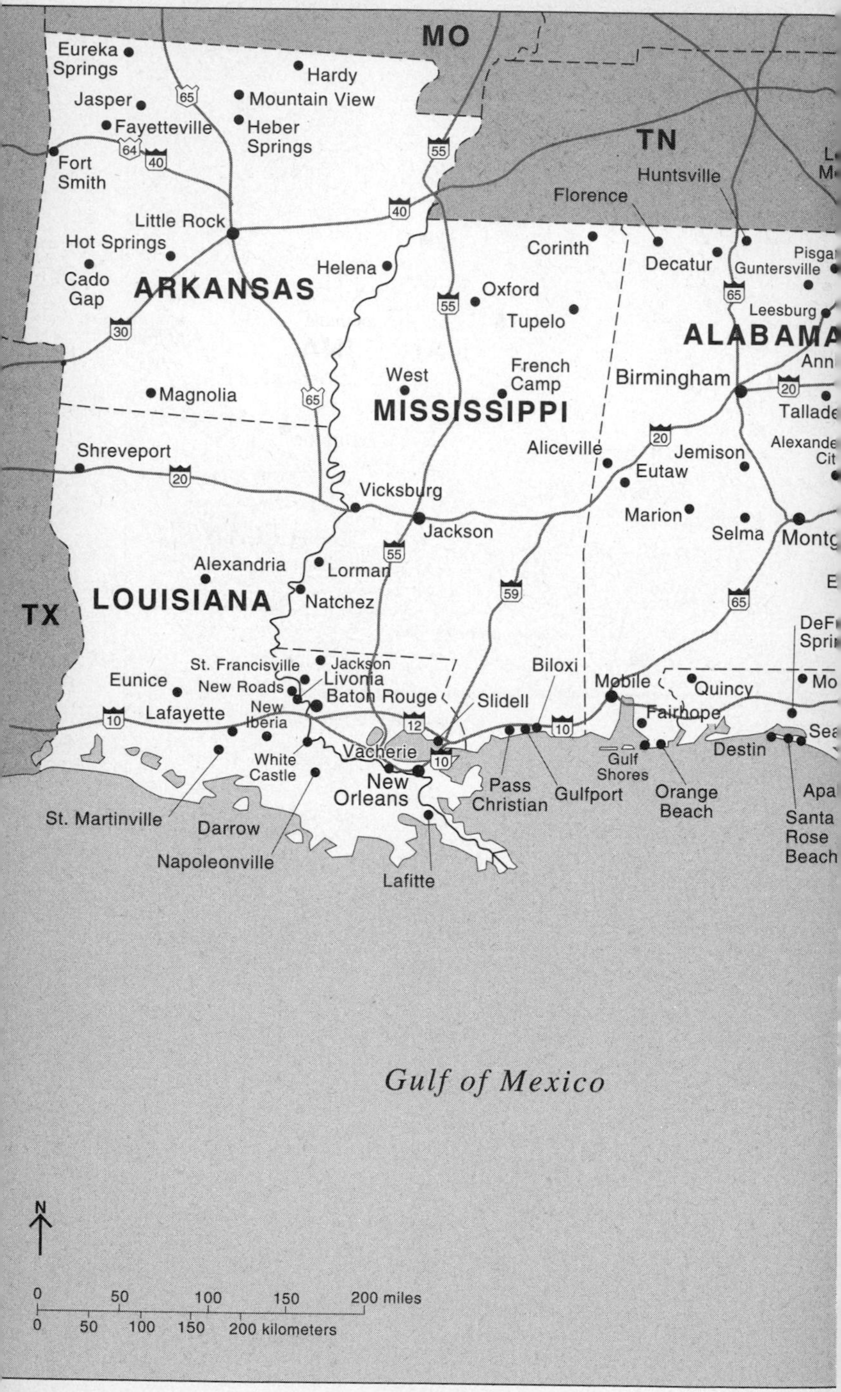

MO
TN
Eureka Springs
Hardy
Jasper
Mountain View
Fayetteville
Heber Springs
Fort Smith
Huntsville
Florence
Little Rock
Hot Springs
Corinth
Decatur
Guntersville
Helena
Cado Gap
ARKANSAS
Oxford
Tupelo
Leesburg
ALABAMA
West
French Camp
Birmingham
Magnolia
MISSISSIPPI
Aliceville
Jemison
Shreveport
Eutaw
Vicksburg
Jackson
Marion
Selma
Alexandria
Lorman
LOUISIANA
Natchez
TX
St. Francisville
Jackson
Biloxi
Eunice
New Roads
Livonia
Baton Rouge
Slidell
Mobile
Quincy
Lafayette
New Iberia
Fairhope
Destin
Vacherie
White Castle
New Orleans
Gulf Shores
Pass Christian
Gulfport
Orange Beach
St. Martinville
Darrow
Napoleonville
Lafitte
Santa Rose Beach
Gulf of Mexico
N

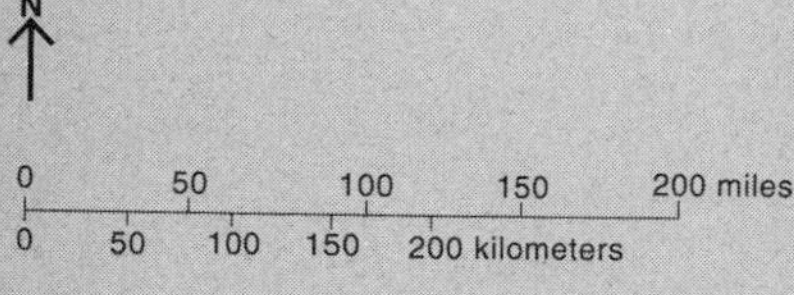

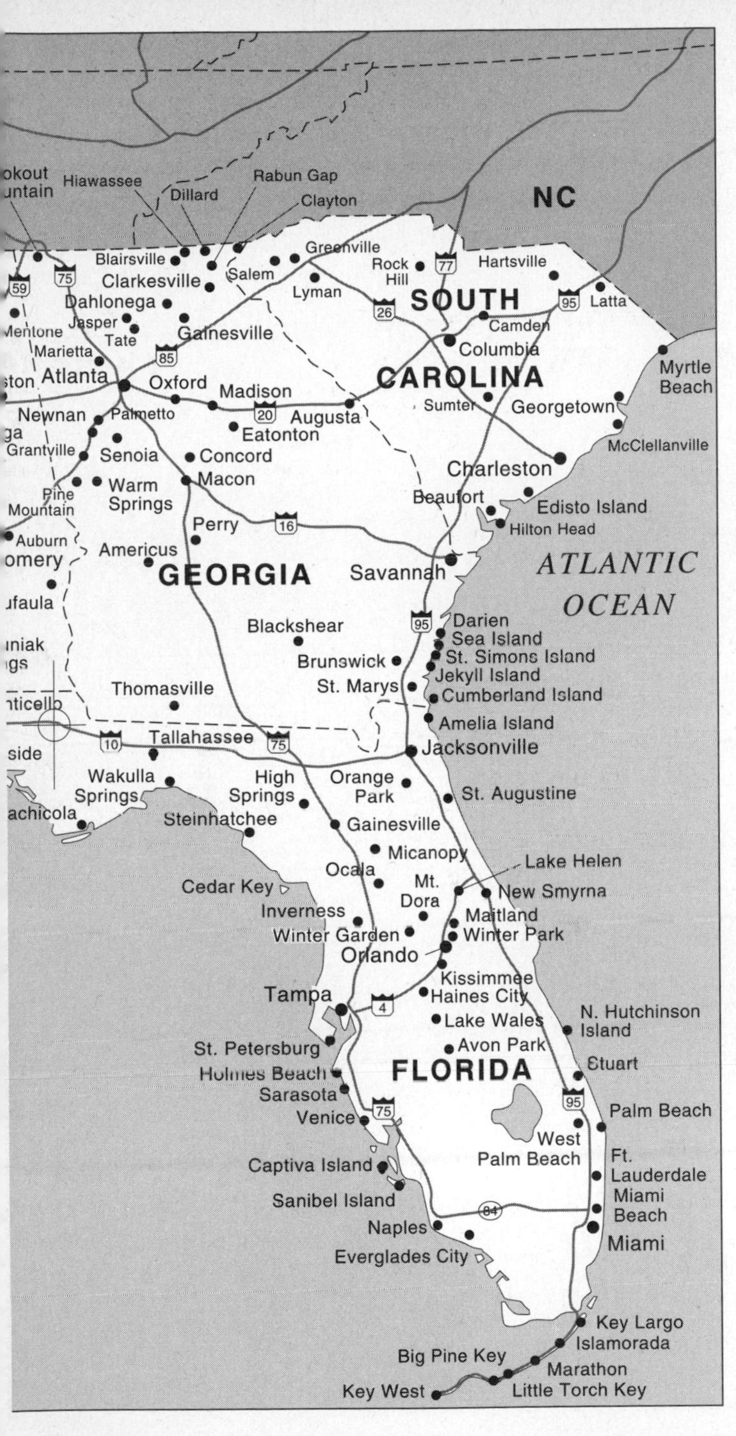

Hiawassee
Rabun Gap
Dillard
Clayton
NC
Blairsville
Greenville
Rock Hill
77
Hartsville
59
75
Salem
Clarkesville
Lyman
SOUTH
Dahlonega
26
95
Latta
Jasper
Mentone
Tate
Camden
Gainesville
Marietta
85
Columbia
Myrtle Beach
Atlanta
Oxford
CAROLINA
Madison
Newnan
Palmetto
20
Augusta
Sumter
Georgetown
Eatonton
Grantville
Senoia
Concord
McClellanville
Macon
Charleston
Pine Mountain
Warm Springs
Beaufort
Edisto Island
Perry
16
Hilton Head
Auburn
Americus
ATLANTIC
GEORGIA
Savannah
OCEAN
95
Darien
Blackshear
Sea Island
St. Simons Island
Brunswick
Jekyll Island
St. Marys
Cumberland Island
Thomasville
Amelia Island
10
Tallahassee
75
Jacksonville
Wakulla Springs
High Springs
Orange Park
St. Augustine
Steinhatchee
Gainesville
Micanopy
Ocala
Lake Helen
Cedar Key
Mt. Dora
New Smyrna
Inverness
Maitland
Winter Garden
Winter Park
Orlando
Kissimmee
Tampa
4
Haines City
Lake Wales
N. Hutchinson Island
St. Petersburg
Avon Park
Holmes Beach
FLORIDA
Stuart
Sarasota
75
95
Venice
Palm Beach
West Palm Beach
Captiva Island
Ft. Lauderdale
Sanibel Island
Miami Beach
84
Naples
Miami
Everglades City
Key Largo
Islamorada
Big Pine Key
Marathon
Key West
Little Torch Key

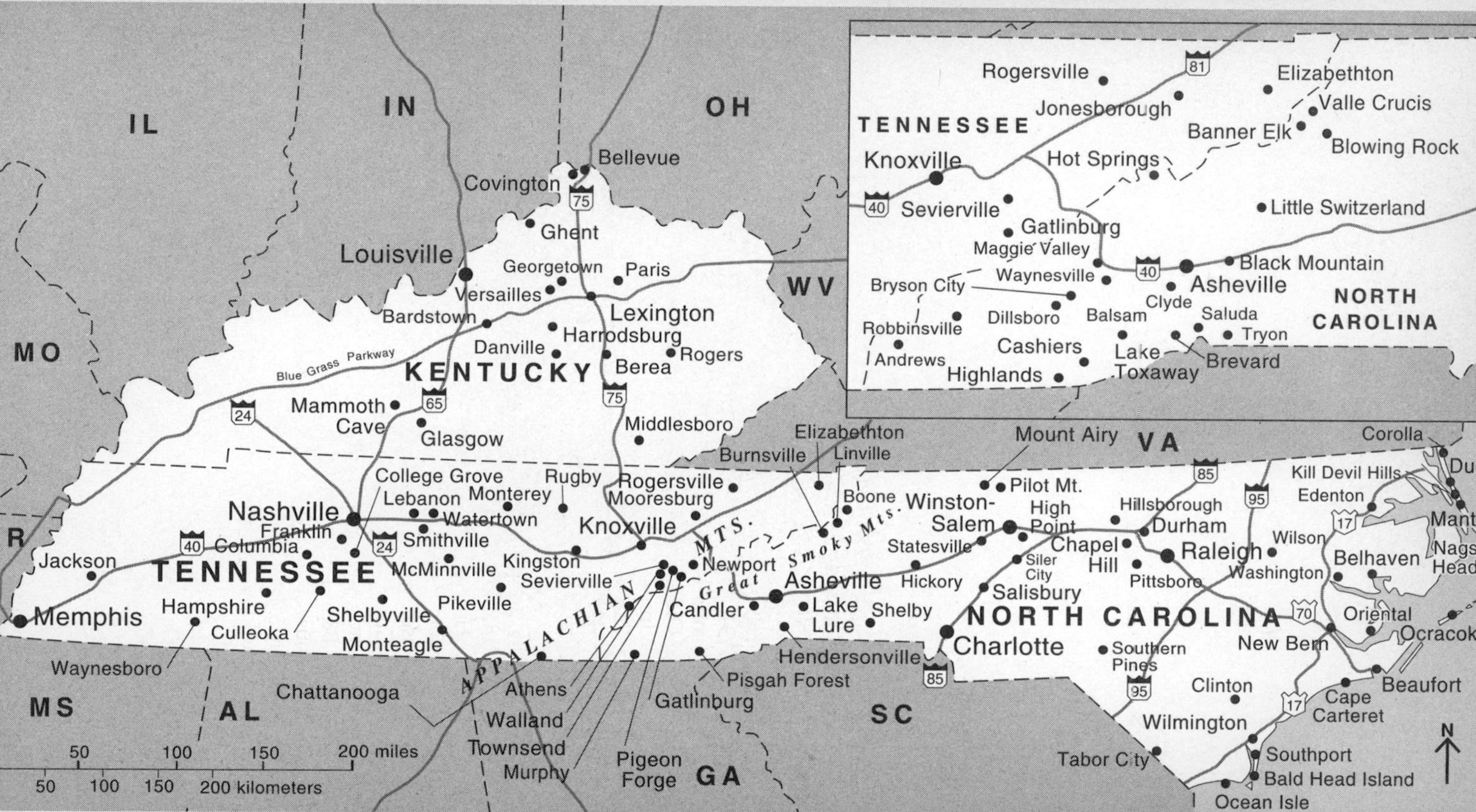
IL
IN
OH
MO
WV
VA
AR
MS
AL
GA
SC
KENTUCKY
TENNESSEE
NORTH CAROLINA
Louisville
Covington
Bellevue
Ghent
Georgetown
Paris
Versailles
Bardstown
Lexington
Harrodsburg
Danville
Rogers
Berea
Blue Grass Parkway
Mammoth Cave
Glasgow
Middlesboro
Memphis
Jackson
Hampshire
Culleoka
Waynesboro
Columbia
Franklin
Nashville
College Grove
Lebanon
Watertown
Monterey
Smithville
McMinnville
Shelbyville
Pikeville
Monteagle
Chattanooga
Rugby
Rogersville
Mooresburg
Knoxville
Kingston
Sevierville
Newport
Athens
Walland
Townsend
Murphy
Pigeon Forge
Gatlinburg
Candler
Pisgah Forest
Hendersonville
APPALACHIAN MTS.
Great Smoky Mts.
Burnsville
Elizabethton
Linville
Boone
Asheville
Lake Lure
Shelby
Hickory
Statesville
Mount Airy
Pilot Mt.
Winston-Salem
High Point
Salisbury
Siler City
Charlotte
Chapel Hill
Hillsborough
Durham
Raleigh
Pittsboro
Southern Pines
Wilson
Washington
Corolla
Kill Devil Hills
Duck
Edenton
Manteo
Nags Head
Belhaven
Oriental
Ocracoke
New Bern
Beaufort
Cape Carteret
Clinton
Wilmington
Tabor City
Southport
Bald Head Island
Ocean Isle
0
50
100
150
200 miles
0
50
100
150
200 kilometers
N
TENNESSEE
NORTH CAROLINA
Rogersville
Jonesborough
Elizabethton
Valle Crucis
Banner Elk
Blowing Rock
Knoxville
Hot Springs
Sevierville
Little Switzerland
Gatlinburg
Maggie Valley
Waynesville
Black Mountain
Asheville
Bryson City
Clyde
Robbinsville
Dillsboro
Balsam
Saluda
Tryon
Andrews
Cashiers
Lake Toxaway
Brevard
Highlands

Index of Accommodations

Hotel/Inn Report Forms

The report forms on the following pages may be used to endorse or critique an existing entry or to nominate a hotel or inn that you feel deserves inclusion in the next edition. Don't feel you must restrict yourself to the space available; feel free to use your own stationery or e-mail. All nominations (each on a separate piece of paper, if possible) should include your name and address, the name and location of the hotel or inn, when you have stayed there, and for how long. Please report only on establishments you have visited in the last eighteen months, unless you are sure that standards have not dropped since your stay. Please be as specific as possible, and critical where appropriate, about the character of the building, the public rooms, the accommodations, the meals, the service, the nightlife, the grounds, and the general atmosphere of the inn and the attitude of its owners. Comments about area restaurants and sights are also appreciated.

Don't feel you need to write at length. A report that merely verifies the accuracy of existing listings is extremely helpful, i.e., "Visited XYZ Inn and found it just as described." There is no need to bother with prices or with routine information about the number of rooms and facilities, although a sample brochure is very helpful for new recommendations.

On the other hand, don't apologize for writing a long report. Although space does not permit us to quote them in total, the small details provided about furnishings, atmosphere, and cuisine can really make a description come alive, illuminating the special flavor of a particular inn or hotel. Remember that we will again be awarding free copies to our most helpful respondents—last year we mailed over 500 books.

Please note that we print only the names of respondents, never addresses. Those making negative observations are not identified. Although we must always have your full name and address, we will be happy to print your initials, or a pseudonym, if you prefer.

Reports should be sent to P.O. Box 150, Riverside, CT 06878, ssoule@msn.com.

To: *America's Favorite Inns, B&Bs, and Small Hotels,*
P.O. Box 150, Riverside, CT 06878 or ssoule@msn.com.

Name of hotel ____

Address ____

Telephone ____

Date of most recent visit ___________ Duration of visit ___________

☐ New recommendation ☐ Comment on existing entry

Please be as specific as possible about furnishings, atmosphere, service, and cuisine. If reporting on an existing entry, please tell us whether you thought it accurate. Unless you tell us not to, we shall assume that we may publish your name in the next edition. Thank you very much for writing; use your own stationery if preferred:

I am not connected with the management/owners.
I would stay here again if returning to the area. ☐ yes ☐ no
Have you written to us before? ☐ yes ☐ no

Signed ____

Name ____
(Please print)

Address ____
(Please print)

____

SO98

FAX TO: 1-801-321-6301

InnPoints Enrollment Application

PERSONAL INFORMATION

Code AFI

Title (Mr/Mrs/Ms etc.)

Last Name

First Name Initial

Company

Home Phone — —

Office Phone — —

Fax Number — —

MAILING INFORMATION

Address

City State

Zip Code

YOUR P.I.N. NUMBER

(For internal verification purposes only)

Choose a Personal Identification Number (P.I.N.) that only you will know and remember.

(Use numbers only, please.)

–OR–

Mother's Maiden Name

OR MAIL TO: P.O. Box 510605, Dept. AFI
Salt Lake City, UT 84151-0605